Touring Guide to Britain

AA

Set between peaceful Coniston Water and the rugged Langdale Pikes, the lakes and forests of Tarn Hows offer some of the finest scenery of the English Lakes.

CONTENTS

This edition produced for Dolphin Publications, Bridge Mills Business
Park, Langley Road South, Pendleton, Salford M6 6EL

Produced by the Publishing Division of the Automobile Association
Editor Russell P O Beach
Art Editor Dave Austin
Assistant Editor Michael Cady
Assistant Designer Robert Johnson
Design concept by M A Preedy, MSIAD

Tour routes compiled and driven by the Publications Research Unit of the
Automobile Association
Index compiled by Linda Beach
Photographs by: Martyn Adelman, Martin Boddy, the British Tourist Authority
S & O Mathews, Jarrold Colour Publications Ltd, and Woodmansterne Ltd

All maps by the Cartographic Department, Publishing Division of the
Automobile Association
Based on the Ordnance Survey Maps, with the permission of the Controller
of HM Stationery Office
Crown Copyright Reserved

Phototypeset by Senator Graphics of London, England
Printed and bound by New Interlitho SpA, Milan, Italy
Colour separations by Rito of Zurich, Switzerland

KEY TO TOURS AND TOUR REGIONS

The Touring Guide to Britain contains 112 selected tours in some of the most picturesque and interesting places accessible to the motoring public. It is divided into the six geographical regions shown on the key maps here and overleaf, and has been designed for ease of use in a moving vehicle. Included in each self-contained tour are a colour map, photographs of interesting places on the route, and text presented in a way that makes this book different from any other of its kind. Places of interest, shown as black type on the maps, are described as they occur on the road and linked in sequence by route directions. This precise wayfinding information is set in *italic* type so that the navigator can easily identify it from the rest of the text. Castles, stately homes, and other places of interest described in the tours are not necessarily open to the public, although they may have been at the time of publication. Properties administered by the National Trust, National Trust for Scotland, and Ancient Monuments Scheme (NT, NTS, and AM) are usually open most times of the year, but there are many exceptions. It is a good idea to check that such places still receive visitors before planning a stop.

THE WEST COUNTRY
PAGES 8-43

SOUTH AND SOUTH EAST ENGLAND
PAGES 44-87

SYMBOLS AND ABBREVIATIONS

MAPS

Main Tour Route	
Detour/Diversion from Main Tour Route	
Motorway	
Motorway Access	⑥
Motorway Service Area	Ⓢ
Motorway & Junction Under Construction	
A-class Road	A466
B-class Road	B423
Unclassified Road	unclass
Dual Carriageway	A48
Road Under Construction	:=====:

Airport	✈
Battlefield	⚔
Bridge	⌒
Castle	♖
Church as Route Landmark	✝
Ferry	—ⓥ—
Folly/Tower	⛫
Forestry Commission Land	
Gazetteer Placename	*River Leven*/Chelford
Industrial Site (Old & New)	
Level Crossing	

Lighthouse	
Marshland	
Memorial/Monument	
Miscellaneous Places of Interest & Route Landmarks	
National Boundary	
National Trust Property	N
National Trust for Scotland Property	NT
Non-gazetteer Placenames	*Deddingto*
Notable Religious Site	
Picnic Site	

WALES AND THE MARCHER LANDS
PAGES 88-127

CENTRAL AND EASTERN ENGLAND
PAGES 128-165

Prehistoric Site

Racecourse

Radio/TV Mast

Railway (BR) with Station

Railway (Special) with Station

River & Lake   *River Arun*

Scenic Area

Seaside Resort

Stately Home

Summit/Spot Height   CLEEVE CLOUD 1049 ▲

Viewpoint

TEXT

AM   Ancient Monument

c   *circa*

NT   National Trust

NTS   National Trust for Scotland

PH   Public House

RSPB   Royal Society for the Protection of Birds

SP   Signpost (s) (ed)

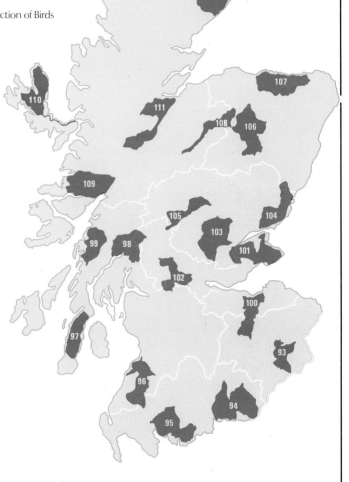

THE NORTH COUNTRY
PAGES 166-201

SCOTLAND
PAGES 202-243

Ruined engine houses, like the one at Wheal
Coates near St Agnes, are forceful
reminders of the men who once struggled to
extract precious mineral ores from primitive
mines deep beneath the rural landscapes of
Cornwall.

The West Country

PENZANCE, Cornwall

The most westerly town in England, Penzance enjoys a mild climate all year round. The town grew to prosperity through tin mining, and possibly smuggling, and was immortalized by Gilbert and Sullivan in *The Pirates of Penzance*. Evidence of its popularity in Regency times can be seen in the fine period buildings still standing in Chapel Street. Also here is a maritime museum with exhibits from 18th-century British warships wrecked off the Scilly Isles. There is a natural history museum in Penlee Park, and many exotic plants grow in Morab Gardens. About 2 miles inland are the Trengwainton Gardens (NT), with their exceptional collections of magnolias, rhododendrons and other shrubs. It was here that magnolias flowered for the first time in the British Isles.

MOUNT'S BAY, Cornwall

Mount's Bay curves in a series of wide coves and inlets between the Land's End peninsula in the west and The Lizard in the east. In spite of playing host to many visitors each year it is still a place of isolated bays and deserted, cliff-fringed beaches.

Leave Penzance on the A3077 'Newlyn', road skirting the harbour to Newlyn.

NEWLYN, Cornwall

This busy fishing port used to be famous for its artist colony. Many of the painters moved north to St Ives, but a few still live and work among the quaint old cottages and fish-cellars. The Passmore Edwards picture gallery shows some of the colony's work.

Cross a river bridge and immediately turn left on to an unclassified road which hugs the coast to Mousehole.

THE PENWITH PENINSULA

Storm-tumbled cliffs haunted by gulls and mermaid legends guard the wild Atlantic shoreline of Penwith. On the other side of Land's End is the great bight of Mount's Bay, where the 'nightmen' of folksong fame crept from secluded coves with 'baccy for the parson and brandy for the squire'.

The fairytale structure of St Michael's Mount dominates Mount's Bay.

MOUSEHOLE, Cornwall

Largely unchanged by time, Mousehole preserves the original character of old Cornwall in its granite houses and working harbour.

Turn left, drive to the harbour, and turn right then right again SP 'Paul', turn inland, and climb to Paul.

PAUL, Cornwall

Dorothy Pentreath, one of the last people to speak the ancient Cornish language is buried here. Inside the 15th-century church are several pieces of old armour.

Keep forward past Paul Church and after ½ mile meet a T-junction. Turn left on to the B3315 and continue for 2½ miles. A detour can be taken from the main route by turning left here on to an unclassifed road through the Lamorna Valley to Lamorna Cove.

LAMORNA COVE, Cornwall

Huge granite boulders and the rocky outcrops of this spectacular cove contrast with the gentler surrounding countryside. A granite quay and pier were built here in the last century to export granite from the quarries near by. Nowadays the cove is visited for its lovely scenery by tourists and artists.

Continue on the B3315 and in 3¼ miles, at a T-junction, turn left. Descend steeply, then climb to the edge of Treen.

TREEN, Cornwall

This tiny village lies near the fortified headland of Treryn Dinas on which stands Treen Castle (NT). Outside the local inn is a sign telling how in 1824 a nephew of Oliver Goldsmith overturned the 60 ton Logan Rock, a famous rocking stone on the headland, and how he was made to replace it at his own expense.

TREEN CASTLE (NT) Cornwall

It is believed that the defences of this excellent Iron-Age cliff castle were started between the 3rd and 2nd centuries BC. A huge bank and ditch cuts off the headland, and at the extreme tip of the rocks jutting out to sea is a bank faced with heavy masonry. Access is by footpath from Treen.

LOGAN ROCK, Cornwall

Pronounced 'loggan', the name of this curious rocking stone is derived from the Cornish verb *log*, meaning to move. It is reached by footpath from the village of Treen.

From the edge of Treen, remain on the B3315. In ¾ mile a detour from the main route can be taken by turning left on to an unclassified road for Porthcurno and the Minack Theatre.

PORTHCURNO AND THE MINACK THEATRE, Cornwall

The first transatlantic cable was brought ashore in this village. Porthcurno has an exceptionally good beach of almost white sand, and just to the south is the unique Minack Theatre — built out of living stone on the edge of the cliffs by Miss Rowena Cade in 1931. The auditorium is formed from ridges cut into the sloping rock, with the natural bedding adapted to make seats facing south and east over a stage right on the cliff edge.

Continue with the 'Land's End' road and after ½ mile turn right still with the B3315. After 2 miles turn left on to the A30 'Land's End' road, and drive to Land's End.

LAND'S END, Cornwall

Famous as England's most westerly point, Land's End is about 873 miles from the equally famous John O'Groats in Scotland. On a fine day the Isles of Scilly are visible 28 miles away to the west. A leisure and exhibition complex outlines the natural history of the area.

LONGSHIPS LIGHTHOUSE, Cornwall

Some 2 miles out to sea from Land's End the Longships Lighthouse rises 50ft high from a 60ft rock. Waves have been known to lash as high as the lantern during severe storms.

Wave torn rocks and the distant Longships Lighthouse starkly outlined against sunset at Land's End.

A short detour can be taken by turning left in St Just on to an unclassified road to Cape Cornwall.

CAPE CORNWALL, Cornwall
Features of this headland, the only 'cape' in England or Wales, include a mine chimney, prehistoric burial ground and a ruined chapel.

From St Just continue on the St Ives road B3306 to Pendeen.

On the headland at St Ives is a fishermen's chapel.

Ruined mine buildings, like the Carn Galver Mine at Morvah, add much to Cornwall's landscape.

Lanyon Quoit is situated in an area rich in prehistoric remains.

Leave Land's End and return along the A30, past the 'Porthcurno' road, to Sennen.

SENNEN, Cornwall
According to legend Sennen, a small village with a past rich in local history, was the battleground for the last Cornish fight against invading Danes. The 15th-century church contains a medieval statue of the Virgin Mary and is the most westerly church in England. Sennen Cove offers good sand, excellent bathing, and superb scenery.

Continue on the A30. After 1¾ miles turn left on to the B3306, SP 'St Just' and pass Land's End Airport. After 3 miles turn left on to the A3071 and enter St Just.

ST JUST, Cornwall
Also known as St Just-in-Penwith, this village is noted for the contents of its old church. Among these is a wall painting, an interesting inscribed stone of 5th-century date, and the shaft of a 9th-century Hiberno-Saxon cross. St Just itself is enchanting.

PENDEEN, Cornwall
Around the village are derelict remains of old mine workings; one that survived until 1986, the Geevor Mine, has an impressive tin-mining museum (may not re-open after 1986). The village church is a copy of Iona Cathedral in Scotland.

Leave Pendeen and continue along the B3306 to Morvah.

MORVAH, Cornwall
This little farming and former mining village is set on the edge of the Penwith moorland. About 1 mile south of the village are Chun Castle and Chun Quoit, respectively a circular Iron-Age fort built of stone and the remains of a large Neolithic dolmen, or tomb chamber.

Shortly beyond Morvah a detour can be taken right along an unclassified road for 2 miles to Lanyon Quoit.

LANYON QUOIT, Cornwall
Perhaps the best known and most visited of Cornwall's megaliths, this neolithic tomb (NT) resembles a huge three-legged stone table.

Remain on the B3306 through rocky and barren countryside, with occasional views of the coast; skirt the village of Zennor.

ZENNOR, Cornwall
The 15th-century church in this former tin-mining community is famous for the mermaid bench end. The writers Virginia Woolf and DH Lawrence both lived in the village in the 1920s. A folk museum here is well worth visiting.

Continue on B3306 to St Ives.

ST IVES, Cornwall
Until her recent death the sculptress Barbara Hepworth was the leading light in a famous artists' community that lived in this attractive fishing port and major holiday resort. Quaint old houses, narrow streets and alleys cluster beneath the 120ft granite tower of the 15th-century church. There are two fine sandy beaches (one for surfing), and a semi-circular harbour. Of interest are the St Ives Museum (civil and maritime history) the Barnes Museum of Cinematography, Barbara Hepworth Museum and Sculpture Garden, St Ives Society of Artists Gallery, Penwith Galleries and the Bernard Leach Pottery.

Leave St Ives on the A3074 and follow SP 'Hayle'. Pass through Carbis Bay and continue into Lelant.

LELANT, Cornwall
Lelant, on the Hayle estuary has a Norman and Perpendicular-style church with a 17th-century sundial and the Cornish Heritage Leisure Park.

At Lelant turn right and in 1 mile at a roundabout take 3rd exit A30 SP 'Penzance'. One mile beyond Crowlas take 2nd exit at roundabout onto the 'Marazion' road unclassified. Shortly turn left and cross a railway bridge to Marazion.

MARAZION, Cornwall
Good bathing and fishing can be enjoyed in this ancient port, and the marshland between Marazion and Ludgvan is the habitat for many species of bird. Marvellous views of famous St Michael's Mount can be enjoyed from here.

ST MICHAEL'S MOUNT Cornwall
This little granite island (NT) rises to a 250ft summit from the waters of Mount's Bay and is accessible by foot via a causeway at low tide, or by boat, from Marazion. Its splendid castle (NT) and priory (NT), both founded by Edward the Confessor in the 11th-century, stand high above a small harbour and hamlet. Inside the 14th-century chapel is an excellent collection of armour and furniture.

Return along the unclassifed road and turn left for Long Rock to rejoin the A30 for Penzance.

COVES OF THE LIZARD

Wreckers once used the jagged reefs and towering cliffs of the Lizard to cripple their prey. All round the peninsula's coast are stern little villages in rocky bays, towering stacks and pinnacles of multi-hued serpentine, and the constant boom of waves crashing into hidden caves.

HELSTON, Cornwall

In Elizabethan times Helston was one of Cornwall's 4 stannary or coinage towns, where all the smelted tin mined in the area was brought to be tested for quality and taxed. Even earlier it had been a busy port, until the Loe Bar formed across the mouth of the Cober River in the 13th century. Well-preserved Regency houses can be seen along Cross Street, and behind the early Victorian Guildhall is an interesting museum with many old implements, including a cider press. Local people would say that May 8 is the best day to visit the town, for that is the time of the Furry, or Floral Dance. From early in the morning the inhabitants dance through the winding streets and in and out of houses to celebrate the time a dragon dropped a rock on the town without causing any damage. About 1¼ miles south west of Helston, on the B3304, is a footpath leading left to Loe Pool.

CORNWALL AERO PARK & FLAMBARDS VICTORIAN VILLAGE, Cornwall

This is an award winning all-weather family leisure park with a large exhibition hall set in beautiful landscaped gardens. Flambards is an authentic life-size Victorian village. A special display covers Britain in the Blitz. The Aero Park has historic aircraft, vehicles, helicopters, Battle of Britain gallery, Concorde flight deck and an SR2 simulator.

Leave Helston on the A3083 SP 'Lizard'. Pass Culdrose Airfield and turn left on to the B3293, SP 'St Keverne'. The road to the viewing area is on the left in ½ mile.

CULDROSE ROYAL NAVAL AIR STATION, Cornwall

Navy search aircraft operate over a wide area of sea around Cornwall from this helicopter base. The public are only admitted to an aircraft viewing area.

Continue to the Mawgan Cross war memorial and branch left over crossroads on to an unclassified road to Mawgan. Continue on the 'Manaccan, Helford' road, through St Martin's Green to Newtown. Keep left, then in 250yds turn left again. After another 1½ miles meet crossroads and go forward, then in ¾ mile turn left and descend to Helford.

HELFORD, Cornwall

This lovely little village on the wooded banks of the Helford River is a favourite haunt of anglers and yachtsmen. The river is dotted with small villages and creeks, and a passenger ferry sails from here to Helford Passage – where there is a bright, attractive inn.

Leave Helford and return along the same road for ¾ mile. Turn left for St Anthony.

The sheltered waters and hidden creeks of Helford River once made ideal bases for the secret activities of smugglers.

ST ANTHONY, Cornwall

The church of St Anthony in Meneage stands only 30yds from the creek. Its chancel and parts of the south wall are Norman, and tradition holds that it was built by shipwrecked Norman sailors as a thank-offering to St Anthony for saving them from drowning. The tranquil scenery of Gillan Creek presents a charming, timeless picture of Cornish maritime life.

Leaving St Anthony drive alongside the creek and after 1 mile turn left, SP 'St Keverne'. Climb to the edge of Gillan, keep right and follow signs for St Keverne.

A fisherman's cottage in Cadgwith.

ST KEVERNE, Cornwall

At first glance St Keverne could be mistaken for a town rather than a village, on account of its large windswept square and church. The latter dates from the 15th century and carries an unusual octagonal spire which has been a welcome landmark for sailors for hundreds of years. Just 1 mile offshore are the treacherous Manacle Rocks, which have made shipwrecks a gruesome part of the village's history. Over 400 victims are buried at the church, including 126 people who died when the *Primrose* was wrecked in 1809. Two miles south-west is a Bronze-Age burial chamber known as the Three Brothers of Grugwith.

Leave St Keverne on the B3293 'Coverack and Helston' road. After 1¼ miles turn left on to an unclassified road and later join the B3294. From here descend into Coverack.

COVERACK, Cornwall

Smugglers once frequented this small fishing village, and wreckers lured unsuspecting vessels on to the Manacle Rocks to plunder their cargoes. Coverack formerly had a lifeboat station that was established after a particularly bad series of disasters. The harbour is overlooked by thatched cottages.

Climb out of Coverack on the B3294 'Helston' road, then join the B3293, and in 2½ miles at crossroads turn left on to an unclassified road SP 'Cadgwith'. Views to the right take in Goonhilly Downs Satellite Communications Station.

GOONHILLY DOWNS, Cornwall

Goonhilly Downs, a small windswept moor only about 7 square miles in area, was once covered by oak forests. Nowadays there is nothing here but a bleak stretch of gorse and heather dominated by the huge radio aerials of the Satellite Communications Station.

Drive over Goonhilly Downs for 3 miles and at Kuggar meet a T-junction. A detour from the main route leads left to Kennack Sands.

Goonhilly Downs Satellite Communications Station receives signals from all over the world.

KENNACK SANDS, Cornwall

Wide firm sands, wave-ribbed and dotted with large shallow pools at low tide, make this a perfect beach for families with children.

Turn right and in ¾ mile at crossroads, turn left for Ruan Minor. At the village turn right and make descent (1 in 4) to Cadgwith.

CADGWITH, Cornwall

Cadgwith's attractive thatched cottages overlook a stone strand dotted with beached boats and the paraphernalia of a working fishing community. All along the coast are sandy coves, and to the south is the great tidal chasm the Devil's Frying Pan. This was formed when a vast sea cave collapsed, and is at its scenic best in stormy weather.

Leave Cadgwith, continue with an unclassified road SP 'Lizard', and ascend. In ¾ mile turn right, then after another ¾ mile turn left on to the A3083 for Lizard.

LIZARD, Cornwall

A mile from Lizard is the headland of Lizard Point, the southernmost tip of a lovely peninsula that has become famous for its outstanding natural beauty (NT). In the heather and bogs of the interior rivulets and streams rise to chatter down to the beach through small valleys and, occasionally, as miniature falls over the edge of the cliffs. Many rare plants grow here, and some of the

area is leased to the Cornwall Naturalists' Trust. Splendid walks extend along the clifftops of the Point. To the east the countryside is sheltered from the full force of Atlantic gales and is lush and green, but round the Point to the west everything becomes wilder and more desolate. Much of the land on this side is pitted with holes left by people digging for the mineral serpentine, a lovely stone prized for the rich shades of greens, reds and purple released by cutting and polishing. Magnificent views from Lizard Point extend many miles along the Cornish coast to Rame Head, (near Plymouth), and when ideal conditions prevail, as far as Bolt Head in the South Hams district of Devon. This superb vantage point forms an ideal site for the Lizard Lighthouse.

Leave Lizard by returning along the A3083 SP 'Helston'. After ½ mile a detour can be made from the main route along a toll road to breathtaking Kynance Cove.

KYNANCE COVE, Cornwall

Serpentine is seen at its very best in Kynance Cove, where spectacular formations of the mineral rise in pillars, stacks, and pyramids from a flat surface of firm sand. An infinity of shades from red through to green, blue and purple lace exposed rock surfaces and ornament the insides of sea-bored caves. High above the surrealistic beach is a stark promontory that affords wonderful views along the coast. Slightly inland is a softer landscape of grass and flowers alongside small streams that eventually trickle from the cliff edge to the beach far below.

Continue with the main tour route on the A3083, and after 3¼ miles turn left on to the B3296 for Mullion. From Mullion a possible detour from the main route leads left along the B3296 to lovely Mullion Cove.

Sea, rocks, and sand combine to create a spectacular seascape at Kynance Cove.

MULLION COVE, Cornwall

Almost as dramatic as Kynance, this superb cove is fringed by steep, cave-pocked cliffs that form a splendid counterpoint to rocky Mullion Island, just offshore. The small harbour (NT) here is used by local fishermen and visiting skin divers.

MULLION, Cornwall

Here the local rock changes from the colourful serpentine to greenstone, a very hard mineral that will spark when struck with steel. The village itself is large, with several shops, and boasts a fine 15th-century church. Notable bench ends inside the latter date from the 16th-century and depict a jester, a monk, Instruments of the Passion, and a few profiles.

At Mullion keep left (one-way) then turn right down an unclassified road for Poldhu Cove.

Mullion Cove is protected from Atlantic breakers by its sturdy harbour walls.

POLDHU COVE, Cornwall

A pleasant beach fringes the sheltered waters of this inlet. On top of the cliffs, which are composed of an unstable slate and clay mixture known as killas, the Marconi Memorial commemorates the first successful transatlantic radio signal in 1901. Some 22 years later this same spot was used for the testing of a short-wave beam system. At the beginning of the century the headland was covered in masts, aerials, wire, and sheds. All that remains now is the simple stone memorial and a few foundations.

Continue from Poldhu Cove, cross a bridge, and ascend to Cury.

CURY, Cornwall

The village church of St Corentin is set in a high windy churchyard and probably dates back to Norman times. It has since been added to.

Continue through the village and in ¼ mile turn left, SP 'Helston'. In 1¾ miles turn left again to rejoin the A3083. Return to Helston.

NEWQUAY, Cornwall

Magnificent beaches, fine scenery, and a wide range of amenities for the holiday-maker have made Newquay one of the most popular seaside resorts in Cornwall. The original Iron-Age settlement was to the north east at Porth Island, where today's tourists admire the grand cliffs and splendid caves. Since the first train arrived here in 1875 tourism has been the main factor in Newquay's growth. The railway originally came to bring china clay and tin to the port, but the harbour proved too small and shallow for large cargo ships. Because of this the harbour has retained some of its original character and preserved a number of old structures. Another area of historic charm is St Columb Minor, once the mother parish of Newquay but now just a suburb. Amongst its old and attractive cottages is the church of St Columba, whose 115ft pinnacled and lichen-covered 15th-century tower is considered one of the finest in the country. Visitors can enjoy the amusement park in Trenance Garden, which also boasts the only zoo in Cornwall, and the mile-long main beach is close to the town. Between Newquay and the surfing beach at Fistral is the rock-strewn promontory of Towan Head, which affords magnificent views.

Leave Newquay on the A392 SP 'Bodmin' and continue to Quintrell Downs. Drive over a level crossing, then at roundabout SP 'St Austell' go forward on to the A3058. After ¾ mile turn right on to a narrow unclassified road SP 'Newlyn East'. Continue for 1 mile to Trerice Manor, on the right.

TRERICE MANOR, Cornwall

With its grey curving gables and E-shaped entrance front, Trerice Manor (NT) has hardly changed since it was first built by Sir John Arundell in 1573. Sir John, a member of an old and influential Cornish family, spent a great deal of time soldiering in the Low Countries. When he returned to his native Cornwall he did not entirely forget foreign parts, as the design of the house shows. Excellent plasterwork on the ceilings and fire-places is acknowledged as the most outstanding feature of the interior.

Continue for 1 mile then at crossroads turn left. In ½ mile at a T-junction turn right. A detour can be taken from the main route by turning left and driving for ½ mile to the Lappa Valley Railway.

LAPPA VALLEY RAILWAY, Cornwall

This 15-inch gauge line built on part of the former Great Western route between Newquay and Chacewater runs through a 2-mile circuit of valley scenery. A stop is made at East Wheal Rose Halt, where passengers can disembark to explore a children's leisure park and the site of an old silver and lead mine.

Continue to St Newlyn East.

ATLANTIC SEASCAPES

Long, foam-capped rollers crash on to ideal surfing beaches between the craggy headlands and promontories of Cornwall's Atlantic coast. Away from the shore is the gentle rise and fall of downland, scored by deep lanes and scattered with the beautifully decayed remains of mine buildings.

ST NEWLYN EAST, Cornwall

Known as St Newlyn East to distinguish it from the port of Newlyn near Penzance, this attractive village was probably the original settlement of Saint Newelina, the Cornish martyr to whom the parish church is dedicated. Beautiful examples of Norman and medieval carving can be seen inside the church, including particularly fine pieces of 14th-century work.

The estuary of the River Gannel opens out to form Crantock Beach.

Follow signs 'Truro', and continue for 1 mile to Fiddler's Green. Turn left, then after 1¼ miles meet crossroads. Go forward SP 'Zelah' then turn right on to the A30. Go through Zelah and in ½ mile turn left on to an unclassified road SP 'Shortlanesend'. Continue for 2 miles to reach the Shortlanesend Inn, and join the B3284 for Truro.

TRURO, Cornwall

Cathedral city of Cornwall and the county's unofficial capital, Truro stands where the rivers Allen and Kenwyn join to form the large Fal-estuary inlet known as the Truro River. Until 1752 the town was one of Cornwall's 4 stannery or coinage towns, to which all smelted tin had to be brought to be tested for quality and taxed. During this time it developed into an important centre for the export of mineral ores, and in the 18th century it became a focus of social life to rival even Bath, the country's then most fashionable town. Among the fine Georgian structures surviving from the period is the outstanding Lemon Street, which was laid out c1795 and is complemented by Walsingham Place, a beautiful early 19th-century crescent just off Victoria Place. The former Assembly Rooms date from c1770 and were the main gathering place for 18th-century society. One of Cornwall's oldest and most famous potteries, Lake's, still works in Chapel Street, and is open to visitors. Edward VII, then the Prince of Wales, laid the cathedral's foundation stone in 1880. Various types of Cornish granite were used in the building's construction, and it stands on the site of the 16th-century church of St Mary. Part of the older building is retained in the east end. The Truro Museum, in River Street, is considered to be the finest in Cornwall and has a number of exhibits depicting the history of the local mineral industries.

Leave Truro following SP 'Redruth' on the A390. In 4 miles meet a roundabout and take the 2nd exit. Continue for a further 2¼ miles to another roundabout and take the 3rd exit on to the B3277 SP 'St Agnes'. Continue to St Agnes.

One of the Wheal Coates engine houses on the cliffs at Chapel Porth near St Agnes.

Atlantic waves have sculpted the natural arch at Perranporth.

Terraced gardens surround Trerice Manor, which became National Trust property in 1954. The house itself shows considerable Dutch influence, brought from the low countries by its builder Sir John Arundell.

Truro Cathedral is a good example of 19th-century church architecture.

ST AGNES, Cornwall

St Agnes is one of those Cornish villages that has retained its charm and character despite the burden of two centuries of mining and one century of tourism. Decaying engine houses and wildflower-covered burrows bear silent witness to the mineral booms of years gone by, and ¼ mile north is Trevaunance Cove – a lovely place with excellent sands. Many futile attempts have been made to build a harbour here, and remains of 18th-century piers from the last try can be seen at the western end of the cove. St Agnes itself fits snugly round the parish church, which was rebuilt in Cornish style during the mid-19th century but is unusual in having a slender spire. Among the pleasant streets and by-ways of the village is the quaint Stippy-Stappy, a steep and stepped row of slate-roofed cottages leading down Town Hill. The well-known beauty spot of St Agnes Beacon lies to the west. Also of interest are the St Agnes Leisure Park with five different themes, and the Little Puppet Theatre.

ST AGNES BEACON, Cornwall

It is said that 32 church towers and 23 miles of coast can be seen from 628ft St Agnes Beacon (NT), perhaps the most prominent landmark in the area. Much of the surrounding area (part NT) has been worked for minerals in times past, but the many mining scars and old buildings add a melancholy beauty rather than the sense of desecration that usually pervades industrial sites. Bolster's Dyke, a 2-mile earthwork on the Beacon, is named after a legendary giant who is supposed to have lived there in ancient times.

WHEAL COATES ENGINE HOUSE, Cornwall

One of the Wheal Coates engine houses, (NT) stands precariously on a forbidding cliff to the west of St Agnes Beacon. It contained a pumping engine for the Towanroath shaft and from a sea-cave below it is possible to look up one of the shafts beneath the pump-house.

Leave St Agnes on the B3285 Perranporth road and continue through Trevellas, then in 1 mile descend into Perranporth.

PERRANPORTH, Cornwall

Terraces of hotels and guesthouses rise from the sea-level centre of this popular resort which was formerly a mining centre. Even though it lacks the quaint cottages and blue-jerseyed fishermen the public expect of the west, visitors find a more than ample attraction in the magnificent bay that sweeps away to the north. This boasts a 3-mile stretch of smooth golden sand, and is reputed to be where surfing was introduced into Britain. Penhale Point offers spectacular rock scenery, and the sands at this end of the beach have been blown into large dunes. Near by, on the road to Goonhavern, is the 2,000-year old hilltop enclosure of St Piran's Round (AM).

ST PIRAN'S CHURCH, Cornwall

Perranporth is in the parish of *Perranzabuloe* which means 'St Piran in the Sand'. St Piran is thought to have come to Cornwall from Ireland in the 6th-century, and legend has it that he wasn't always sober. However, he is said to have taught the Cornish the art of smelting and was adopted as the patron saint of tinners. He built his church north of Perranporth on the Penhale Sands, but by the 11th century shifting dunes had closed in and completely enveloped the little building. It wasn't until the 19th century that it was excavated, and nowadays it is housed in a concrete shell to protect it from further damage. The mile-long walk over easy ground to see the church is well worth the effort.

Leave Perranporth on the B3285 SP 'Newquay' and in 2 miles at Goonhavern turn left on to the A3075. In 2½ miles turn left on to an unclassified road for Cubert.

CUBERT, Cornwall

High above the sandy landscape round Cubert is the spire of the church, a local landmark. Although restored in 1852 the interior of the church preserves fine Norman and 14th-century carvings and a font. In a café in the village centre are the granite remains of a 17th-century Cornish cider press.

A pleasant detour from the main route can be taken to Holywell, some 1¼ miles beyond Cubert.

HOLYWELL, Cornwall

The large beach at Holywell Bay is quieter than most on this coastline and offers good bathing except at low tide. At the north end is a freshwater spring that gave the place its name, one of the holy wells of Cornwall. It can only be reached at low tide via steps cut into the cliff. Magnificent views can be enjoyed from Penhale Point.

Leave Cubert by the Crantock road. Continue for 1½ miles to reach Crantock.

CRANTOCK, Cornwall

A plaque records that the old stocks in the churchyard here were last used in 1817 on a 'Smuggler's son and a vagabond'. This is not surprising since the village was once notorious for its involvement in contraband. The church itself is a showpiece of Edwardian restoration. Attractive countryside (NT) lines the steep-sided estuary of the River Gannel which flows past the popular sands of Crantock Beach.

Leave Crantock on an unclassified road SP 'Newquay'. In ¾ mile turn left on to another unclassified road and continue for 1 mile to the A3075. Turn left and return to Newquay.

BETWEEN BODMIN AND THE SEA

Majestic cliffs indented by tiny harbours are typical of north Cornwall. So also are the long sands of Bude Bay, the eerie enchantment of Arthur's Castle at Tintagel, and the dark counterpoint of Bodmin Moor rising inland.

WADEBRIDGE, Cornwall
One of the finest medieval bridges in England can be seen here. Built c 1485 and widened in 1849, it spans the River Camel with 17 arches and measures 320ft long. It is thought that packs of wool may have been sunk into the river bed to make firm bases for the piers.

Leave Wadebridge on the A39 'Bude' road. Cross the bridge and turn left, then in ½ mile turn left on to the B3314 SP 'Port Isaac'. After 3 miles turn left again on to an unclassified road SP 'Rock'. In a further 1½ miles turn left into Pityme then take the next turning right SP 'Polzeath'. A detour from the main route can be made by continuing ahead for 1 mile to Rock.

ROCK, Cornwall
Rock lies opposite Padstow on the lovely Camel Estuary. The small Church of St Michael, at nearby Porthilly, was dug from drifting sand and houses a simple Norman font.

Continue along the main tour route and pass through Trebetherick to reach Polzeath.

POLZEATH, Cornwall
Safe bathing and excellent sands that offer some of the best surfing in Cornwall are the main attractions of Polzeath. The village stands on Padstow Bay and the wide Camel estuary, within easy reach of beautiful walking country (NT) round Portquin. Fine views over Portquin Bay can be enjoyed from Pentire Head, to the north.

Tintagel Castle is divided in two by a breathtaking chasm.

Leave Polzeath and ascend sharply. After 2 miles branch left SP 'Port Isaac'. In ½ mile turn left on to the B3314 for St Endellion.

ST ENDELLION, Cornwall
Although inland from sheltered Portquin Bay, St Endellion occupies an exposed site and often feels the full force of the gales for which this part of the country is known. Its beautiful compact church was built from Lundy Island granite. Inside, under the 18th-century tower arch, are several quaint bell-ringer's rhymes. A number of amusing and somewhat irreverent Georgian epitaphs can be seen on old gravestones in the churchyard.

Continue along the B3314 for 1 mile, then turn left on to the B3267 for Port Isaac.

PORT ISAAC, Cornwall
In the old part of this outstandingly picturesque fishing village the houses huddle together along a steep coombe and down to the harbour.

Turn right onto an unclassified road and descend to Port Gaverne. Pass through the village and climb inland. After 2½ miles rejoin the B3314 and continue to Delabole.

DELABOLE, Cornwall
At one time most of the roofs in Cornwall came from the ancient slate quarry in this village, which is estimated to have been worked continuously for at least 350 years. Britain's deepest man-made hole, it has a depth of 500ft and a circumference of 1½ miles.

Since the 19th century Boscastle has declined as a port but developed as a resort.

Continue on the B3314 for 1¾ miles, then turn left on to an unclassified road SP 'Tintagel'. After ½ mile keep forward to join the B3263 then keep left. Just before the village of Trewarmett a road to the left offers a pleasant detour to Trebarwith Strand.

TREBARWITH STRAND, Cornwall
The good beach in this cove is crossed by a natural slate causeway, which leads down to the water's edge from the high-water line.

Continue through Trewarmett on the main tour route and drive to Tintagel.

TINTAGEL, Cornwall
The name Tintagel is highly evocative of the Arthurian legends, but the only King Arthur's Hall here nowadays is the modern home of the Fellowship of the Round Table. The local post office (NT) is a superb slate-built structure that dates from the 14th century and was originally a small manor house. Norman workmanship is very evident in the local church, but its origins are probably farther back in Saxon times. A Norman font and Roman milestone can be seen inside.

TINTAGEL CASTLE, Cornwall
Near Tintagel is the romantic ruined castle (AM) that, according to legend, was the birthplace of King Arthur. Its remains post-date that giant of Western folklore by some 7 centuries, but traces of a Celtic monastery (AM) founded early enough to have accommodated him can be seen close by. The castle itself was built on its wave-lashed promontory, now almost cut in half by the sea, by Reginald, Earl of Cornwall and illegitimate son of Henry I, in the 12th century. Views from here take in the entire North Cornish coast from Pentire Point to Hartland Point.

From the Wharncliffe Arms Hotel in Tintagel follow the B3263 'Boscastle' road, and shortly pass through Bossiney. Continue for another ½ mile to reach Rocky Valley.

The ancient slate post office at Tintagel.

```
mls  0   1   2   3   4   5
kms  0   2   4   6   8
```

Slate from the vast quarry at Delabole has roofed buildings throughout the West Country.

Rockpools are a feature of Widemouth Bay, which is situated to the south of Bude.

ROCKY VALLEY, Cornwall

Trees, stone, and water all contribute their own particular magic to the wonderful scenery of Rocky Valley, a deep cut sloping down to the sea. About 1 mile along the valley is its most magnificent feature, the 40ft waterfall of St Nectan's Kieve. Nectan (or Knighton) was a Celtic hermit saint said to have had an oratory beside the kieve (basin).

Continue on the B3263, pass through Trethevey and after 1¾ miles turn left with the B3263 SP 'Bude'. Descend steeply through a hairpin bend to Boscastle.

BOSCASTLE, Cornwall

The tiny harbour here is at the head of a deep S-shaped inlet between high cliffs, and the combined Valency and Jordan rivers meet incoming tides with dramatic effect when the moon is full and the rivers are running at full spate. Even on a calm day the sea can be impressive. A local blowhole amply demonstrates the force of the water. Boscastle itself is an attractive village arranged round a long, broad street that climbs steeply through woodland. Close to the harbour is a witches' museum of interesting (and often gruesome) relics associated with magic and witchcraft. At one time the local seal population was severely reduced by hunters, but this industry is now controlled.

Leave Boscastle, cross a river bridge, and ascend (1 in 6). After 2¾ miles turn left and immediately turn left on to an unclassified road SP 'Crackington Haven'. Later descend steeply into the village of Crackington Haven.

CRACKINGTON HAVEN, Cornwall

This tiny seaside village stands on a rugged stretch of coast and has a good surfing beach. High Cliff, to the south, drops 700ft in a series of weathered faces and terraces.

Leave Crackington Haven and ascend. After 3 miles reach the village of Wainhouse Corner and turn left on to the A39 SP 'Bude'. Continue past Treskinnick Cross, then 1¼ miles farther turn left on to an unclassified road SP 'Widemouth'. After ¾ mile follow the wide sweep of Widemouth Bay to Bude.

BUDE, Cornwall

This small resort near the mouth of the River Neet was once the port for the Bude Canal which ran inland to Launceston. The town's history is displayed in the Historical and Folk Museum on the canal wharf. Also in the town is the World of Nature Exhibition covering local natural history and geology and including an aquarium.

Leave Bude on the A3072 'Bideford' road. After 1¼ miles turn left on to the A39, and in ¼ mile, turn right rejoining the A3072, SP 'Holsworthy'. Drive into Stratton.

STRATTON, Cornwall

This picturesque grouping of attractive houses and thatched cottages has a peaceful atmosphere that belies its turbulent history. In 1643 a Civil War battle was fought here and is re-enacted every May by the Sealed Knot Society. The Tree Inn was the headquarters of Sir Bevil Grenville before he led his Cavaliers to victory at Stamford Hill, just north of the village. Local legend recalls Anthony Payne, a 7ft giant who was born in the Tree Inn and was a retainer in Sir Bevil's household. The village church dates from the 15th century and houses good 16th-century brasses.

Continue on the A3072 'Holsworthy' road. After 2¾ miles at the Red Post Cross turn right on to the B3254 SP 'Launceston'.

Drive along the B3254 to Whitstone and ¾ mile beyond the village turn right on to an unclassified road SP 'Week St Mary'. Continue for 1¼ miles, meet crossroads, and drive straight on towards Canworthy Water. After 2 miles on this narrow road turn right for Canworthy Water. Here keep straight on and after 1 mile ascend to Warbstow.

WARBSTOW, Cornwall

Warbstow Bury is one of the finest Iron-Age hillforts in Cornwall. Situated at 750ft it provides extensive views in all directions except the south-west.

Continue to Hallworthy, turn right on to the A395, and in another 2¾ miles turn left on to the A39 SP 'Wadebridge'. Continue to Camelford.

CAMELFORD, Cornwall

One of the more obscure Arthurian legends places Camelford as having been the site of Camelot, the fabulous city of King Arthur and his Knights of the Round Table. Slaughter Bridge, which crosses the Camel River 1 mile north of the town, is one of several contenders for the title 'Arthur's last battleground'.

The North Cornwall Museum and Gallery contains many items on Cornish rural life.

Leave Camelford on the A39 and keep straight on. Pass through Helstone, crossing the River Allen at Knightsmill, and continue to St Kew Highway.

ST KEW HIGHWAY, Cornwall

Old stocks are preserved in the porch of the village church, and inside is a very fine Elizabethan pulpit decorated with ornamental panels. Also here is a stone inscribed with characters of the Celtic Ogham script, an ancient form of writing.

Remain on the A39 and return to Wadebridge.

PLYMOUTH AND THE WESTERN MOOR

This is the country of Drake and Raleigh, of large adventures in small boats and salty tales that the historians have somehow missed. North are the water-sculpted tors and heathy slopes of western Dartmoor, a place of vast spaces patterned with the shadows of clouds.

PLYMOUTH, Devon

Sandwiched between the estuaries of the Plym and the Tamar, this popular yachting resort and important maritime city is the venue for national sailing championships and a stop-off point for round-the-world yachtsmen. It has been a naval base since the 16th century, and in the 17th the Pilgrim Fathers sailed from its Sutton Harbour to the New World of America in the *Mayflower*. Today Sutton Harbour is busy with large and small boats, and the craft and antique shops, pubs and restaurants of the Barbican make it an exciting district of modern Plymouth as well as a fascinating historic memorial. Most of the city centre was rebuilt after appalling war damage, and the area where Royal Parade is bisected by spacious Armada Way includes a fine shopping complex. The 200ft-high Civic Centre affords excellent cross-town views from its roof deck. A prominent statue of Sir Francis Drake shares the Hoe with Smeaton's Tower (open), which is the re-erected base of the old Eddystone Lighthouse and the impressive Naval War Memorial. Near by are the 17th-century Royal Citadel (AM) and the outstanding aquarium of the Marine Biological Association. Rising from the waters of the sound, almost in front of the Hoe, is the rocky, tree-scattered hump of Drake's Island (NT). The city's Church of St Andrew is the largest in Devon and dates from the 15th century. Close by are Prysten House, the city's oldest building (open), the Victorian Guildhall and the Elizabethan Merchant's House (open). Also of interest are the Elizabethan House and Wall Mural in the Barbican, Charles Church (city war memorial) and the Museum and Art Gallery containing works by Reynolds. Across the estuary is Mount Edgcumbe, which can be reached via the Cremyll Passenger Ferry from Plymouth.

MOUNT EDGCUMBE HOUSE & COUNTRY PARK, Cornwall

This beautiful Tudor mansion (open) was severely damaged during World War II but has since been completely restored. Its lovely gardens and parkland offer extensive views of Plymouth Sound.

DEVONPORT, Devon

Although Devonport started life with an identity of its own, the establishment of the important naval dockyard on the Hamoaze in 1691 resulted in its rapid development into the navy quarter of neighbouring Plymouth. Its fine 19th-century town hall was by the architect John Foulston, and older foundations include the Gun Wharf of 1718 and the Royal Naval Hospital, also of the 18th century.

THE TAMAR BRIDGES, Devon Devon

Spanning the Tamar river north-west of Plymouth city centre are two famous bridges that have opened up the West Country to tourism. The oldest is the Royal Albert, a railway bridge designed by the brilliant engineer Brunel and completed in 1859. Close by is a modern, single-span suspension road bridge opened in 1961 with a lightness and grace that contrast sharply with the heavy solidity of its elderly neighbour.

From Plymouth follow SP 'Exeter' to reach Marsh Mills roundabout. Take 3rd exit onto the Plympton road B3416 and cross the River Plym. Shortly on the left is a road to the Plym Valley Railway then in ½ mile pass a road on the right leading to Saltram House.

Monuments to their times — these two handsome bridges span the Tamar at Saltash.

Sir Francis Drake's statue stands on Plymouth Hoe.

SALTRAM HOUSE, Devon

This fine Tudor house (NT) has an 18th-century façade and contains a saloon and dining room by designer Robert Adam. Features of the lovely garden include an 18th-century summer house and a quaint orangery dating from 1773.

Continue on the B3416 for a further ¾ mile and meet a mini-roundabout. A short detour from the main route to the centre of Plympton can be made from here by keeping forward.

PLYMPTON, Devon

In medieval times Plymouth was an insignificant little hamlet called Sutton, and Plympton an important town with a wealthy priory. Since then the elder community has

become a suburb of the successful younger. A Norman keep on a mound affords goods views. There are two medieval churches, a 16th-century guildhall, and an old grammar school where the painter Sir Joshua Reynolds, who was born in the town, was educated. At the Plym Valley Railway project (no trains running at present) a varied collection of locomotives can be seen.

From the mini-roundabout on the main route turn left SP 'Exeter', and in another ½ mile turn left again SP 'Sparkwell' and 'Cornwood'. In ¼ mile at a mini-roundabout turn right, and continue to Sparkwell. Beyond the village reach the Dartmoor Wildlife Park on the left.

DARTMOOR WILDLIFE PARK, Devon

A fine collection of British and European animals can be seen in this 25-acre zoo park. Excellent all-round views of the grounds are afforded by a tall observation tower.

Continue through Lutton to Cornwood.

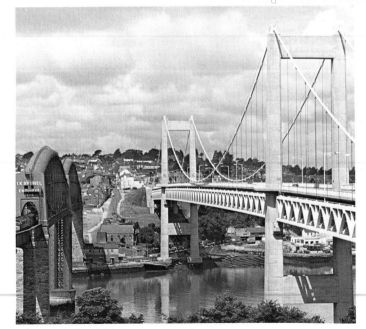

CORNWOOD, Devon

The Hawns ravine on the River Yealm is a feature of this attractively situated village. Dendles Wood incorporates a national nature reserve, and there are numerous Bronze-Age enclosures and hut circles in the district. Fardell and Stert, family seats of the Raleighs and Drakes lie 1½ miles south.

At crossroads turn left SP 'Tavistock'. Begin a gradual ascent with Penn Beacon prominent on the right before skirting the industrial features of Lee Moor village.

Tunnel on the Tavistock Canal above Morwellham Quay.

LEE MOOR, Devon

Colossal conical mountains of white waste dominate the landscape here, proclaiming Lee Moor as Devon's principal source of china clay.

Continue, with wide views, to a crossroads and turn right. In 1¾ miles reach Cadover Bridge on the River Plym and bear left. Trowlesworthy Warren nature trail is to the right here.

TROWLESWORTHY WARREN, Devon

This 1¾-mile nature trail flanks the south-west corner of Dartmoor alongside the River Plym. Prehistoric hut circles can be seen near the river's headwaters.

Ascend, and at the summit turn right SP 'Sheepstor, Meavy'. Descend into Meavy Valley, crossing the river to reach the edge of Meavy. A short detour can be made into the village by turning left here.

MEAVY, Devon

The stream from which this delightful village takes its name winds through woodlands over a rocky bed and pours over a small waterfall. Beside the Norman church on the village green is an ancient oak which is traditionally held to be the church's contemporary.

Cox Tor is situated north of the B3357 road between Tavistock and Merrivale.

Continue forward on the main drive SP 'Princetown' and in ½ mile turn sharp right SP 'Burrator'. In ¾ mile turn right again SP 'Sheepstor' and cross the dam of Burrator Reservoir. In another ¾ mile turn left. A short detour to Sheepstor village can be made by bearing right here.

SHEEPSTOR & THE BURRATOR RESERVOIR, Devon

This enchanting hamlet is centred round an appealing little granite church. The picturesque Burrator Reservoir offers a dramatic backcloth, its sparkling waters reflecting the height of Sheeps Tor and the wooded slopes that rise from the opposite shore.

Skirt the reservoir on a narrow road and after 3 miles turn sharp right SP 'Princetown'. Ascend, and in ¾ mile meet crossroads and turn right again on to the B3212. Climb on to the wide, open moorland of Dartmoor National Park to reach Princetown. On the approach to Princetown are views left of 1,695ft North Hessary Tor and a BBC transmitter.

DARTMOOR NATIONAL PARK (WEST), Devon

Much of this tour is in the south-western part of this vast area, and near Princetown it climbs on to the rugged uplands of the moor itself. The landscape is dramatic and full of contrast, where jagged granite tors rise, from heather and bracken-clad slopes and peat bogs constantly replenished by the highest rainfall in Devon, though here and there great plantations of conifers are helping to dry the ground and bring back the forests that once stood here. Prehistoric crosses and hut circles are common in these parts.

PRINCETOWN, Devon

Sir Thomas Tyrwhitt founded the great convict prison here in 1806 and named the town in honour of his friend, the Prince Regent. Forced labour built many of the roads that allow modern motorists to tour comfortably through remote parts of the moor, and the town church was built by prisoners in 1883.

Turn left on to the B3357 'Tavistock' road, shortly passing the prison, then in 1 mile meet a T-junction and turn left again. Great Mis Tor rises to 1,768ft to the right, and views ahead encompass the Tamar valley and Bodmin Moor. Gradually descend from Dartmoor itself and pass Merrivale Quarry in the Walkham Valley to leave the Dartmoor National Park and enter Tavistock.

Buckland Abbey contains many items connected with Sir Francis Drake, including a portrait of Elizabeth I in panelled Drake's Drawing Room.

TAVISTOCK, Devon

There is an imposing town hall and remains of an abbey founded in the 10th-century. St Eustace's church, 15th-century, has interesting monuments and there is a statue of Sir Frances Drake born at Crowndale just south of the town. Light engineering and timber-working firms in this pleasant market town continue an industrial tradition that started at least as far back as the 14th century. Despite this activity the town remains unspoilt, an ideal touring base on the western fringe of the extensive Dartmoor National Park.;

Leave Tavistock on the A390 'Liskeard' road. In 2½ miles reach the Harvest Home PH and branch left on to an unclassified road SP 'Morwellham'. In 1 mile meet crossroads and go forward, SP 'Morwellham'. Follow a long descent to Morwellham Quay.

MORWELLHAM QUAY, Devon

This quay was once a busy copper-loading port on the River Tamar. Surviving installations now form part of a major industrial museum featuring the history of the port in particular and the development of the Devon copper mines in general.

Return to the crossroads and turn sharp right SP 'Bere Alston'. Continue along a high ridge between the Tamar and Tavy valleys, and after 2¾ miles turn sharp left SP 'Denham Bridge, Plymouth'. After a long descent cross the River Tavy at Denham Bridge and immediately turn right SP 'Plymouth'. Ascend to a T-junction and turn right SP 'Buckland Abbey'. In ½ mile meet crossroads and turn right, passing the entrance to Buckland Abbey on the right, then immediately left.

BUCKLAND ABBEY, Devon

Originally built by Cistercian monks in 1278, Buckland Abbey was considerably altered and adapted as a dwelling place by the Grenville family. The present house (NT) was sold to Sir Francis Drake in 1581, and nowadays contains a Drake Museum full of relics associated with the great sailor.

In 1¾ miles drive to crossroads at the edge of Roborough Down and turn left. Meet a T-junction and turn right on to the A386 (no SP) for Plymouth. Pass through Roborough, and Plymouth Airport on the return to the city centre.

DARTMOOR NATIONAL PARK (EAST), Devon

The south-eastern edge of the vast national park that surrounds Dartmoor proper is a kinder country than the wild, high plateau farther inland. Here are wind-haunted heathlands clad with bracken and heather, where granite outcrops raise strange weathered silhouettes against the sky and the remains of prehistoric settlements survive underfoot. Country lanes strung with picturesque villages of thatch and stone lead into lush river valleys.

ASHBURTON, Devon

Once an important tin and cloth centre on a popular coaching route, Ashburton makes an ideal base from which to tour this side of the national park. Its narrow streets and old tile-hung houses impart their own particular charm to the town, and the fine local church features a characteristic Devon stair turret. The local museum includes American Indian antiques.

From Ashburton follow SP 'Buckland' along an unclassified road and shortly turn left across the River Ashburn. Ascend, and pass beneath the slopes of Buckland Beacon.

BUCKLAND BEACON, Devon

At the summit of this 1,282ft hill, which commands good all-round views, is the Ten Commandments Stone, carved by a local stonemason.
Continue to Buckland-in-the-Moor.

BUCKLAND-IN-THE-MOOR, Devon

Although visited by many people as one of the county's show villages, Buckland-in-the-Moor remains unspoilt. Its 15th- and 16th-century church contains a notable rood-screen, and the church clock has an unusual dial on which the hours are marked by the letters 'My Dear Mother' instead of numbers.

Continue and in 1 mile at a T-junction, turn left SP 'Widecombe'. Descend into the attractive East Webburn Valley and cross the river, then ascend to another T-junction. Turn right, and in 1 mile enter Widecombe-in-the-Moor.

WIDECOMBE-IN-THE-MOOR, Devon

Probably the best known and by far the most commercialized of the Dartmoor villages, Widecombe stands at 800ft and is dominated by the 120ft tower of its fine 14th-century church - often referred to as the Cathedral of the Moor. Adjacent are the Church House (NT) and the green, where the Widdecombe Fair of song fame is held on the second Tuesday in September.

Leave by the 'Bovey Tracey' road, bearing right past the green, and ascend on to open moorland. Later pass 1,560ft Rippon Tor on the right and enjoy magnificent views over South Devon to Torbay. To the left are 1,350ft Saddle Tor and the famous Haytor Rocks (1,490ft).

BELOW THE HIGH MOOR

Below the desolate summits of the high moor is a gentler country, where small rivers tumble through deep wooded valleys, and mellow old towns maintain a pace of life long gone elsewhere in England. Here were the tin, wool, and market centres of Dartmoor - the focuses of Devonshire life.

Ancient farmsteads shelter in many of Dartmoor's deep coombs.

HAYTOR ROCKS, Devon

These rocks rise 100ft above the surrounding moorland heights and form one of the most spectacular crags in the national park. They are easily accessible by car, simple to climb, and afford superb views as far as the coast and the rich, cultivated lowlands of Devon. During the 19th century stone worked from nearby quarries was loaded on to a tramway and hauled some 6 miles to a canal wharf at Teigngrace by horses. The route is still visible in places.

The church at Widecombe-in-the-Moor.

Descend to the Bovey Valley and after 3 miles at crossroads by the Edgemoor Hotel turn left, and in ½ mile turn left again on to the B3344 SP 'Manaton'. Shortly pass the Yarner Wood National Nature Reserve on the left.

YARNER WOOD NATIONAL NATURE RESERVE, Devon

This reserve protects the mature stands of oak, holly, birch, and rowan that make up an unspoilt woodland rich with birdlife. A nature trail has been laid out here, and details are available from the entrance lodge.

Continue a winding climb across the slopes of Trendlebere Down and enter dense woodland surrounding Becka Falls.

BECKA FALLS, Devon

Best seen after heavy rain, these falls are created by the picturesque Becka Brook as it leaps and plunges 70ft down a series of great boulders.
Continue on the B3344 to Manaton.

MANATON, Devon

Once the home of novelist John Galsworthy, Manaton is a scattered hamlet with a typical 15th-century church. A notable feature of the latter is its fine rood-screen, which extends right across the building. There is a pleasant green surrounded by trees and overlooked by the thatched Church House. About 1½ miles south west of Manaton is Hound Tor, where there is a medieval settlement of long houses inhabited from Saxon times to cAD1300. Bowerman's Nose, an outcrop of rock weathered into a curiously distinctive shape, can be seen ¾ mile to the south.

Continue for ¾ mile from Manaton Church and at a T-junction turn right on to the unclassifed 'North Bovey' road. Descend steeply, and after 1½ miles cross the River Bovey. Ascend into North Bovey.

NORTH BOVEY, Devon

Many people consider this east Dartmoor village to be the most picturesque in Devon. The River Bovey countryside that surrounds it is enchanting, and the unspoilt village green is complemented by the delightful Ring of Bells Inn. Inside the church is a fine screen with statuettes.

Follow SP 'Postbridge' and in ½ mile at crossroads turn left. In ¾ mile meet a T-junction and turn left on to the B3212 SP 'Princetown'. Later ascend on to open moorland, passing an unclassified left turn leading to Grimspound and 1,737ft Hameldown Tor.

GRIMSPOUND, Devon

This fine example of a Bronze-Age shepherd settlement consists of 24 small hut circles in a walled enclosure with a paved entrance. Sir Arthur Conan Doyle used the brooding atmosphere of the area in *The Hound of the Baskervilles*.

Continue on the B3212 and climb to a road summit of 1,426ft near the Warren House Inn.

WARREN HOUSE INN, Devon

A traditional welcome in the form of a peat fire that has been burning continuously for over 100 years waits here. The inn takes its name from one of the park's many rabbit warrens. A footpath leads to the headstream of the West Webburn and the remains of artificial ravines dug by tin miners long ago.
Continue to the village of Postbridge.

Bowerman's Nose stands south of Manaton

Grimspound was home for prehistoric shepherds.

Follow SP 'Buckfastleigh' along a narrow road and in ½ mile bear right. In a further ½ mile descend (1 in 5), and at the bottom keep left. In 1¼ miles meet crossroads and turn left SP 'Buckfast, Totnes'. In ¼ mile bear right then immediately left, and in ¾ mile enter Buckfast village to pass the famous abbey.

mls 0 1 2 3
kms 0 1 2 3 4

Turn left on to the B3357 'Ashburton' road and after 4¼ miles descend steeply to the picturesque Dartmeet Bridge.

DARTMEET BRIDGE, Devon
Here, where the East and West Dart Rivers join forces to descend through a deep valley to Dartmouth, is one of the most popular beauty spots in the national park. Footpaths which wind through the valley allow some of the spectacular gorge-like scenery to be seen at close range.

Continue on an unclassified road and ascend (1 in 5) to the neighbourhood of 1,250ft Sharp Tor for fine views down the valley, and continue to Poundsgate. Descend steeply to cross the river at Newbridge, where there is a picnic site, and enter the woods of Holne Chase. In ½ mile turn right on to an unclassified road. (A detour from the main route to the River Dart Country Park can be made here by continuing forward for 1¾ miles).

RIVER DART COUNTRY PARK, Devon
Oak coppice, marshland, and valley bogs make up the varied landscape of this country park, which adjoins Holne Woods (NT) and occupies both banks of the River Dart.

Continue on the main route and in ½ mile turn right again to Holne.

HOLNE, Devon
In 1819 the attractive late-Georgian rectory was the birthplace of the novelist Charles Kingsley. Holne Church dates from c1300 and houses a good screen featuring a wealth of detail. An hour glass is incorporated in the carved pulpit. A fine walk leads west of the village along the Sandy Way to the source of the River Avon.

BUCKFAST ABBEY, Devon
Buckfast Abbey was founded in the 10th century, refounded 2 centuries later, and rebuilt on the old foundations by the Benedictine monks themselves between 1907 and 1938. A magnificent mosaic pavement has been laid inside the church. Near by is the House of Shells museum, which demonstrates the use of shells in arts and crafts.

Continue for ¼ mile to meet a T-junction. A short detour can be made from the main route by turning right into Buckfastleigh here.

BUCKFASTLEIGH, Devon
A long flight of steps leading to the church in this old wool town affords excellent views. Inside the church, which has an Early-English chancel, is a notable Norman font.

DART VALLEY RAILWAY, Devon
The northern terminus of this revived steam line, originally built in 1872 to serve the mining and farming industries, is in Buckfastleigh. Great Western rolling stock and a number of locomotives from that company can be seen here. The 14-mile round trip to Totnes BR station affords excellent views of the superb Dart Valley countryside.

Follow the main route by turning left at the T-junction before the detour. Cross the River Dart by Dart Bridge, turn left again, and in 1¾ miles meet a T-junction. Turn left then shortly right to re-enter Ashburton.

Buckland-in-the-Moor's cottages are built to weather the roughest storms.

POSTBRIDGE, Devon
A small touring centre for the moor, Postbridge derives its name from a bridge that once carried the earliest Dartmoor post road between Exeter and south Cornwall across the East Dart River. A few yards south is the largest and by far the most impressive of Dartmoor's clapper bridges. This primitive-looking structure is massively constructed from huge granite slabs, and is thought to have been built when the inner moor was opened up for mining and farming some time during the 13th century.

Beyond the bridge a detour can be taken from the main route by turning left along an unclassified road and passing Bellever Wood to reach Bellever picnic site and nature trail.

BELLEVER, Devon
Numerous hut circles and other prehistoric monuments survive in this area. Also here are 2 fascinating nature trails laid out for visitors by the Forestry Commission.

Continue with the B3212 and reach the edge of Two Bridges.

TWO BRIDGES, Devon
An hotel and little else stands at this junction of the only 2 major routes across central Dartmoor. North east is Crockern Tor, where the so-called Tinners' Parliament met at irregular intervals to enact special laws governing the stannary towns where tin was valued and taxed. Wistman's Wood, a forest nature reserve some 1½ miles north near the West Dart River, features a mature stand of rare dwarf oaks.

21

THE HILLS OF EAST DEVON

East Devon is a mild, well-rounded collection of contrasts. Gracious Regency coastal resorts rub shoulders with simple picturesque villages, sub-tropical gardens grow alongside native woodlands, and little stone farms fringe the parkland estates of grand country houses.

The Exeter Ship Canal has carried water-borne traffic since 1566.

Ottery St Mary's 14th-century church.

HAYES BARTON, Devon

1 mile west of East Budleigh is the thatched 16th-century house of Hayes Barton (not open), birthplace of the famous adventurer Sir Walter Raleigh in 1552.

At the church turn right and shortly rejoin the A376. Proceed to the next crossroads, where there is an obelisk.

EXMOUTH, Devon

Situated on the estuary of the River Exe, this pleasant town and small port is the oldest and one of the largest seaside resorts in Devon. Most of its sandy beaches offer safe and sheltered bathing, and there are extensive coastal views. Local tourist facilities include swimming pools, the town museum and the Country Life museum. Good Georgian houses can be seen in The Beacon, and a picturesque group near by includes quaint almshouses and a tiny chapel. A passenger ferry makes frequent estuary crossings between Exmouth and Starcross.

A LA RONDE, Devon

This unusual circular house (open) stands east of the Exeter road and was built in 1798 by a Miss Jane Parminter. Its rooms are arranged around an octagonal hall, and the curious Shell Gallery is imaginatively decorated with shells, feathers, and fascinating pictures made from a variety of natural objects.

Leave Exmouth on the Budleigh Salterton road A376 and pass through attractive woodland scenery to Budleigh Salterton.

BUDLEIGH SALTERTON, Devon

During the 13th century this Ottermouth town was a salt-panning community supplying the local priory. At the mouth of the river is a shingle beach backed by red sandstone cliffs, and less than a mile away are the challenging fairways of

the best golf course in east Devon. Several Georgian houses can be seen in the town, and a small but interesting museum called the Fairlynch Arts Centre is in an 18th-century thatched house.

Keep forward through the town and then ascend and turn left. In 2 miles at crossroads turn left into East Budleigh.

EAST BUDLEIGH, Devon

Typical of many Devon communities, this charming little village has delightful thatched cottages and seems hardly to have been touched by time.

A miniature railway provides a mobile viewpoint from which to enjoy the varied scenery of Bicton Gardens.

THE OBELISK, Devon

This curious and rather attractive brick and stone cross is dated 1743 and carries route directions couched in biblical terms and phrases.

A possible detour leads 1 mile to the right, across the River Otter, to Otterton.

OTTERTON, Devon

Fine thatched cottages and a handsome chestnut grove combine to make this one of the most picturesque villages in the area. Restored Otterton Watermill is now an interesting craft centre.

Keep forward on the A376 and after ½ mile reach the entrance to Bicton Park on the left.

BICTON PARK, Devon

The gardens here are among the most beautiful in Britain. Le Nôtre, the designer of the superb gardens of Versailles in France, laid out the fine lawns of the Italian Garden in 1735 and there is an extensive pinetum. Other features include a narrow-gauge woodland railway, countryside and transport museums, the World of Tomorrow and World of Yesterday entertainment themes, and a large adventure playground.

After 1½ miles turn right on to the A3052 and enter Newton Poppleford. Cross the River Otter and ascend alongside Harpford Wood. Shortly turn right on to the B3176 SP 'Sidmouth' and skirt Bulverton Hill on the right before descending into Sidmouth.

SIDMOUTH, Devon

Created as a resort from almost nothing in the 18th century, Sidmouth has a shingle beach backed by spectacular red cliffs and is still a popular holiday town. Rows of Regency terraces are reminders of the prosperous recent past, while elsewhere are the more ancient Old Chancel and Manor House. The former incorporates medieval parts of the old parish church, and the latter now houses a museum. On either side of the town are Peak Hill to the west and Salcombe Hill to the east, both of which offer exceptional views of the coastline. Peak Hill shelters the Royal Glen, a former residence of Queen Victoria. Every August the town is a host to a well-known International Folk Song and Dance Festival.

Follow SP 'Honiton' B3175 and drive to Sidford.

SIDFORD, Devon

Although rebuilt and widened in 1930, Sidford's bridge still displays the pleasing lines of the old high-backed packhorse bridge that stood here from c1100. Porch House, which dates from the 16th century, is said to have hidden Charles II after the Battle of Worcester.

Turn right on to the A3052 and climb Trow Hill, which offers magnificent views across the Sid Valley. Shortly beyond the summit bear left then after ¼ mile turn right on to an unclassifed road for Branscombe.

BRANSCOMBE, Devon
It is difficult to find the centre of this village, which sprawls along steep lanes in a wooded valley, but its situation makes it one of the loveliest in Devon. Features of the upper village include thatched roofs, an old smithy, and a Norman to later church. Some 300 acres of the beautiful Branscombe Estate is owned by the National Trust.

Pass the Mason's Arms PH then follow SP 'Beer', reach to the top of an ascent, and turn left SP 'Honiton'. Continue for 1 mile then turn left on to the A3052. After ¾ mile pass the Three Horseshoes Inn before turning right on to the B3174. After 2½ miles pass the road to the Farway Countryside Park on the right.

FARWAY COUNTRYSIDE PARK, Devon
Much of this 189-acre park is preserved in its natural state, though one or two places have been prepared as picnic sites. Attractions include pony rides, nature trails and a rare breeds farm.

In ¾ mile bear right on to an unclassified road SP 'Farway' and cross Farway Hill, with fine views into the Coly Valley on the right. After ¾ mile keep forward on the 'Honiton' road. Reach a golf course and turn left, then descend into Honiton.

HONITON, Devon
This town gave its name to Honiton lace, a material which is now produced in neighbouring villages and can still be bought in some local shops. Examples can be seen in a small museum housed in the old chapel beside the towered church. Marwood House, Honiton's oldest building, dates from 1619 and contains one of many antique shops that thrive in this acknowledged centre of the trade. A 17th-century black marble tomb to Thomas Marwood, physician to Queen Elizabeth I, can be seen in the parish church above the town. Visitors to the local pottery can watch work being thrown on the wheel and hand painted. An unusual building known as Copper Castle stands by the side of old toll gates on the eastern outskirts.

Turn left into Honiton High Street (the Exeter road), and in ¾ mile turn left on to the A375 SP 'Sidmouth'. Ascend Gittisham Hill and continue to crossroads at the Hare and Hounds Inn. Turn right on to the B3174 SP 'Ottery' and descend into Ottery St Mary.

OTTERY ST MARY, Devon
Various literary figures are associated with this pleasant River Otter town. The poet Samual Taylor Coleridge was born here in 1772, and satirist William Thackeray set his novel *Pendennis* here (though he changed the name to Clavering St Mary). The magnificent collegiate church was modelled on Exeter Cathedral by Bishop Grandisson, and dates largely from 1337. Notable features include twin 14th-

Branscombe Mouth is an unspoilt beach protected by the National Trust.

century stalls and a curious Elizabethan clock. An annual carnival is held in the town on November 5.

Go forward through the town and at the end turn right onto the B3176 SP 'Fairmile'. Cross the river to reach Cadhay House.

CADHAY HOUSE, Devon
This fine Tudor and Georgian courtyard manor house dates mainly from 1550 and is open during the summer.

Continue to Fairmile, cross the A30, and follow SP 'Clyst Hydon'. Continue through farming country to Clyst Hydon and at the end of the village turn right SP 'Cullompton'. In ¾ mile turn left on to an unclassified road. SP 'Hele' then after a further 2 miles meet a junction with the B3185 and turn left then immediately right for Hele. Pass under the M5 motorway, drive over a level crossing and the River Culm, to enter Hele

Portuguese fishing boats are displayed along with many other vessels at Exeter's Maritime Museum.

then turn left. SP 'Silverton'. In ½ mile turn left then in 1¼ miles at crossroads go forward onto the B3185 SP 'Broad Clyst' and recross the River Culm near paper mills. Skirt Killerton Gardens on the right.

KILLERTON GARDENS, Devon
The Georgian Killerton House containing a fine collection of period costumes stands in magnificent 300-acre grounds covering a hilltop. There are many ancient beech trees and a fine 15-acre garden of rare trees and shrubs.

Follow SP 'Poltimore' then 'Exeter' and descend into the city of Exeter.

EXETER, Devon
With a population of 96,000 is the county town, and administrative and commercial centre of Devon. Founded by the Romans at the lowest crossing point of the River Exe, it is one of the oldest cities in England. The cathedral, with unusual Norman twin transeptal

towers, is mainly 14th-century, and the ancient guildhall has an elaborate late 16th-century facade. The modern university is on a hilltop site on the north side of the city and, despite the depredation of wartime bombing, attractive Georgian and earlier houses may still be found in many streets. The maritime museum at the head of the Exeter Canal on the south side of the city is of great interest, as are the Royal Albert Memorial Museum, the Devonshire Regiment Museum, 15th-century Tucker's Hall, St Nicholas's Priory (AM), Rougemont House Museum, and the underground passages. Part of the Norman Rougemont Castle has survived, and stretches of the ancient city walls can still be seen.

Recross the M5 and turn right onto the B3181 SP 'Exeter'. Proceed through Broad Clyst to Pinhoe. Keep forward SP 'Ring Road' and in 1 mile at traffic signals bear left (Exeter City Centre is to the right) and at the next roundabout take 2nd exit SP 'Torbay, Plymouth'. Keep forward to reach Countess Wear Roundabout then take 1st exit unclassified SP 'Topsham'. In 1¼ miles pass under the M5 Exe Estuary viaduct and shortly enter Topsham.

TOPSHAM, Devon
Once an important seaport, Topsham stands on the Exe estuary and features 17th- and 18th-century Dutch-gabled houses. These fine buildings, mainly in the Strand, are reminders of a flourishing trade with Holland. One of them contains a local history museum in its sail loft.

Turn left, (for town centre keep forward) go over a level-crossing then bear right. Shortly cross the River Clyst then at the George Dragon PH turn left on to the A376 and continue to reach a roundabout at Clyst St Mary, and take the 3rd exit on to the A3052 'Lyme Regis' road. In 4¾ miles reach the Halfway Inn and turn right on to the B3180 for the return over Woodbury Common to Exmouth.

BUDE, Cornwall

One of Bude's main attractions is its huge surfing beach, where strong winds that have caused hundreds of wrecks over the centuries provide a constant supply of rollers ideal for the sport. The town itself is sheltered from the full force of the weather by ridges of downland between it and the sea. Visitors interested in sun and sea bathing are catered for by Summerleaze beach, a sheltered area of sand at the mouth of the River Neet. Here a large swimming pool is naturally refilled every high tide. A notable 3-mile scenic walk extends along clifftops south of Bude, visiting Compass Point and Efford Beacon for their excellent views. Bude Castle was built in 1840 and now houses the local council offices.

Leave by the A3072 'Bideford' road. After 1¼ miles turn left on to the A39, pass the edge of Stratton, and drive to Kilkhampton.

KILKHAMPTON, Cornwall

The main feature of the village is the 12th- to 15th-century church, which contains no fewer than 157 carved bench-ends dating from the 16th century. The Norman doorway is elaborately carved, and there is a splendid barrel roof. Three miles east are the Tamar lakes with various leisure facilities.

Continue for 3 miles. A detour from the main route can be made by turning left here on to an unclassified road to reach Morwenstow.

MORWENSTOW, Cornwall

Henna Cliff rears 450ft above the waves about ¼ mile from Morwenstow village church, on the other side of a grassy coomb. It is the highest cliff in Cornwall and forms part of an awesome range that once proved useful to the wreckers, who signalled ships on to the rocks in order to plunder their cargoes. The Norman church itself stands a little aloof from the tiny village, and features attractive Romanesque zig-zag work over the porch and carved bench ends. During the 19th century the local vicar, Robert Hawker, wrote the ballad *Song of the Western Man.*

Continue on the A39 for 2 miles to Welcombe Cross. A detour can be made from the main route to reach Welcombe and Welcombe Mouth by turning left on to an unclassified road.

WELCOMBE, Devon

Situated near the Cornish border, this village stands in a remote glen that leads to a wild stretch of cliff-bound coast at Morwenstow Bay. The cliff strata here has been violently contorted by unimaginable stresses to form really spectacular coastal scenery. A fine waterfall can be seen at Marsland Mouth, and picturesque Welcombe Cove is well worth visiting.

A small stream tumbles into Bideford Bay at Buck's Mills.

NORTH DEVON CLIFFTOPS

Bude's long beach is a brief calm before the great geological storm that lies ahead. Just north are soaring cliffs violently twisted and fractured by massive forces, where small streams from the lush hinterland plunge hundreds of feet to the shore as waterfalls, or dash over boulder beds through deep wooded ravines.

Atlantic waves break constantly on Bude's magnificent beach, creating ideal conditions for surfers.

From Welcombe Cross proceed on the A39 for 1 mile to pass the West Country Inn, then branch left on to an unclassified road SP 'Elmscott'. Cross a short stretch of moorland to reach Tosberry Cross, and bear left then right for Stoke, 3 miles further on.

STOKE, Devon

Hartland's 14th-century church stands here, raising its magnificent tower 128ft into the air to form a local landmark. Inside are a carved Norman font and a fine screen.
Continue for ½ mile and descend steeply to Hartland Quay.

HARTLAND QUAY, Devon

The quay that stood here has long since been washed away by storms, but the rocky shore is a constant attraction. Some of the most exciting shorescapes of the north Devon and Cornwall coasts are formed by the strangely twisted and fractured strata of the local cliffs. The interesting Hartland Quay Museum has sections on geology, natural and coastal history, and shipwrecks. A clifftop path leads 1 mile south to Speke's Mill Mouth waterfall, perhaps the most spectacular of several cliff waterfalls in the district.

Return to Stoke and follow SP 'Hartland, Bideford'. After ½ mile a road to the left leads to Hartland Point.

HARTLAND POINT, Devon

Although only 3 miles from Hartland Quay, the beautiful 350ft cliffs here are red instead of grey. This spectacular coast has an ugly history and has been the death of many a helpless and storm-battered ship. Because of this the point carries a small white lighthouse which emits the strongest light of any on Britain's coast.
Return to Hartland.

HARTLAND, Devon

To the west of this pleasant village is the 18th-century house of Hartland Abbey. The abbey itself was founded in the 12th century and has entirely vanished. A coomb leads from here to the sea.

From Hartland proceed on the B3248 'Bideford, Clovelly' road for 3 miles and turn left on to an unclassified road. After another ⅓ mile turn left again on to the B3237 and drive to the carpark for Clovelly.

CLOVELLY, Devon

Clovelly is one of the West Country's most picturesque fishing villages. No cars are allowed here because the steep cobbled street, lined with lovely old houses, descends 400ft to the sea in a series of steps. Donkeys are used to transport visitors' luggage, and zig-zag steps allow pedestrian access down the wooded cliffs to the tiny quay and a pebble beach. The idyllic surroundings of the village tend to soothe away the normal healthy respect for the open sea, but a local lifeboat station that has saved 350 lives is a sobering reminder that the tranquillity is not permanent. The village, discovered by holidaymakers in the mid-19th century, is popular with artists and enjoys a climate as mild as that of the south Devon coast. Local gardens bloom well beyond their normal season. An attractive 2-mile walk leads west from the harbour to a magnificent range of 400ft cliffs.

Return along the B3237, then in 1¼ miles turn left on to the A39 'Bideford' road to reach Buck's Cross. An unclassified road to the left leads through a wooded glen to Buck's Mills.

BUCK'S MILL, Devon

This unspoilt fishing village of thatched cottages lies at the bottom of a wooded valley, on a section of coast noted for its picturesque cliff scenery.

Continue along the A39 and in 5½ miles at a roundabout take 1st exit on to an unclassified road to reach Abbotsham.

ABBOTSHAM, Devon

Abbotsham Church features a good 15th-century barrel roof bearing trade emblems and coats of arms, and preserves carved bench-ends and a Norman font.

Some of the most rugged coastal scenery in North Devon can be seen near Hartland Quay.

Morwenstow Church contains superb Norman arches and over 100 beautifully carved bench-ends.

Continue and in 1¼ miles turn left on to the B3236 to reach Westward Ho!

WESTWARD HO!, Devon
Named after the famous novel by Charles Kingsley, this seaside resort offers a well-known golf course and 3 miles of sandy beach. West of the town the sands merge into rocks scattered with teeming pools, ideal ground for the infant naturalist. North-east is the 650-acre expanse of Northam Burrows, which now includes a country park and is protected from the Atlantic by a remarkable pebble ridge.

Follow signs Bideford and continue to Northam.

NORTHAM, Devon
Northam village lies close to the attractive Torridge Estuary. An inscribed stone at Bloody Corner recalls King Alfred's successful last battle againt Hubba the Dane in the 9th century.

A detour can be made to Appledore by turning left on to the A386.

APPLEDORE, Devon
Cobbled streets leading to a quay and a sandy beach contribute to the great charm of this village, which has several attractive Georgian houses and cottages. Its tranquility is somehow maintained despite the establishment in 1970 of one of Europe's largest covered shipbuilding docks, on the Torridge estuary. A maritime museum displays North Devon's shipping history.

Follow the main route on the A386 and drive to Bideford crossing the approach to the new by-pass bridge over the Torridge.

BIDEFORD, Devon   SS42
Between c1550 and 1750 this town was the principal port of north Devon and the home of a renowned

ship-building industry. Sir Richard Grenville, who obtained a charter for the town from Queen Elizabeth I, crewed his ship *Revenge* entirely with Bideford men. That brave little vessel will always be famous for its stand against 15 Spanish ships in the Azores. The mile-long, tree-lined quay remains lively, and the estuary is popular with yachtsmen and small-boat sailors. Bridgeland Road preserves evidence of a once prosperous past in the shape of 17th-century merchants' houses. Pre-dating these is the bridge over the River Torridge, a 15th-century structure unusual in that none of its 24 arches is of the same width. It has been considerably renovated and widened to take the burden of 20th-century traffic. The Royal Hotel, across the river, was originally a merchant's house and dates from 1688. It was here that Charles Kingsley wrote part of *Westward Ho!*

Leave Bideford following SP 'Torrington' and drive beside the River Torridge to reach Great Torrington.

GREAT TORRINGTON, Devon
The church in this hilltop market town was rebuilt in 1651, 6 years after it and 200 Royalist soldiers imprisoned inside were blown up by gunpowder. The tragedy was caused by Roundhead troops using the church as a gunpowder store as well as a prison. A fine 17th-century pulpit can be seen inside the building. The well-known Dartington glass is made in the town, and visitors to the factory can watch the highly skilled glassblowers at work. About 1 mile south-east of Great Torrington is Rosemoor Garden (open), where hybrid rhododendrons, eucalyptus, roses, and ornamental trees and shrubs can be seen. Within easy reach are two magnificent vantage points. The castle mound by the town centre stands on a steep hillside high above the Torridge and 1 mile north-west across a ravine the crag of Furzebeam Hill juts out above the meandering river.

From the Bideford end of the town follow SP 'Holsworthy, Bude' B3277 and cross the river into Taddiport. After 6 miles enter Stibb Cross, then forward on to the A388 for Holsworthy.

HOLSWORTHY, Devon
This bustling market town has a dubious claim to fame as the last place in England where a man was punished by being sent to the stocks. The mainly 13th-century church here has a pinnacled 15th-century tower and a carillion which plays one of a number of tunes on the hour.

Leave Holsworthy on the A3072 SP 'Bude'. Later cross the River Tamar into Cornwall and 4 miles further on reach Stratton.

STRATTON, Cornwall
An ancient town that was probably founded by the Romans, Stratton is made up of old and sometimes thatched buildings lining a steep main street. The Tree Inn was once a manor, and in 1643 it served as the home and headquarters of Sir Bevil Grenville before he led the Royalists to victory at the battle of Stamford Hill, ½ mile north-west. Features of the local church include a pinnacled 15th-century tower, a barrel roof with carved bosses, a fine 16th-century brass, and a window by the talented artist and designer Burne-Jones.

Follow SP 'Bude' on the A3072 for the return to Bude.

Clovelly is one of the most popular of Devon's picturesque fishing villages.

ALONG THE EXE VALLEY

From its wild moorland source the Exe struggles through a mile of peat before finding its deep valley to the fertile lands of North-east Devon. All along its route are little red-stone villages that burst into activity once a week when the local hunt meets.

BAMPTON, Devon

This small market town is situated by the River Batherm near its junction with the Exe. Ponies culled from the wild herds that roam the moor are sold in the October Pony Fair. The excellence of the limestone quarried to the south of the town is almost legendary. Today these quarries are of geological rather than commercial interest, and their situation affords fine views of the town. St Michael's Church, built c1300, was rebuilt with a north aisle in the 15th century. Inside are notable carved rood and tower screens and a pulpit dating from the 16th-century.

Leave Bampton on the B3222 SP 'Dulverton', and at Exe Bridge turn right A396 then almost immediately left to rejoin the B3222. Cross the River Exe and proceed through the valley of the River Barle to Dulverton.

DULVERTON, Somerset

The River Barle is spanned here by an attractive 3-arched bridge and is known for its excellent trout and salmon fishing. Dulverton itself is a shopping centre and the general administrative centre for the south-east area of Exmoor, a status that makes it a prime touring base. Everywhere is the sight and sound of water, a fact succinctly commented upon by Lord Tennyson in 1891 when he called Dulverton 'a land of bubbling streams'. Fine views of the town are available from the shade of a giant sycamore, which is some 250 years old and obscures a modest church. Local painters exhibit their works each summer in Exmoor House by the bridge.

Turn left on to the B3223 'Lynton' road and enter the Exmoor National Park.

EXMOOR NATIONAL PARK (SOUTH), Devon & Somerset

Much of this tour runs through the southern area of the Exmoor National Park, a place of dense mixed forests and wild open moors dominated in the north by the River Exe and in the south by the River Barle. Once a year the Exmoor ponies are herded and culled, some being freed and others taken to be sold at the famous local pony fairs. Pure-bred Exmoors are bay, dun, or brown, with no white or other markings of any kind, and have a characteristic oatmeal colour to the muzzle and inside ears. These animals, untainted by domestic stock, are hardy, agile creatures. The possibilities for recreation in the park are unlimited. Superb walks start from almost any point along the route, and those worried about getting lost in the vast expanse of the moor can follow specially marked trails. Care must be taken to avoid the deep, sphagnum-filled bogs; broken-in Exmoor ponies are good for trekking the moor because they know the area and recognize the smell of the boglands. The only other large herd animal found here is the red deer, a lovely, shy animal which is best sought for in secluded spots during the early morning or late evening.

Continue on the B3223. After 4½ miles reach a left turn leading to Tarr Steps for a pleasant detour from the main route.

TARR STEPS, Somerset

Tarr Steps (AM, NT) is the local name for a superb old clapper bridge. Situated on the edge of Exmoor, near Dulverton, it spans the tumbling River Barle and comprises 20 piers topped by a stone footway raised some 3ft above water level. The piers are large blocks of stone placed on the river bed, and the top is made up of several giant slabs that must have taken incredible effort to position. This fascinating monument to the ingenuity of ancient man is believed to have been built before the Norman Conquest. A car-park is provided on the approach.

Back on the main route, continue along the B3223 to reach Winsford Hill and the Caratacus Stone, on the right.

Tarr Steps' enormous slabs have been washed away many times, but have always been replaced in their original positions.

WINSFORD HILL & THE CARATACUS STONE, Somerset

Heather-clad Winsford Hill (NT) rises between Exmoor's two major rivers. Its wooded lower slopes rise to a clear summit from which the marked contrast between the River Barle woodlands and the empty slopes that rise from the Exe can be truly appreciated. The Caratacus Stone, an inscribed tablet on the hill, is thought to date from the dark ages of paganism that followed the departure of the Romans. Its inscription is ambiguous because it is incomplete, and is translated as either 'Kinsman of Caratacus' or 'Caranacus'.

Continue 1¼ miles beyond the Winsford Hill road summit to a left turn that offers a pleasant detour to Withypool.

WITHYPOOL, Somerset

Beautifully situated on the River Barle and much favoured by game anglers, this tiny village has one of the two legal commons existing in the national park (the other is at Brendon). A fine old bridge spans the river here, and nearby Withypool Hill features a stone circle among neolithic burial mounds.

Continue on the main route and after 1½ miles at crossroads turn right on to an unclassified road and descend into Exford.

Exmoor is a beautiful mixture of rolling farmland and open moor.

EXFORD, Somerset

Hunting and horses are the bread and butter of this well-kept Exe-Valley village. The kennels of the Devon and Somerset Stag Hounds are based here, and horses are very much in evidence at all times. Exford's annual Horse Show is generally held on the 2nd Wednesday in August. The nucleus of the village is an attractive grouping of cottages, shops, and hotels around the local cricket and football field. Other buildings are dotted amid the rural outskirts, and the modest little church contains an interesting 15th-century screen.

Follow the B3224 'Lynton' road for 1 mile, rejoin the B3223, and continue to Simonsbath.

Dulverton's Market House dates from 1866.

SIMONSBATH, Somerset

Sited 1,100ft above sea level, Simonsbath is the highest village in the park and stands at the centre of what used to be the Royal Exmoor Forest. Deer were once commonplace here, but today these timid creatures are rarely seen. The 100-year-old church administers the largest parish in the park.

Turn left on to an unclassified road SP 'South Molton' and climb to 1,500ft. After 8 miles join the B3226, and in 1½ miles join the A361 and proceed to South Molton.

SOUTH MOLTON, Devon

Known to have existed as a Saxon colony cAD700, this lovely little town lies just south of Exmoor and is an agricultural centre for the region. Between the Middle Ages and the mid-19th century it became a thriving wool town; it was also a coach stop on the route to Barnstaple and Bideford, and the nearest town to the iron and copper mines of North Molton. A square of elegant Georgian houses is complemented by the town's grand 18th-century Guildhall and 19th-century Assembly Rooms, all built with the profits from wool and minerals. Disaster struck when the industries collapsed, and the town's population was reduced by half. Since 1961 it has been the centre for a busy livestock market. Opposite the square an avenue of pollarded lime trees leads to the local church, which houses an excellently-carved pulpit and carries a 15th-century tower. A small museum behind the Guildhall displays examples of pewterware, a cider press, and an intriguing old fire engine dating from 1736. Also of interest here is the Quince Honey Farm.

Continue on the A361 'Bampton, Taunton' road and cross the rivers Mole and Yeo to Bish Mill. Branch right on to the B3221 SP 'Tiverton' and continue through woodland and hilly farming country to Tiverton.

TIVERTON, Devon

This prosperous industrial and agricultural town stands on the River Exe and its tributary, the River Lowman. After the conquest of the south-west in the 7th century it became one of the first Saxon settlements, and later during the 17th- and 18th-century heyday of the clothing industry the town became the principal industrial area in the county. Architecturally, the town has benefited greatly from the

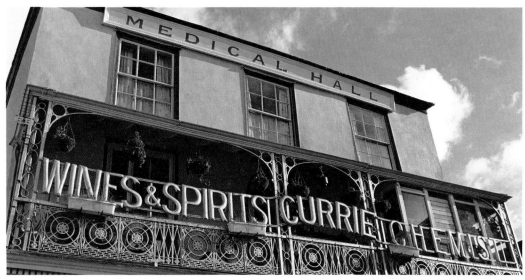

The Medical Hall in South Molton.

prosperity of its inhabitants. Rich wool merchants have bequeathed such fine buildings as St Peter's Church, Blundell's School, and three sets of almshouses. The church, particularly noted for the richly-carved Greenway Chapel and its organ, stands in front of a 12th-century castle (open) which preserves its towers and gateway despite being incorporated in a private house. Blundell's School is famous in having taught such illustrious persons as R D Blackmore, author of *Lorna Doone*, and Frederick Temple, Archbishop of Canterbury from 1896 to 1902. St George's Church was built in 1773 and is reputed to be one of the finest Georgian churches in Devon. Also of interest is the large and very comprehensive museum, including a GWR locomotive, housed in a 19th-century school building. The 19th-century Grand Western Canal

Exford is the most important stag hunting centre on Exmoor.

begins at the south-east edge of the town and extends for 11 miles. It was originally intended to link the Bristol Channel with the English Channel, but the project was never completed. The towpath now forms a famous scenic walk and there are horsedrawn barge trips.

From Tiverton take the A396 'Bampton' road and continue to Bolham. Turn right here for a short detour to Knightshayes Court.

KNIGHTSHAYES COURT, Devon

The 19th-century house (open) that stands here is pleasant enough to look at, but it is totally put in the shade by some of the most beautiful gardens in Devon. Protected by both the National Trust and Knightshayes Garden Trust, the grounds have a woodland theme and are particularly noted for their splendid rhododendrons.

On the main route, continue along the A396 for the return to Bampton.

LYNTON, Devon

This pleasant and very popular resort is sited high on a cliff some 500ft above its sister village of Lynmouth. Tree-covered Summerhouse Hill shields it from the blustery sea gales, and a solid ring of hills protects it from the worst of Exmoor's rain. The Victorians were quick to recognize these attributes as being suited to seaside holidays, and since then the resort has attracted a constant stream of visitors. Victorian architecture predominates here, and a typical eccentricity of that era is the water-powered cliff lift. This was donated by a lawyer named George Newnes in 1890, and has been restored to working order. Newnes also built the Town Hall, behind which rise the flower-strewn slopes of viewpoint Hollerday Hill. Miles of coastline and the Exmoor hills can be seen from here. Other features of Lynton include a Catholic church containing rare and beautiful marble work, and the Lyn and Exmoor Museum in old St Vincent's Cottage. The local cliffs afford views across the Bristol Channel to Wales, and the magnificent Valley of the Rocks is accessible by footpath.

VALLEY OF THE ROCKS, Devon

The poet Robert Southey described this fantastic place of jagged tors and breathtaking coastal scenery with the words '. . . rock reeling upon rock, stone piled upon stone, a huge terrific reeling mass'.

Descend Lynmouth Hill (1 in 4) to Lynmouth and turn right on to the A39 'Barnstaple' road for Watersmeet.

WATERSMEET, Devon

As its name suggests, this National Trust beauty spot is the place where the tumbling waters of the East Lyn River converge with the Hoaroak Water, which cascades down a rocky bed in a series of waterfalls. It is best to leave the car and explore the cool beauty of this wooded gorge on foot.

Continue alongside the Hoaroak Water for ½ mile then turn left on to the B3223 SP 'Simonsbath'. Cross Hillsford Bridge, and in ¾ mile go round a hairpin bend and drive forward on to an unclassified road SP 'Brendon Valley'. Pass Brendon Church, with views of the tree-covered slopes that characterize this area, then descend through the oak-wooded valley of the East Lyn River for Brendon.

BRENDON, Devon

This picturesque village is situated on the banks of the East Lyn, which is spanned here by an attractive medieval packhorse bridge.

Continue alongside the East Lyn River to Malmsmead

MALMSMEAD, Devon

Ponies can be hired here for a 2½ - mile trek along the deep valley of Badgworthy Water, leading to the legendary Doone Country. The journey can just as easily be undertaken on foot.

INTO THE DOONE COUNTRY

Before they come here many people half believe Blackmore's romantic novel 'Lorna Doone' to be a true historical account. By the time they leave, the region's gorse and heather covered moors, wooded ravines, and exquisite little stone villages have convinced them of it.

DOONE VALLEY, Devon & Somerset

R D Blackmore immortalized isolated and beautiful Hoccombe Combe as 'Doone Valley' in his famous novel *Lorna Doone*. Thanks to his brilliantly emotive style this has become one of the most romantic places in the country, and many visitors go away firmly believing that the whole tale was actually a true historical account. Tales of a villainous Doone family who terrorized the moorfolk have been told here since 1790. It appears that Blackmore seized on these as a handy base for his novel, and although he did not concentrate on authentic landscape description, several features can be identified from his text. Lanke Combe enters the valley from the west and has miniature versions of features attributed to Doone Valley by the author, including the famous waterslide. Records show that the remains of several buildings in this area belonged to a medieval settlement, but the name Doone is not mentioned. With or without the legend, this is a beautiful area that should not be missed.

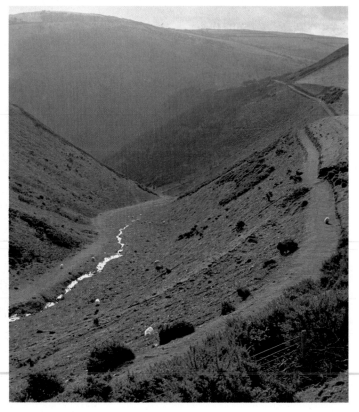

EXMOOR NATIONAL PARK (NORTH), Devon & Somerset

In its northern reaches this vast national park meets the sea with magnificent results. Rugged hogsback cliffs stretch continuously from Lynton to Porlock, falling steeply to the waters of the Bristol Channel and affording views across to the coast of South Wales. Lush coombs wind deep into rambling moorland, scattered here and there with tiny hamlets and picturesque villages. The burgeoning life of the valleys makes a striking contrast with the remote and heather-clad wastelands through which they cut, but together these opposites form a landscape that could be nowhere else but Exmoor. Agriculture and forestry play a large part in the park's life, and the rich patchwork of farmland in areas like the Porlock Vale are sharp reminders that this is more than just a place of outstanding natural beauty. Wildlife abounds on Exmoor. The shy red deer that haunt its wooded coombs are unique in being direct descendants of the wild deer that once roamed prehistoric Britain. Common mammals thrive in a variety of habitats, and the park boasts many species of birds. Vestiges of prehistoric ages can be found in the form of earthworks, tumuli, standing stones, and barrows. Of particular note is the stone circle on Porlock Hill, but there are many other fascinating examples easily reached from Lynton.

From Malmsmead cross a river bridge into Somerset and continue to Oare.

OARE, Somerset

This tiny Oare Valley hamlet stands by the Oare Water and has strong connexions with the fiction of R D Blackmore. It was here that his heroine Lorna was married, and here that she almost met an untimely end. The village church is a lovely little 15th-century building well suited to the magical tale that has been woven around it. Inside are 19th-century boxpews and a curious piscina shaped like a man's head. Exceptionally fine coomb scenery with wooded valleys and steep screes surrounds the area.

Follow the road SP 'Oareford, Robber's Bridge' for 1½ miles. Cross the bridge and continue the steep ascent to join the A39. Proceed along a scenic moorland road, with fine views across the Bristol Channel, and reach Porlock Hill.

PORLOCK HILL, Somerset

The notorious incline of this hill as it rises from Porlock is one of the steepest in Britain, and the breathtaking view from its summit surpasses many. A prehistoric stone circle survives close by.

Make a steep and winding descent (1 in 4) into Porlock.

Rain and mist add extra dimensions of beauty and mystery to Northern Exmoor.

PORLOCK, Somerset

Saxon Kings chose the site of this enchanting coastal village as a base from which to hunt in Exmoor Forest, and nowadays it serves as an ideal touring centre. A famous riding school is established here, and it is difficult to venture far without meeting horses and riders. Notable buildings in Porlock include 15th-century Doverhay Manor House and a mainly 13th-century red-stone church containing the tomb of one John Harrington, who is said to have fought at Agincourt. This remarkable monument is topped by almost life-size effigies of Harrington and his wife. Like many of its neighbours Porlock attracted an artistic following bent on recording its delights in paint and verse. Robert Southey the poet was obviously disenchanted with the weather when he stayed at the Ship Inn and wrote: 'Porlock, I shall forget thee not, here by the unwelcome summer rain confined . . . .'

Leave the village on the B3225 and drive to Porlock Weir.

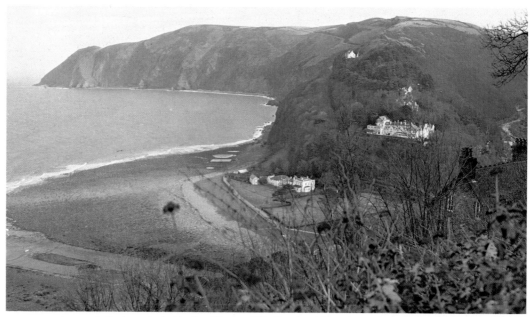

Lynmouth Bay is overlooked by the cliff mass of Blackhead and the ancient earthworks on Wind Hill.

Culbone Church occupies a delightfully wooded position beside a stream.

PORLOCK WEIR & CULBONE CHURCH, Somerset

In years gone by Porlock was a thriving port, but all that remains today is the miniature harbour of this unique little Porlock Bay hamlet. Pleasure craft make good use of its sheltered waters, and its shingle beach is backed by cliffs cloaked with thick woodland. A pleasant walk leads from here to Culbone, where can be seen the smallest English church still in regular use. The building displays Norman and later styles, and measures only 33 by 13½ft. Inside are old benches and a 14th-century screen, while all around are woods and pits once used by a charcoal-burning community.

Return to Porlock and take the 'Lynmouth' road, then branch right on to an unclassified road SP 'Alternative Route via Toll Road' and climb gradually to open moorland. Meet a main road and turn right on to the A39, re-entering Devon at County Gate with a picnic site to the left. After another 2¼ miles reach a footpath leading right to Foreland Point.

Out of season Porlock Weir once more becomes a quiet fishing hamlet.

FORELAND POINT AND LIGHTHOUSE, Devon

The footpath to this lighthouse runs through magnificent coastal scenery (NT) and affords extensive views of the Bristol Channel.

Continue to Countisbury Hill.

COUNTISBURY HILL, Devon

Stagecoach drivers had to change horses at the ancient inn on top of this exceptionally steep hill. West of the inn prehistoric earthworks (NT) overlook the sea and superb cliff walks can be made beyond the small local church.

Descend Countisbury Hill (1 in 4) to Lynmouth.

LYNMOUTH, Devon

In 1812 the poet Shelley and his 16-year-old bride were captivated by the beautiful little fishing village that stood here. Since then tourism and a rash of boarding houses have given it a new lease of commercial life, but the basic framework of towering cliffs and swirling river valleys remains. Disastrous floods that made national headlines in 1952 swept away part of the quay, a great deal of the resort, and a curious edifice known as the Rhenish Tower. Afterwards the East and West Lyn rivers were widened, and strong walls built to prevent a recurrence of the tragedy. This tidying up included the rebuilding of the tower, which is supposed to resemble a type found in Germany and was originally constructed to store salt water for indoor bathing. The picturesque lower town is a medley of colour-washed cottages clustered amid gardens bright with roses, fuchsias, and other shrubs.

Ascend Lynmouth Hill and return to Lynton.

THOMAS HARDY'S WESSEX

Hardy's novels featured many places, thinly disguised, from his beloved Dorset. Here the visitor can find his barren island and wind-blasted heaths, earthworks overlooking thatch and stone villages from the tops of green downs, and salt lagoons held behind by giant shingle banks.

Chesil Bank stretches for 12 miles from Fortuneswell on the Isle of Portland to Abbotsbury.

WEYMOUTH, Dorset

Weymouth's early claim to fame was as the only safe port for miles around, but the town became fashionable for seaside holidays after King George III began coming here in 1789. Georgian terraces still line the wide Esplanade, and quaint little back streets wind round the old harbour. Known for years for the comings and goings of cross-Channel ferries, cargo boats, and pleasure craft, the resort offers sun and sea bathing. Among Weymouth's places of interest are the Museum of Local History and No. 3 Trinity Street. The latter is actually two 17th-century cottages with contemporary furnishings (open).

Leave Weymouth by the A354 SP 'Portland'. Cross Small Mouth, the only outlet for the waters of the Fleet, with Chesil Bank (or Beach) to the right.

CHESIL BANK, Dorset

This 20- to 30ft-high pebble ridge is 200yds wide and extends approximately 12 miles from Portland to Abbotsbury. It is separated from the mainland by a channel and tidal lagoon called the East and West Fleet, and joins the mainland at Abbotsbury. Severe storms are commonplace along the coast here, and bathing from the bank is dangerous.

Weymouth Harbour was used extensively by cargo and passenger vessels for many years.

ISLE OF PORTLAND, Dorset

Dorsetman Thomas Hardy referred to this small, almost treeless limestone peninsula as 'The Rock of Gibraltar' and used it in his novels as the 'Isle of Slingers'. Up until the 19th century it was of small importance, but then convict labour from the local prison was used to build the important naval harbour and breakwater that stand here today. The prison is now a Borstal institution. An old lighthouse on Portland Bill now serves as a bird-watching station. The interior of the island is pitted with excavations left by the extraction of the prized Portland Stone, which was used by Wren for St Paul's Cathedral. All round the coast are the deserted quays where it was loaded before road transport became a practicable possibility.

Continue on the A354 to Fortuneswell and Portland Castle.

FORTUNESWELL, Dorset

East of the village high cliffs drop to the waters of Portland Harbour. Close by is the highest spot in the peninsula, a 490ft eminence bristling with the 19th-century forts and batteries of the vast Verne Citadel.

PORTLAND CASTLE, Dorset

Built by Henry VIII in 1520, this fortress (AM) was part of a defensive chain that stretched from Kent in the east to Cornwall in the west. Its 14ft thick walls were built to absorb cannon fire.

The statue of Thomas Hardy in Dorchester.

At roundabout take 2nd exit then climb steeply through Fortuneswell with SP 'Portland Bill'. Fine views can be enjoyed from the car park at the top of the ascent. Reach Easton.

EASTON, Dorset

Thatched Avice's Cottage, a 17th-century Portland Island dwelling now containing a museum, was featured as the heroine's home in Thomas Hardy's novel *The Well Beloved*. Near by is the single pentagonal tower of Bow and Arrow Castle, said to have been built by William Rufus in the 11th-century. It derives its name from the many small loopholes which pierce the walls. Pennsylvania Castle was built during the 19th century for the Governor of Portland.

Bear left unclassified and proceed to Southwell. At the Eight Kings (PH) turn left for Portland Bill.

PORTLAND BILL AND LIGHTHOUSE, Dorset

This barren mass of limestone drops to only 20ft above the sea at the southern tip of the Isle. Nearby Pulpit Rock is a pinnacle rising from the sea in a series of crags and caves. For years its labyrinthine tunnels were used by smugglers.

Return to the Eight Kings (PH) and turn left to reach Weston, passing one of the Portland stone quarries on the way.

WESTON, Dorset

Portland stone, a superb material made famous by architect Sir Christopher Wren while he was rebuilding London after the Great Fire, is quarried near this village.

Drive through Weston, climb to the top of Portland Hill, and turn left. Descend into Fortuneswell and cross to the mainland. After 1 mile turn left on to the B3157 SP 'Bridport' and proceed through Charlestown and Chickerell to reach Portesham.

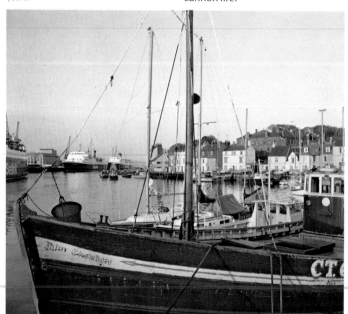

PORTESHAM, Dorset

This village has an attractive green and stands at the foot of hills dotted with ancient monuments. Those nearest include burial mounds and standing stones.

Proceed on the B3157 to reach Abbotsbury.

ABBOTSBURY, Dorset

This very attractive stone-built village has a notable 15th-century tithe barn and gateway from an ancient Benedictine monastery and a 15th- to 16th-century church with a pulpit bearing the marks of Civil War bullets. Abbotsbury Gardens, 20 beautiful acres of rare sub-tropical plants are 1½ miles west of the village. Excellent views are afforded by Chapel Hill, named after the 15th-century chapel standing on its exposed summit.

ABBOTSBURY SWANNERY, Dorset

Swans, once considered a table delicacy, were bred here as long ago as 1393 to provide food for the monastery at Abbotsbury village. The swannery (open) lies ½ mile south of the village in the lagoon formed by Chesil Bank. Some 560 swans and various species of geese, ducks, and other water birds live here.

Continue on the 'Bridport' road and ascend steep Abbotsbury Hill for excellent views over low-hedged fields to the sea. Pass through Swyre to reach Burton Bradstock.

BURTON BRADSTOCK, Dorset

The restored 15th-century church in this picturesque thatched village has an embattled central tower. Unusually stratified cliffs of geological interest can be seen to the east.

Leave Burton Bradstock and proceed for 2 miles; a short detour can be made to West Bay.

WEST BAY, Dorset

A port since the 13th century, West Bay is still used for fishing but additionally caters for small cargo boats and pleasure craft. At one time it served as a harbour for Bridport, which lies 1½ miles north, but nowadays it supplements its port business with resort facilities.

Continue on B3157 to reach Bridport.

BRIDPORT, Dorset

For over 750 years Bridport has been associated with rope and net making, and it is still Europe's principal centre for the production of fishing nets, lines, and cordage. These fascinating local trades are featured in a permanent exhibition at Bridport Museum and Art Gallery. Also here are exhibits showing the archaeology, geology, and natural history of the area. After the battle of Worcester in 1651 Charles II came here to hide, rather incautiously, at the best inn in town; this is now a chemist's shop.

Excavations at Maiden Castle in 1937 revealed the bones of men killed whilst defending the fort against the Romans.

Leave Bridport on the A35 'Dorchester' road and enjoy fine views from Askerswell Down. Proceed to the Nine Stones.

NINE STONES, Dorset

This ancient stone circle (AM) beside the A35 ½ mile west of Winterbourne Abbas is the most notable of many tumuli and configurations of stones in the Dorchester area.

Continue through Winterbourne Abbas. At the end of the village bear right on to the B3159 SP 'Weymouth', then right again on to an unclassified road SP 'Hardy Monument'. Climb on to heathland and turn left to reach the monument.

Dorchester Museum displays many exhibits in elegant Victorian surroundings.

HARDY MONUMENT, Dorset

Admiral Hardy, who was beside Lord Nelson at his death during the battle of Trafalgar, is commemorated here by an obelisk on top of Black Down. Tremendous views can be enjoyed from the hill top (NT).

Continue for 2 miles to a T-junction, and turn right on to the B3159 to enter Martinstown. Drive to the end of the village and branch left on to an unclassified road. In 1¼ miles at a T-junction turn right on to A35. Continue to Dorchester.

DORCHESTER, Dorset

Thomas Hardy was born 2 miles north-east of Dorchester in a cottage (NT, open by appointment), at Higher Bockhampton. The town itself is featured in several of his novels as 'Casterbridge', and the original manuscript of *The Mayor of*

Casterbridge can be seen among other relics in the County Museum. Excellent finds from periods before and after the Romans founded their major walled town of *Durnovaria* here c AD43 are also displayed, and foundations of a Roman villa complete with tessellated pavement can be seen at Colliton Park. After the Monmouth rebellion Judge Jeffries held his notorious 'Bloody Assize' at the Antelope Hotel in 1685, sentencing 292 local men to various degrees of punishment for their treachery. Up to 74 of them were hanged in the town, and their heads were impaled on the railings of St Peter's Church as a grim warning against treason. The rest were deported. Much later in 1834 the infant trades union movement was dealt a public blow at the trial of 6 agricultural workers later to become known as the Tolpuddle Martyrs. They were tried in the courtroom of the old Shire Hall, now a Tolpuddle memorial (open), and were sentenced to transportation for joining forces to request a wage increase for local farmworkers. Also of interest in the town are the Dorset Military Museum, the Dinosaur Museum, and the 17th-century Napper's Mite almshouses.

Leave Dorchester on the A354 'Weymouth' road. An unclassified road on the right leads to Maiden Castle.

MAIDEN CASTLE, Dorset

Situated 2 miles south west of Dorchester, this vast prehistoric hillfort (AM) occupies 120 acres of land and is the finest of its kind in Britain. It was large enough to have accommodated 5,000 people, and probably developed from a simple bank and ditch defence against neighbouring tribes. After successfully storming it the Romans used the castle as a base and built a temple c AD367 within its ramparts.

Continue along the A354 and drive over downland. Pass through Broadwey and return to Weymouth.

SHAFTESBURY, Dorset
Situated on the edge of a 700ft plateau, Shaftesbury is an ancient town full of quaint corners and little eccentricities. Its most famous street, cobbled Gold Hill, plunges down the hillside with a graceful abandon. Thomas Hardy used the original town name Shaston when featuring it in his novels. Shaftesbury's history began with the abbey established here c880, a foundation that became the burial place of Edward the Martyr and grew to be one of the richest in the area until destroyed at the Dissolution in the 16th century. Only slight remains now exist (AM, open sometimes), but various relics are preserved in the Abbey Ruins Museum. In the Grosvenor Hotel is the famous Chevy Chase sideboard, which was carved from a single piece of oak in the 13th century.

Take the A30 'Sherborne, Yeovil' road and descend to the Blackmoor Vale. In 5 miles at East Stour, turn left on to the B3092 SP 'Sturminster Newton' and enter the Stour Valley. Continue to Marnhull.

MARNHULL, Dorset
Thomas Hardy called this village Marlott and made it the birthplace of his heroine in *Tess of the d'Urbervilles*. The 14th-century church has an attractive pinnacled tower overlooking Blackmoor Vale.

Continue to Sturminster Newton.

STURMINSTER NEWTON, Dorset
Important livestock markets are held in this southern Blackmoor Vale town. A fine six-arched medieval bridge spans the Stour, and both Sturminster Mill and the 14th-century Fiddleford Mill one mile to the east have been restored to working order.

Sherborne Abbey has beautiful 15th-century fan vaulting in the choir.

FARMLAND AND FOREST
Gentle hills and farmland watered by several rivers characterize the fertile Blackmoor Vale. In contrast are the rolling grass and woodlands of Cranborne Chase, a vast area that was once the private hunting preserve of kings.

Gold Hill, Shaftesbury's most picturesque street, overlooks the Blackmoor Vale.

Continue through Sturminster Newton on the 'Blandford' road. Cross a bridge and turn right on to the A357 SP 'Stalbridge' then pass through agricultural country to reach Lydlinch Common. Continue for ¾ mile and turn left on to an unclassified road SP 'Stourton Caundle'. Pass the edge of Stourton Caundle and proceed to Purse Caundle.

PURSE CAUNDLE, Dorset
Purse Caundle Manor is an excellent medieval house (open), notable for its great hall and chamber, and beautiful oriel window.

Proceed for ¼ mile and turn left on to the A30 SP 'Sherborne'. Continue to Milborne Port.

MILBORNE PORT, Dorset
Although stone is the predominant building material in this area, beautiful Venn House was brick built in Queen Anne style c1700. The local church preserves Saxon work, and a fine tympanum over the south door.

Proceed on the A30 to Sherborne. (For the town centre turn left)

SHERBORNE, Dorset
Winding streets of mellow stone-built houses dating from the 15th century onwards weave a fascinating web across this beautiful and historic town. From AD705 to 1075 Sherborne was a cathedral city, but the great church was adopted by a slightly later monastery that flourished until the Dissolution in the 16th century. Many of the foundation's buildings were adopted by other bodies and survive in a good state of preservation. Some were occupied by the famous Sherborne School, and the Abbey Gatehouse now accommodates the Sherborne Museum of local history. Over all stands the Norman to 15th-century Abbey Church, a magnificent building best known for its superb fan vaulting. The older of the town's two castles stands ½ mile east and dates from the 12th and 13th centuries. It was reduced to a picturesque heap of ruins (AM) in the Civil War. Sherborne's 16th-century castle was built for Sir Walter Raleigh, and contains fine furniture, paintings, and porcelain (open). It is set in 20-acre grounds designed by the 18th-century garden landscaper Capability Brown.

Follow SP 'Dorchester' to leave Sherborne on the A352. Pass through wooded country and continue through Middlemarsh. Make a winding ascent on the outer slopes to 860ft High Stoy to pass through a gap in the hills and reach Minterne Magna.

MINTERNE MAGNA, Dorset
Features of the attractive wild shrub garden that occupies 29 acres of ground round Minterne House (open) include bamboo-lined walks, great banks of Himalayan and Chinese rhododendrons, and a beautiful collection of azaleas.

Continue for 2 miles and branch left to enter Cerne Abbas. The turf-cut Giant can be seen to the left.

CERNE ABBAS GIANT, Dorset
This 180ft long figure (NT) is believed to be associated with fertility rites and may date from before the Roman occupation.

CERNE ABBAS, Dorset
The village of Cerne Abbas derives its name from a Benedictine abbey founded here in 987. Remains of this include a beautiful 15th-century guesthouse, and the contemporary tithe barn has been converted into a house. Early examples of heraldic stained glass can be seen in the windows of the local church.

In Cerne Abbas centre turn left on to an unclassified road, then in ¼ mile turn right on to the 'Piddletrenthide' road to reach that village.

PIDDLETRENTHIDE, Dorset
Attractive yellow-stone houses are scattered for nearly a mile along the banks of the River Piddle, or Trent. The 15th-century church has one of the finest towers in Dorset.

Turn right onto the B3143 and continue through Piddlehinton. Continue for 1½ miles and turn left on to the Puddletown road B3142 to pass Waterston Manor and reach Puddletown.

PUDDLETOWN, Dorset
Thomas Hardy's Weatherbury in *Far from the Madding Crowd*, this village is one of the most attractive in Dorset and features a beautiful 15th-century church with an unusual panelled roof. Elizabethan and later Waterston Manor stands 2 miles northwest and was described by Hardy as Bathsheba's house in *Far from the Madding Crowd*. Between the village and Wareham are stretches of moorland that were part of the novel's Egdon Heath.

ATHELHAMPTON HOUSE, Dorset
Dorset
Standing in 10 acres of formal landscape and water gardens about 1 mile east of Puddletown is the notable 15th- and 16th-century Athelhampton House, one of England's finest medieval houses (open).

Leave Puddletown by turning left on to the A354 SP 'Blandford'. Continue to Milborne St Andrew, then take an unclassified valley road to the left and drive to Milton Abbas.

BULBARROW HILL, Dorset ST70

Excellent views over much of Dorset can be enjoyed from this 902ft hill, which is an official AA Viewpoint and one of the highest summits in this part of the country.

Follow SP 'Blandford', and in ½ mile bear left. In 3½ miles turn right and at the edge of Winterbourne Stickland turn left. In 4 miles cross the River Stour into Blandford Forum.

Milton Abbas was built by the owner of Milton Abbey to replace a village which he demolished because it spoilt his view.

Bulbarrow Hill is situated in a part of Dorset which is designated as an area of outstanding natural beauty.

Leave Blandford Forum on the B3082 then A350 SP 'Warminster'. Continue along the Stour Valley and pass through Stourpaine. Just past the village on the left are the hills of Hambledon and Hod.

HAMBLEDON AND HOD HILLS, Dorset

Grass-covered Hambledon Hill rises to 622ft and is topped by earthworks raised at various times between the stone age and the Roman conquest. Its steep flanks, worth climbing for the tremendous views, were used by General Wolfe to train troops before embarking to take Quebec. To the south east is slightly lower Hod Hill, which features ancient earthworks and traces of a Roman camp that was built and manned cAD63.

Continue to Iwerne Minster.

IWERNE MINSTER, Dorset

The local Norman to 17th-century church has an attractive stone spire. Just outside the village is the site of a Roman villa.

From Iwerne Minster war memorial turn right on to the unclassified 'Tarrant Gunville' road. Climb on to the heights of Cranborne Chase and turn left on to the Shaftesbury road. Excellent views across Blackmoor Vale can be enjoyed from this section of route. Continue for 1¾ miles and at crossroads turn right for Ashmore.

ASHMORE, Dorset

Georgian houses mingle with flint, stone, and brick cottages round a duckpond and 19th-century church in this charming village. The village itself stands at 700ft in the chalk hills of Cranborne Chase and is the highest in Dorset. To the north is a summit, topped by a prehistoric earthwork, which commands views across the Chase to the Solent channel and the Isle of Wight.

Keep left of Ashmore village pond and in 1 mile join the B3081 to enter Wiltshire for a short distance. On the right is tree-capped Win Green, a 910ft hill which is accessible by track and is the highest point on Cranborne Chase. Re-enter Dorset and descend Zig-Zag Hill to enter Shaftesbury.

The atmosphere of rural tranquillity at Ashmore is enhanced by a duckpond.

MILTON ABBAS, Dorset

Set in unspoilt rural surroundings, this peaceful village of thatched and whitewashed cottages was designed and built from scratch during the 18th century. It was probably the first integrally planned village in Britain. The Brewery Farm Museum is housed in the old brewery and contains antique agricultural implements, bygones, old photographs, and other relics.

From the foot of the village follow the 'Hilton' road past Milton Abbey.

MILTON ABBEY, Dorset

The beautiful abbey church dates from the 14th and 15th centuries and stands in front of a hill surmounted by a Norman chapel. Next to Milton Abbey is 15th-century Abbot's Hall, which was incorporated in a mansion by architects Sir William Chambers and James Wyatt. The huge 18th-century mansion here now is of exceptional interest and houses a school. It is open during the summer months.

Reach Hilton and in ¾ mile turn right and shortly right again for Bulbarrow Hill.

BLANDFORD FORUM, Dorset

All but 50 or so of the town's houses were destroyed by a terrible fire in 1731, which explains why handsome brick and stone architecture of the late 18th century is so much in evidence. Earlier survivals include the Ryves Almshouses of 1682, Dale House of 1689, and the early 17th-century Old House. Much of the countryside round Blandford is rich arable and dairy-farming land, watered by the beautiful River Stour to the south and fringed by the lovely countryside of Cranborne Chase to the north and west.

CRANBORNE CHASE, Dorset

Now an area of rolling grasslands scattered with fine beechwoods, the Chase covers over 100 square miles between Shaftesbury and Salisbury and was once a royal hunting forest. Subsequently the local hunting rights passed into the hands of the earls of Salisbury and Shaftesbury.

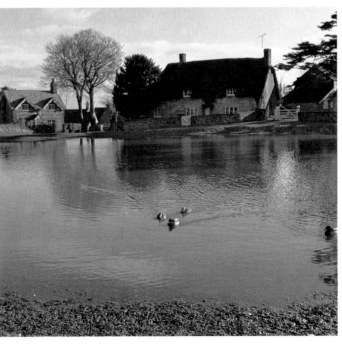

THE ISLE OF PURBECK

Superb views over this exceptionally beautiful peninsula can be enjoyed from high downs that drop sheer to the sea as massive limestone cliffs on the south side. East is the superb haven of Poole Harbour, which insinuates little creeks between heathery promontories and long, tree-covered spits.

THE ISLE OF PURBECK, Dorset

Most of this tour stays within the confines of the Isle of Purbeck, a wild and lovely peninsula that extends from Poole Harbour to Lulworth Cove and is crossed to the west by the Purbeck Hills. Like much of Dorset this is Thomas Hardy country, and reminders of the author and his many novels are everywhere. It is also a designated area of outstanding natural beauty.

SWANAGE, Dorset

This busy resort stands between towering downs that end as cliff-girded promontories on both sides of the sandy bay. Winding, switchback streets weave down to a shopping and amusement area concentrated on the only level piece of ground in the town – the sea front. Farther round the bay is the small pier and quay, where the Bournemouth ferry docks and anglers fish. An attractive group of old buildings clusters round the Mill Pond, off the Main Street and near the parish church is the town museum.

DURLSTON COUNTRY PARK, Dorset

Accessible from Swanage by road or a 1-mile footpath, this fascinating area of wild clifftop has many unusual features. Imposing Durlston Castle is built of Purbeck stone and occupies a lovely site near the headland. On Durlston Head itself is a 40-ton globe map of the world, fashioned from Portland stone quarried in the district, and $\frac{1}{4}$ mile away near the Anvil Lighthouse are the Tilly Whim caves – old quarries once used by smugglers.

Leave Swanage on the A351 SP 'Wareham'. In 1½ miles turn left on to the B3069 SP 'Kingston' to pass through Langton Matravers, a picturesque hillside village of local stone. At the end of the village turn left on to an unclassified road for Worth Matravers.

WORTH MATRAVERS, Dorset

This village is an enchanting combination of steep streets and stone cottages. A rough road south leads to the tiny Norman chapel and fine views on lonely St Alban's (or Aldhelm's) Head, while a toll road to the west leads to the cliff-encircled Chapman's Pool.

From Worth Matravers take the Corfe Castle road and in 1¼ miles at a T-junction turn left to rejoin the B3069. Continue to Kingston, with good views to Corfe Castle.

KINGSTON, Dorset

Features of 19th-century Kingston Church, considered one of the finest in the area, include black Purbeck marble pillars and a beautiful stone-vaulted chancel.

From Kingston a pleasant detour from the main route can be taken via a toll road to 600ft Swyre Head. In clear weather both the Isle of Portland and Isle of Wight can be seen from here. On the main route, bear right with the B3069 and make a sharp, winding descent to meet the A351. Turn left to enter Corfe Castle.

CORFE CASTLE, Dorset

Dominated by the picturesquely ruined stronghold from which it takes its name, this Purbeck-stone village owes its existence to the curiously symmetrical hill on which the castle stands. The mound rises exactly in the centre of a gap in the Purbeck Hills and was probably first fortified by King Alfred against the Danes. When the Normans came they occupied the site and began the magnificent 12th- to 15th-century castle (open) whose remains can be seen today. After the Civil War Cromwell made sure that it could never again be used against him by blowing it up with gunpowder. A river curls round the

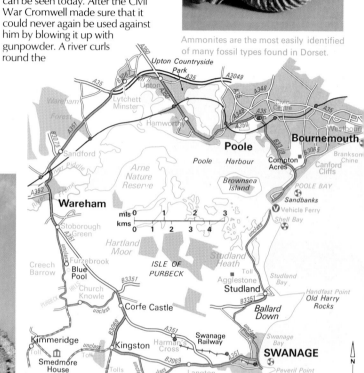

Ammonites are the most easily identified of many fossil types found in Dorset.

Corfe Castle dominates its surroundings.
The River Frome flows to the south of Wareham

base of the steep hill. On the village side is a deep moat spanned by a bridge, and in a garden off the main street is a perfect replica of the village and castle in miniature. Various old relics from the village can be seen in the local museum, and an interesting (though very informal) fossil museum occupies a shed near the castle gates.

Continue along the 'Wareham' road and just past the castle turn left on to an unclassified road and skirt the castle hill to reach Church Knowle. Drive through Church Knowle and meet crossroads. A detour can be taken from the main route by turning left and following toll roads through the estate of Smedmore House to Kimmeridge and Kimmeridge Bay.

KIMMERIDGE, Dorset

Thatched and slate-roofed cottages make up this tiny village, which is situated near the shallow bay from which it takes its name. A toll road leads to the coast.

KIMMERIDGE BAY, Dorset

Very low cliffs of black shale ring this wide, sandless bay, and the beach is littered with great chunks of rock literally packed with fossil ammonites. A condition of entry to the beach nowadays is that hammers and chisels should be left behind. A well sunk here in 1959 produces some 10,000 tons of crude oil each year.

SMEDMORE HOUSE, Dorset

Nearly all the land round Kimmeridge village and bay forms part of the Smedmore estate, and it is by permission of the big house that visitors are allowed on to the toll roads that lead to the attractive coast. The house itself (open) shows a combination of Jacobean, Queen Anne, and Georgian styles. Inside is a good collection of antique dolls.

To continue on the main route, turn right at the crossroads outside Church Knowle and cross the Purbeck Hills. Left are views of Creech Barrow and to the right is the attractive Blue Pool.

BLUE POOL, Dorset

Once an ugly scar left by the extraction of clay, this flooded pit (open) has been transformed into one of the county's most famous beauty spots by the re-establishment of coniferous woodland on its banks. Particles of clay suspended in the water make it brilliant blue when conditions are right. A short distance to the north is Furzebrook where a rail-connected terminal exports oil from the Wych Farm oil-field beside Poole Harbour.

Continue to Stoborough Green and turn left on to the A351 to reach Wareham.

WAREHAM, Dorset

Situated between the tidal River Frome and the River Trent (or Piddle), this quiet port has an ancient quay which now serves anglers and pleasure craft. In Saxon times the settlement was defended by earthworks, and their grass-covered remains still almost encircle the town. Much of Wareham was rebuilt after a great fire in 1762, which explains why so many attractive Georgian houses can be seen here. The parish church preserves original Saxon work and contains an effigy of Lawrence of Arabia. To the north of the town are the sandy heathlands and coniferous plantations of 3,500-acre Wareham Forest.

From Wareham go forward SP 'Poole' and at all roundabouts follow signs 'Poole'. After 4½ miles at the A35 roundabout take the 2nd exit SP 'Lytchett Minster B3067' and pass through Lytchett Minster to reach Upton. Here turn right on to the A350 SP 'Hamworthy'. The road ahead at this point leads to the Upton Country Park.

Continue on the A350 and pass through residential Hamworthy before crossing a bridge to reach Poole Old Town.

POOLE, Dorset

Elizabeth I granted Poole county status which it kept until the late 19th century, and today it is a busy mixture of industrial centre and tourist resort. Its good beach and sheltered harbour have made it popular with holidaymakers, and its position close to a lovely and historic area of heaths and pinewoods makes it ideal as a touring base. Many fine old buildings stand in Poole's historic precinct, including the 18th-century Guildhall and a medieval merchant's house called Scaplen's. Both buildings contain local interest

Kimmeridge Bay, which is famous for its fossils, is overlooked by a ruined tower that was built in the early 19th century.

museums. Poole has a well-known pottery and also the RNLI Headquarters which has a small museum. There are also a maritime museum, aquarium, zoo and the rock and gem centre.

POOLE HARBOUR & BROWNSEA ISLAND, Dorset

Archaeological evidence suggests that Phoenician sailors were using this vast harbour as early as 800BC. It is the second largest natural harbour in the world, and has a coastline that measures over 100 miles if all its indentations are considered. Its largest island is Brownsea, which is accessible by boat from Poole Quay

and is famous as the site of Lord Baden-Powell's first scout camp. Part of its wild heath, wood, and reed-fringed marshland is protected as a nature reserve (NT) and is a haven for many forms of wildlife, including the rare red squirrel.

Follow signs 'Bournemouth' at all roundabouts and continue to follow 'Bournemouth' signs to reach the Poole Civic Centre gyratory system. From here follow signs 'Sandbanks' B3369 to skirt Poole Harbour. In 2½ miles a short detour to Compton Acres Gardens at Canford Cliffs can be made by turning left on to the B3065 and following the signs.

COMPTON ACRES GARDENS, Dorset

These famous private gardens (open) are amongst the finest in Europe and cover some 15 acres overlooking Poole Harbour, Brownsea Island and the Purbeck Hills beyond. There are seven separate and secluded gardens; English, Heather, Japanese, Italian, Roman, Rock and Water, each with its own individual beauty. Most of them contain a priceless collection of bronze and marble statues from all over the world. The careful lay-out of the gardens also include paths, bridges and stepping stones over streams and ponds.

On the main route continue with the B3369 to Sandbanks.

SANDBANKS, Dorset

The sandy beaches of this mile-long peninsula are backed by large houses and a car ferry operates from Haven Point for Studland and Swanage.

At the one-way system join the ferry lane and cross the entrance of Poole Harbour by ferry, then follow an unclassified road to Studland.

STUDLAND, Dorset

Built mainly of red brick, this village contains a fine Norman church and offers 2 miles of sandy beach sheltered by dunes. Moorland extends west from here to Wareham, and on the heathland 1 mile north west is a 500-ton ironstone rock known as the Agglestone.

BALLARD DOWNS AND OLD HARRY ROCKS, Dorset

Views from Studland Bay extend to the headland of Handfast Point and the isolated chalk stacks of the Old Harry Rocks. A little farther south the great bulk of Ballard Down dominates Swanage and offers good coastal views.

From Studland turn inland on the B3351. In 1 mile turn left on to an unclassified road SP 'Swanage' and climb round Ballard Down to return to Swanage.

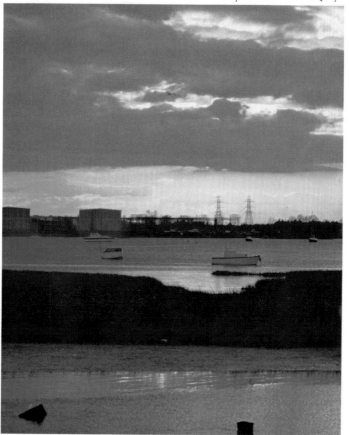

The less sightly aspects of 20th-century life are softened by sunset at Poole Harbour.

35

MINEHEAD, Somerset

The natural beauty of its surroundings combined with its delightful situation and mild climate have made this a popular seaside resort with holidaymakers from all over the country. The Esplanade commands a wide sweep of the bay, where the sands are good and bathing is safe. A prominent feature of the high ground behind the town is North Hill, which overlooks the quaint little harbour some hundreds of feet below and affords fine views across the Bristol Channel. On the landward slope is the parish church, where years ago a light burned constantly to guide travellers on the moor and lead ships to the harbour. During these times Minehead harbour was a busy Channel port second only to Bristol, but now it is just the pleasant holiday town it appears to be. Among its attractions are the beautifully-kept Blenheim Gardens, where there is a model town which is floodlit in the evening.

WEST SOMERSET RAILWAY, Somerset

Britain's longest private line, this railway was re-opened in 1976 and runs 20 miles from the coast at Minehead to Bishop's Lydeard. Steam and diesel trains provide a nostalgic way to enjoy the scenery. Refreshments and souvenirs are available at the Minehead terminus.

Leave Minehead on the A39 'Porlock' road and enter the Exmoor National Park area. In 2¼ miles turn right on to an unclassified road and drive to Selworthy.

EXMOOR NATIONAL PARK (EAST), Somerset

East Exmoor and its associated area is a gentler landscape than the rugged central moor. Open moorland contrasts colourfully with the intensively farmed Brendon slopes, and both natural and planted forests lap occasional rocky summits that afford good all-round views. To the north is the beautiful Bristol Channel coast, while inland are National Trust villages that include some of the most picturesque communities in the entire west country.

SELWORTHY, Somerset

This charming village (NT) is one of the most frequented beauty spots in north Somerset, and is grouped round a walnut-shaped green attractively edged with flowers and overlooked by several old cottages. Also of note are the 15th-century almshouses and an old tithe barn, while over all is the sturdy square tower of the 16th-century church. This handsome building is renowned for the particularly fine wagon roof in its south aisle. Majestic Selworthy Beacon (NT) rises to 1,012ft north of the village and is a good viewpoint.

Return to the A39 'Porlock' road, turn right, and in ½ mile pass the edge of Allerford.

OVER THE BRENDON HILLS

Where Exmoor merges into the Brendon Hills the landscape changes from wild heathland to a tapestry of fields and forest. Wooded byways and patches of moor open on to panoramic seascapes fringed with busy resorts and unspoiled villages.

Beyond Luccombe well-tended countryside gives way to open moorland which rises to the summit of 1,705ft Dunkery Beacon.

ALLERFORD, Somerset

Quaint cottages and the remains of a manor house can be seen here; of particular note is Allerford's much-photographed double-arched packhorse bridge.

Continue on the A39 and in ½ mile turn left on to an unclassified road SP 'Luccombe'. Pass several packhorse bridges to the right and in ¾ mile at crossroads turn right SP 'Dunkery Beacon'. A detour to Luccombe village can be taken from the main route, by keeping straight ahead.

LUCCOMBE, Somerset

Access to this secluded little village (NT), whose name means 'closed-in combe', is by a narrow winding lane. The village church has a good tower, and the churchyard is entered through a charming lychgate.

On the main route, begin the long ascent of Dunkery Hill and bear left at the fork.

HOLNICOTE ESTATE, Somerset

The rolling moorland and dense forest round Dunkery Hill are part of the Holnicote Estate (NT), which incorporates some of the loveliest scenery in the Exmoor National Park. About half its 12,443 acres fall within the Exmoor boundaries, and the whole forms a band 6 miles deep along the Bristol Channel coastline. Features include various prehistoric remains, 4 ancient packhorse bridges, and such notable villages as picturesque Selworthy and Luccombe (both NT).

Continue the ascent of Dunkery Hill through progressively wilder scenery and reach a road summit of 1,450ft. A footpath leads from the carpark here to the 1,705 ft viewpoint of Dunkery Beacon.

DUNKERY BEACON, Somerset

Dunkery Beacon (NT), the highest point on Exmoor, is surrounded by some of the most breathtaking scenery in the national park. It was once a link in a chain of fire-beacon sites across the west country. The top is nowadays shared by a cairn commemorating the gift of the hill to the National Trust, the remains of several tumuli, and an official AA viewpoint marker. The Cloutsham Nature Trail (open all year) starts from Webber's Post and covers some 3 miles of varied habitat.

Stay on the unclassified road and descend for 2½ miles, then go forward on to the B3224 to reach Wheddon Cross. Go forward with the B3224 SP 'Taunton' and ascend on to the Brendon Hills.

BRENDON HILLS, Somerset

Undulating slopes with a rich patchwork of forest and farmland are the distinctive characteristics of this gentle range. Farmers, and more recently the Forestry Commission, have transformed the landscape from moorland into a semi-cultivated countryside of symmetrical fields bordered by beech hedges and interspersed with acres of dark conifers. In earlier times small hillside mining villages sprang up to work local deposits of iron ore, but the last Brendon iron mine closed down in 1883. Vestiges of an even earlier age can be seen along the Ridgeway, which is studded with round barrows dating from the Bronze Age.

After 1¾ miles reach Heath Poult Cross and turn right on to an unclassified road. Continue for 5 miles, along a ridge above the Exe Valley then descend into the Valley and turn left on to the A396, SP 'Tiverton'. In 2½ miles at Exebridge turn left on to an unclassified road SP 'Morebath'. After 1½ miles turn left on to the B3190 'Watchet' road, and shortly pass Morebath; 3 miles beyond the village a car park for Wimbleball Lake lies to the left.

The packhorse bridge at Allerford.

Exmoor National Park

The moorland ridges of Dunkery Hill rise beyond Selworthy's thatched cottages.

Watchet Harbour is used by small vessels of all descriptions.

WIMBLEBALL LAKE
Somerset
Great care has been taken to blend this River Haddeo reservoir project with the countryside of south Exmoor. New plantations of trees native to the area have been established right down to the water's edge, and a small area of bank has been given over to leisure facilities for angling, small-boat sailing, and riding. Amenities include a carpark, a picnic area, and planned woodland walks.

Continue on the B3190 through Upton, then in 2 miles at crossroads turn right on to an unclassified road SP 'Wiveliscombe'. After a further 1 mile branch left and drive over crossroads to skirt Clatworthy Reservoir.

CLATWORTHY RESERVOIR,
Somerset
Like its close neighbour Wimbleball, this beautiful upland reservoir has been integrated with the local scenery and is a haven for all kinds of wildlife. A large carpark gives access to a 10-acre public viewing area with picnic facilities.

*Continue, and on the descent turn left and shortly right before crossing the River Tone and reaching Clatworthy. Keep left through the village SP 'Brompton Ralph', and after 1 mile at crossroads, turn left SP 'Raleigh's Cross', then after a further 2 miles meet a T-junction and turn left on to the B3224. Reach Raleigh's Cross Hotel and turn right on to the B3190 SP 'Watchet'. There are excellent views of the Bristol Channel at first before the long descent to crossroads at Fair Cross.
Here turn left on to an unclassified road SP 'Washford', and in 1 mile pass the entrance to Cleeve Abbey.*

CLEEVE ABBEY, Somerset
Remains of this 13th-century Cistercian abbey (AM), founded in 1188, include a refectory with traceried windows, a timbered roof, and some fine wall paintings. The picturesque gatehouse and painted chamber are of particular note.

The ancient village of Dunster is dominated by its romantic castle.

Continue to Washford, then turn right on to the A39 Bridgwater Road. In ¾ mile at crossroads turn left on to the B3190 for Watchet.

WATCHET, Somerset
Coleridge found the main character for his long, moralistic poem *The Rime of the Ancient Mariner* in this historic seaport, which now doubles as a popular resort. The Esplanade offers a grandstand view of the harbour, and the local beaches offer plenty of opportunities for the fossil hunter. Behind the town are the lofty heights of the Brendon and Quantock hill ranges.

Leave Watchet on the B3191 and continue, with views of the Bristol Channel, to Blue Anchor.

BLUE ANCHOR, Somerset
In front of this small hamlet is a clean white beach which sweeps round the alabaster rocks of Blue Anchor Bay in a brilliant arc. The area is well known for its fossils.

Continue on the B3191 to Carhampton.

CARHAMPTON, Somerset
This little village dates back to 833, when it was the site of a Danish victory. Its restored church contains a magnificent painted screen which dates from the 15th century and stretches across the entire breadth of the building. Each January the villagers re-enact the old ceremony of Wassailing the Apple Trees, an ancient custom involving a toast to the largest apple tree in the cider orchards and a libation of cider thrown on its trunk. The whole procedure has more than a suggestion of ancient fertility rites. Close to the church lychgate is an old pub called the Butcher's Arms, which has the date 1638 worked in sheep's knuckle bones in the cobbled floor.

At Carhampton turn right on to the A39 'Minehead' road and after 1½ miles turn left on to the A396 SP 'Tiverton' to enter Dunster.

DUNSTER, Somerset
Dunster is a beautiful medieval village that has often been described as a 'perfect relic of feudal times'. Its unspoilt condition is largely due to its constant ownership by one family, the Luttrells, for some 600 years until 1950. The Norman castle (NT) was the family seat and is well worth visiting. Its oak-panelled halls display magnificent ceilings and fascinating relics. In the centre of the village is the octagonal Yarn Market, which was built in 1609, when Dunster was an important cloth centre. Not far away is the lovely Luttrell Arms, which is said to have stood for three centuries and was originally the house of the Abbot of Cleeve. Among its many features are an interesting 15th-century porch and a fine chamber displaying a wealth of carved oak. The parish church is by far the finest in this part of the country. Both it and its associated buildings are of particularly warm pink sandstone, and the whole harmonious group is set in a tranquil rural scene. Nearby the River Avill is spanned by the ancient Gallox packhorse bridge (AM).

Return along the A396 for ½ mile and turn left to rejoin the A39. Return to Minehead.

WELLS, Somerset

Wells is a delightful cathedral city situated at the foot of the Mendip Hills. The west front of its fine 13th-to 15th-century cathedral is adorned with statues, and inside are a graceful branching staircase and a 14th-century clock. With its associated buildings the cathedral forms part of England's largest medieval ecclesiastical precinct. The Vicar's Close preserves picturesque 14th-century houses, and across the cathedral green is the moated Bishop's Palace (open), where Wells' famous swans ring a bell near the drawbridge for food. Other interesting old buildings include a medieval tithe barn (AM) and the 15th-century parish church. Wells Museum includes a display on the Mendip Caves.

An interesting detour from the main route to the caves of Wookey Hole can be made at Wells: leave the city on the A371 'Cheddar' road and in ¼ mile turn right on to the unclassified 'Wookey Hole' road. Continue for 1½ miles to Wookey Hole. Please note that route directions for the main tour start after the following entry.

WOOKEY HOLE, Somerset

Inhabited for some 650 years from 250BC this gigantic system was hollowed out of the Mendip limestone by the River Axe. Finds relating to the period of habitation can be seen in the associated museum. The old mill at the cave entrance demonstrates the art of paper making, and is a store for Madame Tussaud's waxwork museum and Lady Bangor's fairground collection.

Leave Wells by the A39 'Glastonbury' road and proceed to Glastonbury.

GLASTONBURY, Somerset

High above the skyline of this ancient town is the 520ft pinnacle of Glastonbury Tor, a place associated in myth with fabulous Avalon and the Celtic Otherworld. Glastonbury was probably founded in Celtic times, but according to legend it was created by Joseph of Arimathea. Other traditions connect St Patrick and King Arthur with the abbey, and it is said that Arthur is actually buried here. The well preserved remains that exist today date from the 12th and 13th centuries, and include St Mary's Church, the abbey church, and a number of monastic buildings (open). By far the best preserved is the superb Abbot's Kitchen. Features of the town itself include 2 medieval churches, the George and Pilgrim Inn, a 15th-century abbey courthouse known as the Tribunal (open) containing late prehistoric finds from lake dwellings at Meare and Godney and the Abbey Barn which houses the Somerset Rural Life Museum.

Leave Glastonbury on the B3151 'Meare' road and proceed through low-lying country to Meare.

38

THE POLDEN AND MENDIP RANGES

Low-lying areas of unpopulated countryside are dominated by the bare Mendip summits and lower Polden Hills. Here are the cradle of early English Christianity, the supposed site of King Arthur's fabulous Camelot, and old battlefields that have seen decisive turning points in the country's history.

MEARE, Somerset

From c300BC to cAD100 a lake settlement of houses on stilts and brushwood existed here. Few traces of this survive, but excavations have yielded many interesting finds that are displayed in Taunton and Glastonbury Museums. A 14th-century building known as the Fish House (AM) was used by the monks of Glastonbury to house their fishermen, and the contemporary manor house was a summer residence for the abbots.

Over 400 statues survive on the west front of Wells Cathedral. They were made during the 13th century and were inspired by sculpture in Continental cathedrals.

Continue on the B3151 for 1¼ miles and turn left on to an unclassified road SP 'Shapwick'. Meet a T-junction and turn left again. Continue across level wooded countryside to Shapwick. By Shapwick Church turn right on to the 'Bridgwater' road and ascend the gradual slope of the Polden Hills.

THE POLDEN HILLS, Somerset

These low hills (part NT), rising to less than 300ft at their highest point, extend from Glastonbury to a point near Bridgwater and dominate the surrounding marshy levels.

About ¾ mile from Shapwick cross a main road, then continue for ⅓ mile and turn right on to the A39. Proceed along a low ridge for 5 miles, then descend and bear sharp left over the King's Sedgemoor Drain. Cross the M5 and enter Bridgwater.

BRIDGWATER, Somerset

It was here that the Duke of Monmouth proclaimed himself King in 1685, prior to suffering a crushing defeat at nearby Sedgemoor. Of interest are the town's wide main street, the tall spire of St. Mary's church and the Admiral Blake Museum.

From Bridgwater follow SP 'Langport' on the A372 and recross the M5. Drive across Sedgemoor.

SEDGEMOOR, Somerset

In 1685 the last battle on English soil took place here when James II defeated James Duke of Monmouth. The King won a decisive victory at the expense of the lives of some 1,400 of Monmouth's followers. The rebels who survived were subsequently dealt with by the travelling 'Bloody Assize' of the notorious Judge Jeffries.

Continue through Weston Zoyland, then after another 2¼ miles skirt Middlezoy. In 1 mile turn right on to the A361 and follow SP 'Taunton to enter Othery. Continue on to Burrow Bridge.

BURROW BRIDGE & BURROW MUMP, Somerset

Wide views are afforded by the hill, or mump (NT), here; an extensive collection of Victorian engines is housed in an old pumping station (open) opposite the Mump.

Cross the River Parrett and immediately turn left (no SP) on to an unclassified road. Follow SP 'Stathe, Langport', reach Stathe, and follow SP 'Curry Rivel'. After ¾ mile branch right, and in 1 mile ascend Red Hill (NT) for excellent views over Sedgemoor. At the road summit bear right and in ¾ mile turn left on to the A378 to enter Curry Rivel. In ¼ mile turn right on to an unclassified road SP 'Drayton, Muchelney'. Proceed through Drayton to reach Muchelney.

MUCHELNEY, Somerset

The Benedictine abbey whose extensive remains (AM) survive here was not the first foundation on the site. Excavations have revealed a rare Saxon chapel, dating from around the 7th century, beneath ruined Norman monastic buildings. Priest's House is a good 14th-century thatched building (NT).

Leave Muchelney by bearing left with SP 'Langport'. Continue for 1 mile, meet a T-junction, and turn right to enter Huish Episcopi.

Wells Cathedral's 14th-century astronomical clock.

Turn right by Somerton Church into unclassified New Street SP 'Ilchester, Yeovil'. Continue for ⅓ mile and turn right on to the B3151. After 2¾ miles turn right then left across the A372. In 1½ miles at the edge of Ilminster reach a mini-roundabout and take the 1st exit SP 'Yeovilton'.

ILCHESTER, Somerset
In Roman times this quiet River Yeo town was an important military station. Its superb Town Hall houses a 13th-century mace - the oldest staff of office in England.

Wookey Hole was formed by the River Axe.

The Market Cross in Somerton was rebuilt in 1673.

HUISH EPISCOPI, Somerset
Glass by Burne-Jones and a fine Norman doorway are features of the local church, but its crowning glory is a 15th-century tower considered to be the finest in the county.

Turn right on to the A372 'Wincanton, Yeovil' road, and later pass the edge of Long Sutton.

LONG SUTTON, Somerset
This attractive village is grouped round a notable 15th-century church and boasts a 17th-century manor house.

In ½ mile turn left on to the B3165 SP 'Somerton', and in 2¼ miles turn right SP 'Ilchester' to enter Somerton.

SOMERTON, Somerset
Somerton was the capital of Somerset under the West Saxons and is particularly known for its attractive market place. All around the square and along the back streets are handsome old buildings, including the Town Hall of c1700 and the 17th-century Hext Almshouses. Somerton Church carries a magnificent tie-beam roof dating from the 15th century.

On the main route, continue for 1½ miles and pass the entrance to the Royal Naval Air Station for the Fleet Air Arm Museum, Yeovilton.

YEOVILTON, Somerset
Yeovilton's Fleet Air Arm Museum portrays the development of naval aviation since 1903 and displays over 40 historic aircraft.

Proceed for ¼ mile and turn right on to an unclassified road SP 'Queen Camel'. In 2½ miles go forward on to the A359 SP 'Sparkford, Frome' to enter Queen Carmel. Proceed for ¾ mile and turn right on to the A303 to enter Sparkford. Here a detour to Cadbury Castle can be taken. Proceed along the A303 for 1½ miles and turn right on to an unclassified road for South Cadbury.

CADBURY CASTLE, Somerset
Once it was thought that the myths linking this hilltop fort with King Arthur's Camelot had been disproved by excavations revealing evidence of Stone- and Bronze-Age occupation. However, digging in 1966 suggested that the site had been re-defended during Arthur's period. The Saxon King Ethelred (the Unready) established a mint here.

From Sparkford bear right to cross a railway bridge, then turn immediately left on to the A359 'Frome' road passing the Sparkford Motor Museum. Continue for 3 miles and branch left on to the B3152 SP 'Castle Cary'. Continue 1½ miles to enter Castle Cary.

CASTLE CARY, Somerset
Several fine old houses and a pretty duckpond are grouped together at the heart of this pleasant small town. The local lock-up, an unusual circular structure once used for the restriction of petty mischief makers, dates from the 18th century.

Leave Castle Cary with SP 'Bath, Bristol (A371)'. After 1 mile turn left on to the A371 SP 'Shepton Mallet'. Shortly bear right across a railway bridge, then proceed for ½ mile to the Brook House Inn and turn left on to an unclassified road SP 'Alhampton'. In 1 mile enter Alhampton and turn right SP 'Ditcheat'. Proceed to Ditcheat and at a T-junction turn left (no SP). Continue to the Manor House Inn and turn right, then shortly bear left SP 'East Pennard'. Proceed to Wraxall, and at crossroads turn right on to the A37 'Shepton Mallet' road. Ascend Wraxall Hill and at crossroads turn left on to an unclassified road SP 'East Pennard'. In ½ mile turn right SP 'Pilton' to reach Pilton.

PILTON, Somerset
One of the most picturesque villages in the area, lovely Pilton has an ancient cruciform tithe barn (AM) and a church with a magnificent 15th-century roof.

Meet crossroads and turn left, then descend to the church and turn left SP 'Shepton Mallet'. Meet a T-junction and turn right on to the A361. Proceed for 1 mile, then turn left on to the B3136 for Shepton Mallet.

SHEPTON MALLET, Somerset
Wool from flocks grazing the windswept Mendip Hills made the fortune of this pleasant market town. Several good 17th- and 18th-century buildings survive from this period, plus a fine church with an intricately carved nave roof.

Leave the town with SP 'Wells A371' to enter Croscombe.

CROSCOMBE, Somerset
Steep wooded hills surround this stone-built village, which has an old church containing amazing 17th-century pastoral and heraldic carvings in rich black oak.

Continue along the A371 to re-enter Wells.

FROM THE CITY OF ELEGANCE

High in the hills that provided the stone for Britain's most elegant city are the Cotswold wool towns. Sturdy manor houses and fine churches seem to grow from the mellow rock, and everywhere are the grass-grown scars of old quarry workings.

BATH, Avon

Justly spoken of as England's most elegant city, Bath is a spa resort of Georgian terraces, crescents, and squares arranged round spacious landscaped parks in the Avon Valley. Warm local stone is set off by trim lawns and mature trees, and the source of the city's prosperity still bubbles into cisterns and baths built by the Romans some 2,000 years ago. Many centuries after the invaders left *Aquae Sulis* to salvage their crashing empire, the dandified high society of Georgian England resumed the sophisticating process. Beau Nash and other arbiters of fashion came here to gossip with royalty and 'take the waters', and the legions of the wealthy occupied magnificent houses built for them by John Wood and his son. Bath today mainly reflects the cultured tastes of the 17th and 18th centuries, but it also contains relics from more distant periods. The ancient baths themselves receive half a million gallons of water at a constant 49°C each day, and their history is interestingly related in an associated museum. Overlooking the baths is the city's splendid 15th-century Abbey Church, while near by is the Pump Room (open) where people came to cure everything from boredom to gout. Rebuilt in 1795, this popular meeting place offers a choice of coffee or spa water in a genteel atmosphere heightened by chandelier lighting, chamber music, and the occasional sedan chair. The work of the Woods is everywhere, but some of the best examples can be seen in the Circus, the superb Royal Crescent (No. 1 is open), and

the Assembly Rooms (open). A very good museum of costume is housed in the latter. Several museums and similar foundations can be visited in the city, and amongst these are the Holburne of Menstrie Museum, the Victoria Art Gallery and the Bath Carriage Museum.

Leave Bath on the A4 'Chippenham' road and follow the Avon Valley to Batheaston, with views of Little Solsbury Hill to the left.

LITTLE SOLSBURY HILL, Avon

A fine Iron-Age hillfort (NT) featuring ramparts faced with dry-stone walling, stands on this flat-topped 625ft hill.

Beyond Batheaston branch right on to the A363 'Bradford-on-Avon' road. Skirt Bathford and climb along wooded slopes before crossing pleasant farmland to reach Bradford-on-Avon.

BRADFORD-ON-AVON & BARTON FARM COUNTRY PARK, Wilts

The disused Kennet and Avon Canal connects here with the River Avon, which itself is spanned by a 17th-century bridge incorporating a small contemporary lock-up. A tall but tiny Saxon church rescued from obscurity here in the 19th century has turned out to be one of the most important buildings of its age in Britain. Old weavers' cottages stand in Dutch Barton Street, and Barton Farm Country Park contains a superbly preserved 14th-century tithe barn (AM). The Park itself is an unspoilt area of country between the canal and the river.

Bradford-on-Avon's tithe barn houses a collection of agricultural machinery beneath its enormous roof timbers.

Leave the town on the B3109 'Chippenham, Corsham' road. After 1 mile reach the Plough Inn and turn right on to an unclassified road SP 'Great Challield, Holt'. After another 1 mile branch left on to a narrow road through attractive farmland. The road to the right offers a pleasant detour to Holt.

John Wood the Younger built Bath's magnificent Royal Crescent, which is a half-ellipse of 30 houses, between 1767 and 1774. The overall style is based on the drawings of the architect Palladio.

HOLT, Wilts

Local weavers once brought their disputes to The Courts to be settled, but this 17th-century building now enjoys a peaceful retirement amid fine gardens (NT). Features of the latter include topiary work, a lily pond, and an arboretum.

Proceed for 1 mile to Great Challield Manor.

GREAT CHALFIELD MANOR, Wilts

Built in the 15th century, this magnificent stone-built house (NT) features a great hall and is encircled by a moat.

Continue to a T-junction and turn right (no SP) to enter Broughton Gifford. Pass the large village green on the left, then bear left on to the 'Melksham' road. Proceed for 1¼ miles and turn left on to the B3107. After ½ mile at the edge of meet a roundabout and take the 1st exit A350 SP 'Chippenham'. For Melksham town centre take the 2nd exit.

MELKSHAM, Wilts

The River Avon is spanned here by an 18th-century bridge, and an attractive group comprising a converted tithe barn and 17th- and 18th-century houses stands near the church. Nowadays the town is an expanding industrial centre.

Continue with SP 'Chippenham A350', passing through Beanacre with 17th-century Beanacre Manor on the left. Proceed for 1¼ miles and turn right on to the unclassified 'Lacock' road to enter Lacock, then turn right SP 'Bowden Hill, Calne'.

LACOCK, Wilts

A wide architectural range from medieval times to the 18th century has been preserved in the stone, half-timbered, and thatched buildings of this delightful village (NT). Its abbey was the last religious house to be suppressed at the Dissolution in 1539, and was later converted into a private dwelling incorporating many of its medieval buildings. Over the centuries its ancient structure has acquired an octagonal Tudor tower and 17th-century gothic hall. The abbey gatehouse contains a museum of work by W H Fox-Talbot, a 19th-century pioneer of photography who once owned the abbey. Elsewhere in the village is a great tithe barn with 8 massive bays, and a small 14th-century lock-up known as the Cruck House.

About ¼ mile past Lacock Abbey cross the River Avon and begin the ascent of 580ft Bowden Hill. Proceed, with fine views of the Avon Valley, and meet a T-junction on the outskirts of Sandy Lane. Turn left on to the A342 and continue for 1½ miles to pass the entrance to Bowood House.

BOWOOD HOUSE, Wilts

The magnificent Georgian house of Bowood, with its superb art collection, is complemented by its extensive grounds, laid out by Capability Brown.

Descend to join the A4, and drive along the Avon Valley to Chippenham.

CHIPPENHAM, Wilts

Situated on the River Avon near the edge of the Cotswold Hills, this pleasant industrial town was a market centre for centuries. Several attractive half-timbered houses and an old lock-up are preserved here.

Leave Chippenham on the A4 'Bath' road, and proceed for 3½ miles. Meet crossroads and turn left on to an unclassified road for Corsham, on the edge of the Cotswold Hills.

THE COTSWOLDS

The Cotswolds extend from north of Bath to north of Oxfordshire, nowhere exceeding 30 miles in breadth but rising to 1,000ft in some places. From the 12th century the whole area benefited from the profits of wool, and a legacy of that wealth survives in the beautiful old cottages, houses, mansions, and churches which are such a feature of the district.

CORSHAM, Wilts

This developing town has an old heart of Bath limestone and a scattering of buildings from various periods. Of particular note are the 16th-century Flemish Cottages and 17th-century Hungerford Almshouses. Magnificent Corsham Court (open) was extended in Georgian times and shows work by architect John Nash and by Capability Brown, better known as a brilliant landscape gardener. Inside are good pieces of Chippendale furniture and superb paintings.

Leave Corsham with SP 'Chippenham' and after ½ mile meet crossroads. Drive forward over the A4 on to the 'Biddestone, Yatton Keynell' road, and proceed for 1¾ miles to enter Biddestone.

BIDDESTONE, Wilts

Stone houses surround an attractive green and pond in this pretty Cotswold village. The 17th-century manor house (not open) has a brick gazebo, or garden house, and can be seen from the road.

Bear right on to the 'Yatton Keynell' road and after ¾ mile cross the main road SP 'Castle Combe'. After another 1¼ miles enter Yatton Keynell, turn left on to the B4039 and follow SP 'Castle Combe'. Proceed for 1¾ miles, and turn left again on to an unclassified road for Castle Combe village. Parking in the village is severely restricted, so it is advisable to stop at one of the car parks along this road and walk.

Weathered stone houses are grouped around an ancient market cross in Castle Combe.

CASTLE COMBE, Wilts

Built of Cotswold stone deep in a stream-threaded combe, this old weaving centre is acknowledged as one of England's most picturesque villages. Numerous old buildings unalloyed by the brashness of concrete and brick present a homogeneous completeness round the canopied 13th-century market cross. Close to the centre is the 17th-century manor house, now an hotel. The village was transformed into a harbour (by means of damming the stream) for a scene in the film "Dr. Doolittle'.

Return to the B4039 and turn left SP

Winter sunlight on Biddestone Village.

'Acton Turville'. *Proceed for 2½ miles to pass through Burton, and at the end of the village turn left on to the unclassified 'Pucklechurch' road. Continue for 4¼ miles and meet crossroads. Turn left here on to the A46 SP 'Bath' and in ¾ mile pass on the right the entrance to Dyrham Park.*

DYRHAM PARK, Avon

Dyrham Park (NT) was built on the site of a Tudor house between 1692 and 1702 for William Blathwayt, Secretary of State and Secretary for War. Dyrham is barely glimpsed in its vale from the entrance gate, and disappears altogether as the drive descends a steep hillside of rough pasture dotted with trees before it turns along the valley floor to the house. The east front, which then greets the visitor, is a great wall of Bath stone blocking the valley with neat rows of tall, narrow many-paned windows. The interior is laid out as apartments, late 17th-century rooms of sensible and sober taste, influenced by the Dutch — William often went to the Netherlands on business. The furniture, paintings and pottery he collected are all still part of the house. A Dutch-style garden of parterres, terraces and detailed formal designs surrounded Dyrham until about 1800, when it fell to the 'modern' taste for landscaped gardens — the style of 'Capability' Brown, which survives today.

Proceed for 1¾ miles, pass through Pennsylvania, then in ¼ mile meet traffic lights and turn right on to the A420 'Bristol' road. In ¾ mile reach the start of a descent, meet crossroads, and turn left on to an unclassified road (no SP). In 1 mile descend steeply, then near the top of the following ascent turn left SP 'Lansdown, Bath'. Reach the top of a 700ft ridge and pass Bath racecourse. Return to Bath.

WESTON-SUPER-MARE, Avon
Good beaches and lavish entertainment facilities are features of this large Bristol Channel resort. Among many places of interest are a marine lake with boating, an aquarium, and a model village. The resort's wide seafront road is lined by several public gardens and overlooks the low Flat Holme and Steep Holme offshore islands. Both these are particularly rich in birdlife. An Iron-Age earthwork (AM) can be seen 1 mile north on Worlebury Hill.

Leave Weston-super-Mare on the A370 'Bristol' road. Pass through suburbs and cross the M5 then flat countryside to reach Congresbury. Turn left, cross the River Yeo, then turn left again on to the B3133 SP 'Yatton, Clevedon'. Proceed through Yatton then cross and pass through Kenn. Cross the M5 and in ½ mile reach the Clevedon Distributor Road. For a detour to visit Clevedon Court and Clevedon Craft Centre turn right and follow signs. For a detour to Clevedon town centre keep forward.

CLEVEDON COURT, Avon
This superb 14th-century house (NT) is one of the oldest of its type to have survived anywhere in Britain. It carries an even older 13th-century tower and is considered typical of its period, with a screen passage dividing the buttery and kitchen from the great hall and the lord of the manor's living quarters. During the 18th and 19th centuries it became a popular meeting place for the avant-garde of the day. Clevedon Craft Centre lies ½ mile to the south and visitors can watch displays of wood carving and turning here at the weekends.

CLEVEDON, Avon
Situated at a junction of hill ranges, Clevedon is a quiet Severn estuary residential town and resort. The pier, designed to cope with the 40ft tidal range in this area is being restored

The main route turns left SP 'Sea Front' on to an unclassified road and in 1¼ miles turn left on to the B3130 for the front. In a further ½ mile bear left, pass the pier, and keep forward for 1½ miles to meet a T-junction, then turn left on to B3124, SP 'Portishead'. In ½ mile at the Walton-in-Gordano crossroads turn left on to an unclassified road (no SP). Continue high above the shores of the Bristol Channel, then enter a built-up area and turn left into Nore Road (no SP). Continue above the coast and in 1¼ miles pass the AA Portishead viewpoint. Pass Battery Point and descend into Portishead.

PORTISHEAD, Avon
Portishead is a residential town, small resort and former port situated on the lower slopes of a wooded hillside overlooking the Bristol Channel.

BEACHES AND GORGES
In many ways tiny Avon is the envy of much larger counties. Its port city of Bristol is one of the most historic in England, its resort offers miles of sandy beaches, and its interior is riddled by limestone cave systems that extend deep into Somerset.

Birnbeck Pier at Weston-super-Mare.

Leave Portishead on the A369 'Bristol' road. After 2¾ miles reach the M5 junction roundabout and take 4th exit SP 'Clifton' (toll) to enter hill country. Continue through Abbot's Leigh. Proceed for 1¼ miles and turn left on to the B3129 SP 'Clifton'. In ½ mile reach the Clifton Suspension Bridge.

CLIFTON SUSPENSION BRIDGE AND AVON GORGE, Avon
Here, where the sheer limestone cliffs of the Avon Gorge constrict that river to a silver ribbon some 245ft below, is the spectacular suspension bridge by the brilliant engineer Isambard Kingdom Brunel. Started in 1836, it was not completed until 1864, 5 years after his death.
Cross the bridge and in 200yds turn left SP 'Motorway M5'. After a short distance turn left again into Clifton Down Road. After ¼ mile meet crossroads and turn left on to the B4468 SP 'Weston'. The right turn here leads to Bristol Zoo. Descend Bridge Valley Road into the Avon Gorge. At the bottom turn left on to

Clevedon Court, though much altered, preserves many 14th-century features, including the south entrance.

the A4, pass underneath the suspension bridge, and after ¼ mile keep left SP 'City Centre' to remain in Hotwell Road. Enter Bristol city centre.

BRISTOL, Avon
During the 16th century ships out of Bristol sailed to every part of the known world opening up international trading routes in a way never before imagined. In 1843 Brunel launched his SS *Great Britain*, the largest iron ship of the time, and in 1970 its rusting hulk was rescued from the Falkland Islands and returned to the Bristol dry dock in which it was originally built. Extensive renovation has restored it as a proud memorial (open) to its great designer and the city of its birth. Nowadays the city's dock areas are at Avonmouth and Portbury which are more fitted to coping with the vast ships of 20th-century world traffic. Bristol's many lovely old buildings include a cathedral that contains examples of Norman, Early-English, Gothic and Victorian architecture. St Mary Redcliffe, one of the city's finest churches, was built and extended between the 13th and 15th centuries and carries a massive tower with a 285ft spire. The 16th-century Red Lodge (open) houses interesting work carvings and furnishings of contemporary and later date, and the Georgian House (open) features furniture from the 18th-century. Outside the Corn Exchange are the original metal 'nails' upon which merchantmen once put their payments, hence the expression 'to pay cash on the nail'. Various displays and exhibitions can be seen in St Nicholas' Church Museum and the City Museum and Art Gallery.

Other features of the Floating Harbour area are the Bristol Exhibition and Watershed Arts Complexes, the Arnolfini Gallery, National Lifeboat Museum and Bristol Industrial Museum, and the Maritime Heritage Centre.

Follow SP 'Weston (A370)' and in 1½ miles cross the impressive Cumberland Basin and Avon bridges, then keep forward to join the A370 'Long Ashton' bypass. Proceed through pleasant countryside and pass the villages of Flax Bourton and Backwell (Farleigh), then 1½ miles beyond Backwell (West Town), meet crossroads, and turn left on to an unclassified road SP 'Bristol Airport'. Ascend deep and thickly-wooded Brockley Combe, then emerge and in 1½ miles meet a T-junction. Turn right on to the A38 'Taunton' road and pass Bristol Airport on the left. Descend Red Hill, cross the River Yeo, then in ½ mile branch left on to an unclassified road SP 'Burrington, Blagdon'. Ahead are views of Beacon Batch Hill. After 1 mile turn right on to the A368 SP 'Burrington Combe' then take the 2nd turning left on to the B3134. Ascend Burrington Combe.

mls 0 1 2 3 4 5
kms 0 2 4 6 8

The SS *Great Britain* at Bristol.

Cheddar Gorge was formed when a great mass of limestone collapsed on to the bed of an underground river.

BURRINGTON COMBE, Somerset
High above Burrington village is 1,065ft Beacon Batch, the summit of Black Down and the highest point of the bleak Mendip range. The dramatic gorge of Burrington Combe inspired the Rev. Toplady to write the hymn *Rock of Ages*.

Climb to over 900ft, with glimpses to the left of Blagdon Lake, then cross high farmland for several miles. Meet crossroads and turn right on to the B3371 SP 'Cheddar'. Proceed through open scenery, then descend into a shallow valley and turn right on to the B3135. Make the long winding descent of Cheddar Gorge.

CHEDDAR GORGE & VILLAGE, Somerset
Every year many thousands of people come here to drive through the spectacular rock scenery of Cheddar Gorge. Curiously weathered limestone outcrops, softened in many places by the foliage of precariously rooted shrubs, hang over the road from 450ft cliffs. Underground the region is honeycombed by caves and potholes, many of which feature weird crystalline formations created by water action. Particularly good examples can be seen in Cox's and Gough's caverns (open). Various archaeological finds are displayed in the Cheddar Caves Museum.

Leave Cheddar with SP 'Bristol' and 'Weston-super-Mare' and in 1 mile turn left and immediately right on to the A371, SP 'Axbridge, Weston'. On the left is the popular yachting centre of Cheddar Reservoir. Branch left and drive into Axbridge.

AXBRIDGE, Somerset
Among many interesting and attractive old buildings in this Mendip town is King John's Hunting Lodge (NT), which dates from early Tudor times. The local manor house (not open) is also of note.

Drive to the end of Axbridge and follow SP 'Taunton, (A38)'. In ½ mile turn left on to the A38 and proceed across the flat ground of the Axe Valley. Views of 690ft Wavering Down and 628ft Crook Peak can be enjoyed to the right. Continue to Lower Weare.

LOWER WEARE, Somerset
Collections of waterfowl and a variety of small pets can be seen here at the Ambleside Water Gardens and Aviaries. Particular features of the gardens are their attractive ponds and varied shrubs.

Continue and pass through Rooks Bridge with the isolated 457ft mound of Brent Knoll increasingly prominent ahead. Cross the M5, then in ¼ mile meet a roundabout and keep left. In 1½ miles at the next roundabout take the 3rd exit on to the B3140 SP 'Burnham-on-Sea'. Proceed for 1½ miles, then meet another roundabout and keep forward to enter Burnham-on-Sea.

BURNHAM-ON-SEA, Somerset
This red-brick town is expanding to cope with holidaymakers who come to enjoy its miles of sandy beaches in larger numbers every year. Bridgwater Bay Nature Reserve lies a little to the south west.

Turn right SP 'Berrow, Brean'. After 1¼ miles reach Berrow and turn right SP 'Weston-super-Mare'. A detour from the main route to Brean can be made here by keeping forward on to an unclassified road and in ½ mile turning left.

Evening light on the vast sands at Burnham-on-Sea.

BREAN & BREAN DOWN, Somerset
At the base of 320ft Brean Down (NT), adjacent to 7 miles of sandy beaches, is the Brean Down Bird Sanctuary (open). Many species from all over the world can be seen here.

On the main route, proceed to Brent Knoll.

BRENT KNOLL, Somerset
This village takes its name from a nearby 457ft hill surmounted by an ancient camp. Inside the 15th-century church are bench ends bearing animal carvings that depict the tale of a greedy abbot who once tried to seize revenue from an unfortunate parish priest.

Meet a T-junction in the village and turn left. Skirt the base of Brent Knoll to reach East Brent, then at crossroads turn left on to the A370. Continue for 3 miles to re-enter Avon and pass the edge of Bleadon. After 2 miles meet a T-junction, turn right and return to Weston-super-Mare along the sea-front.

Rye, one of the most picturesque towns on the south coast, was an important Cinque Port until its harbour silted up. It remains as a superb example of a medieval maritime town, with many of its oldest buildings intact in quaint old streets that have changed little in generations.

South and South East England

SALISBURY, Wilts

The ancient city of Salisbury first came to importance following the abandonment of nearby Old Sarum in the 13th century. The bishop's see was transferred from the old to the new site, and in 1220 the cathedral was refounded in an early-English style that made it seem to soar from the ground rather than sit solidly on it. This illusion is accentuated by numerous slim columns of Purbeck stone and a magnificent 404ft spire that was added in the 14th century and is still the tallest in the country. The Cathedral Close preserves a beauty and atmosphere all of its own, and contains fine buildings dating from the 14th to the 18th centuries. Elsewhere in the town are 16th-century Joiner's Hall (NT), the 14th-century Poultry Cross (AM), and a great number of old inns. Interesting displays illustrating local history can be seen in the Salisbury and South Wiltshire Museum.

From Salisbury follow SP 'Yeovil A30' and drive to Wilton.

WILTON, Wilts

Wilton is an interesting town best known as an important carpet-making centre. Good Georgian houses can be seen in Kinsbury Square, and a curious country cross stands near the market house of 1738. Wilton House (open) was built on the site of Wilton Abbey in the 1540s, but was completely rebuilt by Inigo Jones after a serious fire. Subsequent work includes alterations by architect James Wyatt. Features of the lovely grounds (open) include fine cedars and a Palladian-style bridge over the Nadder.

At roundabout take the 1st exit, passing Wilton House on the left. In ½ mile reach the end of the village and turn right on to an unclassified road SP 'Great Wishford'. Go forward for 2¾ miles, with Grovely Woods to the left, then turn right into Great Wishford.

ON THE WILTSHIRE DOWNS

The grandeur of this tour is in the cathedral city of Salisbury and some of the county's finest stately homes. The beauty is in its fertile river valleys, and soft downland slopes that enfold timeless villages and open up panoramic views from their tree-crowned summits.

Salisbury's cathedral has been a source of inspiration for many artists, including John Constable.

The bridge in the grounds of Wilton House was built in 1737 to a Palladian pattern.

HANGING LANGFORD, Wilts

Hanging Langford clings precariously to the lower flanks of hills at the edge of Grovely Wood. Some 2 miles south west of the hamlet is an earthwork that has yielded evidence of prolonged occupation.

Keep forward and drive to Wylye.

WYLYE, Wilts

Lovely flint-and-stone chequerwork cottages dating from the 17th century can be seen in this village, which stands on the Wylye River at the edge of Salisbury Plain.

SALISBURY PLAIN, Wilts

Most of the undulating 240 square miles of this windswept plateau is under cultivation, although some parts have been given over to military use. Many of its low chalk hills feature prehistoric burial mounds and other monuments. The borders of the plain are defined by the rivers Avon, Bourne, and Wylye. See tour 22 for Stonehenge.

From Wylye keep forward on the unclassified road SP 'Sutton Veny'. Drive along the Wylye Valley to Stockton.

STOCKTON, Wilts

Stockton boasts thatched cottages, an Elizabethan mansion, and an Elizabethan farmhouse with a great barn. Attractive almshouses are grouped round a common courtyard reached via an arched entry.

GREAT WISHFORD, Wilts

This delightful village is set in the Wylye Valley and has a church with a 15th-century crenellated tower. On Oak Apple Day (May 29) the villagers reaffirm their right to collect kindling from Grovely Woods.

Drive to the village church, turn left, and shortly afterwards turn right. Continue to Little Langford.

LITTLE LANGFORD, Wilts

Noted architect T H Wyatt rebuilt the local church in 1864, using material from the previous building. About ½ mile south west of the village is the notable iron-age hillfort of Grovely Castle.

Continue to Hanging Langford.

After 1 mile cross the railway line and turn right for Boyton.

BOYTON, Wilts

Flint and stone chequerwork common to this area can be seen in 13th-century and later Boyton Church, which was restored by the 19th-century architect T H Wyatt.

Drive through Corton and Tytherington, then keep left for Sutton Veny.

SUTTON VENY, Wilts

The ruined church of Sutton Veny dates from the 13th century and lies east of its 19th-century successor. Also here is a manor house dating from the 14th century.

At crossroads at the far end of the village turn left on to the B3095. Drive to Longbridge Deverill.

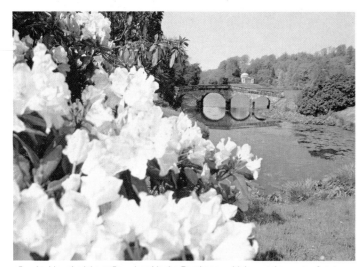

Overlooking the lake at Stourhead is the Pantheon, which contains casts of statues.

LONGBRIDGE DEVERILL, Wilts
John Thynne of Longleat House built the charming group of 17th-century almshouses here. His funeral helm hangs with two others in the tower of the local church.

At crossroads turn right on to the A350. In ½ mile turn left on unclassified road SP 'Crockerton' and then turn left SP 'Horningsham'. Continue through woodland passing Shear Water on the right. After 1¼ miles at T-junction turn right. Take the next turning right SP 'Longleat' to the outskirts of Horningsham. (To avoid Longleat Park toll continue forward through to Horningham/Bath Arms PH) turn right passing the Heavens Gate viewpoint and running alongside Longleat Estate. After 1¼ miles, before the A362 turn left to enter Longleat Park (toll).

LONGLEAT HOUSE, Wilts
This great Elizabethan mansion (open), the seat of the Marquess of Bath, stands on the site of a 13th-century priory and is a treasure house of old furniture, paintings, books, and interior decoration. It was one of England's first unified designs, and the grounds were landscaped by the brilliant 18th-century designer Capability Brown. The estate includes a large safari park (open), the first of its kind in Europe.

Leave the park with SP 'Way Out' and 'Warminster' via the Horningsham Gate.

HORNINGSHAM, Wilts
The thatched noncomformist Meeting House here, said to be one of the oldest of its kind in England, may date from the 16th century.

Drive to the Bath Arms (PH), meet crossroads, and go forward SP 'Shaftesbury' and 'Maiden Bradley'. In 1½ miles at a T-junction turn right for Maiden Bradley.

MAIDEN BRADLEY, Wilts
Wooded downland hills rise to 945ft Long Knoll above this pretty village, in which may be seen a number of attractive old houses.

At crossroads turn left on to the B3092 SP 'Mere', then pass the outskirts of Stourton.

STOURTON, Wilts
Good paintings and Chippendale furniture can be seen inside Stourhead House (NT), but this famous 18th-century mansion is best known for its superb grounds. These were laid out by Henry Hoare, who owned the estate, and show one of Europe's finest layouts of this period. In the park are classical garden temples and a delightful lake.

Continue for 1¼ miles, then turn right and then turn left SP 'Andover' to join the A303. Continue through open countryside for 3½ miles then turn right on to the B3089 SP 'Salisbury'. Continue to the A350 and turn left, then turn immediately right for Hindon.

HINDON, Wilts
Created by bishops of Winchester in the 13th century, this village was handsomely rebuilt by Wyatt after a fire and is an example of good 19th-century restoration.

Proceed from the Grosvenor Arms Hotel and turn right on to an unclassified road SP 'Tisbury'. Meet crossroads and turn right (no SP). Follow a narrow byroad to Newtown. Turn right SP 'Semley', then turn left SP 'Donhead' and 'Wardour'. Descend, and in ½ mile cross a railway. Shortly turn left SP 'Tisbury' and continue past the grounds of Wardour Castle.

WARDOUR CASTLE, Wilts
New Wardour Castle (open), the largest Georgian house in Wiltshire, was begun in 1769 for the 8th Lord Arundell. Its private chapel is larger than many a parish church, and very richly decorated.

WARDOUR OLD CASTLE, Wilts
Wardour Old Castle (AM) dates from the end of the 14th-century. It stands on a wooded bank overlooking an 18th-century artificial lake and is uniquely hexagonal in shape.

Keep forward for Tisbury.

TISBURY, Wilts
In the 7th century this village stood on an important Saxon track. Its cruciform church dates from the 12th century and shares the churchyard with a giant yew, 36ft in circumference, that is reputed to be more than 1,000 years old.

Turn right at the post office SP 'Salisbury'. Continue to the end of the village and turn right again. Proceed for ¼ mile and branch left SP 'Chilmark', passing Place Farm on the left.

PLACE FARM, Wilts
Formerly an abbey grange, this farm comprises a group of 14th to 15th-century domestic buildings. The 200ft-long tithe barn, is one of the largest in England.

Drive to Chilmark.

CHILMARK, Wilts
The creamy stone from Chilmark's quarries (closed) was used in Wilton House, Salisbury Cathedral, and the spire of Chichester Cathedral.

Turn left SP 'Salisbury', then right. Continue to the main road and turn right again, on to the B3089 for Teffont Magna. Keep right into the village, drive to the Black Horse (PH), and turn right on to an unclassified road. Continue with SP 'Tisbury' into Teffont Evias.

TEFFONT EVIAS, Wilts
Twin Teffont Magna and Teffont Evias stand close together in the beautiful Nadder Valley. The former boasts the delightful Fitz House of 1700, and the latter a Tudor mansion that was once the home of Sir James Ley, who became Lord Chief Justice of England and was immortalized by Milton in a sonnet.

In ¼ mile turn left with SP 'Salisbury' and cross a river bridge. Ascend to a main road and turn right to re-join the B3089. After ¾ mile at crossroads (the outskirts of Dinton) turn right on to an unclassified road for Fovant. A slight detour can be made to Philipps House by turning left at the crossroads.

PHILIPPS HOUSE, Wilts
Designed by Sir Jeffry Wyatville in 1816, this splendid neo-Grecian mansion (NT) stands in 200-acre Dinton Park and is let to the YWCA (open by appointment).

DINTON, Wilts
Three notable National Trust properties are to be found on the outskirts of this hillside village. Besides Philipps House there is the Tudor to 18th-century Hyde's House (not open) and ivy-covered Little Clarendon, which dates from the 15th-century (open on application).

On the main route, continue into Fovant.

FOVANT, Wilts
Huge regimental badges were cut in the chalk downs by soldiers stationed here during World War I. A memorial brass of 1492 can be seen in the local church.

Drive to the end of the village and turn right on to the A30. In ¼ mile turn left on to an unclassified road SP 'Broad Chalke'. Ascend on to the downs, and after 1½ miles turn left. Drive to Broad Chalke, bear right then left through the village, and proceed to Bishopstone.

BISHOPSTONE, Wilts
Remarkable furnishings can be seen inside the local church, a beautiful cruciform building with superb stone vaulting and windows.

Continue to Coombe Bissett.

COOMBE BISSETT, Wilts
Just downstream from the fine 18th-century bridge that spans the river here is a picturesque packhorse bridge. Its wooden parapets are new, but the mounting stone is very old. Traces of every century from Norman times to the present day can be seen in the fabric of the attractive local church.

Turn left on to the A354 and return to Salisbury.

A picturesque old mill stands beside the River Ebble in Coombe Bissett.

IN SEARCH OF ANCIENT MAN

Near Uffington the great turf-cut figure of a horse leaps across a downland slope beneath the ramparts of a prehistoric hillfort. Elsewhere in the Vale of the White Horse are the massive stones of Wayland's Smithy, the enigmatic mound of Silbury Hill, and dozens of hilltop tumuli.

Tithe barns like the one at Great Coxwell were specially built to store the tithe, or one tenth of all produce, which was once levied from all land holders.

SWINDON, Wilts

In 1900 Old and New Swindon were combined to form Wiltshire's largest town. The small old town is still recognisable in fragments such as the remains of Holy Rood Church in the grounds of a 17th-century house, The Lawn, the old Town Hall and the Market Square. New Swindon grew out of the Great Western Railway's decision to site its repair and locomotive works here, and much of its history is detailed in the fascinating Great Western Railway Museum, the Railway Village House has been refurbished to show life at the turn of the century.

Leave the County Roundabout with SP 'Oxford A420'. In 1¼ miles after two roundabouts turn left on to the B4006 SP 'Stratton'. At traffic signals in Stratton St Margaret turn left, then turn right, and continue to Highworth.

HIGHWORTH, Wilts

Several 17th-century houses and an impressive church with a good west tower are features of this old hilltop village.

Continue on the A361. Later pass the village of Inglesham and a riverside park on the left.

INGLESHAM, Wilts

The tiny church in Inglesham stands where the River Thames meets the derelict Severn Canal and the River Coln. Inside are attractive box pews, a 15th-century screen, and a beautiful late Saxon carving of the Madonna and Child.

Wayland's Smithy is one of many outstanding prehistoric monuments which stand near the Ridgeway.

Continue on the A361. Cross the Thames via the old Halfpenny Bridge and drive into Lechlade.

LECHLADE, Glos

Lechlade marks the upper limit for large craft using the River Thames. The old Halfpenny Bridge spans the river here, and St John's Bridge stands ½ mile to the east. The local church is noted for the curious figures on its tower buttresses.

Turn right, then right again, on to the A417 Faringdon road. In ¾ mile by the nearside of the Trout Inn, turn left on to the B4449 SP 'Bampton'. A detour from the main route can be made here to Buscot village and Buscot Park by keeping forward on the A417.

BUSCOT, Oxon

Almost 4,000 acres of Buscot village and Park, including lovely woods and farmlands that run down to the Thames, are owned or protected by the National Trust. The late 18th-century house contains a noted collection of paintings, and the attractive grounds feature a water garden by landscaper Harold Peto. The Old Parsonage is an early 18th-century house in 10-acre grounds.

Continue along the unclassified road crossing the River Leach. After 1¼ miles turn right leading to Kelmscott village.

KELMSCOTT, Oxon

Poet and painter William Morris lived in Kelmscott's Elizabethan manor house and is buried in the local churchyard. The village itself is a charming collection of greystone buildings standing on the banks of the upper Thames.

Continue for a further 2¾ miles and meet a T-junction. Turn right on to the A4095 SP 'Faringdon' and shortly cross the historic Radcot Bridge.

RADCOT, Oxon

Many centuries ago the forces of Richard II and Henry IV met in battle at the 14th-century bridge here, and 300 years later Prince Rupert's cavalry defeated Cromwell's parliamentarian horsemen in nearby Garrison Field.

Continue to Faringdon.

FARINGDON, Oxon

Poet Laureate Henry Pye built Faringdon House in 1870, and Lord Berners added a folly to its park in 1935 to help relieve local unemployment. Faringdon Church lost its spire in the Civil War. The town itself is a market centre known for its dairy produce.

Follow SP 'Swindon A420', and after ¼ mile turn right into Highworth Road (B4019). After another 1¼ miles turn left on to an unclassified road for Great Coxwell.

GREAT COXWELL, Oxon

William Morris thought the great 13th-century tithe barn (NT) at Coxwell's Court Farm 'as noble as a cathedral'. Measuring 152ft long by 51ft high and 44ft wide, this huge stone building is certainly one of the finest of its kind in England today.

Turn left (no SP), then in ½ mile at a T-junction turn right, then turn left on to the A420. Take the 1st turning right on to an unclassified road for Little Coxwell, and continue to Fernham. Turn left on to the B4508, then in ¼ mile branch right on to an unclassified road for Uffington, in the Vale of the White Horse.

UFFINGTON, Oxon

Good views can be enjoyed from here of the famous 374ft-long prehistoric white horse cut into the chalk slopes of 856ft White Horse Hill.

Drive to the nearside of the village and turn right, then take the 2nd turning right SP 'White Horse Hill'. In 1 mile cross the main road and ascend White Horse Hill to reach Uffington Castle and associated monuments.

UFFINGTON CASTLE, THE RIDGEWAY, & WAYLAND'S SMITHY, Oxon

The iron-age hillfort (AM) of Uffington stands on the ancient Ridgeway above the famous White Horse in the Berkshire Downs. The Ridgeway is a pre-Roman track that follows the crest of the downs and is now the route of a long-distance footpath. Just off it in a grove of trees is the megalithic long barrow of Wayland's Smithy (AM). This excellent example has lost part of its earth mound, so its chambers are open to view. Wayland is a smith in Norse mythology, and tradition was that anyone who left a horse and coin here overnight would find his mount shod in the morning.

It is quite likely that the exact reason for the construction of henge monuments like Avebury will never be known.

Follow exit signs from Uffington Castle, descend to a main road, and turn right on to the B4507 with further views of the White Horse to the right. After another 2 miles meet crossroads and turn right on to an unclassified road SP 'Lambourn'. Ascend on to the Berkshire Downs in 4¼ miles turn right on to the B4001 for Lambourn. Continue across the Lambourn Downs to Lambourn.

LAMBOURN, Berks
Racehorses are trained on downland gallops near this lovely village, and the crystal Lambourn River is everything a chalk trout stream should be. The local cruciform church, which dates from Norman times, houses several old brasses and the village stocks.

Meet crossroads and turn right on to the B4000, then drive to the next turning left SP 'Baydon'. A short detour can be made from the main route to Ashdown House by keeping straight ahead on the B4000 for 3¼ miles.

ASHDOWN HOUSE, Oxon
Ashdown House (NT) was built from chalk-rock blocks in the latter half of the 17th century. More than a quarter of its interior is taken up by a magnificent staircase.

On the main route, turn left from the B4000 on to the 'Baydon' road and in 2¼ miles meet a T-junction. Turn right and continue to Baydon.

BAYDON, Wilts
A 13th-century font can be seen in Baydon Church, which has Norman origins but acquired its west tower later. Baydon House farmhouse is of mid 18th-century date.

Turn left and continue to the downland village of Aldbourne.

ALDBOURNE, Wilts
Aldbourne, one of Wiltshire's most attractive villages, lies south east of a one-time hunting area known as Aldbourne Chase.

Turn left on to the B4192 SP 'Hungerford', then in 1¾ miles turn right on to an unclassified road and continue to Ramsbury.

RAMSBURY, Wilts
Excellent Jacobean and Georgian buildings can be seen in this charming River Kennet village, and the church contains ancient sculptured stones.

Turn right and keep forward through the village to Axford and Mildenhall.

MILDENHALL, Wilts
Mildenhall, pronounced 'Minall', lies on the River Kennet to the north of Savernake Forest. A late Celtic vessel known as the Marlborough Bucket was unearthed at Folly Farm, which stands near by on the site of the Roman town *Cunetio*.

Continue to Marlborough.

MARLBOROUGH, Wilts
High downs rise to the north and south of this historic River Kennet town. Legend has it that Merlin, the magician of King Arthur's court, was buried under the town's castle mound. The town may well be old enough for this claim, but many of its more ancient foundations were damaged or destroyed by a series of bad fires and by the Civil War. Its High Street, one of the widest in England, is a reminder of the way things used to be. William Morris was a pupil at the famous 19th-century Marlborough College.

Leave Marlborough on the A4 SP 'Chippenham' and drive to Fyfield.

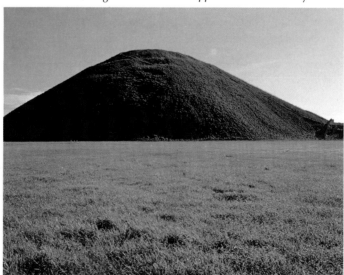

FYFIELD, Wilts
To the north of this attractive village is the high Fyfield Down nature reserve, which is as much protected for its prehistoric monuments as for its abundant wildlife. South of Fyfield are the sarsen stones of the Grey Wethers (NT), and about 1 mile north east of the village at Lockeridge Dene is a dolmen known as the Devil's Den.

Continue on the A4 to Silbury Hill.

SILBURY HILL & THE WEST KENNET LONG BARROW, Wilts
Situated close to the A4 road near Avebury, these superb prehistoric monuments are among the best known in Europe. Silbury Hill (AM), an enormous artificial mound that covers almost 6 acres, is still as enigmatic as when 18th-century Cornish miners employed to explore it by the Duke of Northumberland emerged baffled and empty-handed. A footpath from the A4 leads ¾ mile to the West Kennet Long Barrow (AM), the finest monument of its kind in England. Excavations during the 19th century uncovered skeletons and pottery in the tomb's passage and end chamber, but the side chambers remained undiscovered until 1955.

Drive to the Beckhampton roundabout and take the 3rd exit to leave by the A4361 SP 'Swindon'. In 1 mile keep left for Avebury.

AVEBURY, Wilts
Many experts consider Avebury the most significant prehistoric monument (AM) in Europe. It is certainly one of the largest stone circles in the world, comprising 100 standing-stone positions enclosing some 28 acres of land. Inside the large outer circle, which has quite a few gaps due to superstitious destruction in the past, are two smaller rings about 300ft in diameter. At one time a 50ft-wide avenue of stones ran 1 mile to connect with a pair of concentric circles on Overton Hill. The village itself is a collection of handsome old buildings between the stones and the banks of the monument, featuring a small museum of archaeology, the Great Barn and Museum of Wiltshire Folk and a multi-period church. Avebury Manor is a 16th-century house (open) (NT).

Continue on the 'Swindon' road to Winterbourne Monkton, with views of the Marlborough Downs to the right. Later descend to Wroughton.

WROUGHTON, Wilts
South of the village stands Barbury Castle an ancient hill fort dating from AD 566. The 130 acres of surrounding countryside is a country park.

Drive to the end of the village and turn left for the return to Swindon.

Enigmatic Silbury Hill keeps the secret of its purpose.

COWES, Isle of Wight

This busy island port has a good harbour on the River Medina and is connected to East Cowes by floating bridge and ferry. The headquarters of the Royal Yacht Squadron is based at Cowes Castle, and the town is well known as England's premier yachting centre.

Leave Cowes following SP 'Gurnard' on the B3325. In ¾ mile keep forward on to an unclassified road for Gurnard. Reach a church and keep forward, then meet a T-junction and turn right into Lower Church Road. Continue to the next T-junction, turn left SP 'Yarmouth', and in a further 1½ miles meet another T-junction. Turn right and in another 1½ miles turn right again for Porchfield. Continue through wooded countryside and after 1½ miles turn right for Newtown.

NEWTOWN, Isle of Wight

Sited midway between Newport and Yarmouth, Newtown was created in the 13th century by the bishops of Winchester and stands on the beautiful Newtown River estuary (NT). The 18th-century Old Town Hall (NT) is notable.

In ⅓ mile meet a T-junction and turn right, then in another ¾ mile meet another T-junction and turn right again on to the A3054. Proceed to Shalfleet.

SHALFLEET, Isle of Wight

Shalfleet's church displays very strong Norman features, particularly in the squat west tower and the good south doorway with its contemporary tympanum.

Continue to Yarmouth.

YARMOUTH, Isle of Wight

This Yar-estuary town is better known as a sailing centre than as a resort. Henry VIII built one of his many coastal defence forts (AM) here, and the triangular Fort Victoria of 1853 stands in the grounds of the Fort Victoria country park.

Following SP 'Freshwater', cross the Yar bridge, and in 1 mile bear right. Pass through Colwell Bay and continue to the small resort of Totland. Join the B3322 'Alum Bay' road and in ¼ mile reach a war memorial. Bear right to Alum Bay.

ALUM BAY & THE NEEDLES, Isle of Wight

Sandstone cliffs famous for their multi-coloured strata fringe this lovely bay. The isolated rock stacks of The Needles stretch out into the sea to the south-west, with Scratchell's Bay and a 200ft chalk arch beyond.

Return, and in ¼ mile branch right on to an unclassified road SP 'Freshwater Bay'. To the right is Tennyson Down (NT), one of the West Wight Downs.

WEST WIGHT DOWNS, Isle of Wight

The high, gentle folds of the West Wight Downs (NT) occupy most of the island's south-west corner.

A MINIATURE LANDSCAPE

The Isle of Wight has everything offered by the mainland, but smaller. Here are high downs and soaring cliffs; long beaches fringed by farm and forestland; fishing villages and resorts popularized by royalty in the past and popular with sun seekers today.

The brass cannons overlooking the Solent at Cowes are fired to start yacht races.

Continue to Freshwater Bay and join the A3055 SP 'Chale'. Bear right and ascend, skirting Compton Bay, and drive along a beautiful clifftop road that affords some of the finest views in the island. Later pass the edge of Brook village.

BROOK, Isle of Wight

Brook House dates from the 18th century, and Brook Chine (NT) is a beautiful cleft with 40 acres of grazing and 300 yards of superb seashore.

Continue through pleasant open country with good views. In 2¼ miles pass thickly-wooded Grange Chine to the right, with Brighstone Forest to the left and Brighstone Bay to the right. St Catherine's Point and St Catherine's Hill are prominent ahead before the tour enters Chale.

CHALE, Isle of Wight

Chale Abbey preserves a 14th-century hall, and the local church commands fine views of The Needles.

Drive to Chale Church and keep forward SP 'Ventnor'. In ½ mile turn right on to the B3399 road for Blackgang. A footpath from this point leads to Blackgang Chine.

BLACKGANG CHINE & ST CATHERINE'S HILL, Isle of Wight

It is thought that this dramatic chine derived its name from a gang of smugglers, but nowadays it harbours nobody more sinister than tourists visiting the Theme Park. Inland is 773ft St Catherine's Hill (NT), which affords excellent views and features 14th-century St Catherine's Oratory.

From Blackgang Chine return to the main route and turn right on to the A3055 SP 'Ventnor'. Pass under St Catherine's Hill and continue along the undercliff to St Lawrence.

Turn right (in Niton) and continue along Undercliff to St Lawrence.

ST LAWRENCE, Isle of Wight

Old St Lawrence's was Britain's smallest church until it acquired a porch and bell tower in 1842. Tropical Bird Gardens and glass makers are situated in the 20 acres of Old Park.

Continue to Ventnor.

VENTNOR, Isle of Wight

A paper recommending the local climate for the cure of certain illnesses transformed Ventnor from a fishing village to a focus of 19th-century society. Within the Botanic Gardens is the History of Smuggling Museum.

Follow SP 'Shanklin' and ascend, with fine sea views to the right. In ¾ mile a detour can be made from the main route to the delightful village of Bonchurch by turning right on to an unclassified road.

BONCHURCH & ST BONIFACE DOWN, Isle of Wight

The writers Dickens, Thackeray, and Macaulay all stayed in this delightful village, and the poet Swinburne lived at East Dene House. The village itself stands just below the island's highest point, 785ft Boniface Down (NT), and has a Victorian church.

Continue on the main drive, pass the Landslip viewpoint to the right of the road and reach Shanklin.

SHANKLIN, Isle of Wight

A group of thatched buildings, the Crab Inn, and St Blasius's Church are all that remain of the fishing village that stood here before the seaside holiday fad took over. The town's excellent sea-bathing, superb sandy beach, and good sunshine records attract increasing numbers of visitors every year. Shanklin Chine has a spectacular 45ft waterfall.

Continue through Shanklin and Lake to Sandown.

SANDOWN, Isle of Wight

The assets that contributed to the development of Shanklin have also made Sandown a popular holiday resort. Additional attractions include the Museum of Isle of Wight Geology and a good zoo.

Turn right on to the B3395 SP 'Bembridge' and drive to Yaverland.

YAVERLAND, Isle of Wight

Yaverland Manor House (not open) is the finest 17th-century building of its kind in the island.

Meet a T-junction and turn right. In ¼ mile it is possible to make a detour from the main route by turning right to the downs of Culver and Bembridge.

Until its collapse in 1764 one of the Needles was 120ft high.

Alum Bay is famous for its multi-coloured cliffs.

BEMBRIDGE, Isle of Wight

Yachtsmen favour the nearby natural harbour at the mouth of the Eastern Yar. Numerous displays of nautical heritage from the early days of sail to the present time, are to be found in the Maritime Museum.

Follow the B3395 'St Helens' road and in 1½ miles meet a T-junction. Turn right on to the B3330 into St Helens, then turn left SP 'Ryde' for Nettlestone. At Nettlestone branch right on to the B3340 SP 'Seaview'. On the right is the entrance to Flamingo Park. In ½ mile keep left, then meet a T-junction and turn left, then immediately left again. Turn right into Seafield Road for Seaview.

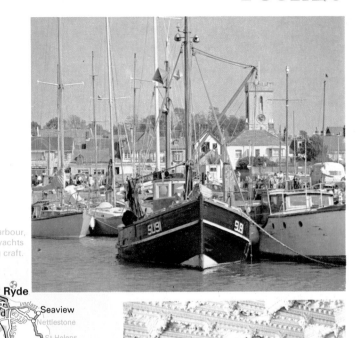

Yarmouth Harbour, crowded with yachts and other sailing craft.

The Indian-style Durbar Room at Osborne House was built in 1891 to accommodate state banquets.

Whippingham's Germanic-looking church.

CULVER & BEMBRIDGE DOWNS, Isle of Wight

Covering some 104 acres of east Wight, these fine downs (NT) rise to a 343ft summit and drop sharply towards the coast. Culver Down features a bronze-age round barrow.

Continue with the main tour to skirt Bembridge Airport and at the far side meet crossroads. Turn left on to an unclassified road and in ¼ mile pass a footpath on the left leading to Bembridge Windmill.

BEMBRIDGE WINDMILL, Isle of Wight

Situated near one end of Bembridge High Street, this stone-built mill (NT) has a wooden roof and was erected c1700. Today it is the only windmill left on the island, and is maintained in working order, but last used in 1913.
Continue into Bembridge.

SEAVIEW, Isle of Wight

Much of the unspoiled fishing village is still evident in Seaview, a quiet resort offering good beaches and excellent shore angling.

Continue to a T-junction and turn right, then keep left on to an unclassified road and drive along the shoreline. In ¼ mile pass through a toll gate, and 1 mile farther turn right on to the B3330. After a short distance turn right on to the A3055 for Ryde.

RYDE, Isle of Wight

Most visitors to the island enter at Ryde, a busy port that was a small fishing and smuggling village until the 18th century.

Follow SP 'Newport' to join the A3054 and pass through Binstead.

BINSTEAD, Isle of Wight

New Quarr Abbey stands near the 12th-century remains of its predecessor at Binstead, and the local church still shows some of its 13th-century origins in spite of Victorian restoration.

Keep forward through Wootton Bridge. In 1½ miles turn right SP 'East Cowes'. Meet a T-junction and turn right on to the A3021, then in 1¾ miles turn left on to an unclassified road SP 'Whippingham Church'. Continue to Whippingham.

WHIPPINGHAM, Isle of Wight

Prince Albert built the ornate church here in 1860, and Queen Victoria was a regular member of the congregation whenever the Royal Family was in residence on the island.

Pass Whippingham Church and continue to a T-junction. Turn left into Victoria Grove, then at the next T-junction turn left again to join the A3021 for East Cowes. Return along the A3021 'Ryde' road, passing the entrance to Osborne House to the left on the outskirts of the town.

OSBORNE HOUSE, Isle of Wight

Queen Victoria and the Prince Consort built Osborne House as a retreat from the pomp and ceremony of Windsor, and Her Majesty died here in 1901. The State apartments (open) remain as they were in her day.

Continue, and in 2 miles keep right SP 'Newport', and after another ¼ mile turn right on to the A3054. Proceed to Newport.

NEWPORT, Isle of Wight

Situated at the head of the Medina estuary, this town is the capital of the island and stands on a site that has been occupied at least since Roman times. Mighty Carisbrooke Castle stands on the foundations of a Roman fort 1 mile south west. The 12th-century remains of the castle include a Norman keep and a 16th-century treadmill that used to be worked by prisoners to raise water. Today it is turned by a donkey for display purposes, and forms a fascinating exhibit in the Isle of Wight Museum.

Follow the A3020 'Cowes' road and pass Parkhurst Prison, backed by Parkhurst Forest.

PARKHURST FOREST, Isle of Wight

Parkhurst Forest is the largest stretch of woodland on the island, and one of the last British refuges of the native red squirrel.

Drive to Northwood and branch left on to the B3325. Continue to a T-junction and turn right to return to Cowes.

LYMINGTON, Hants

Early wealth came to Lymington from its saltworks, but these were closed in the 19th century and the town now makes a comfortable living as a busy holiday resort, yachting centre, and Isle of Wight ferry terminal. Its wide High Street, lined with 18th- and 19th- century houses, climbs from the waterfront to a church with a huge tower crowned by an exotic cupola of 18th century date.

Follow SP 'Beaulieu B3054', cross the Lymington River, and climb into the New Forest. Cross Beaulieu Heath to the pleasant picnic spot of Hatchet Pond. Turn right, then 1 mile farther turn sharp right again on to the unclassified 'Buckler's Hard' road.

BUCKLER'S HARD, Hants

This small Beaulieu River village thrived for several centuries as a shipbuilding yard. A fascinating little maritime museum recalls those times, and the deep estuary is put to peaceful use by yacht owners. The short village street of 18th-century houses was the creation of the 2nd Duke of Montagu, who planned a town and docks here to receive produce from his own extensive foreign estates.

THE SOLENT, Hants

Much of this tour is in sight of The Solent, a narrow and very busy channel that separates the coast of Hampshire from that of the Isle of Wight. It was formed by the submersion of an ancient river valley whose headstream was the Frome and tributaries the Itchen and Test. Most of the coast on the Hampshire side is designated an area of outstanding natural beauty.

Return along the 'Beaulieu' road and after 2 miles turn right on to the B3054. Enter Beaulieu.

BEAULIEU, Hants

Beaulieu's idyllic position among the woods and hills of South Hampshire is enhanced by the superb ruins of its abbey (open). Largely destroyed at the Dissolution, this important foundation retains a beauty that 'mocks the spoilers still' and preserves its great gatehouse (open) as the home of Lord Montagu. Ruined walls pierced by graceful door and window apertures surround trim lawns that were once the floors of large monastic buildings. Elsewhere in the grounds is the well-known National Motor Museum (open), which features an excellent collection of veteran and vintage cars, cycles, and motorcycles.

Continue through woodlands along the B3054 'Hythe' road for 1 mile, then turn right and immediately right again on to the unclassified 'Lepe' road, passing through woodland, and after 2½ miles enter Exbury.

Huge timbers from New Forest trees were once left to weather in the wide street at Buckler's Hard before being used to build ships.

THE FOREST AND THE SEA

Here the woods and heaths of the New Forest meet the lovely Solent shore. Ponies and semi-wild cattle graze through oak-fringed glades where kings once hunted, and wander at will wherever there are no grids to bar them entry.

A beech glade near Knightswood Oak.

EXBURY, Hants

The gardens of Exbury estate are famous for their magnificent rhododendron and azalea displays in late spring (house not open). The village itself stands near the creeks and saltmarshes of the Beaulieu River estuary, in an area of the Solent shore designated as being of outstanding natural beauty.

Turn left into the village and after another 2 miles bear left, with views across The Solent to the Isle of Wight. Continue along the foreshore at Lepe, now part of a country park, then turn inland. After ¾ mile turn right on to the Calshot road. Drive for another 2½ miles, meet a T-junction, and turn right on to the B3053 to enter Calshot.

CALSHOT, Hants

Immediately obvious in this otherwise pleasant little place is the intrusive chimney of its power station. Rather more pleasing to the eye is the low, round tower of Calshot Castle, a coastal fort built by Henry VIII. It occupies a commanding position on a promontory at the end of a long shingle beach. Calshot foreshore is part of a country park.

Return along the B3053 SP 'Southampton' and drive to the edge of Fawley.

SOUTHAMPTON WATER, Hants

Between Calshot and Eling, the route of this tour is never far from the shores of Southampton Water, a maritime highway busy with the traffic of tankers, tugs, liners, ferries and pleasure craft. Southampton port, at its head, has long been one of the most commercially and strategically important harbours in the country. The Crusaders embarked here, the *Mayflower* set sail from the local docks, and Philip II of Spain landed here on his way to marry Mary Tudor in Winchester Cathedral. Today the Water guides great vessels from all over the world into the haven of England's premier cruise passengers port.

FAWLEY, Hants

Esso's petroleum refinery, which dominates Fawley, is an unlovely building but has some claim to fame through sheer size.

Drive to the next roundabout and follow SP 'Hythe' on to an unclassified road. After 1 mile turn right into Frost Lane and descend, over a level crossing, to the shores of Southampton Water. Continue to Hythe.

HYTHE, Hants

Excellent views of Southampton docks and the shore are afforded by the Hythe ferry. Ship-spotting enthusiasts will find the village pier a handy vantage point.

Leave Hythe Pier with SP 'Totton', then after ¼ mile meet a T-junction and turn right. Continue for 2 miles, then on the nearside of the next roundabout turn sharp right on to the 'Marchwood' road. Continue through Marchwood and after 2 miles at staggered crossroads turn right on to the 'Eling' road and continue to Eling.

ELING, Hants

Situated on a creek off the head of Southampton Water, this ancient port has a toll-bridge reputed to be the smallest of its kind in Britain and a working tide mill (open).

Cross the toll-bridge and follow SP 'Lyndhurst' to join the A35, and follow to Ashurst.

ASHURST, Hants

The New Forest Butterfly Farm has an extensive display of tropical butterflies in large glasshouses.

THE NEW FOREST, Hants

This district between the River Avon and Southampton Water comprises some 92,000 acres of undulating forest and heathland threaded by small streams and scattered with ponds. Many species of trees thrive in the mixture of clays, peat, and gravels here, affording cover to various species of deer and the famous New Forest ponies. Parts of the forest are nature reserves.

Continue over heathland to Lyndhurst.

Exhibits on display at the Montagu Motor Museum include historic record-breakers.

The boats in Lymington Harbour sprout a forest of masts.

An excellent way of seeing the Solent shipping is to take the ferry from Hythe to Southampton.

The Knightswood Oak stands near Lyndhurst.

LYNDHURST, Hants
Lyndhurst is the capital of the New Forest and an extremely popular tourist centre. Woodlands lap the boundaries of the town, and it is not unusual to meet one of the area's semi-wild ponies or cows ambling through the streets. The Victorian parish church features stained glass by Burne-Jones, William Morris and others, and a large mural by Leighton. Alice Liddel, on whom the heroine of *Alice in Wonderland* was based, is buried here. West of the church is the Queen's House, where the Verderers' Court still sits to administer the forest.

Follow the 'Bournemouth' road to the Swan Inn and turn right on to the unclassified 'Emery Down' road. After ¼ mile reach the New Forest Inn and turn left SP 'Bolderwood'. Continue along one of the forest's most attractive byways. After 3 miles pass the Island Viewpoint and a common on the left, then turn sharp left (no SP) to re-enter fine woodlands along the Bolderwood Ornamental Drive. After a further 2 miles reach the Knightswood Oak on the left.

KNIGHTSWOOD OAK, Hants
The huge Knightswood Oak has a girth of more than 21ft and is thought to be 600 years old.

Keep forward from the Knightswood Oak and cross a main road to drive along the Rhinefield Ornamental Drive, bordered by fine conifers and rhododendrons. Cross heathland and pass through the outskirts of Brockenhurst. Turn left across a ford and drive to the town centre.

BROCKENHURST, Hants
Many people find this handsome, lively village an ideal base from which to explore the New Forest. The local church is of Norman origin and claims to be the oldest foundation in the forest. *Domesday* records a church on this site, and the enormous yew in the churchyard may well have been planted over 1,000 years ago. Brusher Mills, a famous New Forest snake-catcher responsible for the demise of over 3,000 adders, is buried here.

Recross the ford and follow SP 'Burley' across wide heathland with picnic areas and good views. Pass Hinchelsea Viewpoint on the right and in 4¾ miles enter Burley.

BURLEY, Hants
Nearby Castle Hill rises to 300ft and affords good views over this pretty village. An intriguing collection of souvenirs, trophies, and weapons can be seen in the local Queen's Head Inn.

Take the 'Bransgore' road, cross more heathland, and reach the Crown Inn in Bransgore. Turn left here SP 'Lymington' and cross pleasant countryside. After 2 miles turn left and right across a main road, with the Cat and Fiddle Inn on the right. Drive beyond Walkford and turn left on to the A337. After ¾ mile turn right on to the unclassified 'Barton on Sea' road. Continue for ½ mile and turn left, then meet a T-junction and turn right to enter Barton on Sea.

BARTON ON SEA, Hants
This resort's low clay cliffs form part of the Barton Beds, a geological series noted for its fossil shell, bone, and shark remains. Good views from the clifftop greensward extend to the chalk stacks of the Needles, and Isle of Wight.

Reach the end of the Promenade and turn left to follow SP 'Milford on Sea' across heaths and commons. Turn right on to the B3058 and drive to Milford on Sea.

MILFORD ON SEA, Hants
A popular resort since Victorian times, Milford on Sea offers good bathing from its sand and shingle beach and excellent views across the Solent to the Isle of Wight. All Saints' Church has a picture by Perugino at the west end of the south aisle. On a promontory about 2½ miles south east is Hurst Castle.

HURST CASTLE, Hants
Built by Henry VIII in 1544, this fort (AM) was later occupied by Cromwell's forces and served as a prison for Charles I in 1648. Restoration work was carried out in 1873, and access today is by foot along a shingle promontory or by boat from Keyhaven.

From Milford on Sea, continue along the B3058 'Lymington' road and turn right on to the A337 before re-entering Lymington.

SANCTITY IN STONE

Centuries before Christianity the primitive peoples of England raised the huge megaliths of Stonehenge. Much later came the cathedrals, the Norman permanence of Winchester and soaring early-English completeness of Salisbury.

WINCHESTER, Hants
Venta Belgarum to the Romans, this one-time capital of Wessex boasts an 11th-century and later cathedral that is the second longest in Europe. Inside are richly-carved chantry chapels, the oldest iron grille in England, and coffins holding the bones of Saxon kings. Survivals from the distant 13th century include excellent stretches of the city walls, the hall of Pilgrims' School, and the 13th-century and later Deanery. Winchester College, founded by William of Wykeham in 1382, retains much of its original structure and stands near the ruined Bishop's Palace of Wolvesey Castle. Castle Hall dates from the 13th century, and 16th-century Godbegot House stands on the site of a palace built by King Canute. Close to the centre of town the River Itchen rushes through a lovely old mill (NT) of 1744 before winding through attractive gardens alongside the medieval walls.

Follow SP 'Stockbridge' to leave Winchester on the A272, and in 4¾ miles reach the Rack and Manger Inn. Turn right on to an unclassified road SP 'Crawley'. After another 1 mile reach a pond and turn left into Crawley village.

CRAWLEY, Hants
Almost too perfect to be true, this picture-book village has timber-framed cottages, an old pub, and a duckpond. Its homely church has Norman features, and its Court dates from the late 19th century.

Drive to the far end of the village and keep left, then in 1¼ miles turn right to rejoin the A272. Proceed to Stockbridge Down.

STOCKBRIDGE DOWN, Hants　SU33
Situated on the north side of the A272, this lovely area of open downland (NT) features a group of bronze-age round barrows and the south-west ditch and rampart of iron-age Woolbury Camp hillfort.

Later descend and enter the Test Valley, then continue to the edge of Stockbridge.

STOCKBRIDGE, Hants
People from all over the world come here to fish the Test, one of the most sought-after game rivers in the country. Stockbridge itself is a one-street town of mainly Victorian buildings. The Town Hall, the Grosvenor Hotel, and the White Hart Inn are all early 19th-century, and only the 13th-century chancel of the old church remains.

Meet a roundabout and take the 2nd exit on to the A30, then drive to the next roundabout and branch left on to the A3057 SP 'Andover'. In 1 mile turn left on to an unclassified road SP 'Longstock', then cross a bridge and cross the River Test to Longstock.

LONGSTOCK, Hants
Thatched cottages strung out along a narrow, winding lane form the spine of this pretty village. Medieval tiles can be seen behind the altar of the 19th-century church, which is also notable for its beautiful chancel arch.

Turn left, then at the end of the village turn right (no SP) on to a narrow by-road. In ¾ mile meet a T-junction and turn right. Continue across open downland, then in another ¾ mile keep forward SP 'Grateley'. Pass Danebury Ring on the left.

DANEBURY RING, Hants
At the top of a 469ft hill is Danebury Ring, an iron-age camp that has been thoroughly excavated in recent years. It has been acquired by the County Council as a Heritage Site and public amenity area.

In 2 miles meet a main road and turn left on to the A343. Pass the Army Aviation Museum, then after 1½ miles reach Middle Wallop. Meet crossroads and turn right on to the B3084 for Over Wallop.

OVER WALLOP, Hants
Although St Peter's Church in Over Wallop displays 12th- and 13th-century traces, much of its old structure has been hidden by Victorian restoration. Inside is a 15th-century font.

In 2¼ miles enter Grateley, keep forward on the B3084 passing Quarley Hill on the right, in 1¾ miles at a T-junction turn left on to the A303 SP 'Amesbury'. After ¾ mile at a roundabout take 2nd exit A303 SP 'Amesbury and Exeter', join the dual carriageway and after 5 miles bypass Amesbury before reaching a roundabout.

Danebury Ring consists of three lines of ramparts and ditches and encloses 13 acres.

In Saxon times Winchester was the capital of England.

The church at King's Somborne.

AMESBURY, Wilts
At Amesbury the Avon is crossed by a five-arched Palladian bridge which complements the stately flow of the river. Amesbury Abbey is of the 19th century and stands in a park in which beech clumps have been planted to represent the positions of English and French ships at Trafalgar. The Church of SS Mary and Melor is a flint-built Norman structure containing a contemporary font fashioned from Purbeck marble.

At the roundabout keep forward then in 1¾ miles turn right on to the A344 SP 'Devizes'. Continue to Stonehenge.

STONEHENGE, Wilts

Almost nothing is known about this most famous of all prehistoric megalithic monuments. From time to time the public imagination is caught by theories of sun-worship rites and primitive astronomical computers, but it is likely that these have as little factual base as the neo-druidical ceremonies enacted here every Midsummer's Night Eve. Originally Stonehenge (AM) comprised an encircling ditch and bank dating from the stone age, but this simple base was later developed into circles of sarsen stones around a horseshoe of trilithons enclosing the enigmatic Welsh bluestones (see tour 42). Several stones still stand where they were first erected thousands of years ago, and the largest measures almost 30ft high from its deeply buried base to its top. Much of the surrounding land belongs to the National Trust.

Continue on the A344 and in 1½ miles turn left on to the A360 SP 'Salisbury'. In 1 mile meet a roundabout and keep forward, passing Normanton Down.

NORMANTON DOWN, Wilts

In the Normanton Down area there are no fewer than 26 round barrows of various types, and a single long barrow dating from an earlier period. Excavations of this remarkable group have shown them to be Wessex Graves dating from the early bronze age. Hundreds of other examples survive near Stonehenge.

Follow an undulating road across part of Salisbury Plain, and after 3 miles meet crossroads. Turn left on to an unclassified road SP 'The Woodfords'. Continue to Middle Woodford.

MIDDLE WOODFORD, Wilts

Most of Middle Woodford Church was rebuilt in Victorian times, though the great flint and rubble tower is a survival from earlier days. Heale House, where Charles II once hid and from which he rode forth to view Stonehenge, only the eight acre gardens are open.

At Middle Woodford meet a T-junction and turn right to follow the River Avon to Lower Woodford.

Stonehenge is probably the most famous prehistoric monument in the world.

LOWER WOODFORD, Wilts

High downs rise on either side of this tiny village, which is the lowest of three Woodfords strung along the Avon Valley. The only building of any real note here is the manor house (not open), but the local countryside is enchanting.

In 2 miles cross a river bridge and turn left, then immediately right and shortly pass the earthworks of Old Sarum.

OLD SARUM, Wilts

In Roman times this important centre was linked by the Port Way to *Calleva Atrebatum*, a significant garrison town near Silchester in Hampshire. After a while Old Sarum became the site of a great cathedral, but a combination of water shortage, military troubles, and exposure to inclement weather prompted a move to Salisbury in 1220. The cathedral was demolished in 1331 and the materials transported to the new site for the superb building that stands today.

The River Test is renowned for its trout fishing.

Reach the main road and turn right on to the A345. Continue to Salisbury.

SALISBURY, Wilts

Salisbury's 404ft cathedral spire, the tallest in England, dominates most approaches to this lovely city. The cathedral itself is a perfect example of early-English architecture, set amid an enchanting medley of houses in the ancient cathedral close. Many other old buildings survive in the city.

From Salisbury follow SP 'Southampton' to leave on the A36. In 2¼ miles at the start of the dual carriageway, turn right on to an unclassified road SP 'Alderbury', continue into Alderbury.

ALDERBURY, Wilts

Alderbury House is said to be built of stone from the old belfry of Salisbury Cathedral. The small farm at nearby Ivychurch is on the site of a Norman priory, and local St Mary's Church is of Victorian date.

At Alderbury continue to the end of the village, cross bridge and follow SP 'West Grimstead'. Drive to that village and keep forward SP 'West Dean', and in 3 miles meet a junction and turn right for West Dean.

WEST DEAN, Wilts

Half hidden among trees at the top of a hill are remains of the old St Mary's Church of West Dean. New St Mary's was built of flint and brick in 1866. Close to the ruins is a good 16th-century barn.

Turn right SP 'Lockerley', then beyond East Dean go over a level crossing and continue to Lockerley. In ½ mile bear right, and ¼ mile farther pass under a railway bridge. Drive to the nearside of a green and turn left SP 'Dunbridge'. At Dunbridge turn left on to the B3084 and drive over a level crossing and river bridge. In ½ mile turn right on to an unclassified road SP 'Mottisfont Village'. Meet a T-junction and turn right. Pass the entrance to 18th-century Mottisfont Abbey.

MOTTISFONT, Hants

Remains of a 12th-century priory are incorporated in 18th-century Mottisfont Abbey (NT), which houses an excellent collection of paintings by Rex Whistler.

Cross the River Test then later meet the main road and turn left on to the A3057. Follow the Test Valley to King's Somborne.

KING'S SOMBORNE, Hants

A ring of bells in the Church of SS Peter and Paul is inscribed 'completed in the Jubilee Year of Queen Victoria, 1887'. The building itself is of ancient foundation but was much restored in 1885. The architect Sir Edwin Lutyens designed modern Marsh Court.

In King's Somborne turn right on to an unclassified road SP 'Winchester', then take the next turning left. After another ¾ mile turn right SP 'Farley Mount' then climb through well-wooded country to Farley Mount. This country park has an excellent picnic site. Meet a fork junction and bear left to follow a pleasant by-road. Go forward over all crossroads for 3 miles, then turn left on to the A3090 to re-enter Winchester.

PETERSFIELD, Hants

In its early years Petersfield's prosperity was based on the wool trade, but as this began to decline it became an important coaching centre on the busy London to Portsmouth road. Today it is a thriving country town full of fine old houses in evocatively-named streets. A once-gilded equestrian statue of William III guards the central square, where a market is held every Wednesday and Saturday. The extensive waters of Heath Pond lie south east of the town on the B2146.

Leave Petersfield on the A3 'Guildford' road and continue to Durford Heath.

DURFORD HEATH, W Sussex

The 62-acre expanse of Durford Heath (NT) includes 4 acres of Rogate Common with its abundance of wildlife.

Continue along the A3 for ¾ mile. Reach the Jolly Drover Inn and turn right on to an unclassified road SP 'Rogate' to enter Sussex. After ¼ mile turn left on to the Fernhurst road and drive through wooded country to Milland.

MILLAND, W Sussex

Although close to the Portsmouth road, this straggling village preserves an air of remoteness and seclusion. St Luke's Church of 1878 stands in front of the primitive Old Church which it replaced.

Continue beyond Milland for 1½ miles and turn right with SP 'The Old Cottage'. Ascend to Woolbeding and Pound Commons (NT).

WOOLBEDING COMMON, W Sussex

Woolbeding Common, part of a 1,084-acre estate (NT), includes some 400 acres of common heath and woodland open to public access.

Descend past Woolbeding's Saxon church.

Midhurst's mainly 19th-century church looks over a town that preserves beautiful buildings from many periods of architecture.

HAMPSHIRE DOWNS AND SUSSEX LANES

West of Petersfield are the rolling chalk downs of Hampshire, bare summits rising from wooded flanks watered by trout streams. East are the great wooded commons, winding lanes, and picturesque villages of Sussex.

Cowdray House was built c1500.

WOOLBEDING, W Sussex

Domesday describes Woolbeding as 'a perfect manor containing a church, mill, meadow, and wood.' The mill has gone, but the village is as delightful as that ancient description suggests. All Hallows' Church boasts a good Saxon nave.

Cross the River Rother, meet the A272, and turn left to enter Midhurst.

MIDHURST, W Sussex

This small market town stands on the south bank of the River Rother, at the centre of one of Sussex's most beautiful regions. South lie the downs, and north are the picturesque ruins of Cowdray House (see Easebourne).

Leave Midhurst by the A286 'Guildford' road, cross the river, and turn left through Easebourne.

EASEBOURNE, W Sussex

Formerly more important than Midhurst, immaculate Easebourne is very much an estate village. Among its many well-kept houses are Sycamore Cottage in Easebourne Lane, and The Priory, attached to the south side of St Mary's Church. Tudor Cowdray House (not open) was ruined by fire in 1793.

Leave Easebourne and climb through woodland to the 530ft Henley Common viewpoint. Continue to Fernhurst.

FERNHURST, W Sussex

Almost certainly the last stronghold of the Sussex iron-smelting industry, this large village has settled into attractive rural retirement amid the woods and valleys of the Weald.

Meet crossroads in Fernhurst and turn left on to an unclassified road. Drive through wooded country with SP 'Linchmere', and after 1 mile branch right SP 'Liphook'. Enter Linchmere.

LINCHMERE, W Sussex

Linchmere boasts a tiny green outside the enlarged hill chapel that serves as its church. Magnificent views from here extend over a deep valley flanked by steep slopes.

After Linchmere turn left on to the B2131 to re-enter Hampshire. Enter Liphook.

LIPHOOK, Hants

Most of Liphook straggles untidily along the main Portsmouth road, but here and there it preserves something of a village atmosphere. Bohunt Manor (open) stands in a lovely woodland and water garden.

A detour from the main route can be made here by turning left on to the unclassified 'Midhurst' road and driving for 1½ miles to Hollycombe.

HOLLYCOMBE, W Sussex

The Hollycombe Working Steam Museum and Woodland Garden (open) has a remarkable collection of equipment ranging from old fairground rides to a 2ft-gauge railway through woodland banks of rhododendrons and azaleas. Attractions include traction engine rides and demonstrations of steam ploughing, threshing, and rolling.

At the Royal Anchor Hotel in Liphook (on the main route) at mini roundabouts turn right then sharp left SP 'Greatham' passing Longmoor Camp and Woolmer Forest. Continue to Greatham. In Greatham turn left on to the A325 and follow SP 'Alton'. Reach a church and after another ¼ mile turn right on to the B3006 and drive on to the east Hampshire Downs for Empshott. Continue along the B3006 to Selborne.

SELBORNE & SELBORNE HILL, Hants

It is not just the beauty of its scenery or the architectural distinction of some of its houses that have made this lovely village famous. It is also featured in Gilbert White's classic field study entitled *The Natural History of Selborne*. White, who was born in the Vicarage in 1720, made one of the first and best studies of wildlife inter-action within a defined area. He died in The Wakes, a fine house that now contains a library and the Gilbert White Museum (open). Visitors today can still see the church meadows and high beech hangers where he made many of his observations, and climb the steep Zig-Zag Path to the excellent viewpoint of Selborne Hill (NT).

In 3½ miles turn left on to an unclassified road for Chawton. A short detour can be made from the main route here by keeping forward on the A32 to Alton.

The Gilbert White Museum at Selborne.

MID HANTS RAILWAY, Hants

The original Watercress Line, as this railway has come to be known, was threatened with closure in 1973 and initial efforts to keep the whole line open were not successful. In 1975 the Winchester & Alton Railway Company raised enough money to open 3 miles of track between Alresford and Ropley. All associated buildings in the 10 miles to Alton were also acquired.

New Alresford's Broad Street, said to be the finest village street in Hampshire, is lined with attractive Georgian houses and lime trees.

Jane Austen lived at Chawton Cottage with her mother and sister.

ALTON, Hants

In years gone by this historic market town grew quietly prosperous on brewing and the manufacture of woollen cloth. Fine Georgian buildings grace the main street, and a Tudor cottage that was once the home of the poet Spenser is in Amery Street. Exhibits in the Curtis Museum include a collection of craft tools and other bygones.

Continue back to the main tour route and enter Chawton.

CHAWTON, Hants

In Chawton is the unassuming 18th-century house where novelist Jane Austen once lived. Now a Jane Austen Museum (open), this was her home from 1809 till her death, and all her later books were written here.

Reach a roundabout at the end of Chawton and take the 2nd exit on to the A31. Climb to 600ft at Four Marks continue on the A31 to roundabout, take 3rd exit and follow into Alresford.

NEW ALRESFORD, Hants

During the medieval period New Alresford grew to be one of the 10 greatest wool towns in the country. Aptly-named Broad Street, considered the finest village street in Hampshire, leads downhill to scattered Old Alresford. At the north-west end of the village is the large and picturesque lake.

A short detour can be made from the main route by turning left into Station Road to visit the Mid Hants Railway.

Leave Alresford on the Winchester road and after ½ mile meet crossroads. Turn left on to an unclassified road to Tichborne.

TICHBORNE, Hants

Tichborne is a delightful collection of thatched 16th- and 17th-century houses with an unspoilt little church and a 19th-century manor house. Some 800 years ago the ailing lady of the manor, distressed by the poverty of the villagers, begged her husband to help them. Mockingly he agreed to set aside part of his estate to provide corn for the poor in perpetuity, but that would be only so much land as she could crawl round while one torch burned. Tradition has it that she managed to encompass an amazing 23 acres of ground before the flame – and her life – expired. The land concerned still known as The Crawls, and every year the villages receive a dole of 30cwt of flour blessed by the local priest.

Continue for 1 mile past the village, meet a T-junction, and turn right on to the B3046 for Cheriton. Follow SP 'Petersfield' for ½ mile, then cross a main road on to the unclassified 'Droxford' road. Drive through Kilmeston, climb rolling hills, then later turn left on to the 'Warnford' road for a descent to the Meon Valley. Continue to Warnford.

WARNFORD, Hants

This beautiful Meon Valley village has a 12th- to 17th-century church with a massive Norman tower. Ruins of a 13th-century building, misleadingly known as King John's House, is located at Warnford Park.

Meet a T-junction and turn right on to the A32 'Fareham' road. Cross the River Meon and continue into Corhampton.

CORHAMPTON, Hants

This pleasant River Meon village boasts a rare Saxon church with a contemporary sundial. The walls of the ancient nave slant crazily to the south, but the building is quite safe.

After another mile turn left on to the B2150 'Waterlooville' road, then pass the Hurdles Inn and take the next turning left (no SP). Follow SP 'East Meon' over crossroads and after another ½ mile bear left. Cross downland to meet a T-junction and turn left again on to the 'West Meon' road. Continue to the slopes of Old Winchester Hill.

OLD WINCHESTER HILL, Hants

Why this noted beauty spot should be so named is a mystery, for the city of Winchester lies a good 12 miles to the west. The hill's windswept summit rises to nearly 700ft, affording excellent views over half the county, and a 1¾-mile nature trail has been laid out on its flanks.

Branch right on to a narrow road and later turn right on to the A32. Drive into West Meon and turn right on to the unclassified 'East Meon' road. Continue along the attractive Meon Valley to the edge of East Meon.

EAST MEON, Hants

'Father of angling' Izaak Walton once fished here, and the village is still a popular trout centre. The Norman church is arguably the finest of its kind in Hampshire.

Follow SP 'Petersfield' and in ½ mile turn left on to the narrow 'Lower Bordean' road. Later cross the A272 into the very narrow 'Colemore' road and follow SP 'Petersfield' to a T-junction. Turn right, descend the attractive Stoner Hill, and return to Petersfield.

IN THE NORTH DOWNS

Some of the finest views in the south of England can be enjoyed from the great chalk ridge of the Hog's Back, which itself can be seen across miles of flat farm land scattered with small woods and copses. This is the country of the yellowhammer and skylark, of thorn-covered slopes and the gnarled creepers of old man's beard.

GUILDFORD, Surrey

Medieval kings built a great castle in this ancient town and merchants later developed it into an important centre of the wool industry. Nowadays the castle has vanished except for a 3-storey keep (open) in flower gardens, but the prosperity of wool is reflected in many fine old buildings. Charles Dickens thought the steep High Street 'the most beautiful in the kingdom'. At its summit is the 16th-century Grammar School, the contemporary Abbot's Hospital, and an 18th-century church. Farther down, the ornate clock of the 17th-century Guildhall hangs over the pavement near the Saxon tower of St Mary's Church, and the 19th-century Church of St Nicholas makes an interesting contrast at the bottom of the hill. The River Wey features an interesting 18th-century riverside crane powered by a 20ft treadmill. New buildings include Sir Edward Maufe's controversial cathedral on Stag Hill.

Leave Guildford town centre with SP 'Other Routes' and after 1 mile turn left on to the bypass SP 'Petersfield' then join the A3. After 2¼ miles drive under a road bridge, and in another mile pass the turning for Compton and Loseley House on the left. A short detour from the main route can be taken along the B3000 in the pleasant village of Compton and Loseley House.

The Hog's Back is criss-crossed by quiet country lanes.

COMPTON, Surrey

A gallery devoted entirely to Victorian painter and sculptor G F Watts displays some 200 of his works in this small village. He is commemorated by a mortuary chapel which features vivid interior decoration by his widow.

LOSELEY HOUSE, Surrey

Sir William More, a kinsman of the ill-fated Sir Thomas More, used stone from Waverley Abbey to build this magnificent Elizabethan mansion (open) near Compton. Fine ceilings are complemented by panelling from King Henry VIII's Nonsuch Palace, and every room is appointed with furniture and hangings from many periods.

Continue along the A3 for another ½ mile, then turn right on to the B3000 SP 'Farnham'. Proceed to Puttenham.

PUTTENHAM, Surrey

A handsomely aged church with a 15th-century tower enhances the quiet charm of this small village.

In the village turn left on to an unclassified road and continue along the southern slopes of the Hog's Back to Seale.

THE HOG'S BACK, Surrey

At its highest point this great whaleback ridge of chalk, an outlier of the North Downs, rises to 505ft above sea level. It stretches from Guildford to Farnham, with several parking areas along its length.

Guildford's fine 17th-century clock hangs high above the main street and can be seen for many yards in both directions.

Drive past the church in Seale and turn left. Proceed for ½ mile and meet crossroads, then turn left for The Sands. Cross a main road SP 'Tilford' and pass 534ft Crooksbury Hill on the left. Continue to crossroads and turn left again SP 'Elstead'. After a short distance turn left on to the B3001 and take the next turning right on to an unclassified road for Tilford.

TILFORD, Surrey

Features of this pleasant village include two partly medieval bridges over the River Wey, and a huge old tree known as King John's Oak. The latter is said to be many centuries old. The village is noted for its Bach music festivals. One mile west is the Old Kiln Agricultural Museum.

Cross the River Wey twice with SP 'Frensham' and after ¼ mile turn left. Continue for another 1¼ miles and turn left on to the A287 SP 'Hindhead'. Proceed through Frensham.

FRENSHAM, Surrey

Frensham's lovely ponds are surrounded by woods and heathland on the Hampshire-Surrey border. The Great Pond covers 108 acres, and the Little Pond is resplendent with water lilies in late spring and summer. The 900-acre gorse and heather common (NT) features a line of large prehistoric bowl barrows, and much of the area is now protected as a country park. Frensham's restored church has a Norman font and, under the tower, a great copper cauldron reputed to be over 400 years old. Tradition holds that it belonged to a local witch called Mother Ludlam, and an 18th-century writer tells of it having been filled with ale to entertain the village 'at the wedding of poor maids'.

Cross Frensham Common to reach Frensham Great Pond and Country Park. Proceed for ¾ mile and turn left on to an unclassified road SP 'Thursley'. After 1½ miles reach the Pride of the Valley Hotel. Cross the main road and after 1¾ miles turn right for Thursley.

THURSLEY, Surrey

Old houses and charming cottages straggle along a winding lane to the village church which has a sundial on its shingled spire. A curious epitaph to an unknown sailor murdered by three ruffians at Hindhead in 1786 can be seen on a tombstone in the churchyard.

In ½ mile turn left and ½ mile further turn right on to the A3 'Hindhead' road. Drive over Hindhead Common, with the Devil's Punch Bowl on the right and Gibbet Hill, a picnic site, and Witley Forest on the left. Enter Hindhead.

Four great beams inside Thursley Church support its shingled steeple.

HINDHEAD, Surrey
Founded in the 19th century on the highest town site in Surrey, Hindhead offers some of the most beautiful surroundings in the county. The noted viewpoint of Gibbet Hill (NT) rises to 894ft in the north east, the deep combe of the Devil's Punch Bowl (NT) cuts through a sandstone ridge near by, and all around is Witley Forest. Off the B3002 1½ miles south west is the beauty spot of Waggoner's Wells (NT).

Follow SP 'Haslemere, A287' and descend to Shottermill, then keep forward on the B2131 for Haslemere.

HASLEMERE, Surrey
Haslemere stands in dense woods at the northern foot of 918ft-high Blackdown. For centuries the town has been a centre for craftsmen, and today the tradition is maintained at the Dolmetsch musical instrument workshops and museum (open). Aldworth, home of the great 19th-century poet Tennyson, stands on the slopes of Black Down. A number of 17th-century tiled houses survive behind a raised walk in the town, and the 19th-century Educational Museum of Sir John Hutchinson stands in the High Street (open). The town's annual music festival, usually held in July, is invariably devoted to the Baroque period.

Leave Haslemere on the B2131 SP 'Petworth', with Black Down (NT) on the right. After 2½ miles bear left SP 'Chiddingfold', and after a further ¾ mile meet a T-junction. Turn left on to the A283 for Chiddingfold.

Tree-shrouded Silent Pool is connected in legend with King John.

CHIDDINGFOLD, Surrey
In medieval times this large village was very famous for its fine quality glass. Despite its large size it is one of the loveliest Wealden villages. At its heart is a pretty green with a thorn tree said to be 500 years old, a pond complete with ducks and water lilies, and the delightful 14th-century Crown Inn.

Drive to the Crown Inn and turn right on to an unclassified road SP 'Dunsfold'. Reach the far side of the green and bear right, then continue for 1 mile, turn left, and proceed to Dunsfold.

DUNSFOLD, Surrey
A modern lychgate and a tunnel of clipped yews lead to Dunsfold Church, which dates from the 13th century and has an attractive Tudor porch. Its pews may be the oldest still used in England.

One mile beyond Dunsfold turn right on to the B2130 SP 'Cranleigh'. Continue for 1 mile, then bear left and after ¼ mile turn right. Drive over staggered crossroads and continue for 1¼ miles. Turn right on to the B2128 and drive into Cranleigh.

CRANLEIGH, Surrey
Cranleigh is more than a village, and yet not quite large enough to call a town. Its pleasant green has a rural aspect, but the long main street lined with maples planted by Canadian soldiers in World War I might have been borrowed from a much larger place. In 1859 a surgeon called Napper and the local rector together founded the first cottage hospital.

Clandon Park was designed by a Venetian architect in the Palladian style.

Drive to the end of the village and turn left on to the B2127. After 2¼ miles turn left again into Ewhurst.

EWHURST, Surrey
Climbers come to Ewhurst to test their mettle on Pitch Hill, a sandstone outcrop that rises 1 mile to the north of the village. Ewhurst Mill has not worked for a century and was once a haunt of smugglers.

Keep forward in Ewhurst, on to the unclassified 'Shere' road. After ¾ mile bear left and cross Pitch Hill, with Winterfold Forest on the left, and drive into Shere.

SHERE, Surrey
Situated on the River Tillingbourne under the edge of the North Downs, this enchanting village has long

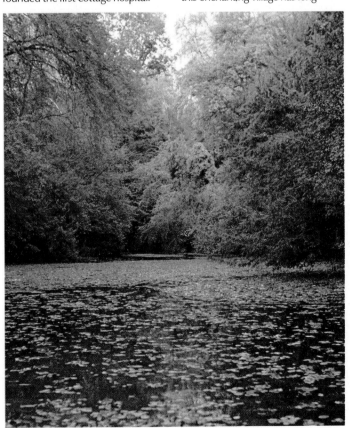

proved an attraction to artists. The church, which figures in the *Domesday Book*, has a Norman tower with a medieval shingled spire. The White Horse Inn has a frame of ancient ship's timbers.

Drive to a T-junction and turn left SP 'Guildford'. Continue to the next T-junction and turn left again to join the A25. After ½ mile, off the main road to the right, is the Silent Pool.

SILENT POOL, Surrey
According to legend King John watched a local girl bathing here. She drowned herself in a fit of shame, and anybody visiting this quiet, tree-encircled water might easily imagine that her spirit lingers here still.

Ascend to Newlands Corner.

NEWLANDS CORNER, Surrey
This famous 567ft high North Downs beauty spot offers views across the Weald to the South Downs.

At Newlands Corner keep right on the A25. Descend for 1 mile and meet crossroads. Turn left on to the A25. By keeping straight ahead a short detour can be taken from the main route to Clandon Park.

CLANDON PARK, Surrey
Built in the early 1730s, this classical mansion (NT) features noteworthy plaster decoration, and stands in gardens refashioned by Capability Brown. A famous collection of china, furniture and needlework bequeathed to the nation by Mrs Hannah Gubbay in 1969 is displayed in these elegant surroundings.

Continue on the A25 to Merrow.

MERROW, Surrey
A footpath that starts between the church and inn at Merrow runs across gentle downland to a summit which affords views into 8 or 9 counties, depending on the weather.

Forward along the A246 returning to Guildford.

WOKINGHAM, Berks
Wokingham boasted a bell foundry in the 14th century, and the silk industry flourished here in Elizabethan days. Rose Street preserves timbered houses and the Rose Inn, where poets Dean Swift, Pope, and Gay spent a wet afternoon together. Gay utilized the time in composing verses to the landlord's daughter, Molly Mog. Several almshouses exist in and around the town, and Lucas Hospital of 1665 – at Luckely – is considered particularly fine.

Follow SP 'Reading, A329' to leave Wokingham via Broad Street. In ¼ mile approach the clock tower, then turn left on to the B3349 SP 'Arborfield' and go over a level crossing. After 2⅓ miles turn right for Arborfield Cross.

ARBORFIELD CROSS, Berks
To the left of Arborfield Cross, off the A327, is Arborfield Garrison. Within the complex is the Royal Electrical and Mechanical Engineers Museum, which is open to the public most weekdays.

Turn right and immediately left on to an unclassified road SP 'Swallowfield'. Continue for 2 miles and turn right. Swallowfield Park is on the right.

SWALLOWFIELD PARK, Berks
Swallowfield Park lies almost on the Hampshire border, at the meeting of the rivers Loddon and Blackwater. Swallowfield Park house was rebuilt in the late 17th century and remodelled by William Atkinson in 1820.

At the park gates turn left across the Blackwater River to reach Swallowfield. Turn left SP 'Basingstoke', at T-junction turn left on to the main road B3349 for Risely. Bear right and in ½ mile at T-junction turn right and at roundabout take 1st exit SP 'Basingstoke' A33. A detour from the main route can be made by taking 2nd exit unclassified road for 2 miles at T-junction turn left and left again for entrance, for Stratfield Saye Park. Then return to the main route.

STRATFIELD SAYE PARK, Hants
This rather unstately stately home (open) was built in the reign of Charles I and purchased by the 1st Duke of Wellington in 1817. The duke intended to use the £600,000 voted to him by a grateful nation to build a new house in the superb park, but funds did not permit this and so the great soldier set about making the existing building as comfortable and convenient as he could. Central heating was installed in the passageways, and there were 'new-fangled' water closets of blue-patterned china in every room. It has been the home of the dukes of Wellington ever since.

On the main route, drive to the Wellington Monument and turn left on to an unclassified road, SP 'Hook

ROYAL PARKS AND HAMPSHIRE WOODS

Close to Windsor is the semi-cultivated countryside of royal parkland; farther away, near the Duke of Wellington's country estate, are dark ranks of conifer plantations and the lighter greens of oak and birch tangled with honeysuckle.

EVERSLEY
– EFOR'S LEIGH –
FIELD of the WILD BOAR

Eversley's ancient origins are suggested by the picturesque nameplate on its village green.

& Eversley', cross Heckfield Heath, and continue for ½ mile. At roundabout take 2nd exit B3011, then after ½ mile branch left on to an unclassified road. Continue, cross the River Whitewater, then after 2½ miles meet crossroads and drive forward. A short detour can be made to the village of Eversley by turning left here and continuing for ½ mile.

EVERSLEY, Hants
St Mary's Church at Eversley was built in the 18th century, and is distinguished in having had naturalist Charles Kingsley as rector. The north aisle was built in his memory. Bramshill House, a Jacobean

mansion regarded as one of the finest in the country, is now the Police Staff College.

Join the A327 for Eversley Cross and drive to The Chequers (PH). Turn left on to the B3016 SP 'Wokingham' and continue to Finchampstead.

FINCHAMPSTEAD, Berks
Finchampstead's pride is the splendid avenue of Wellingtonia pines which runs 1 mile east to Crowthorne. Its church has a white-painted body of Norman date and carries an 18th-century tower built in red brick. The whole building stands on a prehistoric earthwork, as if aloof from the village.

Turn right, then after ¼ mile meet a war memorial and turn right on to the B3348 SP 'Crowthorne'. Pass Finchampstead Ridges on the right.

FINCHAMPSTEAD RIDGES, Berks
This 60-acre heather and woodland National Trust property offers excellent views over Berkshire, Hampshire, and Surrey countryside.

Continue, enter a roundabout, and take the first exit on to the A321. After 1 mile at roundabout take 3rd exit B3430 on to Nine Mile Ride.

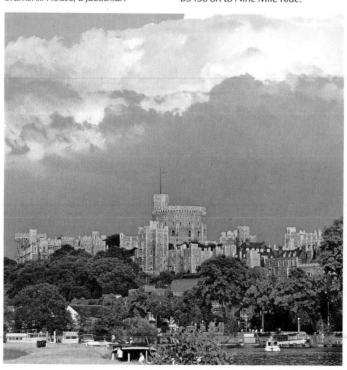

NINE MILE RIDE, Berks
Nine Mile Ride follows the line of a Roman road through delightfully wooded country. At the Bracknell end, to the south, is the 20-acre iron-age hillfort of Caesar's Camp, part of which is now a public recreation ground with a picnic site.

After 2¾ miles at roundabout take 2nd exit SP 'Bagshot'. Continue passing Caesar's Camp (see Nine Mile Ride) and at roundabout take 2nd exit on to the A322. Proceed for 1½ miles on to the A332 'Ascot' road. Continue for 1¾ miles and bear right. Approach a roundabout and leave by the 3rd exit on to the A329, with Ascot racecourse on the left, and enter Ascot.

ASCOT, Berks
Ascot has strong Queen Anne connections. It was she who instituted the Royal Ascot race meeting in 1711, a fashionable event still held in June and patronized by members of the Royal Family. The Ascot Gold Cup was presented for the first time in 1807.

Continue to Virginia Water, which can be seen on the left.

VIRGINIA WATER, Surrey
This 1½-mile-long artificial lake, laid out by Thomas Sandby for George III, is situated at the south-east corner of Windsor Great Park and is well known for its beauty. Colonnades brought from the Roman port of Leptis Magna stand on its bank in contrast to a 100ft totem pole set up in 1958 to mark the centenary of British Columbia. The nearby Valley Gardens are most inviting.

Continue at T-junction and turn left on to the A30. Pass the Wheatsheaf Hotel and proceed for 1¼ miles, then turn left on to an unclassified road for Savill Gardens (left).

THE SAVILL GARDENS, Berks
Windsor Great Park is noted for its magnificent horticultural areas, but none is more popular than the wooded 20-acre Savill Gardens. Its variety of flowers provide a wealth of colour throughout the seasons.

Continue to The Sun (PH) and go forward for ¼ mile before turning right for Englefield Green.

ENGLEFIELD GREEN, Surrey
This large residential district lies within easy reach of delightful Windsor Great Park. Its 250-year-old Barley Mow Inn was once a popular coaching stop. Late 19th-century Royal Holloway College stands among gardens and playing fields between Englefield Green and the railway. It was one of the first women's colleges ever built and became a constituent college of London University in 1900.

Cross a main road and pass a left turn to Cooper's Hill RAF Memorial.

Windsor Castle has dominated its surroundings ever since William the Conqueror started it in the 11th century.

An equestrian statue of George III by sculptor Richard Westmacott stands on a granite base at the end of the Long Walk in Windsor Great Park.

Return along the A308 SP 'Windsor'. In 1 mile meet a roundabout and take the 3rd exit to pass Runnymede.

RUNNYMEDE, Surrey

About ½ mile north-west of Egham are the 60-acre riverside meadows of Runnymede. It was here in 1215 that King John was prevailed upon by his barons to seal the draft of Magna Carta, from which seed – almost by accident – grew the English ideal of personal liberty. Overlooking the meadows is Cooper's Hill, which is crowned by the RAF Memorial and has the American Bar Association's Magna Carta Memorial at its foot. Halfway up its slopes is a memorial to the assassinated US President, John F Kennedy.

Continue through Old Windsor.

OLD WINDSOR, Berks

Old Windsor parish stretches from the River Thames to Virginia Water, including the semi-wild countryside

An immense variety of trees and shrubs is displayed in the magnificent formal landscapes which surround Virginia Water.

Sumptuously decorated rooms full of splendid furniture are features of the seat of the dukes of Wellington, at Stratfield Saye Park.

COOPER'S HILL RAF MEMORIAL, Surrey

The Commonwealth Air Forces Memorial on Cooper's Hill commemorates 20,000 allied airmen who died, with no known grave, in World War II. The site, which gives views of Windsor Castle and seven counties, overlooks Runnymede.

Return to main route then after 300 yards bear left and descend Tite Hill to the edge of Egham. Enter a roundabout and leave by the 1st exit to rejoin the A30. After another ¾ mile enter another roundabout and leave by the 3rd exit on to the A308. Continue to Staines.

STAINES, Surrey

The old market town of Staines, at the junction of the rivers Colne and Thames, is entered via a superb road bridge built by Rennie and opened by William IV. The by-pass & M25 crosses by a modern bridge. West of the local church the London Stone marks the limit of the City of London's former jurisdiction. Sir Walter Raleigh was brought here to be tried because at that time London was in the grip of the plague.

of the Great Park and parts of Windsor Forest. Edward the Confessor had his palace here before the new Windsor of today existed, and William the Conqueror held a Great Council (Witan) here in 1070 – just 4 years after the Norman invasion of Britain.

At roundabout take 1st exit A308; to the left lies Windsor Great Park. Later enter a roundabout and leave by the 3rd exit, into King's Road, to enter Windsor.

WINDSOR, Berks

Windsor is a largely Georgian and Victorian town that owes its existence to its magnificent castle. William the Conqueror first appreciated the site's strategic importance over Old Windsor and built a palisaded fort within a moat. Practically every English monarch who has taken the throne in the 900 years since then has contributed to its development, and today it is the largest inhabited castle in the world.

Leave the town with SP 'Bagshot A332', to return along King's Road. In ¾ mile enter a roundabout and leave by the 2nd exit to enter Windsor Great Park.

WINDSOR GREAT PARK, Berks

Within the boundaries formed by Home Park and the castle to the north, and by all that remains of Windsor Forest's royal chase to the south and west, Windsor Great Park encompasses an area of almost 5,000 acres. Ancient King's Oak, near Forest Gate, is claimed to be the largest in the park. Legend has it that antlered Herne the Hunter meets here with his ghastly pack before chasing across the night skies. Most of the park is accessible by well-kept footpaths.

Continue for 4 miles before bearing right, then turn left SP 'Ascot'. After another ¼ mile meet crossroads and

turn right on to the B3034 SP 'Winkfield'. After ¾ mile turn left on to the A330 SP 'Ascot'. After ⅛ mile turn right on to the B3034, then go forward over all crossroads to join the A3095. Continue for ¼ mile then turn left to rejoin the B3034 and continue for 1 mile. Cross a humpback bridge, keep left, and enter Binfield.*

BINFIELD, Berks

Alexander Pope sang in the choir of the local church as a boy. Among the church's treasures is a fine old hour glass.

Approach crossroads and turn left on to an unclassified road. After ½ mile bear right. Continue, at T-junction turn right on to the B3408, in 1 mile at roundabout take 2nd exit A329 to return to Wokingham.

THE EDGE OF THE NORTH DOWNS

Much of this is National Trust country, protected for its outstanding beauty. Valley woodlands and high, empty commons in Surrey rise to soaring outliers of the West Sussex downs, which roll summit after windy summit into the chalklands of south Kent.

EPSOM, Surrey

In the 18th century this pleasant market town was famous for the medicinal springs that gave their name to Epsom Salts; even before that it was known for horse racing. The popularity of the spa has waned, but that of the turf is still in good heart. Among the town's more notable buildings are 19th-century Durdans and 17th-century Waterloo House.

Leave Epsom from the southern end of the High Street, enter a roundabout, and take the 2nd exit to join the B280. Cross Epsom Common, with a picnic site to the right, and after 1¼ miles approach traffic lights. A detour from the main tour route can be made by turning right at these lights for Chessington Zoo.

CHESSINGTON ZOO, Gt London

In 1931 Reginald Stuart Goddard founded this famous zoo in the grounds of Burnt Stub Manor, the successor to a house burned by Cromwellian troops. The grounds cover 65 acres and contain a large variety of birds, animals, and a children's zoo.

On the main route, continue forward from the traffic lights for 2 miles and turn left on to the A244 for Oxshott. Then turn right on to an unclassified road for Stoke D'Abernon.

STOKE D'ABERNON, Surrey

Preserved in the local church is Sir John d'Abernon's brass of 1277, thought to be the earliest memorial of its kind in the country. The old manor house is Tudor at heart, but received a brick face-lift sometime during the 18th century.

Turn right on to the A245 for Cobham.

A fine example of the screenwork at the church in Charlwood

COBHAM, Surrey

An inscription on the bridge here tells of an earlier structure raised by Queen Matilda, wife of Henry I, because one of her ladies drowned while crossing the pool.

At Cobham, turn left on to an unclassified road SP 'Downside and Ockham'. Cross the river bridge, then turn right and follow SP 'Ockham'.

OCKHAM, Surrey

Hidden among the trees of Ockham Park, close to the great house, is the village church. This is well known for its lovely 13th-century east window of 7 lancets, sometimes known as the Seven Sisters.

Drive to the war memorial and turn right on to the B2039. Take the next turning left on to an unclassified road. Meet crossroads and go forward for 3 miles to East Clandon.

Robert Adam was responsible for many of the fine rooms in Georgian Hatchlands, near East Clandon.

EAST CLANDON, Surrey

Timber cottages and large old barns give this place an enviable air of timelessness and peace, but the mainly 13th-century church has been poorly restored. Admiral Boscawen built 18th-century Hatchlands (NT) for his retirement, but died before he could enjoy it.

Turn left to join the A246 and continue to West Horsley.

WEST HORSLEY, Surrey

A church stood at West Horsley before the Normans came, but the massive tower dates from the 12th century. The body of the building shows traces of almost every subsequent century, including very good 15th-century screens. Sir Walter Raleigh's remains are said to lie under the south chapel.

Continue to East Horsley.

EAST HORSLEY, Surrey

The curious 19th-century mansion known as East Horsley Towers houses the Electricity Council's Staff College. Much older is the local parish church, which was altered considerably in the 13th century and restored almost out of recognition in the 19th. Beautiful recumbent figures of Thomas and Catherine Cornwallis and several old brasses can be seen inside.

Left: Leith Hill Forest is a delightful mixture of woodland and heath.
Below: 18th century Leith Hill Tower.

Continue for ⅓ mile, turn right on to an unclassified road SP 'Shere', and after another ⅓ mile bear left with SP 'Dorking'. Ascend through woodland to the summit of the North Downs, and after 1⅓ miles meet crossroads and turn right SP 'Abinger'. Descend (1 in 6) White Downs Hill and continue for 1 mile, then turn left on to the A25. After ⅓ mile turn right on to an unclassified road and ascend for 1¼ miles. A short detour can be made from the main tour route by turning sharp left to Friday Street.

NORTH DOWNS
This range of chalk hills starts near Farnham in Surrey and extends across Kent to the white cliffs of Dover, culminating in a 900ft summit near Woldingham.

FRIDAY STREET, Surrey
Old cottages and a single street leading to a lake fringed with pine and oak are the main features of this village. The Stephen Langton Inn recalls a prelate of that name who played a leading role in the signing of Magna Carta. Severell's Copse (NT) comprises 59 acres of woodland stretching from the lake to Leith Hill.

Return to the T-junction on the main route, turn left, then keep forward SP 'Leith Hill'. After 1¼ miles pass a footpath leading left to Leith Hill.

LEITH HILL, Surrey
Much of the wooded countryside south of Friday Street is protected by the National Trust, including Leith Hill, Duke's Warren, and the estate of Leith Hill Place. The hill itself carries a picturesque tower whose top is 1,029ft above sea level – the highest point in Surrey.

Continue for 1¼ miles to join the B2126, then keep left for Ockley.

OCKLEY, Surrey
The local village green is sited on the course of the great Roman Stane Street. The local church enjoys a delightful setting and its tower dates from the 18th-century and a timbered porch is of 15th-century origin.

Turn left on to the A29. After the Kings Arms turn right on to the B2126. Continue for 1½ miles, then cross over the A24 to enter Capel. Turn right on to unclassified road SP 'Newdigate' in ½ mile turn left then turn right and enter Newdigate.

NEWDIGATE, Surrey
Typical of Wealden villages in general, Newdigate stands in an area that was once covered by dense forest. The forest has all but disappeared, but some of the great oaks that grew hereabouts can be traced to the massive pillars and arches of the local church tower.

Turn right and drive to Rusper.

RUSPER, W Sussex
Several half-timbered and tile-hung cottages survive in this pretty village, and St Mary Magdalene's Church boasts a sturdy 16th-century tower.

Bear left SP 'Crawley', continue for ¼ mile, then turn right for Faygate. At Faygate turn left SP 'Crawley'. Meet a main road turn left on to the A264. To the right is St Leonard's Forest.

ST LEONARD'S FOREST, W Sussex
The forests of St Leonard's and Worth, along with various scattered woodlands, are among the only sizeable remnants left of the vast prehistoric Forest of Anderida.

After 2¾ miles turn left on to the A23 Crawley bypass. Follow SP 'London' through Crawley suburbs.

CRAWLEY, W Sussex
The planning of this new town is not without merit. Its industrial estates are well separated from the residential areas, and some of the worst effects of high-density building have been avoided by the imaginative use of open spaces. Some 2½ miles north of Crawley is the Greyhound Hotel, Tinsley Green, the venue for the international marbles championship, which began as a competition between two local men for the hand of a girl in marriage.

Continue with the A23 SP 'London' to pass Gatwick Airport.

GATWICK AIRPORT, W Sussex
London's second airport after Heathrow, provides many scheduled and charter flights. The spectators' viewing area is in the terminal.

Continue for 1 mile, enter a roundabout, and leave by the 1st exit on to an unclassified road leading to Charlwood and Leigh. A detour can be made from the main tour route by taking the 3rd exit from this roundabout into Horley.

HORLEY, Surrey
A knight's effigy of c1315 and a 15th-century brass can be seen in the local church, and the half-timbered Six Bells Inn dates from the 15th-century.
Continue to Charlwood.

CHARLWOOD, Surrey
The 11th- to 15-century church in Charlwood is noted for its screen work and wall paintings. The privately-run Gatwick Zoo & Aviaries covers 10 acres, with many of the animals and birds in natural settings.
Continue to Leigh.

LEIGH, Surrey
Charming old houses in this village are complemented by a green and a 15th-century church famous for its memorial brasses. Particularly good examples of the latter are those to the Ardernes, who lived in the area during the 15th century.

Pass through Leigh and after ¼ mile turn right at the Seven Stars (PH) for Betchworth, crossing the River Mole.

The lake at Friday Street is part of the National Trust property of Leith Hill.

BETCHWORTH, Surrey
High trees border the River Mole here, and the church preserves a great Norman chest of solid oak beneath its tower.

Meet a T-junction and turn left then right SP 'Walton-on-the-Hill'. Continue to a roundabout and take the 2nd exit on to the B2032. Climb (1 in 6) Pebble Hill to the downs. At the summit turn left on to the B2033 SP 'Box Hill'. Then bear left on to an unclassified road for Box Hill Country Park and picnic site.

BOX HILL, Surrey
Named after the box trees that grow on its flanks, 563ft Box Hill (NT) is a noted viewpoint and designated area of outstanding natural beauty, including both wood and downland scenery and a Country Park.

Descend to the bottom of the hill. Approach a T-junction and turn right SP 'Mickleham' B2209. Within ¼ mile turn right again on to an unclassified road SP 'Headley'. A detour can be made from the main tour by driving ahead for Mickleham.

MICKLEHAM, Surrey
Playwright George Meredith was born here in 1864. Yews from a Druid's Grove folly stand in the grounds of 18th-century Norbury Park.

Meet a T-junction and turn right on to the B2033. Headley Heath (NT) lies away to the right. Ascend and turn left on to an unclassified road for Headley SP 'Epsom'.

HEADLEY, Surrey
Yews mark the spot where Headley's 14th-century church was pulled down in the last century, and the spire of its 19th-century successor serves as a Surrey landmark. The church bell is a good 500 years old.

After 1¾ miles meet crossroads and turn right. Pass Epsom Downs racecourse.

EPSOM DOWNS RACECOURSE, Surrey
The course here has been the home of good racing since the reign of James I, and has been the venue for the Derby since 1780 perhaps one of Britain's most famous races.
Turn left on to the B290 and return to Epsom.

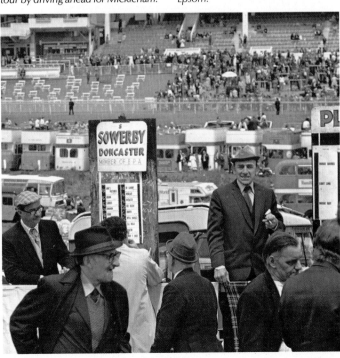
Derby Day at Epsom racecourse attracts racing enthusiasts from all walks of life.

RESORTS AND DOWNLAND VILLAGES

High above the bright, mercurial resorts of the Sussex coast are the tranquil hamlets of the South Downs. Here change is gradual, a process to be approached with the caution born from centuries of experience.

WORTHING, W Sussex

Until the 1760s Worthing was little more than a fishing hamlet, but by the end of that century the patronage of George III's family had encouraged the smart set and the inevitable speculators to take an interest in the new town. Sadly there were no lasting major developments of any great merit, although the usual 18th-century terraces preserve something of the old gentility. Today Worthing is a popular seaside resort with a pier and an extensive pebble beach.

Leave Worthing by the A259 'Brighton' road, with occasional views of the sea to the right. Pass through South Lancing and by Shoreham Airport. Cross the River Adur and enter Shoreham-by-Sea.

Continue along the A259 to Portslade-by-Sea.

PORTSLADE-BY-SEA, E Sussex

The 'by Sea' part of Portslade is a fairly recent seaside development of the original village, which lies 1 mile inland and has a church with Norman origins. North of the churchyard are remains of a 12th-century flint-built manor house.

Continue along the A259 to Hove.

built for the Prince Regent by Henry Holland in 1787. Various museums, galleries, and theatres exist in the town, and visitors are offered all the usual distractions of the British seaside holiday. An excellent aquarium can be visited near Palace Pier, and the Volk's Electric Railway – the first of its kind in the world – runs from here to the Black Rock area. Old Brighton is preserved in the winding streets of The Lanes, which contrast with the new conference centre and up-to-the-minute marina development.

Return along the seafront towards Hove, passing the King Alfred Sports Centre, and meet traffic lights. Turn right here into Hove Street and follow SP 'London'. After 1 mile cross over main A27 and in another ¾ mile at West Blatchington turn right on the A2030.

WEST BLATCHINGTON, E Sussex

An early 18th-century windmill and 19th-century St Peter's Church are all that remain of the village that originally stood in this highly-developed area.

Warehouses and sea-going vessels of all descriptions are an integral part of Portslade-by-Sea's character.

Brighton's elegant pier dates from the 19th century.

SHOREHAM-BY-SEA, W Sussex

Sand at low tide, good fishing in the River Adur, and a busy harbour are features of this popular seaside town. Saxon workmanship can be seen in the mainly Norman structure of St Nicholas' Church. An old chequered-flint house in the town contains the Marlipins Museum of local relics.

Continue on the A259 to Southwick.

SOUTHWICK, W Sussex

Situated on the eastern part of Shoreham Harbour, with the South Downs to the north, Southwick forms part of the Shoreham conurbation and has all but lost its own identity. Roman artefacts excavated from a villa ¼ mile north of the station can be seen in the museum at Hove.

HOVE, E Sussex

Elegant Hove is so much a part of Brighton these days. It has a good beach, several excellent Regency terraces, a museum and art gallery and the British Engineerium with a Victorian water pumping station.

Continue into Brighton.

BRIGHTON, E Sussex

This famous resort developed as a result of the 18th-century health fad for sea bathing. Its success was assured by the patronage of George IV in 1784, and the many superb terraces preserved there today prove its continued prosperity. As with all playgrounds of the wealthy the town has a number of eccentricities. The most impressive of these is the Royal Pavilion, a magnificent Oriental-style palace

Brighton Pavilion has been remodelled several times since it was first built. Architect John Nash was largely responsible for its final appearance.

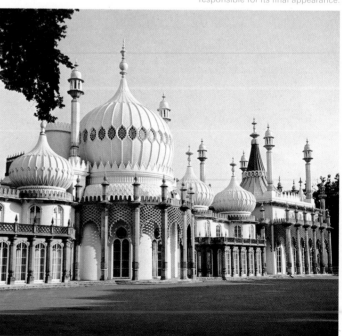

Continue to ascend the A2038. Meet crossroads and turn left on to an unclassified road SP 'Devil's Dyke'. After ½ mile keep left and ascend through open downland to Devil's Dyke.

DEVIL'S DYKE, W Sussex
Devil's Dyke is a cleft in the 711ft crest of the South Downs (see below). According to local legend the devil tried to carve a large nick to let the sea in, but failed. The spot has become popular with hang-glider enthusiasts.

THE SOUTH DOWNS
Stretching west from Beachy Head into Hampshire, the South Downs range is all that remains of a huge chalk backbone that connected England with the Continent. Some 7,000 years ago the Atlantic forced its way through to join up with the North Sea. Access for rambling and riding is available via numerous footpaths and bridleways.

Return, and after ½ mile turn left SP 'Poynings' to pass the Dyke Golf Club. After ¾ mile turn left, with views of 664ft Newtimber Hill on the right. After a further ½ mile turn sharp left and descend into Poynings.

Mosiac pavements are a feature of the Roman remains at Bignor.

POYNINGS, W Sussex
Poynings is a charming downland village with an old church that was endowed by Michael de Poynings, who died in 1369. The Rectory is of early 19th-century date.

Turn left and follow the foot of the South Downs to Fulking.

FULKING, W Sussex
Flocks of sheep graze the sides of the downland fold in which this ancient hamlet stands, and slake their thirsts at a chalk spring. A like service is offered to humankind by the pleasant Shepherd and Dog Inn.

Continue to Edburton.

EDBURTON, W Sussex
A spectacularly sheer downland escarpment towers above this tiny place, making it seem even smaller than it is. The village boasts a privately-owned craft pottery and a salmon-smoking concern. Prehistoric Castle Rings stands on Edburton Hill.

Leave Edburton with 708ft Truleigh Hill to the left and continue to the A2037. Turn left on to the A2037 for Upper Beeding.

UPPER BEEDING, W Sussex
Upper Beeding lies at the north end of a gap in the downs made by the River Adur. It has a narrow main street lined with old cottages.

Leaving Upper Beeding, turn right on to the unclassified road SP 'Steyning', and cross the River Adur into Bramber.

BRAMBER, W Sussex
Before the River Adur silted up this place was a large port. Its massive Norman castle was dismantled after the Civil War, leaving only a gateway and easily-traceable sections of wall (NT). An unusual museum is the House of Pipes, which features some 35,000 tobacco pipes from all over the world.

Continue to Steyning.

STEYNING, W Sussex
Steyning enjoys a magnificent position at the foot of the South Downs and has a late-Norman church. In Mouse Lane is a 15th-century poorhouse, and an old market house stands in the High Street. The Grammar School of 1614 can be seen in Church Street.

Leave Steyning to join the A283. On the left is Steyning Round Hill, which gives views over the Adur Valley. Continue skirting Wiston Park and Wiston.

WISTON, W Sussex
It is well worth stopping in this lovely village at the foot of downland near Chanctonbury. Unfortunately its 14th-century church was badly treated by the 19th-century restorers, but the overall atmosphere of peaceful antiquity.

Continue on the A283. In 1 mile pass an unclassified left turn leading along a wooded glade to the footpath for Chanctonbury Ring.

CHANCTONBURY RING, W Sussex
The extensive prehistoric earthworks of Chanctonbury Ring occupy a 783ft downland summit which affords views over some 30 miles of countryside.

Continue along the A283 to the edge of Washington, enter a roundabout, and leave by the 2nd exit for Storrington. Left of the road are 626ft Chantry Hill and 549ft Harrow Hill.

STORRINGTON, W Sussex
Kithurst Hill rises to 697ft above this straggling village and forms an excellent viewpoint. Celtic field patterns are preserved on its slopes, is the 28-acre Sullington Warren (NT). A large tithe barn of 1685 stands at Manor Farm.

In 1 mile pass an unclassified left turn leading to Parham House.

The nave of Steyning's parish church is a superb example of Norman architecture.

PARHAM HOUSE, W Sussex
This delightfully unpretentious Elizabethan house has a 158ft long gallery and contains fine furnishings and pictures (open).

Continue on the A283 for 1 mile farther then turn left on to an unclassified road SP 'Greatham'. In 2¼ miles cross the River Arun to Coldwaltham. Turn left on to the A29 into Watersfield, then in ½ mile turn right on to the B2138 'Petworth' road. Take the next turning left on to an unclassified road for West Burton, then turn right for Bignor.

BIGNOR, W Sussex
Several notable old houses here include the famous Old Shop, an unusual yeoman's house of the 15th century. The Roman villa sites here are one of the largest and best known in the country.

Return to West Burton then, turn left SP 'Bury' and in 1 mile turn right on to the A29 SP 'Bognor'. Ascend Bury Hill, meet a roundabout and take 1st exit into Amberley.

AMBERLEY, W Sussex
The old lime quarries now have a new lease of life as the Chalk Pits Museum, with many attractions on its industrial past.

Return to roundabout take 1st exit A284 SP 'Littlehampton'. Skirt the grounds of Arundel Park and in 2¼ miles turn left on to an unclassified road to enter Arundel.

ARUNDEL, W Sussex
Looming large over Arundel to guard a gap made in the downs by the River Arun valley is ancient and much-restored Arundel Castle, seat of the Duke of Norfolk. Behind its heavy grey walls are rooms rich in furnishings and art treasures, many of which are open to the public. A prominent town existed here before the Norman conquest, but comparatively few ancient houses remain. The only real rivals to the castle are the 14th-century Church of St Nicholas and the superb Church of Our Lady and St Philip Neri.

Continue on the A27 'Worthing' road, and in 5 miles pass an unclassified right turn to Highdown Hill.

HIGHDOWN HILL, W Sussex
Between the South Downs and the sea, about 1 mile south of the A27, is 266ft Highdown Hill (NT). This 50-acre site is of great archaeological importance for its late bronze-age, early iron-age and Saxon cemeterys, nearby is Highdown Hill Gardens.

Continue on the A27 towards Worthing. Meet a roundabout and take the 2nd exit. After ¾ mile meet another roundabout and take the 3rd exit for the return to Worthing.

Arundel Castle, one of the most impressive Norman and medieval strongholds in the south of England, is the home of the dukes of Norfolk, hereditary Earls Marshal of England.

EASTBOURNE, E Sussex
Consistently top of the seaside sunshine league tables, the thriving resort of Eastbourne has been popular since the beginning of the 19th century.

Leave Eastbourne seafront along the B2103 'Beachy Head' road, with fine views towards the cliffs of Beachy Head. Ascend, and turn left on to an unclassified road to reach the summit of this cliff range.

BEACHY HEAD, E Sussex
Beachy Head, the vast chalk promontory that marks where the South Downs are halted by the sea, is the starting point of the South Downs Way. This path runs west to beyond South Harting on the Hampshire border.

Continue past the Belle Tout lighthouse to Birling Gap.

BIRLING GAP, E Sussex
For centuries Birling Gap was a landing place favoured by smugglers but today the rocky shingle and sand beach is more popular with bathers. Between Birling Gap and Seaford are the great chalk cliffs known as the Seven Sisters.

Follow the tour inland to Eastdean.

EASTDEAN, E Sussex
Cottages and a small shop overlook Eastdean's sloping triangular green, and the local church houses a curious copy of a Norman font.

Turn left on to the A259 'Seaford' road, ascend steeply, then at the summit turn right on to the unclassified 'Jevington' road for Friston.

FRISTON, E Sussex
This downland village lies in a hilly area now popular with glider pilots. At one time its small Church of St Mary served as a landmark for mariners and smugglers alike.

Continue, with downland to the right and Friston Forest to the left. Also to the right is 659ft Willingdon Hill. Reach Jevington.

JEVINGTON, E Sussex
A sturdy Anglo-Saxon tower is carried by Jevington's flint-built church, and in the churchyard is the copper model of a square-rigged schooner once sailed by a Chinaman buried here.

Beyond Jevington descend through Wannock, with 702ft Windover Hill to the left.

WINDOVER HILL, E Sussex
A gentle climb to the summit of this hill is rewarded by excellent views, not the least of which takes in the prehistoric Long Man of Wilmington. Nobody knows who or what this giant turf-cut figure represents.

Continue to Polegate.

POLEGATE, E Sussex
Victorian St John's Church, like much of the rest of Polegate's architecture, is unremarkable but homely. The most notable building here is an early 19th-century windmill with all its sails intact.

At Polegate turn left on to the A22, SP 'London'. Pass through the flat countryside of Wilmington Wood. In 2¼ miles a detour from the main route is possible by turning right on to the A295 and driving to Hailsham.

HAILSHAM, E Sussex
The market at Hailsham is one of the largest in Sussex and continues a tradition that reaches back to Norman times.

In ¼ mile (beyond the Hailsham turning) turn left on to an unclassified road to Michelham Priory. Cross the River Cuckmere before reaching the priory.

MICHELHAM PRIORY, E Sussex
Remains of this small Augustinian priory (open), founded in 1229 for 12 canons and a prior, include a Tudor mansion, a 14th-century gatehouse, and an attractive bridge over the moat.

Continue and shortly turn right, and then turn immediately left, SP 'London'. Turn left on to the A22, then shortly right on to the unclassified 'Horam' road. Join the A267 and enter Horam. Continue on the 'Tunbridge Wells' road and pass through woodland scenery before reaching Cross-in-Hand, on The Weald.

Towering chalk cliffs dwarf the lighthouse at Beachy Head.

TOUR 28   80 MILES

THE SUSSEX WEALD
Suspended between the North and South Downs is the high, broken patchwork of the Sussex Weald, a place of charming towns and villages on hillsides once cloaked by the vast, prehistoric Forest of Anderida.

THE WEALD
The Weald is a high area of broken country suspended between the hills of the North and South Downs. Its towns and villages are rightly famous for their great character and beauty, and several wooded areas exist as reminders of the great Forest of Anderida that once cloaked these long, grassy slopes.

CROSS-IN-HAND, E Sussex
A working windmill stands in this charming village, which is sited at over 500ft on the Sussex Weald. Holy Cross Priory is partly in use as an old people's home, the house and grounds could be visited.

Cross high wooded country to Five Ashes. After ¼ mile (beyond Five Ashes), turn left on to an unclassified road. Later join the B2101 and enter Rotherfield, at the edge of Ashdown Forest.

ROTHERFIELD, E Sussex
Situated at the edge of Ashdown Forest, this village stands at 500ft near the source of the River Rother.

Keep forward, then branch right on to an unclassified road to leave by North Street. Drive to the A26. Turn right SP 'Tunbridge Wells', and pass through Eridge Green.

ERIDGE GREEN, E Sussex
Pretty estate cottages stand behind the local Victorian church, and near by is the sandstone outcrop of Bowles Rocks where trainee mountaineers practise.

Continue for 1 mile through Broadwater Forest, then turn left on to an unclassified road SP 'Groombridge'. After ¼ mile turn right SP 'High Rocks', then in a further ¼ mile bear right and pass High Rocks on the right.

HIGH ROCKS, E Sussex
Perhaps the largest sandstone outcrop in the area is High Rocks, which is used extensively by climbers.

Continue for 1¼ miles. Meet crossroads and turn right on to Major York's road. On the far side of Tunbridge Wells Common turn left on to the A26 and enter Royal Tunbridge Wells.

ROYAL TUNBRIDGE WELLS, Kent
In 1606 Lord North discovered chalybeate springs in the forest that stood here. Subsequently the town of Tunbridge Wells was founded, though building did not begin in earnest until the 1630s. By the end of that century it was a flourishing spa, and has remained so to the present day. Visitors to the picturesque raised parade known as the Pantiles may still 'take the waters'.

From the town follow SP 'Eastbourne A267' and re-enter E Sussex for Frant.

FRANT, E Sussex
Houses cluster round a large green here, and the 19th-century church contains fine stained glass of earlier date.

Turn left on to an unclassified road SP 'Bells Yew Green' and at the latter turn right on to the B2169 'Lamberhurst' road. Return to Kent. Drive through woodland, then pass a left turn leading to the ruins of Bayham Abbey.

BAYHAM ABBEY, E Sussex
Claimed to be the most impressive group of monastic remains in Sussex, this picturesque ruin (NT) dates from the 13th century and comprises a church, monastery buildings, and the former gatehouse – all easily identifiable (open).

After a further ¼ mile pass a left turn leading to The Owl House.

THE OWL HOUSE, Kent
Once the haunt of wool smugglers, this small half-timbered building (open) dates from the 16th century and stands in beautiful grounds. Features of the latter include woodland lakes and splendid collections of flowering shrubs.

In 1¼ miles turn left on to the B2100 and enter Lamberhurst.

LAMBERHURST, Kent
Although strung out along the busy Tunbridge Wells to Hastings road, this old village has managed to retain its own identity and features a fine 14th-century church.

About 1 mile south, off the A21, is Scotney Old Castle.

The weathered and fissured surfaces of such sandstone outcrops as Bowles Rocks, near Eridge Green, make ideal nursery faces for trainee mountaineers. All round the rocks are expanses of sand that have been worn from their surfaces.

Rudyard Kipling lived at Bateman's from 1902 until his death in 1936. The interior of the house is preserved much as he left it.

High Rocks is one of many sandstone outcrops situated near Tunbridge Wells.

SCOTNEY CASTLE, Kent

Ruins of this 14th-century tower and an attached 17th-century house (NT) stand in a landscaped and moated garden planted with trees and flowering shrubs (open). Apart from the interest of the buildings themselves, the gardens are among the finest in the country.

From Lamberhurst return along the B2100 'Wadhurst' road and re-enter E Sussex. In 3 miles turn left on to the B2099 to visit Wadhurst.

WADHURST, E Sussex

The churchyard of SS Peter and Paul features 30 iron grave slabs, a powerful indication of Wadhurst's one-time importance as an iron-smelting centre.

In 1¼ miles turn right on to an unclassified road SP 'Burwash Common'. Pass through woodland to Stonegate.

STONEGATE, E Sussex

This small village has a modern church and is attractively grouped round a junction of minor roads and lanes.

In Stonegate turn left on to the 'Burwash' road and after another ¾ mile turn right. Drive over a level crossing and cross the River Rother to enter Burwash.

BURWASH, E Sussex

In Burwash churchyard is a cast-iron grave slab that is claimed to be the oldest in the country. Pleasant old buildings in the High Street include timber-framed cottages.

Meet a junction with the A265 and turn right. Reach the war memorial and turn left on to an unclassified road SP 'Woods Corner'. In ½ mile pass a right turn leading to Bateman's.

BATEMAN'S, E Sussex

Built in 1634 for a local ironmaster, this lovely house (NT) is best known as the one-time home of writer Rudyard Kipling. Much of the neighbourhood is featured in his *Puck of Pook's Hill*.

Climb to 646ft, cross the River Dudwell, and drive through Dallington Forest. Reach Woods Corner, and at the Swan Inn turn right then left on to the 'Pont's Green' road. Later follow SP 'Ninfield' and descend. Meet the B2204 and turn right SP 'Hailsham'. Later turn right on to the A271 for Boreham Street.

BOREHAM STREET, E Sussex

This village has an appealing character enhanced by attractive houses and the White Friars Hotel. Inside the latter is a 16th-century chimney breast.

Continue through Boreham Street and in ½ mile turn left on to an unclassified road passing Herstmonceux Castle.

HERSTMONCEUX CASTLE, E Sussex

Herstmonceux Castle, a fortified 15th-century moated manor house, was for a time a ruin, before being carefully restored in the 1930's. From 1948 to the mid eighties it was the home of the Royal Greenwich

Observatory before its move to Cambridge. In the Sussex Farm Heritage Centre are some award-winning shire horses plus historic farm associated machinery.

Go forward to Wartling.

WARTLING, E Sussex

Wartling boasts a church with box pews, an 18th-century pulpit, and a wealth of fascinating Georgian monuments.

At Wartling bear right on to the 'Pevensey' road and cross the flat Pevensey Levels. Meet the A27 and turn right into Pevensey.

PEVENSEY, E Sussex

William the Conqueror disembarked here in 1066, and later built a stout castle within ancient Roman walls that had once been shaded by the

vast Forest of Anderida. The village itself preserves Tudor buildings. The old Mint House contains a small museum.

Continue along the A27 to Westham.

WESTHAM, E Sussex

It is probable that the local church was once part of the ancient Hospital of St Cross, most of which stood outside the west gate of Pevensey Castle. Close by is a pair of 15th-century houses.

Turn left on to the B2191 SP 'Eastbourne'. Drive over a level crossing and later join the A259 to return to Eastbourne.

Herstmonceux Castle was built when brick was newly fashionable in England.

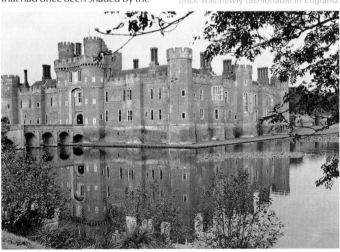

THE WEALD OF WEST KENT

Since medieval times the wealthy have come to West Kent to build their great houses amongst the woods and weathered rocks of the High Weald. Below is a different world of rich valleys full of twisty lanes, fruit orchards, and the smell of growing hops.

SEVENOAKS, Kent
Tradition has it that this town was named from a clump of 7 oaks that once grew here. The original trees have long gone, but in 1955 new ones were taken from Knole Park and planted on the common. It was Knole Park that brought prosperity to Sevenoaks in the 15th century when Archbishop Bourchier acquired it and rebuilt the manor house (NT) as a palace for archbishops of Canterbury. Nowadays the town is largely residential, with an air of confident ease typical of long-established communities. Cricket has been played on The Vyne wicket since 1734.

Leave Sevenoaks with SP 'Westerham' (A25). After 1 mile turn left on to the A25. There are fine views towards the steep wooded escarpment of the North Downs to the right. Continue into the village of Sundridge.

SUNDRIDGE, Kent
Sundridge's pride is the 15th-century timbered hall-house in its main street. The great hall is several storeys high, and its original stone hearth is still to be seen. The house was restored in 1923. Nearby Ovenden House dates from 1745, and 13th-century Sundridge Church contains a number of good brasses.

Keep forward and enter Brasted.

BRASTED, Kent
In spite of traffic the main village street still retains much of its character. At one point it opens on to a small green fringed by half-timbered houses. Brasted Place, in a fine park adjoining the village, was built by Robert Adam in 1784 and subsequently became the home of Napoleon III. About 1½ miles south of the village is 600-acre Brasted Chart (NT), which offers pleasant walks and drives.

Continue along the A25 to Westerham, passing Quebec House on entering the village.

QUEBEC HOUSE, Kent
On the eastern outskirts of Westerham village is early 17th-century Quebec House (NT), famous as the boyhood home of General Wolfe. Relics of this hero of the Battle of Quebec, who died winning the victory that made Canada British, are preserved inside the house. His statue stands in Westerham High Street.

Continue into Westerham village.

WESTERHAM, Kent
General Wolfe was born in the vicarage here in 1727. He stayed at the George and Dragon in 1758, during what was to prove his last visit to the town. Another famous person with Westerham connexions was Sir Winston Churchill, whose statue stands on the tiny green. Westerham Hill is an 800ft- high viewpoint crossed by the Pilgrims' Way.

Continue on the 'Redhill' road. At the end of the village turn left on to the unclassified road for Squerryes Court.

SQUERRYES COURT, Kent
The Warde family have lived in this 17th-century mansion from the time of General Wolfe to the present day, and it was here in 1741 that Wolfe received his commission. A room is set aside for Wolfe mementos, and other parts of the house feature fine paintings and tapestries.

This statue of General Wolfe stands on the green in Westerham.

Left: care was taken to preserve the appearance of Hever Castle during restoration. Below: beautiful Italian statuary is a feature of the grounds at Hever Castle.

Ascend through thickly-wooded country and turn left on to the B269 'Edenbridge' road, with fine views across the Weald. In ¾ mile turn left on to the B2026 'Westerham' road. Climb on to wooded Crockhamhill Common. After the common turn right on to an unclassified road to Chartwell.

CHARTWELL, Kent
Chartwell will always be associated with Winston Churchill. It was his country home from 1922 until his death, and part of it now houses a Churchill museum. Other rooms are arranged much as they must have been in his lifetime. The Churchilliana on display include photographs illustrating every stage of his life, gifts given to him by other world leaders, and his Nobel Prize. A good many of his paintings are to be seen in the house, and in his studio at the end of the garden.

Beyond Chartwell descend to the Eden Valley and turn left on to the B269 'Tonbridge' road. At Four Elms turn right on to the B2042 SP 'Edenbridge', and shortly join the B2027. After 1½ miles turn left on to the B2026 into Edenbridge, and drive along the main street.

EDENBRIDGE, Kent
Several old buildings survive in Edenbridge main street, particularly between the 16th-century Crown Hotel and the bridge over the River Eden. The mainly 13th-century church carries a massive tower crowned by a spire of later date.

Cross the River Eden, take the first turning on the left, and proceed along an unclassified road to Hever Castle.

HEVER CASTLE, Kent
In Tudor times 13th-century Hever Castle was the home of the Boleyns, whose daughter Anne married Henry VIII and bore him the future Queen Elizabeth I. The building began life as a fortified farmhouse, but was made into a crenellated mansion at the beginning of the 15th century. The fortunes of the house waned with the fall of the Boleyns, and by the beginning of this century it had once more reverted to use as a farmhouse. It took a wealthy American, William Waldorf Astor, to restore it to its present magnificence. The superb gardens feature Tudor-style flower beds and a 35-acre lake. Both house and gardens are open to the public.

Leave the castle and continue to Bough Beech. A detour can be made from here to Bough Beech Reservoir: turn left on to the B2027, cross a railway bridge, then turn right on to an unclassified road to the reservoir.

BOUGH BEECH RESERVOIR, Kent
This reservoir is the haunt of migrant waders, ducks, wintering divers, grebe and geese. Access is by written permission only.

Leave Bough Beech and join the B2027 for 200 yards, then turn right on to the unclassified 'Chiddingstone' road. Drive to crossroads and turn left for Chiddingstone. Ahead, at the crossroads, is the entrance to Chiddingstone Castle.

CHIDDINGSTONE, Kent
Chiddingstone, a National Trust village, has a beautifully preserved street lined with half-timbered 16th- and 17th-century houses that were probably built with iron-industry money. At the top of the street is 19th-century Chiddingstone Castle. The Chiding Stone, from which the village takes its name, is a large sandstone rock behind the street. Nagging wives were once brought here to be chided by the assembled village population.

After ½ mile (beyond the village) branch left. In 1¾ miles turn right on to the B2027 for Chiddingstone Causeway. Pass the local church and turn right to follow the B2176. Enter Penshurst.

PENSHURST, Kent
At the centre of Penshurst, behind a screen of tall trees, is 14th-century Penshurst Place. The Sidney family and their descendants have lived here for more than 400 years, and Sir Philip Sidney – diplomat, courtier, and poet – was born here in 1554. The family became Earls of Leicester, and the village contains the original Leicester Square.

Leave Penshurst and follow the B2188 'Tunbridge Wells' road through the Medway Valley to Fordcombe.

FORDCOMBE, Kent
This 19th-century picture village of half-timbered and tile-hung cottages is grouped round a pleasant green. It was built at the instigation of Lord Hardinge, whose seat was near by at South Park.

Beyond Fordcombe turn left on to the A264. Cross Rusthall Common and note a left turn leading to Toad Rock.

TOAD ROCK, Kent
Amongst the many eroded sandstone outcrops in the Tunbridge Wells area is Toad Rock, on Rusthall Common, which has been weathered to look like a toad. Other unusual rock formations are to be found at nearby Happy Valley.

In ¼ mile reach the Spa Hotel and turn right on to Major York's road. Proceed to the far side of the common (carpark for the Pantiles) and turn left on to the A26 into Royal Tunbridge Wells.

ROYAL TUNBRIDGE WELLS, Kent
Extensive parks and gardens impart a quiet charm to this elegant Regency town. The 17th-century Church of St Charles the Martyr is the oldest here and Holy Trinity dates from the 19th century. The latter was built by Decimus Burton, who also laid out lovely Calverley Park. Medicinal waters discovered by Lord North in 1606 – the main reason for the foundation of the town – may still be drunk at the Pantiles, an 18th-century raised promenade fringed with lime trees.

Leave the town with SP 'Hastings' to join the A264. Later turn left on to the A21 'Sevenoaks' road. Pass woodland and branch left on to the A2014. Later turn right and enter Tonbridge.

TONBRIDGE, Kent
A settlement has existed here at least since Anglo-Saxon times. The River Medway played an important part in the town's early prosperity, and the later introduction of the railway increased its importance as a centre of communication. Today Tonbridge is a mixture of market town and rail depot built round a ruined Norman to 14th-century castle on a mound.

Cross the River Medway and follow SP 'Gravesend, A227'. Ascend to Shipbourne.

Kent is renowned for oast houses like this one near Bough Beech.

The variety of architectural styles in the houses at Chiddingstone creates a beautiful village landscape.

SHIPBOURNE, Kent
Most of the Victorian village that makes up Shipbourne lies to the west of the green. St Giles' Church was reconstructed in the 1880s.

Beyond the village pass Fairlawne House.

FAIRLAWNE HOUSE, Kent
Situated just ¾ mile north of Shipbourne, this splendid house (unfortunately not open to the public) dates from the 18th century and features a Great Room designed by the architect Gibbs.

Pass Fairlawne House and ascend. At the top of the hill turn left on to an unclassified road SP 'Ivy Hatch'. Take the next turning left and descend a narrow lane to Ightham Mote.

IGHTHAM MOTE, Kent
Medieval Ightham Mote, a small manor house set in lovely meadowland, is considered to be the most complete of its kind in Britain (open at certain times). Its low bulk is encircled by a moat, and its fine wooded grounds feature a tree-fringed lake. Peacocks are kept in the gardens.

Return to Ivy Hatch and keep left on the 'Seal' road. After a short way turn left again and drive to the village of Stone Street. Bear left on the 'Fawke Common, Riverhill' road and continue through heaths and woodland. Later cross Fawke Common, meet a main road and turn right on to the A225. Descend, and reach the entrance to Knole Park on the right.

KNOLE PARK, Kent
In 1456 Thomas Bourchier, then Archbishop of Canterbury, bought an ordinary manor house called Knole Park. He and his successors developed this humble beginning into a great palace, but when Archbishop Warham died in 1532 Henry VIII seized the estate for himself. Elizabeth I granted it to Sir Thomas Sackville in 1566, who died while improvement work on the interior of the house was still in progress. Knole Park (NT) (open) looks much as it must have done then.

Return to Sevenoaks.

ASHFORD, Kent

For hundreds of years Ashford has been a market town for Romney Marsh and the Weald of Kent. Its prime situation at the meeting of the two rivers Stour (East and Great) has made it a natural focus in the past, and its proximity to London has meant new growth as a population 'overspill' town. Today it is an important shopping and touring centre a mere 14 miles from the ancient city of Canterbury and within easy reach of the south Kent beaches. The town's industrial development began in the 19th century with the establishment of large railway works, which have closed. Future development with the channel tunnel project could increase Ashford's importance as a railway interchange. Medieval, Tudor and Georgian houses have survived despite development, and the 15th-century parish church retains much of its original character. The Intelligence Corps Museum at Templar Barracks displays a fascinating array of mementos.

Leave Ashford on the A28 'Tenterden road, after 1 mile at roundabout take 3rd exit on to an unclassified road to reach Great Chart.

GREAT CHART, Kent

A 14th-century church with a 16th-century pest house in the south corner of its churchyard can be seen here. This long, narrow structure is a timber framed building once used to isolate victims of plagues. Court Lodge, a complete 13th-century stone house, stands near the church.

Continue through the village to rejoin the A28 to Bethersden.

BETHERSDEN, Kent

Marble from this village was used for the altar stairs at Canterbury Cathedral, but many humbler buildings also display its splendour. The quarries are now worked out. Brass memorials to forbears of the 17th-century poet William Lovelace can be seen in the local 14th-century church.

Continue through High Halden to Tenterden.

TENTERDEN, Kent

Typical Wealden houses, *ie* buildings faced with tiles and weather boards, line the broad, grass-verged High Street of this delightful town. Its high situation makes its 15th-century church tower (made of the famous Bethersden marble) visible across the Weald and from many miles out to sea. At one time the tower was used as a beacon to guide shipping. In the 15th century Henry VI admitted Tenterden to the Confederation of Cinque Ports, but the course of the River Rother later changed and the town port was replaced by nearby Smallhythe. Shipbuilding became a major local concern in the 16th century. The museum has various exhibits on the history of local trades

AMONG THE COASTAL MARSHES

Towards the sea the Wealden hills flatten to Romney Marsh, a place of frogs and sheep where church towers can be seen for miles and the threat of flood is constant. At the sea's edge England's Napoleonic defences crumble peacefully, while massive walls repulse the ocean's eternal barrage.

Attractive gardens stretch along the banks of the River Rother at Rye.

and industries. Tenterden is the terminus for the preserved Kent and East railway.

Continue on the A28, drive over a level crossing, and pass the Rolvenden station of the Kent and East Sussex Railway on the left. Drive into Rolvenden.

ROLVENDEN, Kent

Surrounded by well-wooded country, this pleasant combination of weather-boarded (Kentish clad) houses and grass verges is typical of the county. The large 14th-century church preserves two squire's pews, and the restored postmill is a perfect example. Great Maytham Hall, now converted into flats, was designed by Sir Edwin Lutyens in 1910 and stands in gardens that were laid out by landscaper Gertrude Jekyll.

Drive to the church and turn left on to the unclassified 'Wittersham' road. Pass through Rolvenden Layne and cross the Rother Levels. Climb on to the Isle of Oxney, an isolated area of high ground. A detour can be made from the main tour route by turning left on to the B2082 to reach Smallhythe Place. Otherwise turn right on to the B2082 and drive to Wittersham.

SMALLHYTHE PLACE, Kent

Half-timbered Smallhythe Place dates from 1480 and was once the home of actress Dame Ellen Terry. It is now a museum displaying her personal relics (NT). The adjacent 15th-century Priest's House shares its grounds with the Barn Theatre.

WITTERSHAM, Kent

Wittersham is a quiet, charming village on the central ridge of the Isle of Oxney, between the River Rother and the Royal Military Canal. During the middle ages the tower of its 14th-century church was used as a shipping beacon. Inside the church is a finely carved lectern of late medieval origin. Wealden buildings comprising a windmill, oast houses, and a timbered cottage make an attractive group 1 mile east.

Proceed on the B2082 to cross the River Rother and continue over the Rother Levels. Pass through Iden, meet the A268, and pass through Playden to reach Rye (near the Royal Military Canal).

ROYAL MILITARY CANAL

Originally a defence against an expected Napoleonic invasion, this canal between Rye and Hythe now offers peaceful towpath walks and boat-hire facilities.

RYE, E Sussex

On a small hill rising out of fenland by the River Rother, this collection of attractive old buildings and cobbled streets was one of two Ancient Towns attached to the Cinque Ports. As such it was heavily fortified against the medieval French. This maritime importance seems odd today, but at that time Rye was almost encircled by sea. Its influence declined when the harbour silted up in the 16th century, and today the sea has receded. Many historic buildings have survived here, the oldest being probably the Norman and later church, which features a 16th-century clock with an 18ft free-swinging pendulum. Near by is the 13th-century Ypres Tower, which was built as a castle and used as a prison from the 16th to 19th centuries. Nowadays it holds nothing more sinister than a museum of local history. Weather-boarded and tile-hung houses, generally with timber frames, can be seen in Mermaid Street, Church Square, Watchbell Street, and High Street. The Mermaid Inn opened in 1420 and is possibly the oldest in the country. From the same century are The Flushing Inn, Stone House, Old Hospital, and Fletcher's House. Peacock's School was built in 1636, and 18th-century Lamb House (NT) was the home of novelist Henry James. Parts of the town walls remain, but 14th-century Landgate (AM) is the only original entry. The town stands on a small hill.

A detour can be made from the main tour route to Camber Castle by taking the A259 'Hastings' road.

CAMBER CASTLE, E Sussex

This ruined 16th-century coastal defence fort was one of several built in Kent by Henry VIII as a deterrent to the French navy.

The weather-boarded buildings in Tenterden's superb High Street are typical of the Kentish Weald.

DUNGENESS, Kent
This desolate shingle promontory is the site of a nuclear power station that can be seen for miles over featureless Denge Marsh. A slender lighthouse was built here in 1961 because the old one would be obscured by the power station. The original still stands, slightly inland from its successor. Much of the promontory is taken by a 12,000-acre nature reserve frequented by seabirds and shoreline wildlife.

Rolvenden's painstakingly restored windmill.

Innumerable drainage ditches prevent Romney Marsh reverting to its natural state.

From Rye follow SP 'Folkestone A259' to reach Brookland, crossing the flat expanse of Walland Marsh on the way. Water is drained from the land by channels that crisscross the area on both sides of the route.

BROOKLAND, Kent
The 13th- to 15th-century church at Brookland displays an unusual wood and shingle belfry, and houses a Norman font thought to be unique in Britain. The latter is decorated with signs of the Zodiac and little vignettes depicting various seasonal activities.

Continue on the A259 for 1½ miles, meet crossroads, and turn right. In 4 miles turn right again on to the B2075 'Lydd' road to reach Lydd.

LYDD, Kent
Like Rye, Lydd was once a coastal town, but it now lies a good 3 miles inland. Its 14th-century church has a 130ft tower and has been described as the 'Cathedral of Romney Marsh'. A 140-acre water sports centre is on the outskirts of the town.

Proceed to the edge of Lydd, cross a railway bridge, then branch left on to the unclassified 'Dungeness' road. Shortly turn left again. To the right of the road are Denge Marsh and Denge Beach. After 3 miles (beyond Lydd) turn right to reach Dungeness.

ROMNEY, HYTHE, AND DYMCHURCH RAILWAY, Kent
Dungeness is the southern terminus of a 13½-mile narrow-gauge line which is claimed to be the world's smallest public railway. Steam trains run from Hythe, through New Romney, and along the seaward fringe of Romney Marsh to Dungeness.

Return along the unclassified road for 1 mile, then turn right and follow SP to reach Greatstone and Littlestone-on-Sea. At Littlestone-on-Sea turn left on to the B2071 to reach New Romney.

NEW ROMNEY, Kent
One of the ancient Cinque Ports but now 1 mile inland from the sea, New Romney's harbour was destroyed in 1287 by a violent storm which changed the course of the River Rother. Thanks to William Morris the town's Norman and later church was rescued from insensitive restoration in 1878.

Continue through New Romney and turn right on to the A259 'Folkestone' road to cross Romney Marsh.

ROMNEY MARSH, Kent
Most of this 204-square-mile tract has been reclaimed from the sea by drainage work started in Roman times. Flooding is an ever-present threat, as much of the area is still below sea level at high tide, but the land is too fertile to waste and the Marsh is famous for its wool. Tulip-growing is a newly developed local industry.

Continue through St Mary's Bay to reach Dymchurch.

DYMCHURCH, Kent
Situated on the edge of Romney Marsh, this old port is guarded by an ancient sea wall and was once a centre for smugglers. It is now a resort with vast stretches of sand and a variety of historic buildings. One of several Martello towers (AM) along the coast, built as defences against Napoleon, has been restored and houses a small exhibition site.

Continue beside the sea wall to Hythe.

Amongst the steam locomotives which operate on the Romney, Hythe, and Dymchurch Railway are two miniature versions of Canadian Pacific engines.

HYTHE, Kent
This Cinque Port is now a well-known resort. Just north is Saltwood Castle, a well-preserved medieval garrison fort complete with battlement walk, undercroft, armoury, and torture chamber See also tour 31.

Leave Hythe by the A261 'Ashford' road and in 1 mile turn left on to the B2067 'Lympne' road. Proceed to Lympne.

LYMPNE, Kent
Views over Romney Marsh and the Channel extend from Lympne Castle, which was built and variously extended from Norman times to the 15th century. The Port Lympne Zoo Park, Mansion and Gardens affords an interesting visit.

Leave Lympne on the 'Tenterden' road B2067 and in 2½ miles bear right on to the unclassified 'Aldington' road. Continue to Aldington and turn right in the village on to the B2069 'Ashford' road passing pleasant woodland and cross a railway. After ¾ mile (from the railway) turn left on to the A20. Follow SP 'Ashford' to finish the tour.

FROM THE SEA TO THE NORTH DOWNS

At Dover soaring cliffs of dazzling white chalk mark the end of the North Downs' rolling march to the sea. Inland the massive towers of Canterbury Cathedral commemorate the halt of paganism, and the rebirth of Christianity in Kent.

FOLKESTONE, Kent

A popular holiday resort and a harbour for cross-Channel ferries, this ancient port still has a fishing fleet and fish market. A wide grassy promenade known as The Leas extends along the cliff top, and attractively wooded walks slope down to the beach. Spade House, the one-time home of writer H G Wells, now contains a museum.

Follow SP 'Hythe, A259' to Sandgate.

SANDGATE, Kent

The castle here belongs to a series built by Henry VIII after his religious break with Rome, when the threat of invasion seemed very real. Shorncliffe Camp, established on the plateau above Sandgate at the beginning of the 19th century, was founded to cope with the later threat of Napoleon's navy.

Continue to Hythe.

HYTHE, Kent

This ancient Cinque Port was very prosperous in the 12th and 13th centuries; its wealth today is assured by its popularity as a resort. Near by is the Royal Military Canal, which was built in 1804 as a defence against Napoleon but nowadays serves as a valuable leisure amenity. A terminus of the Romney, Hythe, and Dymchurch narrow-gauge railway is in the town.

Follow SP 'Ashford' and 'London' to Hythe Station, past the Royal Military Canal. Return along the 'Folkestone' road, before taking the B2065 'Elham' road and climbing to high ground. Fine views of the North Downs can be enjoyed from here. Continue, and cross the M20 and at roundabout take 2nd exit B2065 to Lyminge.

LYMINGE, Kent

There has been a Christian community at Lyminge since 633, when King Ethelbert's daughter and Bishop Paulinus founded their abbey here. Fragments of walling from the original buildings are incorporated in the Church of SS Mary and Ethelburga. Most of Lyminge is Victorian; the half-timbered Old Robus and 18th-century Old Rectory are notable exceptions.

Drive to the far end of the village take 2nd left on to an unclassified road SP 'Rhodes Minnis' passing through Sibton Park. In ¼ mile (beyond Rhodes Minnis) branch left and climb through Lyminge Forest on to the North Downs. Cross the B2068 and turn right for Elmsted.

ELMSTED, Kent

Flint-built St James's Church in Elmsted is of Norman and later date and carries a medieval west tower. Inside is a late medieval half-timbered altar screen.

At Elmsted Church turn left, SP 'Wye', and continue to Hastingleigh.

HASTINGLEIGH, Kent

Norman and later St Mary's Church stands aloof from the village, half hidden from view by the fall of the downs.

Continue on the 'Wye' road to Wye Downs nature reserve.

WYE DOWNS AND NATURE RESERVE, Kent

Wye and Crundale Downs rise some 2 miles south-east of Wye and form part of the North Downs. The escarpment, covered with shrubs and woodland, is a nature reserve.

Continue to Wye.

THE NORTH DOWNS

This chalk range runs west from the White Cliffs of Dover to the Hog's Back near Guildford, and culminates in a 900ft hill at Woldingham.

WYE, Kent

Archbishop of Canterbury John Kempe founded a college of priests here in 1447, but King Henry VIII put paid to its religious teaching and it later served as a grammar school. Since 1900 it has been the agriculture school of London University. Other features of the town include a racecourse, a Georgian mill house, and 18th-century Olantigh—a venue for summer music festivals.

Follow SP 'Ashford' and cross the Great Stour River. Drive over a level crossing and turn right on to the 'Canterbury' road. After ¾ mile turn right on to the A28 and drive along the Great Stour Valley to Godmersham.

Exquisite stained glass in Canterbury Cathedral depicts Thomas à Becket and the miraculous cures associated with his name.

GODMERSHAM, Kent

A monument to Edward Knight, a close relative of novelist Jane Austen and owner of 18th-century Godmersham Park, can be seen in the local Norman and later church. Landscaped grounds surround the big house.

Continue to the outskirts of Chilham.

CHILHAM, Kent

Chilham village is gathered respectfully around a square at the gate of its castle, which was built for Henry II in 1174. The 300-acre grounds (open) feature wood and lakeside walks, gardens, plus medieval jousting displays.

Continue to the edge of Chartham.

CHARTHAM, Kent

This large Stour valley village is a well-known angling centre. St Mary's Church is of 13th-century date and boasts one of the oldest sets of bells in the country. East of the village is a ruined medieval chapel on a farm.

Continue to Canterbury.

Fishermen take aboard a net on the beach at Hythe.

CANTERBURY, Kent

When the Romans came here they took over a Belgic Stourside community and developed it into the town of *Durovernum Cantiorum*, later to become a Christian community. When the Romans left the area was swept by waves of invaders who had little time for Christianity, but in the year 597 St Augustine's mission arrived to convert King Ethelbert of Kent and restore the town's dilapidated churches. Shortly afterwards Canterbury became the Metropolitan City of the Church of England. Long stretches of the city wall survive on Roman foundations, and the present cathedral dates from 1070. This fine structure is best known as the place where Archbishop Thomas à Becket was murdered for his denial of the king's authority over the church. Canterbury Castle has the 3rd largest Norman keep in Britain. King's School is thought to be the oldest extant.

Follow SP 'Dover' then 'Sandwich' to leave Canterbury on the A257. Continue to Littlebourne.

LITTLEBOURNE, Kent

Close to the local flint church is an ancient thatched barn. Neat single-

A number of Chilham's ancient houses were partly refaced in brick during the 18th century.

This portrait of the 1st Earl of Sandwich hangs in the Guildhall at Sandwich.

storey cottages dating from the 17th century stand at the end of the village green.

Continue to Wingham.

WINGHAM, Kent
Interesting buildings in this town include Debridge House and Wingham Court, both of which date from the 18th century. Many of the local buildings are picturesquely half timbered, and the Red Lion dates from the 15th century.

Turn right on to the B2046 'Folkestone' road, and in 1 mile turn left on to an unclassified road SP 'Chillenden'.

CHILLENDEN, Kent
The local church retains a good many Norman features. Chillenden Windmill, built in 1868 and restored in 1958, stands ½ mile north of the village.

Meet crossroads, turn left, and leave Chillenden by the 'Woodnesborough' road.

WOODNESBOROUGH, Kent
The church here suffered heavy restoration in the 19th century, but it retains a charming 18th-century cupola on the west tower. South-east of the church is a 17th-century brick cottage.

Continue to Sandwich.

SANDWICH, Kent
This, the oldest of the Cinque Ports, is now separated from the sea by 2 miles of sand-dunes. Among its many outstanding old buildings are the medieval Barbican, Fishgate, and a variety of houses and inns. St Bartholomew's Hospital guest house dates from the 15th century, and both the Guildhall and Manwood Court were built in the 16th. The Old House is a fine example of Tudor design. Much of the old beach between the town and Sandwich Bay is occupied by Sandwich Golf Course, which is famous the world over.

Leave Sandwich by the A258 'Dover' road and later turn left on to the A258 'Deal' road. Enter Deal.

Below: Dover's wonderfully preserved Roman lighthouse is thought to date from the 1st century. Right: the unmistakable White Cliffs of Dover would have been a familiar landmark to Roman sailors.

DEAL, Kent
Henry VIII built a castle (AM) in the shape of a six-petalled flower at Deal, though considerable protection was already offered by the notorious Goodwin Sands. These vast, shifting beds lie just 5 miles offshore and have caused hundreds of wrecks. In its early history the town was a limb of the Cinque Ports, but most of its development dates from the end of the 17th century. Local exhibits can be seen in the town museum, and collections from all over the world are shown in the Maritime Museum.

Proceed along the seafront on the 'Dover' road and branch left on to the B2057, SP 'Kingsdown'. Pass 16th-century Walmer Castle.

WALMER, Kent
The Henrian Castle (AM) here stands in attractive gardens and is the official residence of the Lord Warden of the Cinque Ports. The Duke of Wellington died here in 1852 and a number of his possessions are on display inside. Walmer Lifeboat is famous for the many rescues it has made from the Goodwin Sands.

Continue to the small resort of Kingsdown and turn inland SP 'Dover'. Drive to Ringwould, overlooking The Leas (NT).

RINGWOULD, Kent
Several bronze-age barrows can be seen near Ringwould on Free Down. The 12th- to 14th-century church has an attractive 17th-century tower.

Join the A258 'Dover' road for a short distance and turn left on to the B2058 for St Margaret's at Cliffe.

ST MARGARET'S AT CLIFFE, Kent
A variety of old buildings line the twisty main street. A haven of rural peace can be found in The Pines Garden (NT).

A short detour can be taken from the main route to St Margaret's Bay by keeping forward for 1 mile.

ST MARGARET'S BAY, Kent
This sheltered little bay, completely enclosed by towering chalk cliffs, is a popular starting point for cross-Channel swimmers. A narrow beach peters out to weed-bearded boulders and large pools in the chalk bedrock on each side.

Return to St Margaret's at Cliffe, turn left into unclassified Reach Road, and continue to a fine viewpoint overlooking Dover Harbour. Pass a footpath to the Blériot Memorial and turn left on to the A258. Enter Dover.

DOVER, Kent
Formerly the Roman walled city of *Dubris*, Dover was chief of the Cinque Ports and has a magnificent castle (AM) built on a site occupied since prehistoric times. Its strategic position gives it total command of the harbour, and successive English kings spent vast sums on its development. It was last used for military purposes during World War II. The Pharos, a surprisingly well-preserved Roman lighthouse, stands within the castle walls near the exceptionally fine Saxon Church of St Mary de Castro. Dover Town Hall incorporates the 13th-century Hall of Maison Dieu, and nearby Maison Dieu House dates from 1663. The oldest and best-preserved wall paintings north of the Alps can be seen in the Roman Painted House. A granite memorial in North Fall meadow marks the landing of Louis Blériot in 1909, after his historic cross-Channel flight.

Follow SP 'Canterbury' to leave Dover by London Road (A256). Pass a railway bridge and 1 mile farther on turn left on to the B2060 'Alkham' road, then passing Alkham, climbing through a North Downs valley to Hawkinge.

HAWKINGE, Kent
The Kent Battle of Britain Museum contains the largest and most comprehensive collection of remains of British and German aircraft from the Battle of Britain.

Return to Folkestone on the A260.

EPPING AND THE VILLAGES OF ESSEX

Most of the great forest that covered West Essex in Norman times has been cut down, though Epping and Hatfield remain. The magic of Essex today is its village life, which has a timeless quality that echoes the tranquillity of forest communities in ancient days.

WOODFORD GREEN, Gt London

Sir Winston Churchill was MP for Wanstead and Woodford from 1924 to 1964. His statue on Woodford Green is by David McFall.

From Woodford Green follow the A104 'Epping' road and in ¾ mile turn left on to the A110 SP 'North Chingford'. In another ¾ mile turn right on to an unclassified road into Forest Side. Continue to a T-junction and turn right into Ranger's Road (A1069) to pass the Royal Forest Hotel and Queen Elizabeth's Hunting Lodge.

QUEEN ELIZABETH'S HUNTING LODGE, Gt London

Queen Elizabeth's Hunting Lodge is a wood-and-plaster building thought to have been erected towards the end of the 15th century so that the sovereign of the day could enjoy a grandstand view of the chase. After having served as a keeper's lodge for a number of years it now houses the Epping Forest Museum.

EPPING FOREST, Essex

Epping Forest owes its creation to the Norman Conquest. It was maintained as a royal hunting area through the reigns of various monarchs, and in the reign of King Charles I its bounds were fixed to embrace some 60,000 acres. In 1882 what was left of it was formally opened as a publicly-owned area by Queen Victoria.

Enter Epping Forest and in 1 mile meet a T-junction. Turn left on to the A104 and in 1¼ miles meet a roundabout. Leave by the 1st exit on to an unclassified road SP 'High Beach', then bear right SP 'King's Oak' for High Beach.

HIGH BEACH, Essex

It is arguable whether this village is named 'Beech' after the area's principal tree or 'Beach' denoting a gravel bank. Either would seem to be appropriate. The poet Tennyson spent his early manhood here.

Beyond the King's Oak (PH) the Epping Forest Conservation Centre lies to the right. Continue to the next road junction and turn left, then descend and in ¾ mile cross the main road. Continue for 1 mile and turn right SP 'Epping' to pass through Upshire. Ascend to re-enter the forest, then meet a T-junction and turn left to join the B1393. Continue to Epping.

EPPING, Essex

Epping lies outside the forest and has managed to retain its own identity as a small market town of some charm, despite the proximity of London. Winchelsea House and Epping Place, in the High Road, are both of 18th-century date.

Drive to the green at the end of the town and branch left on to the B181, SP 'Roydon'. In 1¼ miles bear right. After ¾ mile, having passed over Cobbin's Brook, reach a T-junction and turn left. Continue through Epping Green to Roydon.

ROYDON, Essex

About 1½ miles south-west of Roydon are the ruins of Tudor Nether Hall, a Manor house that belonged to the Coltes family. It was here that Thomas More came to woo and win the elder daughter of John Coltes. Preserved in the village itself are the old parish cage, stocks, and a whipping post.

Turn left with SP 'Hertford' and shortly

The two upper floors of Queen Elizabeth's Hunting Lodge were originally designed without infilling between the beams, thus enabling an uninterrupted view of the hunt.

This superb brass is one of 15 preserved in Sawbridgeworth's 14th-century church.

cross the River Stort and a level crossing to enter Hertfordshire. In ¾ mile turn right with SP 'Chelmsford' to join the A414. After 3 miles go forward on unclassified road through High Wych, and at T-junction turn left on to the A1184 to Sawbridgeworth.

SAWBRIDGEWORTH, Herts

A number of fine Georgian and older buildings survive in this small town, and to the south is Pishiobury – a fine house built by James Wyatt in 1782 and now a school. Ancient brasses are preserved in St. Mary's Church.

Meet crossroads and turn right on to unclassified road SP 'Chelmsford'. Turn right onto the A1060 then turn left on to the B183 SP 'Takeley' for Hatfield Broad Oak.

HATFIELD BROAD OAK, Essex

Notable features in this markedly-pretty village include a Norman and later church, 18th-century almshouses, and several distinctive Georgian houses.

Keep left and in 1¼ miles turn left on to an unclassified road SP 'Hatfield Forest'. In ¾ mile keep forward and skirt the Hatfield Forest Country Park.

HATFIELD FOREST, Essex

Once a part of the ancient Royal Forests of Essex, 1,049-acre Hatfield Forest is now protected by the National Trust and offers splendid woodland walks along its chases and rides. Additional amenities include boating and fishing.

Continue, and later turn right on to the A120 for Takeley.

TAKELEY, Essex

Takeley, on the line of the old Roman Stane Street, has an interesting Norman and later church with Roman masonry in the fabric of its walls. Inside is a modern font surmounted by a 6ft-high medieval cover. Good timbered houses and 17th-century barns can be seen in the village.

Drive to traffic signals and turn left off the A120 on to an unclassified road SP 'Broxted'. In 1½ miles note Stansted Airport to the left. In another 1¼ miles turn right into Molehill Green. Continue with SP 'Thaxted' and pass through Broxted.

BROXTED, Essex

Broxted's church shows a happy blend of 13th- and 15th-century styles, with the nave and chancel from the earlier period and a belfry and north aisle from the later. Church Hall is of late 16th- to mid 17th-century date.

Beyond the village join the B1051 for Thaxted.

THAXTED, Essex

Many old houses survive to remind the visitor that this was once a very prosperous town. The 15th-century church was clearly built by a community with a great deal of money to spend. The timbered Guildhall dates from the 16th century and incorporates an earlier ancient lock-up. Several old almshouses and a tower windmill can be seen in the area.

Turn left on to the B184 and continue through the village. At the end meet the Fox and Hounds (PH) and turn right on to the B1051 for Great Sampford.

GREAT SAMPFORD, Essex

This pretty village has attractive gabled houses, and opposite the Bull Inn is an Elizabethan manor house. A large pond and three-cornered green complete the picture.

Turn right again on to the B1053 and continue to Finchingfield.

The massive timbers of Greensted Church are a unique survival.

FINCHINGFIELD, Essex

Possibly the most photographed village in Essex, Finchingfield is a picture-book community complete with a church on a hill, a picturesque windmill, quaint old cottages, and a charming green enlivened by the noisy population of its duckpond. St John's Church has a sturdy Norman tower that indicates its origins, but the main body is an attractive mixture of styles. One mile north west is Spains Hall and Gardens.

Drive to the war memorial and turn right on to the B1057 for Great Bardfield.

GREAT BARDFIELD, Essex

A major feature of this old market town is a restored windmill that goes by the name 'Gibraltar'. A pleasant mixture of old cottages and shops complemented by the mainly 14th-century church is surveyed by a timber-framed 16th- and 17th-century hall from its hill above the River Pant.

Turn right SP 'Dunmow' and continue to Bran End. After 2½ miles turn left on to the A130 and continue to Dunmow.

Epping Forest's many acres of varied scenery provide one of East London's most valuable leisure amenities.

An essential part of Finchingfield's charm is its typically English village green.

Great Dunmow's 16th-century Clock House.

GREAT DUNMOW, Essex

The Dunmow Flitch trial is held here every 4 years to find a man and wife who have not had a domestic brawl or wished to be unmarried for 12 months and a day. A flitch of bacon is presented to the couple able to prove this enviable state of affairs. The town, a quiet enough place even without this incentive, boasts a large church and a rather small square.

Turn left again SP 'Chelmsford', then in ¾ mile turn right on to the B184 SP 'Ongar'. Continue to High Roding and Leaden Roding.

THE RODINGS, Essex

A number of attractive villages in the Roding Valley share this suffix. These include High Roding, with its thatched and gabled cottages and a 13th-century church, and Leaden Roding.

Reach the King William IV (PH) in Leaden Roding and turn right on to the A414. In 1 mile turn left on to the B184 for Fyfield. From Fyfield drive for 2½ miles, enter a roundabout, and leave by the 2nd exit on to the A128 into Chipping Ongar.

CHIPPING ONGAR, Essex

Chipping Ongar began as a market town beneath the walls of a Norman castle. Only the mound and moat of the castle remain, but the contemporary Church of St Martin of Tours still flourishes. Explorer

David Livingstone was a pupil pastor of the town's 19th-century Congregational Church.

Drive to the end of the High Street and turn right on to an unclassified road SP 'Greensted'. Pass the Two Brewers (PH) and after 1 mile pass Greensted Church on the right.

GREENSTED CHURCH, Essex

St Andrew's Church is famous as the only surviving example of a Saxon log church extant. The body of King Edmund is known to have been rested here in 1013, but the building is probably much older than that.

In a further ½ mile turn left SP 'Stanford Rivers' and follow a narrow road, then in 1¼ miles meet crossroads and turn left again. Drive to a T-junction, turn right on to the A113 SP 'London', and in 3 miles enter a roundabout. Leave by the 2nd exit for Abridge and continue to Chigwell.

CHIGWELL, Essex

Novelist Charles Dickens used the 17th-century King's Head in Chigwell as The Maypole in his book *Barnaby Rudge*. The town's grammar school was founded in 1629 by Archbishop Harsnett, whose memorial brass can be seen inside local St Mary's Church.

After another 1¾ miles meet a T-junction and turn right, then in ¾ mile meet traffic signals and turn right again on to the A1009 SP 'Woodford Green'. Return to Woodford Green.

BARNET, Gt London

Several charmingly-rural areas have survived here in spite of the capital's appetite for building land. Mill Hill has picturesque weather-boarded houses set neatly on the green ridge from which it takes its name. A 2-mile expanse of unspoilt countryside extends from Cockfosters to Monken Hadley, and Hadley Woods are delightful.

Leave Barnet Church with SP 'Hatfield, A1000'. After ⅓ mile pass through Hadley Green.

HADLEY GREEN, Gt London

Hadley Common and Hadley Green meet at St Mary's Church, a 15th-century building of flint and ironstone, topped by an 18th-century copper beacon. Various Georgian houses and cottages cluster round the fringes of the green in a very village-like way.

Continue to Potters Bar, passing the Battle of Barnet (1471) Obelisk to the right. Meet crossroads and drive forward to pass the BBC radio station at Brookman's Park. In 2 miles bear left for Hatfield. Then forward at roundabout, in ½ mile bear left for Hatfield, at next roundabout forward passing the entrance to Hatfield House (right).

HATFIELD, Herts

Ancient Hatfield preserves many interesting buildings from its long history as a market town, not the least of which is the Tudor palace of Cardinal Moreton. Even this, however, with its Elizabeth I and Mary associations, is overshadowed by the famous and spectacular pile of Hatfield House (open). A chapel of the owners of the house, can be seen in the local church.

Proceed through Old Hatfield and meet traffic lights. Turn right here SP 'Hertford', then within ⅓ mile cross a flyover and turn left to join the A414. A detour can be made from the main tour route by keeping forward on the A1000 and crossing the River Lee to Welwyn Garden City.

WELWYN GARDEN CITY, Herts

Although not the earliest of its kind in England (that honour belongs to Letchworth), Welwyn Garden City was begun in 1919 and represents an attempt to influence the living conditions of ordinary people.

Continue with the A414. In 2 miles enter a roundabout and leave by the 1st exit. After about 1 mile reach Cole Green and take the 2nd turning left on to an unclassified road SP 'Welwyn, B1000'. Continue for 1¼ miles and turn left to join the B1000. In another ⅓ mile turn right on to an unclassified road across the River Mimram SP 'Archers Green'. At the end of this turn right for Tewin.

AN UNSUSPECTED COUNTRYSIDE

Major highways following ancient Roman routes carry new towns and overspill developments deep into the countryside north of London. Between them, unsuspected by their traffic, are quiet rural areas where wood and parkland insulate splendid mansions from the modern rush.

TEWIN, Herts

Tewin lies in wooded countryside above the charming River Mimram, east of the impressive 19th-century Digswell railway viaduct. Close by is beautifully-preserved Elizabethan Queen Hoo Hall.

Proceed to the green in Tewin and keep left for Burnham Green. Drive over crossroads for Woolmer Green.

WOOLMER GREEN, Herts

Local St Michael's Church, built in the late 19th century, was meant to incorporate a tower that was never erected.

Turn right on to the B197 and follow part of the old Great North Road to Knebworth.

KNEBWORTH, Herts

Several examples of the accomplished early 20th-century architect Lutyens' work can be seen in New Knebworth, including the Church of St Martin, Golf Club House, and 'Homewod'.

Meet crossroads and turn left on to an unclassified road SP 'Old Knebworth'. Pass under a railway bridge and turn right. After 1 mile Knebworth House lies to the right.

KNEBWORTH HOUSE, Herts

Among many fine paintings and relics displayed in this large house (open) are manuscripts belonging to historian Edward Bulwer Lytton, who lived here. The origins of the house itself are in the 15th century, but the building shows later influence. The grounds now form a Country Park.

Keep left with the 'Codicote' road and in ⅓ mile turn right SP 'Kimpton and Whitwell'. Continue, then turn right on to the B656 SP 'Hitchin' and shortly pass the Vanstone Garden Centre on the left. Continue for 4⅓ miles, passing a road on the right leading to St Ippollitts.

ST IPPOLLITTS, Herts

By all accounts St Ippollitts was a man skilled in the treatment of horses. The local church was rebuilt in 1879 from old materials.

Continue into Hitchin.

HITCHIN, Herts

Tilehouse Street and Bridge Street preserve the best of Hitchin's older houses, but many other features survive in this medieval wool town. The ancient market square and moated Hitchin Priory, the latter dating from the 1770s, are reminders of a prosperous past. Features of the town church include a fine old porch and good screenwork.

Leave the town by the A600 Bedford road. Continue to Henlow Camp.

HENLOW CAMP, Beds

Long-renowned as a flying centre, Henlow Camp is an RAF establishment situated some 2 miles south of the village from which it derives its name.

Drive to a roundabout and go forward. In 1¼ miles meet crossroads and turn right on to an unclassified road for Clifton.

CLIFTON, Beds

A large 16th-century alabaster monument to Sir Michael Fisher and his wife is in Clifton Church.

Turn left, then immediately right, SP 'Stanford'. In ¼ mile pass the church and turn left. Cross the River Ivel Navigation, proceed for ⅓ mile, and keep right for Stanford. Turn right on to the B658 SP 'Sandy' and keep straight on for Caldecote. Meet crossroads and turn left on to an unclassified road for Ickwell Green.

ICKWELL GREEN, Beds

Perhaps best known for the May Day revels still held round the enormous maypole that rises from its large green, this pretty village boasts several thatched cottages and a smithy where Georgian clockmaker Thomas Tompion once worked.

Turn left SP 'Old Warden' and in ⅓ mile meet a T-junction. Turn right and pass Old Warden Airfield.

OLD WARDEN AIRFIELD, Beds

Historical aircraft and veteran cars can be seen in the Shuttleworth Collection at this small airfield, and flying displays are given occasionally.
Take the 'Shefford' road through Old Warden.

OLD WARDEN, Beds

The first Warden pear was grown in this pretty village. Old Warden Park house was built for Sir Joseph Shuttleworth in 1872, and is now used as an agricultural college. Nearby is the attractive Swiss Garden.
After ⅓ mile meet a T-junction and turn left. Continue for 1 mile, pass under a railway bridge, and turn left. Follow SP 'Shefford' and eventually rejoin the A600. Cross a river and enter Shefford village.

SHEFFORD, Beds

Southill Park, a notable Regency house to the north of Shefford, was rebuilt by Henry Holland in 1800. It was once the home of Admiral Byng, who was unjustly shot for neglect of duty after losing a battle in 1757.

Proceed to traffic signals and turn right on to the A507 SP 'Ampthill'. In 3¼ miles turn left on to an unclassified road SP 'Silsoe'. In 1 mile turn left on to the A6 for Silsoe.

SILSOE, Beds

Silsoe's church is of early 19th-century date, but is a successful attempt at a traditional English church style. Nearby is Wrest Park House and Gardens (open).

Continue to Barton-in-the-Clay.

BARTON-IN-THE-CLAY, Beds

A 16th-century painting of St Nicholas is preserved in the village church. A viewpoint known as the Clappers, including 136 acres of lovely National Trust property crowned by Clappers Wood, rises to the west.

Turn left on to the B655, SP 'Hexton'. Climb on to the Barton Hills and drive to Hexton.

A winter scene at Hadley Green.

Dramatist and critic George Bernard Shaw lived in this Victorian house at Ayot St Lawrence for 44 years.

The Shuttleworth collection at Old Warden Airfield.

SANDRIDGE, Herts

Roman bricks and masonry were used to build a chancel arch in the local Church of St Leonard. Also in the building is a good 14th-century stone rood screen.

Turn left on to an unclassified road SP 'Colney Heath'. In 1 mile turn left at T-junction, and in ½ mile left again. In 1 mile at roundabout forward. Then in a further mile turn right across the dual carriageway and left on an unclassified road for Colney Heath. At roundabout take the 3rd exit SP 'London Colney' and continue.

LONDON COLNEY, Herts

Situated in Salisbury Hall is the interesting Mosquito Aircraft Museum. This contains 3 Mosquitos plus 18 de Havilland aircraft plus many interesting exhibits.

At roundabout take the 2nd exit SP 'Radlett'. A detour may be made from the main tour route by leaving the last-mentioned roundabout by the 1st exit on to the B556 then driving for ½ mile to Salisbury Hall.

SALISBURY HALL, Herts

Red-brick Salisbury Hall was built by Sir John Cuttes, treasurer to Henry VIII, and is encircled by a moat.

Continue and at 2nd roundabout turn left on to the B5378 for Shenley.

SHENLEY, Herts

Nicholas Hawksmoor, the great architect, lived at Porter's Park until his death in 1736. His house now serves as a hospital. Preserved on the village green is the old parish lock-up, once used for petty criminals.

Drive to the end of the village and go forward on to an unclassified road. In 2¼ miles join one-way traffic and follow SP 'Barnet'. Cross a flyover, then turn right and in 1 mile turn left on to the A411. Return to Barnet.

The pavilion in the grounds of Wrest Park at Silsoe dates from 1709.

HEXTON, Herts

Nature lends a dramatic hand to the appearance of Hexton. All around are the undulating Barton Hills, and in the village itself the main street is lined with laburnums. The 19th-century St Faith's Church is guarded by giant yews.

Meet crossroads and turn right on to an unclassified road leading to Lilley.

LILLEY, Herts

Thomas Jekyll successfully copied a traditional style when he designed the attractive local church in 1870.

Keep forward over all crossroads and enter Whitwell.

WHITWELL, Herts

Brick-and-timber cottages and a charming old inn called The Bull make up this pretty village, set in unspoiled countryside.

Turn right on to the B651 SP 'St Albans', and ascend to the edge of Kimpton.

KIMPTON, Herts

The large flint Church of SS Peter and Paul stands at the north-eastern end of this village and is thought to date from the early 14th century.

Turn left, then right, and in 1 mile turn left on to an unclassified road for Ayot St Lawrence. Turn left into the village, then pass the church and Ayot House on the left.

AYOT ST LAWRENCE, Herts

Author George Bernard Shaw lived at Ayot St Lawrence from 1906 to his death in 1950 and his house – Shaw's Corner (NT) – is preserved as it was in his lifetime. His ashes were scattered in the garden.

Keep right and after 1 mile meet a T-junction. Turn right, then in a further 1¼ miles meet another T-junction and turn right on to the B653. Meet a roundabout and leave by the 1st exit on the B651 into Wheathampstead.

WHEATHAMPSTEAD, Herts

Modern industry has come to Wheathampstead, and many of its old cottages are now shops. Sarah Jennings, later the Duchess of Marlborough, is said to have been born at nearby Water End Farm. Features of the village itself include a 13th-century church and the 15th-century Bull Inn.

Continue along the B651 to Sandridge.

THE BUCKINGHAM CHILTERNS

Great rounded hills crowned with beeches enfold valleys where pure chalk streams are home to the speckled trout. Here and there steeples rise dark against the green flanks, proclaiming downland villages famous for their beauty.

UXBRIDGE, Gt London
Uxbridge stands on the banks of the River Colne and the Grand Union Canal. Its Old Crown and Treaty House featured in an historic meeting between Charles I and Parliament in 1645. St Margaret's Church dates from the 14th and 15th centuries, but its tower was rebuilt in 1820. The Market House dates from 1789.

Follow SP 'Denham' then 'Beaconsfield' to leave Uxbridge on the A4020, crossing the Grand Union Canal and the River Colne. Proceed to the Denham roundabout and take the 3rd exit on to the A40. Denham village lies off the road to the right.

DENHAM, Bucks
Denham is a most attractive village of fine houses, old inns, and ancient brick and timber cottages. St Mary's Church, which dates from the 15th century, contains wall paintings of the Day of Judgement and a 13th-century font. The local Wesleyan Chapel was built in 1820. At the end of the main street is 17th-century Denham Place, which stands in grounds landscaped by Capability Brown. Savay Farm is a 14th-century hall house.

Continue for 2 miles, with the River Misbourne to the right of the road, and meet traffic signals. Turn right on to the A413, SP 'Amersham' and proceed for 2¼ miles. Go forward to skirt Chalfont St Peter.

Go forward to skirt Chalfont St Giles. A detour from the main route to Milton's Cottage can be made by driving to the Pheasant Inn and turning left on to an unclassified road.

MILTON'S COTTAGE, Bucks
Milton lived in this timber-framed and brick cottage (open) during the plague year of 1665. He completed *Paradise Lost* here and began *Paradise Regained*.

CHALFONT ST GILES, Bucks
St Giles' Church has a 13th-century heart in Victorian dress. The village has a small green bordered by ancient brick and timber cottages. Artefacts relating to life in the Chilterns are on show at the Chiltern Open Air Museum.
Continue to Amersham.

Ancient beech trees provide spreading canopies of dappled shade on many of the Chiltern summits.

CHESHAM, Bucks
Chesham stands in the Chess Valley, with attractive Chiltern countryside to the north-west. Georgian houses and cottages exist here. The George Inn in the High Street dates from 1715. A charter granted by King Henry III in 1257 gave Chesham its market, held every Wednesday.

In Chesham bear left then right with one-way traffic SP 'Berkhamsted'. Meet a roundabout, drive forward for about a ¼ mile, and turn right. Continue to a T-junction and turn left. Within ½ mile keep forward to an unclassified road SP 'Tring'. In 1¾ miles bear left to climb on to the Chilterns.

THE CHILTERN HILLS
Wooded in the west but mostly windswept and bare near Ivinghoe in the east, the Chiltern Hills extend in a majestic line from Goring in the Thames Valley to a point near Hitchin, and culminate in 835ft Coombe Hill above Wendover. Many of the chalk 'downs' are crowned with ancient beech groves. The North Bucks Way, a 30-mile walk from Wolverton to Chequers, is open for public use.

Keep forward to Hawridge Common and continue to Cholesbury.

CHOLESBURY, Bucks
Cholesbury Common boasts a fine tower windmill which started life as a smock mill in 1863. Its form was revised after it had been declared unsafe in 1884, and it has now been converted into a private house. Iron-age Cholesbury Camp covers 15 acres near by.

Continue to Buckland Common, then drive to the Horse and Hound (PH) and keep left. Take the next turning right to St Leonards.

Chesham's parish church of St Mary dates mainly from the 19th century, but retains details from earlier periods.

mls 0 1 2 3 4 5
kms 0 2 4 6 8

Meet traffic signals by the Crown Hotel and turn right into Church Street. Within 1 mile approach more traffic signals and turn left on to the A416 for Chesham Bois.

CHESHAM BOIS, Bucks
St Leonard's at Chesham Bois is a 19th-century restoration, but the arch of its south entrance may have been part of a medieval church. Memorial brasses can be seen inside.

Continue on the A416 to Chesham.

CHALFONT ST PETER, Bucks
A complete contrast in building styles is offered by two local churches. One is a Victorianized 18th-century structure and the other a 20th-century creation. The once-fashionable gothic-revival style is evident in Chalfont House, which was built for General Churchill.

AMERSHAM, Bucks
Amersham is a lovely collection of old houses, quaint cottages, and ancient inns in the Misbourne Valley. Sir William Drake built the Town Hall in 1682, some 15 years after the almshouses bearing his name. Beech woods grace the Chiltern countryside around the town.

ST LEONARDS, Bucks

The Church of St Leonard, rebuilt after the Civil War and restored in 1845, has plastered walls and carries a squat bell turret surmounted by a spire.

Follow the 'Aston Clinton' road. Descend Aston Hill through Wendover Woods T-junction A4011. Turn left and continue along the A4011 to Wendover.

WENDOVER, Bucks

Many delightful brick and timber cottages survive here, plus a collection of quaint inns which includes the Red Lion Hotel, where Oliver Cromwell slept in 1642. Bosworth House, in the main street, is of 17th-century origin. Both the local windmill and a watermill have been converted into houses. The ancient Icknield Way crosses the Chilterns near by on its way from east to south-west England.

Turn left on to the A413 SP 'Amersham'. Within ¼ mile turn left again, then continue for 1½ miles and turn right on to an unclassified road. Ascend to Dunsmore, go forward with SP 'Kimble', and follow the narrow road over a shoulder of Coombe Hill.

COOMBE HILL, Bucks

About 1½ miles west of Wendover is Coombe Hill (NT) – 106 acres of downland in the highest part of the Chilterns. Excellent views include Aylesbury and the Chequers Woods.

Descend to Chequers Court.

CHEQUERS COURT, Bucks

Chequers is a notable 16th-century house that was given to the nation by Lord Lee of Fareham, as a thank-offering for the ending of World War I. About 3 miles from Princes Risborough in hundreds of acres of parkland, it is the Prime Minister's official country residence and contains valuable Cromwellian relics.

Turn left SP 'Great Missenden'. In 1¼ miles turn sharp right SP 'Princes Risborough', and in 1 mile descend Longdown Hill. Turn left on to the A4010 for Monks Risborough.

MONKS RISBOROUGH, Bucks

A well-known local landmark is the 80ft chalk cross cut on a slope overlooking the Icknield Way. Its upkeep was traditionally the duty of the earls of Buckingham.

Continue to Princes Risborough.

PRINCES RISBOROUGH, Bucks

Among several picturesque old houses surviving here is a 17th- and 18th-century manor house (NT).

At roundabout take 3rd exit A4129 SP 'Thame'. In 1 mile at roundabout turn left on to the B4009. Proceed to Chinnor along the line of the Icknield Way.

Above: this pastel of John Milton at the age of 62 hangs in Milton's Cottage.
Right: this picturesque, creeper hung cottage is where the poet ended his days in blindness and loneliness, a disillusioned old man.

CHINNOR, Oxon

A Chiltern village with a cement works sounds incongruous, even to 20th-century ears, but Chinnor has just such an industry. Its moated manor house and attractive church are more typical of the area.

Meet crossroads and turn left, then within ¼ mile go forward along an unclassified road with SP 'Bledlow Ridge'. Wain Hill viewpoint lies to the left.

WAIN HILL, Bucks

Cut into the solid chalk slope of Wain Hill is the 75ft-long Bledlow Cross, one of two turf-cut crosses in the county.

In ½ mile ascend Chinnor Hill and turn sharp left for the climb to Bledlow Ridge.

BLEDLOW RIDGE, Bucks

The climb to Bledlow Ridge is steep, but well worth the effort for it commands breathtaking views.

Descend to West Wycombe.

WEST WYCOMBE, Bucks

This town has a beautifully-preserved main street (NT) which enshrines architecture dating from the 15th to 19th centuries. The town's Church of St Laurence stands isolated on a 600ft-high hill at the site of a village which has long gone. Artificial chalk caves in the area once housed the notorious Hell Fire Club founded by Sir Francis Dashwood who owned the mansion in West Wycombe Park (NT). Nearby is a small motor museum.

Join the A40 and drive through the village to High Wycombe.

HIGH WYCOMBE, Bucks

High Wycombe has been important since Roman times, and once earned a very good living from wool and lace. It is now well known for the manufacture of furniture, particularly chairs, and has a museum dealing solely with the craft in Castle Hill House. The Guildhall and octagonal Little Market House are scheduled as Ancient Monuments.

Leave High Wycombe following SP 'Great Missenden, A4128' and cross the River Wye. Within 1½ miles reach Hughenden Manor on the left.

HUGHENDEN MANOR, Bucks

Hughenden Manor was the home of Disraeli, Prime Minister of Great Britain under Queen Victoria. It was remodelled in 1862 but his study still remains as he left it.

After about ½ mile turn right. Ascend for ¾ mile and approach the White Lion (PH). Turn right again into unclassified Cryers Hill Lane and proceed to a T-junction. Turn left SP 'Penn' and in 1 mile turn right. In ½ mile approach traffic signals at Hazlemere and drive straight over crossroads on to the B474 SP 'Beaconsfield'. Go forward to Penn.

PENN, Bucks

Penn is in one of the loveliest parts of the Chilterns. Village inn and church stand side by side overlooking the green in the company of fine Georgian houses, and the view from the churchyard is exceptional.

Continue through Penn to the outskirts of Beaconsfield and Bekonscot Model Village.

BEKONSCOT MODEL VILLAGE, Bucks

Situated in Warwick Road, Beaconsfield New Town, this model has cottages, churches, waterways, a railway, an airport, farms, and fields, at the scale of one inch to one foot.

Continue into Beaconsfield.

BEACONSFIELD, Bucks

Beaconsfield has a green bordered by roads of Queen Anne and Georgian houses, and ancient inns with notable histories. The half-timbered Royal Saracen's Head was once a coaching stop. Although St Mary's Church is medieval in origin it wears a Victorian face; the poet Edmund Waller lies buried here.

At roundabout turn left A40 SP 'London'. Continue for ½ mile, enter a roundabout, and leave by the 1st exit. After another ½ mile at roundabout the unclassified left turn leads to Jordans.

JORDANS, Bucks

The most famous of all Quaker Meeting Houses stands here. It was built in 1688 and is only a few years younger than Old Jordans Farm, where Quaker meetings were held prior to its completion.

Continue along the A40 to the outskirts of Gerrards Cross.

GERRARDS CROSS, Bucks

This largely residential district has a Byzantine-style church of 1859 and a few Georgian houses.

Continue along the A40 and enter Denham roundabout. Leave by the A4020 exit and return to Uxbridge.

A painted ceiling dominates the Blue Drawing Room in 18th-century West Wycombe Park.

OXFORD, Oxon

This ancient and world renowned university town stands on three main waterways – the River Cherwell, the River Thames (known locally as the Isis), and the Oxford Canal. It is first mentioned in the Saxon Chronicle of 912, but all the indications are that there was a thriving community on the site at least 200 years earlier. Organized teaching has existed at Oxford since the 12th century, and the collegiate system became established in the 13th century as the various religious orders consolidated. Town and gown were often at loggerheads in medieval times, particularly when university privileges conflicted with the interests of local merchants. Charles I established his parliament here, and Oxford served as the Royalist headquarters during that troubled time of civil war. The town's street plan forms an intriguing network centred on Carfax, a junction of four streets and the centre of the old community. Perhaps the most notable of the four is High Street, which is known locally as 'The High'. At the east end is Magdalen, one of the richest colleges in Oxford, and a little closer to Carfax is St Edmund Hall – a unique relic of a residential society founded for graduates in 1220. The High's centrepiece is the University Church of St Mary the Virgin, which is instantly recognizable by its beautiful 14th-century spire. Wren designed the Sheldonian Theatre, at the east end of Broad Street, and the 19th-century bulk of Ashmolean Museum displays a varied array of fascinating and often valuable collections.

From Oxford follow SP 'The East A420'. Pass through Headington.

HEADINGTON, Oxon

Stone for many of the Oxford colleges was worked in the once-famous Headington quarries. The village church dates from the 12th century and incorporates a fine Norman chancel arch. Morris dancing is a long-standing local tradition, and Headington's own troupe of dancers performs annually on Whit Monday.

Continue to a roundabout and take the 2nd exit into unclassified Bayswater Road. After ¾ mile turn right, SP 'Stanton St John'. Drive forward to a T-junction and turn right, then left, into Stanton St John.

STANTON ST JOHN, Oxon

John White, the chief founder of Massachusetts in New England, was born here in 1575. Milton's grandfather also lived here. The village has thatched farms, stone cottages, an ancient manor house, and a lovely old church.

Drive to the church, turn left, then follow SP 'Oakley'. Enter that village.

NORTH OF THE SPIRED CITY

Just a few miles from the city of learning and dreaming spires are the vast victory estate of Blenheim, an ancient Saxon demesne that was the playground of the high aristocracy, and the gentle contours of the Vale of Oxford.

OAKLEY, Bucks

Oakley House stands at the south end of the village and is of 17th-century date. Early 13th-century St Mary's Church contains a number of old coffin-lid monuments.

From Oakley approach a main road and turn right on to the B4011. Take the next turning left on to an unclassified road for Brill.

BRILL, Bucks

Isolated Brill is a lovely village which stands at 700ft above the Vale of Aylesbury. Its two greens are fringed with charming cottages and almshouses, and its Tudor manor house radiates the warmth of mellow red brick. Brill windmill (open) dates from 1668 and may be one of the oldest postmills to have survived anywhere in Great Britain.

Proceed to the Sun Hotel, turn left into Windmill Street, and pass the old windmill. Later ascend, then descend to join the B4011 to Blackthorn. After 1 mile turn left on to the A41 for Bicester.

BICESTER, Oxon

The site of Roman Alchester lies a mile to the south of Bicester, and the modern A421 follows the line of an old Roman road close by. No Roman remains have been found at Bicester itself, but the *castra* element in its name suggests that there was once a garrison here. If that was the case then the military tradition continues, for nowadays it is the base for one of the largest army depots in the country. Local roadsides have wide grass verges for the convenience of the many horseriders hereabouts.

Follow SP 'Oxford, A421', then turn right on to the A4095 SP 'Chipping Norton'. Proceed for 1 mile, then go forward on to the B4030 to Middleton Stoney. Cross a main road and continue to the outskirts of Lower Heyford.

LOWER HEYFORD, Oxon

Set on a slope overlooking a wide valley and the River Cherwell, Lower Heyford has a 13th-century church which carries a 15th-century tower and is entered via a 15th-century porch complete with sundial. The font dates from the 17th century.

Cross the Oxford Canal and River Cherwell. (Rousham House is on the left).

ROUSHAM HOUSE, Oxon

Near the River Cherwell is Rousham House, a 17th- and 18th-century building which boasts the only garden layout by William Kent to have survived intact (open).

DEDDINGTON, Oxon

Continue to the Hopcrofts Holt Hotel, and turn right on to the A423 for Deddington.

One of many small towns near the lovely River Cherwell, Deddington is built of honey-coloured local stone and is rich in Civil War associations. Many of these may be 'local colour', but King Charles I is reputed to have slept at 16th-century Castle Farm while in the area. The local church is of 14th-century date and has a very fine north porch. Its tower was rebuilt in 1635 after the first attempt fell down.

Turn left on to the B4031 'Chipping Norton' road and pass through Hempton. After 3 miles keep left and join the A361. After ½ mile turn left on to the B4022 SP 'Enstone'. Continue for 1 mile and turn left again on to an unclassified road for Great Tew.

GREAT TEW, Oxon

Delightful cottages of thatch and stone combine with the old village stocks here to present a truly traditional picture of rural England. A number of interesting monuments can be seen in the church, and the manor house has been rebuilt in its original gardens.

After ½ mile turn right SP 'Little Tew'. Drive to crossroads and turn left to rejoin the B4022. After a further 3 miles drive over staggered crossroads and skirt Enstone. Proceed to Charlbury.

CHARLBURY, Oxon

Set in the Evenlode Valley, Charlbury is a compact little town with many narrow streets containing 18th-century buildings, including shops and inns. Within Wychwood Forest is Cornbury Park, although the Earl of Leicester once resided here when he was a favourite of Elizabeth I, the majority of the building dates from the 17th and 18th centuries. Ditchley Park is a fine 18th-century house by James Gibb, it lies 2½ miles to the north east and is occasionally open in the summer.

Continue along the B4022, crossing the River Evenlode, with Wychwood Forest to the right. Later turn right into Witney.

WITNEY, Oxon

The name 'Witney' is synonymous with blanket making, an industry that has grown from the town's close proximity to rich wool country and the availability of ready power from the River Windrush. *Domesday* records that two mills stood here, and doubtless there were others even before that. The main street extends for almost a mile to a green set with lime trees and graced with fine houses built with the profits of wool and weaving. Prosperity is similarly mirrored in the 17th-century Butter Cross, which stands on 13 stone pillars and displays both a clock tower and a sundial. The old Blanket Hall of 1720 displays a curious one-handed clock. Witney's

The Oxford Canal flows through Lower Heyford.

church carries a 156ft-high spire that serves as a landmark for many miles.

Return along the A4095 'Bicester' road to the outskirts of North Leigh.

NORTH LEIGH, Oxon
Features of North Leigh include a disused windmill and a church with a Saxon tower. Inside the church is a 'doom' painting and an unusual collection of coffin plates. North-east of the village are superb Roman remains (AM) on one of the best villa sites in this country.

Continue on the A4095 and pass through Long Hanborough to Bladon.

BLADON, Oxon
Sir Winston Churchill, his wife, and both his parents are buried in Bladon churchyard. The church itself is a Victorian reconstruction of a building that had previously occupied the site for many centuries.

Drive 1 mile farther and approach a roundabout. Turn left on to the A34 for Blenheim Palace and Woodstock.

BLENHEIM PALACE, Oxon
John Churchill, 1st Duke of Marlborough, won more than a victory when he crushed the French at Blenheim in 1704. Queen Anne awarded him and his heirs forever the Royal Manor of Woodstock with the Hundred of Wootton, while a no

less grateful parliament voted him half a million pounds to pay for the building of Blenheim Palace. The duchess rejected plans for the house drawn up by Wren and chose instead Sir John Vanbrugh's suitably grandiose scheme. The gardens were originally laid out by Henry Wise, and the grounds – later modified by Capability Brown – cover 2,500 acres and include a vast lake, Triumphal Way, and sunken Italian garden. The palace itself is an Eldorado of art treasures and fine furnishings. One-time prime minister and war leader Sir Winston Churchill was born here in 1874.

WOODSTOCK, Oxon
The royal demesne of Woodstock was from Saxon to Tudor times the site of a great country manor that served as the playground of royalty. Various members of the high aristocracy were born here, some installed their mistresses or hunted here, and several died here. Elizabeth I was imprisoned here by Mary for a while, but the tables were resoundingly turned when the Virgin Queen returned in triumph after her accession to the throne. Woodstock House was, unfortunately, a total casualty of the Civil War and has all but vanished. In the town itself is a grand town hall that was built in

Blenheim Palace, which covers 3 acres of ground, was built for the Duke of Marlborough between 1705 and 1722.

1766 by Sir William Chambers with money donated by the Duke of Marlborough. Tradition has it that the very famous Bear Inn dates back to 1237. There are a great number of very old and attractive stone houses in the streets of Woodstock.

Return along the A34 towards Oxford. After 3½ miles meet an unclassified right turn leading to Yarnton.

YARNTON, Oxon
Yarnton's manor house was built in 1612 and has since been well restored. Above its porch are the Spencer Arms. The local church, which dates from the 13th century, carries a 17th-century tower and contains a fine Jacobean screen.

Continue along the A34 for the return to Oxford.

AMONG THE COTSWOLDS

Wool and stone shaped this landscape. Mellow rock torn from hillsides cropped smooth by generations of sheep was built into great churches, houses, towns and villages by local skill applied with the profits from wool, medieval England's greatest resource.

BURFORD, Oxon

Like so many other wool towns in this part of the country, Burford is centred on a charming main street lined with honey-coloured buildings of local stone. The excellence of this building material is apparent in the fact that Sir Christopher Wren would specify no other for St Paul's Cathedral. The town's main street descends a steep hillside and crosses the River Windrush via a fine old bridge. Buildings of particular interest include 15th-century almshouses, the Great House of 1690, and basically Norman church which claims to be the second largest in Oxfordshire. Features of this splendid building include an imposing tower and spire, and somewhat macabre Civil War associations. In 1649 several Cromwellian mutineers were trapped in the building by their own forces, and on capture 3 of the imprisoned men were shot near the churchyard. The history of Burford is shown in the Torsey Museum and set in 200 acres of woodlands is the Cotswold Wildlife Park.

From the Bull Hotel in Burford follow the unclassified road to Asthall.

ASTHALL, Oxon

The banks of the Windrush afford a delightful view of Asthall Manor, a striking Elizabethan house with mullioned windows and an overall atmosphere of permanence. Alongside is the parish church, which is of Norman origin and features two interesting arches in the north chapel.

Meet a T-junction and turn right SP 'Witney'. Ascend, then turn left on to the B4047 and proceed to Minster Lovell.

MINSTER LOVELL, Oxon

Clustered stone-built cottages and the fine, partly-timbered Swan Inn nestle together to form this quaint little Windrush village. Of special note are the ruins of a 15th-century hall (AM), which boasts two gruesome legends. The first is of Lord Francis Lovell, who is supposed to have hidden in a secret room after the Lambert Simnel Rising of 1487. His whereabouts was known to only one servant, who died suddenly leaving the unfortunate Lord Francis incarcerated until his skeleton was reputedly discovered in 1718. A similar tale recounts the story of an unfortunate young Lovell bride who decided to hide in a large chest on her Christmas wedding night and became trapped.

At the White Hart Hotel turn left on to the unclassified 'Leafield' road. Descend and cross the River Windrush and continue to Leafield. Drive to the war memorial, turn left, then continue to the Fox Inn and bear right. Shortly pass the Leafield Radio Station. Continue to Shipton-under-Wychwood and turn right on to the A361 to enter the village.

The peaceful ruins of Minster Lovell Hall are haunted by macabre legends involving death by starvation and suffocation.

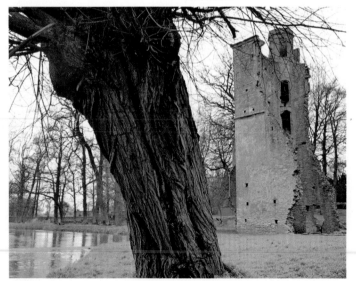

SHIPTON-UNDER-WYCHWOOD, Oxon

Restored Shipton Court is of Elizabethan origin and one of the finest buildings in the village; unfortunately it is closed to the public. More easily accessible is a fountain which was raised to the memory of 19 Shipton men who died in the wreck of the ship *Cosipatrick* in 1874. The Shaven Crown Inn has a Tudor gateway.

The church doorway at Windrush is decorated with the carved heads of many exotic beasts.

mls 0 1 2 3 4 5
kms 0 2 4 6 8

Churchill's ornate fountain stands as a memorial to the founder of the local church.

Cross the River Evenlode and continue to Chipping Norton.

CHIPPING NORTON, Oxon

The 'Chipping' element of this name means 'market', and for a considerable period the 'market at Norton' was the commercial centre for the Evenlode Valley. When the Cotswolds became one giant sheepwalk the town assumed new importance as a gathering place for wool merchants and other traders. Much of the town's attraction today is due to its many survivals from a prosperous past. Among these are numerous 18th-century houses and a 'wool' church that is among the finest in the county; 17th-century Almhouses, The Bliss Tweedmill of

1872, the White Hart and Crown and Cushion were once coaching inns. Four miles north-east is Chas Heton House, which contains tapestries and period furniture.

Follow the B4450 'Stow' road and drive to Churchill.

CHURCHILL, Oxon

Two famous men were born here in the 18th century – William Hastings, 1st Governor-General of India, and 'The Father of Geology' William Smith, who was the first man to map the rock strata of England and identify fossils peculiar to each layer. A restored church of 1826 crowns a nearby hilltop and displays a fine tower which can be seen for miles around. An unusual square-shaped fountain with open arches and pinnacles rising from a basin of flowing water stands as a memorial to Squire Langston, the original builder of the church.

Continue to Bledington.

BLEDINGTON, Glos

Situated near the River Evenlode, Bledington boasts its own Victorian maypole and a fine Norman church containing good examples of old glass. Nearby Maugersbury Hill forms an excellent viewpoint.

Later join the A436 for Stow-on-the-Wold.

STOW-ON-THE-WOLD, Glos

'Stow-on-the-Wold where the wind blows cold' is a local saying that aptly describes this, the highest hilltop town in the Cotswolds. It is set on a ridge between the upper valleys of the rivers Windrush and Evenlode and has an enormous market square with stocks and a 14th-century cross. This is the focal point of the town. Inside the local church is a splendid 17th-century painting of the Crucifixion by Belgian artist, de Craeyer. Hundreds of Royalists were imprisoned here after a Civil War battle fought in 1646.

Follow SP 'Tewkesbury' to join the B4077 and proceed to Upper Swell.

UPPER SWELL, Glos

This charming and unspoilt village comprises a cluster of houses and a tiny church. Its main feature is a fine manor house.

About 4¼ miles farther a road on the left leads to Cotswold Farm Park.

COTSWOLD FARM PARK, Glos

Rare breeds of British farm animals are kept here in an authentic farmyard setting in beautiful countryside on the Cotswold Hills. Major attractions include a pet's corner, young stock, and rides round the park in a pony-drawn trap.

Continue on the B4077 through Ford. Descend to Stanway.

STANWAY, Glos

Magnificent wooded hills surround this attractive small village, which has a tithe barn mentioned in the Domesday Book. Stanway House, a focal point for the community, is approached through an imposing gateway in the style of Inigo Jones.

Meet crossroads and turn right on to an unclassified road, passing the grounds of Stanway House. In 1¼ miles turn right and drive to Stanton.

STANTON, Glos

Larch woods on Shenbarrow Hill shelter this unspoilt village, which is often described as the most attractive in the Cotswolds. Elizabethan Stanton Court and 16th-century Warren House are old manor houses of particular note, and thatched barns add the softness of straw or reed to the picture. Watching over all is the homely sentinel of the restored church.

Return and in ¼ mile bear right SP 'Cheltenham'. In ¾ mile turn left on to the A46 and continue to the Toddington roundabout. Keep forward at the roundabout, then in 1 mile take the 2nd turning on the left on to an unclassified road for Hailes Abbey.

HAILES ABBEY, Glos

For many years the 13th-century Cistercian foundation was a thriving centre of learning and religion, attracting pilgrims from all over the country. Nowadays it is a collection of ruins (AM, NT) with a small site museum in which tiles, bosses, and various early relics are preserved.

Return for 200 yds and turn left on to Roel Hill, which affords fine views of the surrounding countryside. Meet a T-junction and turn left, then turn right and continue to Guiting Power.

GUITING POWER, Glos

This picturesque village is attractively situated on the upper reaches of the River Windrush.

In ¼ mile meet a T-junction and turn right SP 'Andoversford', then take the next turning left SP 'Stow'. Continue along a quiet country road to Lower Swell.

LOWER SWELL, Glos

Huge copper beeches and stone walls line the route into Lower Swell. In the village the small River Dikler flows past attractive bankside cottages and a working smithy. An elegant Georgian pillar topped by an urn stands on the village green and inside the local church are fine examples of Norman carving.

Turn right on to the B4068 SP 'The Slaughters', then turn left on to an unclassified road for Upper Slaughter.

UPPER SLAUGHTER, Glos

An outstanding 3-gabled Elizabethan manor house (open), with 15 tall chimneys and an avenue of mature trees, dominates this beautiful Cotswold village. Also here are a fine 17th-century parsonage and an attractive, partly Norman church.

Lower Slaughter's 19th-century brick mill contrasts sharply with the stone houses elsewhere in the village.

Pollarded willows and the enchantment of running water combine with the mellowness of old Cotswold stone in Burford's ancient river bridge, which spans the Windrush.

Drive to the end of the village and turn left, then continue to the neighbouring village of Lower Slaughter.

LOWER SLAUGHTER, Glos

As the River Eye winds its peaceful course between the rows of charming cottages which flank both its banks in this village it is spanned by many bridges, stone and wooden, and shaded by the dark-green umbrellas of stately yew trees. This scene of rural tranquillity is completed by a church with a 12th-century arcade.

Cross a bridge and turn right, then at the end of the village turn right again on to the A429. In ½ mile turn left on to an unclassified road for Bourton-on-the-Water.

BOURTON-ON-THE-WATER, Glos

This Cotswold-stone village – with its churches, shops, houses, sloping lawns alongside the River Windrush, and watermill – is reproduced at one-ninth actual size in the garden of the Old New Inn. Elsewhere in the village are the Birdland Zoo Gardens, a Village Life Exhibition and the Cotswolds Motor Museum.

Meet crossroads in the village and follow the unclassified 'Sherborne' road. Cross the river and bear right. Ascend, and in 3½ miles turn left for Sherborne.

SHERBORNE, Glos

Number 88, a cottage on the Windrush road, was once an old chapel and retains a fine Norman doorway. Sherborne House shares extensive grounds with Lodge Park, a charming 19th-century building that was erected as a grandstand for the audiences of deer coursing.

Leave Sherborne and continue to Windrush.

WINDRUSH, Glos

This village is named after the River Windrush. The local church faces a triangular patch of green surrounded by tall trees and has a Norman doorway considered to be one of the best of its type.

Keep left and continue for ¾ mile, then meet a T-junction and turn left for Great Barrington. Drive to the war memorial and bear right for Taynton.

TAYNTON, Oxon

Taynton's thatched grey-stone houses nestle together with a 700-year-old church on timbered slopes above the River Windrush. Stone for the building of Blenheim Palace was supplied by the famous quarries in this area.

After the village keep forward for the A424, then the A361. Cross a river and re-enter Burford.

CHELTENHAM SPA, Glos

Cheltenham started life as a typical Cotswold village, but in 1715 a mineral spring was discovered here. A pump room was built in 1738, George III gave the place his personal approval, and within half a century architects were commissioned to design a new town. The result attracted many people of education and means, who came as much for Cheltenham's fashionable elegance and taste as for its water's vaunted medicinal properties. The architect Papworth was responsible for much that is best in Cheltenham, and Forbes built the famous Pittville Pump Room. Schools flourished too, including the Cheltenham College for Boys of 1841, and the Cheltenham Ladies' College of 1853. Composer Gustav Holst was a pupil at the town's grammar school. Each March Prestbury Park is host to the Cheltenham Gold Cup horse race.

GOLD IN THE COTSWOLD COUNTRYSIDE

Here is a mature countryside, first civilized by the Romans, later smoothed by the wealth of medieval clothiers, and finally polished by Regency high fashion. Everywhere is the honey colour of Cotswold stone, giving the name of Gloucestershire's rich Golden Valley another meaning.

Turn right on to the B4070, then turn left. After $\frac{3}{4}$ mile branch right on to the unclassified 'Painswick' road. In $2\frac{1}{2}$ miles meet a T-junction and turn left on to the A46. Continue to Painswick.

PAINSWICK, Glos

Years ago Painswick was an important centre of the cloth industry. This prosperity is evident in

Follow SP 'Cirencester A419' passing the wide expanse of Rodborough Common.

RODBOROUGH COMMON, Glos

Rodborough Common (NT) lies 1 mile south of Stroud. Its 240-acre site includes part of an early agricultural enclosure.

The 19th-century lines of Sudeley Castle are complemented by beautiful formal gardens.

An Ionic temple was the inspiration for Cheltenham Spa's 19th-century Pump Room.

Painswick's carefully clipped churchyard yews were planted at the end of the 18th century.

Follow SP 'Stroud A46' then SP 'Birdlip B4070' to leave Cheltenham, then climb Leckhampton Hill. At the top meet the main road and turn right, then enter a roundabout and leave by the 1st exit on to the A417. The 2nd exit leads to delightful Crickley Hill and can be taken as a diversion from the main tour.

CRICKLEY HILL, Glos

This Country Park (part NT) comprises 36½ acres of beautiful Cotswold escarpment and an interesting Iron Age promontory fort.

Continue along the A417, with magnificent views across the Severn Valley to the Malvern Hills, and enter Birdlip.

BIRDLIP, Glos

Birdlip stands on the edge of the Cotswolds, at an altitude of 900ft. Several mosaic pavements and a well-preserved hypocaust system have been uncovered at the site of a Roman villa to the west.

its many old houses and inns, amongst which are the tall-chimneyed Court House (associated with Charles I) and 18th-century Painswick House. One of the country's few original bowling greens has been preserved at the Falcon Hotel, and a few old cloth mills have survived south of the town. St Mary's Churchyard boasts almost a hundred yews that are kept tidy in a traditional annual clipping ceremony.

Follow the Painswick Valley to Stroud.

STROUD, Glos

Situated on the modest River Frome and the Stroudwater Canal, this town was once reckoned to produce the finest broadcloth in the country. It still makes most of the baize for the world's billiard tables, and has an excellent reputation for its scarlet dyes. A number of 18th-century mills and typical Cotswold cottages have survived. The District (Cowle) Museum contains exhibits of local interest.

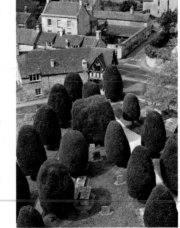

After Rodborough Common continue along the A419 and enter Brimscombe.

BRIMSCOMBE, Glos

Most of the key buildings in Brimscombe are of relatively recent date. Holy Trinity Church was built in 1840, and both Hope Mill and Port Mill are of 19th-century origin. A few earlier buildings survive at Bourne Mill.

Continue along the pleasant Golden Valley to Chalford.

CHALFORD, Glos

Views from Chalford's steep and narrow streets encompass the fertile Golden Valley, the River Frome, and stretches of the disused Stroud Canal. An old round house which originally served as a lock-keeper's cottage now houses an interesting museum of canal relics. Thoughts of past prosperity are woken by the local mills and wool masters' houses.

THE GOLDEN VALLEY, Glos

The original Golden Valley runs from Dorstone to Pontrilas in Herefordshire. The Gloucestershire Golden Valley cradles the River Frome and, like its namesake, is known for peaceful villages and unspoilt countryside.

After 2 miles (from Chalford) reach the White Horse Inn and turn left on to an unclassified road for Frampton Mansell.

FRAMPTON MANSELL, Glos

Important buildings in this village follow Cotswold tradition by dating mainly from the years of wool prosperity. Manor Farmhouse is of the late 17th century, and St Luke's Church was built in 1844.

Continue to Sapperton.

SAPPERTON, Glos

Views from the local churchyard extend along the length of the Golden Valley. Cotswold-stone cottages in the area date back to the 17th century, and Daneway House (1 mile north-west) can claim even greater antiquity, with parts dating at least from the 13th century. The Thames and Severn Canal ran through here via a 2½-mile tunnel through which 18th- and 19th-century bargees propelled their craft by lying on their backs and pushing against the walls or roof with their feet. This was commonly known as 'legging it'.

Turn right, then meet a T-junction and turn left. After 1 mile turn right to Daglingworth.

DAGLINGWORTH, Glos

Saxon work has survived in the local church in spite of major 19th-century rebuilding.

Continue, and ⅓ mile beyond the village turn right on to the A417 for Cirencester.

CIRENCESTER, Glos

In Roman times Cirencester was *Corinium Dobunorum*, the second largest town in England and the focus of several major highways. When the Romans withdrew the town declined, but wool later boosted it and wool money paid for its Church of St John the Baptist, one of the largest of its kind in the country. The town's Corinium Museum contains one of the country's most comprehensive collections of Roman remains, which includes mosaic floors and Romano-British sculpture.

Follow SP 'Burford A433' to leave Cirencester. Drive to Barnsley.

BARNSLEY, Glos

The church at Barnsley was restored in the 19th century, but its 16th-century tower and two ancient carved tables survived. Sir Isaac Newton's library was discovered at Barnsley Park after it had been removed from Thame Park.

Continue to Bibury.

BIBURY, Glos

William Morris thought Bibury 'the most beautiful village in England'. Most of its stone-built houses have gardens that run down to the River Coln, and the Arlington Row (NT) of river-fronted cottages is famous. Near Arlington Mill, which houses a museum, is a bird sanctuary. Bibury Court Hotel is of Jacobean origin, and The Swan – at the end of the street – is a pleasant coaching inn.

Drive to the Swan Inn and take an unclassified road through the Coln Valley to Ablington.

ABLINGTON, Glos

This lovely River Coln community has a late 16th-century manor house with an impressive barn. There is a prehistoric long barrow near by.

After Ablington turn left to cross a river bridge over the Coln. Later turn right and continue to Winson.

WINSON, Glos

Winson Manor dates from 1740, but Manor Farm is of slightly earlier origin. Most of the village cottages are of 17th- or 18th-century date, and the church is early-Norman.

Drive through the village and turn right for Coln Rogers.

COLN ROGERS, Glos

The nave and chancel of local St Andrew's Church are Saxon. Both the Old Rectory, at the south end of the village, and Lower Farm, belong to the 17th century.

Proceed to Coln St Dennis.

COLN ST DENNIS, Glos

Coln St Dennis has a Norman church and a 19th-century rectory. The hotel at Fosse Bridge, a ¼ mile to the north-west, is also of 19th-century date. Colnpen is a 300ft long barrow near by.

Turn left for Fossebridge, left again on to the A429, then right on to an unclassified road. Follow SP 'Chedworth Roman Villa'.

CLEPWORTH ROMAN VILLA, Glos

Chedworth Roman Villa (NT) dates from the 2nd to 4th centuries, and was rediscovered in 1864. It has various rooms and two bath suites laid out around two courtyards. The site has an excellent museum.

Return for 1½ miles into Yanworth.

YANWORTH, Glos

Traces of wall paintings, fragments of medieval glass, and a Norman font can be seen in Yanworth's 12th-century church.

Continue for 2 miles to the main road. Turn left on to the A429 and drive to the outskirts of Northleach.

NORTHLEACH, Glos

Northleach stands on high ground, east of the Roman Fosse Way, between the Coln and Windrush valleys. Its attractive stone-built

Mellow stone houses nestle amongst rolling Cotswold scenery at Bibury.

cottages and almshouses are dominated by a magnificent church. Nearby is the Cotswold Countryside Collection.

Continue to roundabout, turn left on to the A40 'Cheltenham' road, then after 2¾ miles pass the Puesdown Inn. After a further ¾ mile meet crossroads and turn right on to the unclassified 'Brockhampton' road. Proceed for 2¼ miles and cross the main road for Brockhampton. After ¼ mile meet crossroads and turn right SP 'Charlton Abbots'. Drive to the next crossroads, turn right SP 'Guiting Power'. Ascend and, at next crossroads, turn left along Roel Hill, passing Sudeley Castle.

SUDELEY CASTLE, Glos

Catherine Parr, the last of Henry VIII's wives, lived in this medieval castle (open). In 1858 it was reconstructed by Sir Gilbert Scott, who also designed Catherine's tomb to replace one destroyed during the Civil War.

Continue into Winchcombe.

WINCHCOMBE, Glos

Ancient Winchcombe was once capital of the Kingdom of Mercia. The site of its abbey, founded in 797 and destroyed by Henry VIII, is being excavated. Within the town hall is a Folk and Police Museum.

Follow the A46 'Cheltenham' road. After ⅓ mile reach an unclassified left turn leading to prehistoric Belas Knap.

BELAS KNAP, Glos

About 2 miles south-south-west of Winchcombe is the 180ft-long Belas Knap long barrow (AM). This was restored in 1930 and is considered one of the finest of its type extant.

Return and continue along the A46, with extensive views from the highest area in the Cotswolds.

CLEEVE HILL, Glos

Early 20th-century St Peter's Church shares Cleeve Hill with 17th-century Cockbury Court and 18th-century Hayes. The area is dominated by lofty Cleeve Cloud.

CLEEVE CLOUD, Glos

Overshadowing Cleeve Hill is the massive 1,031ft bulk of Cleeve Cloud, one of the highest points in the Cotswolds. Magnificent views can be enjoyed from its summit.

Continue the descent through Prestbury to Cheltenham, passing the racecourse and airfield on the way.

Several architectural styles are incorporated to glorious effect in Cirencester's parish church.

MORETON-IN-MARSH, Glos

Moreton-in-Marsh is a pleasant small market town under the edge of the north Cotswolds. Among many interesting old inns here are the White Hart, where Charles I slept in 1643, and the famous Redesdale Arms coaching stop. The town's curfew tower carries a 17th-century clock. Two miles north west, set in 50 acres, is the Batsford Arboretum.

Follow SP 'A44 Oxford' from Moreton-in-Marsh and continue to the Four Shire Stone, on the left of the road.

FOUR SHIRE STONE, Glos

About 2 miles east of Moreton-in-Marsh is the famous Four Shire Stone, where Gloucestershire met Oxfordshire, Warwickshire, and an isolated part of Worcestershire before the county reorganization of the 1970s.

Pass Four Shire Stone and in ¾ mile turn right on to an unclassified road for Chastleton.

CHASTLETON, Oxon

Chastleton House is of Cotswold stone and was built by wealthy wool merchant Walter Jones in 1603. His descendants are still in ownership. On the top floor of the house are state rooms and a long gallery, which contain many items of original furniture (open).

Go through Chastleton and after ½ mile turn left. Cross a cattle grid and turn right on to the A44. Pass the Cross Hands (PH) and turn left on to an unclassified road. Proceed to the Rollright Stones.

ROLLRIGHT STONES, Oxon

This important bronze-age monument (AM) comprises two configurations of stones. The circle, nicknamed 'The King's Men', measures a full 100ft across and is

close to 'The Whispering Knights' group and an isolated outlier called the 'King's Stone'.

After ¾ mile turn left on to the A34 and descend to Long Compton.

LONG COMPTON, Warwicks

A little thatched gatehouse tops the churchyard gate at Long Compton. The church itself is of Norman and later date and preserves an old stone figure of a lady in the porch.

Continue to Shipston-on-Stour

SHIPSTON-ON-STOUR Warwicks

Situated on the edge of the Cotswolds in the Vale of Red Horse, this old wool town has attractive Georgian houses and inns complemented by a 19th-century church incorporating the 500-year-old tower of its predecessor.

Turn left on to the B4035 'Campden' road. Proceed for 1¾ miles, cross a main road. Continue for 1¼ miles then turn right on to an unclassified road through Charingworth to Ebrington.

EBRINGTON, Glos

Delightful cottages of stone and thatch enhance the undoubted appeal of this beautiful Cotswold village. Ebrington Manor shows a great deal of restoration to its basically 17th-century structure.

TOUR 38   65 MILES

IN THE VALE OF RED HORSE

Relics of ancient man dot the North Cotswold Hills above vales of almost legendary richness, where English fruit and vegetables are raised round villages that grew fat on the profits of wool. Great men lived and died here; great rivers continue to flow.

Drive to the end of the village and keep right, then right again on to an unclassified road SP 'To the Hidcotes'. After 2¼ miles turn right for Hidcote Bartrim.

The Curfew Tower in Moreton-in-Marsh is possibly the oldest building in the town.

HIDCOTE BARTRIM, Glos

Hidcote Bartrim boasts a late 17th-century manor surrounded by lovely formal gardens (open) (NT).

Return to the T-junction and turn left, then take the next turning on the right SP 'Mickleton'. Meet the main road and turn right on to the A46 to enter Mickleton.

MICKLETON, Glos

Medford House is a superb example of Renaissance architecture, and the village itself preserves thatched and timber-framed buildings. Half a mile south east is Kingsgate Court Gardens magnificently situated, affording fine views. St Lawrence's Church dates from the 12th century.

Drive through the village and turn left. After ½ mile continue on to the unclassified road for Long Marston.

LONG MARSTON, Warwicks

King's Lodge in Long Marston has associations with King Charles II, who is said to have come here in disguise after the Battle of Worcester. The bell in the village church hangs in a turret built on great oak beams resting on the floor of the nave. The village itself is a delightful grouping of timber and thatch cottages in leafy country lanes. It has its own traditional morris dancing troupe.

Continue to Welford-on-Avon

WELFORD-ON-AVON, Warwicks

Welford-on-Avon's Norman church has an ancient lychgate and stands among charming timber-and-thatch cottages near a new maypole.

The Rollright Stones have been a Cotswolds feature for thousands of years.

Go forward and later cross the River Avon, then turn left on to the A439 and drive to Bidford-on-Avon.

BIDFORD-ON-AVON, Warwicks

Traditionally this unspoilt village was the birthplace of playwright William Shakespeare. There is little doubt that Tudor Corner House was once the Falcon Inn beloved of both Shakespeare and his contemporary Ben Jonson. Latterly the inn has served as a workhouse and as a group of cottages. A fine 15th-century bridge spans the Avon.

Turn left on to the B4085 SP 'Broadway', and cross a bridge. After ½ mile turn right for Cleeve Prior.

CLEEVE PRIOR, Herefs & Worcs

The name of this village derives from the priors of Worcester, who were once lords of the manor here. Tall chimneys and a priest's hole that once hid Charles I's banker are features of the Jacobean manor house. Stone-built cottages overlook the triangular green, and the 15th-century King's Arms still offers comfort to the traveller.

Continue to South Littleton.

SOUTH LITTLETON, Herefs & Worcs

North, Middle, and South Littleton are a picturesque group of tiny Avon Valley villages. North Littleton has a manor house, a tithe barn, and dovecote, and a church that is considered to be of great architectural merit. South Littleton boasts a beautiful early 18th-century house.

Continue along the same road for a further 1 mile, then go over a level crossing and turn left on to the unclassified 'Bretforton' road. Continue to Bretforton.

BRETFORTON, Herefs & Worcs

Three tributaries of the Avon drain the lovely countryside round this ancient village. Of particular note here are the 600-year-old Fleece Inn (NT) and medieval Grange Farm. The latter, changed greatly from its original form by successive owners, gave shelter to Prince Rupert in 1645. The country's largest collection of dovecotes survives here, including several very old examples and one that has been made into a cottage.

Join the B4035 and continue to Weston-Sub-Edge.

WESTON-SUB-EDGE, Glos

Several appealing 17th-century houses preserved in the main street of this village include Latimer's, a particularly fine example associated with the historic bishop of that name. Bank House and Riknild are also of note. Slightly later than these is the Manor House, and the 'old' Rectory was built in the 19th century.

Meet a T-junction, turn right on to the A46, and pass through Willersey.

Chipping Campden's arched Market Hall was built in 1627.

WILLERSEY, Glos

The 6 bells of Willersey's Church of St Peter were re-cast from the original 3 in 1712 and rung the following year to celebrate the Treaty of Utrecht. Various medieval styles can be seen in the building itself. Willersey House was once a farmhouse in the village, but in 1912 was dismantled and rebuilt at the top of a hill in its present enlarged form and is now the Dormy House Hotel.

Later meet a T-junction and turn right on to the A44 into Broadway.

BROADWAY, Herefs & Worcs

Broadway's wide main street is lined with fine houses and pretty cottages built in Cotswold stone. St Eadburgha's Norman and later church is somewhat self-effacingly hidden away at one end of the community, and the 17th-century Lygon Arms coaching inn shows a narrow frontage to the street.

Drive to the end of the green and turn left on to an unclassified road to Snowshill. Ascend, then bear right into the village.

SNOWSHILL, Glos

Secluded Snowshill is a hillside village of ancient Cotswold cottages grouped round a handsome 19th-century church. Its manor house (NT) dates from the 16th century, but subsequent periods have left their marks in various alterations and additions. Inside are collections of clocks, toys, and musical instruments.

Continue to the church and turn left. Ascend to the top of the incline and meet crossroads. Go forward SP 'Chipping Campden, Broadway Tower'. After 1¾ miles turn left and proceed to Broadway Tower.

BROADWAY TOWER, Herefs & Worcs

Lady Coventry built this picturesque folly tower in the 18th century, and it now forms the nucleus of a 30-acre country park. Its lofty situation at over 1,000ft gives views over several counties, and in very clear weather it is possible to pick out such landmarks as Tewkesbury Abbey, Worcester Cathedral, and Warwick.

Continue for ½ mile, cross a main road with SP 'Mickleton', and after ¾ mile turn right. Continue for 2¼ miles and meet a T-junction. Turn right on to the B4081/B4035 for Chipping Campden.

Welford-on-Avon is a picturebook village set in a pastoral landscape.

CHIPPING CAMPDEN, Glos

Wool made Chipping Campden rich, and the handiwork of the merchants who prospered here can be seen in the fine gabled stone houses, the 14th-century Woolstaplers Hall, and the 15th-century wool church. Near the church are remains of the once-beautiful Campden House, whose owner burned it down in 1645 rather than see it fall into Parliamentarian hands.

Drive through the town and turn left with the B4081 SP 'Broad Campden'. After ¼ mile turn left again on to an unclassified road for Broad Campden.

BROAD CAMPDEN, Glos

Features of this village include an 18th-century Friends' Meeting House that has been restored and the much older Chapel House – a 12th-century chapel converted into a private dwelling.

Keep right through the village then bearing right before the climb to Blockley.

BLOCKLEY, Glos

Blockley's architecture follows the usual basic pattern for the area, with a high street of 18th- and 19th-century houses complementing a Norman church.

Turn left, continue for a short distance, then turn right on to the B4479. Proceed for 1¼ miles, meet a T-junction, and turn left on to the A44. Pass through Bourton-on-the-Hill.

BOURTON-ON-THE-HILL, Glos

A fine example of a Winchester bushel can be seen in Bourton's Norman and later church. The village itself stands on a hill and is made up of cottages standing in attractively-terraced gardens. Bourton House is of 18th-century date and has a superb 16th-century tithe barn.

Return to Moreton-in-Marsh.

Llyn Ogwen lies in a steep-sided valley cut millions of years ago by the immense glaciers which shaped the face of Snowdonia as we see it today. This majestic lake is the gateway to what is surely the most spectacular mountain pass in North Wales.

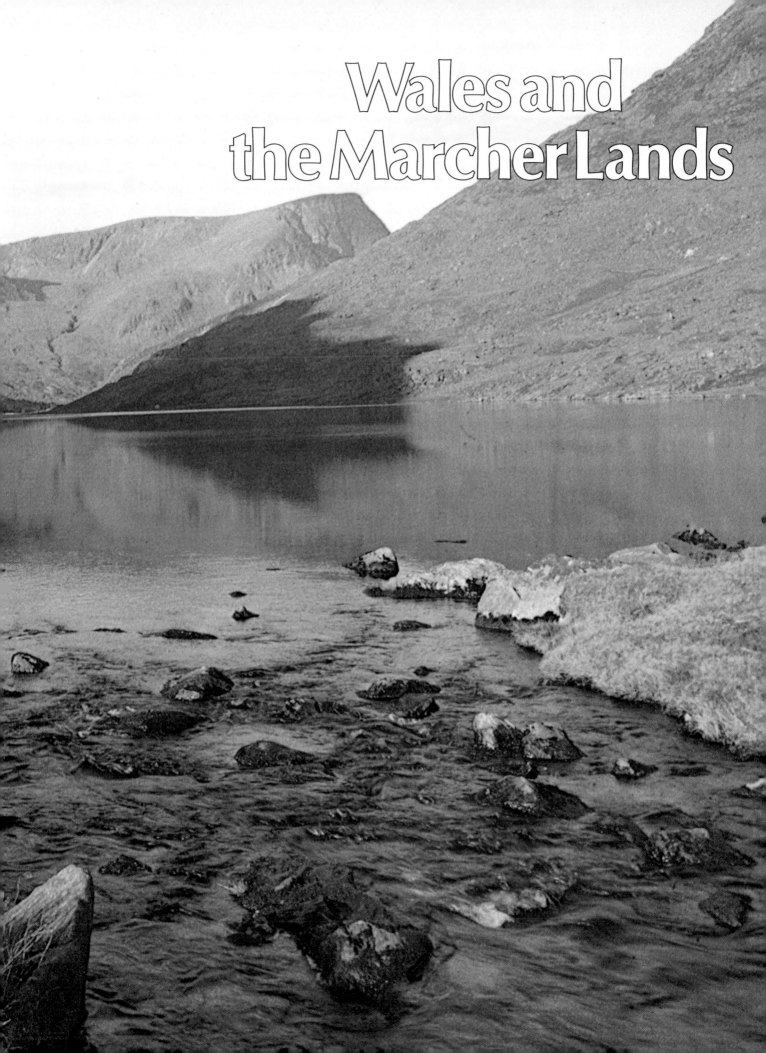

Wales and the Marcher Lands

CARDIFF, S Glam

Utilitarian in parts, though not depressingly so, Cardiff displays the mixture of dignity and pragmatism to be expected from the capital city and cultural centre of Wales. Massive expansion resulted in the city becoming the world's principal coal port by the start of the 20th century, but its present-day appearance is almost totally modern. One family particularly

BESIDE THE BRISTOL CHANNEL

For many centuries the Bristol Channel has admitted traders and invaders to the heartlands of the Severn Valley, and more recently it has provided a route for the export of Welsh coal. Picturesquely ruined castles recall troubled times; great harbours recall the industrial prosperity of the past.

considered to be one of architect William Butterfield's finest achievements. The Turner House Art Gallery, a branch of the National Museum, is in Plymouth Road.

At the roundabout take 2nd exit SP 'Sea Front' on to an unclassified road. Descend to the Esplanade and drive forward into Raisdale Road. Cross a railway bridge and at crossroads, turn left. After ¼ mile turn left on to the B4267 SP 'Sully, Barry'. After 1 mile a detour can be made by turning left on to the unclassified 'Swanbridge' road for Sully Island.

involved in the city's growth was the Butes, who built the vast docks, sank a fortune into the development of the city as a living and working community, and restored the castle. The latter, an appealing mixture of genuine period remains and 19th-century reconstruction, was the brainchild of the 3rd Marquess, working with the architect William Burges. Inside the perimeter walls the handsome Norman keep surmounts a motte surrounded by a defensive moat. In direct contrast, and well distant in a 'gothick' complex, are 19th-century living quarters that reveal the full expression of romantic medievalism so loved by Bute and the famous Burges. Cardiff's principal buildings stand quite close to the castle in Cathays Park and include the City Hall and County Hall, the University College and the National Museum of Wales. The Llandarf district north-west of the city centre can be reached through some of Cardiff's elegant parks. Here, in a village-like setting, is the city's cathedral, an historic building which was almost destroyed by the ravages of war but is now fully restored to its old splendour. Its south-east tower and spire form a delicate and familiar local landmark. Other features in the city include quaint Victorian arcades, the world famous Cardiff Arms Park Rugby Ground, the new St David's concert and conference hall, Welsh Industrial and Maritime Museum and the Bute Road Station Trust.

Leave Cardiff via the A4160 'Penarth' road. After 3 miles at a roundabout take 2nd exit, and at the next roundabout bear right to enter Penarth.

The Norman keep and later, 19th-century, buildings at Cardiff Castle stand within walls that date partly from Roman times.

Real gold adds splendour to the 19th-century buildings at Cardiff Castle.

mls 0   1   2   3   4   5
kms 0   2   4   6   8

Ogmore Castle was founded by a Norman knight called William de Londres.

PENARTH, S Glam

During the second half of the 19th century Penarth was adopted by well-to-do Victorians and transformed into a seaside resort. Gardens and lawns lend quiet charm to the pleasant atmosphere of the town, and the old harbour has found a new lease of life with water ski-ing and sailing enthusiasts. Dangerous currents make bathing hazardous. St Augustine's Church, on the headland, was built in 1865 and is

SWANBRIDGE, S Glam

At low tide Sully Island becomes accessible from here. Views from the island encompass much of the Bristol Channel and are constantly changing with the coming and going of sea traffic.

On the main route pass through Sully and in 1 mile turn left on to the A5055 and enter Barry. After 1 mile turn right under a railway bridge, then keep forward at ensuing roundabouts SP 'Barry Island'. Pass Barry Station, bear left, and shortly turn left to reach Barry Island.

BARRY, S Glam

In the 19th century Barry's population expanded from 500 to a staggering 12,665, and side by side with the development of docks that were to become among the largest in the world came the popularization of the Barry Island holiday resort. Park Road leads to Porthkerry Country Park, passing scant remains of Barry Castle on the way. Scrapped British Rail steam locomotives rust away in a metal breaker's yard here. Over 2,000 birds of prey can be seen at the Welsh Hawking Centre.

Return across the causeway and keep forward then ascend on the A4050 'Cardiff' road. In ½ mile at a roundabout take the 1st exit SP 'Cowbridge'. At the next roundabout take the 1st exit A4226 SP 'Llantwit Major'. After a mile turn left on to the unclassified 'Rhoose' road. In ¾ mile enter a roundabout and leave by the 1st exit. Cardiff (Wales) Airport to the right is the home of the Wales Aircraft Museum. Continue, with views left across the Bristol Channel through Rhoose, dominated by a cement works, to Aberthaw. After ¾ mile meet a T-junction and turn left on the the B4265. Cross the River Thaw and enter St Athan.

ST ATHAN, S Glam
Two 14th-century effigies and a window commemorating the coronation of George VI can be seen in St Athan's medieval church. An RAF airfield lies to the north-west.

Continue on the B4265 to Boverton, turn left on to an unclassified road, for Llantwit Major.

LLANTWIT MAJOR, S Glam
Once this quiet place was one of the most important and influential centres of learning in British Christendom. The school founded here by 5th century St Illtud attracted scholars from distant parts and fostered some of the greatest minds of early Welsh history. A faint echo of the foundation survives in the 13th- and 15th-century Church of St Illtud — a remarkable structure formed by two churches joined end to end. Inside are a richly-carved Jesse Tree, depicting Christ's descent from the line of David, and a collection of ancient stone crosses. Other features of the town include an old dovecote and monastery gateway, a 15th-century town hall, the Old Swann Inn, and the imposing Great House (open to the public on application).

Follow signs Bridgend and at the bypass roundabout take 1st exit rejoining the B4265. Pass through typical Vale of Glamorgan scenery to St Bride's Major. Turn left on to the B4524 'Southerndown' road, and continue to Southerndown.

SOUTHERNDOWN, M Glam
This small resort is a good starting point for exhilarating walks to Ogsmore-by-Sea or the windy

headland of Trwyn-y-Witch (Witches Nose). Curious blowholes and wave-carved caves are features of the local cliffs.

Continue to Ogmore-by-Sea.

OGMORE-BY-SEA, M Glam
Sandy beaches and pleasant cliff walks make this a pleasant Bristol Channel resort; at low tide a more sinister side is revealed in the shape of Tusker Rock — notorious cause of dozens of shipwrecks.

Continue past the Merthyr-Mawr Warren at the mouth of the Ogmore River to reach Ogmore Castle.

OGMORE CASTLE, M Glam
This Norman castle (AM), on the River Ewenny has a somewhat battered stone keep that is one of the earliest of its type.

CANDLESTON CASTLE, M Glam
A footpath and stepping stones across the River Ewenny lead from Ogmore Castle to the tree-shrouded and dilapidated remains of Candleston. During the 15th century it overlooked a wide fertile plain, which has since been overwhelmed by sand dunes.

Continue on the B4524. After 1½ miles meet a junction and turn left on to the B4265, passing the edge of Ewenny.

EWENNY, M Glam
In 1141 Maurice de Londres, of Ogmore Castle, founded a priory here. Its remains (AM) are in beautiful surroundings and comprise the virtually complete 13th-century circuit walls, fragments of various buildings, and a Norman church considered to be the finest of its kind in Wales. Massive defensive details are reminders of the precarious balance that existed between war and peace in medieval Wales.

Cross the Ewenny River and in 1 mile at the roundabout take 3rd exit SP 'Cardiff' on to the Bridgend Bypass A48. At the next roundabout take 2nd exit A473 SP 'Llantrisant' and in a further 1 mile at a roundabout take 2nd exit on to the B4181 SP 'Coity'. Go under the railway bridge then keep forward unclassified for Coity. Turn right on to the 'Bryncethin' road, and pass the entrance to Coity Castle.

COITY, M Glam
Coity Castle (AM) dominates the centre of its namesake village. Nearby St Mary's Church contains several interesting monuments, and features a beautiful east window made by William Morris' company.

Ascend with hill views and cross the M4. Descend to join the B4280, turn right SP 'Blackhill' on to the A4061 under a railway bridge, and bear right into Bryncethin. Continue along the wooded Ogmore Valley to Blackmill, and turn right on to the A4093 'Tonyrefail' road. Continue through farm and moorland scenery to the edge of Tonyrefail. Turn right on to the unclassified 'Thomastown, Llantrisant' road, and after 1¼ miles turn right again. In 1 mile at roundabout take 1st exit on to the A4119. Follow the Ely River, then pass Llantrisant Forest and enter Llantrisant.

LLANTRISANT, M Glam
Both church and castle command dominating hilltop sites above the steep attractive streets of Llantrisant. The Royal Mint was moved here in 1967.

Enter the roundabout in Llantrisant and take the 2nd exit on to the A4119 SP 'Cardiff'. After 1½ miles turn left SP 'Groes-faen'. Pass through Groes-faen and in 3 miles turn right on to an unclassified road SP 'St Fagan's'. In 1¾ miles enter St. Fagan's.

ST FAGAN'S, S Glam
Attractive thatched cottages and a waterside church are charming features of this River Ely village, but St Fagan's is best known for the amazing collection of buildings that has been gathered round its 16th-century castle to form the Welsh Folk Museum. Complete buildings of many different periods have been rescued from all over Wales and painstakingly rebuilt in the grounds. Even the furnished interiors are authentic, and in some cases the buildings still fulfil their original functions.

Turn left, following the river, then keep forward through the Cardiff suburbs to reach the city centre.

SWANSEA, W Glam

Almost three centuries of intensive industrialization have left scars upon the Swansea landscape. The lower Swansea Valley once presented a view of unparalleled devastation, but intensive land reclamation and landscaping is restoring the greenery. Not all of Swansea is built over or barren; over 900 acres of tended parkland bring the country into the city. Bombing during World War II flattened the town's centre and destroyed much of Swansea's tangible history, but scant remains of a 14th-century fortified manor house (AM) can be seen in Wind Street, and 15th-century St Mary's Church was rebuilt in 1955. In 1919 the former Technical College became a university which has since expanded to occupy several buildings in the town. There is a fine Civic Centre, a new Leisure Centre, and a Maritime Museum and Marina.

THE GOWER PENINSULA, W Glam

This small 18- by 5-mile peninsula contains some of the most unspoilt and beautiful scenery in South Wales. Cliffs fringing excellent beaches on the southern coast are considered to be among the finest in Britain, and the soft agricultural landsdcape of the interior is scored by numerous thickly-wooded valleys. Ancient remains point to the Gower's one-time colonization by the Celts and Romans, and reminders of later times are everywhere in the shapes of ruined castles.

Leave Swansea on the A4067 SP 'Mumbles'. Pass the university, and after 1¼ miles follow SP ahead for 'Mumbles'. After 1½ miles reach Oystermouth.

OYSTERMOUTH, W Glam

Picturesque Oystermouth Castle is a 13th-century ruin which occupies the summit of a small hill above a holiday and residential area.

Detour straight ahead on the B4433 to reach The Mumbles seaside resort.

THE MUMBLES, W Glam

In 1807 a horse-drawn tramway was opened between Swansea and The Mumbles as the first passenger-carrying railway in the world. The line was closed in 1960, but The Mumbles remains a popular resort offering a good beach, a pier, and the facilities for a variety of water-based leisure activities. Mumbles Head overlooking Bracelet Bay is a starting point for delightful coastal walks.

From Oystermouth turn right on to the B4593 SP 'Langland'. In ¼ mile reach the church and turn left, then in ½ mile meet crossroads and keep forward along an unclassified road. Descend to Langland Bay.

LANGLAND BAY, W Glam

A sandy beach and views which extend across the Bristol Channel to Somerset are the main features of this popular little bay.

SWANSEA AND THE GOLDEN GOWER

The counties of Glamorgan form an area of contrasts, where astonishing scenes of industrial dereliction rub shoulders with the rural and coastal beauty of the Gower Peninsula, the green lung of Swansea.

Drive to the carpark at Langland Bay and turn right into Brynfield Road. After ½ mile go forward on to the B4593 then turn left. Descend to pass Caswell Bay, then continue forward along an unclassified road and ascend inland. After ¾ mile meet a T-junction and turn left. Follow the road as it turns right to reach Bishopston.

BISHOPSTON, W Glam

An interesting old church survives in this village, but the main attraction here is the local scenery. Lovely Bishopston Valley leads down to Pwil-du Bay and Head, and marvellous cliff ranges extend along the coast (NT) to the west.

Leave Bishopston, and at the T-junction turn left on to the B4436 SP 'Port Eynon'. Drive through Kittle and after ½ mile turn right. After ¾ mile turn left on to the A4118 SP 'Parkmill and Port Eynon'. Continue to Parkmill.

Swansea Docks have their origin in the 14th century, when a charter confirmed the town's right to build ships.

Pennard Castle stands on a rocky outcrop amongst sand dunes near Parkmill.

PARKMILL, W Glam
Ilston Stream flows through Parkmill and continues past the ruins of Pennard Castle to its outlet at beautiful Threecliff Bay (NT). Extensive wind-sculpted sand-dunes hereabouts are known to have buried two churches and threatened to engulf the castle. Near by is the prehistoric Parc Le Breos tomb.

PARC LE BREOS BURIAL CHAMBER, W Glam
This fine example of megalithic tomb architecture (AM) can be reached on foot along a path from Parkmill.

Continue through Penmaen and pass the ridge of 609ft Cefn Bryn on the right. Several paths afford access to this eminence, which makes a fine viewpoint. After 1¾ miles reach the gatehouse of Penrice Castle.

PENRICE CASTLE, W Glam
Open only by written application, ruined Penrice Castle dates from the 13th century and was built to replacve an earlier structure which occupied the mound near Penrice Church.

Turn left here on to the unclassified Oxwich road. Descend through pleasant woods to marshland behind Oxwich Bay.

OXWICH BAY, W Glam
Sand-dunes and marshlands behind Oxwich Bay comprise a large National Nature Reserve which protects a wide variety of flora and fauna. Access is restricted to permit holders, but Oxwich Bay itself has superb sands and excellent scenery that can be enjoyed by anyone.

Continue into Oxwich.

OXWICH, W Glam
Thatched and whitewashed cottages more suggestive of England than South Wales are a feature of Oxwich, and the pleasant local church stands shaded by sycamores at the village edge. Inside the church is the lovely de la Mare tomb, installed by the Norman rooted family who once owned Oxwich Castle (AM). The castle was rebuilt as a Tudor manor house in 1541, but still incorporates relics from the original 14th-century stronghold. At time of publication the structure was closed for repairs.

Drive to the crossroads in Oxwich and turn right. After ½ mile reach a T-junction and turn right SP 'Horton'. After ¾ mile reach another T-junction and turn left SP 'Horton'. After 1½ miles meet crossroads and continue straight across. In ¾ mile turn left on oto the A4118 and descend to Port Eynon.

PORT EYNON, W Glam
Situated at the bottom of a steep hill and noted as a surfing centre, Port Eynon preserves several thatched cottages and lies east of breathtaking

cliff scenery (NT). The churchyard has a fine memorial statue of a lifeboatman.

Return along the A4118 from Port Eynon and after 1¾ miles reach Scurlage. Turn left on to the B4247 and continue to Rhossili, below Rhossili Down.

RHOSSILI AND RHOSSILI DOWN, W Glam
Golden sand stretches round the whole 3-mile arc of Rhossili Bay from spectacular Worm's Head (NT), where there is a large sea-bird colony. Behind the village is Rhossili Down (NT), which rises to 632ft and is known for its distinctive flora.

Return along the B4247 to Scurlage and turn left on to the A4118. After 1 mile go forward along an unclassified road SP 'Burry' and reach Llanddewi.

LLANDDEWI, W Glam
Features of this tiny village are the Gower Farm Museum, a primitive little church which preserves an ancient font and slight remains of a Tudor castle.

Continue, passing through Burry to reach Burry Green. Here turn left for Llangennith.

LLANGENNITH, W Glam
During the 6th century St Cenydd founded a monastery here. This was adopted by Norman monks in the 12th century, and today a few remains of its buildings are preserved in the structures of College Farm. The nearby church is sited on a sloping green and displays the best example of a saddle back-roofed tower in the Gower Peninsula. Llanmadoc Hill, affords excellent views.

Return along the 'Burry Green' road. After 1½ miles turn left SP 'Llanmadoc'. In 1½ miles, just beyond the right turn for Cheriton and slightly off the route, is Llanmadoc village.

LLANMADOC, W Glam
Situated below an Iron-Age fort on the slopes of Llanmadoc Hill this small village has a medieval church displaying many interesting features, not the least of which is a triangular door. Nearby are the wild and wind-haunted expanses of Whiteford Burrows (NT).

On the main route turn right into Cheriton.

CHERITON, W. Glam
David Davis, a former rector, executed much of the woodwork displayed in the local church. Many ancient features are preserved in the structure of the tiny 13th-century building itself.

From Cheriton continue east to Weobley Castle.

WEOBLEY CASTLE W Glam
Medieval Weobley Castle (AM) overlooks Llanrhidian Marsh from a

Planned additions to 14th-century Weobley Castle were never built because of financial difficulties.

lovely setting that belies its war-like function. It was built during the 13th and 14th centuries, and later rebuilt as a fortified manor house.

Continue through Old Walls and enter Llanrhidian.

LLANRHIDIAN, W Glam
A mysteriously-carved stone stands in the church porch here, and near by are two ancient upright stones of equally enigmatic purpose. Llanrhidian Marshes (NT), more typical of East Anglia than Wales, are rich in wildlife.

At the end of the village a detour to Reynoldston can be made by turning right on to the B4271 SP 'Swansea'. After 1¼ miles turn right on to an unclassified road and climb over Cefn Bryn to Reynoldston.

The outline of Worm's Head resembles a recumbent dragon.

REYNOLDSTON AND ARTHUR'S STONE, W Glam
Reynoldston's Victorian church stands on the west flank of the Cefn Bryn ridge and contains various 17th- and 18th-century monuments. Arthur's Stone, on the ridge of Cefn Bryn, is a prehistoric tomb covered by an enormous capstone.

Return to Llanrhidian and turn right on to the B4295. Pass through Crofty to enter Penclawdd.

PENCLAWDD, W Glam
Cockle gathering on the nearby sands is a traditional occupation of the Penclawdd women, but the famous pony-drawn carts on which they carried their spoils are not as much in evidence as they were before the last war.

Continue to Gowerton. Meet crossroads and go forward, then bear right on to the B4296. Reach Dunvant and turn left into the suburbs of Swansea. Follow SP 'Swansea' to Killay and turn left on to the A4118. Continue through Sketty to Swansea town centre.

ON THE BLACK MOUNTAIN

Infinite shades of green colour this tour: pale hillsides rise from ruined Talley Abbey; lush farmland borders the winding Afon Tywi; and the light-shifting subtlety of moorland sedges surrounds the giant Llyn Brianne Reservoir and climbs the Black Mountain.

LLANDEILO, Dyfed
This riverside market town stands amid rich farming land and is a good centre for fishing and touring. Many places of interest exist in the surrounding area. A 19th-century stone bridge in the town arches over the River Tywi in a magnificent single span of 145ft. Llandeilo's church, virtually rebuilt between 1848 and 1851, contains two attractive cross heads of Celtic origin.

Leave Llandeilo on the A40 'Llandovery' road and in ¼ mile reach the B4302 turnoff on the left. This may be taken as a detour to picturesque Talley by turning left SP 'Talley' and driving 6 miles through the hamlets of Maerdy and Hallway.

TALLEY, Dyfed
Neat cottages and an attractive church protectively cluster round the remains of once-famous Talley Abbey (AM) deep in the green folds of the Dyfed hills. Little of the abbey's 12th-century fabric has survived pillaging for building material that has gone on unchecked through the centuries, but an undeniable air of sanctity still exists. A path through the yard of the adjacent church leads to the two lakes of Talley, where clouds of dragonflies hover over the placid waters during the summer months.

On the main route continue along the A40 and pass through pleasant hill scenery to Llandovery.

LLANDOVERY, Dyfed
Llandovery's name means 'Church amid the waters' and derives from its position at the confluence of the Bran, Gwydderig, and Tywi. The town has been a place of some significance at least since Roman

times, a fact highlighted by the siting of Llanfair-ar-y-Bryn Church within the ramparts of a Roman fort. Roman tiles are incorporated in the fabric of the church. A monument to William Williams, a local man who is most remembered as being the composer of the hymn *Guide Me O Thou Great Jehovah* stands in the churchyard. Another notable inhabitant of Llandovery was Rhys Pritchard, who wrote a collection of simple verses collectively called *The Welshman's Candle*. This work became as popular in Wales as Bunyan's *Pilgrim's Progress* did in

England. A reminder of the town's important connexions with cattle droving is the building which houses Lloyd's Bank. Until 1909 this was the Black Ox Bank, founded in 1799 by a drover named David Jones. The nearby Market Hall is a low 19th-century building capped by an extraordinary pepper-pot turret. Llandovery College, a public school founded in 1848, was created for the express purpose of providing an education entirely in the Welsh language. Overgrown remains of a Norman castle surmount a mound above the cattle market.

Coarse grass and moorland sedges blanket the undulating ridges of the Black Mountain, which is traversed by twisting mountain roads.

Rhys ap Gruffydd founded Talley Abbey during the 12th century.

Drive over the level crossing in Llandovery and turn left on to the A483 SP 'Builth Wells'. In ¼ mile meet crossroads and turn left on to the unclassified 'Llyn Brianne' road. One mile farther reach the bridge by Dolauhirion.

DOLAUHIRION BRIDGE, Dyfed
Designed by William Edwards and built in 1773, this splendid bridge spans the Tywi in a single graceful arch of 84ft.

Continue through increasingly spectacular scenery, with Crychan Forest behind a high ridge to the east.

CRYCHAN FOREST, Dyfed & Powys
This large forest is named after the little Afon Crychan. The forest itself extends almost from Llandovery to Llanwrtyd Wells and is bounded in the east by the moorland of Mynydd Eppynt.

About 1¾ miles from Dolauhirion pass a left turn from the main tour rout which leads to Cilycwm village.

Beautiful Dolauhirion Bridge spans the Afon Tywi north of Llandovery.

CILYCWM, Dyfed
Situated in one of the tributary valleys of the Tywi, Cilycwm is surrounded by some of the wildest scenery in South Wales and is noted for the old wall paintings in its 15th-century church. The village chapel is claimed to be the first Methodist meeting place to have existed in Wales.

Continue through Rhandirmwyn on the main route. Three miles on the left is a signposted footpath leading to Twm Sion Catti's Cave.

TWM SION CATTI'S CAVE, Dyfed
A short nature trail up Dinas Hill leads to the one-time hideout of Twm Sion Catti, a famous early 16th-century outlaw whose modern reputation has a lot in common with England's tales of Robin Hood.

Continue through a wooded gorge to reach the carpark and viewing area at Llyn Brianne Reservoir. A narrow but excellently surfaced road may be taken through magnificent scenery to the reservoir's farthest arm and Towy Forest.

LLYN BRIANNE RESERVOIR, Dyfed & Powys
The creation of this huge reservoir in the early 1970s was greeted with mixed emotions, as the area flooded had previously been considered one of the most remote and beautiful in Wales – if not all Britain. New roads to the lake have made it easily accessible, and the spectacular scenery that surrounds its great expanse can be enjoyed by all. The last British nesting sites of the kite exist in closely-guarded and highly-secret locations in this area.

TOWY FOREST,
TOWY FOREST, Dyfed & Powys
On the northern slopes of Llyn Brianne, accessible via the new reservoir road, are the coniferous ranks of Towy Forest. The Afon Tywi has its source some miles north in the wild moors of central Wales.

Return along the Llyn Brianne access road to the crossroads at Llandovery. Turn right on to the A483 and then left on to the A40 SP 'Brecon'. In ¼ mile turn right on to the A4069, SP 'Llangadog', and continue along the Tywi Valley to reach Llangadog.

LLANGADOG, Dyfed
Llangadog was once an important town, with a 12th-century native Welsh castle unusual in that it was probably using defensive techniques learned from the Norman conquerors. The overlords, ever wary of opposition, completely destroyed it in 1277. All that remains today is a mound sited about ½ mile south of the village. Carn Goch, the largest iron-age hillfort in Wales, lies 3 miles south-west at OS SN689243.

At the T-junction turn left, SP 'Brynamman'. Follow the pretty Afon Sawdde Valley with the river on the left and ascend on to the slopes of the Black Mountain. Continue to the 1,600ft viewpoint.

BLACK MOUNTAIN, Dyfed
West from the A4069 viewpoint the Black Mountain falls away in ridges to the fertile Tywi Valley. In the middle distance Carreg Cennen Castle can be seen perched on its craggy limestone cliff, and to the east the grass-covered peaks of 1,987ft Foel Fraith and 2,076ft Gareg Las rise against a long backdrop provided by the ridge of Bannau Sir Gaerfyrddin – The Carmarthen Van. Geologically the Black Mountain is made up of very ancient red sandstone in the north and younger millstone grit in the south, the two beds being separated by a band of limestone. It is a lonely windswept land inhabited only by sheep and a thriving population of indigenous wild animals.

Descend, with views over a partly industrial area, to Brynamman. Turn right for Gwaun-cae-gurwen. On the nearside of the ensuing level crossing turn right again on to the A474 SP 'Ammanford'. Drive through Garnant and Glanaman to Ammanford.

AMMANFORD, Dyfed
Until the late 19th century the Cross Inn at the centre of this town was almost the only building here, but discovery of a local anthracite coalfield quickly brought the mixed blessing of industrial prosperity. Nowadays the area is dotted with slag heaps from the workings, but the essentially agricultural character of the local countryside remains.

At traffic signals turn right on to the A483 SP 'Llandeilo'. Proceed to Llandybie.

LLANDYBIE, Dyfed
This small town stands on the edge of the local coalfield and is justifiably proud of its splendid early Victorian railway station. The church preserves a medieval barrel roof and carries an imposing battlemented tower. Inside are a number of interesting monuments. A lane leads east from Llandybie to beautiful river scenery and the waterfall of Glynhir.

Associated in legend with one of King Arthur's knights, Carreg Cennen Castle is perched dramatically on a limestone cliff overlooking the Black Mountain.

Continue to Ffairfach. A slight detour for splendid Carreg Cennen Castle can be made from here by taking a right turn on to an unclassified road, then turning right again and ascending. Follow the subsequent descent and keep left at the edge of Trapp.

CARREG CENNEN CASTLE, Dyfed
No description of this most romantic of castles can better that given by A C Bradley, who wrote: 'It looks for all the world like an Arthurian Castle one might see in dreams. . . .' A steep approach via a farmyard leads to the imposing pile of walls and turrets perched on a limestone cliff which drops a breathtaking 200ft into the attractive valley below. The existing building fabric dates from the 13th century, but a fortress existed here long before that. The atmosphere of permanence about the castle inspired Dylan Thomas to refer to it reverently, in the prayers of one of his characters, as 'Carreg Cennen, King of Time'.

Return to Ffairfach on the main route and continue to Llandeilo with views to the left of Dinefwr Castle.

DINEFWR CASTLE, Dyfed
As Llandeilo is approached from the south, the ivy-clad tower of a castle can be seen rising from trees on a hill directly west of the town. This is Dinefwr (Dynevor) Castle (AM), which was once the seat of Welsh princes. Ruins comprising the keep and part of the curtain wall are situated in a private park near a 19th-century mansion. The ruins will be open to the public when necessary repairs are completed.

Llyn Brianne serves as a storage reservoir for the Afon Tywi water supply scheme.

THE STONEHENGE QUARRY

Between placid Cardigan and bustling Fishguard is a jagged coast backed by the craggy, rock-strewn block of Mynydd Prescelly. In prehistoric times the great bluestones of Wiltshire's Stonehenge were hewn from these slopes and somehow hauled to Salisbury Plain.

FISHGUARD & GOODWICK, Dyfed

Lower Town, as the oldest part of Fishguard is called, is a delightfully unspoilt fishing village. It was chosen as the setting for the film version of Dylan Thomas' *Under Milk Wood*, and is connected to Upper Town by a steep hill. The square in Upper Town features a Market Hall and the attractive Royal Oak Inn. During the 18th century Fishguard witnessed the signing of a treaty that ended the last invasion of British soil. In reality the so-called 'invasion' was a fiasco perpetrated by a motley band of French soldiers and convicts bent on pillage. Unable to reach and destroy Bristol, which had been their mission, they landed at Carregwastad Bay and quickly discovered large amounts of alcohol from a recent shipwreck. Incapably drunk, the invaders were easily captured by the local militia – aided (it is said) by stout-hearted Welsh women dressed in traditional costumes that the French took to be soldiers' uniforms. Goodwick, almost joined to Fishguard, is a resort with sandy beaches; it is also the embarkation point for one of the principal ferry services to Eire. East and west of Fishguard is the breathtaking seaboard and shore scenery of the Pembrokeshire Coast National Park.

PEMBROKESHIRE COAST NATIONAL PARK (NORTH), Dyfed

Two outstanding features of the northern part of this superb national park are its grand coastal scenery and its rugged upland typified by the Mynydd Prescelly range. Pencaer Peninsula, to the west of Fishguard, is characterized by a wind-torn landscape and precipitous cliffs that make it as daunting as it is exhilarating. Much of Pencaer Peninsula and the northern part of Mynydd Prescelly are made up of volcanic rocks, but farther east at Dinas Head and Cemaes Head are gentler sedimentary rocks from a less traumatic period of the earth's history. National Park information is available in Fishguard.

Leave Fishguard by the A487 'Cardigan' road. Descend from Upper to Lower Town with views across the old harbour to Fishguard Bay. Continue to Dinas.

DINAS, Dyfed

This small village features the handsome Tabor Chapel and is connected to the cove and cliff

scenery of Dinas Island by several little roads and footpaths. The 'island' is isolated only in name nowadays, but at the end of the ice age it was separated from the mainland by a true channel. The local church, at Cwm-yr-eglwys, was built in 1860 after its predecessor was destroyed in a violent storm. The cove here is considered one of the most beautiful in Wales and the tip of the headland falls away in the impressive 500ft cliffs of Dinas Head. Strange impressions found on a slab of rock here are traditionally held to be the Devil's footprints. Seals are very numerous along the coast. Pwllgwaelod, on the west side of Dinas Island, is a quiet bay with an old lime kiln and an inn.

Continue on the A487 for 1½ miles to reach Cerrig-y-Gof.

CERRIG-Y-GOF, Dyfed

Overgrown though this important prehistoric monument may be, it is worth exploring because it is the only one of its kind in England and Wales. It is in a field off the main A458 road (OS ref SN037389), and comprises the remains of five rectangular burial chambers set in a circle. The name can be translated into English as 'Blacksmith's Stones'.

Continue on the A487 to Newport.

NEWPORT, Dyfed

Ever since the 13th century, when this pretty little town received its first charter, the Lord (or Lady) Marchers of Cemais have had the right to select the town mayor. Remains of the original Norman castle were incorporated into a mansion during the 19th century. Newport, as its name implies, was once an important seaport, but today its main function seems to be as a quiet resort taking full advantage of its superb sands. To the west lies Parrog, which once received coastal trade at a quay whose crumbling remains are

Once a haven for small fishing boats, picturesque Fishguard Harbour, situated in Lower Town, now provides safe anchorage for holiday craft.

still visible. Newport is surrounded by reminders of man's prehistoric past, including the remains of an iron-age fort above the town on the peak of Carningli, and a cromlech called Carreg Coetan Arthur, upstream from Gwaun bridge.

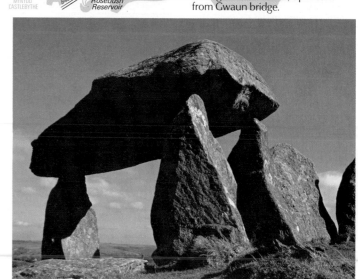

The huge stones which make up the distinctive outline of Pentre Ifan burial chamber were originally covered by a large cairn that has long since disappeared.

By tradition the first cuckoo of spring sings from Nevern's ancient cross.

Continue on the A487 for 2 miles and meet crossroads. Turn left on to the B4582, drive through woodlands, and cross the Afon Nyfer to enter Nevern.

NEVERN, Dyfed
Not only is Nevern one of the most attractive and beautifully-set villages in Wales, it is also the guardian of a great treasure in the shape of a Celtic cross which stands outside the local church. Almost 13ft high and carved with intricate patterns, the cross carries a number of obscure inscriptions that have never been deciphered. Also in the churchyard is an avenue of Irish yews leading to the rugged old building itself, which contains other carved stones. One of the trees exudes a blood-like sap and is known as the 'Bleeding Yew'.

Follow the 'Cardigan' road B4582 between high banks for 5 miles, then meet the A487 and turn left. Descend into Cardigan with panoramic views. Shortly before entering the town the route allows a detour to be made to St Dogmaels via a left turn on the B4546.

ST DOGMAELS, Dyfed
The old Welsh county of Cardiganshire was named after the influential Ceredig, whose descendant St Dogmael founded a hermitage here in the 6th century. The abbey was established in 1115 by Robert Fitz-Martin, Lord of Cemais, and the ruins (AM) that survive today comprise fragments dating from the 14th to 16th centuries. A collection of carved stones is housed on the site of the former abbey infirmary, and other examples may be seen in the adjoining 19th-century parish church. One of these, known as the Sagranus Stone, was inscribed in both Latin and Ogham and proved an invaluable key to mid-19th-century historians working to decipher the ancient Ogham script. The road to St Dogmaels can be followed beyond the village to the excellent beach at Poppit Sands. Good walks from here lead through lovely countryside to the wild cliffs of Cemaes Head.

Enter Cardigan.

CARDIGAN, Dyfed
Poets of all periods have waxed lyrical over the beautiful Afon Teifi, which flows into the sea at Cardigan. The salmon and sea trout that thrive in its tree-shaded waters are fished for from coracles, small traditional craft that have continued to use the river while relative newcomers have been forced elsewhere by the silting of Cardigan's port. The town is no longer of maritime significance, but the observant visitor will find many reminders of its sea-faring past. A fine 17th-century 6-arched bridge spans the Teifi beneath the remains of a Norman castle. Cardigan nowadays has a mainly Victorian character and appearance typified by its notable 19th-century guildhall, the venue for a regular market held among its basement arches.

Recross the Teifi bridge and in ¼ mile branch left on to the A478 'Tenby' road. After 2 miles note a left turn leading to fascinating Cilgerran Castle.

CILGERRAN, Dyfed
Legions of artists have been inspired by the craggy situation and romantic air of Cilgerran Castle. The Afon Teifi, itself the subject of poetry and song, flows beneath the castle walls and once a year is the scene of competitive bustle and the display of ancient skills in a picturesque coracle regatta. The pretty little village of Cilgerran is somewhat overshadowed by its 13th-century guardian (AM). North of the village is the Cardigan Wildlife Park.

On the main route proceed along the A478. After 3 miles turn right on to the B4332 'Fishguard' road and continue with fine views of the Prescelly Mountains. Drive into Eglwyswrw.

EGLWYSWRW, Dyfed
In medieval times the body of St Wrw was entombed in a chantry chapel of the local church, after which the parishioners would allow nobody else to be buried there because they believed that the virgin saint 'would not have any bedfellows' – even in death.

Meet a T-junction and turn left on to the A487 SP 'Fishguard'. After ¾ mile turn left again on the B4329 SP 'Haverfordwest' and drive to Crosswell. Here a detour can be made to Pentre Ifan burial chamber; turn right on to an unclassified road and follow a stretch of the wooded Afon Nyfer, then in 1½ miles turn left.

PENTRE IFAN BURIAL CHAMBER, Dyfed
Undoubtedly one of the finest megalithic monuments in Britain, Pentre Ifan (AM) stands on a slope overlooking vast tracts of the Pembrokeshire National Park and the distant waters of Cardigan Bay. To the west is 1,138ft Mynydd Carningli, on which St Brynach is said to have been ministered to by

Nest, whose beauty was legendary in medieval Wales, was abducted from Cilgerran Castle by one of her admirers.

angels. The monument itself consists of a 16-ton capstone supported by three spindly uprights and is thought to be some 5,000 years old.

On the main route, continue along the B4329. Climb steadily on to high moorland and reach a 1,328ft road summit. This viewpoint affords fine panoramas of the Mynydd Prescelly range.

MYNYDD PRESCELLY, Dyfed
Gentle moorland slopes dotted with outcrops of stone typify the scenery of Mynydd Prescelly, an ancient mountain range which culminates in 1,760ft Foel Cwmcerwyn east of the B4329. Beyond Foel Cwmcerwyn and 1,531ft Foel Feddau is 1,200ft Foeldrygarn, whose slopes are said to have provided the famous blue stones of Stonehenge, in Wiltshire.

The slopes of Mynydd Prescelly rise to rock-strewn summits from 1,535ft Foeleryr.

Descend to Greenway and crossroads at the New Inn. Opposite is Rosebush Reservoir.

ROSEBUSH RESERVOIR, Dyfed
Completed in 1932, this reservoir holds 170 million gallons and is an excellent leisure amenity for fishing and boating enthusiasts.

Turn right on to the B4313 'Fishguard' road. After 1 mile pass an unclassified right turn leading to the delightful countryside of the Gwaun Valley.

GWAUN VALLEY, Dyfed
Words like magical, secret and enchanting come easily to mind when describing the Gwaun Valley. Its little river flows through a thickly-wooded coomb, which rises on the northern side to the lower slopes of the Prescelly Mountains.

Return to Fishguard on the B4313, passing through attractive countryside.

WESTERN BAYS

Retired seamen favour the quiet towns and villages of Cardigan Bay, and their neat cottages fit in well with the pastel shades of the omnipresent Welsh chapels. Inland is neat farming country crossed by small streams that suddenly waken into angry rapids and waterfalls.

LAMPETER, Dyfed

Neat rectangular fields bounded by hedges cover the gentle hills around Lampeter like a giant patchwork quilt. The town itself preserves a distinctive Welsh character coloured by its own personality. Small shops interspersed with dapper private houses, two Georgian hotels, and a proud Victorian town hall occupy the main street under the eye of the parish church. The latter was rebuilt in 1869, but contains memorials from earlier ages. Lampeter is best known for St David's College, which was founded in 1822 so that Welsh students (prohibited by expense from attending Oxford or Cambridge) could acquire a university education. The founder was Thomas Burgess, Bishop of St David's and the son of a Hampshire grocer. Although integrated with the University of Wales in 1971, the college remains a complete university in miniature.

Leave Lampeter on the A482 SP 'Aberaeron'. Drive through pleasant hill country and join the Aeron Valley at the combined villages of Felin Fach and Ystrad Aeron. Continue with the river through wooded country to reach Aberaeron.

ABERAERON, Dyfed

Lampeter is not alone in being connected with that most English of counties, Hampshire. At the turn of the 18th century an Aberaeron heiress called Susannah Jones married a widowed Hampshire curate. Some years later the couple inherited a fortune and commenced to plan and build Aberaeron. The Development, which included the construction of harbours, quays, stores, a town hall, and numerous dwellings, continued well into the middle of the 19th century and resulted in an extremely pleasing Georgian-style town with a charm enhanced by the Welsh habit of highlighting architectural details with brightly-coloured paint. Aberaeron's days as a busy seaport are long gone, and today it performs a useful service as an elegant and unspoilt holiday resort.

Leave Aberaeron on the A487 'Aberystwyth' road. Drive through Aberarth, with glimpses of coastal scenery to the left, and continue to Llanon.

LLANON, Dyfed

Memories of Dylan Thomas' *Under Milk Wood* are awoken here. Like the setting for that famous play, the village seems to be a retirement place for old sea captains with shipshape little cottages named after the craft they once commanded. Llanon is certainly of the sea and grew from the nearby fishing village of Llansantffraid, where the remains of fish traps said to have been constructed by the monks of Strata Florida Abbey can still be seen in places on the beach.

Continue to Llanrhystud.

LLANRHYSTUD, Dyfed

No less than three castle mounds, the best of which is Caer Penrhos, survive near this attractive 19th-century village.

Climb inland and descend through Llanfarian to the Ystwyth Valley. Continue through Rhyd-y-Felin and later cross the Afon Rheidol into Aberystwyth.

ABERYSTWYTH, Dyfed

Seat of government and a holiday resort with a shopping area that serves a large locality, Aberystwyth grew to real importance with the establishment of its Norman castle by Edmund Crouchback in 1277. It is still a place of significance, and opposite the ruins of the castle is a Victorian hotel building that was bought in 1870 to form the nucleus of the University of Wales. Modern university buildings stand east of the town on Penglais Hill and include the National Library of Wales, which houses an incomparable collection of early Welsh manuscripts. Also of interest are the varied exhibits of the Ceredigion Museum. Notable among the many superb 18th- and 19th-century buildings preserved in the town are the fine houses that stand in Laura Place. A Victorian funicular railway operates on Constitution Hill, and echoes from the more distant past are evoked by the well-preserved iron-age earthworks that lie south of the town on Pen Dinas. The church at Llanbadarn Fawr — now a suburb of Aberystwyth — was founded in the 6th century by St Padarn, but the building that now occupies the site dates from the 13th century. Two beautiful Celtic crosses are preserved inside.

VALE OF RHEIDOL LIGHT RAILWAY, Dyfed

British Rail's only narrow gauge line uses steam locomotives along 12 miles of the lovely Rheidol Valley between Aberystwyth and the spectacular Devil's Bridge. Originally opened in 1902 to carry local lead ore and the occasional passenger, the line's route through the breathtaking scenery of the 'Vale' has ensured success as a major tourist attraction and probably assured its future as a centre for steam-engine nostalgia.

To leave Aberystwyth, return over Afon Rheidol on the A487 SP 'Cardigan' and after 1¼ miles branch left on to the A4120 'Devil's Bridge' road. Climb steadily, pass through Capel Seion, then 5 miles beyond the latter reach a 990ft road summit affording splendid views into the thickly-wooded Rheidol Valley. Continue to Devil's Bridge.

DEVIL'S BRIDGE, Dyfed

A spectacular wooded gorge, tremendous waterfalls, and three bridges stacked on top of each other in a 700-year sequence are to be seen here.

Leave Devil's Bridge on the B4343 'Tregaron' road. Continue through hilly country and descend into the Ystwyth Valley. Cross a river and enter Pontrhydygroes.

PONTRHYDYGROES, Dyfed

The neat cottages in this village were once occupied by employees of the important local lead-mining industry. Ruins of the mine buildings stand empty and useless on the surrounding hillsides — a comment on 'robber' mineral industries.

Continue, and at the post office bear right on to an unclassified road SP 'Trawscoed'. Drive along a thickly-wooded valley and pass the Tyn-y-Bedw picnic site. After a short distance turn left on to the B4340 and proceed to Ystrad Meurig.

Whitewashed farm buildings dotted amongst gentle hills typify the countryside of old Cardiganshire.

This staunch little steam engine was specially built for the Vale of Rheidol Railway in 1902.

Little remains of once-powerful Strata Florida Abbey, except a beautiful doorway and these medieval floor tiles.

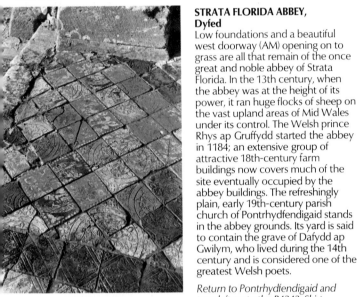

STRATA FLORIDA ABBEY, Dyfed

Low foundations and a beautiful west doorway (AM) opening on to grass are all that remain of the once great and noble abbey of Strata Florida. In the 13th century, when the abbey was at the height of its power, it ran huge flocks of sheep on the vast upland areas of Mid Wales under its control. The Welsh prince Rhys ap Gruffydd started the abbey in 1184; an extensive group of attractive 18th-century farm buildings now covers much of the site eventually occupied by the abbey buildings. The refreshingly plain, early 19th-century parish church of Pontrhydfendigaid stands in the abbey grounds. Its yard is said to contain the grave of Dafydd ap Gwilym, who lived during the 14th century and is considered one of the greatest Welsh poets.

Return to Pontrhydfendigaid and turn left on to the B4343. Skirt Tregaron Bog.

YSTRAD MEURIG, Dyfed

The now closed St John's College had been a famous educational establishment since the mid-18th century. Also of interest here are the slight remains of a Norman castle.

Continue to Caradog Falls, with the extensive Tregaron Bog to the right.

CARADOG FALLS, Dyfed

These picturesque falls are situated on a tributary stream of the Afon Teifi, just south of the tour route.

Continue to Pontrhydfendigaid.

PONTRHYDFENDIGAID, Dyfed

A quaint old bridge spans the Teifi here. Once a year the village is the venue of a popular and well-endowed eisteddfod – a traditional Welsh festival of poetry and music.

Leave Pontrhydfendigaid on the B4343 'Tregaron' road. Cross the Afon Teifi and shortly turn left on to an unclassified road for a detour to Strata Florida Abbey.

TREGARON BOG (CORS TREGARON), Dyfed

The 1,898-acre extent of this National Nature Reserve makes it the largest peat bog in Wales. In spring it is loud with the cries of curlew and plover, in summer it is white with the fluffy tufts of bog cotton grass, and in winter its sedges turn the glowing red that must have inspired its full Welsh name – 'Cors Goch Glanteifi', or the 'Red Bog Along the Teifi'.

Continue to Tregaron.

TREGARON, Dyfed

Dominating the square of this unspoilt Welsh town is a bright-green statue of Henry Richard. Born in 1812, he became the Liberal MP for Merthyr and was such an outspoken supporter of disarmament that he became known as the 'Apostle of Peace'. The church of St Caron dates basically from the 14th century, but was restored during the 19th century. On Tuesdays Tregaron fulfils its prime function as a market town and fills with farmers, traders and sheep.

Leave Tregaron with SP 'Llanddewi Brefi, B4343'. Drive along the Teifi Valley to reach Llanddewi Brefi.

LLANDDEWI BREFI, Dyfed

A great synod was held here in AD 519 to debate the *Heresy of Pelagius*, which denied the biblical doctrine of original sin. One of those refuting Pelagius was St David, beneath whom the ground is said to have risen so that those around could hear what he was saying. The village's 13th-century church stands on a mound which tradition holds to be the same miraculous eminence that provided the saint with his vantage point. Several interesting old stones can be seen inside the church.

Continue on the B4343 SP 'Lampeter' to reach Llanfair Clydogau.

LLANFAIR CLYDOGAU, Dyfed

Sarn Helen, a Roman road, passes through this scattered little parish. The local church stands within a circular graveyard and contains a strangely-carved font. Other features of the village include a handsome bridge and an elegant chapel.

Drive through Cellan, and within 2 miles meet a junction. Turn right on to the A482 and return to Lampeter.

Aberaeron's brightly painted Georgian cottages overlook Cardigan Bay.

AMONG THE BEACONS

High moorland that sweeps north from the industrial valleys of South Wales culminates in the sandstone peaks of the Brecon Beacons. Huge reservoirs built to satisfy industry lie to the south, and the crumbling towers of castles rise above the woodlands of the Usk Valley.

BRECON, Powys

Streets lined with Georgian and Jacobean houses add much to the beauty and character of Brecon, a mid-Wales town that was raised to the status of cathedral city in 1923. It is an ideal centre from which to explore the Brecon Beacons National Park. The cathedral is situated on the northern outskirts and was originally the church of a Benedictine priory. Dating mainly from the 13th and 14th centuries, the building is cruciform in plan and displays a number of outstanding architectural features. Several priory buildings, including a fine tithe barn, have been restored. A charming walk extends along the banks of the Afon Honddu beyond the cathedral. Remains of Brecon Castle have been incorporated into the Castle Hotel, and parts of the medieval town walls can be seen at Captain's Walk, an area named after French prisoners who exercised there during the Napoleonic wars. St Mary's Church is a greatly restored medieval building in the city centre. The fascinating Brecknock County Museum stands in Glamorgan Street, and the regimental museum of the South Wales Borderers is sited on The Watton. Across the 16th-century bridge which spans the River Usk is Christ College, which was originally built as a Benedictine friary. Restored in the 19th century, it is now a public school.

Crickhowell's beautiful 17th-century bridge is framed by an encircling ring of peaks, including the flat summit of aptly named Table Mountain.

Snow and ice add a new dimension of beauty to Llangorse Lake, a place more generally associated with the pastimes of summer.

BRECON BEACONS NATIONAL PARK, Powys

From the Black Mountain in the west to the Black Mountains in the east are the 519 square miles of mountain, moor, and pastoral countryside that make up this valuable conservation area. Much of the underlying rock here is Old Red Sandstone, but to the west and south the landscape is built on younger limestones and grits.

Leave Brecon on the B4601 Merthyr road, cross the River Usk, and after 1 mile cross the Afon Tarell. At the roundabout take 2nd exit A470. Proceed to Libanus and there turn right on to an unclassified road SP 'Mountain Centre'. Ascend to moorland and reach the Mountain Centre.

MOUNTAIN CENTRE, Powys

Magnificent views can be enjoyed from the centre, which functions as a meeting place, refreshment room, lecture theatre and comprehensive information office.

Continue and in ½ mile at a T-junction turn left. After 1¾ miles meet crossroads and turn left on to

the A4215 (no SP), then in ¾ mile keep left. Descend to the Tarell Valley and turn right on to the A470 'Merthyr'. Follow a long, easy ascent to a road summit on 1,440ft and the Storey Arms.

STOREY ARMS, Powys

The outdoor pursuits centre here is one of the most convenient points from which to explore the national park's mountain and moorland scenery. To the south-west is 2,409ft Fan Fawr, the highest point of Fforest Fawr, while inside the tour route to the east are the peaks of the Brecon Beacons themselves (NT).

THE BRECON BEACONS, Powys

When seen from a distance the Beacons (NT) present the extraordinary appearance of long, grass-covered swells that break at their apex like frozen waves and fall away to the north in stunning precipices. The highest point is 2,907ft Pen-y-fan, which affords views to the Bristol Channel.

Continue to the Fawr Reservoirs.

THE FAWR RESERVOIRS, Powys

Strung out along the west side of the A470 and fed by the Taf Fawr river are the three Fawr reservoirs – namely Beacons, Cantref, and Llwyn-on. They were constructed during a period between 1892 and 1927 to supply Cardiff with water. Above the Llwyn-on Reservoir is the Garwnant Forest Centre.

Continue past the reservoirs and reach Cefn-coed-y-cymmer.

CEFN-COED-Y-CYMMER, M Glam

The great Cyfarthfa Ironworks were founded here in 1766 by the Crawshay family and Watkin George, one of the foremost of the early ironmasters. Also here is a fine 19th-century railway viaduct.

To visit Cyfarthfa Castle continue on the A470 for 1¼ miles.

CYFARTHFA CASTLE, M Glam

Built in 1825 for 'Iron King' William Crawshay, this rather extravagant latterday castle now houses a museum and art gallery.

From Cefn-coed-y-cymmer turn left on to the unclassified 'Pontsticill and Talybont' road. In 1½ miles at the Aberglais PH turn left. A detour can be made to Morlais Castle by turning right here.

MORLAIS CASTLE, M Glam
Splendidly situated on a 1,200ft hill which affords excellent views of the Brecon Beacons, Morlais Castle (open) was a borderland stronghold built and defended by Gilbert de Clare.

On the main route, continue through Pontsticill and at the end of the village keep left to follow the shores of Pontsticill Reservoir.

PONTSTICILL RESERVOIR, Powys
Excellent views can be enjoyed from a viewpoint at the south end of this extensive reservoir, which was constructed at the beginning of this century as part of a system designed to supply nearby coalfields. Nearby is the present northern terminus of the narrow-gauge Brecon Mountain railway.

Continue for 2¾ miles and turn right. A detour ahead leads to the Neuadd Reservoirs.

The ruined keep of Tretower Castle saw action in the strife that bedevilled Wales during the middle ages.

NEUADD RESERVOIRS, Powys
The two Neuadd Reservoirs form part of the large Taf Fechan system and are beautifully set in the heart of the Brecon Beacons.

On the main tour route, continue across a river and shortly pass a picnic site on the right. Ascend to reach a 1,400ft road summit offering views of Craig-y-fan-ddu and Craig-y-fan. Descend through woodland to the Talybont Valley and the Talybont Reservoir.

TALYBONT RESERVOIR, Powys
Large numbers of waterfowl and other aquatic wildlife may be seen on this 2-mile long reservoir, which supplies Newport with water.

Continue for 1¼ miles beyond the reservoir and turn right (no SP) for Talybont village.

Panoramic views of the magnificent Brecon Beacon mountains are opened up on the roads which follow the Usk Valley between Llangattock and the cathedral city of Brecon.

TALYBONT & THE MONMOUTHSHIRE AND BRECON CANAL, Powys
Winding serenely from Brecon to Pontypool, the Monmouthshire and Brecon Canal offers a leisurely route from which to enjoy the scenery of the Usk Valley. It was built between 1799 and 1812, principally to supply the iron mines of old Monmouthshire (now Gwent), and was originally planned to stretch from Pontypool to Abergavenny. Within months of its commencement the decision was made to extend it to Brecon. Talybont has a modern bridge crossing the canal and makes an ideal centre from which to walk the towpaths and explore the surrounding countryside. East of Talybont the canal passes through the 375-yard Ashford Tunnel.

Cross the canal bridge at Talybont and turn right on to the B4558. Beyond the village keep forward SP 'Crickhowell'. Drive along the wooded Usk Valley to reach Llangynidr.

LLANGYNIDR, Powys
A fine old bridge of c1600 spans the Usk at Llangynidr, and five of the Monmouthshire and Brecon Canal's six locks are in this village.

Drive 1 mile beyond the canal bridge at Llangynidr and turn right on to the B4560 'Beaufort' road. Climb through sharp bends to 1,460ft for magnificent views. Continue past a quarry and turn left on to an unclassified road SP 'Llangattock'. (For a detour to 1,694ft with superb views continue the ascent on the B4560 for another 1 mile.) Continue on the main route and descend to Llangattock.

LLANGATTOCK, Powys   SO21
St Catwg's Church, on the edge of the village, carries a massive 15th-century tower and contains some interesting memorials. Old limestone quarries exist south on the slopes of Mynydd Llangattock, where there is also a National Nature Reserve.

Turn left into Llangattock then keep forward to the end and turn left on to the A4077. Turn right to cross the Usk into Crickhowell.

CRICKHOWELL, Powys
A magnificent 13-arched bridge dating from the 17th century spans the River Usk at Crickhowell. All that remains of the local castle is a mound and some battered-looking masonry, but there are some attractive houses in the town and the church has a pleasing 19th-century broach spire. Sir George Everest, who gave his name to the Himalayan mountain, was born here in 1790.

Leave Crickhowell on the A40 'Brecon' road. After 1¾ miles the A479 to the right leads to Tretower and its castle.

TRETOWER, Powys
A sturdy keep surrounded by a many-sided stone wall comprises the remains of Tretower Castle (AM), which was usurped as a habitation in the 14th century by nearby Tretower Court (AM). The latter is considered a very fine example of a fortified mansion and was the home of the Vaughan family for three centuries.

Continue on the A40 to Bwlch.

BWLCH, Powys
Fine views of the Usk Valley and the surrounding mountains are afforded from the road as it approaches this little hamlet. The name 'Bwlch' means 'The Pass'.

Drive beyond the war memorial and turn right on to the B4560 'Llangorse' road. Continue to Llangorse.

LLANGORSE, Powys
Restoration and so-called improvement during the 19th century destroyed much of the character of the little local church, but its 15th-century wagon roof has survived. An ancient inscribed stone has been preserved here.

Continue to the end of the village and turn left on to an unclassified road SP 'Brecon'. Shortly pass a road leading to the lovely expanse of Llangorse Lake.

LLANGORSE LAKE, Powys
This, the largest natural lake in South Wales, is a haven for many kinds of flora and fauna. It is also a centre for many water-based leisure activities, including fishing and boating.

On the main route, continue and in 1½ miles turn left into Llanfihangel Tal-y-llyn. Keep forward and after 2½ miles turn left. Go under the road bridge then turn right to join the A40. In ¾ mile at roundabout take 2nd exit B4601 to re-enter Brecon.

The graceful 15-arched viaduct at Cefn-coed-y-cymmer was built in 1866 to carry the Brecon and Merthyr Railway. Today it stands as an impressive example of 19th-century invention and engineering skill.

THE WELSH LAKES

At one time the valleys of the Elan and its tributaries were noted for their beauty, but now they lie under the surface of a massive water storage scheme that has turned the area into the Lake District of Wales. Down-stream on the Afon Rheidol are the stupendous falls of Devil's Bridge.

RHAYADER, Powys

This little market town retains a 19th-century atmosphere even though many of its shops have been modernized. Its old inns include The Triangle, a partly weather-boarded building across the Wye in the Cwmdeuddwr district, and, on the town side of the bridge the Cwmdeuddwr Arms. Both are grand old institutions with histories that stretch back several centuries. All that remains of Rhayader's castle is a large mound between Church Street and West Street, high above a reach where the river flows over boulders and rocky platforms to dash under the bridge in pretty falls. Rhayader was one of the centres of the Rebecca Riots in the first half of the 19th century, when men dressed as women and calling themselves Rebecca's Daughters smashed turnpike gates as a protest against heavy tolls. Some light industry has been introduced into Rhayader in an attempt to curb the depopulation which has bedevilled the region in recent decades.

Leave Rhayader on the B4518 'Elan Valley' road and continue to the edge of Elan village where there is a new visitor centre. Keep forward on to an Caban Coch Dam and Reservoir.

ELAN VALLEY & CABAN COCH RESERVOIR, Powys

Late in the 19th century the Corporation of Birmingham constructed a reservoir system in an area now unofficially known as The Lakeland of Wales. The new landscape is very beautiful and highly popular, but the scheme called for the drowning of a whole valley complete with attractive waterfalls, meadows, farms, houses and a church. Beneath the placid surface of the new lake is a house in which the poet Shelley lived for some time. He wrote appreciatively about the splendid local scenery in a letter to his friend Hogg, suggesting that it had impressed him even though his mind was on higher, less substantial things.

Continue to the Garreg-Ddu viaduct and turn left to cross it. Proceed through pleasant woodland, with the remains of the Dol-y-Mynach Dam on the left, and enter the attractive Claerwen Valley. At an AA telephone box turn right to reach Claerwen Dam.

CLAERWEN RESERVOIR, Powys

The Claerwen project, officially opened by Queen Elizabeth II on 23rd October 1952, is a vast 600-acre lake held back by a massive dam. The Afon Teifi rises in the high moorlands to the west of the reservoir, and the route of an ancient road used by monks travelling from Strata Florida Abbey to Abbey Cwmhir runs through the area.

Return across Garreg-Ddu viaduct and turn left. Follow the wooded shores of Garreg-Ddu Reservoir.

GARREG-DDU RESERVOIR, Powys

A unique submerged dam separates this reservoir from Caban Coch Reservoir. The entire Elan Valley complex supplies Birmingham with an amazing 75 million gallons of water a day and provides a haven for many forms of aquatic and marginal wildlife, including various plants.

From the end of Garreg-Ddu Reservoir ascend a short winding stretch of road to Penygarreg Dam and Reservoir.

PENYGARREG RESERVOIR, Powys

Some 124 acres of lake, unbroken except where a tiny fir-covered islet rises at the centre, backs up the Elan Valley from yet another of the project's great dams. This and the other reservoirs can be fished for trout by permit holders.

Continue alongside Craig Goch Reservoir.

CRAIG GOCH RESERVOIR, Powys

Topmost of the Elan Valley dam and reservoir complex, Craig Goch has a surface area of about 200 acres and may be extended. Plans were prepared to increase the capacity of the lake by allowing it to back up the valley close to the source of the Afon Elan.

At the end of the reservoir cross a bridge and ascend then turn left on to the 'Aberystwyth' road. Continue along the wide moorland valley of the Afon Elan to a road summit of 1,320ft. Descend into the deep and wild Ystwyth Valley, and within 4 miles reach Cwmystwyth.

CWMYSTWYTH, Dyfed

Ruins of mine workings, buildings and cottages in the neighbourhood of this village illustrate the 19th-century's insatiable desire for mineral wealth, but the village itself – no longer a centre of the mining industry – has settled into attractive retirement. Beyond Cwmystwyth, off the Pontrhydygroes road, is a pile of rubble that once stood as the proud mansion of Hafod, built by one Thomas Johnes in the late 18th century. The building was twice burnt down, and each blaze destroyed many priceless works of art and irreplaceable manuscripts. Johnes improved the estate by planting over 2 million trees and introducing new farming techniques, but the fires and the death of his beloved daughter Marianne in 1811 turned the innovator into a broken old man. A charred monument to Marianne in Hafod Church testifies to a final irony – the gutting of the church by fire in 1932.

Beyond Cwmystwyth bear right to join the B4574 'Devil's Bridge' road. Ascend a wooded slope and reach The Arch Picnic Site.

THE ARCH PICNIC SITE, Dyfed

Thomas Johnes of Hafod erected an arch over the road here in 1810 to commemorate the Golden Jubilee of George III. Three Forestry Commission trails lead from the picnic site.

Descend with the Mynach Valley on the right and enter Devil's Bridge.

DEVIL'S BRIDGE, Dyfed

Cwm Rheidol narrows to form a spectacular 500ft-deep wooded gorge at Devil's Bridge, where Afon Mynach adds its own 300ft of impressive waterfalls to the grandeur of the Afon Rheidol's Gyfarllwyd Falls. Excellent views into the gorge can be enjoyed from the road bridge, but the full scenic splendour of the area can only be fully appreciated by a descent into the valley bottom. A flight of 91 steps known as Jacob's Ladder zig-zags down to river level, where a small bridge and platform afford views of five separate waterfalls which make up a superb 300ft cascade. Water erosion has resulted in the formation of curious cavities known as punchbowls at the bottom of the

Penygarreg Reservoir is one of a series created to supply Birmingham with water.

The spectacular 300ft Mynach Falls are set amid trees festooned with moisture-loving ferns and mosses.

An unusual combination of weatherboarding and stone is displayed by the Cwmdeuddwr Arms at Rhayader.

The elegant dam which separates Craig Goch Reservoir from Penygarreg Reservoir.

Spoil tips and deserted buildings are reminders of once-thriving mineral workings at Cwmystwyth.

series. Similarly magnificent views are available from a terrace in front of the Hafod Arms Hotel, which was rebuilt in the 1830s. Of the three bridges stacked on top of each other at Devil's Bridge the oldest is – naturally – the lowest, and is thought to have been built in the 12th century by monks from Strata Florida Abbey. Legend has it that the Devil built it as a complex trick to win a soul, and abandoned it after he failed. The second bridge was built in 1753, and an iron bridge was built above the other two much later in the early part of this century.

VALE OF RHEIDOL LIGHT RAILWAY, Dyfed

British Rail's only narrow-gauge line uses steam locomotives and is an unfailing tourist attraction. Its Devil's Bridge terminus is a charming miniature, attractively laid out and set amid dense rhododendron thickets.

Leave Devil's Bridge village by crossing the Devil's Bridge on the A4120 'Ponterwyd' road. Continue high above the Rheidol Valley and after a short distance reach Ysbyty Cynfyn.

YSBYTY CYNFYN, Dyfed

Several stones of the prehistoric circle in which this immaculate, evergreen-shrouded church stands have survived in place. Many gravestones in the churchyard bear Cornish names and are reminders of the days when West Country miners came to Wales in search of better opportunities. A path leads from the church to a wooded gorge featuring a waterfall and the 'Parsons Bridge', so called because it was built for the convenience of a travelling parson who held services both here and at Llanbadarn Fawr.

Continue and shortly in ½ mile turn right on to the B4343 'Dyffryn Castell' road. In 1¾ miles turn right SP 'Llangurig' on to the A44 and reach Dyffryn Castell.

DYFFRYN CASTELL & PLYNLIMON, Dyfed

A path leads from here to the slopes of Plynlimon, a 2,470ft mountain. The views afforded by its summit are spectacular enough to make the ascent easily worth the effort involved. On a clear day the view encompasses much of Wales, from Cader Idris in the north to the Brecon Beacons in the south-east.

Plynlimon, famous for its wetness, is the source of the mighty Severn, the lovely Wye, and several lesser but equally vigorous rivers. Ascents to the summit can also be made from Eisteddfa Gurig (a little north of Dyffryn Castell) and from Nant-y-Moch Reservoir, which is on the west side of the mountain. The banks of the reservoir afford views of low crags that give Plynlimon a more mountainous aspect than is obvious from other vantage points. It should be stressed that although the ascent of Plynlimon is not difficult, the would-be explorer should wear sensible clothing and beware of the mountain's mercurial moods.

Ascend to Eisteddfa Gurig and a 1,400ft road summit. Continue alongside the Afon Tarenig and reach its confluence with the River Wye. In 5 miles enter Llangurig.

LLANGURIG, Powys

Small and beautiful Llangurig is delightfully set in the upper valley of the River Wye, amid hill ranges. The church of St Gurig owes much of its appearance to J W Lloyd of Llandinam, who commissioned Sir Gilbert Scott to restore the building. Lloyd, famous for his inconstancy, began his career as a curate in Llangurig but later became a Catholic and eventually aspired to become a Knight of St Gregory. In later life he returned to the Anglican faith. Stained-glass windows show scenes from the life of St Gurig, relate incidents associated with the royal families of Wales, and depict members of the Lloyd family.

Leave Llangurig on the A470 SP 'Rhayader' and drive down the attractive Wye Valley, accompanying the river itself for part of the way, and return to Rhayader.

103

MOORLANDS OF CENTRAL WALES

Towns are few and far between in mid Wales, and villages tend to be scattered round chapel or church buildings. Much of the area is open moorland scored by the occasional river valley, a wild, underpopulated region haunted by the cries of curlews and buzzards.

LLANIDLOES, Powys

Tree-lined streets, a happy blend of old and new architecture, and a few venerable shop fronts combine to form Llanidloes' unique character. The 16th-century Market Hall in the centre of the town is a rare survivor of a type of building that was once common all over the country. Its arcaded lower floor is open to the street and once sheltered market stalls. The floor above now houses a folk museum, but has variously functioned as an assize court, Quaker meeting place, Wesleyan and Baptist premises, public library, and working men's institute. John Wesley preached from a stone preserved beside the hall. A beautiful arcade of five bays in the parish church was brought from Abbey Cwmhir at the time of the Dissolution of the Monasteries, and was installed in 1542. Also from the abbey are the timbers of the hammer-beam roof, but the gilded angels are not original and were added to the ends of the beams at the time of their transfer. Llanidloes stands at the confluence of Afon Clywedog and the River Severn.

Leave Llanidloes on the B4518 'Llyn Clywedog' road. Cross the Severn and turn left to follow the Clywedog Valley. After 2 miles, with views of 1,580ft Fan Hill on the right, turn left on to an unclassified road. Cross the valley and ascend to Clywedog Dam.

LLYN CLYWEDOG RESERVOIR, Powys

Excellent views of the reservoir can be enjoyed from the dam, whose curving 237ft wall is the highest of its kind in Britain. The reservoir itself was opened in 1968 and is a popular sailing venue. Nearby Fan Hill commands extensive views to Plynlimon Mountain and south into the old county of Radnorshire.

Continue with the Clywedog Reservoir on the right and Hafren Forest on the left.

HAFREN FOREST, Powys

Comprising large plantations between Clywedog Reservoir and the slopes of Plynlimon Mountain, this forest was started by the Forestry Commission in 1937, and is named from the Welsh equivalent of 'Severn'. The River Severn flows from the eastern flank of Plynlimon, where it rises in company with the Wye and several other vigorous waters. A picnic site is situated in the forest opposite the extreme western arm of the reservoir.

Continue to a T-junction and turn right on to the 'Llanbrynmair' road. After 2½ miles reach the edge of Staylittle.

Bare moorland slopes crossed by winding roads typify the scenery of the mid-Wales wilderness, a place of rolling hills and deep valleys.

The once bare slopes of Plynlimon are gradually being covered by the dark coniferous plantations of Hafren Forest, which was begun in 1937.

STAYLITTLE, Powys

Two local blacksmiths gave this little village its name. It is said that they used to shoe horses so quickly that customers only needed to stay-a-little. On the hillside above the village is a Quaker burial ground with a nearby chapel overlooking the Clywedog Reservoir.

At Staylittle turn left on to the B4518. After 1 mile turn left on to the unclassified 'Machynlleth' road, which is unguarded and must be driven with care. After a short distance pass high above the deep gorge of the Afon Twymyn, and continue to Dylife.

DYLIFE, Powys

A few haphazard ruins, spoil tips, and an air of desolation are all that remain of an enormous lead-mining community that once flourished at Dylife. Huge numbers of men lived and worked here under awful conditions until the 1870s, but all that exist now are an inn and a tiny group of houses set back off the road. A little east of Dylife the infant Afon Twymyn plunges down spectacular Ffrwyd Fawr waterfall.

Continue for about 2 miles to a track leading left from the route to lakes Glaslyn and Bugeilyn.

LAKES GLASLYN & BUGEILYN, Powys

Care should be taken to stay on the footpath access to these two lakes, as the area is made dangerous by deep peat bogs and several precipitous drops. This is a wild and lonely landscape, once extensively mined for lead, but now inhabited only by sheep, birds, and the occasional fox. Glaslyn lies on private land, and Bugeilyn (which means Shepherd's Lake), is situated in the foothills of the Plynlimon range. Small flint arrowheads, presumably once used by people now buried in nearby prehistoric cairns, have been found washed out of the peat.

Continue towards Machynlleth and shortly reach a 1,671ft road summit. Views south and east from here take in extensive moorland, with 1,850ft Foel Fadian to the left and 1,784ft Bryn-y-Fedwen to the right. Descend, with impressive views north-west to Cader Idris and Aran Fawddwy, then drive down a long descent and keep forward at all road junctions to reach Machynlleth.

MACHYNLLETH, Powys

On market days Machynlleth's Maengwyn Street is packed with stalls selling a wide variety of wares. On the north side of the same street is the Owain Glyndwr Institute, which stands on the site of a building where Welsh revolutionary Owain Glyndwr held Wales' last independent parliament in 1404. On the other side of the street is the timbered Court House, with an inscription dated 1628. The road as a whole is dominated by an ornate Victorian clock tower which was erected by public subscription to mark the coming of age of Lord Castlereagh, heir to the Marquess of Londonderry. The marquess owned Plas Machynlleth, a 17th-century

mansion which stands at the end of Pentrerhedyn Street and now houses the council offices. The grounds in which the house stands have been adopted as a public park.

Leave Machynlleth on the A489 'Newtown' road and proceed to Penegoes.

PENEGOES, Powys

A tradition that the head of a Welsh chieftain, executed in this village, is buried under a local tree has proved so tenacious that in 1950 there was a serious proposal to dig for the skull. Penegoes once had a tiny curative bath that was fed from a spring whose waters were said to bring relief from rheumatism. Richard Wilson, painter of landscapes, was born in the village in 1714. His birthplace is said to have been the Rectory, but the building occupying this site now dates only from c 1800.

Follow the Dyfi Valley to Cemmaes Road and turn right on to the A470 'Newtown' road. Continue along the Twymyn Valley to Llanbrynmair.

Situated in the Dyfi Valley, Machynlleth is the principal market town for this part of Mid Wales and has associations with the popular Welsh folk hero, Owain Glyndwr.

LLANBRYNMAIR, Powys

Roughly divided into half old and half new, this small scattered village enjoys a rural setting threaded by little rivers and was the site of an important castle during the 12th century. Only the castle mound survives today. The local church is sited in the old part of the village and contains ancient oak timbers. Abraham Rees, preacher and scholar, was born in the village in 1743. In 1778 he embarked on the preparation of information for *Chambers' Encyclopaedia*, a mammoth task that took 9 years to complete and won Rees election as a Fellow of the Royal Society. He was later made a Doctor of Divinity by Edinburgh University for his work on a further encyclopaedia.

Continue through the wooded gorge of the Afon Iaen to reach a road and rail summit at Talerddig, where there is a natural arch beside the road. Continue to Carno.

Left: the valley at Dylife was once exploited for its mineral wealth. Below: this statue of engineer David Davies stands at Llandinam.

CARNO, Powys

Opposite Carno's church, which contains an ancient cross-incised slab that saw many years' service as a gatepost, is the Aleppo Merchant Inn. This unusual title was given to the pub by a retired sea captain who had been in charge of a ship of that name. A Roman fort was situated here, and later in history several fierce battles between the ruling princes of north and south Wales were fought near Carno.

Drive along the broad valley of the Afon Carno and pass through Clatter and Pont-dolgoch to reach Caersws.

CAERSWS, Powys

Earthworks of a large Roman installation may be seen near the railway here, forming a hub from which the raised causeways of ancient roads still radiate in recognizable form. The village itself is laid out in a typically Roman grid-iron pattern at the meeting of two rivers with the Severn. John Ceiriog Hughes, a famous 19th-century bard, was manager of a narrow-gauge railway here for many years. A memorial plaque marks the house where he lived, and his remains lie north-west at Llanwnog. The latter boasts a fascinating old church.

Continue on the A470 and after ½ mile meet a T-junction. Turn right on to the 'Llangurig' road and shortly go over a level crossing, then follow the River Severn to reach Llandinam.

LLANDINAM, Powys

Green hills rising to the lower slopes of mountains spread from the Severn Valley site of this pretty village. Close to a handsome iron bridge that spans the river is a statue of Llandinam's most famous native, David Davies. After starting from a modest beginning Davies worked to become a railway contractor, then went on to make a fortune with the construction of Barry Docks. The local church has been extensively restored and stands on the site of a hillfort which is still faintly visible. Ancient carvings preserved in the church include an interesting illustration of Adam and Eve.

Remain on the A470 for the return to Llanidloes.

CASTLES ON THE BORDER

South from one of the tortuous meanders carved by the River Severn runs the border between England and Wales – a contentious division guarded by medieval fortresses at Powis, Montgomery, and Clun.

WELSHPOOL, Powys
Prior to the 19th century this 'English town in Wales' was known simply as Pool, a name derived from the marshy nature of the area in which it stood. The 'Welsh' prefix, ironic in the light of the town's hotly disputed position in the borderlands between England and Wales, was added in 1835 to distinguish it from Poole in Dorset. Opposite the town hall is a half-timbered building with a Jacobean staircase, one of several such examples in the town. Severn Road leads to a splendid railway station incorporating many gables, end towers, and a platform canopy resplendent with wrought-iron arcading. Powysland Museum stands in Salop Road and was started in 1874 by Morris Jones, who had previously founded the Powysland Club – claimed to be the oldest archaeological society in Wales.
Also of interest are a restored 18th-century cockpit, the Montgomery Canal Exhibition Centre with narrowboat trips, and the Oriel Gallery.

POWIS CASTLE, Powys
Approached from Welshpool through a magnificently-wooded park, Powis Castle dates originally from the 13th century. Subsequent alterations which continued right up until the end of the last century have changed the building beyond all past recognition, and it now appears as a vast mansion. As an historic treasure Powis is very special because it has been continuously occupied, its present form having gradually evolved through the centuries in response to the tastes of various owners. The 18th-century terraced gardens that complement the building are especially noteworthy, and the interior of the castle is rich with curios including mementos of Clive of India. In 1952 the castle and park were passed over into the protection of the National Trust.

Leave Welshpool on the A483 'Newtown' road and follow the Shropshire Union Canal past the grounds of Powis Castle. After 4 miles turn right on to the B4390 to reach Berriew.

BERRIEW, Powys
Recipient of an award for the best-kept village in Wales, Berriew is a picturesque combination of black-and-white cottages and a few more recent buildings interspersed with trim flower gardens. Pretty fails can be seen near by on the Afon Rhiw, which joins the Severn 1½ miles east.

Leave Berriew by turning left on to the B4385 and cross the Rhiw. Shortly turn left again. Later meet a T-junction and turn right to rejoin the A483 'Newtown' road. Continue to Garthmyl and turn left on to the B4385 SP 'Montgomery'. Cross the Severn and continue to Montgomery.

MONTGOMERY, Powys
Montgomery's superficially Georgian character is shown in the red-brick town hall that dominates Broad Street, a thoroughfare almost as wide as it is long. Elsewhere fine examples of Tudor and Jacobean architecture make surprise appearances round secretive corners or at the tops of quaint slopes and steps. The parish Church of St Nicholas was built just before Henry III granted Montgomery's Royal Charter in 1227. Its best features include 15th-century nave roofs, a double screen, and monuments to the Herbert family. Poet George Herbert was born in the now-ruined castle (AM), built by Henry III to replace a Norman stronghold at Hendomen to the north-west. Also of interest is the Historical Exhibition Centre.

Continue on the B4385 SP 'Bishop's Castle', with views across the River Camlad valley – the only river to flow from England into Wales. Enter Bishop's Castle.

BISHOP'S CASTLE, Salop
This hillside market town stands on the edge of Clun Forest and preserves a number of interesting old buildings, the most picturesque of which is the 16th-century House on Crutches. Its Victorian church retains a Norman tower, and the 18th-century town hall stands over a medieval lock-up.

At the end turn left and in ½ mile at crossroads turn right on to the A488 SP 'Clun'. Continue through wooded hill country to Clun.

CLUN, Salop
Thousands of flint implements displayed in the museum at Clun's 18th-century town hall demonstrate that man has lived in this area for a very long time. Attractive almshouses of 1618 enliven the somewhat stolid appearance of the village. Remains of a Norman castle overlook the River Clun from a small hill, and the large expanse of Clun Forest stretches west as a patchwork of treeless uplands and recent afforestation.

Leave Clun on the A488 'Knighton' road and ascend Clun Hill to a summit of 1,150ft. Slowly descend and cross the River Redlake, then ascend again before skirting Kinsley Wood to reach Knighton.

KNIGHTON, Powys
The Offa's Dyke long-distance footpath was officially opened here in 1971. The dyke itself, built by a king of Mercia in the 8th century, runs through the town. Built largely of local stone, Knighton occupies a delightful hillside position in the Teme Valley and has scant remains of a Norman motte-and-bailey castle. Knighton Railway Station stands on the Central Wales line and is a little gem of Victorian-gothic railway architecture. The town's livestock sales are famous.

Leave Knighton on the A488 SP 'Newtown'. After ¼ mile turn right on to the B4355 to follow the River Teme. Continue to Knucklas.

KNUCKLAS, Powys
Crowning the hill above Knucklas are the remains of a 13th-century castle which is connected in legend with Gwynhwyfar (or Guinevere), whom the heroic folk figure King Arthur married. A beautiful 75ft-high railway viaduct which can also be seen here is of Victorian date and carries crenellated towers.

Continue through pleasant valley scenery to Beguildy.

A ruined keep and two 13th-century towers are the most outstanding features of Clun's impressively sited castle.

Elegant ironwork surrounds the grave of social reformer Robert Owen at Newtown.

Victorian romanticism is reflected in the crenellated towers of the railway viaduct at Knucklas.

BEGUILDY, Powys
Some years ago a would-be benefactor offered to donate a large sum of money to the local school on condition that the village should revert to its correct Welsh spelling of Bugail-dy meaning the 'Shepherd's House'. The offer was declined. Features of the local church include a rood screen with fine tracery and a Jacobean pulpit and altar.

Drive on through Felindre and later ascend on to open moorland; to the right below 1,732ft Cilfaesty Hill is the source of the Teme. Descend into Dolfor.

DOLFOR, Powys
Dolfor stands at an altitude of 1,000ft and affords extensive mountain views to the north west. Views south to the Brecon Beacons range can be enjoyed from the 1,565ft summit of nearby Kerry Hill. The rivers Teme, Ithon, and Mule all rise in the area.

In Dolfor turn right on to the A483, then right again (no SP) on to a narrow unclassified road. Beyond the local church keep forward to a 1,200ft road summit, offering splendid views north over Newtown and the Severn Valley. Continue down a long descent and turn left on to the A489. Enter Newtown and turn right for the town centre.

NEWTOWN, Powys
Robert Owen, a social reformer who became known as the father of trade unionism, was born in Newtown and is buried in the churchyard of the old parish church. Some of the reasons why Owen was such an assiduous campaigner for workers' rights can be understood by a visit to the Newtown Textile Museum, and a museum dedicated to his memory is situated over the Midland Bank. The 15th-century rood screen from the old church has been preserved in a handsome 19th-century successor. Newtown was originally established in 1279, but the 20th century has incorporated it in a designated development area and made it into a new town all over again. Extensive new building has given the community two new bridges over the River Severn plus a theatre and various civic buildings.

Leave Newtown on the B4568, cross the River Severn, and at a roundabout, take the 3rd exit SP 'Bettws Cedewain'. After 2½ miles turn left on to the B4389 'Llanfair Caereinion' road. Proceed to Bettws Cedewain.

BETTWS CEDEWAIN, Powys
Close-knit round a stone bridge spanning the little River Bechan, this attractive village has an interesting 14th-century church which carries a timbered and louvred tower typical of the area. A barrel organ and a pre-Reformation brass, depicting a priest vested for mass, can be seen inside.

Continue for 2 miles and turn right to enter Tregynon. After 1¼ miles cross the Afon Rhiw and enter New Mills. Turn left and make a winding ascent to a road summit of 980ft. Descend into Llanfair Caereinion.

LLANFAIR CAEREINION, Powys
The river at the foot of the hillside on which this quiet little greystone town is built has two names – Banwy and Einion. In the local church, which was rebuilt in 1868, is the 14th-century stone figure of a knight. The ancient doorway of the church is a good example of medieval building.

The charming House on Crutches in Bishop's Castle straddles a passage between the High Street and Market Place.

To leave Llanfair turn right, bear left and cross the Banwy-Einion, then turn right on to the A458 'Welshpool' road. After ¼ mile note the terminus of the Welshpool and Llanfair Railway on the right.

WELSHPOOL AND LLANFAIR LIGHT RAILWAY, Powys
Opened in 1903, this narrow-gauge railway was the only line of its type built in Wales to carry general goods. Passenger services ceased in 1931, but the railway continued to fulfil its original function until it was completely closed down in 1956. Four years later in 1960 the Welshpool and Llanfair Light Railway Preservation Co was formed, and by 1973 was large enough to purchase the line outright. The line has been restored and progressively re-opened, reaching a new terminus on the west side of Welshpool in 1981. A wide variety of locomotives and rolling stock is used to operate the railway.

Continue through pleasant scenery, with the railway to the right, and return to Welshpool.

ROSS-ON-WYE, Herefs & Worcs

High above the roofs of this attractive town rises the splendid 208ft spire of St Mary's Church, the topmost part of which was rebuilt in the 17th century with money donated by the philanthropic John Kyrle. Inside the main church, which dates mainly from the 13th century, are numerous interesting monuments. An important feature of the High Street is the red-sandstone Market Hall (AM) of 1670, which features a Charles II medallion set into the gable overlooking Man of Ross House – where Kyrle lived. The most conspicious reminder of Kyrle's many benefactions is the Prospect – a garden with excellent views over the river. Several ancient and attractive groups of buildings are preserved in the town, including a number of almshouses and the 16th-century Wilton Bridge.

Leave Ross-on-Wye by the B4260 SP 'Monmouth (A40)'. After ¾ mile cross the River Wye into Wilton.

WILTON, Herefs & Worcs

The splendid 16th-century bridge that spans the Wye here features a curiously inscribed sundial which was added in the 18th century. Near by are a group of old buildings and the picturesquely overgrown ruins of a 13th-century castle.

At the roundabout take 1st exit A40 and in 2 miles ascend to Pencraig. Continue for ½ mile, then turn left on to an unclassified road. Proceed to Goodrich.

GOODRICH, Herefs & Worcs

Imposing ruins of moated Goodrich Castle (AM), built in the 12th century as a defence against Welsh raiders, stand on a wooded hill overlooking the beautiful River Wye.

Branch right with SP 'Symond's Yat' then turn right on to the B4229. After ¾ mile turn left on to an unclassified road SP 'Symond's Yat East' and cross Huntsham Bridge. After 1 mile keep left and steeply ascend a narrow road to reach Symond's Yat Rock.

SYMOND'S YAT, Herefs & Worcs

This famous beauty spot lies in a narrow loop of the River Wye. An AA viewpoint at the summit of 473ft Yat Rock affords magnificent views over the Yat (gap or 'gate') itself, and of the river as it winds through the rich woodlands of its deep valley.

Join the B4432 SP 'Coleford' and continue to Christchurch, then turn right on to the B4228. After ½ mile meet crossroads and turn right on to the A4136 SP 'Monmouth'. Proceed to Staunton.

STAUNTON, Glos

Fine views of the Wye Valley can be enjoyed from many vantage points around this old village. The local

THE FOREST OF DEAN

Carpets of daffodils in spring and a leafy canopy in summer provide a backcloth for the one-man craft industries for which the forest is famous. West are the silvery coils of the majestic River Wye, which borders this outstanding region and divides England from Wales.

The Forest of Dean is a place of beauty and interest at all times of the year.

church has Norman origins and is often referred to as the 'Mother Church of the Forest of Dean'. An isolated rock known as the Buckstone makes a fine viewpoint. It used to move to the touch, but after having been dislodged in 1885 it was firmly fixed in its original position.

Descend into Wales through beautifully wooded scenery and after 4½ miles turn left on to the A466 SP 'Chepstow'. A short detour to Monmouth can be made by remaining on the A4136.

MONMOUTH, Gwent

Strategically placed where the rivers Wye and Monnow meet, this ancient town played a vital role in subjugating South Wales from the Roman period till the Middle Ages. The outstanding reminder of these troubled times is a unique fortified bridge (AM) which has spanned the Monnow and guarded the town since 1260. The once-powerful castle (birthplace of Henry V) preserves an interesting 12th-century building among its remains. Near by is the Great Castle House (exterior AM), a 17th-century structure noted for its fine interior decorations. Other historic buildings include a ruined priory, several fine churches, an 18th-century shire hall, and venerable houses of the Tudor and Georgian periods. The Monmouth Museum in the Market Hall contains notable Nelson relics. East of the town is wooded Kymin Hill (NT), an excellent viewpoint which carries an 18th-century Naval Temple at its summit.

Shots from a cannon called Roaring Meg battered Goodrich Castle into submission during the Civil War.

Continue along the Wye Valley and pass through Redbrook, where the river forms part of the border between England and Wales. East of the road are traces of Offa's Dyke.

OFFA'S DYKE, Gwent etc

King Offa of Mercia constructed the banks and ditches of these extensive earthworks some time during the 8th century. The dyke, broken in places, stretches from Chepstow to Prestatyn and for many centuries was accepted as the boundary between England and Wales.

Cross Bigsweir Bridge and drive through Llandogo. Continue to Tintern Abbey.

TINTERN ABBEY, Gwent

Set amid the soft hills of Gwent and surrounded by the remains of ancient monastic buildings is the beautiful roofless church of Tintern Abbey. This once-important Cistercian foundation was created in 1131, and its size gradually increased along with its influence and importance – mainly in the 13th and 14th centuries. Close by is the little village of Tintern Parva.

Continue along the A466 and after 3 miles pass a path on the right leading to Wyndcliff Viewpoint. Drive through St Arvans and pass Chepstow Racecourse on the left. At the roundabout take the first exit into Chepstow.

CHEPSTOW, Gwent

Spectacularly perched above a bend of the Wye are the extensive remains of Chepstow Castle (AM), a massive fortification that was begun in stone only a year after the Norman invasion of England. The quaint old town, includes many old houses. A fine 18th-century house contains the town's museum, and the West Gate (AM) of the town wall still survives.

Leave Chepstow on the A48 SP 'Gloucester' and cross the River Wye into England. Ascend, and after ¼ mile at crossroads turn left on to the B4228, SP 'Coleford'. Continue to the edge of Hewelsfield.

HEWELSFIELD, Glos

Norman workmanship is evident in the fabric of Hewelsfield Church, which is said to be one of the oldest in the Forest of Dean.

Continue, with views of the River Severn to the right, and later turn left into St Briavels.

ST BRIAVELS, Glos

During the Middle Ages this quiet little village was the administrative centre for the Forest of Dean. Its church was built in 1089 and maintains a custom in which small cubes of bread and cheese are distributed among the parishioners after evening service on Whit Sunday. This practice is probably 700 years old. St Briavels Castle, now a youth hostel, has a magnificent 13th-century gatehouse and a 12th-century great hall.

Ruardean's parish church has a fine tympanum made by a local school of sculptors.

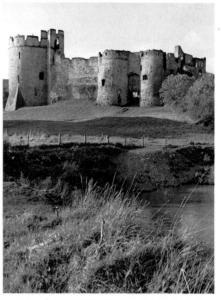

Chepstow was one of the earliest stone castles to be built in Britain.

The tower on Monnow Bridge was built as a fortified entrance to Monmouth.

The writer C S Lewis was so moved by the majestic roofless ruin of Tintern Abbey that he wished all churches were open to the sky.

Keep forward through St Briavels and after ¼ mile reach crossroads and turn left rejoining the B4228. After 1¾ miles turn left on to the B4231 and after ¼ mile turn right to rejoin the B4228. After ¾ mile turn right on to an unclassified road SP 'Parkend', and after 1 mile meet a T-junction. Turn right on to the B4431 and continue to Parkend.

PARKEND, Glos
This rather undistinguished village has an interesting 'gothicky' church dating from 1822. Close by is the Dean Forest Railway.

DEAN FOREST RAILWAY, Glos
Plans are underway to open a working steam railway from Lydney to Parkend in the near future. A collection of locomotives and rolling stock is kept at the Norchard Railway Centre north of Lydney.

Continue on the B4431, and after 1¼ miles turn left on to an unclassified road SP 'Speech House'. Approach Speech House through the Forest of Dean.

FOREST OF DEAN, Glos
Within the boundaries of this historic area – the first National Forest Park to be created in England – is some of the finest woodland scenery to be found anywhere in Britain. Since 1016 the forest has been Crown property (although it is now cared for by the Forestry Commission) and it is

famous for a number of privately run industries, including coal mining and traditional charcoal burning. Specially laid-out forest trails and a forest drive help visitors appreciate the best that the area has to offer.

SPEECH HOUSE HOTEL, Glos
This handsome building succeeded St Briavels to become the administrative centre for the Forest of Dean, on its completion in 1676 it now serves as an hotel, but the old Verderers Court of Foresters is still held there.

Turn right on to the B4226 and pass a picnic site on the left. Continue to the edge of Cinderford.

CINDERFORD, Glos
Typical of early 19th-century development, this village was largely created to house the workforce required to operate the Forest Vale Ironworks.

Continue on the B4226 and ascend. After ¾ mile turn right on to the A4151 SP 'Gloucester' and proceed to Littledean.

LITTLEDEAN, Glos
Features of this small place include an attractive old church, an 18th-century gaol which now serves as a police station, and Littledean Hall (open), incorporating Roman, Saxon and Norman work, with a museum, watergardens and a large Roman temple.

At the T-junction turn right SP 'Newnham' on to an unclassified road. Descend to Newnham-on-Severn.

NEWNHAM-ON-SEVERN, Glos
Many old houses survive in this pleasant little town, which has a grassy bank down the centre of its high street. The local church affords enchanting views across the River Severn to the Cotswold Hills.

Turn left on to the A48 'Gloucester' road. After 2 miles turn left on to an unclassified road SP 'Mitcheldean'. Continue to Flaxley.

FLAXLEY, Glos
Unspoilt Flaxley is a cluster of houses with an unpretentious church and an historic abbey. The latter was originally created in the 12th century, but after a great fire in 1777 much of the monastic complex was rebuilt in the Georgian style. It is now used as a private dwelling.

Continue and in 1 mile turn right. Two miles farther cross a main road to enter Mitcheldean.

MITCHELDEAN, Glos
The beautiful 18th-century spire of Mitcheldean Church rises grandly over the roofs of much older half-timbered cottages in the village.

At Mitcheldean Church turn left for Drybrook. At Drybrook crossroads go straight across, then keep left. In ¾ mile meet a T-junction and turn right on to the B4227. Continue to Ruardean.

RUARDEAN, Glos
Above the inner doorway of Ruardean's notable church is a beautifully-preserved Norman tympanum depicting St George's battle against the dragon.

Bear right and descend, and after 1½ miles turn right on to the B4228 SP 'Ross'. Follow the River Wye and drive through Kerne Bridge to reach Walford.

WALFORD, Herefs & Worcs
This Wye-side village has a 13th-century church and stands on the site of a Roman camp.

Continue on the B4228 to return to Ross-on-Wye.

HEREFORD, Herefs & Worcs

Once the capital of Saxon West Mercia, this ancient town is at the centre of a rich agricultural district and is especially noted for the production of cider. There has been a cathedral in the city since the 7th century, but the present building dates mainly from the 12th and shows a variety of later alterations. It is dedicated to St Mary and to St Ethelbert, a king of East Anglia who was murdered near Hereford in AD 794. His tomb later became a famous shrine. Other notable relics in the cathedral are the 14th-century *Mappa Mundi* (Map of the World), King Stephen's 800-year-old chair, the best library of chained books in the country, and many monuments and tombs. Cloisters leading to the ancient Bishop's Palace contain a rare 12th-century timbered hall, and the College of Vicars Choral dates from the 15th century. There is another chained library in All Saints Church. The 11th-century St Peter's Church is the oldest in Hereford. A wealth of half-timbered buildings is preserved here, including the outstanding early-15th-century Old House, now a museum. In Widemarsh Street is the St John Coningsby Museum, which incorporates a 12th-century chapel and hall with 17th-century almshouses. Preserved main-line steam locomotives are maintained at the Bulmers Railway Centre. The lovely Wye flows under the ancient Wye Bridge, past the cathedral grounds and castle ruins. Also to be seen are the Museum and Art Gallery, the Churchill Gardens Museum in a fine Regency house, the Cider Museum with a reconstruction of a cider factory, and the Waterworks Museum containing a collection of pumping engines. There are also some remains of the medieval city walls.

Leave Hereford on the A438 SP 'Brecon'. After 5 miles reach The Weir on the left.

THE WEIR, Herefs & Worcs

Fine views of the Wye and the Black Mountains can be enjoyed from this steeply sloping riverside garden (NT, open). The house (not open) dates from the 18th century.

Continue to Letton, with occasional views of the Wye, and 1¾ miles beyond the village turn left and pass through Willersley and Winforton. Proceed to Whitney-on-Wye.

Follow the Wye to enter the Welsh county of Powys. Continue, with views of the Black Mountains to the left, to reach the outskirts of Clyro.

CLYRO, Powys

Francis Kilvert the diarist was curate of this quiet little village between 1865 and 1872. His notes and records paint a highly detailed picture of life in the Radnorshire hills during the 19th century, and have been the subject of a television series. The local church was rebuilt in 1853 but

RIVERS OF THE SOUTH

After looping from its mid-Wales source the magical Wye swings in great curves down to Hay, Ross, and the cathedral city of Hereford. West of the Wye the River Dore flows gently through its fertile valley to join the Monnow, a Wye tributary overlooked by ruined border fortresses.

Hereford Cathedral's massive sandstone tower was designed and built at the beginning of the 14th century.

retains some of its original 13th-century structure. There are slight remains of a Norman castle, and to the east, of a Roman fort.

Turn left on to the B4351, shortly cross the Wye, then turn right into Hay-on-Wye.

HAY-ON-WYE, Powys

Book lovers are in their element here, for Hay has more than its fair share of book shops. Narrow streets winding through the old town are full of fascinating small shops, and on market day are alive with bustling activity. William de Braose, one of the most ruthless of the Marcher Lords, built a castle here to replace one burned down by King John. Folk hero Owain Glyndwr destroyed the later castle during the 15th century, but a fine gateway, the keep, and parts of the wall remain. Alongside the ruins is a Jacobean house.

At the Blue Boar Inn turn left on the B4348 'Peterchurch' road and re-enter England. After 2¼ miles turn right SP 'Ross' and continue to the edge of Dorstone.

DORSTONE, Herefs & Worcs

Thomas de Brito, one of the four knights who murdered Thomas à Becket in Canterbury Cathedral, founded the local church. Although largely rebuilt in 1889 it retains a 13th-century tower arch. A lane from Dorstone leads 1 mile north to Arthur's Stone, a prehistoric tomb (AM) dating from c 2000 BC. The view from here is magnificent.

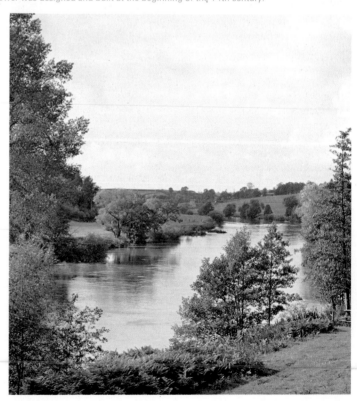

Winding its way from its mountain source, the River Wye sweeps in great loops into the rolling farm and pasture lands at How Caple.

Continue and in ¼ mile at crossroads turn right. Drive along the Golden Valley to Peterchurch.

PETERCHURCH, Herefs & Worcs

Situated in the heart of the lush Golden Valley, Peterchurch has a large and exceptionally well-preserved Norman church. A wooden panel representing a fish with a chain round its neck hangs over the south door. Wellbrook Manor (not open) is one of the best examples of a 14th-century hall-house in the country.

After 2 miles turn right on to the B4347 SP 'Pontrilas', still following the River Dore; later enter Abbey Dore.

c 1070, but it was largely rebuilt during the reign of Henry III. Owain Glyndwr, the Welsh partisan, took the castle in 1410 but was ousted by Harry Monmouth (who was later to become King Henry V). This was Glyndwr's last recorded battle.

Continue through pleasant hill country and after 4¼ miles turn left on to the B4521 SP 'Ross'. Reach the edge of Skenfrith.

Ross-on-Wye is dominated by its 13th-century church.

Prehistoric Arthur's Stone is situated near Dorstone.

Jerusalem is the centre of the world on the *Mappa Mundi*, in Hereford Cathedral.

The craggy ruins of Skenfrith Castle stand near the River Monnow.

ABBEY DORE, Herefs & Worcs

The meadows and orchards of the Golden Valley surround this little village, which is famous for its parish church. In 1174 an abbey was founded here, but after the Dissolution of the Monasteries its buildings were neglected. In 1633 Lord Scudamore commissioned the brilliant craftsman John Abel to rebuild the church. Much of the original fabric was restored; additions by Abel included the fine wooden screen. Court Gardens (open) across the river have 4 acres of walled and river gardens and exotic plants.

Continue to Ewyas Harold.

EWYAS HAROLD, Herefs & Worcs

An important Norman castle stood here during the 13th century, but only the mound has survived to the present day. The church, partly rebuilt in 1868, retains its impressive 13th-century tower.

Bear left over a river bridge. After ¾ mile cross the A465 and the River Dore, then turn right SP 'Monmouth'. After 1½ miles turn right to re-enter Wales and ascend to Grosmont.

GROSMONT, Gwent

This small old-world town, set amid beautiful scenery by the River Monnow, was a borough until 1860. Inside its massively towered church is a huge, flat-faced stone knight of ancient origin. The castle (AM) here was one of 3 erected in the vicinity to protect the border between England and Wales, the others being Skenfrith and White Castle. It is quite likely that the first on this site was built as early as

SKENFRITH, Gwent

Remains of 13th-century Skenfrith Castle (AM, NT), one of a trio built to defend the English border, include a central keep enclosed by a four-sided curtain wall and a moat. In its western range is a flight of stone steps leading down to a central room which contains a fireplace with beautifully carved capitals. The local church also dates from the 13th century and has an impressive partially-timbered tower.

Cross the River Monnow, re-enter England, and after 1¾ miles at Broad Oak crossroads turn right on to an unclassified road SP 'Welsh Newton'. After 1½ miles reach the entrance to Pembridge Castle.

PEMBRIDGE CASTLE, Herefs & Worcs

Dating originally from the 13th

century, this castle (not open) has a 16th-century chapel and a 17th-century hall. Some of the structure was restored during this century, and the buildings are partly used by a local farmer.

Continue and in 1 mile reach the A466, and turn right into Welsh Newton. Take the next turning left on to an unclassified road SP 'Llangarren' and after 1¾ miles turn right to enter Llangrove. Continue and descend into Whitchurch.

WHITCHURCH, Herefs & Worcs

Roman remains were found on the outskirts of this village in the 19th century. The Church of St Dubricius is set beside the River Wye and contains a Norman font. Nearby are the Jubilee Maze and Museum of Mazes.

Follow SP 'Ross' to join the A40 and continue through Pencraig, with occasional views of the Wye. Later reach Wilton.

WILTON, Herefs & Worcs

The splendid bridge and nearby buildings here are described in tour from Ross-on-Wye.

At the roundabout take 3rd exit B4260 into Ross.

ROSS ON WYE, Herefs & Worcs

A handsome market hall standing in the centre of this town is just one of many attractive buildings preserved here. Overlooking all is the fine 13th-century church.

Follow SP 'Ledbury' and after 1 mile at roundabout take 2nd exit on to the A449. At the next roundabout take 1st exit SP 'Worcester'. After 1¾ miles branch left to join the B4224 SP 'Hereford'. In ¼ mile turn left and proceed to Fownhope.

FOWNHOPE, Herefs & Worcs

Wooded hills, leafy lanes with grassy verges, and old timbered buildings exist in a magical combination in and around this picturesque Wye-side village. The church has a Norman tower and preserves a contemporary tympanum which depicts the Virgin and Child.

Continue to Mordiford

MORDIFORD, Herefs & Worcs

Parts of the beautiful bridge that spans the Lugg here date from the 14th century. Near by, making a delightful group, are the partly-Norman church and a Georgian rectory. The Palladian mansion of Sufton Court to the north is open occasionally.

Keep left and cross the River Lugg and continue through Hampton Bishop to re-enter Hereford.

111

KIDDERMINSTER, Herefs & Worcs

Carpets were the foundation of Kidderminster's prosperity, and the carpet-weaving industry that was introduced here in 1735 continues to be a major concern. The town's architecture is homely rather than distinguished, although handsome St Mary's Church and the cluster of Georgian buildings in Church Street have much to offer the eye.

Leave Kidderminster on the A456 'Leominster' road and shortly reach the West Midlands Safari Park.

WEST MIDLANDS SAFARI PARK, Herefs & Worcs

Giraffes, elephants, and many other exotic beasts can be seen in the 200 acres of this interesting wildlife park. Other attractions include a pets' corner for the children, a 'boat safari', bird gardens, and a complete dolphinarium.

Cross the River Severn via Telford's bridge and enter Bewdley.

BEWDLEY, Herefs & Worcs

Telford's fine bridge spanning the Severn at Bewdley was built in 1795. Severnside is a beautiful street lined with 17th- and 18th-century houses. An elegant parade of Georgian and earlier buildings line both sides of Load Street, which is eventually closed off by a large Georgian house and 18th-century St Anne's Church. Bewdley's more distant history is represented by several excellent half-timbered buildings. Past industries of the town are demonstrated at the museum housed in 18th-century buildings called The Shambles, and

ANCIENT TOWNS

From Kidderminster this tour visits the handsome Georgian streets of Bewdley, the purpose-built canal town of Stourport, and delightful Ludlow – an ancient gem in the English landscape. Scattered between are villages, each one unique in its character.

a craft centre in Lax Lane specialises in brassrubbing. Overlooking the town is Tickenhill House, and period mansion refaced in 1738 and incorporating a royal palace.

Bridgnorth's Town Hall, built between 1648 and 1652, straddles the town's High Street.

Leave Bewdley on the B4194 SP 'Ribbesford'. Drive along the west bank of the River Severn, and after 2¾ miles meet crossroads. Turn left on to the A451 to enter Stourport-on-Severn.

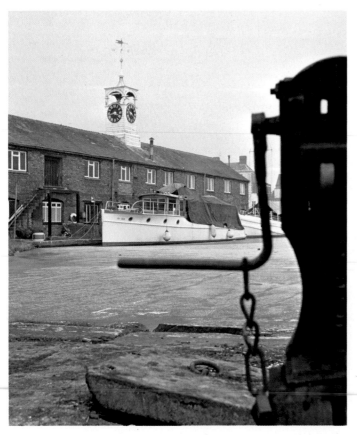

STOURPORT-ON-SEVERN, Herefs & Worcs

After the opening of the Staffordshire and Worcestershire Canal, built by the engineer James Brindley in 1766, Stourport became a major canal port. It has survived to the present day as the only example of a purpose-built canal town in England.

Return along the A451 SP 'Great Witley' and recross the River Severn. After 4½ miles reach Great Witley.

GREAT WITLEY, Herefs & Worcs

Entry into Great Witley's Chapel of St Michael transports the visitor from the English countryside to some remote part of Italy. Rich rococo decoration completely alien to rural Britain assaults the eye – not unpleasantly – from skilfully-patterned walls and painted ceiling panels. Close to the chapel, which was consecrated in 1735, is the ruined shell of 17th-century and later Witley Court.

At the end of the village turn right on to the A443. SP 'Ludlow'. After 1 mile branch right on to the B4202 SP 'Cleobury Mortimer'. Shortly reach the edge of Abberley.

Winter holds the canal basin at Stourport-on-Severn in an icy grip. A Georgian warehouse stands in the background.

ABBERLEY, Herefs & Worcs

Overlooked by 930ft Abberley Hill, this peaceful little village is centred on the ruins of a Norman church that was replaced by a handsome Victorian successor. The clock tower of Abberley Hall is visible for miles.

Continue, and gradually ascend to Clows Top for good all-round views. Meet crossroads and turn left on to the A456 SP 'Leominster'. Descend with distant views into Mamble.

MAMBLE, Herefs & Worcs

Mamble's church dates almost entirely from the beginning of the 13th century and carries an unusual timber bell turret.

Continue to Newnham Bridge and turn right then follow the Teme Valley to the edge of Tenbury Wells.

TENBURY WELLS, Herefs & Worcs

Mineral springs discovered here in 1839 brought instant fame as a spa town to Tenbury, and the Pump Room and Baths from this period can still be seen. 'Taking the waters' has long since ceased to be fashionable, and nowadays the town fulfils a quiet rôle as a little market centre for the surrounding countryside. Half-timbered buildings make a pleasant contrast with two fine churches dating from the 19th century.

Take 2nd main turning on to the B4214 SP 'Cleehill' and proceed through hilly country to Cleehill.

CLEEHILL, Salop
Just east of Cleehill on the A4117 is an AA viewpoint which affords superb views to the east and south. North is 1,750ft Titterstone Clee Hill, whose bare slopes rise to a summit crowned by the vast 'golf ball' of a satellite tracking station.

Turn left on to the A4117 and descend then cross the bypass into Ludlow.

LUDLOW, Salop   SO57
Ludlow is a latterday Camelot on the banks of the Corve and Teme, among the gentle Shropshire hills. High above the town's roof tops soars the 135ft tower of the parish church, while on the ground the lovely River Teme adds its own enchantment to the picture-book quality of Ludlow Castle. The church, mainly of 15th-century date, is the largest in the county and preserves contemporary choir stalls. The ashes of poet A E Housman are kept here. Near by are the beautiful black-and-white Reader's House (open on application), and the 17th-century Feathers Hotel. These are possibly the best of many half-timbered buildings preserved in the town. Georgian architecture testifies to the continued popularity of Ludlow and is epitomized in the elegant Butter Cross, which now houses a museum. Broad Street, lined with many fine dwellings from the same period, extends from the Butter Cross to Ludlow's sole surviving medieval gate, the Broad Gate. The town's earliest structure is, of course, the castle. From as early as 1085 this occupied a strategic position in the contentious England/Wales border country known as the Marcher Lands. The town was actually planned round the castle in the 12th century. John Milton's 'Comus' was given its first performance here in 1634. Ludford Bridge (AM) spans the Teme and is of medieval origin.

To leave Ludlow return along the A4117 'Kidderminster' road and pass under a railway bridge. Immediately turn left into unclassified Fishmore Road. After 1 mile branch right SP 'Hayton's Bent'. Ascend, with views to Corve Dale, Wenlock Edge, and the Clee Hills, and follow SP 'Clee St Margaret' to reach that village.

CLEE ST MARGARET, Salop
Remotely set in the Clee Hills by the Clee Brook, this little village is built mainly of stone and is centred on a church with a Norman nave.

Cross a ford and turn left SP 'Abdon'. After ⅓ mile meet crossroads; a detour (SP 'Bouldon') may be taken left from here across pleasantly rural Shropshire countryside to visit Heath Chapel.

Scenes such as this, of the steam-operated Severn Valley Railway, were once commonplace throughout Britain.

HEATH CHAPEL, Salop
This simple, barn-like building stands on its own in a field and is a perfect example of Norman ecclesiastical architecture. It contains a Norman font and various furnishings dating from the 17th century.

Continue on the main route to Abdon.

ABDON, Salop
Bracken-covered slopes rise from this village to Abdon Burf, a tract of rough country that culminates in the dominating eminence of 1,790ft Brown Clee Hill. Excellent views across to Wenlock Edge are afforded by this high region.

The impressive remains of Ludlow's castle are reflected in the waters of the River Teme near 15th-century Dinham Bridge.

Turn right SP 'Ditton Priors' and after 1 mile turn left then in ¾ mile bear right SP 'Cleobury North'. Skirt the north side of Brown Clee Hill, and after 1½ miles turn left and descend to a T-junction. Turn right and continue for ½ mile, then turn left on to the B4364 SP 'Bridgnorth'. Enter Cleobury North.

CLEOBURY NORTH, Salop   SO68
Wooded Burwarton Park adds much to the charm of this village, which boasts a large and picturesque Norman church that was carefully restored by architect Sir Gilbert Scott in the 19th century.

Continue on the B4364 to the

outskirts of Bridgnorth, then turn right on to the A458 to enter the town.

BRIDGNORTH, Salop
Shropshire has more than its fair share of lovely old towns, and Bridgnorth vies with the best of them. It is divided into two parts — Upper Town and Lower Town — by a steep ridge which is negotiated by a twisty road, several flights of steps, and a funicular railway with a breathtaking gradient of 1 in 2. In Lower Town is Bishop Percy's House, a fine half-timbered building of 1580 which is possibly the oldest structure in Bridgnorth. Upper Town is on the site of the original settlement and though much of it burned down during the Civil War the High Street is still straddled by its picturesque town hall (AM). The half-timbered upper storey of this building was made from a barn after the old town hall became a battle casualty. Many fine inns can be found in the High Street as it leads to the ancient North Gate, and at the other end are the elegant Georgian houses of East Castle Street. A precariously leaning tower (AM) is all that remains of Bridgnorth Castle. Nearby St Mary Magdalene's Church was built by engineer and architect Thomas Telford in 1794, and St Leonard's Church stands at the heart of a charming mixture of buildings dotted among grassy verges. The Hermitage (AM) is one of several local caves inhabited until fairly recent times. The station and engine shed at the northern terminus of the Severn Valley Railway provide much interest. East of the town on the Stourbridge road the Midland Motor Museum has over 90 exhibits.

THE SEVERN VALLEY RAILWAY, Salop
Steam locomotives operate between Bridgnorth and Kidderminster over one of Britain's best preserved railways, following the Severn Valley and providing a mobile viewpoint through the beautiful countryside of the area. Trains run most months in the year.

Leave Bridgnorth on the B4364 'Cleobury Mortimer' road and drive to Kinlet. Turn left on to the B4363 SP 'Bewdley', then shortly meet a T-junction and turn left on to the B4194. Continue through Wyre Forest.

WYRE FOREST, Salop, Herefs & Worcs
This one-time royal hunting forest covers an extensive area of mixed heath, scrub, and woodland. During the spring its many wild cherry trees make a picture of white blossom, and in summer the forest is a great attraction to walkers and picnickers. Knowles Mill, a National Trust property set in an orchard, stands close by off the B4194.

Enter Bewdley and turn left for the return to Kidderminster.

POETRY AND SHROPSHIRE IRON

Inspiration lives in the Shropshire hills and along Wenlock Edge. Housman captured its essence in the lovely poems of 'A Shropshire Lad', and the early ironmasters distilled it in a graceful bridge that was to herald the industrial revolution.

SHREWSBURY, Salop
Superbly set in a huge loop of the Severn, this beautiful and unspoilt town is famous for its half-timbered buildings and picturesque streets. Also here are many excellent examples of 18th- and 19th-century architecture. Traditionally founded during the 5th century by the Romans, Shrewsbury has been occupied by various peoples interested in its strategic position. Two notable 18th-century bridges span the Severn into the town centre, and the remains of a castle that defended the vulnerable north-eastern entrance dominate the imposing railway station. Fortification of the castle site was begun in the 11th century, but the remains date mainly from the 13th and were incorporated in a private house about 200 years ago. Near by are the 17th-century buildings of old Shrewsbury School, which now houses the civic library. Outstanding churches in Shrewsbury include the Norman and later Abbey Church, 12th- to 17th-century St Mary's, and mainly 18th-century St Julian's, with its ancient towers. Amongst the outstanding buildings are Rowley's Mansion, which houses a museum of local history and art; Whitehall of 1582; the gateway of the Council House; the Lion Coaching Inn; and the small complex of 14th-century cottages, shops and fine old hall called Bear Steps.

Leave Shrewsbury on the A49 'Leominster' road, and ½ mile beyond Baystonhill turn left on to an unclassified road to reach Condover.

CONDOVER, Salop
Pink sandstone was the predominant material used to build both the 17th-century local church and Condover Hall (open on application), a splendid example of Elizabethan architecture.

At Condover turn left SP 'Pitchford' and after ¼ mile bear left. After 1½ miles meet crossroads and turn right to enter Pitchford.

PITCHFORD, Salop
Half-timbered Pitchford Hall (not open) is a perfect example of a 16th-century black-and-white building, and the adjacent church retains good Norman details.

Continue to Acton Burnell.

ACTON BURNELL, Salop
Edward I held what is said to have been the first English parliament here in 1283. Ruined Acton Burnell Castle (AM) dates from the 13th century and was built by Robert Burnell, Bishop of Bath and Wells, partly as a castle and partly as a palace.

Meet crossroads, turn right SP 'Church Stretton', and after 2 miles bear right. Enter Longnor.

LONGNOR, Salop
In a grove of trees here is a perfect 13th-century church with 18th-century furnishings. Longnor Hall (not open) stands in a large deerpark and dates from 1670. Near by is black-and-white Moat House.

Continue, and after a short way turn left on to the A49. Enter Leebotwood.

Winter sunshine on Wenlock Edge.

LEEBOTWOOD, Salop
The finest of several half-timbered buildings in this village is the thatched Pound Inn. A 1,236ft hill known as The Lawley rises high above the village nearby.

Continue, with Caer Caradoc Hill to the left and the Long Mynd moorland to the right.

CAER CARADOC HILL, Salop
Earthworks of an iron-age hillfort said to have been defended by King Caractacus crown this miniature mountain, which is only 1,500ft high.

Amongst Shrewsbury's many beautiful half-timbered buildings is the Old Council House gateway.

THE LONG MYND, Salop
Rising like the armoured back of some prehistoric monster from the ordered fields of lowland Shropshire, the Long Mynd is a heather-covered mass of ancient grits and shales, largely owned and protected by the National Trust. Where the moorland hills fall towards Church Stretton they are scored by numerous ravines; the lovely Cardingmill Valley is possibly the most beautiful.

Continue and meet crossroads. Turn right on to the B4371 SP 'Town Centre' and enter Church Stretton.

CHURCH STRETTON, Salop
During the late 19th century the district around Church Stretton became known as 'Little Switzerland', and the town itself developed into a popular inland resort. Red-brick and half-timbered Victorian villas mingle with older black-and-white buildings to create a pleasant character complemented by the Church of St Lawrence, which has been adapted through many periods. Above the Norman north doorway is a Celtic fertility symbol. There are three Strettons in the valley – Church Stretton at the centre, All Stretton to the north, and Little Stretton to the south. The latter has many half-timbered buildings.

Return to crossroads and turn left on to the B4370. Pass through the pretty village of Little Stretton. Turn right on to the A49, and continue to Craven Arms.

CRAVEN ARMS, Salop
Originally the hamlet of Newton, this 19th-century town development was renamed after a coaching inn that just preceded its expansion. Today it is an important centre for livestock auctions.

A detour of ¾ mile from the main tour route can be made by continuing on the A49 to Stokesay Castle.

STOKESAY CASTLE, Salop
Wooden beams, overhanging walls, steep roofs, and decorated woodwork, make Stokesay a picture-book castle. It is of the oldest surviving examples of a fortified manor house set in a romantic setting with a quaint Elizabethan gatehouse and dating from c 1280. The castle (AM) owes its superb condition to a singularly uneventful history. Beyond the moat is a church that was damaged during the Civil War and subsequently refurbished during the Commonwealth. Interior furnishings and fittings of that time remain intact.

Leave Craven Arms on the B4368 SP 'Bridgnorth' and enter Corve Dale. Shortly reach Diddlebury.

DIDDLEBURY, Salop
Diddlebury enjoys a picturesque setting beside the river in Corve Dale, beneath the high ridge of beautiful Wenlock Edge. Saxon masonry in the local church includes attractive herringbone work on the north wall.

Continue to the White House at Aston Munslow.

THE WHITE HOUSE, Salop
Many periods are represented in the complex of buildings associated with this mansion, and the house itself has a 14th-century hall and 16th-century cross-wing. A fascinating museum of country life accommodated here displays a variety of farm relics.

Continue through Munslow, with Wenlock Edge to the left and the River Corve to the right. Reach Shipton.

SHIPTON, Salop
Famous and beautiful Shipton Hall (open) is the focal point of this Corve Dale village. Built in c 1587 and enlarged at the back during the mid-18th century, it comprises a large range of buildings, including a fine stable block which dates from the 18th century.

At Shipton bear left on to the B4378 SP 'Much Wenlock' and continue to Much Wenlock.

MUCH WENLOCK, Salop
Poet A E Housman celebrated the beauty of this region in his collection *A Shropshire Lad*. The town is a charming little market centre with

The traceried stonework of Wenlock Priory is echoed in the symbolic design of Much Wenlock's attractive town nameplate.

many excellent half-timbered and other buildings, including such notable examples as Raynald's Mansion, the Manor House, and the Guildhall. Remains of Wenlock Priory (AM), which was founded in the 7th century and became a Cluniac house in 1080, include beautiful interlocking Norman tracery. Near by is splendid Priors Lodge of 1500.

Leave Much Wenlock on the A458 'Bridgnorth' road and continue to Morville.

MORVILLE, Salop
Morville Hall (NT) was rebuilt in the 18th century, and the local church contains a wealth of details from many periods.

Continue and later at roundabout take the 1st exit to join the B4364 and enter Bridgnorth.

BRIDGNORTH, Salop
Bridgnorth is an ancient town, with many interesting buildings.

Leave Bridgnorth on the B4373 and after 5½ miles bear right SP 'Wellington'. Descend into the Severn Gorge and cross the river to reach a T-junction. Turn left and in ¼ mile at roundabout join the A4169 to enter Ironbridge.

IRONBRIDGE, Salop
Across the River Severn here is a splendid iron bridge that was built in

Right: Abraham Darby designed the revolutionary bridge at Ironbridge in the 18th century, unconsciously creating a memorial to the British industrial revolution. Below: a detail of the bridge's ironwork.

1779, the first of its kind in the world. This must surely be the most beautiful monument there is to the industrial revolution, which had its birth in this area. The Ironbridge Gorge Museum, covering six square miles, includes a reconstructed Victorian village and museums of iron and steel making and of the Coalport China Company and a visitor centre. The streets and buildings of Ironbridge itself cling to the sides of the Severn Gorge.

Beyond Ironbridge keep forward on to the B4380 SP 'Shrewsbury'. Continue to Buildwas.

BUILDWAS, Salop
Concrete cooling towers looming from a local power station otherwise hidden by trees make a controversial counterpoint to the 12th-century remains of Buildwas Abbey (AM), near the River Severn. Stone from the ruin was incorporated in the local church. North of the hamlet is the 1,334ft bulk of The Wrekin.

Continue through Leighton, along the Severn Valley, to the edge of Wroxeter.

WROXETER, Salop
During Roman times the important town of *Uriconium* stood here. Excavated remains (AM) include the baths and fragments of other buildings. Near by is a church which incorporates Roman bricks and masonry in its fabric, and displays architectural features from many ages. Inside are several very fine monuments and memorials.

Continue on the B4380 and after ¾ mile turn left on to the A5. Enter Atcham.

ATCHAM, Salop
Spacious wooded parklands and two 18th-century bridges are the main features of this pretty, village which also has a church uniquely dedicated to St Eata. The Myton and Mermaid Inn is of Georgian origin, and Longer Hall was built in 1803 to designs by John Nash. Humphrey Repton laid out the grounds of both Longner and nearby Attingham Hall (NT) (open), a magnificent house of 1785.

Cross the Severn and return to Shrewsbury.

TO THE VALLEY OF SONG

Walled Chester stands on the edge of England like the medieval guardian it once was. Across the border in Wales a natural wall of mountains encloses Llangollen, in a valley that rings with song during the International Eisteddfod.

Victorian architect W H Kelly designed this building, which stands in Park Street, Chester, in a convincing half-timbered style.

CHESTER, Cheshire

Founded nearly 2,000 years ago by the Romans, Chester boasts some of the richest archaeological and architectural treasures in Britain. It is the only city in England to have preserved its Roman and medieval walls in their entirety, and today they provide a 2-mile circular walk which affords excellent views of both the city and its surrounding countryside. At one point the walls overlook the Roodee, a racecourse where the Chester Cup has been run every May since 1824. Chester, or *Deva* as it was once known, remained a principal military station and trading town until the Romans withdrew from Britain, then was probably re-occupied by the Saxons to prevent the Danes from using it as a stronghold. It gradually regained its position as a place of importance, and after it had fallen to the Normans in 1070 became the capital of a county Palatine whose earls were almost as powerful as the king. The medieval town flourished as a port until silting of the Dee during the 15th century brought a decline in trade prosperity. The city continued as a commercial centre, however, and its fortunes largely revived during the rich 18th and 19th centuries. Much survives from all periods of Chester's history, but the source of its distinctive character is undoubtedly the galleried tiers of shops known as The Rows. The beautifully restored sandstone cathedral dates mainly from the 14th century. It incorporates extensive Benedictine monastic

remains, and is especially noted for its richly carved woodwork, the Lady Chapel, the refectory, and the cloisters. Partly ruined St John's Church retains excellent Norman workmanship. Most of Chester Castle now dates from the 19th century, but its 13th-century Agricola Tower is largely original. The castle contains the Cheshire Military Museum encompassing four separate regiments. Black-and-white buildings abound in Chester — God's Providence House, Bishop Lloyd's House and Old Leche House being outstanding — and there are also many timbered inns. The city's history is illustrated in the Heritage and Visitor Centres and the Grosvenor and Guildhall museums. Other museums located on the city walls are at the Water Tower and the King Charles Tower. There is also a Toy Museum in The Rows. Chester Zoo offers a variety of exhibits second only to London.

Leave Chester on the A483 SP 'North Wales' and cross the River Dee via Grosvenor Bridge. Reach a roundabout and take the 4th exit on to the A549 SP 'Saltney'. Reach Saltney and cross into Wales. In 2½ miles at Broughton roundabout take 2nd exit A5104 SP 'Corwen'. After ¾ mile turn left and 1¼ miles further left again. In 1 mile turn left into Penyffordd. In ¼ mile turn right and after 2 miles cross the River Alyn to pass through Portblyddyn.

The gates at the entrance to Chirk Castle are an outstanding example of wrought-iron work by the Davies brothers of Wrexham.

Panoramic views of Eglwyseg Mountain are afforded from the Horseshoe Pass near Llangollen.

At the Bridge Inn turn left then immediately right and ascend. Proceed, with mountain views, through the village of Llandegla.

Turn right then immediately left, then after ¾ mile reach a roundabout and take the 1st exit on to the A542 'Llangollen' road. Ascend to the Horseshoe Pass.

HORSESHOE PASS, Clwyd

Fine views of the surrounding mountain scenery can be enjoyed from this 1,367ft pass. North-east is 1,844ft Cyrn-y-Brain, topped by Sir Watkin's Tower, and west are the slopes of Llantysilio Mountain.

Descend along the Eglwyseg Valley to Valle Crucis Abbey.

VALLE CRUCIS ABBEY, Clwyd

Pleasantly wooded hills frame the view from the picturesque ruins of this ancient abbey, which was founded in 1201 and has left extensive remains (AM). 'Valle Crucis' means 'Vale of the Cross' and derives from nearby Eliseg's Pillar (AM), which was erected to commemorate a nobleman of ancient times.

After a short distance reach the Horseshoe Falls.

HORSESHOE FALLS, Clwyd

Not a natural cascade but a beautifully curving weir with a fall of 18 inches, this lovely River Dee feature was built to feed water into the Llangollen Canal.

Continue with Castell Dinas Bran to the left.

CASTELL DINAS BRAN, Clwyd

Ramparts of an Iron-Age fort partly surround this ruined 13th-century stronghold, which occupies a hilltop site overlooking Llangollen.

Turn right to cross the Dee and enter Llangollen.

LLANGOLLEN, Clwyd

This small town's world-wide reputation as a centre of Welsh culture and music comes from the International Eisteddfod held here for one week in July. During this time the small streets are transformed by a riot of colourful national costumes and chatter of foreign tongues, while the surrounding hillsides echo to the sound of great international choirs and poets performing in a huge 1,000-seat marquee. Plas Newydd (open) is a black-and-white house on the edge of the town which was, for many years, the home of the 'Ladies

Valle Crucis Abbey was founded by Madog ap Gruffyd, a prince of Powys, during the 13th century.

of Llangollen' who arrived here in 1779, entertained a string of celebrities and generated endless gossip with their lifestyle. Transport enthusiasts are covered by the Canal Museum and Passenger Boat Trip Centre with horsedrawn trips along the Shropshire Union Canal, and by the Llangollen Railway.

Follow the A5 'Shrewsbury' road through the winding valley of the Dee to Froncysyllte.

FRONCYSYLLTE, Clwyd

Thomas Telford's amazing 120ft high Pontcysyllte Aqueduct and the longest in the United Kingdom, was built to carry the Shropshire Union Canal over the deep ravine of the River Dee. It can be seen by turning left. Downstream is a railway viaduct whose impressive design is almost as remarkable.

Continue to Chirk.

CHIRK, Clwyd

An interesting section of the Shropshire Union Canal in this well kept village includes a long, damp tunnel which opens into a wide basin before the canal is carried high across the Ceiriog Valley.

CHIRK CASTLE, Clwyd

Outside Chirk behind superb 18th-century wrought-iron gates (AM) is Chirk Castle, a 13th-century border

Poets, artists, and writers have praised Llangollen's hospitality since the early 19th century.

fortress in a commanding position above the Ceiriog Valley. Unlike many of its contemporaries this stronghold has been continuously inhabited since it was built, and considerable structural changes have been made to suit the tastes of successive owners.

Cross the River Ceiriog into England, and after 1¼ miles turn left on to the B5070 SP 'Overton'. In 1 mile reach St Martin's.

ST MARTIN'S, Salop

The interior of the beautiful 13th-century local church preserves Georgian furnishings which include boxpews and a double-decker pulpit. Attractive almshouses stand near by.

Join the B5069 and cross undulating countryside to re-enter Wales. Reach the A528 and turn left to enter Overton.

OVERTON, Clwyd

Very old churchyard yews in this pleasant small town are traditionally held to be among the 7 greatest wonders of Wales.

Keep forward on the B5059, SP 'Bangor' then turn right. Continue with views of the Dee and Bangor racecourse, to Bangor-is-y-Coed.

BANGOR-IS-Y-COED, Clwyd

An ancient stone bridge is the dominating feature of this picturesque village. At one time a monastery stood near by, but the buildings were destroyed and its monks slaughtered by order of King Aethelfrith of Northumbria in AD 615. Little survives today.

Turn right SP 'Wrexham' and shortly right again then in ¼ mile turn right on to the bypass A525. After 1¾ miles turn right on to the B5130 SP 'Wrexham Industrial Estate' then keep forward, no SP. In 5½ miles turn left then right across the bypass to enter Holt. Bear right then keep forward.

HOLT, Clwyd

Slight remains of a Norman castle can be seen near the 8-arched 15th-century bridge that spans the Dee here. The local church is a fine building which dates originally from the 13th century but was rebuilt in the 15th. Inside is an elaborately decorated font.

Cross the Dee on to the B5434 to Farndon and re-enter England.

FARNDON, Cheshire

In Farndon attractive houses group round a large church that was rebuilt after Civil War damage. An unusual feature of the church is a stained-glass window depicting a troop of Royalist soldiers.

Turn left on to the B5130 SP 'Chester' and continue through wooded scenery to 'Aldford.

ALDFORD, Cheshire

Earthworks of a Norman motte-and-bailey castle may be seen north of Aldford's Victorian church.

Return to Chester.

LLANDUDNO, Gwynedd
Justifiably known as the 'Queen of Welsh Resorts', Llandudno developed in the 1850s from a cluster of fishermen's cottages to a Victorian seaside resort which is a classic of its kind. The town was the brainchild of Liverpool surveyor Owen Williams, who planned the great sweep of the Promenade and the majestically wide streets. Great Orme's Head, with its gardens, cable railway, an ancient church, and windswept grassy slopes, separates the resort's two superb beaches.

Leave Llandudno on the A546, SP 'Deganwy'. Pass through Deganwy and in 1¼ miles reach a roundabout and take the 1st exit on to the A55 'Betws-y-coed'. A detour to Conwy may be made from the main route by crossing the Afon Conwy from this roundabout.

CONWY, Gwynedd
Three bridges span the Conwy estuary for access to the town, which is squeezed between the mountains and the sea. The oldest of the bridges was built by Thomas Telford in 1826 to carry traffic previously forced to use the perilous ferry. In 1848 Stephenson built a tubular railway bridge across the estuary, and in 1958 a new road bridge took the load from Telford's original. All three bridges seem to lead straight into Edward I's magnificent castle, which, along with the complete town walls, is a supreme example of 13th-century defensive architecture (all AM). The original medieval street plan is preserved, but only a few old buildings survive. Outstanding amongst these are Aberconwy (NT), which was built in 1400, and houses the Conwy Exhibition and the lovely Tudor house of Plas Mawr. Also of interest are the Visitor Centre, and 'Britain's Smallest House'.

Continue on the main route through Llandudno Junction. After ¾ mile at

NORTHERN RESORTS AND MOUNTAIN LANES

Children's laughter is as common as the cries of gulls on the North Wales coast, but away from the sea the sounds diminish and change till all that is heard is the breeze through sedges and the murmur of mountain streams.

The weathered rock of Great Orme's Head is typical of limestone scenery.

roundabout follow signs Betws-y-coed on to the A470. Drive through Glan Conwy, pass the Felin Isaf Watermill (open) and 1¼ miles farther reach the entrance to Bodnant Gardens.

BODNANT GARDENS, Gwynedd
The finest garden in Wales, and one of the best in Britain, Bodnant (NT) occupies a superb terraced site on the east side of the Conwy Valley and is open from March to October. It is best seen early in the year when its celebrated azaleas and rhododendrons are in bloom. The gardens were first laid out in 1875 by Henry Pochin, and have been considerably extended since.

Follow the beautiful Vale of Conwy to Llanrwst.

LLANRWST, Gwynedd
A graceful 3-arched bridge that spans the Conwy here is dated 1636 and (probably wrongly) attributed to architect Inigo Jones. Near by is Ty Hwnt i'r Bont, a 15th-century house (NT) which is open as a café. In the parish church are an elaborate 15th-century rood loft and screen which were brought from Maenan Abbey at the Dissolution. Across the river are the beautiful Gwydir Chapel of 1633, which houses memorials to one of Wales' greatest land-owning families, the Wynnes, and the Tudor

Gwydir Castle (open), which was once one of their family seats.

Continue on the A470, cross a railway bridge then turn left on to the B5427 SP 'Nebo'. In 3½ miles reach a T-junction and turn right on to the B5113. Pass through Nebo and later descend into Pentrefoelas.

PENTREFOELAS, Clwyd
Mountain scenery starts to give way to moorland near this hamlet. An 8ft-high inscribed pillar known as the Levelinus Stone marks the spot where Llywelyn ap Sisyll, a prince of Gwynedd, fell in battle in 1023.

Turn left on to the A5, and after ¼ mile turn left again on to the A543 'Denbigh' road. Ascend on to the Denbigh Moors.

DENBIGH MOORS, Clwyd
Forestry plantations and huge reservoirs have dramatically changed the character of this moorland region in recent years. The latest enterprise is the construction of the vast Brenig Reservoir.

Continue past the lonely Sportsman's Arms – the highest inn in Wales – and drive through Bylchau to reach Denbigh.

DENBIGH, Clwyd
Overlooking the town's attractive streets are the ruins of Edward I's great castle (AM). It was begun in 1282 with the construction of town walls that have remained remarkably intact to the present day. Perhaps the most impressive feature of the fortress is its tripartite gatehouse. Inside the town walls are remains of St Hilary's Tower (AM), which formed part of the original garrison chapel, and Leicester's Folly (AM). The latter is part of a church that was to have replaced the Cathedral of St Asaph, but was never completed. In the lower part of the town are the remains of a Carmelite friary (AM).

Continue on the A525 'Rhyl' road, with the ridge of the Clwydian Range prominent to the right. Enter Trefnant.

Conwy Castle is arguably one of the greatest works by Edward I's military architect, Master James of St George.

TREFNANT, Clwyd

Church, parsonage, and school here were built by architect Sir Gilbert Scott during the 19th century. The capitals of the columns inside the church are decorated with carved leaves typical of tree species found in the countryside round Trefnant.

Keep forward for St Asaph.

Delightfully naive 17th-century paintings decorate the roof of Gwydir Uchaf Chapel at Gwydir Castle, Llanrwst.

ST ASAPH, Clwyd

Both a village and a city, little St Asaph stands beside the River Elwy and has a cathedral that was founded by St Kentigern in AD 560. This has subsequently been rebuilt several times, and major restoration work was carried out during the 19th century by architect Sir Gilbert Scott. The building, no bigger than a large parish church, is the smallest cathedral in England and Wales.

Follow SP 'Rhyl', and after ¾ mile meet a roundabout and keep forward. A detour to Bodelwyddan can be made from the main route by turning left on to the Conwy road A55.

BODELWYDDAN, Clwyd

Rising gracefully above the village roof tops like the tip of a giant white spear is the 202ft spire of the parish church. Its prominence as a landmark that can be seen miles around must have been planned by Lady Margaret Willoughby de Broke, who built it in 1856 as a giant memorial to her husband. The interior of the building has earnt it the name 'The Marble Church', for no less than 14 different kinds of that stone were used in its construction.

Continue on the main route and turn right into Rhuddlan.

RHUDDLAN, Clwyd

The princes of Wales and their Norman conquerors recognised Rhuddlan's position in the Vale of Clwyd as being of military significance, and both forces built castles here. The mound, or motte (AM), of the first invasion stronghold

still exists but it is the great castle of Edward I (AM) that really captures the eye. This was his headquarters whilst conducting the campaign to conquer Wales, and it was the Statute of Rhuddlan that confirmed his sovereignty in 1284. The parish church dates originally from the 13th century, and the bridge (AM) over the Clwyd has 16th-century arches.

At the roundabout take the 1st exit for Rhyl.

RHYL, Clwyd

'Sunny Rhyl' offers 3 miles of sandy beach and almost all the entertainments expected of a seaside resort as popular as this. Few other British holiday towns cater better for the family holiday, and Rhyl has been a confirmed success ever since its development from a pair of fishermen's cottages in 1833.

Leave Rhyl promenade on the 'Abergele' road and shortly turn right on to the A548. Follow the coast through Kinmel Bay and Towyn to Pensarn.

PENSARN, Clwyd

This resort, linked with Abergele, is at the centre of a 5-mile sand and shingle beach.

Reach a roundabout and turn left to enter Abergele.

ABERGELE, Clwyd

No longer simply a market town but also a busy resort, Abergele is surrounded by caravan sites, chalets, and all the paraphernalia associated with the seaside. Its Tudor church features a double nave.

Turn right on to the A547 'Conwy' road and pass the road to Gwrych Castle.

Partial demolition after the Civil War reduced Rhuddlan Castle's 13th-century fabric to a picturesque ruin.

GWRYCH CASTLE, Clwyd

This mock-Norman extravagance with castellated walls and fairy-tale turrets was built in 1814. It now serves as a holiday centre, offering medieval banquets and jousting among its attractions.

Continue to Llanddulas.

LLANDDULAS, Clwyd

Llanddulas is both a holiday village and a loading point for limestone worked in local quarries.

Remain on the A547 SP 'Old Colwyn' and continue to Colwyn Bay.

COLWYN BAY, Clwyd

Lovers of Victorian architecture will find much to please them in Colwyn Bay. The resort is hardly more than a century old, and is somewhat more restrained in character than many of its neighbours. Excellent parks soften the character of the town, and the Welsh Mountain Zoo is a post-war development featuring a good variety of wild animals.

Continue forward and follow signs 'Rhos on Sea' then 'Llandudno' on to the B5115. Pass through Rhos then cross Little Orme's Head and return to Llandudno.

Fish eagles, hawks, and many other birds of prey can be seen at Colwyn Bay's Mountain Zoo.

The graceful lines of the bridge at Llanrwst have led to its being attributed to Inigo Jones.

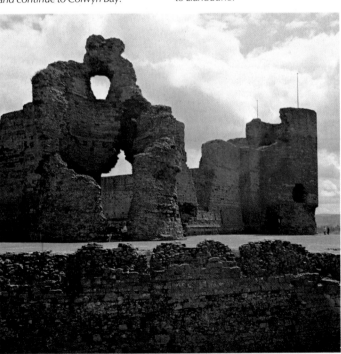

LAKES AMONG THE FORESTS

Rarely level and often winding, the roads taken by this tour
ascend the rocky clefts of mountain streams to summits that
give panoramic views across forest-clad mountains and
tree-bordered lakes. Everywhere is the sparkle
and chatter of water.

BALA, Gwynedd

Behind Bala's cheerful and
unassuming tree-lined High Street is
Tomen-y-Bala, the mound of a
Norman castle. During the 18th
century this was a popular spot for
the local folk to do their knitting.
Hand-knitted stockings from Bala
were once famous, and George III
would wear no others. In the High
Street is a statue of Tom Ellis, a
farmer's son who became Liberal
Chief Whip and a tireless
campaigner for Welsh home rule.
Cyffdy Farm Park (open) is a rare-
breed centre for North Wales.

SNOWDONIA NATIONAL PARK

Much of this route is within the
boundaries of the 845-square-mile
Snowdonia National Park, which
contains some of the most dramatic
and beautiful scenery in Britain and is
famous for its mountain ranges.
The breath-taking valleys between
mountains are often graced by
lovely lakes and reservoirs, or
enlivened with the sound of running
water. In the south are old mine
workings where prehistoric and
modern men have searched
for gold.

*Leave Bala on the B4391 'Llangynog'
road and skirt the northern extremity
of Bala Lake. Cross the River Dee and
follow its valley for several miles.
Climb on to open moorland and the
slopes of the Berwyn Mountains.*

THE BERWYN MOUNTAINS

Stretching from Llangollen to Lake
Vyrnwy, this mountain range is
gradually being changed in
appearance as vast forests of
conifers swallow up its slopes. Views
from the two highest peaks – 2,712ft
Cadair Berwyn and 2,713ft Moel
Sych – open up outstanding
panoramas in all directions.

*Descend into the Eiarth Valley and
enter Llangynog.*

LLANGYNOG, Powys

Remains of once-important slate
quarries and lead mines may be seen
in this area. The church is dedicated
to St Cynog, who was the eldest son
of Brychan, a prince of one of the
ancient Welsh kingdoms.

*Follow SP 'Llanfyllin' along the Tanat
Valley to Penybontfawr.*

PENYBONTFAWR, Powys

Picturesquely set on the southern
slopes of the Berwyn Mountains,
this village has a handsome
Victorian church and a charming
school building. All around is
beautiful countryside.

*Turn right on to the B4396 SP 'Lake
Vyrnwy' and continue along a narrow,
winding road through wooded
country to Llanwddyn.*

The valley which romantic Lake Vyrnwy
occupies was created by a glacier
during the ice ages.

During the 16th century these hills near Dinas Mawddwy were the haunt of
notorious brigands.

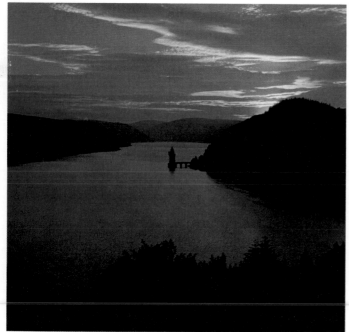

LLANWDDYN, Powys

Built to replace the old village of
Llanwddyn, which now lies under
the waters of artificial Lake Vyrnwy,
this village stands in a countryside
dominated by rank upon rank of
dark green coniferous forest. Such
rare creatures as the pine marten
and polecat have been able to make
a comeback because of the new
habitats provided by afforestation,
and are increasing in numbers.

*Turn right on to the B4393 to reach
Lake Vyrnwy. Turn left across the dam
and skirt the wooded south shores of
the lake.*

LAKE VYRNWY, Powys

This lake is 4¾ miles long and was
created in the late 19th century to
supply Liverpool with water. The
gothic water tower on its north-east
side, and thick forests that clothe its
banks to the water's edge, seem to
suggest the depths of the German
Black Forest rather than Wales.

*Continue the circuit of the lake and
return to Llanwddyn. Two alternative
routes leading from the north end of
the lake to Bwlch-y-Groes and
through the Hirnant Pass to Bala
respectively are described at the end
of this tour. Follow the 'Llanfyllin' road
and in 4 miles turn right on to the
B4395 SP 'Pont Llogel'. Later skirt
Dyfnant Forest and cross the Afon
Vyrnwy. Continue to the edge of
Llangadfan. Turn right on to the A458
'Dolgellau' road and climb gradually
out of the Banwy Valley. Descend
along the wooded Dugoed Valley to
Mallwyd.*

MALLWYD, Gwynedd

Mallwyd is set beside the Afon Dyfi
and is the haunt of both artists and
anglers. The rib of a prehistoric
animal handg over the church
porch.

*Turn right on to the A470 and reach
Dinas Mawddwy.*

DINAS MAWDDWY, Gwynedd

During the 16th century this very
Welsh village was at the centre of a
region notorious for its bandits.
Remains of old mines and quarries
dot the area, and one group of
quarry buildings now houses the
Meirion Woollen Mill (open). (An
alternative route to Bala over the
spectacular Bwlch-y-Groes Pass
starts from Dinas Mawddwy and is
described at the end of this tour.)

*Continue on the A470 and climb the
bleak 1,170ft Bwlch Oerddrws Pass.
Descend, with views of Cader Idris
mountain. Beyond the Cross Foxes
Hotel a detour may be taken right on
the B4416 to Brithdir.*

BRITHDIR, Gwynedd

The startling 19th-century church
here was built in memory of Charles
Tooth by his widow, and was
designed so that it appeared to
spring from the soil rather than sit
solidly on it. The interior is simple,
but glows with reflected light from
the beaten copper of the altar and
pulpit. On the approach to the
village is the beautiful Torrent Walk.

*Descend and branch left into
Dolgellau.*

DOLGELLAU, Gwynedd
Granite and boulder stone from the surrounding mountains are the principal materials from which Dolgellau is built. Its narrow, twisting streets are set in a fine position beside the Afon Wnion, and to the south green slopes rise to the craggy summits of Cader Idris. St Mary's

Church was built in 1716 against a plain medieval tower. Wooden columns support the nave roof, and the interior is lit by windows with excellent stained glass. Beautiful Precipice Walk, which lies north of the town and is approached from the Llanfachreth road (off the A494), affords superb views throughout its 7-mile length round the rugged slopes of Foel Cynwch. Gold for the Queen's wedding ring came from old mines in the tree-clad hillsides above Dolgellau's rooftops.

From Dolgellau follow signs 'Bala'. Cross the river then turn right. Later join the A494 and climb the wooded Wnion Valley. To the west is 2,409ft Rhobell Fawr.

RHOBELL FAWR, Gwynedd
Composed of solidified lavas from ancient volcanoes, this 2,409ft mountain is the highest point in the wedge of land between the Wnion and Mawddach Valleys. Fine views

afforded from its summit take in the Rhinog Mountains to the west and the Arans to the east.

COED-Y-BRENIN FOREST, Gwynedd
This Forestry Commission enterprise embraces all the woodlands around and to the north of Dolgellau. It covers an area of nearly 16,000 acres, and access to the woodland and its varied mountain scenery is provided by 100 miles of forest roads; the public is warned against the dangers of leaving litter and especially, carelessly discarded cigarette stubs.

Descend to Llanuwchllyn and the southern end of Bala Lake.

LLANUWCHLLYN, Gwynedd
A road-side memorial here commemorates two great champions of the Welsh language, Sir O M Edwards and his son Sir Ifan ab Owen Edwards. Sir Ifan founded the Welsh League of Youth in 1922. The nearby lakeside mansion of Glanllyn is used as a centre for the league's activities.

ALTERNATIVE ROUTES
At the north-western end of Lake Vyrnwy are 2 mountain roads. One of these can be taken through the Hirnant Pass to Bala, and the other leads up Cwm Eunant to Bwlch-y-Groes. The latter is described under the Dinas Mawddwy alternative route, which follows later.

HIRNANT PASS, Gwynedd
This alternative route is well worth driving for its scenery. From Lake Vyrnwy it climbs steeply along the valley of the little Afon Nadroedd to a 1,641ft summit at the Hirnant Pass before descending along Cwm Hirnant through the Penllyn Forest to Bala.

From Dinas Mawddwy an alternative route may be taken back to Bala via Llanymawddwy and Bwlch-y-Groes. Leave Dinas Mawddwy by turning right on to an unclassified road and ascend the valley of the Afon Dyfi to Llanymawddwy.

Dolgellau's narrow streets are divided by the Afon Wnion, which is spanned here by an ancient 7-arched bridge.

Near Brithdir is spectacular Torrent Walk, which follows the Afon Clywedog.

Bwlch-y-Groes, the Gap of the Cross, is the highest mountain pass in Wales.

BALA LAKE or LLYN TEGID, Gwynedd
Largest natural lake in Wales, Bala is over 4 miles long and in some places measures some 150ft in depth. It is surrounded by mountain scenery and is a popular venue for water-based sports. The narrow-gauge Bala Lake Railway runs along its south-eastern bank from Llanuwchllyn station to Bala, providing a mobile viewpoint from which to enjoy the superb waterside scenery. Originally the route was owned by British Rail, who closed it down in 1965 and sold it to the local council. The potential of the lake-side section was quickly recognised, and a number of steam locomotives were acquired to provide a tourist service.

Return to Bala.

LLANYMAWDDWY, Gwynedd
This remote and mountain-encircled hamlet has a tiny church with an attractive old bellcote.

Ascend a 1 in 4 road to Bwlch-y-Groes.

BWLCH-Y-GROES, Gwynedd
At 1,790ft this is the highest mountain pass in Wales. A road east descends to Lake Vyrnwy through Cwm Eunant, and the road to Bala follows the spectacular and precipitous Cynllwyd Valley.

THE ARANS, Gwynedd
To the west of Bwlch-y-Groes rise the twin peaks – 2,970ft Aran Fawddwy and 2,901ft Aran Benllyn – of the Aran range. Aran Fawddwy is the highest mountain in Wales outside the Snowdon range.

Descend along the Cynllwyd Valley to join the B4403 and drive along the south-eastern shores of Bala Lake to reach the B4391 and Bala.

THE LLEYN PENINSULA, Gwynedd

In many respects the Lleyn is similar to the other western peninsulas of St David's in South Wales and Cornwall in England. All three were settled by Iberian peoples in prehistoric times, and their cultures are still strongly Celtic in character. Their coastlines are rugged and invariably magnificent, and their inland hills are scored by numerous small river valleys. The great mountain barrier at the eastern end of Lleyn has enabled the peninsula to preserve more of its own special character than was possible for the others.

PWLLHELI, Gwynedd

Seaside resort and market town, Pwllheli is the unofficial capital of the Lleyn Peninsula and has an old harbour that was once busy with sea-going craft. Even now it provides a safe haven for small boats, but is frequented more by holiday-makers than ancient mariners. Butlins Holiday Camp lies 3 miles east.

Leave Pwllheli on the A497 'Criccieth' road and continue to Llanystumdwy.

LLANYSTUMDWY, Gwynedd

This village is assured of a permanent place in history because of its association with David Lloyd George, the small-town solicitor who became Prime Minister. His childhood was spent in a roadside cottage here (open), and his body was brought back to lie beside the River Dwyfor. Interesting items are displayed in the Lloyd George Museum.

Continue to Criccieth

CRICCIETH, Gwynedd

Waves break constantly on the rocks beneath the ruins (AM) of a fortress built here by the princes of North Wales in the 13th century. The castle was enlarged by Edward I after he had occupied the region. Victorian charm and a relaxed atmosphere supplement the obvious amenity of the resort's excellent sun and sea-bathing beach.

Leave by the B4411 SP 'Caernarfon' and in 4½ miles turn left on to the A487 for Bryncir.

AN ARM IN THE OCEAN

The coast of the lovely Lleyn Peninsula is a confusion of wide sands and massive cliffs. Vagrant lanes run through fields cut from the flanks of mountains, and ancient churches mark a pilgrim's way to Bardsey – burial place of a thousand saints.

The eastern peak of Yr Eifl, a forked mountain on the north coast of the Lleyn Peninsula, is crowned by a magnificent hillfort called Tre'r Ceiri.

BRYNCIR, Gwynedd

Good-quality cloth is sold from the working woollen mill in this Dwyfach Valley village. A 6th-century tombstone stands at Llystyngwyn Farm.

Continue to Llanllyfni.

LLANLLYFNI, Gwynedd

The Afon Llyfni flows north of this Victorian quarryman's village from its source at Llyn Nantlle Uchaf, among disturbingly derelict slate workings. Of the several old chapels in Llanllyfni, only Ebenezer has retained its 19th-century interior.

Continue to Penygroes.

PENYGROES, Gwynedd

This colourful quarryman's town grew from its sister community of Llanllyfni with the development of the slate industry during the 19th century.

From Penygroes turn left on to an unclassified road SP 'Clynnog and

Porth Dinllaen was considered as a possible rail terminus for Ireland in the 19th century.

Pwllheli'; After 2 miles meet a T-junction and turn left on to the A499. Drive through Pontllyfni and enter Clynnog-fawr.

CLYNNOG FAWR, Gwynedd

St Beuno founded a monastery here in AD 616, and is buried in a chapel connected to the local church by a passage. His tomb was once reputed to hold great curative value. The church itself, a magnificent structure with a massive tower, was an important stopping place for pilgrims to the monastery on Bardsey Island. Between the main road and the sea is a well-preserved prehistoric tomb called Bachwen.

Continue for 3½ miles and turn right on the B4417, SP 'Nefyn', and pass a lay-by under the slopes of Yr Eifl.

Welsh architect Clough Williams-Ellis designed David Lloyd George's memorial at Llanystumdwy.

YR EIFL, Gwynedd

Englishmen know the triple peaks of this 1,849ft mountain as 'The Rivals', but a more accurate translation of the Welsh name is rendered 'The Fork'. Footpaths lead to the summits. The mountain is the haunt of cuckoos in spring, and its rock-strewn and heather-clad peaks afford stunning views in the crystal conditions that often prevail at that time of year. One of the finest iron-age hillforts (AM) in Wales, with mighty stone walls defending an interior crowded with hut circles, is sited on the eastern peak. It is possible that the complex was inhabited until cAD 400.

Descend through Llithfaen to Nefyn.

NEFYN, Gwynedd
At one time it was claimed that Nefyn sent more of its men to sea than almost any other British town. In 1284 Edward I celebrated his conquest over the Welsh here, and in 1353 the Black Prince made the town one of the 10 royal boroughs of North Wales. Today Nefyn enjoys a genteel retirement from politics and makes the most of the resort possibilities offered by its fine sands.

Turn right on to the 'Aberdaron' road and enter Morfa Nefyn.

MORFA NEFYN, Gwynedd
Rugged headlands shelter a long sweep of sandy beach at Morfa Nefyn, and an unclassified road leads right from the tour route to the picturesque hamlet of Porth Dinllaen. This small community was once considered as a rail terminus point for Ireland; some might think it had a lucky escape.

Continue on the B4417 and pass through Edern to reach Tudweiliog.

TUDWEILIOG, Gwynedd
The coast near this village is indented by many small sandy coves, backed by formidable cliffs pocked with caves. Architect Sir Gilbert Scott designed the simple but effective local church in 1850.

Continue and in 4¼ miles turn right on to the B4413. After ¼ mile the route allows a possible detour to Porth Oer:, turn right on to an unclassified road.

PORTH OER, Gwynedd
Famous for its Whistling Sands, which really do whistle when trodden on, Porth Oer is a sheltered little bay offering cliff walks and fine seascapes.

Continue to Aberdaron on the B4413.

ABERDARON, Gwynedd
Last stop on the old route for Bardsey Island, Aberdaron is an attractive village with a café reputed to have been a pilgrim's halt. The name of the café, Gegin Fawr, means Big Kitchen. A large church on the site of a foundation established by St Hywyn in the 6th century probably sheltered pilgrims as they waited for a boat to take them across to the island, the burial ground of saints.

BRAICH-Y-PWLL, Gwynedd
A spectacular 500ft cliff dramatically ends the Lleyn here. Views inland extend along the whole peninsula to Snowdonia, and a little over a mile out to sea is the holy island of Bardsey, destination of pilgrims since

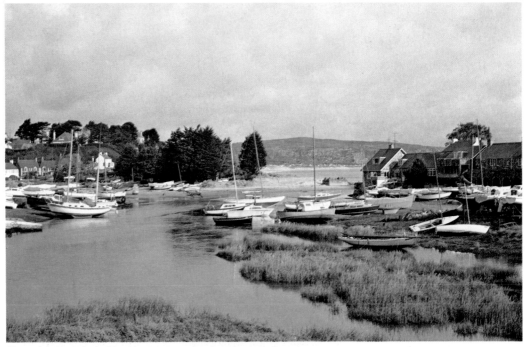

Abersoch is a popular holiday resort with a sheltered harbour.

the 6th century. Most of this magnificent coastline is protected by the National Trust.

Continue from Aberdaron on an unclassified road to Rhiw.

RHIW, Gwynedd
The scattered cottages and 18th-century church of this village do little to obstruct views of the magnificent South Lleyn coast (NT). The village itself is windswept and exposed, but 1,000ft Mynydd Rhiw shelters the house and gardens of nearby Plas-yn-Rhiw from the Atlantic weather.

PLAS-YN-RHIW, Gwynedd
This charming house, built in the 16th century and modernized in Regency times, is surrounded by nearly 60 acres of woodland and garden. The whole property and large areas of beautiful coastline were given to the National Trust in 1952 by the Misses Keating. Views from the house embrace an incomparable panorama extending across Hell's Mouth and Cardigan Bay to the enigmatic mountain of Cader Idris.

Keep forward on the 'Abersoch' road to reach Llangian.

LLANGIAN, Gwynedd
Neat cottages with well-tended gardens full of flowers have helped this lovely place win the coveted Best-kept Village in Wales Award.

Turn left, then ascend and turn right to descend to Abersoch.

ABERSOCH, Gwynedd
Smart villas, expensive-looking yachts, and plush hotels are the typical signs of fashionable affluence displayed by this resort. Its popularity can be mostly attributed to its sandy beaches, mild climate, and safe bathing, but lanes leading to the windswept headland of Trwyn Cilan are also a major attraction.

ST TUDWAL'S ISLANDS, Gwynedd
Seen from the coast at Abersoch, these two grass-covered islands are named after a saint who came to live on one of them in the 6th century. They are privately owned, but trips can be made round their coasts by hired boats from Abersoch.

Follow the Pwyllheli road A499 along the coast to Llanbedrog.

LLANBEDROG, Gwynedd
Excellent sandy beaches and attractive cliff walks have assured Llanbedrog's popularity as a resort. The parish church is embowered in trees and preserves a medieval screen. Fragments of ancient glass can be seen in the east window. Above the village is a hill which features a ruined mill (NT) and affords good views.

Continue through low-lying countryside and in 3 miles join the A497 to re-enter Pwyllheli.

Clynnog Fawr's magnificent church dates from the 16th century, and is the burial place of St Beuno.

SNOWDON AND THE SEA

The name Gwynedd lives again as a modern county.
Gwynedd the fortress, the strong land dominated by the great
star of Snowdon and moated by the Menai Strait, has never
died. It is still as majestically severe as it was
under the Celtic princes.

CAERNARFON, Gwynedd

Workaday Caernarfon is a comfortable small town which has become the most important tourist centre in Snowdonia. Above its jumbled roofs rise the massive towers of Edward I's 13th-century castle (AM), acknowledged as the finest of its type in Britain, while nearby is the old walled town and, in the harbour area, a maritime museum. East of the town centre is the Roman fort of Segontium, with its own museum. Although host to thousands, the town preserves a parochial 'Welshness' that is implicit in the gesticulating statue of Lloyd George opposite the castle balcony from which newly invested Princes of Wales greet their subjects. The sheltered waters of the Menai Strait abound with small craft from the town's sailing clubs, and offer some of the finest fishing in Britain.

Leave Caernarfon on the A487 SP 'Bangor', and drive alongside the Menai Strait to port Dinorwic.

PORT DINORWIC, Gwynedd

Once a busy port concerned with the export of Dinorwic slate, it is now a well-known yachting centre with a large marina.

Continue and in 1½ miles at a roundabout take 1st exit SP 'Holyhead'. In ¾ mile at another roundabout take 1st exit to join the A5. Cross the Britannia Bridge into Anglesey and immediately branch left then turn right A4080 to reach Menai Bridge town. Here follow signs Bangor and cross Telford's suspension bridge then at roundabout take 1st exit A5122 to enter Bangor.

BANGOR, Gwynedd

Old Bangor is a delightfully undistinguished maze in which the Cathedral of St Deiniol (claimed to be the oldest bishopric in Britain) crouches with unassuming modesty. The handsome buildings of the University College of North Wales were officially opened in 1911. There is a town museum and art gallery. On the seaward side Bangor's streets dip down to the city shore and a superb pier.

Leave Bangor on the A5122 'Betws-y-coed' road and continue to the entrance of Penrhyn Castle Estate.

PENRHYN CASTLE, Gwynedd

Although the site of Penrhyn Castle (NT) can lay claim to antiquity, the improbable extravaganza that rears its battlements above the park's

Caernarfon Castle, one of a series built to subjugate the Welsh, is arguably the finest example of medieval fortification in Britain.

wooded acres has its roots set firmly in 19th-century gothic fantasy. Parts of the edifice bear more than an accidental likeness to other great houses, and the combinations of revived styles favoured by architect Thomas Hopper are bewildering but effective. Inside are interesting exhibits, displays, and impressive chambers open to the public.

In ¾ mile at roundabout take 2nd exit A5 and almost immediately turn right on to the B4409 'SP Caernarfon'. In 3½ miles at a roundabout turn left on to the B4547 SP 'Llanberis'. After 2 miles turn right and descend to a T-junction with the A4086. A detour can be taken from here by turning right on the A4086 to the edge of Llanrug, then left on to an unclassified road for Bryn Bras Castle.

BRYN BRAS CASTLE, Gwynedd

Bryn Bras Castle (open) is a piece of 19th-century romanticism which presides over Llanrug village . It stands in grounds noted for their peaceful lawns and embowered walks through tranquil mature woodland.

The main drive turns left on to the A4086 to skirt the shore of Llyn Padarn.

LLYN PADARN, Gwynedd

Once part of a much larger water, Llyn Padarn is separated from its sister lake Peris by a natural dam formed by the gradual accumulation of material washed down in a mountain stream. Its north-eastern shore carries the narrow-gauge line of the steam-powered Llanberis Lake Railway, whose predecessor transported slate from the Dinorwic

slate quarries to Port Dinorwic. There is also a country park.

Shortly branch right into Llanberis.

LLANBERIS, Gwynedd

Terraced houses built on sites blasted from the rock huddle together to form Llanberis, a typical village of the slate-working communities of North Wales. A

route which ascends to the main summit of Snowdon from here is considered the easiest of the mountain's 3 main paths. Close to the village is the lower terminus of the Snowdon Mountain Railway. Also here is the Oriel Eryn Welsh Environment Interpretation Centre, and across the valley at Gilfach Ddu is the Welsh Slate Museum housed in the works buildings of the former Dinorwic Quarry. This is also the starting point of the Llanberis Lake Railway.

SNOWDON MOUNTAIN RAILWAY, Gwynedd

Unlike its close neighbour, the Llanberis Lake Railway, Snowdon's hard-working little rack-and-pinion steam line was created as a tourist aid and owes nothing to heavy industry. It was an enormous success during the 19th-century tourist boom, and still carries a huge number of armchair mountaineers. About ½ mile or so from the lower terminus is Ceunant Mawr, one of the finest waterfalls in North Wales, and by the second viaduct the River Arddu twists in a 120 ft fall from the lip of a spectacular gorge.

Continue along the A4086. Pass Dolbadarn Castle and skirt Llyn Peris.

DOLBADARN CASTLE, Gwynedd

The 13th-century castle represented by these gaunt, strangely attractive ruins (AM) was a stronghold of the Welsh princes and has nothing to do with Anglo-Norman design. Its task was to guard the entrance of brooding Llanberis Pass; its bloody history testifies to the single-mindedness with which its native garrisons fulfilled this rôle.

LLYN PERIS, Gwynedd

Smaller and narrower than Padarn, Llyn Peris is a secretive place entirely dominated by the moonscape devastation of the enormous Dinorwic slate workings.

Llyn Padarn is one of many jewel-like lakes which encircle Snowdon.

The Great Hall at Penrhyn Castle displays the mixture of styles favoured by romantic Victorian architects.

Radiating from the main peak of Snowdon are the knife-edged ridges of Crib Goch and Y Lliwedd.

This view from Snowdon's summit encompasses the lesser peak of Yr Aran and distant Moel Hebog.

Since it was opened in 1896 the Snowdon Mountain Railway has carried millions of passengers to the mountain's summit.

DINORWIC SLATE QUARRY, Gwynedd

The vast disused Dinorwic slate quarry rises terrace upon grey terrace from the shore of gentle Llyn Peris, a large monument to the scale of disruption caused by man in the search for materials. The effects of slate extraction might be considered appalling, but workings such as these provided much-needed employmemt.

Continue past Nant Peris and ascend to the summit of Llanberis Pass.

LLANBERIS PASS, Gwynedd

Snowdonia's great mountain masses tower above this narrow pass. To the north are the Glyders, whose highest point is 3,279ft Glyder Fawr, and to the south is the Snowdon massif, crowned by 3,560ft Yr Wyddfa.

PEN-Y-PASS, Gwynedd

Situated at the 1,169ft summit of the Llanberis Pass, this is the starting point of the Miner's Track nature trail and path to Snowdon.

SNOWDON, Gwynedd

Snowdonia National Park covers some 845 square miles and comprises large tracts of mountain and moor divided by deep valleys. Within this area is the star-like Snowdon range, with Snowdon itself culminating in the peak of Yr Wyddfa

– the highest land south of the Scottish border. Radiating from the main peak are the knife-edged summits of Crib Goch and Y Lliwedd, which encircle lakes Glaslyn and Llydaw. Although all the paths to Snowdon are well trodden, no walker should set out without being properly dressed and equipped as sudden changes in the weather can prove fatal, even to the experienced.

Descend to the Pen-y-Gwryd Hotel situated at the head of the Gwryd Valley, and at the T-junction turn right on to the A498, SP 'Beddgelert'. Continue to the viewpoint above Llyn Gwynant.

LLYN GWYNANT AND NANT GWYNANT, Gwynedd

From the viewpoint Llyn Gwynant appears as a jewel surrounded by the tree-covered flanks of mountains, with the craggy, waterfall-threaded slopes of 2,032ft Gallt-y-Wenallt on the north side. Nant Gwynant, which connects lakes Gwynant and Dinas, is often described as the finest mountain valley in Snowdonia. From its northern side the Watkin Path winds up a wooded valley on to open mountainside to reach the summit of Snowdon.

Continue along the valley and reach Llyn Dinas.

LLYN DINAS, Gwynedd

Beautiful Llyn Dinas derives its name from the ancient fort of Dinas Emrys, which stands near the lake's west end, and is traditionally associated with Merlin the magician. Legend has it that the true throne of Britain is hidden in the waters of the lake, and will one day be revealed by a youth treading on a certain stone. Rising to the north-west is 2,451ft Yr Aran, which is a superb pinnacle from which to appreciate the majesty of the Snowdon range.

Skirt the shores of Llyn Dinas and continue to Beddgelert.

BEDDGELERT, Gwynedd

Alpine-style Beddgelert is completely surrounded by mountains and echoes their permanence in the solid stone of its architecture. Its name (Gelert's Grave) refers to the legend that Welsh hero Llywelyn the Great killed his dog Gelert because he thought that it had savaged his son. In fact the dog had just saved the baby boy from wolves. Historians have thoroughly debunked this story, which has since been laid at the door of an inventive local innkeeper, but its telling rarely leaves a dry eye in the schools of North Wales. Moel Hebog—The Mountain of the

Hawk'—dominates the landscape to the south-west of Beddgelert.

Keep forward on the A4085 'Caernarfon' road and reach Beddgelert Forest and picnic site.

BEDDGELERT FOREST, Gwynedd

Attractive trails laid out by the Forestry Commission lead up through varied stands of conifers to tree-shrouded Llyn Llywelyn from the picnic site here.

Continue past Llyn-y-Gadair to Rhyd Ddu, where a path leads to Snowdon. Skirt Llyn Cwellyn and follow the Afon Gwyrfai (known for its excellent game fishing). Pass through Betws Garmon and Waunfawr to re-enter Caernarfon.

THE ISLE OF ANGLESEY, Gwynedd

Isolated Anglesey, in which this tour is contained, is separated from the rest of Wales by the Menai Strait and presents a landscape of low, undulating hills unlike anywhere else in the Principality. First impressions are deceptive, however, for much of the coast is as wild and rugged as any to be found in the British Isles. The family holidaymaker will find good facilities and amenities here, and the lone wanderer can find all the solitude he desires. In prehistoric times the island was *Mona*, 'The Mother of Wales', and visible remains of the cultures that flourished here are everywhere.

MENAI BRIDGE, Gwynedd

This largely Victorian town, named after Thomas Telford's superb bridge, is clustered round the Anglesey end of the crossing. Places of interest here include the Tegfryn Art Gallery and a fascinating Museum of Childhood, in which many rare and valuable exhibits illustrate the interests of children over the last 150 years.

Leave Menai Bridge on the A545 'Beaumaris' road and drive alongside the Menai Strait.

MENAI STRAIT, Gwynedd

This 14-mile stretch of water, flowing from sea to sea between Anglesey's wooded shoreline and the sloping pastures of the mainland, might be considered the major geographical feature of North Wales. Its beauty matches the splendour of Snowdon, and its sheltered reaches provide a testing venue for the water-sports enthusiasts who flock here in the summer months. Both banks – island and mainland – offer superb walking country where seabirds and rabbits are more common than people. Above Port Dinorwic are the remains of Stephenson's amazing 19th-century tubular rail bridge; farther up is the graceful suspension bridge that has carried the A5 road since 1826.

Continue to Beaumaris

THE ISLE OF ANGLESEY

Today Anglesey is known for its quiet resorts and sandy beaches, its spectacular cliffs and a gentle interior threaded by narrow lanes. At one time it filled the bellies of North Wales with wheat and was known, almost reverently, as 'Mona', the Mother.

Beaumaris Castle is one of the best examples of concentric fortification in Britain.

BEAUMARIS, Gwynedd

The biggest attraction of Beaumaris is undoubtedly the castle (AM), an unfinished masterpiece that was the last in a chain built by Edward I to subjugate the Welsh people. A measure of the success with which this aim was achieved is the fact that the castle has never seen any military action and was never completed, the walls not being built to their intended height. The town contains much of interest, including the early 17th-century Court House and 15th-century Tudor Rose House, the Beaumaris Gaol and Exhibition, and the Museum of Childhood. Several excellent inns include the Bull's Head, which was visited by Dr Johnson and Charles Dickens. The church is of 14th-century origin.

Turn inland on the B5109 'Pentraeth' road and cross rolling countryside to pass through Pentraeth.

Turn right on to the A5025, and continue with fine views of attractive Red Wharf Bay.

RED WHARF BAY, Gwynedd

More than 10 square miles of sand are revealed here at low tide, so it is not particularly surprising that the bay was once famous for its cockles. During the last century a small local shipyard built boats for the Amlwch copper trade.

Continue to Benllech.

BENLLECH, Gwynedd

Perhaps the most popular seaside resort on the island, Benllech offers 2 miles of golden sand and safe bathing.

Continue with the Amlwch road and in 2 miles at a roundabout take the 1st exit. A detour from the main route can be made by keeping forward on to an unclassified road for Din Lligwy.

DIN LLIGWY BURIAL CHAMBER, Gwynedd

This important Bronze-Age tomb (AM) consists of a huge capstone resting on a number of uprights and horizontals. Much of the chamber is cunningly hidden in a rock-cut pit.

DIN LLIGWY ANCIENT VILLAGE, Gwynedd

Some of the ancient enclosed dwellings on this remarkable site (AM) still stand to a height of 6ft, and date from around the early Roman period. The surrounding wall was built in the late 4th century. Near by is the beautiful ruin of a 14th-century chapel.

Continue on the main drive to Amlwch, with Parys Mountain rising to the left.

One of engineer Thomas Telford's finest works, this suspension bridge carries the London to Holyhead road over the Menai Strait and has a central span of 579ft.

PARYS MOUNTAIN, Gwynedd
Now desolate and scarred, 419ft-high Parys Mountain was exploited for its copper in a small way by the Romans, but in 1768 came a boom. Fortunes were made and for a while Anglesey was the copper centre of the world, but by 1820 it was all over. Falling prices and the exhaustion of the ore forced the industry into collapse.

AMLWCH, Gwynedd
At the height of the copper boom Amlwch was a major port and shipbuilding centre. Now an oil terminal and chemical industries provide the town's employment.

Continue on the Cemaes road to Bull Bay.

BULL BAY, Gwynedd
Sheltered rocky coves and a good beach are the main attractions of this little holiday resort.

Continue to Cemaes Bay.

The Marquess of Anglesey's tall statue overlooks the Menai Strait.

CEMAES BAY, Gwynedd
Cottages cluster round a small harbour in this quaint little fishing village. Spectacular cliff walks lead in both directions from the bay, and on the headland to the west is Wylfa nuclear power station (open).

Continue with signs for Valley to Llanrhyddlad.

LLANRHYDDLAD, Gwynedd
Llyn Llygeirian and a large number of prehistoric sites are situated north of this hamlet.

Continue to Llanfaethlu.

LLANFAETHLU, Gwynedd
Distant views of Snowdonia can be enjoyed from this village, and secluded bays and rocky headlands are features of the nearby coast.

Continue through Llanfachraeth and Llanynghenedl to Valley.

VALLEY, Gwynedd
Plane spotting enthusiasts can see RAF jet trainer aircraft and the occasional rescue helicopter operating from the base near here.

Meet traffic signals, turn right on to the A5, and cross the Stanley Embankment to Holy Island.

HOLY ISLAND, Gwynedd
The silhouette of a giant aluminium plant dominates the approach across the Stanley Embankment these days, but 720ft Holyhead Mountain still exercises a compulsive attraction as the highest point on the island. Many prehistoric monuments survive here.

Continue to Holyhead.

HOLYHEAD, Gwynedd
This, the largest town in Anglesey, is a major ferry terminal for Ireland and is constantly busy with the jostling of travellers, seamen, and holidaymakers. The old parish church of St Cybi is built within the walls of a Roman fort, and the flank of Holyhead Mountain – which towers over the town – is scattered with the remains of prehistoric huts. Beyond the mountain a yawning chasm separates South Stack Lighthouse from the rest of the island.

Return along the A5 and shortly branch right on to the B4545 to reach Trearddur Bay.

TREARDDUR BAY, Gywnedd
This fashionable Anglesey resort has fine sandy beaches broken up by occasional rocky outcrops.

Cross Four Mile Bridge and return to Valley. Meet traffic signals and turn right on to the A5. Pass through Bryngwran, and in 1 mile at crossroads turn right on to the A4080 SP 'Rhosneigr'. Continue through open country, and at Llanfaelog turn right for Rhosneigr.

RHOSNEIGR, Gwynedd
Cheerfully unpretentious, Rhosneigr is an ideal spot for holidaymakers who like the quiet life.

Continue on the A4080 and in 1¼ miles turn right 'SP 'Aberffraw' to reach Barclodiad-y-Gawres.

BARCLODIAD-Y-GAWRES, Gwynedd
The carved stones of this megalithic passage grave (AM) are among the finest of their kind in Britain.

Continue to Aberffraw.

ABERFFRAW, Gwynedd
Aberffraw is a grey, somnolent village which has little to show of its historic past. Between the 7th and 13th centuries it was the capital of the Kingdom of Gwynedd, but no trace of the palace or associated buildings survives. A rocky islet to the south-west features an ancient church which is accessible at low tide.

Proceed for 3 miles to Malltraeth.

MALLTRAETH, Gwynedd
In c1800 a high embankment was built here to stop the incursion of the sea. Before this the estuary of the Cefni penetrated far inland, nearly cutting Anglesey in two. The village is well known for its fine sands and bird-haunted salt marshes.

Skirt Malltraeth Sands and continue through Newborough Forest to reach Newborough.

Holyhead Mountain's 720ft height offers superb views over the island.

NEWBOROUGH, Gwynedd
Former inhabitants of Llanfaes, ousted by Edward I, founded this English-sounding village in 1303. A national nature reserve covers 1,566 acres of duneland and rocky coast to the south of the village, and Newborough Forest is constantly being extended to fix the dunes in the north part of the sanctuary. Three nature trails enable casual visitors to see much of the natural beauty of the area, but access to unmarked parts of the reserve is by permit only. Nearby Llanddwyn Island is accessible except at times of very high tide.

In ½ mile at a roundabout turn left and 2 miles beyond Bryn-Siencyn reach a road on the left which leads to Bryn-celli-ddu.

BRYN-CELLI-DDU, Gwynedd
This is a magnificent Bronze Age passage grave (AM) of a type more usually found in Ireland. It consists of a passage leading to a polygonal chamber beneath a large mound.

Continue on the A4080 and shortly reach the entrance to Plas Newydd.

Llanfair PG's full name contains 59 letters and is the longest in Britain.

PLAS NEWYDD, Gwynedd
Rebuilt by architect James Wyatt in the 18th century, this fine mansion (NT) overlooks the Menai Strait and is famous for the Rex Whistler mural in its dining room.

At the edge of Llanfair PG turn right.

LLANFAIR PG, Gwynedd
The full name of this village, Llanfairpwllgwyngyllgogerychwyrn-drobwyllllantysiliogogogoch means 'Church of St Mary in a hollow of white hazel near to a rapid whirlpool and to St Tysilio's Church, near to a red cave' and was invented by a tailor who combined the business of tourism with this wry joke against the tourists. George Stephenson's famous tubular railway bridge over the Menai Strait has been replaced by steel arches and road deck after being damaged by fire in 1970, and an unassuming tin hut in the village was where the Women's Institute formed its first branch in the early 20th century. Overlooking the bridge, the village, and the Strait the splendid Marquess of Anglesey Column affords remarkable views for anybody with the stomach to climb it.

Return to Menai Bridge on the A5080.

Tissington, which enjoys an idyllic situation in glorious Derbyshire countryside, is a traditional village grouping of cottages, hall, and church set round a delightful pond.

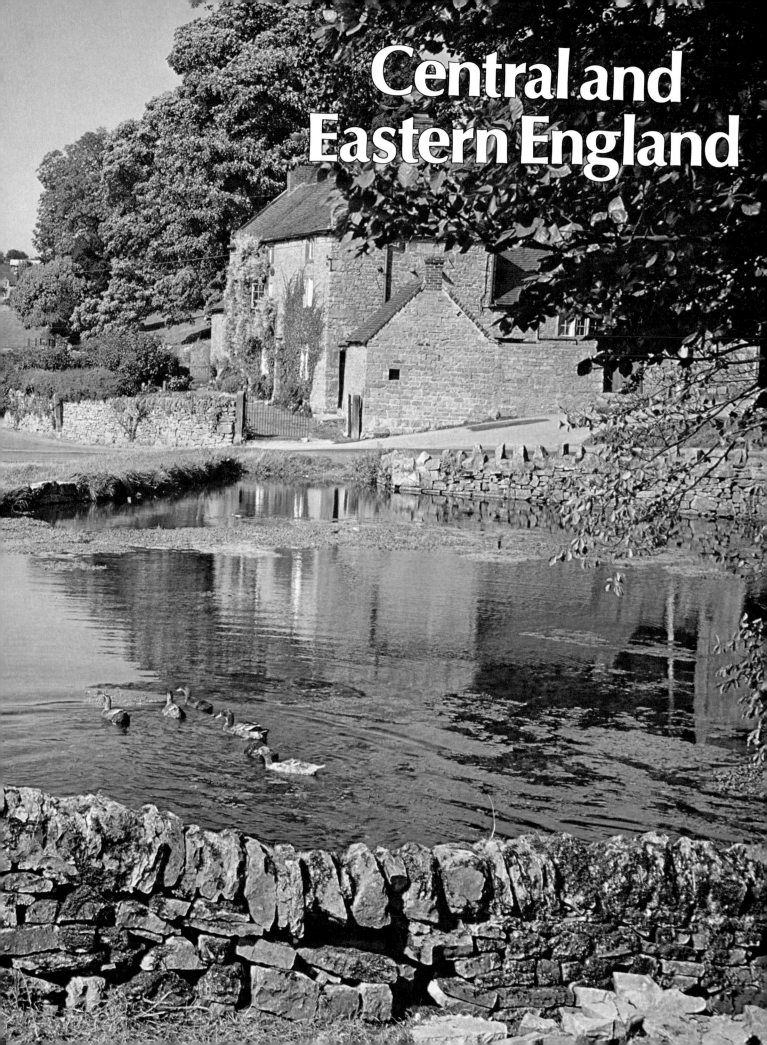

Central and Eastern England

WARWICK, Warwicks

Imposing Warwick Castle is one of the finest medieval strongholds in Europe. It stands on a Saxon site above this compact River Avon town, and its exceptional Norman and later structure hides an interior completely rebuilt during the 17th century. The castle is still occupied, but visitors have access to the state rooms, torture chamber, silver vault, ghost tower, and Avon-side grounds that were landscaped by Capability Brown. Also in the town are the remains of town walls, two gates, and a great number of building styles ranging from half-timbered to the conscious starkness of the 20th century. Lord Leycester's Hospital was founded as a guildhall in 1383 and converted to almshouses in 1571 (open), and the 18th-century Shire Hall is considered an excellent example of its type. Elizabeth Oken's House contains a Doll Museum, and 17th-century St John's House features both a museum of crafts, costume, and furniture, and the Museum of the Royal Warwickshire Regiment. The 18th-century Court House is an Italianate building.

Leave Warwick on the A425 'Banbury' road and continue for 2¼ miles to join the A41. Proceed for 1¼ miles and turn right on to the B4087 SP 'Wellesbourne'. Continue to Wellesbourne.

A magnificent collection of armour is housed in Warwick Castle.

WELLESBOURNE, Warwicks

Georgian houses and a Hall dating from *c*1700 are the main features of this pleasant village.

Follow SP 'Stratford B4086' for 1 mile and turn right on to the B4088 SP 'Charlecote' to reach the village of Charlecote.

CHARLECOTE, Warwicks

Charlecote Park (NT) is a fine Elizabethan house with a great hall and museum. The Avon flows through grounds where Shakespeare is said to have been caught poaching deer. Attractive old cottages survive in the village.

In Charlecote turn left on to the unclassified 'Hampton Lucy' road and cross the River Avon. Continue to Hampton Lucy.

SHAKESPEARE COUNTRY

England's heartlands are watered by the Avon and Stour, great rivers that wind through charming Elizabethan villages, country estates graced by stately houses, and historic towns where Shakespeare drew inspiration from the comedy and tragedy in the lives of his contemporaries.

The River Avon formed an essential aspect of Warwick Castle's defences.

HAMPTON LUCY, Warwicks

Of particular interest here is a cast-iron bridge that was built in 1829.

On entering Hampton Lucy bear left SP 'Stratford'. Proceed for 1½ miles, bear left again, and in ¾ mile turn left on to the A46 for Stratford.

STRATFORD-UPON-AVON, Warwicks

William Shakespeare was born here in 1564. His childhood home contains a museum relating to his life, and the old Guildhall that housed his school still stands. A picturesque Elizabethan knot garden can be seen near the foundations of New Place, where he died, and his remains lie in Holy Trinity Church. A lovely thatched and timbered cottage (open) in the nearby village of Shottery is where his wife Anne Hathaway was born, and gabled Hall's Croft (open) was the home of their daughter Susanna. Many of the great man's works are staged in the Royal Shakespeare Theatre, which was built on an Avon-side site in 1932; it incorporates a museum and picture gallery (open). Among many 15th- and 16th-century buildings preserved in the town are several lovely half-timbered houses and the 14-arch Clopton Bridge over the Avon. Harvard House was the home of the grandparents of John Harvard, founder of the US university of the same name. The World of Shakespeare specializes in scenes from Elizabethan England, the Motor Museum preserves a number of veteran and vintage cars, and an Arms and Armour museum exhibits some 800 pieces.

Leave the town by the A34 'Oxford' road and later pass Alscot Park to the right. Proceed to Alderminster.

ALDERMINSTER, Warwicks

Views across the Stour valley to Meon Hill and the Cotswolds can be enjoyed from the 13th-century church here.

The Guildhall schoolroom, where the poet and dramatist William Shakespeare took his first steps in learning.

Remain on the A34 to reach

Newbold-upon-Stour. At the end of that village turn right on to an unclassified road and drive to Armscote. Turn right and continue to Ilmington.

ILMINGTON, Warwicks

Situated at the east foot of the Cotswolds, this village has several picturesque cottages and an old tithe barn. The rectory and manor house both date from the 16th century. Above the village is 854ft Ilmington Down, one of the highest points in Warwickshire.

Turn left and follow SP 'Campden' to climb Ilmington Down. Descend, meet crossroads, and turn left to reach Ebrington.

EBRINGTON, Glos

Delightful stone and thatched cottages complement a church with a fine Norman doorway in this lovely Cotswold village.

Join the B4035 and drive to Shipston-on-Stour.

SHIPSTON-ON-STOUR, Warwicks

Once one of the most important sheep markets in the country, this mainly Georgian town lies at the edge of the Vale of Red Horse.

Follow SP 'Banbury', cross the River Stour, and proceed for ¾ mile to crossroads. Turn left on to the unclassified 'Honington' road, then in ¾ mile turn right SP 'Tysoe' and proceed for 2¾ miles. Meet crossroads and drive forward. In ¾ mile a detour from the main route can be made by turning right to reach Compton Wynyates.

COMPTON WYNYATES, Warwicks

The estate in which this exceptional Tudor house stands has been in the same family since the 13th century. Sir William Compton built the magnificent red-brick extravagance that stands here today, and the interior has remained largely unaltered since Tudor times (not open). Close to the house the wild hillside parkland has been cultivated as a modern topiary garden.

Continue to Upper Tysoe.

UPPER TYSOE, Warwicks

One of a trio of villages named from the Norse God Tiw, this little place has a 16th-century manor house and stands in the Vale of Red Horse. The Vale itself derives its name from a turf-cut figure on Rising Hill, due east of Lower Tysoe. Until 1800 this was scoured annually, but it is now scarcely visible.

In Upper Tysoe turn left SP 'Kineton', then right SP 'Shenington' and 'Banbury'. Ascend Tysoe Hill, meet crossroads, and turn left to follow the ridge of Edgehill. Continue for 2 miles and drive forward on to the A422. A short detour from the main route can be made by continuing on the A422 for ½ mile to Upton House.

The superb Tudor architecture of Compton Wynyates.

Anne Hathaway's Cottage at Shottery.

UPTON HOUSE, Warwicks
Good views can be enjoyed from the lovely terraced gardens of this impressive 17th-century house (NT). Inside are collections of porcelain, pictures, and various pieces of 18th-century furniture.

On the main route, continue for ¼ mile after joining the A422 and bear left on to an unclassified road for Edgehill village.

EDGEHILL, Warwicks
An 18th-century folly which now forms part of a pub in the village affords extensive views over the countryside. North, on private ground by the B4086, is the field where the first major battle of the Civil War was fought in 1642. Here the horizon is dominated by the attractively wooded 700ft ridge of Edgehill, which extends for 3 miles.

Leave Edgehill village and in 1 mile bear left on to the B4086 SP 'Kineton'. Descend to Kineton with the Edgehill battlefield to the left.

KINETON, Warwicks
Near Kineton station are the remains of a motte and bailey castle, and ¾ mile north west is a sail-less tower windmill. The church has a splendid 13th-century doorway.

Turn right on to the B4451 SP 'Southam' and proceed to Gaydon. Turn right on to the A41 SP 'Banbury'. Proceed for 2 miles and turn left on to the unclassified 'Fenny Compton' road, then keep forward SP 'Burton Hills'. Ascend the Burton Hills (a country park) and pass the isolated village of Burton Dassett to the right.

BURTON DASSETT, Warwicks
Church Hill rises to 689ft above this pretty village and is surmounted by a lookout tower that may once have been part of a medieval windmill. The hill's summit, used as a beacon site during the Battle of Edgehill in 1642, is now a country park.

Continue for 1 mile to reach crossroads and turn right to descend to Avon Dassett. Drive to the end of the village and keep forward. Enter Farnborough.

FARNBOROUGH, Warwicks
Notable Farnborough Hall (NT) dates from the 17th and 18th centuries and features excellent rococo stucco-work with panels of scrolls, rays, shells, fruit and flowers. Delightful grounds include landscaped terraced lawns which afford superb views to the ridge of Edgehill. A classical air is given the gardens by a small Ionic temple and an oval pavilion.

Keep left through Farnborough and at the end of the village turn left on to the A423 SP 'Coventry'. In 2 miles it is possible to make a detour from the main route to Wormleighton by turning right on to an unclassified road.

WORMLEIGHTON, Warwicks
Prince Rupert slept at Wormleighton Manor the night before he gave battle to parliamentarian cavalry at Edgehill. The reputedly lovely house was destroyed later in the Civil War, but the imposing gateway survives, complete with its carved crests.

On the main route, proceed on the A423 to the edge of Southam.

SOUTHAM, Warwicks
At one time this ancient town was famed for a mineral spring and healing well which were both claimed to have wide-ranging medicinal powers. The Reverend Holyoake, a rector of the local 15th- and 16th-century church, compiled the first dictionary of the English language.

At the edge of Southam turn left on to the A425 SP 'Leamington' to reach Ufton.

UFTON, Warwicks
Views from this 380ft-high village extend beyond the ancient Fosse Way and River Avon to the distant Malvern Hills, known for their mineral springs. Inside the village church, which dates from the 13th century but has been extensively restored since, is a good 16th-century memorial brass.

Continue and pass through Radford Semele to reach Leamington Spa.

Fine views of Edgehill can be enjoyed from this folly built in the 18th century.

LEAMINGTON SPA, Warwicks
In the 18th century it was claimed that mineral springs in this lovely old town were beneficial in the treatment of various complaints. As the high-society fashion for taking the waters blossomed so also did Leamington, and today it boasts many grand old buildings that recall the prosperity of those times. The Pump Room of 1814, rebuilt in 1925, is an excellent focus for the terraces of Regency, Georgian, and Victorian houses that grace the streets around it. Between the buildings are wide parks and open spaces, the carefully tended Jephson Gardens, and the vagrant windings of the River Lea. The Warwick Art Gallery and Museum exhibits a good selection of paintings and examples of 18th-century glass.

Continue along the A425 and return to Warwick.

131

NORTHAMPTON, Northants

One of the largest market towns in England, Northampton is the administrative centre of its county and is noted for its high number of fine churches. Among the finest is Holy Sepulchre, a rare round church that was founded in 1110 and has been variously adapted through the ages. Inside is a 6ft-tall brass which dates from the 17th century and is one of the largest in England. Other old buildings include 17th-century Haselrigg House, the 16th-century Welsh House. Abington Park has landscaped surroundings, and a 15th- to 18th-century house containing a museum. The Northamptonshire Record office is housed in Delapre Abbey, a 19th-century building on the site of a Cluniac nunnery. The main industry of the town used to be shoe manufacturing whose history is displayed in the Museum of Leathercraft. One of the Eleanor Crosses erected by Edward I, can be seen on the town's southern outskirts.

Leave Northampton on the A4500 'Wellingborough' road and drive to Ecton.

ECTON, Northants

Features of this village include a 13th- and 14th-century church, a gothic-revival hall, and an elegant 17th-century manor house.

From Ecton drive for 1¼ miles and turn right on to the B573. Enter Earls Barton.

EARLS BARTON, Northants

The magnificent Saxon church tower here was built about 1,000 years ago and may once have been incorporated in the defences of a nearby Norman castle.

Continue through Great Doddington and in 1¼ miles meet traffic signals. Continue forward to Wellingborough.

WELLINGBOROUGH, Northants

Situated at the junction of the rivers Ise and Nene, this old market centre is now a rapidly developing town serving numerous light industries.

The Welland Valley near Harringworth is dominated by a stupendous railway viaduct.

TOUR 59   *95 MILES*

NORTHAMPTONSHIRE RIVERLANDS

Between the meanderings of the Welland and Nene are forests and farms, water meadows loud with the calls of wildfowl, and villages of stone and thatch clustered round elegant church spires. Much of the countryside was once held by squires, and many of their sturdy farms survive.

Fotheringhay's church is an imposing survival of a much larger structure.

Follow SP 'Peterborough' to join the A510, and continue to Finedon.

FINEDON, Northants

Curiously decorated ironstone houses and cottages gather beneath the graceful 133ft spire of an ironstone church in this large village. The church dates from the 14th century, but most of the houses were built by the village squire in Victorian times.

Proceed for 3¼ miles and turn right on to the A604. In 3½ miles cross the River Nene into Thrapston.

THRAPSTON, Northants

The device from which the American Stars and Stripes were derived can be seen on a tablet to Sir John Washington in the village church. A nephew of Washington emigrated to America and was the great-grandfather of the first US president.

Return across the River Nene and turn right on to the A6116 to reach Islip.

ISLIP, Northants

Brasses re-created by the Reverend H Macklin, author of a standard book on this type of memorial, can be seen in Islip Church.

Proceed to Lowick.

LOWICK, Northants

Lowick's notable church has a 15th-century tower and 14th-century windows featuring 16 beautiful figures worked in stained glass.

Drive through Sudborough and on approaching Brigstock turn right on to a narrow unclassified road SP 'Lyveden'. Proceed for 2¼ miles; ¼ mile to the right of the road is Lyveden New Bield.

LYVEDEN NEW BIELD, Northants

When Sir Thomas Tresham's family became involved in the Gunpowder Plot he had to stop building this ambitious house, which was begun in 1600 and still remains as a shell (NT). Its plan was meant to symbolize the Passion of Christ.

Continue for 2⅔ miles and turn right on to the A427 to enter Oundle.

OUNDLE, Northants

Set in pleasant countryside by the River Nene, this stone-built town is a place of narrow streets and alleys between rows of old houses broken by the occasional tiny cottage or inn. Its well-known public school was founded in the 16th century by William Laxton, a grocer who was born here and eventually became Lord Mayor of London. Latham's Hospital dates from 1611. The Norman and later St Peters' has a magnificent 280-foot spire.

Leave Oundle and follow the 'Peterborough' road for 1¼ miles, then turn left on to an unclassified road SP 'Fotheringhay' and pass Cotterstock village on the left.

COTTERSTOCK, Northants

The poet John Dryden wrote his *Fables* in an attic room of 17th-century Cotterstock Hall while staying with his cousin, who owned it. Beautiful gardens lead from the house to the banks of the River Nene. In the village are a fine church, a 14th-century rectory, and an 18th-century mill with later mill cottages.

Drive through Tansor and continue to Fotheringhay.

FOTHERINGHAY, Northants

A mound here once carried the grim castle in which Mary Queen of Scots was imprisoned before her execution in 1587. Nowadays the mellow old cottages and willow-hung banks of the Nene create a tranquillity in which such macabre associations become difficult to believe. The imposing church was a gift from Edward IV.

Take the 'King's Cliffe' road and pass through Woodnewton to reach Apethorpe.

APETHORPE, Northants
Stone-built Apethorpe boasts a very large Tudor and later hall, and an imposing 13th- and 17th-century village church, now a museum.

Proceed to King's Cliffe.

KING'S CLIFFE, Northants
Features of this beautiful little village include 17th-century almshouses, a church with a Norman tower and 13th-century spire, and lovely surroundings.

Turn right to follow the 'Stamford' road and later turn left on to the A47. In ¾ mile turn right on to an unclassified road and drive to Collyweston.

COLLYWESTON, Northants
Stone roofing slates have been quarried here for many years. The church has a Saxon chancel wall, and a Dovecote dates from the 16th century.

Turn left on to the A43; and at roundabout take 3rd exit then shortly left into Duddington.

DUDDINGTON, Northants
Thatched cottages and a medieval 4-arched bridge across the River Welland help to make this one of the prettiest villages in the area. The picture is completed by a 17th-century watermill and mansion.

Drive through Duddington to rejoin the A43. In ¾ mile turn right on to the unclassified 'Wakerley' and 'Harringworth' road. Drive past extensive ironstone workings to reach Harringworth.

HARRINGWORTH, Northants
A spectacular feature of this village is the 82-arch brick-built railway viaduct that spans the Welland Valley here. This magnificent feat of engineering was built between 1874 and 1879.

Proceed south to Gretton.

GRETTON, Northants
Stocks and a whipping post still stand on the green in this attractive hilltop village, and fine views extend into the Welland Valley. A few 17th-century houses and a church with Norman origins are reminders of its long history.

Drive along the 'Weldon' road for 1¼ miles and turn left. In ¾ mile a detour may be made from the main route by turning left; this leads to Kirby Hall in ¾ miles and Deene Park in 2¼ miles.

Duddington's famous watermill was built in 1664.

NORTHAMPTON

Edward I erected this cross at Geddington in 1290, as a memorial to Queen Eleanor.

KIRBY HALL, Northants
This magnificent old house (AM) was begun in 1572 and bought by Sir Christopher Hatton, a favourite of Queen Elizabeth I. In the 17th century its appearance was completely changed by the architect Inigo Jones.

DEENE PARK, Northants
A little farther along the detour route from Kirby Hall is the 16th-century mansion of Deene Park (open), which stands in a lake-watered estate known for its rare trees.

Proceed along the main tour route to Weldon.

WELDON, Northants
The fine lantern tower carried by Weldon Church was once an invaluable landmark for travellers in thickly-wooded Rockingham Forest. An old lock-up once used for petty criminals stands on the green.

On entering Weldon turn right into Chapel Road then right at T-junction. At roundabout take 1st exit A43 for Geddington. Meet crossroads and turn left on to an unclassified road to enter the village.

GEDDINGTON, Northants
One of the three surviving Eleanor Crosses stands in the main square of this lovely stone and thatch village, a reminder of the grief experienced by Edward I at the loss of his queen some 7 centuries ago. Of later date is the medieval bridge that spans the River Ise here, and ¾ mile south is 15th-century Boughton House (open), a monastery enlarged to its present magnificent proportions in the 16th and 17th centuries. Inside are art collections and sumptuous old furnishings, while all around are beautifully planned and tended gardens.

Return to the crossroads and drive forward on to the unclassified 'Newton' and 'Rushton' road. After Newton turn right then left under a railway. Continue to Rushton.

RUSHTON, Northants
Triangular Lodge (AM), a famous curiosity in the grounds of 15th-century Rushton Hall, is far more than a mere folly. Its peculiar design, in which the number three is depicted time and again, is a devout symbolization of the Trinity, disguised to fool religious persecutors during a time of repression. The village is a cluster of golden ironstone houses on the banks of the River Ise.

In Rushton turn right SP 'Desborough'; at Desborough turn left on to the A6 to reach Rothwell.

It is thought that Inigo Jones may have been responsible for the ornamental garden gateway of Kirby Hall.

ROTHWELL, Northants
Inside the mainly 13th-century church of this old industrial town is a charnel containing thousands of bones. The centre of Rothwell is graced by the elegant 16th-century Market House (AM).

Turn right on to the B576 and proceed to Lamport.

LAMPORT, Northants
Mainly 17th- and 18th-century Lamport Hall (open) is set in an attractive park featuring an early alpine rock garden. Inside the house are paintings by Van Dyck and other artists, and an excellent collection of china and furniture.

In Lamport turn left on to the A508 and drive to Brixworth.

BRIXWORTH, Northants
Local Roman buildings were cannibalized to provide materials for a fine church raised here in the 7th century. The skill of the Saxon builders has been well proved, because today the church survives as one of the finest of its type.

Pass the Red Lion (PH) and turn left on to the unclassified 'Sywell' road. Later cross the Pitsford Reservoir into Holcot, meet crossroads, and turn right SP 'Northampton' to reach Moulton. In Moulton turn left and shortly right onto the A43 to return to Northampton.

CAMBRIDGE, Cambs

This famous and attractive university town started life as a small Celtic settlement on the marshy banks of the Cam. In 1209 a split in the Oxford community resulted in a migration of students and scholars to Cambridge, and the establishment of a university that was to rival its unwilling parent in wealth and prestige. Traces of the first foundation – which was Peterhouse in 1284 – are largely disguised by later work, but 14th-century Clare College occupies buildings that were part of a 12th-century nunnery. Most of the other colleges show similar mixtures. King's College, founded by Henry VI in 1441, has an outstanding chapel that overlooks the Cam and is famous for some of the finest gothic fan vaulting in Europe. Corpus Christi is unique in having been founded by two town guilds, and lovely half-timbered Queens' of 1346 is by far the most picturesque. Much more can be learned about the university and its superb buildings, and the interested visitor is advised to invest in a guide booklet. The town itself is a delightful collection of old streets and houses alongside the river. Peaceful lawns and meadows slope down to the water's edge as grassy quays for summer punters, in marked contrast to the busy activity of the excellent shopping areas in the middle of town. Not surprisingly the city has several good museums. Extensive art and archaeological collections are housed in the Fitzwilliam, the Scott Polar Research Institute has many relics relating to famous expeditions, and the Sedgwick displays fossils from many different parts of the world. Cambridge and County Folk Museum is packed with domestic and agricultural bygones.

Leave Cambridge on the A1303 'Bedford' road and drive for 2½ miles to reach Madingley Postmill.

BETWEEN THE OUSE AND THE CAM

West of Cambridge and the willow-shaded Cam a countryside of orchards and pasture stretches flatly to low Fenland horizons. Here and there the skyline is interrupted by a windmill or church tower, the roofs of an ancient riverside town, or the bushy crown of an occasional copse.

Trinity College Bridge in Cambridge leads to the famous 'Backs'.

MADINGLEY POSTMILL, Cambs

The body of this restored windmill pivots on a central post so that the sails can be turned into the wind. Originally from Huntingdonshire, this interesting industrial relic was moved to its present site in 1936.

Continue for ¼ mile to reach the American Cemetery.

AMERICAN CEMETERY & CHAPEL, Cambs

The War Memorial Chapel that stands here is a striking example of modern architecture. Inside is a 540-square-foot map showing Atlantic sea and air routes used by American forces during World War II.

Continue and at roundabout take 4th exit on to an unclassified road to reach Madingley.

MADINGLEY, Cambs

Just outside this attractive village is Madingley Hall, a fine Elizabethan house that stands in a wooded park and serves as a hostel for university students. Both Edward VII and George VI lived here when they were undergraduates at Cambridge.

Continue to the A604 and turn left. Proceed for 4 miles, turn right on to an unclassified road, and drive to Swavesey.

SWAVESEY, Cambs

Attractively situated close to fenland, this long, narrow village has a good 14th-century church with notable window tracery. Inside the building are bench-ends with animal carvings.

Proceed to Over.

OVER, Cambs

This pretty fenland village stands in orchard country to the east of the River Ouse, a popular venue for boating and angling. Its pleasant church contains a bell that was cast some 600 years ago.

Drive to Willingham.

WILLINGHAM, Cambs

The local windmill and the impressive tower of Willingham's 14th-century church are prominent landmarks in the flat farmlands that surround this village. The church nave has a notable 15th-century hammerbeam roof adorned with over 50 carved angels.

Turn left on to the B1050 and reach the River Ouse. Follow the river and turn left on to the A1123 to enter the village of Earith. Continue through Needingworth, and after 1½ miles turn left on to the A1096 to enter St Ives.

ST IVES, Cambs

In 1110 King Henry I granted St Ives the right to hold a fair. The town grew up around its fairground and its annual market became established as one of the largest in England. The River Ouse runs through the town and is spanned here by a narrow 6-arched bridge (AM) that dates from the 15th century. The Norris Museum situated in the Broadway contains a comprehensive collection of Huntingdonshire history.

Follow the A1096 south and cross the river. After ¼ mile turn right on to an unclassified road and continue to Hemingford Grey.

HEMINGFORD GREY, Cambs

A moated mansion in this lovely village dates back to the 12th century and is thought to be the oldest inhabited dwelling in England. The 12th-century church is picturesquely sited in a bend of the River Ouse.

Turn left and shortly right, proceed to Hemingford Abbots, and follow SP 'Huntingdon' to join the A604. Drive for 1 mile and branch left. Meet a roundabout and turn right on to an unclassified road to reach Godmanchester.

GODMANCHESTER, Cambs

The site of this ancient town was once occupied by a Roman military station. Nowadays it is a treasure-house of varied architectural styles. Island Hall is a mid-18th-century mansion set in a tranquil riverside setting (open).

Turn right on to the B1043, crossing a 14th-century bridge (AM), and enter Huntingdon.

HUNTINGDON, Cambs

Both Oliver Cromwell and the diarist Samuel Pepys were born here and attended the town's former grammar school. Parts of the building date back to Norman times, and today it houses a museum of Cromwellian relics.

Leave Huntingdon on the A141 'Kettering' road and drive to Hinchingbrooke House.

King's College Chapel, a medieval masterpiece, is one of the principal glories of Cambridge.

HINCHINGBROOKE HOUSE, Cambs

Now restored and in use as a school, this Tudor and later mansion (open) has been home to the Cromwells and the Earls of Sandwich. It incorporates parts of a medieval nunnery.

Continue on the A141 'Kettering' road to Brampton.

BRAMPTON, Cambs

Pepys House in Brampton is a lovely old gabled cottage that was the home of the diarist's parents, and was owned by him from 1664 to 1680. The stalls in the local church display excellent carving.

Leave Brampton and in 2 miles join the A1 for the outskirts of Buckden.

The Great Ouse at Hemingford Grey.

Britain's oldest surviving postmill at Bourn resembles those seen in illuminated manuscripts.

BUCKDEN, Cambs

Considerable remains of Buckden Palace, a former residence of the bishops of Lincoln, comprise a fine Tudor tower and an inner gatehouse of *c*1490 (open). The buildings are well restored and in use as a school. The local church is known for its notable spire and carvings.

Continue to a roundabout on the A1 and take the B661 'Kimbolton' road to reach Grafham Water.

GRAFHAM WATER, Cambs

This 2½-square-mile reservoir supplies drinking water for 1½ million people and is a valuable leisure amenity offering long bankside walks and facilities for boating and trout fishing. Several picnic sites have been laid out around the edge.

Continue to Great Staughton.

GREAT STAUGHTON, Cambs

Opposite 14th-century and later Great Staughton Church, which has a fine tower and contains good monuments, is a mansion with a pair of picturesque timber-framed barns. The village cross dates from the 17th century and features a sundial.

A rare medieval chapel survives in the centre of the 15th-century bridge over the Great Ouse at St Ives.

At Great Staughton turn left on to the A45 and continue for 4 miles, crossing the A1. Cross the River Ouse and enter St Neots on the B1428.

ST NEOTS, Cambs

The great charm of this ancient market town is its compactness. Interesting old inns can be found in many of its secretive back streets, and attractive buildings cluster round three sides of the Ouse-side market square.

Leave St Neots by turning right on to the B1043 crossing the A45 and after 3 miles join the A1. Turn left on to the B1042 and drive through Sandy.

SANDY, Beds

Low wooded hills that rise to the east of this large River Ivel village make a pleasant change from the flat countryside crossed by much of the tour. About 1 mile east is the 100-acre Lodge Nature Reserve, which is the HQ of the Royal Society for the Protection of Birds. A nature trail offers public access.

Continue along the B1042 and pass a TV mast to the left before reaching Potton. At Potton take the B1040 'St Ives' road through Gamlingay to Waresley, then drive forward on to an unclassified road for Great Gransden. Turn right, then shortly left into the village. Follow SP to Caxton and turn right then left for 'Bourn' to reach Bourn Postmill.

BOURN POSTMILL, Cambs

Although the working parts of this remarkable windmill have been replaced from time to time, the base and outer structure date back at least to 1636. It is claimed to be the oldest example in England.

Continue for 1 mile, meet a T-junction and turn right to reach Bourn.

BOURN, Cambs

Red-brick Bourn Hall has Jacobean origins but has been restored. Between it and the attractive little Bourn Brook is a church with a fine 13th-century tower.

Drive through Bourn and join the B1046. Continue through Toft and Comberton to reach Barton, and turn left on to the A603. Proceed for 1 mile, at roundabout take 3rd exit on to the unclassified 'Trumpington' road, and continue to Grantchester.

GRANTCHESTER, Cambs

Rupert Brooke immortalized this beautiful village of thatched and lime-washed cottages in his poem *The Old Vicarage, Grantchester*. He lived here for a while after leaving King's College in nearby Cambridge, and wrote of the village as 'the lovely hamlet'.

Cross the Cam and continue to Trumpington.

TRUMPINGTON, Cambs

Inside the elaborate local church is England's second oldest memorial brass. It is dated 1289 and was raised to Sir Roger de Trumpington, whose local associations are obvious in the name. Other features of the village include a 16th-century inn and two 18th-century halls.

Join the A1309 and return to Cambridge.

HADLEIGH, Suffolk

Many fine Georgian and Victorian houses are preserved in this River Brett market town, and the High Street shows a remarkable architectural mixture of timber, brick, and plaster-faced buildings. Some of the plasterwork has been raised in decorative relief, known as pargetting, and most of the structures are excellent examples of their type. The fine 15th-century Guildhall (open) has two overhanging storeys and has been a school and an almshouse. Also of note is the imposing Deanery Tower, a remnant of the medieval palace of Archdeacon Pykenham. Features of the local 14th- to 15th-century church include a bench-end that depicts the legend of a wolf which found and guarded the decapitated head of St Edmund.

Leave Hadleigh on the A1071 'Sudbury' road. At the edge of the town turn right on to the A1141 'Kersey, Lavenham' road and follow the shallow valley of the River Brett for 1¼ miles. Meet crossroads and turn left on to an unclassified road for Kersey.

CONSTABLE LANDSCAPES

Here is the country of John Constable, who immortalized much of its rural beauty in his paintings. Here also are the ragged estuaries of the Stour and Orwell, which carve the coastline into a confusion of small bays, sheltered shingle beaches, and reed-covered marshes.

Hadleigh's superb timbered Guildhall has been well restored and extended. The ground floor originally formed almshouses.

Wildlife of all kinds and restored Thames barges co-exist on the Orwell estuary.

SUDBURY, Suffolk

Sudbury stands on the River Stour and is famous as the birthplace of painter Thomas Gainsborough in 1727. His house at 46 Gainsborough Street is now a local arts centre and museum containing a selection of his work, and he is commemorated by a bronze statue on Market Hill. Novelist Charles Dickens referred to the town as 'Eatanswill' in *Pickwick Papers*. St Peter's Church was built in the 15th century as a chapel of ease and contains a fine painting by a local artist named Robert Cardinall. St Gregory's is much older, having been built on the foundations of an old college by the Archbishop of Canterbury c1365. In 1381 he was brutally murdered in the Peasants' Revolt, and his skull is preserved as his memorial in the vestry. Other features of the building include beautifully carved choir stalls and one of the finest 15th-century font covers in the country. Also in the town is the notable Corn Exchange, containing the Quay Theatre and Arts Centre.

Leave Sudbury on the B1508 SP 'Bures' and continue to Great Cornard.

GREAT CORNARD, Suffolk

Although almost a suburb of nearby Sudbury, the nucleus of this village is still centred on its charming church and preserves an identity entirely separate from its large neighbour.

Stay on the B1508 and drive through the Stour Valley to Bures.

BURES, Suffolk

Fine half-timbered houses and an elegant church dating from the 13th to 15th centuries are the main features of this pretty little village, which stands on the banks of the River Stour. Inside the church is a font adorned with painted shields and a private chapel containing a monument dated 1514. Chapel Barn is an ancient thatched building that was once attached to the former Earl's Colne Priory.

Drive to Bures Church and turn left on to an unclassified road SP 'Nayland'. Follow the Stour Valley for 3¾ miles to reach a right turn that can be taken as a short detour to Wissington.

KERSEY, Suffolk

Shakespeare mentioned the cloth once made in this beautiful old weaving centre in his plays *Measure for Measure* and *Love's Labours Lost*. Nowadays Kersey's Brett Valley position, sloping streets, and numerous half-timbered buildings make it known as one of the most picturesque places in Suffolk. The local church is a gem of 14th- and 15th-century architecture on a site mentioned in the *Domesday Book*.

Drive to the church in Kersey and follow the 'Boxford' road. Continue to Boxford.

BOXFORD, Suffolk

This quaint old village takes its name from an attractive stream that runs close to its timber-framed cottages. Its church features an unusual wooden porch that may be the earliest of its kind in the country, and contains an unusual 17th-century font with doors.

Leave Boxford on the A1071 'Sudbury' road and continue for 2¼ miles. Turn right on to the A134 and drive to Sudbury.

WISSINGTON, Suffolk
Many people come to this attractive village to see the famous series of 13th-century wall paintings in St Mary's Church, a well preserved Norman building with later additions. Close by is an 18th-century house built by architect Sir John Soane.

On the main route, continue with the 'Nayland' road and in 1 mile meet staggered crossroads. Drive across on to the B1087 to enter Nayland at the start of Dedham Vale.

The Chapel Barn near Bures preserves several alabaster tomb chests.

NAYLAND, Suffolk
Alston Court, an attractive half-timbered courtyard house, is one of many 15th-century buildings to be seen in this River Stour village. John Constable painted the altar piece in the local church.

DEDHAM VALE, Essex
This area of outstanding natural beauty stretches from Nayland village to Flatford Mill, and is familiar to many people through the paintings of John Constable.

From Nayland continue on the B1087 to reach Stoke-by-Nayland.

STOKE-BY-NAYLAND, Suffolk
Visitors who are also lovers of John Constable's paintings will recognise the lofty 120ft tower of Stoke-by-Nayland's handsome church. Entry to the south end of the building is through magnificently carved doors, and inside are many notable monuments. Close by are the timber-framed Maltings and the Guildhall, both superb survivals from the 16th century.

Leave Stoke-by-Nayland on the B1068 'Ipswich' road and drive to Thorington Street.

THORINGTON STREET, Suffolk
Early 18th-century additions are evident in the mainly 16th-century structure of Thorington Hall (NT), a fine house that completely dominates this tiny village.

Continue on the B1068 and later cross the River Brett to enter Higham.

HIGHAM, Suffolk
Attractive St Mary's Church and 19th-century Higham Hall preside over this pleasant little village, which has a number of good timber-framed cottages.

Leave Higham on the B1068 and after 2 miles meet the A12. Turn left then in ¼ mile turn left again onto the B1070 'East Bergholt' road. Continue for 1 mile into East Bergholt.

EAST BERGHOLT, Suffolk
In 1776 the great landscape painter John Constable was born here, and speaking of the area he once said 'These scenes made me a painter.' Clustered round the 14th-century church are mellow Elizabethan cottages set amid beautiful gardens. Separated from the church but close by is a unique timber-framed belfry. Stour, home of the late Randolph Churchill, stands near by in the gardens which he created (open).

Drive to East Bergholt Church and bear right to reach Flatford Mill.

FLATFORD MILL, Suffolk
Perhaps the most famous and admired of all Constable's landscape subjects, Flatford Mill (NT) is picturesquely situated on the River Stour and serves as a field-study centre. Both it and nearby Willy Lott's Cottage (NT) attract legions of artists every summer.

Leave Flatford Mill and bear right along a one-way street. After ½ mile meet crossroads and turn right. Continue for ¼ mile to meet the B1070 'Manningtree' road, then drive forward and continue for another 1½ miles to the A137. Turn left here SP 'Ipswich' to reach Brantham.

BRANTHAM, Suffolk
Inside Brantham Church is an altarpiece with a painting by John Constable.

Leave Brantham on the A137. Continue for 1 mile, reach the Bull Inn, and turn right on to the B1080 'Holbrook' road. Continue to Stutton.

STUTTON, Suffolk
Architecture from many periods survives in the church, and there are a number of notable private houses in the neighbourhood. Among these is Stutton Hall (not open), which dates from 1553.

Drive forward for 1 mile and pass through the grounds of the Royal Hospital School.

ROYAL HOSPITAL SCHOOL, Suffolk
An impressive tower with a white stone pinnacle that can be seen for miles around marks the location of the Royal Hospital School, which was founded in 1694 for the sons of seamen. The present group of buildings was occupied when the school moved from Greenwich in the early part of this century.

From the school continue for ½ mile and turn right on to an unclassified road for Harkstead.

Dark-framed and pastel-tinted weavers' houses line Kersey's pretty main-street, which runs down to a small ford.

HARKSTEAD, Suffolk
Notable features of this solitary 14th-century church are its contemporary tower and fine Easter Sepulchre. The building as a whole is an interesting example of medieval architecture.

Continue on the winding 'Shotley' road and drive through Erwarton.

ERWARTON, Suffolk
Red-brick almshouses are a striking feature of this pretty village, which also has an Elizabethan hall with a fine gateway.

Leave Erwarton and pass the gatehouse of Erwarton Hall. Continue to Shotley and turn right on to the B1456 for Shotley Gate.

SHOTLEY GATE, Suffolk
Views of the busy shipping traffic into Harwich and Felixstowe can be enjoyed from this promontory. Close by is the former naval training centre HMS Ganges.

Return along the B1456 'Ipswich' road, pass through Chelmondiston, and reach Woolverstone.

The scene at Flatford Mill has changed little from the days when it was the subject of Constable's famous pictures.

WOOLVERSTONE, Suffolk
Imposing Woolverstone Hall, built in the 18th century by William Berners, is beautifully situated overlooking the attractive Orwell estuary. It now houses a school.

Continue along the B1456 beside the River Orwell, then later turn right on to the A137 and drive to Ipswich.

IPSWICH, Suffolk
Modern commercial development has made this major port and agricultural centre into the largest town in Suffolk. In spite of this it has managed to preserve a number of historic buildings. See tour 63 for fuller details.

Leave Ipswich with SP 'Colchester', then join the A1071 'Sudbury' road. Cross the River Gipping and proceed to Hintlesham

HINTLESHAM, Suffolk
The Great Hall was recently owned by the internationally famous chef Robert Carrier, but is now a Hotel. The building itself has an Elizabethan core behind a fine Georgian acade and features a drawing room with an exceptional filigreed plaster ceiling. Inside the local church are notable monuments to the Timperley family.

Leave Hintlesham on the A1071 and return to Hadleigh.

EAST ANGLIAN HEARTLANDS

The last king of East Anglia ruled from Bury St Edmunds in the 9th century. Today the town is an important market centre for east Suffolk, a focal point for farming communities made rich by a flourishing wool trade in medieval times.

BURY ST EDMUNDS, Suffolk

Edmund, the last king of the East Angles, was killed by the Danes c869 and was subsequently hailed by his people as a martyr. In 903 his body was moved from its resting place at Hoxne to Bury, then known as *Beodricsworth*, which became an important religious centre and place of pilgrimage. The abbey that grew here prospered until it was burned by the townsfolk in 1465. Its rebuilding resulted in one of the architectural glories of England, but it became too powerful and, like many of its contemporaries, was broken at the Dissolution. Today its former splendour can be judged by extensive ruins that form a focal point for a country park. Two gates still stand, and the precincts are made splendid by the Cathedral Church of St James. A large graveyard separates this fine building from 15th-century St Mary's Church, which is known for its magnificent hammerbeam roof and the grave of Mary Tudor. Mary's life is illustrated in a window given by Queen Victoria. Bury St Edmunds itself is an attractive market town which retains its 11th-century street plan and many fine old buildings. Moyse's Hall dates from the 12th century and contains a museum, and the lovely Guildhall and Cupola House are both of 15th-century origin. Excellent Georgian shop fronts are preserved in some streets, and the Town Hall of 1771 was designed by Robert Adam. Also from this period are a brick-built Unitarian chapel with an exceptionally

well-preserved interior, and the Angel Corner (NT) is a Queen Anne house, now containing a collection of clocks and watches. The Theatre Royal (NT) build in 1819 is a rare example of a Georgian playhouse. The 18th-century Angel Hotel was the scene of Mr Pickwick's meeting with Sam Weller in Charles Dickens' *Pickwick Papers*.

Some 2½ miles south west of the town, off the A143, is Ickworth House.

Once a rich and splendid monastery, the abbey at Bury St Edmunds is now an extensive ruin.

ICKWORTH HOUSE, Suffolk

Started by Frederick Harvey, 4th Earl of Bristol and the Bishop of Derry, this 18th-century house (NT) is one of the most remarkable in England and an apt memorial to its builder's eccentricity. The Earl Bishop intended to fill it with works of art collected during his extensive travels, but in Rome he was imprisoned by Napoleonic troops and his enormous collection confiscated. He died in 1803, with only half his dream actually realized in bricks and mortar. Visitors today can see the full glory of the strange elliptical rotunda that grew from plans by the Italian architect Asprucci. Inside the house is a fine collection of 18th-century and French furniture. Part of the 2,000-acre grounds (NT) were landscaped by Capability Brown.

Leave Bury St Edmunds on the A134 'Sudbury' road. Drive through the villages of Sicklesmere and Bradfield Combust, and ¾ mile beyond the latter pass an unclassified right turn leading through Hoggards Green to the village of Stanningfield. This offers a pleasant detour from the main route.

STANNINGFIELD, Suffolk

Stanningfield Church has two fine Norman doorways, one within a timbered porch, and the 13th-century chancel preserves notable features. West of the village is Elizabethan Coldham Hall, which has a dovecote of the same period.

Continue on the A134 and approach Long Melford with the grounds of Kentwell Hall to the right.

KENTWELL HALL, Suffolk

Access to this mellow Elizabethan manor (open) is through a 300-year-old avenue of lime trees and over a moat. The combination of water, tree-shaded grass, and old brick forms a tranquil beauty that is a rarity in the 20th century.

Fine medieval houses in Lavenham reflect the wealth brought by the wool trade.

LONG MELFORD, Suffolk

Perhaps the stateliest village in Suffolk, Long Melford has an impressive main street lined by fine old buildings and dominated by a magnificent church. The latter dates from 15th-century reconstruction and occupies the site of a Roman temple. Its many windows give the interior an airiness accentuated by soaring columns and slender pillars. The Lady Chapel of 1496 can almost be considered as separate from the main building, though attached in mortar if not in style to the east end. The well-proportioned tower is a sensitive addition dating from 1903. Interesting monuments include a carved 15th-century piece in the Clopton Chantry and a number of contemporary brasses that illustrate clothing and hairstyles of the period. Leading down towards the village from the church is a triangular green fringed by the 18th-century wall of the Congregational churchyard, the 15th-century Bull Hotel and 16th-century Trinity Hospital. The latter was founded by Sir William Cordell and greatly restored in the 19th century. Dominating the village is Melford Hall (NT), one of the finest Elizabethan manors in England. It occupies three sides of a lovely old courtyard and carries a splendid array of turrets.

Drive to the Bull Inn and turn left on to the unclassified 'Lavenham' road. In 1¼ miles continue forward to Acton.

ACTON, Suffolk

Inside Acton Church is an excellent brass, the most famous military memorial of its type in the country. It was raised to Sir Robert de Bures *c*1302 and depicts a knight in chain mail holding a shield. A notable sculpture of a reclining man with his wife at his feet carries the date 1722 and has been attributed to Thomas Green of Camberwell.

From Acton turn left with SP 'Lavenham'. In 2¼ miles join the B1071 and continue to Lavenham.

LAVENHAM, Suffolk

Easily one of the most outstanding villages in East Anglia, Lavenham has hardly changed in appearance since its heyday as an important wool town in the 14th and 15th centuries. Its dozens of immaculately preserved buildings include timber-framed houses, the Guildhall (NT), and the Wool Hall. Slightly apart from the village is the local church, a superb building that is considered a complete work of art in itself. It carries a 141ft tower resplendent with shiny knapped flint, and was built with money donated by a family of clothiers. Other reflections of prosperous times are 15th-century Little Hall, the old Town Cross (AM), and The Priory. An 18th-century hand-operated fire engine is preserved in the village.

Leave Lavenham on the A1141 'Hadleigh' road. After 2 miles turn left on to an unclassified road and enter Brent Eleigh.

One of the many superb old buildings preserved in Long Melford is Elizabethan Melford Hall.

BRENT ELEIGH, Suffolk

Fine wall paintings have been discovered in the 14th-century Church of St Mary here, and Jacobean woodwork is much in evidence on the pulpit, south door, and box pews. Elizabethan Brent Eleigh Hall has modern additions by architect Sir Edwin Lutyens.

Return to the A1141 and turn left for Monks Eleigh.

MONKS ELEIGH, Suffolk

This pleasant little village has a good church with a notable tower and a carved pulpit. An attractive weatherboarded mill and Georgian millhouse stand near by.

Drive to the end of the village and bear left on to the B1115 'Stowmarket' road. Continue to Chelsworth.

CHELSWORTH, Suffolk

An attractive double hump-backed bridge spans the small River Brett here, and the village features many lovely timber-framed houses.

Stay on the B1115 and turn left for Bildeston.

Moated Kentwell Hall dates from the 16th century and stands in lovely grounds about 1 mile north of Long Melford.

BILDESTON, Suffolk

Many notable half-timbered cottages survive here, and the village church is reached by a footpath across pleasant farming country.

From Bildeston continue on the B1115 to Hitcham.

HITCHAM, Suffolk

A 15th-century hammerbeam roof can be seen in Hitcham Church, which is comfortable rather than outstanding and forms a natural focus for this delightful village. Many of the local cottages are half timbered.

Continue on the B1115 and drive through Great Finborough to reach Stowmarket.

STOWMARKET, Suffolk

Poet John Milton visited this busy Gipping Valley market town many times to see his tutor Thomas Young, who lived at the vicarage. Most of the buildings are of fairly recent date, like the good Georgian and Victorian houses round the market square. Inside the town church, which displays a variety of styles, are an old organ and a rare wigstand. A large open-air museum relating to East Anglian Life has an attractive riverside setting here, with frequent demonstrations from craftsmen.

Leave the town on the A1302 'Bury St Edmunds' road. In ¾ mile join the A45, and after another 1¾ miles branch left on to an unclassified road. Continue to the village of Haughley.

HAUGHLEY, Suffolk

A Norman castle that once stood here has entirely vanished, but its mound remains as a monument to the village's previous importance. There are 30 18th-century leather buckets in the church porch, possibly a hangover from early fire precautions, and the nave has a good roof. New Bell's Farm is an experimental station of the Soil Association.

In Haughley turn left and continue to Wetherden. In the latter village turn left again, then in a further ½ mile turn right and pass the grounds of Haughley Park on the left.

HAUGHLEY PARK, Suffolk

Characteristic stepped gables and elegant octagonal chimneys are dominant features of this lovely old house, built in 1620 and restored in recent years. It stands in beautiful grounds and is open to the public on Tuesdays May to September.

After 1¼ miles rejoin the A45. In ½ mile branch left, then turn left on to an unclassified road. A short detour can be made from the main route to passing over the A45 to join the A1088 'Thetford' road and driving for 2½ miles.

NORTON, Suffolk

Excellent examples of old woodcarving, including misericords and a notable font, can be seen inside the local church. Nearby is the partly 18th-century Rectory and The Norton Bird Gardens set in 4 acres of gardens with a variety of species.

On the main route, continue to Woolpit.

WOOLPIT, Suffolk

At one time wolves were brought here to be destroyed and buried, hence the name. A local legend tells of the Green Children, a boy and girl who suddenly appeared in some obscure period of village history and were remarkable for their distinctive colour. The story goes on to say that they claimed to be from underground St Martin's Land, a place of perpetual twilight, and that the boy died but the girl married and had a family. The local church boasts a rare brass-eagle lectern and double-hammerbeam roof.

Leave Woolpit on the unclassified 'Bury St Edmunds' road and in ¾ mile rejoin the A45. In 1¼ miles turn left for Beyton.

BEYTON, Suffolk

Good Norman features of Beyton Church include a pleasing round tower and an attractively simple doorway.

After village rejoin the A45 for the return to Bury St Edmunds.

TOUR 63   70 MILES

FARMLANDS OF SUFFOLK

This corner of rural Suffolk is the England of the romantics, an ideal of pastoral beauty hauntingly captured in the paintings of John Constable. It is a place of rolling meadows and tiny rustic villages, where life moves at an easy pace and the air of timelessness can almost be touched.

The Ancient House in Ipswich displays fine decorated plasterwork known as pargetting.

This rare old mill on the river Deben at Woodbridge is operated by the rise and fall of water between tides. Records of East Anglian mills worked in this way date back as far as the 12th century.

IPSWICH, Suffolk
Centuries of development have made this major port the largest and one of the most successful towns in Suffolk. It is the main centre of employment in the eastern part of the county, and despite continued expansion has managed to keep many relics of its eventful past intact. A red-brick gateway bearing royal arms survives from the unfinished Cardinal College of St Mary, which was founded by Cardinal Wolsey – a native of the town – in the 16th century. The Ancient or Sparrowe's House of 1567 stands in the Buttermarket and is noted for its exterior decoration of intricate patterns and features carved in plaster, an outstanding example of the East Anglian art of pargetting. Original oak panelling and heavy carved beams can be seen by visitors to the bookshop which it now houses. Close by are the Great White Horse Hotel, which features in Charles Dickens' *Pickwick Papers*, and many old streets lined with well-preserved timber-framed houses. Christchurch Mansion (open) was built by a Tudor merchant and is isolated in an oasis of parkland near the centre of town. It contains fine collections of furniture and paintings. Exhibits relating to local history and wildlife can be seen in the Ipswich Museum of Archaeology and Natural History, which stands in the High Street. The number of good

churches in the town reflects its former importance and prosperity. Among the best are: St Margaret's, with a fine hammerbeam roof; St Peter's, with an impressive black Tournai font; and St Mary-le-Tower, which boasts a lovely pulpit carved by Grinling Gibbons. A remarkable 16th-century Unitarian Meeting House stands in Friar Street.

Leave Ipswich on the A1156 with SP 'Felixstowe' and in 5 miles reach an unclassified right turn leading to Levington. A short detour can be taken to Levington from here.

LEVINGTON, Suffolk
This attractive small village stands on the banks of the Orwell and is the base for the Suffolk Yacht Harbour. Its church dates from the 16th century.

On the main route, continue along the A45 and after 5 miles follow SP 'Town Centre' to enter Felixstowe.

FELIXSTOWE, Suffolk
Towards the end of the 19th century this sheltered spot on the Suffolk coast was developed as a seaside resort. It attracted fashionable society, including the German Kaiser, and acquired a 2-mile length of promenade bordered by delightful flower displays and beautifully tended lawns. Long before this a 16th-century stronghold which became the Landguard Fort (AM) was defending the sea approach to

Harwich. A later period of insecurity this time generated by Napoleon's hold on Europe, resulted in the building of a Martello tower c1810. Felixstowe Dock is an important container port. A modern leisure centre offers all year round entertainment.

Leave Felixstowe on the A45 'Ipswich' road and in 7 miles turn right on to the A12 SP 'Woodbridge' and 'Gt Yarmouth'. After 4 miles reach a roundabout and go forward, passing the Post Office Research Station on Martlesham Heath. In ¾ mile turn right on to the A12 to reach Martlesham.

MARTLESHAM, Suffolk
Martlesham village is picturesquely sited on a creek of the River Deben and features a church with an unusual 7-sided wagon roof. The local Red Lion Inn displays a curious sign that was taken from a Dutch ship in 1672.

Continue on the A12 to the end of Martlesham, drive under a railway bridge, then turn right on to the B1438 to reach Woodbridge.

WOODBRIDGE, Suffolk
Attractive houses of major historical interest surround the old market square round which this port has grown. Many date from the 16th century, and the entire group is centred on the superb Shire Hall, which features work from the 16th to 19th centuries and picturesque Dutch-style gables. Multi-period Woodbridge Church carries a tall, flint-flushwork tower and contains a seven sacrament font. One old mill, a rare example which depends on the tide, is open. The port's status as a busy centre of ocean trade declined a long time ago, but today it is a popular sailing centre with a fine riverside park at Kyson Hill (NT).

From Woodbridge continue on the B1438 to Melton.

140

MELTON, Suffolk

A small colour-washed brick building known as Friar's Dene was once the village gaol. Melton Church has a handsome tower with an attractive broach spire.

From Melton turn right on to the A1152 SP 'Orford'. Cross the railway line and the River Deben, then bear left and in ¾ mile keep forward on to the B1084. After a short distance enter part of Rendlesham Forest, which contains a picnic site, and continue to Butley.

BUTLEY, Suffolk

An Augustinian priory founded here in 1171 has vanished but its superb 14th-century gatehouse has survived as one of the finest medieval buildings of its kind in Suffolk. Particularly notable are the heraldic designs cut into its stonework.

Leave Butley, remaining on the B1084, then skirt part of Tunstall Forest and pass through Chillesford. In 1¾ miles meet crossroads and turn right to reach Orford.

The finely-preserved postmill at Saxtead Green is typical of many in Suffolk.

ORFORD, Suffolk

In 1165 Henry II built a moat-encircled castle with an 18-sided keep here in an attempt to establish Norman power over the peoples of East Anglia. Today the building (AM) that developed from these early beginnings contains a collection of arms and affords excellent views of the picturesque houses and fishermen's cottages below its walls. On the seaward side of the village the River Alde is separated from the sea by Orford Ness.

ORFORD NESS, Suffolk

This long strip of coastal marshland is occupied by the Orford Ness and Havergate national nature reserve, one of the few places in England where the rare avocet can be seen.

From Orford return along the B1084 and in 1¼ miles drive forward on to the unclassified 'Snape' road. Skirt another part of Tunstall Forest for nearly 4 miles and join the B1069. Pass The Maltings, cross the River Alde, and enter Snape.

Tudor Helmingham Hall's moat is spanned by two drawbridges.

SNAPE, Suffolk

The magnificent Maltings concert hall, built on the site of old maltings where barley was stored prior to export, is the yearly venue for the famous Aldeburgh Music Festival. Its situation on the banks of the River Alde adds an extra dimension to its pleasing architecture. Snape Church houses a richly carved 15th-century font, and close to the village are slight remains of an ancient Benedictine priory.

Leave Snape, continue for ¾ mile, then meet the A1094 'Ipswich' road and turn left. In 2 miles turn left on to the A12 and pass through Farnham for Stratford St Andrew.

STRATFORD ST ANDREW, Suffolk

Close to this pleasant little village is 17th-century Glemham Hall (open), an impressive red-brick mansion standing in 350 acres of beautiful parkland. Inside are panelled rooms appointed with fine paintings and Queen Anne furniture. The village church contains Norman workmanship and houses a 13th-century font.

Remain on the A12 and in 1 mile, at an entrance to Glemham Hall, turn right on to the unclassified 'Parham' road. In a further 1 mile turn right, then in a short distance turn left and continue to Parham.

PARHAM, Suffolk

Tranquilly set in the upper valley of the River Alde, this little village has a church where the village stocks and a beautiful 14th-century screen are preserved. Just to the south-east is 16th-century Moat Hall, a picturesque timber-framed house that is encircled by a moat and nowadays serves as a farm.

Leave Parham on the B1116 and continue to Framlingham.

FRAMLINGHAM, Suffolk

Framlingham's superb Norman castle (AM) was started in 1190 and represented an important advance in castle design. Fragments of the Great Hall are incorporated in picturesque 17th-century almshouses, and the towers carry distinctive Tudor chimneys. Monuments to the Howard family, who took possession in the 15th century, can be seen in the local church. The town itself is a historic market centre with many old houses and a well-known college.

From Framlingham follow the B1119 SP 'Stowmarket' to reach Saxtead Green.

Thames barges moored on the Orwell estuary near Ipswich are reminiscent of a maritime past when the elegance of sail was commonplace.

SAXTEAD GREEN, Suffolk

One of the finest postmills (AM) in Suffolk with its wooden superstructure and brick round house stands here. Stones and machinery inside are in excellent working order. It was first recorded in 1706 and substantially rebuilt at least twice during its working life. Today it stands 46ft high and carries sails with a span of almost 55ft.

Leave Saxtead Green on the A1120 'Stowmarket' road and continue to Earl Soham.

EARL SOHAM, Suffolk

Old cottages and Georgian houses face rows of allotments across a long street in this somewhat rambling village. The local church carries a 15th-century tower and contains several good monuments.

Drive to the end of Earl Soham village and turn left, then in 3 miles turn left again on to the B1077 'Ipswich' road. In 1 mile pass another fine windmill on the left, then in a further 1¼ miles reach Helmingham Hall on the right.

HELMINGHAM HALL, Suffolk

Every night the two drawbridges that span the moat to this lovely manor house are raised, though more for the sake of tradition than against rival lords or jealous monarchs. Home of the Tollemache family since the 16th century, the hall has Georgian additions with crenallations by John Nash and stands amid beautiful gardens (open) in an ancient deer park. More than 500 red and fallow deer share the estate with herds of Highland cattle. Visitors may recognise parts of the grounds from John Constable's great landscape painting *Helmingham Dell*.

Continue to Ashbocking.

ASHBOCKING, Suffolk

The medieval church in this village carries a 16th-century tower which is contemporary with Ashbocking Hall, an attractive timber-framed building near by.

Continue to Witnesham.

WITNESHAM, Suffolk

Situated near a tributary of the River Deben, this peaceful little village has an Elizabethan hall and a good church. The hall includes a few Victorian additions and the church, which contains an 8-sided font, has an excellent hammerbeam roof.

Continue on the B1077 to Westerfield.

WESTERFIELD, Suffolk

Westerfield Hall is a 17th-century building with attractive Dutch gables. The local church dates from c1300 and features a nave window in which pieces of a Norman doorway have been re-used. The roof in both the chancel and nave is of hammerbeam construction.

Leave Westerfield and drive through built-up areas to re-enter Ipswich.

NORWICH, Norfolk

Once an important centre of the worsted trade, this county town stands on the River Wensum and boasts a cathedral with one of the finest interiors in the country. It dates from Norman times and contains the oldest bishop's throne still used in England. Other major features include a fine presbytery, a beautiful cloister, and a magnificent nave roof featuring many of the 800 roof bosses to be found in the cathedral. Access to the building is by two fine gates, the Erpingham of 1420 and St Ethelbert's of 1272 (both AM). Close to a former water gate on the river are Pull's Ferry and the Barge Inn, two reminders of the city's antiquity, and amongst the many other fine old buildings are no less than 30 parish churches. The largest and finest of these is St Peter Mancroft, which carries a notable tower, but all the others have particular details that make them worth a visit. St Andrew's dates from the 15th century and displays a remarkable series of carved shields, and St Michael-at-Coslany has fine flintwork in the Thorpe Chapel. Norwich Castle (open) was started c1130, but its Norman origins have been heavily disguised by 19th-century refacing. Survivals from the medieval city and later are many. Flint-faced Bridewell is a 14th-century merchant's house that now contains a museum; the Cow Tower (AM) dates from the same period and formed part of a defensive system along the river bank. Slightly later is the St Peter Hungate Church, a 15th-century building which carries a fine hammerbeam roof and now houses a museum. In the 1920s a chapel was converted to house the well-known Maddermarket Theatre. The most famous of the city's many picturesque streets is Elm Hill, a cobbled road lined with old colour-washed shops and houses, while the most outstanding of its lay buildings are the 15th-century Suckling House and chequered-flint Guildhall. In 1978 the supermarket magnet Sir Robert Sainsbury presented the University the Sainsbury Centre for Visual Arts, which is housed in an outstanding modern building. The colourful open-air market has been a weekday occurrence since Norman times.

Leave Norwich on the A47 'Yarmouth' road and pass through Thorpe St Andrew to Blofield.

BLOFIELD, Norfolk

Blofield Church, an impressive building that forms a landmark visible for miles round the village, is noted for its tall west tower. Inside is an 8-sided font ornamented with various scenes in relief.

Continue to Acle.

ACLE, Norfolk

This well-known touring centre is within easy reach of the lovely Norfolk Broads and is a good base from which to explore the area. Its unusual church has a picturesque thatched roof and a round tower

AMONG THE NORFOLK BROADS

Close to the great cathedral city of Norwich are marshlands, meres, and lakes in a landscape dotted with the stark shapes of old wind pumps. Hidden canals link vast acreages of water drained from the local countryside, offering ideal highways by which to explore the broadlands.

Norwich Castle rises high above the city from a landscaped hilltop.

that dates from the 12th century. East of the village, on the tour route, are several windpumps that have survived from the days when many such machines were built to pump excess water from the reclaimed marshlands.

Continue along the A47 to Great Yarmouth.

GREAT YARMOUTH, Norfolk

Holiday amenities in this important oil and fishing port include 5 miles of seafront fringed by excellent sands and backed by colourful gardens. Its situation on Breydon Water, the combined estuaries of the Bure, Waveney and Yare, gives it an

Ormesby, one of Broadland's loveliest stretches of water.

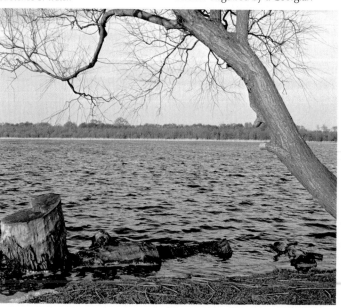

aspect that suits both the holidaymakers and the busy maritime traffic that uses its harbour. The town is very old and has managed to retain many historic features. Most of these can be seen in the South Quay area, where there are remains of the town walls and the notable Custom House. Leading from the town wall to the quay are the Rows, a number of narrow lanes where the 300-year-old Merchant's House (AM) can be seen. Close by is the 14th-century Greyfriar's Cloister (AM). The Elizabethan House Museum has a largely 16th-century interior disguised by a Georgian

façade. Exhibits include furniture from that and later periods, and a fascinating collection of Victorian toys. The 13th-century building that houses the Tollhouse Museum is one of the oldest in Great Yarmouth and incorporates ancient dungeons. Close to England's largest parish church is Anna Sewell House, a 17th-century building that was the birthplace of the authoress of *Black Beauty*. The House of Wax museum features various historical figures and scenes , and the Maritime Museum of East Anglia illustrates life saving and marine oil exploration. Near Wellington Pier in an acre of landscaped garden is the quaint Merrivale Model Village.

Leave Great Yarmouth on the A149 SP 'Caister'. In 2 miles meet a roundabout and drive forward to enter Caister.

CAISTER-ON-SEA, Norfolk

Remains of town walls and a gateway (AM) survive from the time when this popular little resort was a Roman settlement. Much more recent is the 15th-century castle (open), whose remains now house a museum of veteran and vintage cars.

From the town centre turn left on to the A1064 'Acle' road and pass the remains of Caister Roman Town on the right. Meet a roundabout and take the 2nd exit. In $\frac{3}{4}$ mile turn right on to an unclassified road SP 'Great Ormesby', and in 1 mile turn left on to the A149 to enter Ormesby St Margaret – at the edge of the Broads country.

THE BROADS, Norfolk

More than 30 large and very beautiful sheets of water, often linked by navigable channels, are contained in a triangular area between Norwich, Lowestoft, and Sea Palling. These, together with many rivers, lakes, and canals, provide some 200 miles of water for cruising and sailing. The essential character of the Broads can only be properly appreciated from a boat, and there are hire firms and tour operators in such centres as Wroxham, Horning and Potter Heigham. Angling permits are available from tackle shops in these and other towns.

A short and very pleasant detour from the main route can be made by staying on the A149 and continuing to Ormesby Broad.

ORMESBY BROAD, Norfolk

The main road between Ormesby St Margaret and Rollesby crosses this vast expanse of water and offers some of the best broadland views available to the motorist.

On the main route, drive to the war memorial in Ormesby St Margaret and turn right on to an unclassified road alongside the green, SP 'Scratby'. Meet a T-junction and turn right SP 'Hemsby'. At Hemsby, drive to the end of the village and turn left on to the B1159 SP 'Mundesley'. Continue along a winding road to Winterton.

WINTERTON-ON-SEA, Norfolk

Much of the countryside round this little fishing village is included in a 260-acre nature reserve.

Continue to West Somerton.

WEST SOMERTON, Norfolk

Situated at the weedy eastern end of Martham Broad, this quiet village is an excellent angling base and a good place to see how the marshes were drained. A maze of streams and man-made ditches still carries excess water into the main broads, and two windpumps that were used to pump from one level to another can be seen near by.

Continue with SP 'Cromer' to Horsey Mere.

Horsey Church is noted for its thatched roof and unusual stained-glass windows.

HORSEY MERE, Norfolk

Access to this important breeding ground for marshland plants and animals is restricted to naturalists and permit holders. The mere's drainage windmill (NT) was built in 1912 and has been well restored.
Continue to Horsey.

HORSEY, Norfolk

Despite frequent incursions of the sea since it was built, the thatched village church has retained its Norman round tower.
Continue to Sea Palling, then in 1¾ miles turn left B1151 to Stalham.

STALHAM, Norfolk

Two miles south east of Stalham is the Sutton windmill, the tallest windmill in the country built in 1789 it has nine floors plus a cap floor, and a museum.
Return to B1159 turn left and continue to Lessingham, then Happisburgh.

HAPPISBURGH, Norfolk

Offshore shipping is warned away from the treacherous Haisboro' Sands by a lighthouse, but the same drifts provide sun and sea bathers with a superb dune-backed beach. The name of this pretty little fishing village is pronounced Hazeborough.

In 1¼ miles meet crossroads and turn right for Walcott. Continue to Bacton.

BACTON, Norfolk

Easy access to the broad local beach of shingly sand and pebbles is via a high sea wall. The village itself is an attractive little place that grew up alongside Broomholm Priory, a 12th-century foundation that claimed to possess a piece of the True Cross and became a great centre of pilgrimage. Remains of the priory, which was mentioned by Chaucer, include the gatehouse, north transept, chapter house, and refectory.

Drive past a windmill to Mundesley.

West Somerton was the haunt of smuggling gangs in the 18th century.

The best way to appreciate the Norfolk Broads is by boat.

MUNDESLEY, Norfolk

This quiet resort has a gently shelving sand beach backed by cliffs. It is associated with the poet William Cowper.

Continue to Trimingham.

TRIMINGHAM, Norfolk

Some of the highest cliffs in Norfolk overlook a good bathing beach here. A painted screen can be seen in the local church.

Continue to Overstrand.

OVERSTRAND, Norfolk

Pleasant cliff walks lead from here to the nearby resort of Cromer, and safe bathing can be enjoyed from the local sands. The 14th-century Church of St Martin was built after the old parish church fell into the sea.

Continue to Cromer.

CROMER, Norfolk

Although a bustling resort mainly occupied with the needs of holidaymakers, Cromer still has a small fishing fleet and has the reputation for supplying the best crabs in England. Its sandy beach is backed by lofty cliffs, and its many amenities include a zoo and boating pool. The 15th-century parish church carries one of the tallest towers in Norfolk. Close to Cromer is Felbrigg Hall (NT), a fine house that dates from the 17th century.

Leave Cromer on the A149 'Norwich' road and in 2¼ miles bear left SP 'North Walsham'. Continue to Thorpe Market and North Walsham.

NORTH WALSHAM, Norfolk

Homely buildings and winding little lanes make this beautiful market town well worth a pause in any journey. Its fine church is given an air of gothic mystery by a ruined tower that fell in 1724. Inside are a painted screen, a tall 15th-century font cover, and various monuments. The local grammar school was founded in the early 17th century.

Follow SP 'Norwich' on the B1150. Pass Westwick Park and drive beneath an arched gateway which spans the road; continue to Coltishall.

COLTISHALL, Norfolk

This shooting and angling centre is situated on the River Bure and enjoys a genteelly relaxed atmosphere imparted by many 18th-century buildings.

Cross the River Bure to Horstead.

HORSTEAD, Norfolk

Horstead Church carries a slender west tower that dates from the 13th century. The delightful village mill stands opposite the miller's house.

Drive through wooded countryside and return to Norwich.

SALTINGS ON THE WASH

Along the sweeping coastline of the Wash are wide sandy bays backed by wild salt marshes populated by wildlife suited to the open surroundings. Here and there the flint tower of a medieval village church breaks the skyline, providing a landmark for travellers on both land and sea.

The creek at Burnham Overy Staithe is very popular with yachtsmen.

KING'S LYNN, Norfolk

Two markets were founded here in Norman times, medieval merchants came here to build warehouses on the River Ouse, and 20th-century industry has continued the town's long history of commercial significance. Everywhere are survivals from periods that the settlement has grown through, and its medieval buildings are some of the finest in the country. Traces of the ancient walls show how the town has expanded since the troubled times in which they were built, and the superb Hanseatic Warehouse of 1428 recalls full-sailed barques laden with exotic goods. To complement the two market places are two guildhalls, both of which date from the early 15th century. The biggest of these (NT) is the largest medieval guildhall extant and is now used as a theatre. The other contains old town regalia, including a 14th-century vessel known as King John's Cup. Both the last-mentioned building and the much more recent Town Hall of 1895 display a striking flint-chequerwork design. The superb Custom House, perhaps the most outstanding building in the town, was built by architect Henry Bell while he held office as mayor in 1683. Many other of the town's old buildings have ancient roots but have been changed over the centuries. Clifton House dates originally from the 14th century but has later additions; Hampton Court shows period work from the 14th to 18th centuries; and Dutch-gabled Thoresby College of c1500 now reflects the tastes of the 17th century. The huge parish church contains two outstanding memorial brasses that are the biggest and most famous in England. Red Mount Chapel of c1485 is an octagonal building with beautiful fan vaulting.

Leave King's Lynn by the A47 'Swaffham' road and continue to Middleton.

Dutch influence is evident in King's Lynn's charming Custom House.

MIDDLETON, Norfolk

Major Everard-Hutton, one of the famous Six Hundred who fought at Balaclava, is commemorated by a memorial in the local church. Some 3 miles north west is Middleton Tower, a splendid red-brick gatehouse of mainly 19th-century date.

Pass Walton Common, then cross the River Nar to enter Narborough.

NARBOROUGH, Norfolk

Several fine brasses and a standing effigy can be seen in the local church.

Continue, and later pass Swaffham Heath to reach Swaffham.

SWAFFHAM, Norfolk

Legend tells of the 'Pedlar of Swaffham', who travelled to London to throw himself into the Thames but was dissuaded by a man he met on London Bridge. This stranger related a dream in which he found treasure in a remote village garden – a garden that the pedlar recognised as his own. He hastened home to find two pots of gold; an image of the pedlar is now incorporated in the town sign. The triangular market place has a domed rotunda built by the Earl of Oxford in 1783 as a market cross. Features of the local church include a splendid angel-carved double-hammerbeam roof and a fine 16th-century west tower.

Leave Swaffham on the A1065 'Cromer' road. In 2¾ miles turn left on to an unclassified road for Castle Acre.

CASTLE ACRE, Norfolk

This aptly-named village lies within the outer bailey of an 11th-century castle, of which only the earthworks and a 13th-century gateway remain. Impressive ruins of an 11th-century Cluniac priory, including fine Norman arcading (AM) and a Tudor gatehouse, can be seen near by.

Continue through the village and turn right SP 'Newton'. Rejoin the A1065 'Cromer' road and drive to Weasenham.

WEASENHAM, Norfolk

Prehistoric barrows in all shapes and sizes, including bell, bowl, disc, and saucer types, can be seen in the countryside round Weasenham Plantation.

Continue to East Raynham.

EAST RAYNHAM, Norfolk

Raynham Hall, a magnificent 17th-century building which has been ascribed partly to Inigo Jones, was once the home of the agricultural innovator nicknamed Turnip Townshend.

In 2½ miles turn right SP 'Town Centre' for Fakenham.

FAKENHAM, Norfolk

This attractive market town dates from Saxon times and was a Royal Manor until the 17th century. Its Market Place has two old coaching inns, both showing traces of earlier work behind Georgian façades, and the parish church has a commanding 15th-century tower.

From Fakenham town centre follow SP 'King's Lynn' to join the A148. In ¼ mile turn right on to the B1105 SP 'Walsingham' and descend into East Barsham.

EAST BARSHAM, Norfolk

East Barsham is known for its brick and terracotta manor house, a splendid example of early Tudor work. Fine chimneys typical of the style rise high above the rooftops, and the approach is guarded by an imposing two-storeyed gatehouse.

Continue for 1 mile to Houghton St Giles.

HOUGHTON ST GILES, Norfolk

On the far side of the Stiffkey river, about 1 mile south west of this attractive village, is the last in a chain of wayside chapels which once lined the Walsingham Way. It is known as the Slipper Chapel because pilgrims to the shrine of Our Lady at Walsingham would remove their shoes here before completing their journey barefoot. It is now the official Roman Catholic Shrine of Our Lady.

Continue to Walsingham, also known as Little Walsingham.

The legendary Pedlar of Swaffham is commemorated by the town sign.

WALSINGHAM, Norfolk

The shrine at Walsingham, a place of paramount importance to the pilgrims of the middle ages, was founded in the 11th century. Virtually every English king from Richard I to Henry VIII came here, and the last-named had the shrine robbed when he dissolved the monasteries. In the 19th century the pilgrimages were revived, and a new Shrine of Our Lady was built for the Anglican Church in the early part of the 20th century. Remains of what was once a giant concourse of buildings date mainly from the 13th and 14th centuries, and include the superb east wall of the priory.

Continue on the B1105 'Wells' road and skirt Wighton to meet the A149. Turn left, then right, with SP 'The Beach'. Enter Wells-next-the-Sea.

WELLS-NEXT-THE-SEA, Norfolk

Old houses and the picturesque quayside make a charming group in this small resort and port. Bathing may be enjoyed in a nearby creek.

Leave the resort on the A149 'Hunstanton' road and drive to Holkham.

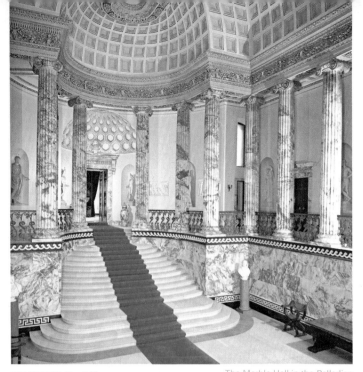

The Marble Hall in the Palladian mansion of Holkham exemplifies William Kent's lavish style.

HOLKHAM, Norfolk

Holkham Hall (open), a vast Palladian mansion, is one of the show-pieces of the county. The present house was rebuilt in the 18th century to plans by William Kent, who also designed much of the furniture to be seen inside. Experts consider the entrance into the wonderful alabaster hall to show Kent's genius at its peak, and all the rooms are sumptuously decorated in the fashion of the day. An impressive art collection is displayed in the house, and the library has an excellent collection of 18th-century books. The lake-watered grounds were laid out by Capability Brown in 1762.

Continue to Burnham Overy Staithe.

BURNHAM OVERY STAITHE, Norfolk

Close to this tiny village are a water mill (NT) and tower windmill (NT), both in a good state of preservation. Neither is open to the public at time of publication.

After a short distance cross the River Burn and continue to Burnham Deepdale.

BURNHAM DEEPDALE, Norfolk

Inside the local church, which carries a rare Saxon round tower, is an outstanding Norman font.

Continue to Brancaster Staithe.

BRANCASTER STAITHE, Norfolk

A boat service operates from here to Scolt Head Island, where there is a bird sanctuary (NT) and nature reserve.

Continue for ⅓ mile to Brancaster.

BRANCASTER, Norfolk

This one-time Roman station is now a golfing resort. A lane leads from the church to a pebble beach which, though not as attractive as its large sandy neighbour, is far safer for bathing.

Continue through Titchwell to Thornham.

THORNHAM, Norfolk

A rectangular earthwork on a slope overlooking the waters of the Wash here was excavated in 1960, revealing the remains of an iron-age village. The complex, thought to date from cAD40, measures 133 by 175ft and includes a defensive ditch cut into the soft chalk.

Drive through Old Hunstanton and ½ mile farther turn right on to an unclassified road SP 'Sea Front'. Continue into Hunstanton.

A peaceful atmosphere pervades Wells-next-the-Sea.

HUNSTANTON, Norfolk

Hunstanton is the largest seaside resort in west Norfolk and the only East Anglian coastal town to face west. Great stretches of sand are backed by cliffs of mixed chalk and sand rising 60ft above the beach.

Pass the Pier, bear right into Westgate, and in ⅓ mile meet a roundabout. Take the 1st exit SP 'King's Lynn', then meet the main road and turn right on to the A149 to reach the outskirts of Heacham.

HEACHAM, Norfolk

Pocahontas, the Red Indian princess who married John Rolfe at Heacham Hall in 1614, is commemorated in both the village sign and a memorial in the local church. Her son founded a line which was to include the wife of US president Woodrow Wilson.

Continue to Snettisham.

SNETTISHAM, Norfolk

One of the finest churches in Norfolk stands here. Its lofty spire can be seen for many miles across the flat local countryside, and its superb west front is reminiscent of Peterborough Cathedral. Also in the village is attractive Old Hall, an 18th-century house with Dutch gables.

Continue through Ingoldisthorpe to Dersingham. Turn left on to the B1440 SP 'Sandringham'. Ascend through wooded country and in ⅓ mile pass the gates of Sandringham House.

SANDRINGHAM, Norfolk

Included in this 7,000-acre estate, owned by the Royal Family, are a 19th-century house and museum (open), the farms and woodlands of 7 parishes, and a 300-acre country park. The park church is of exceptional note and contains an organ that was the last gift of King Edward VII. Many superb royal memorials enrich the interior, and the nave is roofed in English oak.

In 1 mile turn right on to the B1439 into West Newton. Continue to the main road and turn left to rejoin the A149. In 1 mile turn right on to an unclassified road for Castle Rising.

CASTLE RISING, Norfolk

The sea has long withdrawn from this one-time port, but the Norman castle (AM) built to protect it still stands. It occupies a Roman site and has a great keep in which a fascinating sequence of rooms, galleries, and minor stairs are reached by a single dramatic staircase. The local Church of St Lawrence is famous for its Norman west front, which has a fine doorway on the lower level and houses a richly carved square font on a circular shaft. Bede House or Trinity Hospital dates from the 17th century and is an almshouse charity for elderly ladies.

Continue to South Wootton, meet traffic signals, and drive over crossroads. After another 1½ miles meet a T-junction, turn right, and return to King's Lynn.

SPALDING, Lincs

This historic fenland town stands on the banks of the Welland in an area of drained marshland where market gardeners and bulb growers raise crops in soil of almost legendary richness. In springtime the district is glorious with tulips, daffodils, narcissi, and hyacinths that form a carpet of blazing colour comparable only with the bulb fields of Holland. Every May the town holds a spectacular Flower Festival that attracts visitors from all

BULB FIELDS IN THE FENS

Spring in the Fens is an explosion of colour. Daffodils, tulips, and hyacinths cover acre after flat acre of reclaimed land, stretching away from the bulb towns in gloriously-variegated carpets reminiscent of the Dutch countryside rather than rural England.

mutiny. He became a pioneer of Australian exploration and wrote a book about his voyages. He died in 1814, on the day that his book was published.

Continue through fenland along the A52.

THE LINCOLNSHIRE FENS, Lincs

The Fens of Lincolnshire covered an area that is barely above sea level and have been reduced by centuries of land reclamation. The Romans built the first sea wall here and drained the land behind it; in subsequent centuries their work was continued, and much later the expertise of Dutch engineer Vermuyden was used to make many acres of ground into rich arable land. A giant reclamation scheme begun in the 17th century used the talents of such famous men as Rennie and Telford, and was largely responsible for the shape of the landscape as it exists today. Everywhere the flat fields and pastures are criss-crossed by drains and dykes that stretch away to an almost treeless horizon.

Continue along the A52, with Swaton Fen on the right and Horbling Fen to the left. In 4 miles turn left on to the B1177 'Bourne' road and proceed to Horbling.

HORBLING, Lincs

Spring Well, situated a little way north of Horbling's Norman and later church, was once a communal washing trough. The village itself is a charming collection of mainly Georgian houses.

Proceed along the B1177 to Billingborough.

BILLINGBOROUGH, Lincs

The local church carries a 150ft spire that can be seen for a long way over the surrounding flat countryside. An unusual façade is displayed by the George and Dragon Inn, which dates from the 17th century.

Continue for $\frac{3}{4}$ mile by Billingborough Fen and pass a track leading right to the site of Sempringham Abbey.

SEMPRINGHAM ABBEY, Lincs

Sir Gilbert of Sempringham founded the Gilbertine order here c1130. He was the son of the local lord, and the Gilbertines were the only monastic order to have been founded in Britain. Close to the site an uneven area of grassland covers the remains of the village, but the superb Norman church survives as an outstanding example of its period.

Continue along the B1177 and drive through Pointon to Dowsby.

DOWSBY, Lincs

Dowsby Hall was built c1603, and the local church contains many fine moulded arches.

Stay on the B1177 through Dunsby, passing Dowsby Fen and Dunsby Fen on the left. Join the A15, with Bourne North Fen to the left, and continue to Bourne.

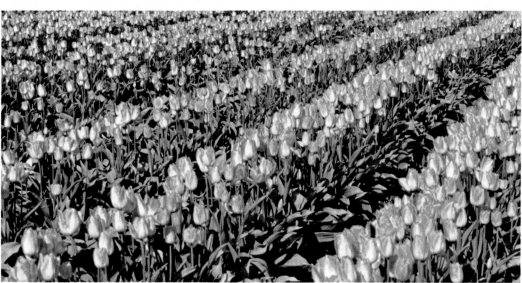

The area around Spalding is ablaze with tulips in the spring.

over the country. On the eastern outskirts are the beautiful Springfield Gardens, 25 acres of lawns and water features designed to show over a million bulbs to their best advantage. In summer the early freshness of the bulbs is replaced by the mature beauty of more than 80 species of rose in the magnificent Summer Rose Garden. The town itself has many old buildings in charming streets on both banks of the river, including several good examples of 18th-century design. One of the oldest is the greatly restored Ayscoughfee Hall, which dates from the 15th century and now houses a museum of local history. Its mellow stone and graceful lines are complemented by well-kept lawns enclosed by yew hedges. A small museum in Broad St (open by appointment) was founded by the Gentleman's Society in 1710. Spalding has many good churches, but the best is the late 13th-century Church of SS Mary and Nicholas. This has an angel-carved hammerbeam roof in the nave and was extensively restored by the Victorian architect Sir G G Scott.

Leave Spalding on the A16 'Boston' road and drive to Pinchbeck.

PINCHBECK, Lincs

Situated on the River Glen in a bulb-growing district, this village has preserved its old wooden stocks and has a restored church with a leaning tower. A fine 18th-century group of buildings includes the rectory and a stable block.

Continue on the A16 to Surfleet.

SURFLEET, Lincs

The spire on the church in this fenland village leans 6ft out of true – considerably more than the tower at Pinchbeck. Naturalist Gilbert White described a local heronry in his early work *Natural History*, but this has since been abandoned.

Cross the River Glen and proceed along the A16 to Gosberton.

GOSBERTON, Lincs

An outstanding feature of this pleasant little village is its cruciform church, which displays a curious tower gargoyle fashioned in the shape of an elephant.

Fleet Fen is part of Lincolnshire's extensive 17th-century drainage works.

Leave Gosberton, keep forward on the A152, and continue to Donington.

DONINGTON, Lincs

In Roman times the area around Donington was drained in the first of many attempts to reclaim agricultural land from the Fens. Much later the town was a centre of the flax and hemp industry, and nowadays it is a popular touring base. Its cobbled market square is surrounded by pleasant Georgian buildings, and its church carries a fine tower surmounted by an elegant spire. Inside is a tablet commemorating Captain Matthew Flinders, a great sailor who was born in Donington and travelled with Captain Bligh after the *Bounty*

The beautiful water gardens near Peakirk are the home of various water birds, including trumpeter swans.

BOURNE, Lincs

Bourne is an ancient market town and reputedly the birthplace of Hereward the Wake, the last Saxon to resist the invading Norman army. The town was the former manufacturing base of the BRM racing car and is renowned for the purity of its water. The many watercress beds in the area are ample proof of the latter. Good domestic architecture in the town includes attractive Tudor cottages in South Street and a generous scattering of Georgian houses and shops. The Burghley Arms Hotel was the birthplace of Sir William Cecil, Lord High Treasurer to Elizabeth I, in 1520. Other famous natives of the town include Frederick Worth, founder of the House of Worth in Paris, and Robert Mannying, who founded an Augustinian abbey here in the 13th century. Remains of the monastic buildings are incorporated in the nave of the parish church. A Roman canal known as the Car Dyke runs close to the town, and castle earthworks can be seen a little way south.

Continue along the A15 'Peterborough' road and drive through Thurlby. Cross the River Glen and continue through Baston and Langtoft to Market Deeping.

MARKET DEEPING, Lincs

Several fine old houses testify to the one-time prosperity and importance of this ancient market town, situated on the River Welland at the edge of the Fens. Its restored church has an unusual rood loft doorway, and the 13th-century parish rectory is thought to be the oldest inhabited parsonage in England.

Leave Market Deeping on the A15, cross the River Welland, and pass the village of Northborough. Proceed to Glinton.

GLINTON, Cambs

Among the pleasant stone cottages of this attractive village is a fine 17th-century manor house; the entire group is centred on the slender spire of the local church.

Leave Glinton and turn left on to the B1443 'Thorney' road. Continue to Peakirk.

PEAKIRK, Cambs

A rare 14th-century lectern and numerous paintings can be seen in Peakirk's church, the only one in Britain dedicated to St Pega. Close to the village is the Wildfowl Trust gardens.

Leave Peakirk and continue east for 4 miles, then turn left on to the A1073. After another 2 miles turn left again on to an unclassified road and drive into Crowland.

CROWLAND, Lincs

One of the most interesting features of this pleasant little town is its unique Triangular Bridge (AM), which was built in the 14th century to span several streams of the River Welland. Its three arches, which meet at an angle of 120 degrees, now stand on dry land. In 1720 a carved figure of the Virgin Mary was taken from the partly ruined abbey that now serves as the parish church and placed on the bridge. The original abbey was founded in 716 by King Ethelbald in memory of St Guthlac.

From Crowland follow the B1040 to Thorney.

THORNEY, Cambs

It was here that the Saxon hero Hereward the Wake made his last stand against the invading Norman armies under William the Conqueror. Remains of a 12th-century abbey built by William after his victory can be seen near by, and the restored abbey church shows Norman and later workmanship. Abbey House is a largely 16th-century building with 17th-century additions. A good 18th-century windmill stands in the grounds.

From Thorney turn left on the A47 'Wisbech' road and in 1½ miles turn left again on to the B1167 SP 'Gedney Hill'. Continue for 4½ miles, then turn left on to the B1166 to Gedney Hill. At Gedney Hill turn left and continue to Holbeach Drove, then turn right on to the B1168 with Fleet Fen to the right. Meet crossroads 1 mile beyond Holbeach St Johns and turn right on to the B1165 for Sutton St James. Drive to the end of this village, turn left on to the B1390 to Long Sutton.

LONG SUTTON, Lincs

Many different architectural periods are represented in the fabric of this pretty market town's church, but the main feature is its detached, 162ft tower. This has a lead and timber spire that is considered one of the finest in Britain.

Leave Long Sutton on the A17 SP 'Sleaford', passing Gedney to the left.

Whaplode Church never came to the attention of 19th-century restorers, whose enthusiasm often outstripped their ability.

GEDNEY, Lincs

The fine marshland church in Gedney features a notable west tower and contains a 14th-century brass. Also inside are a number of alabaster effigies.

Leave the village and in a short distance turn left on to the A151 'Spalding' road, passing through Fleet Hargate into Holbeach.

HOLBEACH, Lincs

One of the county's major bulb-growing centres, this ancient market town boasts many good Georgian houses and a 14th-century church with a lofty spire and fine traceried windows. William Stukely, a founder of the Society of Antiquaries, was born here in 1718.

Proceed along the A151 to Whaplode.

WHAPLODE, Lincs

The splendid Norman and later church in this little marshland village has a presence that is out of all proportion to the size of the community that it serves. Inside is a notable 17th-century monument to Sir Anthony Irby.

Continue along the A151 for the return to Spalding.

Large stone warehouses testify to Market Deeping's former prosperity, which has left a fine architectural heritage.

LINCOLN AND THE WITHAM VALLEY

The proud triple towers of Lincoln Cathedral can be seen for many miles across the flat lands of the Witham Valley, a fertile area of farms and fens whose threatened monotony is relieved by picturesque villages of honey-coloured stone.

Lincoln Cathedral's striking position is emphasized by its impressive west front.

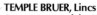

LINCOLN, Lincs

Historic Lincoln rises majestically from the north banks of the River Witham, on a slope crowned by its beautiful triple-towered cathedral. This splendid building, the third largest of its type in England, completely dominates the city and overlooks miles of countryside. Its 11th-century origins are largely hidden by extensions and additions from subsequent periods, and its many ancient treasures include the best preserved of four existing copies of *Magna Carta*. In the Library are first editions of *Paradise Lost, Don Quixote*, and part of Spenser's *Faerie Queen*. Amongst many other interesting churches in the city are St Benedict's and St Peter at Gowt's, both of which include a great deal of Saxon work. Newport Arch (AM), the only surviving Roman gateway to span an English street, is a relic of the ancient walled city of *Lindum Colonia*. The Close, also known as Minster Yard, contains a superb collection of buildings including a fine tithe barn of 1440 and the ancient Bishop's Palace (AM). Lincoln Castle was founded by William the Conqueror in 1068 and over the centuries has grown into the impressive structure that occupies some 6 acres of city ground today. Its main features include 14th-century Cobb Hall, which was once a place of punishment, the Observatory Tower, and a fine Norman keep. Other old buildings in

the city include the Jew's House, a fine example of 12th-century domestic architecture, and nearby Aaron's House – a product of the prosperous wool age and the oldest inhabited dwelling in England. Timber-framed 16th-century houses line the High Street as it crosses High Bridge, preserving in miniature the appearance of old London Bridge before it was destroyed in the Great Fire that razed the capital in 1666.

148

From Lincoln follow SP 'Sleaford A15' and ascend to Bracebridge Heath. Turn right on to the A607 SP 'Grantham' and after a short distance pass the large RAF base at Waddington on the left. Continue past Harmston Heath (on the left) and the village of Harmston in attractively wooded countryside to the right. After a short distance pass Coleby on the right, with Coleby Heath stretching away to the left.

Much of the medieval street plan is preserved in Lincoln.

COLEBY, Lincs

Interesting old buildings in this pleasant village include the church and 17th-century Coleby Hall. The former is of Norman date and incorporates a Saxon tower, and the latter shares attractive grounds with the Temple of Romulus and Remus, by Sir William Chambers.

Continue on the A607 into Navenby, with Navenby Heath on the left.

NAVENBY, Lincs

Stone and pantiled houses form charming architectural groups in this pleasant little village, and the restored church rises grandly above their rooftops to complete the picture. Inside the church is a notable Easter Sepulchre decorated with carved figures.

Beyond Navenby turn left on to an unclassified road SP 'Ancaster, Sleaford'. Continue for 2¼ miles and meet crossroads. A detour from the main route can be made here by turning left and driving for 2¼ miles to Temple Bruer; access is via a road through Temple Farm.

TEMPLE BRUER, Lincs

A preceptory of the Knights Templar was founded here during the reign of Henry II, and the restored 13th-century tower (AM) of their church can still be seen. Very few of their distinctive round churches survive in the British Isles.

On the main route, continue for 1¾ miles and meet more crossroads. Turn right on to the A17 SP 'Newark' and descend into Leadenham.

LEADENHAM, Lincs

Leadenham Old Hall (not open) is a beautiful building of c1700 built entirely of golden ironstone. One of its main features is a delightful rustic doorway. The village itself is dominated by its lovely church spire and boasts a 19th-century drinking fountain beneath a hexagonal canopy.

Meet traffic lights in Leadenham and turn left on to the A607 SP 'Grantham'. Continue to Fulbeck.

FULBECK, Lincs

A delightful combination of woods and farmland surrounds this pretty village. The hall, dating from 1773, contains fine period furniture and is set in an 11-acre garden.

Proceed on the A607, passing the edge of Caythorpe.

CAYTHORPE, Lincs

The characteristically utilitarian appearance of Caythorpe's village architecture is lifted by the mellow gold of local ironstone. Notable Ivy House dates from 1684 and has projecting wings with gables. The local church features a good tower.

Drive ½ mile beyond the Caythorpe crossroads and turn right on to an unclassified road for the village of Hough-on-the-Hill.

HOUGH-ON-THE-HILL, Lincs

As its name suggests, this village occupies a lofty site that makes it an excellent viewpoint. The local church is noted for its tower, which features a curious Saxon turret containing a newel stairway.

Beyond the local church turn left SP 'Barkston, Grantham' and proceed to Barkston.

BARKSTON, Lincs

Barkston Church features a good ironstone tower. Close by is a group of almshouses that reflect a style uniformly applied to the buildings of the local Belton estate.

From Barkston turn left on to the A607, with Syston Park ahead. After ¾ mile drive forward on to the A153, skirting Honington.

North Kyme Fen typifies the Kesteven area of Lincolnshire

HONINGTON, Lincs

About ¾ mile south-east of this village is Honington Camp, one of the few major hillforts built in this part of the country. It is of iron-age date and was probably manned to defend the Ancaster Gap. During the 17th century an urn of Roman coins was found here, which seems to suggest that the inhabitants of nearby Ancaster found the camp useful. Honington Church contains some good Norman work.

Continue on the A153, passing Honington Camp, and proceed for 2¼ miles. Turn left on to the B6403 to Ancaster.

ANCASTER, Lincs

Sited on the old Roman road of Ermine Street, this village is set in pleasantly wooded countryside and stands near the site of Roman *Causennae*. Remains of this ancient camp and posting station can be seen near by, and relics excavated from the area can be seen in Grantham Museum – including mosaic flooring and an altar. Some 2 miles south of the village are quarries where the famous Ancaster stone was worked for many of Lincolnshire's beautiful churches.

Proceed along a modern road that follows the line of Ermine Street.

ERMINE STREET, Lincs

This Roman road, built about 1,900 years ago between London and Lincoln, allowed the occupying forces to reach trouble spots in eastern England with comparative ease. The name is derived from a Saxon tribe who lived near by.

Drive for 3¾ miles beyond Ancaster and turn right on to the A17, then left on to the B1429 SP 'Cranwell', passing the RAF College. Continue to Cranwell.

CRANWELL, Lincs

Traces of Saxon workmanship can be seen in Cranwell's mainly Norman church, which houses a fine old screen. West of the village is the well-known RAF college, which was founded in 1920 and includes a number of well-designed buildings.

In ¾ mile turn right on to the A15 'Sleaford' road and pass the edge of Leasingham.

LEASINGHAM, Lincs

Notable buildings in this old village include the Ancient House of 1658, the 17th-century Old Hall, and Georgian Leasingham Manor. Later additions include Leasingham Hall and Roxholme Hall, both of the 19th century. The local church has a lofty west tower crowned by a spire.

Proceed along the A15 to Sleaford.

SLEAFORD, Lincs

Charmingly situated on the banks of the peaceful River Slea, this pleasant little market town is dominated by a 12th- to 15th-century church with one of the earliest stone spires in England. The building's outstanding window tracery is arguably the best in the country. Early structures in the town include a 15th-century timber-framed vicarage and the Black Bull Inn; a carved stone at the latter is dated 1689 and 1791, and illustrates the old sport of bull baiting. Most of the town's workaday buildings date from the 19th century, including the Sessions House, and the Carre's Hospital.

Leave Sleaford on the A153 'Horncastle' road. After 2¾ miles turn right and proceed to Anwick.

Little survives to tell of the wealth and prestige that came to Bardney Abbey before its downfall and ruin.

ANWICK, Lincs

Just south of Anwick's medieval church are adjoining cottages in the romantic gothic style. One houses the post office and the other is a smithy.

Continue with Anwick Fen on the right, and drive through the village of North Kyme. Beyond North Kyme continue forward on to an unclassified road SP 'Walcot', skirting Digby Fen on the left. In 1¼ miles turn left on to the B1189; proceed for 4 miles and turn right on to the B1191 SP 'Woodhall Spa', driving through Martin and later passing Martin Fen on the left. Cross the River Witham at Kirkstead Bridge, and after another ¾ mile pass a right turn leading to Kirkstead Abbey. It is worth making the short detour to this historic place.

KIRKSTEAD ABBEY, Lincs

Scant remains of a rich Cistercian abbey founded by Hugo Brito in 1139 can be seen here, but the site is most famous for the 13th-century architectural gem of St Leonard's Chapel. This was built outside the abbey gates for lay worshippers, and has survived in a remarkably good state of preservation. Its wooden screen is thought to be the second oldest in England and includes timber work dating from 1210.

Like many of Sleaford's buildings, Carre's Hospital, in Eastgate, dates from the mid-19th century.

Continue along the main route and enter Woodhall Spa.

WOODHALL SPA, Lincs

In Victorian and earlier times this inland resort was famous for its natural springs, and a fine pump room and bathing establishment remain from this period. Nowadays the town is well known as a golfing centre, with Lincolnshire's only championship-standard course.

Continue along the B1191 to Tower on the Moor.

TOWER ON THE MOOR, Lincs

This impressive 60ft tower dominates the local countryside and is a well-known (if enigmatic) landmark. It is thought to have been built in the 15th century.

Continue along the B1191 to Horncastle.

HORNCASTLE, Lincs

Roman *Banovallum*, the 'walled place on the River Bain', stood on the site now occupied by this pleasant little market town. Remains of the ancient fort that guarded the settlement have been incorporated in the modern town library. The local church dates from the 13th century and contains the fine Dymoke Brass of 1519, plus a 17th-century chest and various other relics. A 10-day horse fair was held in Horncastle every August and is featured in George Borrow's *Romany Rye*.

Leave Horncastle on the A158 'Lincoln' road and in ¼ mile turn left on to the B1190 SP 'Bardney'. Drive through Thimbleby, Horsington, and Bucknall, later passing Tupholme Abbey to the left.

TUPHOLME ABBEY, Lincs

Remains of a religious house that was founded c1160 can be seen here, including part of the refectory.

Continue along the B1190 for 1½ miles and turn left into Bardney.

BARDNEY, Lincs

Ethelred, King of Mercia, founded a Benedictine abbey here in the 7th century. It was rebuilt in Norman times by the Earl of Lincoln, and grew to become one of the country's most powerful centres of religion and education. Excavations conducted amongst the extensive ruins in 1912 uncovered many interesting relics, some of which can be seen in the local church. The town itself is a typical fenland community on the River Witham, in an agricultural area.

Leave Bardney and cross the railway and the River Witham. Continue along the B1190, with Branston Fen to the right, and shortly bear right to skirt the Lincoln Edge. In 3 miles reach the Plough Inn and bear right SP 'Lincoln', then drive through Washingborough and return to Lincoln.

SKEGNESS, Lincs

In 1863 a rail service was begun at Skegness, with trains running to and from the teeming towns of the industrial Midlands. The result was a boom in seaside tourism, and the holiday crowds of today continue to enjoy the excellent sands and bathing facilities that prompted the transformation of this one-time fishing village into one of the east coast's most popular resorts. Magnificent seafront gardens border a long promenade where, in simpler days, Lord Tennyson and his brothers strolled to take the bracing sea air. A vast swimming pool, the Natureland Zoo, and various first-class entertainments vie for attention with 6 miles of sandy beach. The Church Farm Museum has the Farmhouse and cottage furnished as it would have been in the 19th century. At the southern end of the beach is Gibraltar Point, where there is a nature reserve and bird observatory.

Leave Skegness on the A158 'Lincoln' road and drive to Burgh-le-Marsh.

BURGH-LE-MARSH, Lincs

One of the main features of this area is a fine 5-sailed tower windmill that is still in working order. The impressive local church has two porches and a tower with 16 iron crosses. Inside is a restored screen.

Drive for 2¾ miles beyond the village and approach a roundabout with Gunby Hall to the left.

GUNBY HALL, Lincs

Lord Tennyson described this imposing red-brick building (NT) as 'a house of ancient peace'. It was built c1700 by Sir William Massingberd and shows the influence of Sir Christopher Wren. Features of the interior include an oak staircase, wainscoted rooms containing portraits by Reynolds, and various pieces of fine furniture. The house and its formal gardens are open by prior written appointment.

Continue along the A158 and drive through Candlesby, with Welton High Wood to the right. Proceed to Scremby.

SCREMBY, Lincs

Notable features of the good 18th-century church in Scremby include a panelled chancel and a monument to Charles Brackenbury.

Beyond Scremby meet crossroads and turn right on to an unclassified road to Skendleby.

SKENDLEBY, Lincs

Attractively set in the Lincolnshire Wolds, this pleasant village features a partly greenstone church and a mid 18th-century hall. Near by is a prehistoric site known as the Giant's Hill, where there are two long barrows. The most prominent measures 200ft long and stands 5ft high; the other has been severely reduced by ploughing.

Drive to the end of Skendleby and bear right SP 'Willoughby', then

BETWEEN THE WOLDS AND THE SEA

Attractive resorts and beaches of fine sand are interspersed with charming little fishing villages on Lincolnshire's holiday coast. Inland are picturesque hamlets clustered round greenstone churches, hills crowned by solitary windmills, and the enchanting lanes of the Wolds country.

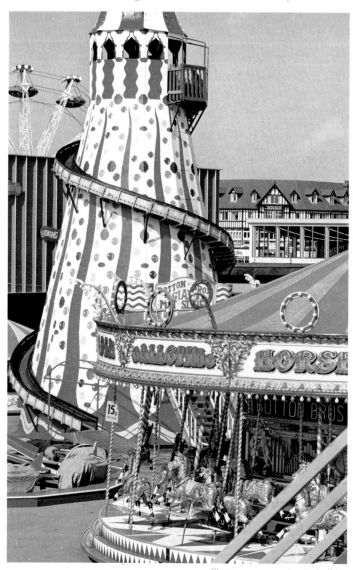

Skegness prepares for the holiday season.

ascend to cross a main road. Descend, and in 1¾ miles turn left on to the B1196 SP 'Alford'. Approach Alford, with Well Vale to the left, and turn sharp left on to an unclassified road to enter the village of Well.

WELL, Lincs

Set on the eastern slopes of the Wolds, in the pastoral beauty of Well Vale, this tiny village takes its name from a spring that bubbles from the chalk to fill two lakes in a closely-wooded valley. Close to the village the beautiful Georgian red-brick building of Well Vale Hall stands in 170 acres of fine parkland.

Return to the B1196 and turn left to enter Alford.

ALFORD, Lincs

One of Lincolnshire's finest windmills can be seen here. Its 6-storey brick tower carries five sails and is topped by an ogee cap. It dates from 1813 and, although intact, is no longer in use. Merton Lodge is a good example of the many Georgian and later houses to be seen in the town.

Leave Alford on the A1104 'Louth, Lincoln' road and ascend. Reach Ulceby; cross a roundabout and take the 2nd exit on to the A16, then in ¼ mile turn right on to the unclassified 'Harrington' road. Continue, with panoramic views, into Harrington.

HARRINGTON, Lincs

Harrington Hall (open) was rebuilt in 1673 and features a good Elizabethan facade and contains fine 17th- and 18th-century paintings, china and furniture and beautiful gardens.

Continue through pleasantly wooded countryside to Somersby.

Burgh-le-Marsh church clock urges a greater regard for time.

SOMERSBY, Lincs

The poet Alfred Lord Tennyson was born in this tiny Wolds village. His house, which still stands but is not open to the public, was adapted by his father to include a dining room with high gothic windows that entirely suited that era of romanticism. Various memorials to the Tennyson family can be seen in the local church, and a fine carved cross stands in the churchyard.

Keep forward into a narrow road for Salmonby and turn left SP 'Horncastle'. Continue for 2 miles, then meet crossroads and turn right SP 'Belchford'. Climb to a road summit of 455ft, with good all-round views, then descend into Belchford and turn right SP 'Alford'. After a short distance ascend Belchford Hill and meet a T-junction. Turn left SP 'Louth' and continue, with magnificent views, to a road summit of 487ft. In 3¼ miles meet crossroads and turn right on to the A153, passing the entrance to Caldwell Park Motor Cycle Racing Circuit on the right. In ¾ mile branch right (no SP) on to an unclassified road and continue to Tathwell.

TATHWELL, Lincs

Attractively situated in a sheltered position above a lake, this village has a good church that features a Norman tower and contains various interesting monuments.

Beyond Tathwell meet crossroads and drive forward SP 'Legbourne'. A short detour from the main route can be taken by turning right at the crossroads and driving to Bully Hill.

BULLY HILL, Lincs

Some of the finest prehistoric barrow groups to have survived in the whole county of Lincolnshire can be seen here. The largest of seven measures 60ft in diameter by 10ft high, and they are thought to date from the late stone or early bronze age.

On the main route, drive 1¼ miles beyond the crossroads and turn right on to the A16. After another 1¼ miles turn left on to the unclassified 'Little Cawthorpe' road, descend through Maltby and Haugham Woods, and turn right at Little Cawthorpe. Reach the village church and turn left (no SP), then pass through a ford and meet a T-junction. Turn right, and in ½ mile turn right again on to the A157. Continue to the end of Legbourne and bear right, then turn left on to the unclassified 'Manby' road. Continue to Little Carlton, turn left to reach Manby village.

mls 0 1 2 3 4 5
kms 0 2 4 6 8

Few windmills are as well preserved as this tower mill at Burgh-le-Marsh. It was built in 1833 and is in good working order.

The solid Norman tower of St Vedast's Church, Tathwell, is well sheltered from the elements.

Gunby Hall's austere face conceals a wealth of fine decoration.

MANBY, Lincs
The greenstone church of this pleasant little village has a tall tower and contains a remarkably well-preserved Saxon slab decorated with a distinctive rope design.

Meet crossroads beyond Manby and turn right on to the B1200. Continue to Saltfleetby.

SALTFLEETBY, Lincs
Close to St Peter's Church in Saltfleetby is the isolated tower of a church that the present greenstone building replaced. The recent building incorporates a few early-English fragments from its predecessor.

Meet a junction with the A1031, turn right, and continue to Theddlethorpe St Helen.

THEDDLETHORPE ST HELEN, Lincs
This tiny coastal village is near a scrub-covered foreshore that forms part of a national nature reserve and is one of the few remaining habitats of the Natterjack toad. This curious amphibian runs instead of hops, and is easily identifiable by the pale stripe down its back. Signposts and warning flags mark the site of an RAF bombing range on the sands.

Proceed along the A1031 for 3 miles, then turn left on to the A1104 into Mablethorpe.

MABLETHORPE, Lincs
Thanks to a highly expensive system of groynes this popular resort boasts a beautiful beach of firm golden sand. In normal weather swimmers can enjoy safe bathing here, but rough conditions make the water treacherous and red flags are flown to warn people away. Low tide reveals old stumps that are the sole remains of a woodland village swamped by the sea in 1289. All that survived was the fine old Church of St Mary, which contains various medieval relics. Today the town is guarded by a concrete promenade.

Leave Mablethorpe on the A52 'Skegness' road and continue to Trusthorpe.

TRUSTHORPE, Lincs
Fine sands and good bathing facilities make this a popular resort, but it is also the base for Humber Radio – an important Post Office link with ships and oil rigs in the North Sea. The tall radio mast dominates the village.

Continue on the A52 and drive into Sutton-on-Sea.

SUTTON-ON-SEA, Lincs
Safe bathing and a level sandy beach are the main features of this little coastal resort. The 4,500-year-old stumps and roots of a forest that was flooded by the sea can be seen at low tide.

From Sutton-on-Sea it is possible to take a pleasant detour from the main route, along the shore below the Sea Bank Dyke. In 1 mile meet a roundabout and turn left on to the unclassified road to Sandilands and drive straight on beside the sea wall. Reach Chapel St Leonards and turn left across a river bridge, then turn right with SP 'Skegness' to rejoin the A52 before Ingoldmells. On the main route, continue along the A52 to Huttoft.

HUTTOFT, Lincs
A tall windmill of the tower type can be seen here, with an interesting early-Victorian grain store.

Continue along the A52 and drive through Mumby to Ingoldmells.

INGOLDMELLS, Lincs
This little resort offers 3 miles of firm golden sand and a host of holiday diversions, including a funfair. Remains of an early iron-age salt-panning site between Ingoldmells and Chapel St Leonards include various structures that can only be seen at low tide.

Continue along the A52 for the return to Skegness.

INSIDE OLD RUTLAND

Tiny Rutland has vanished in name but survives in fact. The towering spires of its churches rise from typically-clustered cottages of thatch and ironstone, and some of England's richest pasture is grown where the stag and hart were hunted in ancient times.

Market Harborough's old grammar school was founded in the 17th century and is a fine example of its type.

MARKET HARBOROUGH, Leics

A market was held here as early as 1203, and over the centuries the town has grown and prospered to become the mature community that exists today. The most recent developments have been industrial, but these have not been made at the expense of many fine buildings from previous, less intrusive periods. The most famous is the former grammar school, a lovely timbered and gabled building of 1614 that stands on wooden pillars above street level. The Three Swans is the largest of many old local inns and displays one of the finest wrought-iron signs in England. The parish church dates from the 13th to 15th centuries and is known for its tower, a beautiful structure crowned by a broach spire that is visible for miles around. Every November the church bells are rung to commemorate the rescue of a merchant lost in the Welland marshes in 1500, and the ringers traditionally receive one shilling for beer. Much of the town's present prosperity is due to the Symington family, who made liberty bodices in a Victorian factory behind the church.

Leave the town on the A427 'Corby' road to reach Dingley.

Rockingham Castle's Panel Room is part of a rich collection of treasures.

DINGLEY, Northants

The most impressive feature of this small village is Dingley Hall (not open), an unforgettable building with a south gateway flanked by polygonal towers.

Continue, and in about 2¼ miles pass the village of Stoke Albany to the left.

STOKE ALBANY, Northants

Features of the fine local church, which dates from the 13th century, include good doorways and windows.

Continue along the A427 beyond East Carlton, then turn left on to the B670 and proceed to Rockingham.

ROCKINGHAM, Northants

Set on a steep hillside overlooking the River Welland, this lovely village of flint-built thatched cottages has a number of new houses that have been built of traditional materials to harmonize with the whole. The summit of the hill is occupied by Rockingham Castle, which was originally built by William the Conqueror, and affords views into 4 counties. The site of the keep is now a rose garden surrounded by yew hedges, but surviving fragments of the old structure include the moat, foundations of the Norman hall, and the twin towers of the gatehouse. King John used the castle both as a fortress and as a hunting lodge for Rockingham Forest, a vast blanket of wood and heathland that once covered much of Leicestershire. The mainly Elizabethan house that stands here today (open) contains collections of paintings and furniture.

Turn left on to the A6003 'Uppingham' road, crossing the River Welland. (To enter Rockingham village turn right here into the A6003 main street.) Continue to Caldecott and drive forward on to the B672, then in 4½ miles pass under the Welland railway viaduct.

WELLAND VIADUCT, Northants

This 82-arch railway viaduct dates from 1874 and is a notable example of 19th-century industrial

architecture. It spans the complete width of the Welland Valley and is a well-known landmark.

In 2 miles turn right, then left, to join the A6121; continue to Ketton.

Naseby was the scene of a decisive Civil War battle.

KETTON, Leics

One of the largest and most attractive of old Rutland's villages, this picturesque collection of butter-coloured buildings is a noted quarrying centre. The local stone is greatly prized as a building material and has been worked at least since Roman times. St Mary's Church has an exquisite spire that rises high above the village's sepia roofs of Collyweston slate, perfectly complementing one of the finest examples of church architecture in the east Midlands. The west front of the building is an excellent example of late 12th-century work, and the rest of the structure dates almost entirely from the 13th century.

Continue along the A6121 and drive through Tinwell to Stamford.

STAMFORD, Lincs

Justly considered one of England's most beautiful towns, stone-built Stamford has a long history that can be traced back as far as the time of Danish settlement. In the 13th and 14th centuries it was important enough to have its own university, and the powerful influence of early Christianity is evident in many fine churches and other ecclesiastical buildings. All Saints' Place is the visual centre of the town and is noted for its outstanding, multi-period architecture. Browne's Hospital has been described as one of the finest medieval almshouses surviving in England, and includes a beautiful Jacobean hall and chapel. Close to the Welland are the ancient Burghley Almshouses. The George Hotel was a coaching inn in the 14th century, and among fine buildings from many periods in St George's Square is a house that has been continuously inhabited since c1350. Even older than that is the Bastion in West Street, a section of the old town wall that has been untouched for 700 years. Close to the town is Elizabethan Burghley House (open) where the well-known Burghley Horse Trials are held. The house itself is considered one of England's greatest mansions and contains many superb rooms. It boasts over 100 works of art and antique furnishings.

Follow SP 'Grantham' and then 'Oakham' to leave Stamford by the A606. Continue to Empingham.

EMPINGHAM, Leics

Dominating this large attractive village is the handsome tower and spire of St Peter's Church, a well-proportioned building with a good west front. Features of the interior include fragments of ancient glass and considerable remains of medieval colour.

Continue, and 1 mile beyond Whitwell reach Rutland Water on the left. Turn right here on to the unclassified 'Exton' and 'Cottesmore' road, entering an avenue of trees. After 1¼ miles reach a right turn that offers a pleasant detour to Exton. The main route skirts Exton Park.

EXTON, Leics

Situated in one of the largest ironstone extraction areas in Britain, this charming village of thatched limestone cottages is well worth the small diversion needed to visit it. The ruined Old Hall, probably built during the reign of Elizabeth I, was burned down in 1810; the New Hall replaced it some 40 years later. Exton's parish church is noted for its remarkable range of monumental sculpture, which illustrates the progress of this art form in England from the 14th to 18th centuries.

On the main route, drive to Cottesmore and turn left on to the B668. Continue to Burley.

This gateway forms an imposing entrance to the mansion at Burghley.

BURLEY, Leics

Burley-on-the-Hill (not open) is considered by many to be the most beautiful country house in the county. Its fine colonnades and exquisitely restrained detail, the work of Joseph Lumley between 1694 and 1705, ornament a small hill that was once an ancient earthwork. The building is best appreciated from the south, looking down a long avenue of trees to the fine lines of the front.

Descend into Oakham.

OAKHAM, Leics

Once the capital of the tiny and now defunct county of Rutland, this well-known hunting centre preserves memories of its former status in the Rutland County Museum. This is housed in the late 18th-century indoor riding school of the Rutland Fencibles. The town's church dates from the 12th to 15th century and features unusual nave capitals. It shares its churchyard with the original grammar school, which was founded in 1584. Remains of Oakham Castle include a beautiful Norman hall (open), where a unique collection of horseshoes is nailed to the wall. These were traditionally contributed to the household by members of the royalty or peerage visiting the lordship for the first time. An old butter cross with stocks has been preserved in the town.

Local stone brings unity to Ketton's interesting old buildings.

Follow SP 'Melton Mowbray', drive over a level crossing, and turn left then left again on to an unclassified road for Braunston.

BRAUNSTON, Leics

This lovely ironstone village stands on a hillside above the valley of the little River Gwash. Inside its distinctive church are traces of a previous building dating from the 12th and 13th centuries.

From Braunston follow the 'Leicester' road, and in 4¾ miles pass 755ft Whatborough Hill to the right. Access to the summit is by a nearby track. Continue to Tilton.

TILTON, Leics

The early-English and later church in this high village is noted for its strange gargoyles.

Join the B6047 'Market Harborough' road and in 2 miles drive over a main road. After another 3 miles reach the top of an ascent and turn right on to an unclassified road SP 'Carlton, Kibworth'. Continue to Kibworth Harcourt.

KIBWORTH HARCOURT, Leics

Examples of architecture from many periods can be seen in this village. Among the most notable are the Old House of 1678, the 18th-century Congregational Church, and 19th-

century Kibworth Hall. Close to the village is the imposing tower of St Wilfred's Church.

Follow SP 'Leicester' to join the A6, then take the 1st unclassified road on the left SP 'Kilby, Wistow'. Cross the Grand Union Canal at a series of locks, continue to crossroads, and turn left for Fleckney and Saddington. Drive to Saddington, turn right, and continue to Mowsley. At Mowsley turn right and right again with SP 'Leicester'. In 1 mile turn left on to the A50, and after a further 1½ miles turn right on to the B5414. Drive to North Kilworth and turn right on to the A427, then turn left with the B5414 for South Kilworth.

SOUTH KILWORTH, Leics

South Kilworth's church is mainly of 19th-century design, although Norman and 14th-century work from a previous building can be seen inside. The font is of 12th- or 13th-century date.

Beyond South Kilworth pass Stanford Reservoir on the left, then turn left on to the unclassified 'Stanford on Avon' road. Descend to Stanford on Avon, passing Stanford Hall and Stanford Park on the right.

STANFORD ON AVON, Leics

Divided between Leicestershire and Northamptonshire by the River Avon, this pleasant village has a good church with a pinnacled 15th-century tower. Stanford Hall (open) is impressively sited in open pasture and stands on the site of an earlier house. The present building dates from the reign of William and Mary, and has an imposing facade that adds a touch of grandeur to its pleasing design. Its rooms contain collections of costumes and furniture, and there is a motor museum in the stable.

In ¼ mile turn left on to the 'Cold Ashby' road and later re-cross the Grand Union Canal. In 1½ miles climb 690ft Honey Hill. Continue to Cold Ashby and turn left on to the B4036, then drive to Naseby.

NASEBY, Northants

A stone column 1½ miles north of this village marks the field where the Battle of Naseby was fought in 1645. The Cromwellian victory heralded a new era of British government and sealed the fate of King Charles I. The Naseby Battle Museum at Purlieu Farm displays layouts of the battleground and various local relics. In Naseby Churchyard is a huge copper ball that is said to have been brought back from the Siege of Boulogne in 1544.

At Naseby turn left then right on to the unclassified 'Sibbertoft' road, and in 1 mile pass the site of the Battle of Naseby on the left. Reach Sibbertoft and turn right for the 'Theddingworth' road, and after 1 mile bear right to Marston Trussell. Return to Market Harborough via Lubenham and the main A427.

LEICESTER, Leics

Situated on the River Soar and Grand Union Canal, this county town and university city has been a thriving centre at least since Roman times. Relics from its very early history include Roman pavements under the former Central Station and below a shop fronting St Nicholas' Church. Other traces of the occupation have been found at the Jewry Wall site, including remains of 2nd-century Roman baths and the wall itself. Various relics from ancient times to the middle ages can be seen in the Jewry Wall Museum and site. The Leicestershire Museum and Art Gallery stands in New Walk, a delightful promenade of elegant houses, mature trees, and carefully preserved Victorian lamp-posts. An ancient city gateway known as The Magazine houses the museum of the Royal Leicestershire Regiment, and the Newarke Houses Museum offers a vivid insight into social history from the 16th century to Victorian times. It is housed in an interesting old Chantry House of 1511, and its immediate neighbour dates from c1600. Wygston's House Museum of Costume is laid out in a 15th-century house, and the Leicestershire Museum of Technology preserves various items of industrial interest in the apt surroundings of Abbey Pumping Station. Among many interesting churches in Leicester is St Martin's, which stands on a Saxon site that was previously occupied by a Roman temple and now enjoys cathedral status. It was largely rebuilt in the 19th century and has a well proportioned tower and spire. Good Norman work is retained by the Church of St Mary de Castro. The city's Guildhall is a fine late 14th-century building with magnificent timbering, and the 17th-century Court House incorporates fragments of a Norman hall. There is also a Norman castle, but very little of it survives. Close to the university is a fine public park and cricket ground, and the University Botanic Gardens are of note.

Leave Leicester on the A46 'Newark' road and after 3 miles branch left on to the B667 into Thurmaston.

THE CRAGS OF CHARNWOOD

Charnwood Forest is a huge upthrusting of rock whose wind-blasted heaths dominate miles of Leicestershire's gentle farming country. Now treeless and pitted with great quarries, it is an eerie place where open moorland flows round fascinating outcrops of rock and the lines of ancient forts.

The small brook at Rearsby is spanned by a quaint medieval bridge.

THURMASTON, Leics

This large suburb of Leicester stands on the east bank of the River Soar and has a number of developing industries. In its older quarter is a fine church with distinctive 13th century nave arcades.

Continue through the town on the B667, reach a roundabout at the far end, and take the 2nd exit on to the A607 SP 'Melton'. Drive through Syston.

SYSTON, Leics

The tower buttresses of Syston Church display curious sculptures of a man and two women, possibly representations of the founder and his wives. Many of the houses in the area are brick-built structures of 18th-century date.

Continue to Rearsby.

REARSBY, Leics

Situated on a tributary of the River Wreake, this village has a good 13th- and 14th-century church with an unusual drum-shaped font. To the east of the church is an attractive 6-arched medieval bridge, and a gabled house of 1661 stands in Mill Road.

Turn right on to the B674 for Gaddesby.

GADDESBY, Leics

One of the largest and most beautiful of Leicestershire's many lovely village churches can be seen here. Its south side is richly decorated with stone carvings, and the south aisle is a showpiece. Inside is an equestrian statue of Colonel Cheney at Waterloo.

Charnwood Forest's windswept character is well appreciated from Beacon Hill.

Stay on the B674, and within 1 mile turn left on to an unclassified road to Great Dalby. Meet a T-junction and turn right into Great Dalby. Pass the village church, turn right on to the B6047, and proceed to Twyford. Turn left on to the unclassified 'Burrough' road and proceed to Burrough-on-the-Hill.

BURROUGH-ON-THE-HILL, Leics

Breached ramparts of an iron-age fort at Burrough Hill are thought to mark the site of a pre-Roman capital. The local church dates from the 13th century and has a good tower.

Continue to Somerby, meet a T-junction, and turn left SP 'Pickwell' and 'Melton'. In 2¼ miles cross the A606 and follow SP for Stapleford. To the right, on the approach to Stapleford, is Stapleford Park.

STAPLEFORD PARK, Leics

Home of Lord and Lady Gretton, this fine old house (open) has an early wing dating from 1500 and was restored in 1633. Its exterior decoration includes an exceptional collection of stone sculptures depicting scenes from history, the scriptures, and legend; inside are rooms that have been attributed to John Webb. As well as fine pictures, tapestries and furniture, the house contains the famous Thomas Balston collection of Victorian Staffordshire pottery figures (NT). In the grounds are a lake with an island bird sanctuary, a miniature steam passenger railway, and many other diversions for both children and adults.

From Stapleford proceed north and after a short distance turn left to join the B676. A short detour from the main route to the village of Saxby can be made by turning right here on to the B676.

SAXBY, Leics

An ancient Saxon cemetery has been discovered at Saxby, and the local rectory and church both date from 1789.

On the main route, continue along the B676 to Melton Mowbray.

MELTON MOWBRAY, Leics

No matter what various sections of public opinion feel about hunting it is still a thriving tradition, and nowhere is it in better health than at Melton Mowbray. Three famous packs meet here, and the district is often loud with the noise of horns, hounds, and horses. The town is internationally famous for Stilton cheese and pork pies, and its attractive situation on the River Eye makes it a popular goal for summer visitors. St Mary's is arguably the stateliest and most impressive of all the county's churches, and beautifully illustrates the early-English, decorated, and perpendicular architectural periods. Anne of Cleves House is of ancient origin. The Melton Carnegie Museum depicts the making of Stilton cheese and pork pies. Attractive parks and gardens border the river.

Leave Melton Mowbray on the A6006 'Loughborough' road, pass Asfordby, and in 3¼ miles turn left on to the B676. After 1½ miles pass beneath the A46, which follows much of the course of the ancient Fosse Way.

FOSSE WAY
Certain stretches of this famous Romanized road are mere tracks, but much of its diagonal route across England from Axminster to Lincoln is followed by modern main roads. Excavations have shown that the courses of earlier paths were adopted by the Roman engineers who plotted the road.

Continue to Burton-on-the-Wolds, turn left on to an unclassified road, then shortly join the B675 and drive to Barrow-upon-Soar.

BARROW-UPON-SOAR, Leics
This attractive and popular village stands on the east bank of the River Soar and has a curious village sign that depicts an aquatic prehistoric reptile. Good local

Kirby Muxloe Castle, unfinished since the 15th century.

Old John Tower in Bradgate Park is an 18th-century folly built on a 700ft hill.

buildings include an old hospital of 1694 and almshouses of 1825.

Drive to the end of Barrow-upon-Soar, at roundabout take 2nd exit then cross a river bridge. Turn right into Quorndon.

QUORNDON, Leics
Valuable Tudor relics are preserved in the 14th-century Farnham Chapel of Quorndon's fine granite church, which also has a fine Norman doorway. The village gives its name to the most famous hunt in England, and has a station on the Great Central Railway. The latter runs 5 miles between Loughborough and Rothley and a 3-mile extension to Birstal is currently undergoing reconstruction.

CHARNWOOD FOREST,
Once an important hunting ground, the bracken-covered summits of Charnwood Forest thrust their bare crags of ancient rock high above the fertile wooded plains of Leicestershire. Their presence in the generally unspectacular Midlands countryside is a startling scenic contradiction, and the fascinating range of geological beds that make

up their bulk is a constant source of interest to geologists. Fine views can be enjoyed from the forest, and its sweeping barrenness gives an invigorating sense of freedom.

At Quorndon, turn left on to the A6 and drive for 200 yards, then turn right on to the unclassified 'Cropston' and 'Anstey' road to skirt Hawcliff Hill and Buddon Wood, on the edge of Charnwood Forest. After 2¼ miles meet crossroads and turn right towards Swithland. After a short distance cross the end of lovely Swithland Reservoir, a noted local beauty spot. Ascend through the village of Swithland.

SWITHLAND, Leics
An attractive village associated with the traditional industry of slate cutting, Swithland stands near the eastern edge of Charnwood Forest in pleasantly wooded surroundings. Good monuments can be seen in the local church.

Drive 1 mile beyond Swithland and turn left for Woodhouse Eaves.

WOODHOUSE EAVES, Leics
Several of the cottages in this picturesque hill village are made of rough stone taken from the slate pits at Swithland. To the west is 818ft Beacon Hill, an AA viewpoint and the site of an iron-age encampment.

Drive to the end of the village and turn left on to the B591; in 1¼ miles pass the Beacon Hill carpark and viewpoint, then in a short distance at crossroads turn left on to the B5330 and meet crossroads. Drive forward on to the unclassified road for Newtown Linford, and pass the main entrance for Bradgate Park on the approach to the village.

BRADGATE PARK, Leics
The 850 acres of untouched heath and woodland that make up this superb country park were given to the city and county of Leicester in 1928 as permanent public space. The area, which extends from Cropston Reservoir to Newtown Linford, offers excellent walks through stands of cedar and oak, and alongside the course of a tiny stream. Bradgate House, now in ruins, was completed c1510. In 1537 it was the birthplace of the unfortunate Lady Jane Grey, who was the uncrowned Queen of England for nine days before being beheaded by order of Mary Tudor. At the highest point of the park is an 18th-century folly tower known as Old John, which was erected to the memory of a retainer who was killed by a falling flagpole.

Continue into Newtown Linford.

NEWTOWN LINFORD, Leics
This village stands on the borders of Bradgate Park and has some attractive old houses, but it is a little too close to the suburbs of Leicester for comfort. Its 18th-century church features painted royal arms.

Follow the B5327 'Leicester' road to Anstey.

ANSTEY, Leics
The 5-arched packhorse bridge that spans Rothley Brook in this Charnwood village is considered one of the finest in England. It dates from the 14th or 15th century and is complemented by some fine old cottages. Anstey was the birthplace of Ned Ludd, who as an apprentice initiated the infamous Luddite riots of 1812 by wrecking machinery that had been introduced to take over his job.

Meet a roundabout and turn right, crossing Rothley Brook with the old packhorse bridge to the right. Continue for 200 yards and turn right on to the unclassified 'Glenfield' road, then after a further 1 mile meet a roundabout and keep forward to enter Glenfield.

GLENFIELD, Leics
Victorian St Peter's was built to replace the old Glenfield Church, which stands in ruins near by. Several architectural features salvaged from the interior of the older structure can be seen inside.

From Glenfield follow SP 'Kirby Muxloe' to Kirby Muxloe.

KIRBY MUXLOE, Leics
Considered an excellent example of its type, this moat-encircled fortified manor (AM) was begun by Lord Hastings in 1480 – towards the end of the Wars of the Roses. The wars ended before the house was completed, and Hastings was executed for treason.

Meet roundabout at the edge of Kirby Muxloe and turn left towards Leicester. In 1 mile meet a roundabout and turn left on to the A47 for the return to Leicester.

NOTTINGHAM, Notts

The growth of this ancient city was influenced by the Saxons, Danes, and Normans, but it was the industrial revolution that made it a thriving commercial centre famous for fine lace. Early prosperity was aided by the natural highway provided by the River Trent, a strategic advantage that may have prompted William the Conqueror to build a strong castle here soon after his invasion of Britain. It was destroyed in the reign of Stephen, rebuilt by Henry II, and throughout the turmoil of the Wars of the Roses remained loyal to the cause of the Yorkists. When the Tudors came to the throne it fell into a slow decline and was reduced to ruins by the time it was bought by the Duke of Newcastle in 1651. The duke converted the soundest parts of the building into a house, but this was gutted by Reform Bill rioters in 1831. Nowadays the castle is the property of the Corporation and houses a museum and art gallery. Among several good churches in Nottingham is St Mary's, a splendid example of 15th-century architecture with excellent windows and a glorious Madonna and Child painted by Bartolommeo. Other notable buildings include the 18th-century Shire Hall, the partly-medieval Trip to Jerusalem Inn, and a wealth of Georgian domestic architecture. The city's natural history museum is in Wollaton Hall, a 16th-century building that stands close to the university campus.

Leave the city with SP 'Loughborough A60' and cross the River Trent. A pleasant detour from the main route to Holme Pierrepont can be made by turning left on to the A6011.

HOLME PIERREPONT, Notts

This early Tudor hall (open) was built to a medieval design c1500 and contains a fine collection of 17th-century English oak furniture. Its grounds include a formal courtyard garden of Victorian date, a country park, and a national and international competition and training centre for water sports.

On the main route, continue along the A60 and pass Ruddington and Bradmore to reach Bunny.

Victorian Belvoir Castle dominates the surrounding landscape.

THE FORESTS OF SHERWOOD

Away from the industry of the coalfields is a picturesque countryside of forests, farms, and villages thick with legends of Robin Hood and his outlaw band. Great oaks grow in Sherwood, and fertile countryside follows the meandering course of the River Trent.

BUNNY, Notts

A great deal of this village was designed in the 17th century by Thomas Parkyns, who did as much as he could to improve the living conditions of his tenants by rebuilding farms and providing four charming almshouses. He lived at Bunny Hall, and his great love for sporting combat earned him the title The Wrestling Baron. This passionate interest is evident in his book *The Cornish Hugg*, and his self-designed graveyard monument shows him in an aggressive stance at the start of a bout. The local church dates from the 14th century and contains several good monuments.

Beyond Bunny turn right on to an unclassified road SP 'Gotham, East Leake' and skirt wooded Bunny Hill. Reach a railway bridge and after another ¼ mile turn left. Continue to East Leake, meet a T-junction, and turn right for East Leake Church.

EAST LEAKE, Notts

Inside the partly Norman church at East Leake is an unusual vamping horn, a type of trumpet that was once used during choir services to 'vamp up' or encourage the singers.

Return to the centre of East Leake and keep straight on to Costock. Cross a main road, continue through Wysall to Keyworth, then turn right and drive to Widmerpool.

WIDMERPOOL, Notts

Some of the county's loveliest woodland scenery makes a perfect setting for this charming little village. The picturesquely ruined church has a 19th-century body with a 14th-century tower and contains an exquisite marble sculpture.

On the nearside of Widmerpool turn left SP 'Kinoulton', and in 1¾ miles cross two main roads. The 2nd of these follows the old Fosse Way.

FOSSE WAY

Much of this ancient Romanized track is followed by modern main roads, though parts are still foot and bridle paths.

In a short distance descend and keep forward into Kinoulton.

KINOULTON, Notts

Glorious views over the rich Vale of Belvoir and mature woodlands known as the Borders can be enjoyed from this high village, which claims to have one of the best cricket grounds in the county. The local church, built in brick by the Earl of Gainsborough c1793, stands opposite a forge.

Meet a T-junction and turn right to Hickling, then drive forward along a winding road for Nether Broughton. Continue with SP 'Melton' to turn left on to the A606, and in 1¼ miles climb Broughton Hill at the northern end of the Leicestershire Wolds. Meet crossroads, turn left on to the unclassified 'Eastwell' road, then in ¼ mile keep forward and meet a T-junction. Turn left SP 'Eastwell', and after 4 miles meet crossroads and turn left again, SP 'Harby'. After a short distance descend 524ft Harby Hill, and continue to Harby. Turn right SP 'Bottesford', and in 4 miles pass a right turn leading to Belvoir Castle. A worthwhile detour can be made from the main route to this historic building.

BELVOIR CASTLE, Leics

Nowadays the superb site overlooking the Vale of Belvoir is occupied by a 19th-century 'castle' by architect James Wyatt, but originally this windy ridge was guarded by a strong medieval fortress that was occupied by the Manners family in the 16th century. This original castle was built in the late 11th century by Robert de Todeni. His coffin is on display in the present castle. The old castle was twice remodelled and finally much of it was destroyed by fire in the 19th century. Its rebuilding and refurbishment were supervised by Sir John Thoroton, friend and chaplain to the Manners family. The present structure (open) is renowned for its pictures, superb Gobelin Tapestries, and a regimental museum of the 17th/21st Lancers. The attractive grounds of the castle contain a number of interesting features including several statues, a mausoleum and a temple.

Continue to Bottesford.

BOTTESFORD, Leics

The church in this village is one of the best in the county and contains an outstanding collection of monuments. Old stocks and a whipping post are preserved near the remains of an old cross, and attractive Fleming's Bridge dates from the 17th century.

In Bottesford turn left on to the A52 and continue to Bingham.

Bottesford still retains its old stocks and whipping post.

BINGHAM, Notts

The most notable building in this village is the church, which boasts a fine tower capped by a spire. Some of its windows date from the 14th and 15th centuries.

Meet traffic signals and turn right on to the B687 SP 'Newark'. In 1 mile meet a roundabout and take the 2nd exit on to the A6097, then after a further 1 mile pass East Bridgford on the right.

EAST BRIDGFORD, Notts

Several good Georgian cottages and houses can be seen in this village, which occupies an attractively wooded site above the River Trent.

Descend and cross the River Trent, then meet a roundabout and take the 2nd exit to skirt Lowdham. In 1¼ miles turn left on to the unclassified 'Woodborough' road. Continue to Woodborough.

WOODBOROUGH, Notts

The broad upper windows in the terraced cottages of this village were once filled by the frames of stocking knitters, for whom the terraces were originally built. Inside the attractive 14th-century church is later monumental sculpture and carving.

Drive to the end of Woodborough, turn left to reach high ground, and in 1½ miles turn right on to the B684. After another 1½ miles turn right on to the A614, then in 3½ miles turn left on to the unclassified 'Kirkby-in-Ashfield' road to enter Sherwood Forest.

SHERWOOD FOREST, Notts

All that remains of the 100,000-acre wood and pasture land that surrounded Nottingham in the 13th century are a few tracts between that city and the Dukeries District. The area is inextricably meshed with the legend of Robin Hood, the philanthropic outlaw who is popularly thought to have been born in Locksley c1160. Tradition has it that Robin of Locksley was the true Earl of Huntingdon, and the legend is perpetuated by many local

Magnificent old oak trees still survive in Sherwood Forest, part of which is now a country park.

PAPPLEWICK, Notts

Papplewick Pumping Station is a fine Victorian building situated in a landscaped park. It contains two Boulton and Watt beam engines and is open most Sundays. On seven weekdays during the year, the boilers are steamed with engines working.

Turn right on to the B6011 SP 'Linby'; continue to Linby.

LINBY, Notts

The combination of red-roofed stone cottages with two crosses and a small stream flowing on each side of the main street makes this one of the county's prettiest villages. East of Linby is Castle Mill, which was rebuilt and castellated in the 18th century by the then Lord Treasurer.

A beautiful example of a James Watt beam engine is preserved at Papplewick.

references. An old oak known as Robin Hood's Larder stands within the boundaries of Sherwood, but the oldest tree in the forest is claimed to be Green Dale Oak, which stands south of Welbeck Abbey and is also said to be the largest in the district. Part of the area has been preserved as the Burntstump Country Park.

In 1¼ miles turn right SP 'Blidworth', and after a further ¼ mile turn left on to the B6020 SP 'Sutton-in-Ashfield', passing through the edge of Blidworth.

BLIDWORTH, Notts

Tradition has it that this colliery village was the home of Friar Tuck and Maid Marian, characters that add the essential ingredients of humour and romance to the Robin Hood legend. The fellow outlaw and friend of Robin, Will Scarlet, is said to be buried in the local churchyard.

In 2½ miles meet crossroads and turn left on to the A60 to pass the entrance of Newstead Abbey on the right.

The superb lake provides a perfect setting for Newstead Abbey.

NEWSTEAD ABBEY, Notts

An abbey founded here in the 12th century was converted into a house in 1550 and later was to be the ancestral home of the poet Lord Byron. In 1931 the house (open) was given to the city of Nottingham, and today it provides a fitting setting for

relics of the poet, and of the explorer Dr Livingstone – who stayed here in 1864. Surviving features of the religious foundation include the west front of the priory church, the cloisters, and the Chapter House.

Continue along the A60 and in ¼ mile turn right on to the B683. Continue to Papplewick.

After a short distance turn right on to the A611. Gradually ascend, skirting the southern part of Sherwood Forest, and after 1½ miles turn left on to the A608. Ascend, cross the M1 motorway, then after another 1½ miles join the B600 SP 'Nottingham' and continue through wooded country. In 2¼ miles pass an unclassified right turn offering a detour to Eastwood.

EASTWOOD, Notts

The house in which D H Lawrence was born in 1885 in this old mining town, has been restored and furnished to depict working class life in Victorian times (open). The sharp contrast between pithead and countryside are reflected in many of his novels.

On the main route, continue along the B600 to Greasley.

GREASLEY, Notts

Handsome Greasley Church has a tall 15th-century tower that serves as a landmark for many miles around.

Drive into a built-up area, then meet a T-junction in Nuthall and turn left. After a short distance meet a roundabout and go forward on to the A610 for the return to Nottingham.

PEAK DISTRICT NATIONAL PARK

Some of England's wildest and most beautiful scenery is protected and made accessible to millions of people in the 542 square miles of this national park, which is mainly divided between the counties of Derbyshire, Cheshire, and Staffordshire. The high, craggy northern region includes gritstone Kinder Scout and various other lofty peaks, but in the south are gentler limestone landscapes that have been sculpted by water and softened by valley woodlands. The undulating White Peak area has thinly-grassed pastures separated by snaking limestone walls, and the lovely River Dove flows through its deep ravine past pinnacles, buttresses, and spires of weathered stone. East are the gritstone uplands and ridges of Millstone Edge, Froggat Edge, and Stanton Moor.

MATLOCK, Derbys

This River Derwent spa town is situated on the eastern edge of the national park, in a high area of gritstone moors and ridges. During the 19th century it was a resort for people following the fashion for taking the waters, and a great hydropathy centre was built at Matlock Bank. This impressive building now houses Derbyshire County Council. Along the banks of the Derwent stretch lovely Hall Leys Gardens.

A detour can be taken from the main route to Matlock Bath by leaving Matlock on the A6 SP 'Derby' and continuing south for 1¼ miles.

MATLOCK BATH, Derbys

Regency visitors popularized the medicinal springs of Matlock Bath, and although the resort declined in Victorian times it remains one of the district's many attractive touring centres. Its Petrifying Wells are very famous and are hung with various objects left by visitors to turn to stone. Every autumn a parade of illuminated and decorated boats is staged on the River Derwent. The resort's charming setting among tree-covered hills is overlooked by the 1,000ft Heights of Abraham, which were worked for lead in Roman times. The Victorian Prospect Tower, on the crest of the heights commands excellent views. In the town is the Peak District Mining Museum, which traces the history of the Derbyshire lead industry.

On the main tour, leave Matlock on the A6 'Buxton' road and drive to Darley Dale.

DARLEY DALE, Derbys

Stone from the quarries near here has long been prized as a building and sculpting material, and can be seen to advantage in many of Britain's large towns. The village church preserves ancient stone coffins and sections of an unusually decorated Saxon cross.

Leave Darley Dale and continue on the A6 to reach Rowsley.

HILLS OF THE SOUTHERN PEAK

This part of the Peak District national park is of gentle aspect, a region of undulating limestone hills scored by the beautifully-wooded Derwent Valley and trout-rich races of the Wye. Curtains of rich foliage screen weathered outcrops, curious stone spires, and the dark mouths of caves.

ROWSLEY, Derbys

Local examples of 17th-century domestic architecture include a fine old bridge over the River Wye and the pleasant Peacock Inn of 1652. More recent survivals include two obsolete station buildings, one of which was designed by Sir Joseph Paxton in 1849.

Drive 1¼ miles beyond Rowsley and turn left on to the B5056 'Ashbourne' road. A pleasant detour from the main route to Haddon Hall can be made by keeping straight ahead on the A6 for ½ mile.

HADDON HALL, Derbys

Medieval architecture can be seen at its best in the peaceful lines of this romantic old house (open). Parts of it date from the 12th century, and although it was originally built as a fortified manor house it has never seen military action. Among its many treasures is a chapel with a Norman font and lovely 15th-century wall paintings, and a long gallery with a painted ceiling and outstanding panelling. Terraced rose gardens are a striking feature of the grounds.

On the main tour, continue along the B5056 'Ashbourne' road and in 1 mile bear right on to an unclassified road SP 'Youlgreave'. A detour to Winster and the Nine Ladies stone circle can be made by driving along the B5056 for a further 2¾ miles, then turning left on B5057 to Winster.

WINSTER, Derbys

Set in the main street of this delightful village is a stone built 17th-18th-century market house (NT).

Return and in 1¾ miles turn right on to an unclassified road, through Birchover to Stanton Moor.

STANTON MOOR, Derbys

The most remarkable of several fascinating prehistoric sites on the moor is the Nine Ladies stone circle (AM), which stands 900ft above sea level in an area that affords splendid views into the Derwent Valley.

On the main tour, continue along the unclassified 'Youlgreave' road, enter the Bradford Valley, and after ¾ mile pass the village of Alport to the left.

Dovedale is said to be the most beautiful of the Derbyshire Dales.

ALPORT, Derbys

Pleasantly sited on a tumbling tributary of the River Bradford, attractive Alport is typical of the area and preserves a number of old houses. The oldest is 16th-century Monk's Hall.

Leave Alport and continue to attractive Youlgreave.

YOULGREAVE, Derbys

Every June, on the Saturday nearest St John the Baptist's Day, the springs and wells of this charming village are dressed with flower pictures as part of an ancient Derbyshire tradition. Today the ceremony is Christian, but it is likely that the ornamentation was once intended to appease the spirits of the springs.

Leave Youlgreave on the 'Ashbourne' road for 4½ miles and meet the A5012. Turn right here, then turn left to join the A515 and continue to the Newhaven Hotel.

NEWHAVEN HOTEL, Derbys

This building, a black-and-white structure with 5 bays, was built by the Duke of Devonshire in the 18th century. About 2½ miles north is the outstanding prehistoric stone circle of Arbor Low (AM).

Continue along the A515 to Alsop Plantation, with lovely Dovedale to the west of the road.

ALSOP PLANTATION, Derbys

The plantation on Alsop Moor is protected by the National Trust and extends alongside the main A515, below a 1,253ft summit. Its presence is an attractive addition to the local limestone scenery.

In 1½ miles pass the edge of Dovedale to the right.

DOVEDALE, Derbys & Staffs

Here the lovely River Dove flows through a 2-mile ravine where spectacular limestone scenery of craggy buttresses and curiously weathered outcrops is clothed and softened by carpets of lush vegetation. Perhaps the most famous of many beauty spots in the national park, the dale (NT) is also noted for trout fishing.

In 2¾ miles turn left on to an unclassified road and continue to the village of Tissington.

TISSINGTON, Derbys

Greystone houses line two sides of the attractive triangular green on which this exceptionally beautiful village is centred; the third side is occupied by a fine Norman and later church. Features of the latter include a good Norman font, an unusual 2-decker pulpit dating from the 18th century, and various monuments. Traditional Derbyshire well-dressing ceremonies are enacted at five different wells on Ascension Day.

Leave Tissington and turn right, then drive through attractive parkland to meet the A515. Turn left and continue to Fenny Bentley.

Beautiful gardens surround romantic Haddon Hall.

MIDDLETON TOP, Derbys
An Engine House with beam engine built in 1829.

Return to main route, then descend through the attractively wooded Via Gellia for Cromford.

SOUTH WINGFIELD MANOR, Derbys
Extensive remains can be seen of a fine 15th-century manor house where Mary Queen of Scots was imprisoned in 1584. Access to ruins is through the Manor Farm.

Continue along the B5035 to Crich and branch right on to an unclassified road SP 'Holloway' for the Crich Tramway Museum.

CRICH TRANWAY MUSEUM, Derbys
Vintage tramcars from all over Britain have been restored to working order and are on display in this fascinating museum, which occupies a disused quarry. An air of authenticity is created by a period setting comprising the reconstructed façade of Derby's Georgian Assembly Rooms and a collection of Victorian Street furniture. An exhibition illustrates the history of lead mining in Derbyshire.

Many Derbyshire wells, such as this example at Tissington, are decorated for thanksgiving ceremonies.

Crich Museum houses many historic trams in working order.

Richard Arkwright's original cotton mill at Cromford was two storeys taller than the present building.

FENNY BENTLEY, Derbys
Features of this pleasant village include the successful amalgamation of a 15th-century manor house with the remains of an ancient tower, and a good Derbyshire church. Inside the latter is a macabre monument commemorating Thomas Beresford, his wife, 16 sons, and 5 daughters.

Leave Fenny Bentley, drive for ½ mile, and turn left on to the B5056 SP 'Bakewell'. Continue to Grangemill. At crossroads turn right on to the A5012 continue for 1¾ miles to reach a right turn B5023. A detour can be made by turning right then sharp left to Middleton. At crossroads turn right and right again for Middleton Top.

CROMFORD, Derbys
The world's first mechanized textile factory was built here by Richard Arkwright, a native of the village, in 1771 (open). The mill is gradually being restored by the Arkwright Society. One of the key figures in England's industrial revolution, he lived in Willersley Castle and built the church in which he is buried. A fine old bridge that spans the River Derwent here carries a rare 15th-century bridge chapel (AM).

Leave Cromford and turn left, then turn right on to the A6 SP 'Derby'. Pass Cromford Canal on the left, then reach Shining Cliff Wood on the right.

SHINING CLIFF WOOD, Derbys
This attractive area of woodland (NT) occupies 200 acres on the west bank of the River Derwent, and is a haven for many forms of wildlife.

Continue along the A6 to reach Ambergate and turn left on to the A610 SP 'Ripley'. Follow the Amber Valley, and after 2 miles turn left on to the B6013 SP 'Chesterfield'. In 3 miles turn left again on to the B5035 to reach South Wingfield Manor.

CRICH STAND, Derbys
High above the Crich Tramway Museum is the 940ft summit of Crich Stand, a lofty vantage point crowned by a monument to the Sherwood Foresters – the Nottingham and Derby Regiment.

Descend to Holloway. Turn right SP 'Riber' and 'Tansley', then in ⅓ mile meet crossroads and drive straight on. In 2 miles meet a T-junction and turn left SP 'Riber Village', and after ¼ mile keep left to reach the Riber Castle Fauna Reserve on the right.

RIBER CASTLE FAUNA RESERVE, Derbys
Near-natural surroundings are provided for comprehensive collections of European birds and animals in the 20 acres of this excellent reserve. Special features include a colony of lynx, and many breeds of domestic animals that have died out elsewhere. Picturesque ruins of 19th-century Riber Castle dominate 853ft Riber Hill.

Descend steeply through hairpin bends, turn right at the bottom, and in ¾ mile turn left on to the A615. Return to Matlock.

AMONG THE HIGH PEAKS

Climbers and walkers come to this part of the national park for the stark ridges of weathered grit, towering rock outcrops, and refreshingly empty moorland. Villages of timbered cottages shelter in the valleys, making a contrast with the huge reflectors of Jodrell Bank's radio telescopes.

THE PEAK DISTRICT NATIONAL PARK

This tour starts west of the Peak District boundary and explores the brownstone towns and villages in the mid western part of the national park. In places massive limestone extraction has taken its toll of the landscape, but the sheep-cropped grass of high gritstone edges still rolls away to close horizons in areas of outstanding natural beauty that have been saved by the Peak Planning Board. Visitors should remember that although the region is protected it is not automatically accessible to the public. Some 40,000 people live and work in the park, and permission should always be sought from farmers and landowners before enclosed land is entered. Information centres are located in Buxton, Castleton, and Edale.

Leave Congleton via West Street and West Road to join the A34 'Newcastle' road. Proceed to Astbury.

ASTBURY, Cheshire

Notable Jacobean and earlier woodwork can be seen in Astbury's 14th- and 15th-century church, and the fine village Rectory dates from the 18th century.

Continue along the A34 to pass Little Moreton Hall.

An attractive aqueduct carries the Macclesfield Canal over the road near Congleton.

Little Moreton Hall is one of the finest medieval houses in Britain.

CONGLETON, Cheshire

This market town stands on a bend on the River Dane and is a dormitory settlement for the vast industrial conurbations of Manchester and the Potteries. Its own industries include the manufacture of artificial yarn for the textile trade. Notable buildings in the town include three half-timbered inns and an 18th-century church with heavy woodwork that seems appropriate to Congleton's solid personality.

THE CLOUD, Cheshire

Some 3 miles east of Congleton a lofty hill known as The Cloud (NT) rises from farmed slopes to a 1,050ft summit offering magnificent all-round views. East are the Staffordshire hills, west the rolling Cheshire Plain, and south the towns and distinctively shaped chimneys of the Potteries.

LITTLE MORETON HALL, Cheshire

Beautiful carved gables and a distinctive black-and-white exterior of Elizabethan wood- and plasterwork have made this splendid 16th-century manor house (NT) one of the most famous examples in Britain. The dazzling effect of symmetrical timber patterns against brilliant white is increased by the reflection of the house in its own lovely moat. Inside are a long wainscoted gallery, a great hall, a chapel, and fine oak furniture.

Continue for $\frac{3}{4}$ mile to the edge of Scholar Green and turn left on to an unclassified road SP 'Mow Cop'. After $\frac{1}{4}$ mile turn left again, and after a further $\frac{1}{2}$ mile cross a canal bridge and drive beneath a railway before ascending Mow Cop.

MOW COP, Cheshire

Rough turf covers this stark limestone ridge for much of its 1,091ft height, but the rugged outcrop of rock known as the Old Man of Mow carries little but a sham ruin built in 1750. Known as Mow Cop Castle, this folly makes a picturesque addition to the distinctive outline of the Old Man.

Continue past a towered church and in 1 mile turn right (no SP) into Mow Lane. Descend through Gillow Heath to the main road and turn left, then in 300 yards turn right on to an unclassified road SP 'Biddulph Moor'. Climb to the village of Biddulph Moor and turn left SP 'Leek'. Take the next turning right, proceed for $\frac{1}{2}$ mile to reach a T-junction, and turn left. Continue for 1 mile and turn right. After $2\frac{1}{4}$ miles glimpse Rudyard Reservoir on the left and descend to Rudyard.

RUDYARD, Staffs

Rudyard Kipling's parents courted and became engaged in this lovely village, and when their talented son was born they named him after it. Attractive woodlands to the north border a 2-mile reservoir formed in 1793 to provide water for the Trent and Mersey Canal. Today the banks of this attractive lake are skirted by a 5-mile footpath dotted with secluded picnic spots near the water's edge. A section of the path follows the trackbed of an abandoned railway, and its route passes caverns, unusual rock formations, and the remains of Roman copper workings.

Continue on the B5331 'Leek' road, meet a T-junction, and turn right on to the A523. Take the next turning left on to an unclassified road SP 'Meerbrook', continue for $\frac{1}{2}$ mile, then turn left again. Approach Meerbrook with Tittesworth Reservoir right.

MEERBROOK, Staffs

Wild upland country popular with climbers and fell walkers surrounds this tiny moorland village. A curious aspect of the area is its naturalized colony of red-necked wallabies. This numbers some 30 strong and began when several of the animals – natives of Australia – escaped from a private estate.

Turn right SP 'Blackshaw Moor, Leek', and after $\frac{1}{4}$ mile meet a main road and turn left on to the A53 'Buxton' road. Climb on to open moors in the Peak District National Park, with a 2-mile stretch of rocky outcrops known as the Staffordshire Roaches to the left. The highest point of the Roaches is 1,658ft; Merryton Low rises to 1,603ft to the right. Pass the Royal Cottage Inn and reach an unclassified left turn leading to the village of Flash. A short detour can be made from the main route here.

FLASH, Staffs
Situated at 1,518ft, Flash is claimed to be the highest village in England and is itself dominated by 1,684ft Oliver Hill to the north.

Later enter Derbyshire and ascend to 1,631ft below the distinctive summit of Axe Edge.

AXE EDGE, Derbys
Rising from an area of fine walking country, this 1,810ft summit is the highest point in the moors from which the rivers Dove, Manifold, Wye, Dane, and Goyt spring.

Proceed to Buxton.

Extremely faint signals from outer space can be detected by the advanced Jodrell Bank radio telescopes.

BUXTON, Derbys
Situated some 1,007ft above sea level, this natural touring centre is the highest town in England and has been known as a spa resort of one sort or another since Roman times. A superb legacy of 18th-century architecture has been left from its most popular period, and the tourists of today are catered for by a large range of entertainment facilities.

Leave Buxton with SP 'Congleton' to return along the A53 'Leek' road, and after 1¼ miles turn right on to the A54. Make a winding ascent with 1,640ft Burbage Edge visible to the right, and after 1 mile enjoy views of 1,795ft Whetstone Edge on the same side. Below these ridges, in the deep Dane Valley, is a junction of Derbyshire, Cheshire, and Staffordshire boundaries in an area known as the Three Shire Heads. Descend from undulating moorland to Allgreave for distant views of a Post Office communications tower, and after passing close to the tower skirt Bosley Reservoir and turn right on to the A523 'Macclesfield' road. Continue for 2 miles to Oakgrove and turn left on to an unclassified road SP 'Gawsworth', immediately crossing the Macclesfield Canal. Proceed to Gawsworth.

GAWSWORTH, Cheshire
Spacious lawns and gardens watered by five lakes grace the grounds of Gawsworth Hall, a beautiful black-and-white timber-framed house (open) dating from Tudor times. Also in the park are rare traces of a tilting ground, where knights once displayed their prowess in jousts and mock battles. At one time the house was the seat of the Fytton family, whose daughter Mary was a favourite maid of Elizabeth I and may have been the 'Dark Lady' of Shakespeare's sonnets. Features of the village itself include the fine Old Rectory and an attractive church, both of the 15th century. The church carries quaint gargoyles and contains a notable range of monuments to the Fyttons. A nearby wood contains the tomb of 18th-century dramatist and eccentric Maggotty Johnson.

At Gawsworth turn left SP 'Gawsworth Church'. Continue to the end of the village and keep right, passing an attractive pond, with views of Gawsworth Hall. Continue along this unclassified road, pass the church, and at the Harrington Arms Inn turn right then right again on to the A536. After ½ mile meet crossroads and turn left on to an unclassified road for Marton.

MARTON, Cheshire
A famous oak tree in this village is said to be the largest in England. The local church is a quaint timbered structure dating from the 14th century.

Drive to a junction with the A34 and turn right SP 'Manchester'. Continue for 3½ miles to reach the entrance to Capesthorne Hall.

Rudyard's extensive reservoir has been planned to cater for a wide variety of leisure pursuits.

CAPESTHORNE HALL, Cheshire
A chapel which adjoins this lovely 18th-century house (open) may be the earliest surviving work of the architect John Wood of Bath. The house itself contains various relics, including pictures, ancient vases, old furniture, and Americana.

Continue along the A34 for 1 mile, meet traffic signals, and turn left on to the A537 'Chester' road. Continue to the Chelford roundabout and turn left on to the A535 SP 'Holmes Chapel' to reach Jodrell Bank.

Ramshaw Rocks are among the most striking gritstone crags in the Peak District.

JODRELL BANK, Cheshire
Manchester University made the name Jodrell Bank internationally famous by building a giant steerable radio telescope here in 1957. Now known as Mark I, the instrument has a 250ft reflector and is still one of the largest of its type in the world. The Mark II was built in the early 1960s and has a 125ft reflector with an advanced form of digital control. Regular presentations of the stars and planets are given in the Planetarium (open), and there are fascinating working models of both the telescopes on view.

Keep forward on the A535. In 3½ miles, near the outskirts of Holmes Chapel, turn left into unclassified Manor Lane (no SP). Continue to the A54 and turn left for the return to Congleton via Somerford.

BUXTON, Derbys

Situated just outside the boundaries of the national park, this is the highest town in England and an ideal base from which to tour the moors and dales of the Peak District. It is sheltered by hills even higher than its 1,007ft site, yet is able to offer gentle scenery more typical of the lowlands alongside sedate reaches of the lovely River Wye. Grinlow Woods lie to the south of the town, Corbar Woods are a mere ½ mile away, and 1 mile east is the enchanting valley of Ashwood Dale. The town itself is built round a spa whose medicinal properties were discovered by the Romans and exploited to the benefit of the town towards the end of the 18th century, when Buxton rivalled the elegant supremacy of Somerset's Bath. The growth of the town during this period was largely due to the efforts of the 5th Duke of Devonshire, who built the beautiful Crescent and Pump Rooms opposite the town's hot springs. The pale blue mineral water of the area still bubbles up from a mile underground at a rate of ¼ million gallons per day and a constant temperature of 82 degrees Fahrenheit and now feeds the local swimming pool. The Pavilion concert hall, theatre, and ballroom stand in 23 acres of lovely gardens featuring a boating lake, bowling and putting greens, tennis courts, and a children's play area. Spa treatment is available from the Devonshire Royal Hospital, which was originally built as the Great Stables and has a superb dome that was added in 1879. The former Pump Rooms now house the Micrarium, a unique opportunity to explore the world of nature using special microscopes. Poole's Cavern is an interesting show cave within the Buxton Country Park.

Leave Buxton on the A6 with SP 'Matlock' and descend through the wooded limestone gorge of the River Wye. Climb away from the valley, with Great Rocks Dale to the left, to reach the edge of Taddington. It is

THE PEAK DISTRICT DALES

Here the great River Wye and its tributaries have carved deep gorges in the soft limestone hills, making secluded pockets of outstanding beauty where the severity of naked rock is softened by water and foliage. The dales themselves are only accessible by foot.

possible to visit this village by turning right from the main route on to an unclassified road.

Buxton built its reputation as a spa, but today it provides facilities for all tastes. The Pavilion Gardens offer a varied and relaxing landscape which enhance the town's appeal.

TADDINGTON, Derbys

Taddington stands at an altitude of 1,130ft in attractive limestone country and is one of the highest villages in England. The slopes of Taddington Wood (NT) face lovely Monsal Dale some 1½ miles east, and to the south-west Taddington Moor rises to 1,500ft at the highest point in the hills south of the River Wye. Close to the summit of the moor is the Five Wells Tumulus, an unusual barrow with two burial chambers. Various interesting prehistoric remains can be found on the moors.

Descend wooded Taddington Dale, with Monsal Dale on the left, and pass Great Shacklow Wood and river valley on right. Take next junction, unclassified road, to enter Ashford-in-the-Water.

ASHFORD-IN-THE-WATER, Derbys

Two ancient bridges span the Wye in this delightful village, one dated 1664 and the other complete with a sheep-dipping enclosure at one end. An interesting well-dressing ceremony is held here on the Saturday before Trinity Sunday. Ashford marble was quarried near by.

Drive to the end of the village and turn right on to the B6465 then at T-junction turn right A6020 after a short distance rejoin the A6 to reach Bakewell.

Dramatic scenery found in the Peak District can be explored from Buxton by following the River Wye as it runs south through spectacular Chee Dale.

BAKEWELL, Derbys

A busy cattle market and the largest town in the national park, Bakewell stands on the wooded banks of the Wye and is sheltered by hills on three sides. Many of its attractive brownstone buildings bear witness to a historic past, and its beautiful 12th-century church is famous for the superb Saxon cross (AM) preserved in its churchyard. The 5-arched medieval bridge (AM) that spans the river was widened in the 19th century, but is basically one of the oldest structures of its type in Britain. Holme Hall and the Market Hall both date back to the 17th century, and the Old House Museum is an early-Tudor house with wattle-and-daub interior walls. Inside the latter are exhibitions of costumes and domestic utensils. The name of the town will always be associated with the Bakewell tart, a dish apparently created by accident when a harassed cook in the Rutland Arms mistakenly poured the egg mixture meant for the pastry of a jam tart into the jam. The unusual dish was very well received by guests, and the cook was instructed to continue making her delicious mistake.

Leave Bakewell on the A6 'Matlock' road to pass Haddon Hall.

HADDON HALL, Derbys

Although originally a fortified dwelling, exquisite 12th- to 15th-century Haddon Hall (open) was never fought over and survives as one of the finest examples of medieval architecture extant. Its peaceful history is reflected in its lovely wood and parkland setting on the River Wye, and its beauty is enhanced by the enchanting rose gardens that ornament its grounds. The romantic feeling of the place is supported by its history, for it was from here that Dorothy Vernon eloped with Sir John Manners in the 16th century.

Continue along the A6 and cross the Wye to enter Rowsley.

ROWSLEY, Derbys

This charming little greystone village stands on a tongue of land at the confluence of the rivers Wye and Derwent. The actual waters' meet is a delightful spot beloved of artists and anglers alike. Sir Joseph Paxton designed the earlier of two obsolete but charming station buildings here, and the beautiful old Peacock Inn was originally a 17th-century manor house.

Pass the Peacock Inn on the left, then in a short distance turn left on to the B6012 SP 'Baslow'. Continue to Beeley.

BEELEY, Derbys

From ancient times this little community was known for the grindstones fashioned by its craftsmen from the local hard grit. A tributary of the River Derwent, which is famous for its trout, runs close to the village.

Chatsworth's superb apartments include the State Bedroom of the ill-fated Mary Queen of Scots.

CALVER, Derbys
Anglers come here for the fine Derwent trout, and the village boasts a good 18th-century cotton mill.

In Calver meet traffic signals and turn left on to the B6001 'Bakewell' road. Continue to Hassop.

HASSOP, Derbys
Situated at the edge of wild Longstone Moor, this little village has a Jacobean hall that was the home of the Earls of Newburgh until 1853. Much of the local countryside has the tended appearance of parkland.

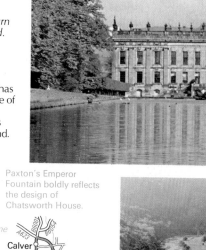

Paxton's Emperor Fountain boldly reflects the design of Chatsworth House.

Beyond Beeley skirt the grounds of Chatsworth House, then cross the River Derwent and enter the park to pass Chatsworth House itself.

CHATSWORTH HOUSE, Derbys
Popularly known as the Palace of the Peak, this magnificent mansion (open) stands in a superb park on the River Derwent and is backed by beautifully wooded slopes. It was built in the 17th century for the 1st Duke of Devonshire and is noted particularly for its superb state apartments and great art collection. An earlier house that stood on the same site was partly designed by the 1st Duke's ancestress Bess of Hardwick, and was occasionally visited by Mary Queen of Scots. Remains of the original Elizabethan park layout can be seen in the old Hunting Tower, which vies as the major focal point with a fountain that is the tallest in Britain. Features of the magnificent park include mature chestnut avenues and the charm of ornamental waters.

Beyond Chatsworth Park join the A619 and enter Baslow.

BASLOW, Derbys
This characteristic gritstone village stands on the River Derwent and is partly built round an old triangular goose green. Most through traffic is taken across the river by a recent bridge, but the old hump-backed crossing survives – complete with tollhouse.

In Baslow turn left SP 'Chapel-en-le-Frith' to join the A623. Continue to the village of Calver.

In Hassop turn right on to an unclassified road and drive to a T-junction in Great Longstone. Turn right for Monsal Head and continue to the Monsal Head Hotel, then turn right again on to the B6465 to pass a magnificent vantage point offering panoramic views across Monsal Dale.

MONSAL HEAD, Derbys
This great rocky prominence affords superb views into Monsal Dale, where the River Wye threads its way between lush slopes punctuated by rocky crags and overhangs of weathered stone. The head and dale together form one of the national park's loveliest beauty spots.

Continue through Wardlow, turn left on to the A623, and in 1¼ miles turn left again to join the B6049. Continue into Tideswell.

TIDESWELL, Derbys
Although this ancient town was granted a market as early as the 13th century, the only notable building to have survived the centuries is the superb Church of St John the Baptist. This is considered the finest building of its type in the county and is popularly known as The Cathedral of the Peak. Local wells and springs are dressed in a traditional ceremony held in Wakes Week, on the Saturday nearest June 24.

Continue with the 'Buxton' road, and after 1 mile pass the Tideswell picnic area (left). Descend into Miller's Dale.

MILLER'S DALE, Derbys
Threaded by a narrow road to Litton Mill, this part of the Wye Valley is enclosed by craggy limestone cliffs that rise high above the river behind dense screens of shrub and woodland. The mill was once used for processing silk.

Beyond a railway viaduct and just before a bridge over the Wye turn sharp right on to an unclassified road for Wormhill. Pass Chee Dale on the left and continue to Wormhill.

WORMHILL, Derbys
Situated high above the river curve that includes Chee Dale, this village is excellently situated for fine views across the River Wye and is popular with walkers. Narrow Chee Dale is only accessible on foot, but it is worth the exercise. One of the village's most notable buildings is a 17th-century hall with mullioned windows.

Pass Wormhill and bear left SP 'Peak Dale'. Continue for ½ mile and turn right for the village of Peak Forest.

PEAK FOREST, Derbys
The name of the medieval hunting ground that covered most of northern Derbyshire is preserved in this attractive little village. A chapel founded here in 1657 was extra-

Native ashwoods fringe the River Wye in picturesque Monsal Dale.

parochial and could issue marriage licences to anybody who applied. Before the building was demolished, Peak Forest gained something of a Gretna Green reputation as a goal for eloping couples. North of the village on the south side of Eldon Hill is a sheer-sided pothole known as Eldon Hole. For many years this was reputed to be bottomless, but modern potholers have discovered it to be a 186ft limestone shaft leading to two caverns which radiate from the bottom. On no account should an attempt be made to descend the hole without proper equipment.

Turn left on to the A623 SP 'Chapel-en-le-Frith', keep left at Sparrowpit, and within 1¼ miles turn left on to the A6. Proceed towards Buxton, passing limestone quarries on the left at Dove Holes. Black Edge rises to the right of the road.

DOVE HOLES, Derbys
Not to be confused with a natural rock formation of the same name north-west of Tissington, this area is the site of vast limestone workings that extend some 4 miles south-east along Doveholes Dale, Peak Dale, and Great Rocks Dale. The quarries are 1,086ft above sea level. A railway tunnel penetrates 1½ miles through bedrock deep beneath the main road here.

BLACK EDGE, Derbys
This high prominence rises to 1,662ft and affords excellent views over much of the national park's finest countryside.

Descend and return to Buxton.

IN THE WOODLANDS OF CANNOCK CHASE

Nowadays the great chase, or hunting ground, of Cannock is a protected area of woodland famous for its superb stands of mature oak and birch. All around are the quaint black-and-white villages typical of the area, guardians of tradition.

LICHFIELD, Staffs

A city of great age and architectural distinction, Lichfield has a fine red sandstone cathedral which carries three tall spires popularly known as the Ladies of the Vale. They form a well-known local landmark easily discernible above the rooftops of the town, and the grand west front of the building carries no less than 113 statues within its arcades and panels. Before the Commonwealth this type of decoration was reasonably common, but Cromwellian troops tracking down the sin of idolatry smashed such work wherever they could. Inside the building is preserved the 7th-century manuscript book of the *St Chad Gospels*, a rare treasure indeed. Other features include beautiful windows, a sculpted group by Chantrey, and numerous good memorials. The Bishop's Palace of 1687 is a lovely old example of its type, and restored Lichfield House dates from the 16th century. An old house in the Market Square was the birthplace of Dr Johnson and now serves as a Johnsonian Museum featuring, amongst other relics, his favourite silver teapot. The Lichfield Heritage Exhibition and Treasury is housed in the ancient Guild church of St Mary's, included is an audio-visual on the Civil War and siege of Lichfield and examples of the silversmith's craft.

Leave Lichfield with SP 'Tamworth A51', passing the Barracks to the left on Whittington Heath.

WHITTINGTON BARRACKS, Staffs

The official museum of the Staffordshire Regiment can be visited at Whittington Barracks, themselves evidence of Lichfield's long association with the military.

Pass a TV mast on the right and descend past Hopwas Hays Wood to Hopwas, then continue to Tamworth.

TAMWORTH, Staffs

Tamworth's fine castle (open) displays an intriguing mixture of architectural styles ranging from the original Norman to the charming pretence of the 19th century. The 10ft-thick walls of the keep are typically Norman, but the less massive warden's lodge and beautiful banqueting hall both show the delicacy of Tudor workmanship. A frieze of 55 oak panels in the state dining room, which is in the north wing, is painted with the arms of the lords of the castle up to 1718. A museum of local history is housed in the castle. Tamworth Church has·a unique square tower with a double-spiral staircase at one corner, and the red-brick Town Hall of 1701 is one of the prettiest in the country.

Follow the A513 'Burton' and 'Alrewas' road, and after 4 miles pass an unclassified left turn that can be taken as a detour from the main route to Elford village.

Rich furnishings in Lichfield Cathedral include an ornate choir screen.

TRENT & MERSEY CANAL, Staffs

Designed by the great engineer Brindley to service the industrial heartlands of England, this canal was begun in the late 18th century and was the first safe means by which fragile goods could be transported from the Potteries district. Josiah Wedgwood, owner of one of the more famous Staffordshire china industries, worked in association with Brindley to produce this undoubted advantage to his interests. Just beyond Alrewas the canal actually joins the Trent by lock, and leaves the river by the same method after 250 yards.

In 1¾ miles at junction turn left on to the B5016 for Barton-under-Needwood. Continue forward SP 'Yoxall', then in 1 mile reach The Bell (PH) and turn right on to the unclassified 'Tutbury' road. In 3 miles cross a main road and continue to Tutbury.

Tranquillity reigns today on the Trent and Mersey Canal, formerly an important route for the pottery trade.

ELFORD, Staffs

Elford Church contains a remarkable collection of heraldic shields, all in excellent condition, and the evocative monument to a child who is said to have been killed after being hit on the temple by a tennis ball in 1460. Many other fine memorials can be seen here.

On the main route, continue along the A513 to Alrewas.

ALREWAS, Staffs

Famous for its River Trent eel fishing and basket-weaving industries, this charming little village of thatched black-and-white Tudor cottages is considered one of the prettiest in the county. Its 13th- and 14th-century church contains a fine font, and its situation on the Trent and Mersey Canal offers fine towpath walks.

Turn right on to the A38 SP 'Burton', and in 1 mile cross the River Trent before continuing alongside the canal.

TUTBURY, Staffs

This picturesque old town stands on the banks of the River Dove and claims to have the finest Norman church in the Midlands. The west front of the building is certainly magnificent. Mary Queen of Scots was twice imprisoned in Tutbury Castle (open), and led a thoroughly miserable existence in the cramped surroundings of a high tower that still stands. Nowadays this sad place is visited for the outstanding views it affords over Needwood Forest. Other remains of the castle, dramatically situated on an isolated outcrop of rock, include 14th-century John of Gaunt's Gateway. The most striking building in the main street of the town is the old Dog and Partridge Inn.

Drive forward into the A50 High Street and cross the River Dove. Continue over a level crossing, then turn left on to an unclassified road SP 'Scropton' and 'Sudbury'. Continue for 2 miles beyond Scropton and turn left on to the A515. A short detour from the main route to attractive Sudbury can be made by turning right here on to the A515, then left on to an unclassified road leading to the village of that name.

Tutbury Castle offers excellent views over Needwood Forest.

SUDBURY, Derbys
Built largely in the 17th century, this village is an excellent early example of unified design being applied to a community rather than being allowed to develop in its own random fashion. Sudbury Hall (NT), seat of the Vernon family, contains exceptional carving by the sculptor Grinling Gibbons. A stained glass window given by Queen Victoria can be seen in the village church.

On the main route, continue along the A515 and recross the River Dove. Reach Draycott-in-the-Clay and ascend, then in ¾ mile meet crossroads and turn right on to an unclassified road for Newborough. Continue to Newborough and turn right on to the B5324 SP 'Abbots Bromley', then cross rolling countryside and turn right on to the B5014 to enter Abbots Bromley.

ABBOTS BROMLEY, Staffs
People from all over the country come to Abbots Bromley on the Monday after September 4, when the curious and ritualistic Horn Dance is performed through the streets and surrounding country lanes. Six of the twelve dancers carry ancient reindeer antlers on their shoulders, a seventh rides a hobby horse, a fool capers along the route in multi-coloured costume, and the entourage is completed by a young girl alongside a boy carrying a bow and arrow. The dance as it is seen today is thought to commemorate the granting of hunting rights to the local people by the Abbot of Bromley in the 12th century. However, it is likely to have been derived from a pagan ceremony with roots far back in prehistoric times. Features of the town itself include many half-timbered houses and a market place with an old butter cross. The 16th-century Church House and Bagot Almshouses are of particular note.

Continue along the B5014 and in ⅓ mile turn left on to the B5013 SP 'Rugeley'. In 1 mile cross the extensive Blithfield Reservoir.

BLITHFIELD RESERVOIR, Staffs
The Queen Mother opened this 4,000 million gallon reservoir in 1953, and today it has become naturalized to such an extent that it is a valuable sanctuary for wildlife. Views can be enjoyed from the road, but a permit is required to visit the banks.

Pass a viaduct to reach Blithfield Hall on the right.

BLITHFIELD HALL, Staffs
Set graciously in the peaceful Blithe Valley, this estate has been the home of the Bagot family and their ancestors for 900 years and includes a fine old house of Elizabethan origin. Additions from later periods are evident in the design of the building, and inside is a magnificent staircase in carved oak. Of particular interest is a unique collection of relics from the Stuart period. Herds of black-necked Bagot goats roam the park.

Continue along the B5013 and in 1¾ miles turn right on to the unclassified 'Stafford' road. A short detour from the main route to the village of Rugeley can be made by keeping forward along the B5013 for a further 2¼ miles.

RUGELEY, Staffs
During the 19th century this village became nationally famous as the home of notorious Dr William Palmer, who was found guilty of poisoning a bookmaker to whom he owed money. On its own this act is not sensational, but it appears that this unfortunate victim was the last in a long line of poisonings by Palmer, including many relatives and friends. The grave of the bookmaker, John Cook, can be seen in the local churchyard. The actual town is a pleasant little place that easily lives down its connexion with the Prince of Poisoners. About 4 miles south-south-east is Hanch Hall of 13th-century origin. House and gardens (open).

On the main route, continue along the unclassified 'Stafford' road and in 1½ miles meet crossroads. Turn left, then left again to join the A51, then cross the River Trent and at roundabout take 2nd exit A513 SP 'Stafford'. Follow the Trent Valley and pass the entrance to Shugborough Hall on the right before reaching Milford.

SHUGBOROUGH HALL, Staffs
Now run by Staffordshire County Council and housing the county museum, this great white mansion (NT) stands in beautiful grounds on the River Sow and contains fine collections of furniture and period bric-à-brac. Access to the gardens is by a bridge over a lovely ornamental lake, and the grounds are scattered with superb classical monuments and follies. The most notable of the latter are the Doric Temple and the Tower of the Winds.

Sudbury Hall is a typical example of 17th-century elegance.

Continue to Milford and turn left on to the unclassified 'Brocton' road. At Brocton drive forward SP 'Stafford', then meet a main road and turn left on to the A34 SP 'Cannock'. In ¼ mile turn left on to the unclassified 'Hednesford' road and climb to Cannock Chase.

CANNOCK CHASE, Staffs
Once the private hunting ground of the kings of England, the 26 square miles of wooded Cannock Chase form a designated area of outstanding natural beauty that is available for everybody to enjoy. Several pine and spruce plantations have been established in the area by the Forestry Commission, but a few of the majestic oaks that were once commonplace can still be seen in Brocton Coppice. The feather-like plumes of birches grace Black Hill, and to the west the bracken-clad forest glades give way to heather and gorse. Among many wild creatures to be seen here are deer and the rare native red squirrel. Good views are afforded by the hilltops of Seven Springs, which culminate in 795ft Castle Ring; the latter is crowned by the ramparts of a good iron-age hillfort.

Continue along the unclassified 'Hednesford' road and pass a German military cemetery on the left. Meet crossroads and ascend, then meet more crossroads and drive forward into the colliery district round Hednesford. In ¼ mile drive forward, descend to crossroads, and keep forward to cross a railway bridge. Turn right on to the A460, drive under a railway bridge, and turn left on to an unclassified road SP 'Rawnsley' and 'Hazelslade'. An alternative return to Lichfield, taking in the Chasewater Park Railway at Brownhills, can be taken by continuing with the A460 and following the route indicated on the tour map. On the main route, continue along the unclassified road and after ¾ mile turn left. Drive over a level crossing and climb through thick woodland to crossroads. Turn right into Startley Lane and descend. Continue, with Castle Ring rising from Cannock Chase to the right, and meet a main road. Turn right on to the A51 for the return to Lichfield.

The Abbots Bromley Horn Dancers performing outside Blithfield Hall.

A total of 48 enormous stones in two configurations make up the megalithic monument of Castlerigg Circle near Keswick. Lake District people have wondered at its significance for thousands of years, ever since its stone-age builders deserted it for reasons that can only be guessed at.

The North Country

BEVERLEY, Humberside

The gothic completeness of medieval Beverley Minster has won it acclaim as one of the most beautiful churches in Europe. Its lovely twin bell towers can be seen for miles across the flat Humberside pastures, and its interior is packed with the monumental art of some 700 years. Here can be seen the full blossoming of the 14th-century stonemason's skill in the magnificent Percy Tomb, the ingenuity of 15th-century glassmakers in the great east window, and the craft of local men in the rich extravagance of carved wood. At the far end of the Main Street is St Mary's Church, a beautiful building that was started in the 12th century as a chapel for its more famous neighbour. Over the years it has been enlarged, with a wealth of excellent architectural detail, and is now independent. One of its more notable features is a 15th-century ceiling painting of the English kings. In early times the town was an important market centre and the capital of the East Riding of Yorkshire, a status that it had to defend with a stout wall pierced by five gates. Subsequent periods saw the community outgrow these confines, and all that remains today is the 15th-century North Bar. Evidence that much of the expansion was in the 18th and 19th centuries can be seen in the many Georgian houses and shopfronts that survive. The ornate market cross dates from c1714, and the Guildhall of 1762 displays a wealth of plasterwork and wood carving by local men. Inside 18th-century Lairgate Hall (open), which houses the council offices, is a Chinese Room with hand-painted wallpaper. Beverley's Art Gallery and Museum displays pictures and relics of local interest.

Leave Beverley and follow SP 'Hessle, A164'. Later reach Skidby Windmill.

SKIDBY WINDMILL, Humberside

Well-preserved Skidby Windmill was built in 1821 and is the only example to have remained intact north of the River Humber and east of the Pennine Chain. Its black-tarred tower and white cap form a striking combination that makes it a prominent local landmark. An agricultural museum has been established inside (open).

At the windmill turn left on to an unclassified road SP 'Cottingham'. Later turn right on to the B1233 to reach Cottingham.

COTTINGHAM, Humberside

Several halls of residence for the students from Hull University are established in this village, which is grouped round a large square. Inside the local church is a fine brass dating from the 14th century.

Continue along the B1233 and drive over a level crossing. Keep forward through 2 roundabouts, then ¾ mile beyond the University of Hull turn right on to the A1079. Proceed to the centre of Hull.

HUMBERSIDE AND HOLDERNESS

Between the River Humber and the sea is a flat peninsula famous for its magnificent churches, whose towers and spires stand high above the surrounding countryside of marshlands and drainage canals. Fishing fleets put out from Hull, and many of the coastal villages have become holiday resorts.

HULL, Humberside

This major industrial and commercial centre is an international port and a fishing base for deep-sea vessels. As such it suffered badly in World War II, but its rebuilding has included a fine shopping precinct scattered with flowerbeds and interspersed with parks and gardens. Docks stretch for a full 7 miles along the north side of the Humber, joined here by the little River Hull, and one of the world's longest suspension bridges at 4,626ft/1,410m — The Humber Bridge. Despite these extensive new developments the city centre still has a few old buildings untouched by bombs or town planning, including the largest parish church in England and 18th-century Maister House (NT). An early 17th-century mansion in which the MP and anti-slavery campaigner William Wilberforce was born in 1759 is now preserved as the William Wilberforce Historical Museum. The Town Docks Museum relates to fishing and shipping, and the Transport Museum has a collection of vehicles including a steam Train Locomotive of 1882. The Archaeology and Natural History Museum has several interesting displays and contains The Hasholme Boat, the biggest surviving prehistoric logboat in the country.

Leave Hull on the A165 with SP 'Hornsea' and 'Bridlington'. In 3¼ miles reach a roundabout. Keep forward to another roundabout and take the 3rd exit on to the B1238 SP 'Aldbrough'. Continue for 1¼ miles and keep forward to reach Sproatley.

SPROATLEY, Humberside

This village is in the heart of the Holderness area, where vast fields, golden with corn in summer, stretch flatly to the horizon or lap the fringes of small copses. Its 19th-century church, given an air of mystery by a cloak of ivy, contains an inscribed coffin lid of the 13th century.

Bear right, drive to the end of the village, and turn left on to an unclassified road to reach Burton Constable Hall.

BURTON CONSTABLE HALL, Humberside

Grand 18th-century state rooms and 200 acres of parkland enchantingly landscaped by Capability Brown are features of this attractive Elizabethan house (open). Lakes covering some 22 acres provide plenty of scope for boating, venue for several rallies and fairs during the summer months.

Return to Sproatley and turn right to return along the B1238. Meet a war memorial and branch left on to the B1240 to Preston. At Preston turn left again to reach Hedon.

The Proud Pharisee is one of many carvings in the nave of magnificent Beverley Minster.

HEDON, Humberside

At one time this small town was a major port connected to the Humber Estuary by canals. It was rich enough to start building the magnificent King of Holderness in the 12th century, and subsequent work on this church shows the prosperity to have lasted at least until the 15th century. Trade has long since filtered away to Hull, but the huge pinnacled tower of the 'King' remains in all its glory. Near by, the Ravenspur Cross commemorates a long vanished village of that name, where Bolingbroke (later Henry IV) landed in 1399 to claim the English throne for the House of Lancaster.

Turn left on to the A1033 SP 'Withernsea'. Pass through flat agricultural countryside crisscrossed by drainage canals to reach Keyingham.

KEYINGHAM, Humberside

An attractive medieval church can be seen in this village, and just to the north west is a tower that was once a windmill.

Drive through Ottringham and continue to the edge of Winestead.

WINESTEAD, Humberside

Features from the Norman and Jacobean periods jostle for attention with others less easy to define in Winestead Church. A good 16th-century brass can be seen inside.

Continue to Patrington.

PATRINGTON, Humberside

Hedon's superb church has a rival here in the Queen of Holderness, a magnificent cruciform building in the decorated style of architecture. Its tower and spire are considered outstanding, and excellent craftsmanship of many kinds can be seen inside. At one time the village was an important market town in the manor administered by the archbishops of York.

A pleasant detour can be taken from the main route by following the B1445 from Patrington to Easington (where there is a natural gas pipe terminal), and continuing through Kilnsea to Spurn Head and the Humber Shore.

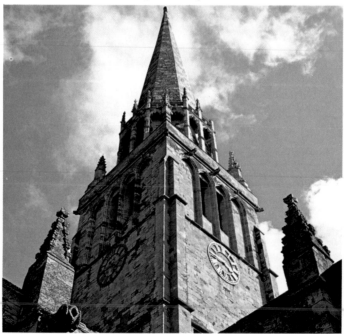

St Patrick's Church in Patrington has the grandeur of a small cathedral.

Hornsea Mere is famous for its huge pike and large flocks of coot.

The poet Andrew Marvell was MP for Kingston upon Hull from 1658 until his death in 1678.

SPURN HEAD, Humberside

Between the North Sea and the Humber estuary is Spurn Head, a narrow hook of sand and shingle that lengthens by about a yard each year as silt from the Humber and aggregate from the Holderness cliffs is deposited at its tip. At present it is about 3¼ miles long and is gradually being stabilized by the tough roots of marram grass. Many migrant species of bird rest in the sanctuary at the end of the peninsula, and their comings and goings are watched from a special observatory. Centuries ago a beacon was burned here to guide shipping through the Humber estuary, but nowadays the steady beam of a lighthouse provides a more dependable warning. A road stretches for about three-quarters of the peninsula's length; the rest, except parts of the bird sanctuary, can be explored on foot.

On the main route, drive from Patrington on the A1033 and continue to Withernsea.

Spurn Head Nature Reserve attracts huge numbers of migrant birds, as well as flocks of waterfowl and waders.

WITHERNSEA, Humberside

This quiet resort offers donkey rides, a reasonable sand and shingle beach, paddling and boating pools, a playground, and various amusement arcades – in fact, many of the diversions associated with family seaside holidays. Sports facilities include bowling greens, a putting course, and an open-air swimming pool. Inland the white 127ft bulk of a disused 19th-century lighthouse rises from a street of houses, and a quirky castellated gateway survives from a pier that stood here in the Victorian heyday of seaside holidays.

Drive to the Spread Eagle (PH) in Withernsea and turn left into Hull Road. Drive to the old lighthouse and turn right on to the B1242 SP 'Roos' and 'Hornsea'. Pass through Roos and in ½ mile turn left. Continue for a further ¼ mile, then turn right and proceed to Aldbrough.

Withernsea lighthouse is now disused but still provides a focal point in this small resort.

ALDBROUGH, Humberside

About 1½ miles from this small village is a pleasant sand and shingle beach backed by small eroded cliffs. In the village itself is a 13th- to 15th-century church with a Norman arch and a sundial bearing a Saxon inscription.

Continue along a flat, winding road and pass through Mappleton to reach Hornsea.

HORNSEA, Humberside

Hornsea has become very well known through its fine pottery, which is made in Rolston Road and can be bought from a seconds shop. More can be learned about the processes and skills involved from a conducted tour, and the company has a special playground and mini-zoo for the children. The resort itself is popular with families and offers excellent sands divided from gardens and amusements by the fine Promenade. Behind the narrow streets and clustered houses of the old village is Hornsea Mere, a 2-mile lagoon formed during the ice ages. Today it is a popular boating venue with a reserve for wildfowl and a 5-mile walk round its wood and reed-fringed banks.

Skirt Hornsea Mere on the B1244 with SP 'Beverley'. Pass through Seaton and Catwick to reach Leven.

LEVEN, Humberside

Between Leven and the River Hull is a 3-mile stretch of canal built in 1802. At one end of the waterway is the Canal House, a fine 3-bay building which incorporates a grand Georgian doorway from a house at Hull. Inside the dignified village church is the shaft of a Saxon cross.

Turn left on to the A165 then after 1 mile meet a roundabout and take the 2nd exit on to the A1035 SP 'Beverley'. Pass through rather featureless countryside and cross the River Hull, and the adjacent Beverley and Barmston drain; re-enter Beverley.

FROM THE COAST TO THE MOORS

Every summer thousands of visitors flock to Scarborough and Whitby, bustling resorts with much to entertain the holidaymaker. Inland are the forest and heather-clad hills of the North Yorks Moors, where the colours are green and brown and silence is broken only by small natural sounds.

Pleasure craft throng Scarborough harbour.

Fylingdales Radar Station keeps a grim vigil on the desolate moor.

Time and war have desecrated Whitby Abbey.

SCARBOROUGH, N Yorks

An important conference centre and one of the most popular seaside resorts in Yorkshire, this charming old town overlooks two sandy bays divided by the massive bulk of a 300ft headland. In Roman times this excellent vantage point was the site of a signalling station, and the foundations of that ancient structure still exist amongst the magnificent 12th-century castle ruins (AM) that stand here today. Views from the 100-acre site, which is accessible through a 13th-century barbican, extend across the red roofs of the medieval old town to the harbour far below. Of particular note among the remains are the fine keep and three medieval chapels. During the 18th and 19th centuries the town became caught up in the fashion for seaside holidays and acquired several fine terraces of hotels and boarding houses, many of which still offer accommodation. The Natural History Museum, Art Gallery, and The Rotunda Museum are housed in notable Victorian buildings, and a museum of general interest can be visited in Woodend, the one-time holiday home of the Sitwell family. Typical resort facilities and amusements offered to the visitor include fine promenades and well-tended seafront gardens, plus a good zoo with a dolphinarium. Views can be enjoyed from pleasant clifftop walks and the 500ft eminence of nearby Oliver Hill.

Leave Scarborough with SP 'North Bay' and join the A165, then in 1 mile meet a roundabout and take the A165 to reach Burniston. Meet a junction with the A171 and turn right SP 'Whitby'. Continue to Cloughton, bear left with the A171, and drive through an afforested area to Fylingdales Moor.

FYLINGDALES MOOR AND RADAR STATION, N Yorks

The huge white domes of Fylingdales Early Warning Station seem a constant reminder of doom in the lonely desolation of the surrounding moor. At one time the area was inhabited, and the intrusive evidence of advanced technology contrasts strangely with prehistoric burial mounds and the Wade's Causeway, which is Roman.

Continue along the A171 for 8¾ miles. A detour from the main route can be made by turning left on to the B1416, driving 1¼ miles, then turning left again on to an unclassified road to reach Newton House and the start of the Falling Fosse Nature Trail. On the main route, continue along the A171 and in ¾ mile turn right on to an unclassified road SP 'Fylingthorpe' and 'Robin Hood's Bay'. Pass a viewpoint and picnic site on the right and

descend (1 in 4) through hairpin bends to reach Fylingthorpe.

FYLINGTHORPE, N Yorks

This residential area of Robin Hood's Bay boasts the fine 17th-century Old Hall, which was built by the Chomley family of Whitby Abbey.

Keep forward to Robin Hood's Bay.

ROBIN HOOD'S BAY, N Yorks

Considered one of the most picturesque villages in England, this charming collection of old houses, shops, and inns occupies a precarious cliff-top site and was once a favourite haunt of smugglers. Its steep flights of steps and narrow passages recall unlit boats at the bottom of the cliffs, and furtive movements between houses where well-disguised hiding places waited to be filled with contraband. It is difficult to establish any real connexion between the village and the folk hero after whom it is named, but it may be that the famous outlaw leader came here to escape by boat to Europe. During the last decade coastal erosion has destroyed two rows of houses, and the sea is so close that at high tide its waves lash the Bay Hotel. Superb sands are revealed at low tide.

Leave the village on the B1447 SP 'Whitby' and continue to Hawsker.

HAWSKER, N Yorks

It is thought that the well-preserved 10th-century cross shaft at Old Hall in Hawsker may mark the site of a medieval church. The intricate design of interlaced knot work and bird figures is typical of traditional Norse design.

Drive through the village, meet the A171, and turn right. Descend to Whitby.

WHITBY, N Yorks

Ruins (AM) of an abbey founded here by St Hilda in 657 can be seen above the town on the East Cliff. Close by is a huge carved cross that was erected in 1898 to commemorate Caedmon, the ancient poet whose *Song of Creation* is considered by some to mark the start of English literature. Below the abbey ruins the River Esk divides the old part of the settlement from the more recent West Cliff area, which is connected to the harbour via a rock-cut passage romantically named after the Khyber Pass. Whitby has always had a strong sea-going tradition and has been the home of many famous maritime figures, including Captain Cook. His house in Grape Street is identified by a plaque, and the stimulus that prompted his nautical career is still a persuasive element in the town's atmosphere – though the 18th-century colliers on which he worked have long since vanished. One of the finest buildings here is St Mary's Church, which stands at the top of a spectacular 199-step flight and contains superb 18th-century craftsmanship. The museum in Pannet Park illustrates fascinating episodes from the town's long history. Local craftsmen have been making ornaments and jewellery from jet, a particularly hard, shiny form of coal found in the area, for hundreds of years. One of the most unusual features of Whitby is a whalebone arch from Norway.

Leave Whitby on the A171 'Teesside' road and in 1½ miles turn left on to the A169 SP 'Pickering'. Drive through Sleights and climb on to Sleights Moor, in the North Yorks Moors National Park.

Old cottages line the hills on both sides of Whitby harbour.

GOATHLAND, N Yorks

All around this greystone moorland village are lovely walks leading past streams that suddenly plunge over rocky lips as spectacular waterfalls. Three superb examples in the immediate neighbourhood are Nelly Ayre Foss, Mallyan Spout, and Thomason Foss, and dozens of others in varying sizes can be visited by the rambler willing to venture a little farther. The village itself is well known for the Plough Stotts, a traditional group who perform sword dances in the area. A well-preserved stretch of Roman Road (AM) can be seen to the south, and the North Yorks Moors Railway is close by.

The Hole of Horcum is a vast bowl of rich grazing land.

Several restored steam locomotives run on the North Yorks Moors Railway.

NORTH YORKS MOORS NATIONAL PARK

Heather-clad moors occasionally scored by fertile valleys are the main ingredients in the startlingly open landscape of this 553-square-mile national park. To the west are the rounded heights of the Cleveland and Hambledon Hills, east the rugged beauty of the Yorkshire coast, and south the lush woodlands of the Vale of Pickering.

Continue across Sleights Moor for 3 miles. A short detour from the main route to Goathland can be made by turning right on to an unclassified road and entering the village.

NORTH YORKS MOORS RAILWAY

Steam railway enthusiasts have restored and re-opened the old British Rail link that connected Grosmont with Pickering, and in doing so have provided a superb mobile viewpoint from which 18 miles of beautiful national park countryside can be enjoyed in comfortable conditions.

On the main tour, follow the A169 over bleak moorland, with views of Fylingdales Early Warning Station, then pass the lovely Saltersgate Inn and ascend to the Hole of Horcum.

HOLE OF HORCUM, N Yorks

This vast natural hollow in the Yorkshire moorlands shelters the farms of High and Low Horcum, forming a lush oasis of pasture in the wilderness of Levisham Moor.

After 4 miles reach the Fox and Rabbit Inn, then turn left on to an unclassified road SP 'Thornton Dale'. After another 2 miles turn left SP 'Low Dalby (Forest Drive)' on to a Forestry Commission toll road. Proceed to the hamlet of Low Dalby and turn left on to the Forest Drive SP 'Bickley'.

DALBY FOREST DRIVE, N Yorks

Some 10 miles of well-surfaced roads offer the motorist a route through the beautiful woodlands of Dalby and Bickley Forests, where conifer plantations and stands of mature deciduous trees provide a vast haven for many species of wildlife. Red squirrels inhabit the conifers, the glades are full of wild flowers in spring and summer, and there is constant activity from such common woodland birds as jays, nuthatches, and the tiny goldcrest. A footpath which starts just beyond Staindale leads left to a curious formation of layered limestone known as the Bridestones. Amenities include numerous parking places, picnic sites, and forest trails, while many footpaths allow an uninhibited appreciation of the area. The Forest Drive is likely to be closed during periods of very dry weather, when the ever-present fire risk is abnormally high.

Continue along the Forest Drive to a fire tower and turn left, then drive for 2 miles to leave the Forestry Commission roads. Descend (1 in 8), and after ¾ mile meet a T-junction and turn right SP 'Scarborough'. Pass the Moorcock Inn at Langdale End and after 1 mile turn sharp right SP 'Troutsdale' and 'Snainton'. Continue along a winding road through Troutsdale; fine views can be enjoyed along the length of this valley, and there is a picnic site near a viewing spot at Cockmoor Hall (not open). Meet a T-junction in Snainton and turn left on to the A170 SP 'Scarborough'. Proceed to Brompton.

BROMPTON, N Yorks

Brompton's greystone Church of All Saints features fine stained glass.

Leave Brompton and continue along the A170 to West and East Ayton.

AYTON, WEST AND EAST, N Yorks

Situated on either side of the River Derwent, the twin villages of East and West Ayton are linked by an attractive 4-arched bridge which dates from 1775. The ruined pele tower of Ayton Castle makes a good counterpoint to the tower of East Ayton's church, on the other bank.

Immediately after crossing the Derwent to enter East Ayton turn left on to an unclassified road. In 2 miles turn right on to a road SP 'Private'. Keep forward at this junction to reach a picnic site and viewpoint. After 2 miles on the private road pass a pond on the right, then after another 1 mile meet a T-junction and turn right to re-enter Scarborough.

IN THE VALE OF YORK

Away from the gothic completeness of York's superb minster are the rolling farmlands of the Vale of York and dry limestone ridges of the Howardian Hills. Everywhere are monuments to the skills of past generations, and close by are the untamed tracts of the Yorkshire Moors and Dales.

York Minster's magnificent proportions are difficult to appreciate except from a distance.

YORK, N Yorks

Capital of a British province under the Romans in AD 71, this ancient centre is still the chief city of northern England and preserves many fascinating reminders of its historic past. The earliest surviving building is the Roman Multangular Tower, though parts of the city walls derive from the same period – particularly in the section south of Monk Bar. The walls themselves complete a 3-mile circuit round the medieval boundaries of the city and are among the finest examples of their type in Europe. Micklegate Bar, one of four main gates giving access through the defences, is traditionally the only one used by royalty. York's chief glory is its magnificent Minster, which towers over the little streets and houses of the old town. It is the largest gothic cathedral north of the Alps, and its fine windows contain more than half of all the medieval glass surviving in England. One reason for the purity of the Minster's architectural style is the speed with which it was built – between 1220 and 1470 – and the consequent absence of modifications brought about by changing ideas in church design. Many people consider the octagonal Chapter House to be the loveliest part of the overall medieval design. In 1984 the South Transept was seriously damaged by fire; fortunately it is now undergoing extensive restoration. As far as fine old churches are concerned, York probably has more than anywhere else in the country except perhaps Norwich. Holy Trinity is of 13th-century date and contains good box pews, All Saints' North Street has medieval glass and carries a beautiful 15th-century tower, and St Mary's Castlegate has a rare Saxon dedication stone. Many of the city's buildings have been standing for 500 years and more, including the lovely Guildhall (AM), the Merchant Adventurers' Hall and Chapel (open), Taylors' Hall (open), and the lovely timbered front and picturesque courtyard of William's College. The latter shows work from later periods, and the 17th-century Treasurer's House (NT) preserves good collections of painting and furniture. Elizabethan King's Manor (open), once the home of the Abbot of St Mary's Abbey, is now owned by York University. It is not surprising that a city with as rich and well-documented history as this should have as many museums as York. York's newest museum is the Jorvik Centre, where time cars take you back in time to a reconstruction of Jorvik 'a viking city'. Relics from the Roman occupation can be seen in the Yorkshire Museum, in the grounds of ruined St Mary's Abbey, and close to the 13th-century fragments of York Castle (AM) is the Castle Museum of Yorkshire life. Close by in the old Debtors' Prison are collections of dolls and militaria,

(continues)

The glorious architecture of the Minster can be glimpsed at the end of many of York's old streets and alleyways.

(continued)
and the National Steam Museum preserves great old locomotives such as the *Mallard*. St Mary's Heritage Centre, in Castlegate, uses audio-visual displays and the work of contemporary artists to describe the city's architectural development. Over all is a sense of permanence fostered by the mellow stone of a city that is more medieval than modern.

Leave York on the A1036 SP 'East Coast' and 'Malton', then in 3 miles at a roundabout take 2nd exit then 1st exit at next roundabout on to the A64 SP 'Malton'. Passing agricultural country and in 7½ miles pass the Spittle Beck Inn. In 1½ miles it is possible to make a short detour from the main route by turning right on to an unclassified road SP 'Kirkham Priory', descending over a level crossing and the River Derwent, and driving to the hamlet of Kirkham.

KIRKHAM, N Yorks

Ruined Kirkham Priory (AM) includes a beautiful 13th-century gatehouse and a lavatorium, where the monks used to wash.

On the main route, continue along the A64 and in 1 mile turn left on to an unclassified road SP 'Welburn, Castle Howard'. Pass through Welburn, meet crossroads and turn right, then drive through an arch and wall gateway to reach Castle Howard.

CASTLE HOWARD, N Yorks

One of the most spectacular houses in Britain, Castle Howard (open) dates from the 17th and 18th centuries and is considered to be the greatest achievement of the architect Vanbrugh. A central dome forms the focal point of the house and is echoed in the 1,000-acre grounds by a circular mausoleum designed by Hawksmoor. Other garden follies include the lovely Temple of the Four Winds, and the huge gatehouse is crowned by a pyramid. Among many treasures inside the house is an extensive collection of period costumes.

The square wooden tower of Raskelf Church, a most unusual feature in this part of England, contrasts pleasantly with the masonry body.

Leave Castle Howard, cross the Howardian Hills, and descend to meet a T-junction at the edge of Slingsby. It is possible to make a detour from the main route to Slingsby by driving forward at the village crossroads.

SLINGSBY, N Yorks

Misnamed and never completed, the 17th-century house known as Slingsby Castle is a picturesque ruin that adds an air of gothic mystery to the countryside round the village. It was originally started for the soldier, philosopher, and mathematician, Sir Charles Cavendish. A feature of the village itself is its maypole, the scene of great celebrations every May 1.

On the main tour, meet the aforementioned crossroads and turn left on to the B1257 SP 'Helmsley'. Continue to Hovingham.

HOVINGHAM, N Yorks

The stone cottages of this lovely little village cluster round the green under the Saxon tower of All Saints' Church and the stately presence of Hovingham Hall. The latter is an unusual building in distinctive yellow limestone, with a gatehouse that was designed as a riding school where horses could be exercised out of the rain (open by appointment only).

In Hovingham turn left on to an unclassified road SP 'Coulton' and 'Easingwold'. Drive through Hovingham High Wood and meet crossroads. Turn right SP 'Gilling' and follow a narrow road for 1½ miles. Meet a T-junction and turn right on to the B1363 to reach Gilling East.

GILLING EAST, N Yorks

It is thought that the architect Vanbrugh may have designed the west front of Gilling Castle (open), though most of the building is much too old for him to have had any hand in its construction. The keep dates from the 14th century, and a well-preserved ribbed plaster ceiling helps to make its dining room one of the finest in England. On either side of the village are the lovely Hambledon and Howardian Hills.

Return south along the B1363 to reach Brandsby.

BRANDSBY, N Yorks

Features of this harmonious hillside village include a woodcarver's shop, an 18th-century hall, and an unusual church with a stone cupola. Neat terraces of cottages complete the picture.

Continue to Stillington, in the Vale of York.

STILLINGTON, N Yorks

The 18th-century writer Laurence Sterne was vicar here for a time, and the lovely old church in which he served features a 12th-century priest's door.

VALE OF YORK, N Yorks

Numerous country lanes bordered by thick hedgerows criss-cross the fertile farmlands of the Vale of York, a large lowland expanse watered by the River Ouse and its many tributaries. Broad water meadows known as 'ings' border the rivers, providing an ideal habitat for marshland wildlife and water loving plants. Here and there large areas of heathland have survived uncultivated, providing ideal hunting grounds for nightjars and vipers.

The Devil's Arrows are a mysterious group of prehistoric standing stones near Boroughbridge.

Drive through Stillington village and pass the church. Keep forward on to an unclassified road SP 'Easingwold', then in 3½ miles meet the A19 and drive forward to enter Easingwold.

EASINGWOLD, N Yorks

An unusual bull ring can be seen in the market place of this pleasant town of red-brick houses and cobbled lanes. The local church contains an ancient parish coffin.

Meet crossroads in Easingwold and turn left on to an unclassified road to reach Raskell.

RASKELF, N Yorks

The 15th-century tower of local St Mary's church is made of wood and is said to be unique in Yorkshire. Parts of the building's main body date back to Norman times.

In Raskelf bear left then right SP 'Boroughbridge', and drive to Brafferton.

Castle Howard is a superb example of Vanbrugh's architectural genius.

BRAFFERTON, N Yorks

Brafferton Church was extensively restored in Victorian times, but still displays good examples of 15th-century workmanship.

In Brafferton village turn right and after 1 mile cross the River Swale and turn left. In 2¾ miles turn left then immediately right, then in 1 mile meet a T-junction and turn left. Continue to a roundabout and take the 1st exit on to the B6265. Cross the River Ure and enter Boroughbridge.

BOROUGHBRIDGE, N Yorks

Three large monoliths known ominously as the Devil's Arrows stand a few hundred yards to the west of Boroughbridge. The largest rises to 22½ft, and it is thought that the group may be some 3,000 years old. On the town side of a fine bridge that spans the Ure is a market place with a 250ft-deep well.

Turn left then keep left through Boroughbridge with SP 'York', and at the far end of the town branch left on to an unclassified road to reach Aldborough.

ALDBOROUGH, N Yorks

This pretty village stands on the site of *Isurium*, the northernmost town to be built without any military motives during the Roman occupation. Remains (AM) revealed through excavation include sections of a boundary wall, two tessellated pavements, and a wide variety of coins, pottery, and artefacts on display in the small site museum. In the village itself are a striking maypole and a cross that probably commemorates the Battle of Boroughbridge, which was fought here in 1322.

Drive to the battle cross and bear right. Pass the church to reach the B6265, turn left to follow the old Ribchester Roman road, and continue to Green Hammerton. Join the A59, and in 1¾ miles cross the River Nidd. Drive through low-lying country for the return to York.

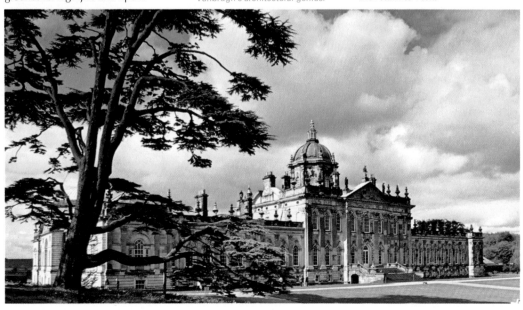

SKIPTON, N Yorks

Attractively situated on the Airedale moorlands at the eastern edge of the Craven district, Skipton is dominated by a medieval castle (open) that was restored by Lady Anne Clifford in 1658. Founded in Norman times, the building was subsequently extended and was strong enough to resist a 3-year siege before falling into the hands of Cromwell's parliamentarian army in the Civil War. The Lord Protector dismantled the castle to make sure that it could never again be manned against him, but thanks to Lady Anne its six massive towers still punctuate the skyline of the town that grew beneath its walls. Opposite the massive castle gateway is the Craven Museum, where exhibits and displays illustrate the geology and folk history of the district. An old four-storey corn mill, on a site where similar buildings have operated since the 12th century, houses the George Leatt Industrial and Folk Museum, where working waterwheels and a collection of carts and horse traps can be seen.

Leave Skipton on the A59 'Harrogate' road. A detour from the main route to the Yorkshire Dales Railway can be made by taking the B6265 from Skipton and turning left on to an unclassified road to Embsay.

YORKSHIRE DALES RAILWAY, N Yorks

This small preserved steam railway with its centre at Embsay, runs on 1¼ miles of track and has over 20 locomotives at various stages of restoration. Existing facilities for visiting enthusiasts include access to the current work, a signal box, and a personalized saloon car.

On the main tour, leave Skipton via the A59 and drive through a countryside of drystone walls and quarries to Bolton Bridge. Reach the Devonshire Arms Hotel and turn left on to the B6160 SP 'Bolton Abbey', then continue to Bolton Abbey.

THE YORKSHIRE DALES

Some of England's most impressive scenery can be seen in the rocky clefts of Airedale and Wharfedale, the superb natural amphitheatre of Malham Cove, and the breathtaking gorge of Gordale Scar. Underground are miles of water-worn tunnels, many resplendent with rock and ice formations.

Augustinian monks selected a magnificent site for their abbey at Bolton.

BOLTON ABBEY, N Yorks

Woodlands and pastures in a bend of the River Wharfe make a fittingly peaceful setting for the remains of this once-powerful 12th-century priory (open). Most of the structure lies in ruins, but the nave has served as a parish church for hundreds of years and the old gatehouse was incorporated into a mansion during the 19th century. The little river can be crossed by stepping stones or a footbridge here, and attractive riverside walks extend from the ruins to The Strid.

Continue through a wooded stretch of Wharfedale to reach The Strid and later Barden Tower.

A man-made order is brought to parts of Wharfedale by a pattern of drystone walls.

THE STRID & BARDEN TOWER, N Yorks

The modern translation of the old English word Strid is Turmoil, which is an apt description of the way in which the River Wharfe boils through a 12ft constriction of its gorge at this point. Farther north are the picturesque ruins of Barden Tower, a 12th-century structure that was restored by Lady Anne Clifford of Skipton Castle in 1659.

Reach Barden Tower and turn right on to an unclassified road SP 'Appletreewick'. Cross the river, and turn sharp right on an ascent with SP 'Hazlewood' and 'Storiths'. Continue along a gated road beneath Barden Fell, descend (1 in 5), and cross a ford. Ascend steeply (1 in 4) from the ford,

passing The Strid again, and meet the A59. Turn left and ascend a winding road on to Blubberhouses Moor. Enter a narrow rocky valley and climb to the edge of Blubberhouses, at the end of Fewston Reservoir. Cross a river bridge and turn sharp left on to an unclassified road SP 'Pateley Bridge'. Continue over high moorland, and turn left on to the B6265. Stump Cross Caverns lie to the left of the road.

STUMP CROSS CAVERNS, N Yorks

Dramatic subterranean formations of ice and eroded rock can be appreciated from a pathway that extends ¼ mile into these caverns.

Continue, with views into beautiful Upper Wharfedale, to Grassington.

GRASSINGTON, N Yorks

The lovely area in which this Upper Wharfedale village stands has been mineral deposits and has been settled since very early times. Many iron-age camps and barrows survive, and during the Roman occupation the area was extensively mined for lead ore. The village itself is a popular tourist centre with a cobbled market square reached via a picturesque medieval bridge. A National Park Interpretation Centre is based here.

Leave Grassington and follow an unclassified road SP 'Conistone' through wooded country, occasionally passing close to the River Wharfe. Reach Conistone and keep left to meet the B6160. Turn right and continue to Kilnsey Crag.

KILNSEY, N Yorks

This village is completely dwarfed by the great limestone scar of Kilnsey Crag, one of the best-known landmarks in Yorkshire.

A pleasant detour can be made from the main route by continuing along the B6160 to Kettlewell.

KETTLEWELL, N Yorks

At one time this attractive Wharfedale village was a small oasis of civilization in a great tract of forest, but nowadays the drystone-scattered expanses of the open moor extend right to its boundaries. Great Whernside rises to 2,310ft in the north-east.

On the main tour, leave Kilnsey on the B6160 and drive north. In ¾ mile branch left on to an unclassified road SP 'Arncliffe' and drive through Littondale to reach Arncliffe.

ARNCLIFFE, N Yorks

Typical greystone houses of the Dales area nestle amongst clumps of mature sycamores in this secluded Littondale community. Evidence of long occupation is apparent in a clearly-defined Celtic field system in the immediate district, and the village church stands on the site of a building dated c1100. South of Arncliffe is the dramatic mile-long cliff of Yew Cogar Scar.

In Arncliffe turn right SP 'Halton Gill' and continue through Littondale.

LITTONDALE, N Yorks
Once a medieval hunting forest, this lovely dale in the national park has avoided the depredations of the early lead miners. It retains extensive areas of wild woodland, and its farmlands show signs of having been cultivated since early times.

Reach Halton Gill and turn left on to a gated unclassified road. Continue, following SP 'Stainforth' and 'Settle', and ascend (1 in 5) to a road summit of over 1,400ft, with views of Pen-y-Ghent to the right.

The classic limestone 'pavement' above Malham Cove stretches away to the moors.

MALHAM COVE & GORDALE SCAR, N Yorks
The huge natural amphitheatre of Malham Cove, fringed by the sheer grey wall of a spectacular 240ft cliff, is one of the finest sights anywhere in the generally remarkable scenery of the national park. It is the source of *(continues)*

the River Aire and forms part of a 22-mile fault that resulted from the intolerable stresses imposed by enormous glaciers during the ice ages. An energetic climb leads to the moorland above and Malham Tarn. Gordale Scar, a precipitous, winding gorge filled with the sound of waterfalls and dashing cascades, can be reached from the cove via a 1½-mile footpath.

MALHAM, N Yorks
In the height of the summer season this little stone village is inundated by visitors who flock to the area for its magnificent scenery. Information about the Malham district is available from the Yorkshire Dales National Park Interpretation Centre, which is based in the village.

THE PENNINE WAY
From its southern extremity in Derbyshire, this 250-mile footpath follows the mountainous spine of England and passes through Malham before crossing Pen-y-Ghent on its way to Kirk Yetholme in Scotland. Prospective walkers should realize that this is a fairly rugged route, particularly in its northern sections, and can be positively hazardous in bad weather.

Leave Malham with SP 'Skipton' and continue to Kirkby Malham.

KIRKBY MALHAM, N Yorks
Close to the local 17th-century vicarage is the charming village church, containing a 12th-century font and family box pews of the Georgian period.

Drive through the village to Airton.

AIRTON, N Yorks
Situated in Upper Airedale, this charming village is on the route of the Pennine Way and boasts several good 17th-century buildings. The most notable are the Manor House, the Friend's Meeting House, and the Post Office.

Leave Airton, continue for ¾ mile, and turn left. Drive through the grounds of Eshton Hall (not open) and turn right to reach Gargrave.

GARGRAVE, N Yorks
Although Gargrave's parish church is mostly Victorian, it retains a 16th-century tower and fragments of several Saxon crosses.

Meet the A65 in Gargrave and turn left to cross the Leeds and Liverpool Canal.

LEEDS & LIVERPOOL CANAL
Wonderful scenery that can only be guessed at by the road-bound tourist is revealed to anybody who takes the trouble to hire a boat on this 127-mile canal. It is one of the longest waterways in Britain, rising to 500ft above sea level as it crosses the high ridge of the Pennine Chain.

Continue along the A65 to re-enter Skipton.

Gordale Scar is an impressive 240ft gorge where the sound of water is ever present.

PEN-Y-GHENT, N Yorks
Potholing enthusiasts come here to dare the uncertainties of aptly-named Hell Pot and Hunt Pot, two entrances to the cave system that riddles Pen-y-Ghent. Above ground, this 2,273ft summit, one of the famous Three Peaks, affords wide views that extend more than 40 miles to Helvellyn in clear weather.

Continue along the gated road and turn left on to the 'Malham' road. Ascend (1 in 5) to cross wild moorland, and in 3 miles bear right to meet crossroads. Drive forward on the gated 'Grassington' road to reach the Malham Tarn carpark.

MALHAM TARN, N Yorks
All around the isolated waters of Malham Tarn (NT) are heathery moorlands and unusual raised bogs. The tarn itself is the habitat of many species of aquatic wildlife, and the serious naturalist can familiarize himself with the area at the Field Centre in Malham Tarn House, on the northern shore. Above the field centre are the high white cliffs of Highfolds Scar and a natural limestone pavement.

Leave the Malham Tarn carpark and descend steeply to pass Malham Cove and Gordale Scar.

RIPON, N Yorks

Popularly known as the Gateway to the Dales, this attractive city stands at the meeting of the Rivers Ure, Skell, and Laver and boasts a small but impressive cathedral. The main features of this lovely 12th-century building include a Saxon crypt that may be the earliest Christian survival in England, a fine early-English west front, and a beautiful 15th-century screen. Excellent examples of local woodcarving are the finely worked misericords and curious Elephant and Castle bench. Every night Ripon's market square is the scene of a 1,000-year-old custom, when the town Hornblower or Wakeman strides out in his tricorn hat and sounds his ancient horn at each corner of a huge 18th-century obelisk. Years ago this sound indicated that the Wakeman had begun his night watch over the town, and that the townspeople could sleep secure in their beds. The half-timbered Wakeman's house, later used by the mayor, dates from the 13th century and now contains a museum. An interesting Prison and Police museum is housed in the old prison building dating from 1686.

Before Ripon is left on the main tour route, a short detour can be made to Newby Hall: follow the B6265 SP 'Boroughbridge' to pass Ripon Racecourse and cross the River Ure, then turn right on to an unclassified road and in $\frac{1}{4}$ mile turn right again to reach Newby Hall.

NEWBY HALL, N Yorks

Some of Robert Adam's finest work can be seen in his additions to this splendid Queen Anne House (open), which contains superb Gobelin tapestries and an important collection of classical sculpture. The beautiful grounds run down to the River Ure and contain a miniature railway.

To leave Ripon on the main tour follow SP 'Pateley Bridge B6265'. In $2\frac{1}{4}$ miles reach Studley Royal and Studley Royal Park.

STUDLEY ROYAL, N Yorks

The fine house that once graced this lovely park burned down in 1945, and the present owner lives in a converted stable block that dates from the 18th century. Attractive estate cottages cluster round a 19th-century church that is considered the ecclesiastical masterpiece of architect William Burges and has a very rich interior. The park (open), landscaped in the 18th century, features many of the conceits of the period, including a temple folly and various statues. Its lakes and woodland combine in a sylvan beauty which is enhanced by grazing herds of deer and livestock, and at one point adjoins the magnificent ruins of Fountains Abbey.

Leave Studley Royal on the B6265 and after $\frac{3}{4}$ mile turn left on to an unclassified road to reach the impressive ruins of Fountains Abbey.

ALONG THE EDGE OF THE DALES

Between York and the deep Dales country is a gentler area of farmland. Here the landscape is dotted with curiously-weathered rocks rising from deep vegetation, peaceful reservoirs, and ancient ruins beside enchanting rivers. A foretaste of the Dales is given in How Stean Gorge.

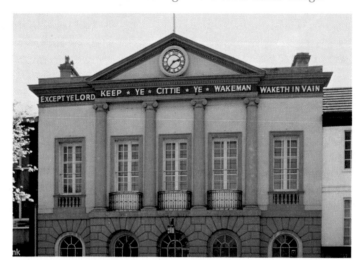

FOUNTAINS ABBEY, N Yorks

Generally considered to be the finest in England, the remarkably well-preserved ruins of this 12th- to 15th-century Cistercian abbey (NT) are part of the Studley Royal estate (open) and clearly demonstrate the layout of a Norman and medieval monastic foundation. Particularly notable are the nave, tower, and lay-brothers' quarters. Opposite the ruins is Fountains Hall, which was built with stone taken from the abbey in the 17th century.

Ripon's Town Hall reminds the citizens of the Wakeman's traditional role.

Return to the B6265 and turn left, drive through wooded countryside, and emerge on to Pateley Moor for views over Nidderdale. A short detour from the main route to Brimham Rocks can be made by driving to the road summit on the moor and turning left.

Fountains Abbey was once the wealthiest Cistercian house in England.

BRIMHAM ROCKS, N Yorks

Thousands of years of wind and rain have sculpted the millstone grit of this group of rocks into a variety of weird and wonderful shapes. The surrounding moorland (NT) offers excellent views and is a popular site for picnics.

On the main tour, continue along the B6265 and later turn right to descend to Pateley Bridge.

PATELEY BRIDGE, N Yorks

Since ancient times this pleasant market town has been a focus for the everyday life of Nidderdale, but nowadays its steep main street is busy as much with tourists as with local traffic. The picturesque ruins of Old St Mary's Church occupy a lofty hillside site, and the Nidderdale Museum displays over 3,000 items relating to life in the Yorkshire Dales. Of particular note are the Victorian Room and a replica cobbler's shop. West of the town are the fascinating Stump Cross Caverns – more than $\frac{1}{4}$ mile of natural passages and caves featuring many strange rock formations (open).

Leave Pateley Bridge and cross the River Nidd, then take the next turning on the right SP 'Ramsgill' to join an unclassified road. Drive for 1 mile to reach Foster Beck Flax Mill.

FOSTER BECK FLAX MILL, N Yorks

Industrial archaeology enthusiasts will find this well-restored flax mill of considerable interest. Now a restaurant, it is built of local stone and features a huge 17th-century water wheel that is the second largest in the country.

Drive alongside Gouthwaite Reservoir and continue to Ramsgill and Lofthouse, at the head of Nidderdale.

NIDDERDALE, N Yorks

Part of the lovely valley of the River Nidd, Nidderdale is rich in mineral deposits and has been mined for lead and iron for many centuries. Its stone has also been in great demand for building, and the landscape is pitted with the overgrown remains of worked-out quarries. All along the river, from its high source in the rugged fell country of Great Whernside to the lush lower parts of its valley, the scenery offers plenty of incentives for the motorist to leave his car and explore on foot.

The huge water wheel at Foster Beck flax mill

LOFTHOUSE AND HOW STEAN GORGE, N Yorks

The pretty Upper Nidderdale village of Lofthouse is a good centre from which to explore the beautiful How Stean Gorge, a 70ft-deep cleft accessible by footpaths that thread their way along its rocky sides and over little bridges. The largest of two interesting caves here is Elgin's Hole, which penetrates nearly a mile into the roots of Middlesmoor Hill.

Return alongside Gouthwaite Reservoir to reach the B6265 and turn left to re-enter Pateley Bridge. Leave the town on the B6165 SP 'Harrogate' to reach Summer Bridge, then turn right on to the B6451 'Otley' road. Follow a long climb past Menwith Hill Wireless Station and turn right on to the A59 'Skipton' road, then proceed to Blubberhouses, at the north-west end of Fewston Reservoir. Drive to the village church, turn left on to the unclassified 'Timble' road, then take the next turning left SP 'Fewston'. Continue through pine forests, cross a dam separating Fewston and Swinsty Reservoirs, and continue to Fewston.

FEWSTON, W Yorks

This charming village faces across Fewston Reservoir to the historic lines of a 16th-century hall (not open). The lovely village church dates from the 17th century.

Keep right through Fewston and cross part of Swinsty Reservoir, then meet the B6451 'Otley' road and turn right to cross Sandwith Moor. Follow a long descent to Lindley Wood Reservoir and enter Otley.

OTLEY, W Yorks

Although largely dominated by modern industry, this old market town on the River Wharfe retains several good buildings as reminders of its long history. Among these are old inns and a fine cruciform church containing fragments of Saxon crosses and a good Georgian pulpit. A curious memorial in the churchyard commemorates the men who lost their lives while working on the Bramhope railway tunnel between 1845 and 1849. Close to the town are the fine Elizabethan halls of Farnley, where the artist Turner was a visitor, and Western. Above the town is the 925ft summit of Otley Chevin, from which panoramic views over the lovely countryside of Lower Wharfedale can be enjoyed.

Leave Otley on the A659 'Tadcaster' road and follow the River Wharfe to reach Pool. Turn left on to the A658 SP 'Harrogate', then cross the river and turn left again on to the B6161 to reach Leathley.

LEATHLEY, N Yorks

Outside the Norman and later church in Leathley are the old village stocks and a mounting block. The local almshouses and hall date from the 18th century.

In Leathley turn right on to the unclassified 'Stainburn' road and follow SP 'Rigton' to reach lofty Almscliff Crag.

ALMSCLIFF CRAG, N Yorks

This high crag affords superb views and has been the training ground for some of Britain's best-known rock climbers. The climbing faces should not be attempted without proper experience and equipment.

Continue to North Rigton and turn left, then right, to meet a junction with the A658. Turn left SP 'Harrogate' and in 1¾ miles turn left again on to the A61 to reach Harrogate.

HARROGATE, N Yorks

One of the chief towns in Yorkshire's old West Riding, Harrogate achieved early fame as a spa resort and nowadays is an important conference centre. Its mineral springs were discovered in the 16th century, and the Royal Pump Room was built as the country's first public baths in 1842. From that time onwards the town's popularity steadily increased, resulting in a wealth of dignified stone buildings and beautiful gardens that have made it known as the Floral Resort of England. The Valley Gardens are particularly notable, and the Harlow Car Gardens contain 60 acres of ornamental and woodland gardens (open). Some 200 acres of commonland known as The Stray, a popular place for walking and picnics, borders the southern boundary of the town. An interesting museum of local history, Victoriana, and costumes is housed in the 19th-century Pump Room.

Beautiful gardens surround the elegant 18th-century mansion of Newby Hall.

Leave Harrogate on the A61 SP 'Ripon' and drive to Killinghall. Continue for 1 mile beyond that village, cross the River Nidd, and meet a roundabout. Take the first exit on to an unclassified road and enter Ripley.

RIPLEY, N Yorks

Much of this attractive village was rebuilt during the 19th century, but it is largely unspoilt and retains an ancient market cross and stocks in its cobbled square. Ripley Castle (open), home of the Ingilby family since 1350, shows workmanship of mainly 16th- and 18th-century date and stands in beautiful grounds landscaped by Capability Brown. Its gatehouse is a fine building of c1450, and one of its floors was made from the timber of a British man-of-war. Oliver Cromwell stayed at the house on the eve of the Battle of Marston Moor in 1644, and armour from the opposing Royalist army is on view. Notable tombs and memorial brasses can be seen in the village church, and the churchyard features a curious weeping cross with eight niches in which sinners could kneel and repent.

Drive through Ripley, meet a roundabout, and take the 2nd exit to rejoin the A61. Return through undulating countryside to Ripon.

'Capability' Brown landscaped the grounds of Ripley Castle.

RICHMOND, N Yorks

Dramatically situated overlooking the River Swale, this attractive and historic town makes an excellent base from which to explore the lovely countryside of Swaledale. The dominant feature of the town is its massive Norman castle (AM), one of the earliest in Britain with 11th-century curtain walls round a splendid keep. In the shadow of its mighty presence are streets of lovely old buildings, all illustrative of important phases in Richmond's past. The cobbled Market Place is one of the largest in the country and is approached along little alleyways known as wynds. Greyfriars Tower is the remnant of an abbey that was founded here many centuries ago, and facing the Market Place is one of the strangest churches in England. Dedicated to the Holy Trinity, its main body and medieval tower are divided from each other by shops and offices actually built into its main structure. Other buildings in this area include several handsome Georgian and Victorian houses. The most outstanding Georgian building in the town is the Theatre Royal (open) of 1788, beautifully restored and the oldest theatre in the country to have survived in its original condition. A Green Howards' Museum displays the colourful and fascinating history of that regiment. Many fine walks can be enjoyed in and around Richmond, but one of the closest and best is along the banks of the Swale to spacious parklands at Lowenthwaite Bridge.

Leave Richmond on the A6108 SP 'Scotch Corner' at roundabout take 1st exit B6274 for Gilling West. Ascend to high ground, turn left on to the A66 'Brough' road, and continue along a pleasant road to Greta Bridge, on the Rivers Greta and Tees, with views across moors and valleys.

GRETA BRIDGE, Durham

Among the many artists and writers who have recognized and recorded the beauty of this charming little hamlet are Dickens, Scott, and Turner. Just to the north is the junction of the Greta with the Tees, and south-west of Greta Bridge the river runs through the lovely woodland of Brignall Banks. Features of the hamlet itself include a picturesque river bridge dating from the 18th century, and the Morrit Arms public house, whose site was once occupied by a Roman fort.

Continue along the A66 'Brough' road for ¼ mile and turn right on to an unclassified road SP 'Barnard Castle'. In 1¼ miles are views ahead of Egglestone Abbey.

EGGLESTONE ABBEY, Durham

The waters of the River Tees add an extra dimension to the picturesque quality of these lovely remains (AM).

Turn right and cross the River Tees to reach the Bowes Museum.

THE NORTHERN DALES

In the northern part of the Yorkshire Dales national park are the great ice-scoured valleys of Wharfedale and Swaledale, carved out to their present size by huge glaciers that flowed across the Pennines over a million years ago. On the moors above are greystone villages and steep, sheep-cropped slopes.

BOWES MUSEUM, Durham

Built in the style of a French château, the building that houses this museum is an architectural surprise to eyes that have come to expect the solid little stone houses of the area. Inside is one of the finest art collections in Britain, featuring fine European paintings, furniture, porcelain, tapestries, jewellery, and dolls.

Continue to Barnard Castle.

BARNARD CASTLE, Durham

Ancient houses and several inns line the main street of this enchanting town, which has grown up round the walls of its ruined medieval castle (AM) and is a busy market centre for its area. See also tour 89.

Leave Barnard Castle with the A67 SP 'Brough, Bowes', re-cross the River Tees, and turn left on to the B6277 SP 'Scotch Corner'. Drive through woodland to meet the A66, turn right, and in ¼ mile turn left on to an unclassified road SP 'Reeth'. A short detour can be made from the main route to Bowes Castle by continuing along the A66.

Below the huge bulk of Richmond's 11th-century castle are picturesque streets displaying an attractive mixture of architectural styles. The abundance of Georgian design is particularly noticeable.

BOWES CASTLE, Durham

Close to the ruined keep of this Norman castle (AM) are the military remains of the Roman fort of *Lavatrae* (AM), which preceded it.

On the main tour, continue along an unclassified moorland road, with occasional steep hills (1 in 4), and drive through the pines of Stang Forest before climbing to a road summit of 1,677ft. Breathtaking views extend into lonely Arkengarthdale, in the vast and very beautiful Yorkshire Dales National Park.

YORKSHIRE DALES NATIONAL PARK

The boundaries of this national park encompass nearly 700 square miles of high dells scored by literally dozens of lovely river valleys that have collectively come to be known as the Yorkshire Dales. Many great dales exist in the region, but Wharfedale and Airedale are probably the most famous. The

desolate rocky scenery in the high part of the first mentioned gradually softens towards its lower reaches, and Airdale opens out into spectacular limestone scenery as it drops towards the village of Malham. In the south are the Three Peaks, well known for their dangerous potholes, while the length of the park is threaded by the Pennine Way long-distance footpath. Movement and sound is brought to the region by delightful waterfalls and lakes fed by rapid streams that rise in the rocky countryside of the high fells. This is one of the many interesting dales tours.

ARKENGARTHDALE, N Yorks

Lead mining was carried on in this lovely valley from the 13th to 19th centuries, and traces can be seen today. The dale itself is a lovely valley that follows the course of the Arkle Beck to impressive Swaledale in the south-east.

Cross Arkle Beck and drive along Arkengarthdale, passing through Langthwaite to reach Reeth.

REETH, N Yorks

During the 19th century this one-time market town became a busy centre of the lead-mining industry of nearby Arkengarthdale. Nowadays it is a peaceful village charmingly grouped round its large green, within easy reach of some of the wildest country in the national park.

In Reeth turn left on to the B6270 'Richmond' road. Continue through pleasant countryside to Grinton.

GRINTON, N Yorks

Grinton Church is a splendid building that has come to be known as the Cathedral of the Dales. It was founded in Norman times and contains an ancient font that is probably its original. Other features include beautiful screenwork and a Jacobean pulpit.

Gradually descend along Swaledale, between moorland heights that rise steeply to over 1,400ft from the river.

SWALEDALE, N Yorks

Among the many relics of 18th- and 19th-century lead mining that still litter this wild and deep valley are remains of some of the 20 smelt mills that were used to process the ore. The valley itself is a deep cleft that runs west from Richmond, and is connected to Wensleydale via the bleak Buttertubs Pass.

Enter woodland and meet the A6108: turn right and follow SP 'Leyburn' to reach Downholme.

DOWNHOLME, N Yorks

This tiny village stands high above the River Swale and has an attractive church that features Norman workmanship.

Proceed along a winding moorland road, passing through Bellerby to reach Leyburn.

This 16th-century porcelain dish is one of many treasures in the Bowes Museum.

Arkengarthdale is one of Yorkshire's more secluded dales.

LEYBURN, N Yorks

The sloping market place in this old town is an appropriate example of the switchback landscape of the local countryside. Its Wensleydale position, above the River Ure, makes it an ideal touring base. Within easy walking distance of the town centre is a 2-mile limestone scar known as The Shawl, which affords excellent views into Wensleydale.

An exquisite setting adds to the enchantment of ruined Jervaulx Abbey, once a powerful monastic centre.

WENSLEYDALE, N Yorks

Dairy herds from the many farms scattered along the length of this fertile valley convert the freshness of its lush pastures into rich milk from which the distinctive Wensleydale cheese is made. The villages of the dale are generally small and without exception charming. Here and there its pastoral solitude is emphasized by the sound of falling water.

To leave Leyburn follow SP 'Middleham' to the end of the town and turn right on to the A6108. Descend and cross the River Ure via an unusual bridge to reach the village of Middleham.

MIDDLEHAM, N Yorks

Once the chief town of Wensleydale, this scenic village is now an important horse breeding and training centre and a good touring base. Its impressive ruined castle (AM) was the seat of the powerful Neville family, who controlled much of the area from the massive keep that still stands at its full height behind well-preserved 13th-century curtain walls. Close by is the curious Swine Cross.

Continue along the A6108 'Masham' road, with moorland to the right and gentle riverside pastures to the left. Continue to East Witton.

EAST WITTON, N Yorks

Most of the houses in this compact village are contained in two main rows facing two 19th-century churches and an attractive 17th-century bridge.

A detour can be made from the main route to Braithwaite Hall by turning right in East Witton and driving in partly-wooded country for 2 miles.

BRAITHWAITE HALL, N Yorks

Now in use as a farm, this fine 17th-century house (NT) stands in attractive pastoral countryside and is open by appointment. Near by a large hillfort occupies a 2½-acre site.

On the main tour, continue along the A6108 to reach Jervaulx Abbey.

JERVAULX ABBEY, N Yorks

Cistercian monks chose this beautiful riverside site as a fitting setting for their abbey in the 12th century. Although it was destroyed in the 15th century, enough remains to show today's visitors the exquisite proportions of their achievement. Particularly notable are the remains of the monks' dormitory, which features a hall and beautiful lancet windows of the period.

Continue along the A6108 and pass the Ellington Firth Picnic Site before entering Masham.

MASHAM, N Yorks

Masham's former importance as a market town can be judged from the huge square which is dominated by a Market Cross. In the churchyard of St Mary's are important remains of a Saxon cross, and the mainly-Norman church carries a beautiful 15th-century spire.

Leave Masham on the A6108 'Ripon' road. Cross the river, then immediately turn left on to the unclassified 'Bedale' road. Follow the river and in 1 mile turn right, then continue for ¾ mile and turn left on to the B6268. Continue to Bedale.

BEDALE, N Yorks

This mainly Georgian town features an old stepped market cross in the main street, and an unusual church whose first floor is reached by a stair guarded by a portcullis. These elaborate precautions were taken against the very real possibility of Scottish raids. Opposite the church is Georgian Bedale Hall (open), a fine house with a museum and a complete ballroom wing.

Continue along the A684 'Northallerton' road and later turn right, following SP 'Scotch Corner' to join the A1. Continue on a fast section of dual carriageway on the Great North Road. After 5 miles bear left, join the A6136 to reach Catterick.

CATTERICK, N Yorks

Known mainly for the military training area on its borders, this delightful little grey-stone village has a good church of c1500. Inside the church are two 15th-century brasses.

Drive through Catterick to Catterick Bridge, on the Swale.

CATTERICK BRIDGE, N Yorks

Most people come here to watch horse racing on the famous local course, but the lovely little local bridge that spans the Swale dates from 1422 and is worth attention. The local scenery is superb.

Turn right and cross the River Swale, then turn left SP 'Richmond' and meet the B6271. On the left are the river and Easby Abbey.

EASBY ABBEY, N Yorks

Picturesque ruins of an abbey founded in 1155 grace the beautiful surroundings of this Swaleside site. The remains (AM) are considerable.

Continue along the B6271 for the return to Richmond.

SOUTHPORT, Merseyside

Particularly well known for its beautifully laid out gardens, this attractive and elegant resort is also noted for its wide range of sporting facilities. It is the home of the Royal Birkdale Golf Club, which has been the venue for Ryder Cup competitions, and is host to county cricket matches, horse jumping trials, and lawn tennis matches. The annual flower show is also a popular event. Amenities for holiday-makers include 6 miles of excellent sands, the largest pier in England, a model village, and boat hire on the 91-acre Marine Lake. The Victorian heyday of seaside holidays is recalled by old salt-water swimming baths and a room of the Botanic Gardens Museum. An interesting collection of fine buildings and shops can be found in Lord Street, which is considered one of the finest thoroughfares in the north of England. Churches in Southport include St Cuthbert's, which displays fine woodwork and a clock of 1739, and a curious red and yellow building in the suburb of Crossens. The latter building shares its churchyard with a very ornate neo-Norman mausoleum. The expanding Steam Transport Museum boasts a fine collection of locomotives, buses, traction engines, and various commercial vehicles. It is planned to become the largest centre of its type in the north west of England, and will be a valuable aid to the understanding of industrial archaeology in transport.

Leave Southport on the A565 SP 'Preston', passing through Crossens. After 3 miles turn right on to the B5246 SP 'Rufford'. Continue through Mere Brow, Holmeswood, and Rufford, and meet the A59 SP 'Preston'. Turn left, and after ¼ mile reach the entrance to Rufford Old Hall on the right.

Unusual 17th-century windows at Astley Hall dominate the exterior.

TO THE WEST PENNINES

Between the elegant seaside resort of Southport and the wild western slopes of the Pennines is the Lancashire Plain, an area of farm and parkland where much of the county's folk history is preserved in picturesque villages, great houses in fine grounds, and fascinating small town museums.

The village cross guards a picturesque approach to St Michael's Church, Croston.

RUFFORD OLD HALL, Lancs

This superb timber-framed Tudor building (NT) stands in 14½ acres of beautiful grounds and is one of the finest examples surviving in England today. Built by the Hesketh family in the 15th century, it was slightly extended during Victorian times but has not been spoilt by 19th-century over restoration. The exterior is a startling combination of decorative black timbers infilled with brilliant white plaster, and the great hall carries an extremely ornate hammerbeam roof. Inside the house is a rare 15th-century screen, and one of the wings contains the Philip Ashcroft Museum of folk crafts and antiquities.

Leave Rufford Old Hall and continue along the A59 for 1 mile, then turn right on to the A581 'Chorley' road. Continue along the A581 to the Leeds and Liverpool Canal.

LEEDS AND LIVERPOOL CANAL, Lancs

As it crosses the rugged Pennine Chain this 127-mile waterway between two of northern England's major cities reaches an amazing 500ft above sea level. The canal took 40 years to build and has many features of interest to naturalists and industrial archaeologists.

Proceed along the A581, crossing the River Douglas, and later turn left over a bridge to reach Croston.

CROSTON, Lancs

Picturesque countryside following the twisting course of the River Yarrow makes a fine setting for this tiny village. Among its most notable buildings are 17th-century almshouses and a 15th-century church containing a curious memorial brass.

From Croston, turn right and in ¼ mile meet a war memorial. Turn left here and in 1 mile meet a T-junction. Turn right and continue along the A581 for 3½ miles. Cross the M6, then meet the A49 and turn left. Turn right on to the A581. Drive for a short distance to reach Astley Hall on the left.

ASTLEY HALL, Lancs

Charmingly set in nearly 100 acres of wood and parkland, this fine 16th-century and later house (open) has a drawing room with lovely tapestries depicting scenes from the legend of the Golden Fleece. Throughout the house are fine collections of furnishings, pottery and paintings, and special exhibitions are frequently mounted in its rooms.

Leave Astley Hall and proceed along the A581 into Chorley.

CHORLEY, Lancs

Industry is this old textile centre's way of life. It was once known for cotton weaving and calico printing, but in recent years these traditional concerns have been largely replaced by a variety of modern enterprises. The town stands at the edge of farming country close to the foot of the Pennines. The area is dominated by the imposing height of 682ft Healey Nab which rises to the east.

Meet traffic signals in Chorley and turn left on to the A6 SP 'Preston'. In 1 mile cross a railway bridge, meet a roundabout, and take the 2nd exit on to the A674 SP 'M61' and 'Blackburn'. Continue, with Healey Nab rising to the right, and drive through Higher Wheelton. In 2 miles meet a roundabout; a detour from the main route can be taken here by following the 1st exit on to the A675 to reach Hoghton Tower.

HOGHTON TOWER, Lancs

Ancestral home of what is claimed to be the oldest baronetcy in England, this fine 16th-century mansion occasionally opens its state rooms, ballroom, Tudor wellhouse, and dungeon to the public. The gardens can also be visited at certain times. In 1617 King James I stayed here, and is said to have been so taken with a loin of beef prepared by the house kitchen that he drew his sword and knighted it, ever since which that particular cut has been sirloin – a charming, if dubious, tale.

On the main tour, take the 2nd exit from the roundabout and continue for ½ mile to a T-junction. Turn right on to A6061 to Fensicowles, then meet the A6062 and turn right SP 'Darwen'. In ¼ mile drive under a railway bridge and immediately turn right on to an unclassified road, then turn left. Continue for 1 mile to the Black Bull (PH), meet crossroads, and drive forward. In 1 mile meet the A666 and drive forward on to the B6231 SP 'Accrington'. In ¼ mile pass a railway bridge and ascend to Guide, then meet crossroads by the King Edward VII (PH). Turn right on to the B6232 SP 'Bury', then keep left and after 2 miles reach the Grey Mare Inn; turn right on to an unclassified road SP 'Edgworth'. Drive to Edgworth, meet crossroads, and continue forward to reach Turton Bottoms. Meet a T-junction with the main road and turn sharp right on to the B6391 SP 'Darwen'. Turton Tower stands to the left.

180

BELMONT, Lancs

Belmont Church is a good example of 19th-century architecture that has been built to serve rather than impress. Its main feature is an attractive 6-light window.

At Belmont meet a T-junction and turn right on to the A675. Take the next turning left on to an unclassified road SP 'Rivington', and drive through open moorland with views of 1,498ft Winter Hill on the left. Descend to a T-junction and turn right, then meet another T-junction and turn left to reach Rivington.

RIVINGTON AND ANGLEZARKE RESERVOIRS, Lancs

These broad sheets of water add an extra dimension of beauty to the somewhat severe moorland countryside around them. They were built in the 19th century to supply Liverpool with water, and have naturalized into perfect habitats for many types of wildlife.

Leave Rivington and drive forward SP 'Adlington', crossing the Rivington Reservoir. Meet a T-junction, turn left SP 'Horwich', and in ¾ mile meet a junction with the A673. Turn right on to the A673 and take the next turning left on to an unclassified road SP 'Blackrod'. In 1 mile meet the A6, drive forward, and in ½ mile turn right. Continue for 1 mile, meet a T-junction with the B5239, and drive forward SP 'Standish'. In 1½ miles meet a T-junction and turn right on to the A5106, then in 200 yards turn left on to the B5239 and continue to the town of Standish.

STANDISH, Gt Manchester

This colliery town stands on the line of a Roman road and features a good church that was rebuilt in the 16th century. Inside the building, particularly in the roof, are good examples of woodwork. The old village stocks are preserved on the steps of a modern town cross.

Meet traffic signals in Standish and drive forward on to the A5209. In 1¼ miles turn right to follow SP 'M6', then meet a roundabout and take the 2nd exit to cross the M6 motorway. Continue to Parbold.

PARBOLD, Lancs

Parbold Hall is a splendid stone-built Georgian house (not open) with a Venetian-style doorway. Excellent views of the surrounding countryside can be enjoyed from the summit of Parbold Hill, which is crowned by the impressive 19th-century building of Christ Church.

Leave Parbold and cross the Leeds and Liverpool Canal, then the River Douglas, to reach Newburgh. Continue to Burscough.

BURSCOUGH, Lancs

Slight remains of a priory lie to the south-west of Burscough, which has a Victorian church with four attractive pinnacled buttresses.

From Burscough, join the A59 SP 'Southport' and in ¾ mile turn right on to the B5242. Continue through Bescar, meet traffic signals, and turn right on to the A570 to reach Scarisbrick and its hall.

SCARISBRICK, Lancs

Designed by the architect Pugin in 1837, ornate Scarisbrick Hall (open on application) is an excellent example of the opulence favoured in the Victorian period. It is gothic in style and was the architect's first major work, taking 4 years to complete. The 150 rooms of the house are now occupied by a school.

Leave Scarisbrick and continue along the A570 for the return to Southport.

Turton Tower features ornate 19th-century timbering.

TURTON TOWER, Lancs

The core of this L-shaped building (open) is a 15th-century pele tower, a type of fortified dwelling that was once common in the north of England. Two wings were added in the 16th century, and the house now contains fine collections of paintings and furnishings, plus a fascinating local history museum.

Good views of Turton and Entwistle Reservoirs can be enjoyed from the Turton to Belmont road.

Continue north along the B6391 with views of the Turton and Entwistle Reservoirs on the right. In 1 mile meet a T-junction and turn left on to the A666 SP 'Bolton'. In ½ mile turn right on to an unclassified road SP 'Belmont', then take the next turning right and descend with views of Delph Reservoir to the left and Belmont Reservoir to the right. After 1 mile drive over crossroads to reach Belmont.

RIVINGTON, Lancs

Rivington Pike rises to a 1,190ft summit above this attractive little moorland village. It is crowned by an 18th-century stone tower and commands excellent views over miles of countryside. In the village itself is a good church housing a fine screen and a 16th-century pulpit. Rivington Hall, which stands in 400-acre Lever Park, was rebuilt in 1744 and contains a general interest museum. Close to the village are the Rivington and Anglezarke Reservoirs.

BEACHES AND THE BOWLAND FELLS

Blackpool is more than the most popular holiday resort in the north; it is also an ideal place from which to tour the rolling, windmill-dotted landscape of the Fylde, its austere little villages, and the high wild moors of the Forest of Bowland.

The packhorse bridge near Hurst Green.

Blackpool's Tower dominates the crowded beach.

BLACKPOOL, Lancs

Every summer Lancashire shuts down its industry for the annual wake, or holiday, and for a brief period Blackpool's resident population of about 152,000 is swelled by an influx of 8 million trippers eager to be entertained. Until the seaside-holiday vogue of the 18th century the town was little more than a cluster of cottages, but it has developed from these small beginnings to become one of the premier resorts in Great Britain. Everything is geared up to the boisterous, fun-fair atmosphere of high summer, and the natural asset of a beautiful sandy beach is supplemented by three fine piers and the splendid dominance of the famous 519ft tower. In the latter are a ballroom that is often the scene of dance festivals and beauty contests, undersea world, amusements, and various facilities for children. The traditional heart of the 7-mile Promenade is the famous Golden Mile, a bewildering collection of novelty shops, ice-cream vendors, and seafood stalls. Blackpool Zoo is one of the most modern in Britain, featuring a unique free-flight bird hall. Some of the other animal enclosures can be visited by miniature railway, and the entire complex is laid out to the best advantage of both visitors and animals. The East Drive area is well known for its richly-planted gardens, and the town's many other parks and public open spaces are green islands of peace amongst the bustle and noise of streets packed with tourist and local traffic. Sporting events held here every year include county cricket, league football, and various other championships associated with the amenities available.

Leave Blackpool and follow the A584 SP 'Lytham St Anne's' along the coast to reach Lytham St Anne's.

LYTHAM ST ANNE'S, Lancs

No less than four championship courses make this popular seaside resort a mecca for golfing enthusiasts. Sand yachting and safe bathing are offered by 6 miles of sandy beach, and the British Sand Yachting Championships are held here every May. The residential part of the resort is laid out on garden-city lines, with many beautiful parks and gardens between streets of pleasant houses. Ashton Gardens and Lowther Gardens are of particular note, and the fascinating Alpine Gardens offer fine walks in landscaped surroundings where little bridges span water and cool hollows. In and between these gardens are many good half-timbered buildings, including the attractive 18th-century structure of Lytham Hall.

Drive through the town to Lytham.

LYTHAM, Lancs

Lytham and St Anne's are incorporated in the borough of Lytham St Anne's, but this is where the similarity stops. The former is a quiet residential town with few of the holiday amusements and entertainments offered by the St Anne's area. A white windmill on picturesque Lytham Green near the shore is typical of many that once operated in the area.

Ribchester's White Bull Inn sports an unusual sign.

THE FYLDE, Lancs

Between the Wyre estuary north of Blackpool and the Ribble estuary in the south is a flat, wind-blown area of land known as the Fylde. This area was once known for its many windmills, and several of these fascinating old structures have survived intact.

Continue along the A584 SP 'Preston' to reach Warton.

WARTON, Lancs

There is a small aerodrome here, and the town has a good church of Victorian date.

Continue along the A584 to Freckleton, then in 2¾ miles meet traffic signals and turn left on to the A583. Take the first turning right on to an unclassified road SP 'Clifton'. Skirt Clifton, and in 2 miles reach the Clifton Arms (PH). Turn right SP 'Broughton' and cross the Lancaster Canal. In 1½ miles meet a T-junction and turn right, then after another ¼ mile turn left. In 1¼ miles join the B5411 and continue to Woodplumpton.

WOODPLUMPTON, Lancs

The 20th-century navigator Henry Foster was born in this village, and his memorial can be seen in the local church. This warm, honey-coloured building is mainly of 15th- to 19th-century date.

Drive to the end of the village and turn right SP 'Broughton', then in a short distance turn right again on to the B5269. Continue to Broughton, meet traffic signals, and drive forward SP 'Longridge'. Proceed through Whittingham to Longridge.

LONGRIDGE, Lancs

High above the roof tops of this pleasant village is the fine steeple of 19th-century St Wilfrid's Church, a symmetrical counterpoint to the nearby craggy bulk of 1,148ft Longridge Fell.

Leave Longridge on the B6243 SP 'Clitheroe' and in ¼ mile turn right with the B6245 SP 'Blackburn'. Later bear left into Ribchester.

RIBCHESTER, Lancs

In Roman times the wild country hereabouts was guarded by a fort that stood on this site for 300 years. Known as *Bremetennacum*, its large remains have been excavated and many of the finds installed in the local Museum of Roman Antiquities. A model displayed here shows what the building must have looked like in its complete state, and among the exhibits are gold coins, pieces of pottery, brooches, oil lamps, and a rare bronze parade helmet. Other remains from the same period have been incorporated in some of the village buildings. Two Roman columns support the oak gallery in 13th-century St Wilfred's Church, and the pillars at the entrance of the White Bull Inn are said to have come from a Roman temple. Just to the north of Ribchester is the Norman Stydd Chapel and a neat row of attractive 18th-century almshouses.

A detour from the main route can be made to Longridge Fell by leaving the centre of Ribchester on an unclassified road SP 'Chipping', then driving for 3¼ miles to the excellent road summit and viewpoint of the fell. On the main tour, leave Ribchester by continuing along the B6254 and in ¼ mile turn left on to an unclassified road SP 'Hurst Green'. In 1¾ miles reach the top of an ascent and turn right on to the B6243 'Clitheroe' road and continue to Hurst Green.

HURST GREEN, Lancs

An attractive feature of this village is the Church of St John the Evangelist, which was built in 1838 and has a castellated tower in keeping with the romantic leanings of the period. In magnificent grounds close to Hurst Green is the imposing building of Stonyhurst, a famous school that was founded in the 16th century.

Leave Hurst Green and continue along the B6243. In 1¾ miles cross the River Hodder, with a 16th-century packhorse bridge visible to the right. In 1¼ miles meet a junction with the unclassified 'Bashall Eaves' road. A short detour can be taken from the main route to Clitheroe by turning right here and driving along the B6243.

CLITHEROE, Lancs

After the Civil War the small Norman keep of Clitheroe Castle (open) was presented to General Monk, and today it still stands in a dominant position on a limestone knoll above the town. Inside is an important collection of fossils from the surrounding district. The town itself is an industrial centre that grew to prosperity through cotton, and at one time it was full of the clatter and noise of textile milling. Sinister Pendle Hill, associated with the notorious trial of several Lancashire women who were said to be witches and accordingly executed, rises to 1,831ft on the east side of Clitheroe. Ironically the founder of the Society of Friends claims to have drawn his inspiration from the same hill.

Refreshing solitude is discovered near Blaze Moss in the Trough of Bowland.

On the main tour, keep forward at the junction and follow the unclassified road to Bashall Eaves. After 1 mile drive over crossroads and follow the Hodder Valley, with Longridge Fell on the left. To the right are views of 1,296ft Waddington Fell and 1,300ft Easington Fell. At Bashall Eaves keep forward, then after 1 mile reach Browsholme Hall.

BROWSHOLME HALL, Lancs

Altered and extended during the 18th century, this basically Tudor mansion contains fascinating collections of tapestry work, armour, furniture, and pictures. It is open by appointment and stands in beautiful gardens that were landscaped in honour of the Prince Regent and Mrs Fitzherbert.

Continue for 1 mile and turn right SP 'Whitewell' via Hall Hill. After ¼ mile an unclassified right turn offers a short detour which ascends for 1 mile to a 960ft viewpoint.

VIEWPOINT, Lancs

One of the best parts of the tour, this high road summit affords magnificent views south to the Hodder Valley, Longridge Fell, and Pendle Hill, with the dark peaks of the Pennine Range in the distance. North and west are the hills of the Forest of Bowland, with 1,629ft Totridge Fell and 1,415ft Burn Fell particularly prominent.

On the main tour, climb to a road summit of 750ft and descend into the Hodder Valley at Whitewell. Turn right SP 'Lancaster' and enter the Forest of Bowland.

FOREST OF BOWLAND, Lancs

In the days when the word 'forest' meant 'hunting ground' this area was the preserve of the kings of England, who regarded the local deer as their own property and were particularly hard on anybody caught poaching. Today the forest is a largely treeless expanse of moorland and steep-sided fells which has been designated as being of outstanding natural beauty. It lies partly in Lancashire and partly in what used to be the West Riding of Yorkshire, and offers excellent riverside walks.

Cross the River Hodder and Langden Brook. Drive through Dunsop Bridge into a deep, narrow valley and climb to the Trough of Bowland.

TROUGH OF BOWLAND, Lancs

Here the road climbs to more than 1,000ft above sea level via steep gradients (1 in 6) through lonely moorland that was once the haunt of highwaymen. Views from the summit encompass 1,383ft Blaze Moss to the south, 1,651ft Whin Fell in the north-east, and 1,567ft Hawthornthwaite Fell in the distance.

Descend from the road summit of the Trough of Bowland to reach the village of Marshaw. After 1¾ miles reach a chapel and turn left on to the 'Preston' road and descend (1 in 5) to Abbeystead. Follow SP 'Preston' and in 3¾ miles reach Dolphinholme. After ¼ mile reach a church and bear right, then in 1¼ miles meet a T-junction and turn left SP 'Garstang'. The revolving restaurant tower of Forton Service Area can be seen on the left as the route reaches Forton village. After the village drive for 1¼ miles and turn left on to the A6 SP 'Preston', then continue for 2¼ miles. A detour from the main route to Garstang can be made by turning left here on to the B6430 and driving into the town itself.

The Forest of Bowland is a lonely area of great beauty.

GARSTANG, Lancs

Among the fine Georgian buildings in this little town, which stands on the Lancaster Canal, are the Town Hall and elegant St Thomas' Church.

On the main tour, continue along the A6 for another 2¼ miles and turn right on to the A586 SP 'Blackpool'. Follow the course of the River Wyre to St Michael's-on-Wyre.

ST MICHAEL'S-ON-WYRE, Lancs

Situated at the junction of the Rivers Calder, Brock, and Wyre, this pleasant village has a lovely church which preserves fragments of 14th-century wall paintings. The rural nature of the community is emphasized by a shearing scene in the church's 16th-century stained-glass window.

Continue along the A586 to reach Poulton-le-Fylde.

POULTON-LE-FYLDE, Lancs

Old fish stones where the prices of fish caught by local boats were once fixed survive here, and the old market place features a set of stocks. Alongside the latter is a whipping post and a stepped Jacobean pillar. Georgian St Chad's Church features a beautiful carved screen and chairs that are prime examples of the wood craftsman's art.

Continue along the A586 to re-enter Blackpool.

GRANGE-OVER-SANDS, Cumbria

This quiet seaside resort is situated on Morecambe Bay. Its shingle and rock shore is scattered with fascinating rock pools at low tide, and is backed by lovely wooded fell scenery that sweeps right down to the sea. Bathing is dangerous. The mile-long promenade offers bracing walks, and the mild local climate has allowed the establishment of flourishing ornamental gardens throughout the town.

Leave Grange on the B5277 'Lindale, Kendal' road and drive through well-wooded countryside with views across Morecambe Bay to the right. Continue, with the Lakeland fells visible ahead, to Lindale.

LINDALE, Cumbria

John Wilkinson, the 18th-century iron master, is appropriately commemorated by a cast-iron obelisk in this pretty village.

In Lindale turn right SP 'Lancaster', and in 1¼ miles meet a roundabout. Take the 2nd exit on to the A590, later pass the craggy cliffs of Whitbarrow Scar on the left, and continue for 1½ miles. Immediately before a river bridge turn left on to the A5074 SP 'Bowness' and follow the lovely Lyth Valley. Continue, with views of the Lakeland fells ahead, and ascend a winding road through picturesque countryside. Drive through Winster, continue for 2 miles to reach crossroads, and turn left on to the B5284. In ¼ mile turn right on to the A592 to reach the town of Bowness-on-Windermere.

LAKE WINDERMERE, Cumbria

The largest and one of the most beautiful lakes in England, Windermere measures 10½ miles long and is only 1 mile wide. Its surface is studded with charming little islands, and its steep banks are cloaked with dense masses of attractive woodland. Water-sports enthusiasts find it suitable for most of their requirements, and at one time it was the regular venue for world water-speed record attempts.

BOWNESS-ON-WINDERMERE, Cumbria

In summer the quaint narrow streets of this pleasant little Lakeland town are busy with anglers, sailors, walkers, and tourists who have come here just for the beauty of the surroundings. Its fine 15th- to 19th-century church has superb examples of medieval stained glass in the east window, and the picturesque quality of local stone can be seen everywhere. Motor launches operate from Bowness Pier to Belle Isle, an enchanting 38-acre island in the middle of Lake Windermere. The house (open) on this unusual estate was the first completely round building of its type erected in England and contains interesting collections of furniture, portraits, and miscellanea.

SOUTHERN LAKELAND

Characterized by narrow switchback lanes and tranquil lakes that recede far into the distance, this part of the Lake District was a favourite haunt of famous poets and artists. Relics of them remain, as does the timeless and indefinable quality of peace that first attracted them.

Return along the A592 SP 'Barrow' and in ¾ mile pass a right turn leading to Lake Windermere Ferry. An alternative route that shortens the tour by 15 miles can be followed by taking the ferry and rejoining the main route at Far Sawrey, on the other bank. On the main route, drive through thick woodland along the east shore of Lake Windermere to reach Fell Foot Park.

FELL FOOT PARK, Cumbria

Attractively situated on the shores of Lake Windermere, this 18-acre park (NT) offer facilities for bathing, boating, picnicking, and many other outdoor pursuits.

Meet a T-junction and turn right on to the A590 to reach Newby Bridge.

NEWBY BRIDGE, Cumbria

This unusual stone bridge dates from the 17th century and spans the River Leven at the southern extremity of Lake Windermere. It is an attractive ingredient of the beautiful local scenery.

Turn right on to an unclassified road SP 'Lakeside, Hawkshead' and follow a winding road along the west shore of Lake Windermere to Lakeside.

LAKESIDE, Cumbria

Steam locomotives run south from here to Haverthwaite on the Lakeside and Haverthwaite Railway, which connects with passenger ferries operating from Ambleside and Bowness-on-Windermere.

Leave Lakeside and after ¾ mile bear right. In 2½ miles reach Graythwaite Hall Gardens.

GRAYTHWAITE HALL GARDENS, Cumbria

In spring and summer the 7 acres of this landscape garden are glorious with the blooms and foliage of many different plants. The Elizabethan hall round which they were created was sympathetically re-modelled in the 19th century.

Leave Graythwaite Hall and branch right SP 'Sawrey'. In ¾ mile descend steeply, then in 1¾ miles bear left and ascend to Far Sawrey. If the alternative route via the ferry has been taken, resume the main tour here.

FAR SAWREY, Cumbria

This beautiful Lakeland village is situated between Lake Windermere and tranquil Esthwaite Water.

Keep left in Far Sawrey, then turn left on to the B5285 SP 'Hawkshead'. Continue to Near Sawrey.

NEAR SAWREY, Cumbria

In 1943 Beatrix Potter, creator of Peter Rabbit and a host of other engaging animals in her children's books, bequeathed Hill Top Farm (open) and about half the village to the National Trust. The 17th-century farmhouse was her home up until her death, and the lovely surroundings of the village must have influenced her enchanting and essentially rural tales.

Lake Windermere is a popular centre for boating and sailing as well as being a magnetic scenic attraction.

Continue along the B5285 and follow the north shore of Esthwaite Water.

ESTHWAITE WATER, Cumbria

Rowing boats can be hired by those wishing to explore this picturesque small lake by water, and its shores offer mountain views in which the 2,631ft peak of the Old Man of Coniston is prominent.

Continue to the edge of Hawkshead. A detour can be made from the main tour route to the Grizedale Wildlife Centre by driving forward, turning left on to an unclassified road SP 'Newby Bridge', then continuing for ¼ mile and turning right SP 'Grizedale'; proceed across Hawkshead Moor to reach Grizedale.

GRIZEDALE, Cumbria

The variety of wildlife to be seen in this region is superbly illustrated in the Forestry Commission's Visitor and Wildlife Centre at Grizedale. The deer exhibit is of particular note, and among the best of several planned walks in the area is the 1-mile Millwood forest trail. Take care against fire in dry weather.

On the main tour, turn right to skirt the village of Hawkshead.

HAWKSHEAD, Cumbria

Hawkshead's distinctive charm comes from its unspoilt stone cottages, courtyards, and narrow winding alleys. The 16th-century grammar school numbers Wordsworth among its past pupils. The poet lodged in Ann Tyson's cottage while he studied there. The cottage still stands and is noted for its unusual outside staircase. The picturesque Courthouse (NT) houses the Folk Museum of Rural Crafts.

Keep forward on to the B5286 SP 'Ambleside' and follow a winding road that affords fine views of the local countryside. Drive through Out Gate, and in 2 miles reach an unclassified right turn offering a detour to impressive Wray Castle.

WRAY CASTLE, Cumbria

Lovely grounds (open) surround the 19th-century extravagance of Wray Castle (not open) on the banks of Lake Windermere, sweeping right down to the water's edge. The castle, estate, and much of the attractive local countryside are protected by the National Trust.

On the main route, continue to the village of Clappersgate.

CLAPPERSGATE, Cumbria

Magnificently situated at the northern end of Lake Windermere, Clappersgate is best known for the beautiful floral displays that can be enjoyed in the White Craggs Garden (limited opening) during spring and summer.

Leave Clappersgate and turn right on to the A593. Continue, with fine views of Wansfell and 1,581ft Wansfell Pike ahead, and cross a river bridge. Turn left to enter Ambleside.

AMBLESIDE, Cumbria

Features of this very popular Lakeland tourist centre include a National Trust information office in tiny Bridge House. Excellent walking and climbing areas are nearby. See tour 86 for more details.

The area around Skelwith Bridge is graced by several lovely waterfalls.

Return along the A593 SP 'Coniston' and pass through Clappersgate. Cross Skelwith Bridge and continue along an undulating road with all-round mountain views. Tilberthwaite High Fells rise to the right, dominated by the strangely-shaped peak of 2,502ft Wetherlam. Continue, later driving below the steep slopes of the Coniston Fells with the Old Man of Coniston towering in the background, to Coniston.

CONISTON, Cumbria

This cluster of whitewashed cottages at the tip of lovely Coniston Water is a bright spot in a landscape dominated in the west by the 2,631ft Old Man of Coniston. A little farther west is the 2,555ft peak of Dow Crag, whose testing faces are popular with climbers. Features of the village itself include Coniston Old Hall, with its typical round Lakeland chimneys, and the Ruskin Museum. John Ruskin, the 19th-century writer and artist, loved this area and is buried in the local churchyard. Although the museum is devoted mostly to him, parts of it recall the death of the famous Donald Campbell.

Leave Coniston and turn left on to the B5285 SP 'Hawkshead' to skirt the northern end of Coniston Water.

CONISTON WATER, Cumbria

One shore of this tranquil 5½-mile-long lake is cloaked in the woodlands of Grizedale Forest, and the lake itself is famous as the place where Sir Donald Campbell died while trying to better the world water-speed record in 1965. Conditions were not ideal during the attempt, but its failure may not have been entirely due to the choppy surface and is still a matter for conjecture.

Keep left and climb through woodland, then in 1¾ miles turn left on to an unclassified road SP 'Tarn Hows'. In ¼ mile turn left again and ascend steeply to reach Tarn Hows.

Marvellous views of the Langdale Pikes and other famous Lakeland features can be enjoyed from the peaceful shores of picturesque Tarn Hows.

Evening gives a dramatic aspect to Morecambe Bay.

TARN HOWS, Cumbria

Arguably the most outstanding of many beautiful areas in the Lakeland region, Tarn Hows (NT) is a group of lakes and woodland in an area ringed by the peaks of mountains. Visitors are catered for with carparks and picnicking facilities.

Descend steeply along a narrow road SP 'Coniston', meet a T-junction, and turn right on to the B5285. Take the next turning left on to an unclassified road SP 'East of Lake' and follow the eastern shore of Coniston Water. In 1½ miles reach Brantwood.

BRANTWOOD, Cumbria

This house (open), once the home of writer and artist John Ruskin, is now a museum containing examples of his work and a variety of personal possessions. The grounds feature fine gardens, a deer trail, and one of the best nature trails in the Lake District.

Continue along a winding road that hugs the shore of the lake, with views of several waterfalls to the right. Above the road to the left are the steep wooded slopes of Grizedale Forest. On the far side of the lake descend into the Crake Valley, passing the wooded Furness Fells on the left, and meet a T-junction. Turn left to reach Spark Bridge, then turn left again and in ¼ mile drive forward over crossroads SP 'Newby Bridge', then bear right and at T-junction turn left on to the A590 SP 'Bowness', then in 1¼ miles meet crossroads and turn right on to the B5278 SP 'Cark'. A detour from the main route to Rusland can be made by turning left at the crossroads instead of right.

RUSLAND, Cumbria

Rusland Hall (open) was built in 1720 and nowadays houses a museum of mechanical musical instruments and early photographic equipment. Its elegant landscaped grounds are the home of white peacocks.

On the main tour, continue along the B5278 to reach Haverthwaite.

HAVERTHWAITE, Cumbria

Steam-hauled trains on the standard-gauge Lakeside and Haverthwaite Railway connect with passenger steamers on Lake Windermere, at the other end of the line, and run 3½ miles through some of Lakeland's finest scenery.

Drive beyond Haverthwaite and bear right, then continue along the B5278 through thickly wooded countryside to reach Holker Hall.

HOLKER HALL, Cumbria

Originally built in the 16th century, this house (open) contains fine furniture and exquisite woodcarvings by local craftsmen. A motor museum exhibits over 100 cars and motorcycles, and the grounds include a deer park featuring a number of different species. During the summer Holker Hall is the scene of many local shows and events.

Proceed to Cark.

CARK, Cumbria

One of the main features in this pleasant little village is its 16th-century hall, which has mullioned windows and a grand 17th-century doorway.

Drive to the Rose and Crown Hotel and branch left on to an unclassified road. Continue to Cartmel.

CARTMEL, Cumbria

Little remains of the great priory (NT) that made this pleasant old town one of the most important religious centres for miles around, but the exceptionally beautiful priory church has survived. This large building was extended at various times up until the dissolution of the monasteries, after which it was left to decay until its restoration in 1618.

Keep forward, pass a school, and turn right SP 'Grange'. In 1 mile turn left into Grangefell Road and descend, with fine views over Morecambe Bay, for the return to Grange-over-Sands.

AROUND THE THREE PEAKS

High fells and isolated dales sheltering the stone houses and outbuildings of hill farms surround Yorkshire's Three Peaks, rugged summits whose flanks are riddled with caves and pounded by the constant drop of lovely waterfalls. The roads are narrow and hilly, but the scenery is spectacular.

SEDBERGH, Cumbria
This market town lies below Howgill Fells, a range of rounded bracken-topped hills which links the Yorkshire Dales with the edge of the Lake District. A famous public school for boys was founded here in 1525, but the majority of the town's buildings are 19th-century and the general feel of the place is very Victorian. Permanent displays relating to the topography of the area can be seen in the National Park Centre.

Leave Sedbergh on the unclassified 'Dent' road and follow the River Dee through beautiful Dentdale. Continue through pleasant countryside to Dent.

DENTDALE, Cumbria
Lower Dentdale is a broad and well-wooded valley that narrows to a gorge and mountain pass beyond Dent village. Dent marble, a particularly hard form of limestone prized as a building material, is found in small quarries along its length, and beautiful fell scenery rises from both banks of the Dee.

DENT, Cumbria
In the heart of Dentdale is the attractive old village of Dent, a picturesque collection of houses and cottages centred on the twisting course of a cobbled main street. The village drinking fountain commemorates Alan Sedgwick, a pioneer geologist born here in the 19th century.

Drive to the George and Dragon Inn in Dent, turn right, and after 1 mile turn right again SP 'Ingleton'. Follow a narrow winding road into Deepdale, with Whernside rising on the left.

WHERNSIDE,
Cumbria & N Yorks
Whernside, the cave-riddled flanks of Pen-y-Ghent, and lofty Ingleborough are neighbouring summits of a massive millstone-grit formation known as the Three Peaks. The first-named rise to 2,419ft above sea level. The area's many potholes and tunnels should not be entered by any but the most experienced and well-equipped explorers.

Ascend steeply along a gated road to White Shaw Moss and a road summit of 1,553ft. Descend through Kingsdale, on either side of which runs a lofty limestone scar, and reach Thornton-in-Lonsdale. Turn left over a railway bridge, then left again. After a short distance turn left to enter the Dales centre of Ingleton.

INGLETON, N Yorks
This popular dales centre is a good rambling and touring base situated close to several beauty spots. Waterfalls in the area include 40ft Thornton Force and Pecca Falls, and lovely rock and river scenery can be enjoyed on a 2¼-hour round walk that follows the enchanting Doe Valley and returns alongside the River Twiss. The summit of Ingleborough is less than 4 miles from the village.

INGLEBOROUGH, N Yorks
Ingleborough is the second highest of the Three Peaks, and its 2,373ft summit forms a curious 15-acre plateau that was once guarded by an ancient stronghold. All that remains of the fortification today is a low rampart pierced by three openings. A well-known section of the massive cave systems that riddle the local limestone is known as the White Scar Caves (open). Potholers come from all parts of the country to explore its tunnels, where an underground river flows amongst strange rock formations into a sunless lake. Farther east is Gaping Gill, an awesome pothole whose 360ft shaft leads to a main chamber that extends a full 500ft below ground. It has the longest shaft in Britain and is a severe test of nerves and skill for the experienced climbers that attempt it.

Leave Ingleton and follow SP 'Settle' to join the A65. Drive through farming country and after 4 miles turn left on to the B6480 to enter Clapham.

CLAPHAM, N Yorks
A Yorkshire Dales National Park centre is based in this attractive little village, and the local caves attract potholing enthusiasts from all over Britain. About 1 mile north is the entrance to Ingleborough Cave (open), which runs for 900 yards and is noted for its splendid stalagmites and stalactites. The village is a charming collection of greystone houses and whitewashed cottages on the banks of Clapham Beck.

The windswept character of the Yorkshire Dales is particularly striking near Muker.

Leave Clapham on the 'Settle' road to join the A65, then in ¼ mile turn left on to an unclassified road for Austwick village. In ¾ mile reach Austwick.

AUSTWICK, N Yorks
Many of the Craven District's outstanding geological features lie close to this village. Of particular interest is a series of perched boulders, huge rocks left in precarious positions by the melting glaciers of the ice ages.

Leave Austwick by returning to the A65 and later pass beneath Giggleswick Scar to reach the edge of Giggleswick.

GIGGLESWICK, N Yorks
A well-known public school founded here in 1553 occupies impressive 19th-century buildings, but the early history of Giggleswick is best represented by its old market cross, stocks, and tithe barn. The local church features an ancient reading desk and a carved pulpit of 1680.

Leave Giggleswick and proceed to the town of Settle.

Adventurous visitors can follow a footpath behind the stupendous Hardrow Force waterfall.

HAWES, N Yorks

This sheep-marketing centre is the focal point of Upper Wensleydale life and a major supplier of the distinctive Wensleydale cheese. Within the old station buildings are a National Park Centre and the Upper Dales Folk Museum, which depicts life and trades in the dales.

In Hawes turn left on to the unclassified 'Muker' road and cross the River Ure. Reach a T-junction and turn left, then take the next turning right. A short detour can be made from the main route to Hardrow Force waterfall by keeping forward with SP 'Hardrow Force'.

HARDROW SCAR & FORCE, N Yorks

Considered one of the most spectacular in England, this magnificent waterfall plunges 90ft over the limestone rim of Hardrow Scar into a glen that was once used for brass band contests because of its superb acoustics. Access to the falls is by foot only, through the grounds of the Green Dragon Inn.

On the main tour, climb through the fine scenery of Buttertubs Pass.

BUTTERTUBS PASS, N Yorks

This 1,726ft pass links the lovely valleys of Swaledale and Wensleydale, and is named after deep limestone shafts that pock the countryside a short distance from the road. It is thought that these may have been dug by farmers and used to cool and harden butter that had got too warm on the way to market.

Continue along Buttertubs Pass and meet the B6270. A detour from the main route to Muker can be made by turning right here and driving for 1¼ miles through fell country.

Pen-y-Ghent, one of the impressive Three Peaks that rise above the national park.

MUKER, N Yorks

Set among the high moors and fells of Upper Swaledale, this remote little cluster of greystone houses is attractively set below the 2,340ft summit of Great Shunner Fell.

On the main tour, turn left on to the B6270 to Thwaite and later skirt the village of Keld.

KELD, N Yorks

Lovely Kisdon Force is one of several attractive waterfalls to be seen near this village, and the desolate area of Birkdale Common lies to the west.

Beyond Keld drive along a narrow hilly road through Birkdale Common, climbing to a road summit of 1,698ft on the Cumbrian border. Descend steeply (1-in-5) with views over the Eden Valley to reach Nateby, and turn right on to the B6259. Later turn right on to the A685 to enter Kirkby Stephen.

KIRKBY STEPHEN, Cumbria

This picturesque little market town is attractively set amongst moorland in the Eden Valley, and features a fine parish church containing several ancient carved stones. To the south the River Eden rises from its remote source in the wild Mallerstang Valley.

Leave Kirkby Stephen on the A685 SP 'Kendal' and after 2 miles turn left on to the A683 'Sedbergh' road. Continue among high fells along the attractive Rawthey Valley to reach the Cross Keys Inn.

CROSS KEYS INN, Cumbria

Originally built c1600, this inn (NT) was altered somewhat in the 18th and 19th centuries but is still a fine building. The impressive 600ft waterfall of Cautley Spout is accessible by footpath from here.

Leave the Cross Keys Inn and continue along the A683 to re-enter Sedbergh.

SETTLE, N Yorks

The charm of this small Ribblesdale market town is in its narrow streets of unpretentious buildings and secluded courtyards. Folly Hall, also known as Preston's Folly, is an unfinished 17th-century house with an elaborate front that contrasts severely with a very plain back. In many ways this sudden difference reflects the startling changes of the local countryside. In Victoria Street is an interesting museum of North Craven life.

Return through Settle along the A65 and turn right on to the B6479 SP 'Horton in Ribblesdale' to begin a drive through scenic Ribblesdale. After a short distance reach Langcliffe.

LANGCLIFFE, N Yorks

In 1838 a chance discovery of the feature now known as Victoria Cave led to the retrieval of many fascinating prehistoric remains, including the bones of animals long extinct in the British Isles.

Leave Langcliffe and proceed on the B6479 to reach Stainforth.

STAINFORTH, N Yorks

A 17th-century packhorse bridge that spans the River Ribble here is said to have replaced a similar structure built by monks in the 14th century. Some 300 yards downstream is the impressive waterfall of Stainforth Force. The lovely Ribblesdale Valley extends north and south along the river's rambling course.

From Stainforth, continue to Horton in Ribblesdale.

HORTON IN RIBBLESDALE, N Yorks

Alum Pot, one of the best-known potholes in the Craven district, lies 4 miles north-west of this picturesque moorland village.

Continue past Horton-in-Ribblesdale, with views of Pen-y-Ghent (right).

RIBBLESDALE, N Yorks

This long, wide valley of the Ribble cuts through a varied landscape and is popular with walkers, climbers, and potholers. The railway line from Settle to Carlisle runs through Ribblesdale and is considered one of the most scenic routes in the country.

PEN-Y-GHENT, N Yorks

One of the famous Three Peaks, this mountain rises to 2,273ft and is known for its potholes. In clear weather the views from its summit extend as far as Helvellyn, some 45 miles away.

Continue along the B6479 through desolate countryside beside the Leeds–Carlisle railway line to Ribblehead. A fine railway viaduct can be seen on the left, and 2,419ft Whernside rises straight ahead. Meet a T-junction and turn right on to the B6255 SP 'Hawes'. Ascend Redshaw Moss to a road summit of 1,434ft, then later descend through the steep fell country of Widdale. Meet the A684 and turn right to enter Hawes.

AMBLESIDE, Cumbria

This popular tourist centre of grey slate houses stands near the northern end of Lake Windermere and is popular with anglers, fell walkers, and climbers. The waters of the lake are alive with fish large enough to satisfy the most discriminating fishermen, and the rugged countryside of the Coniston Fells is only 3 miles away. The beautiful scenery of the lake shores is best appreciated from the water, and regular boat tours can be joined at Waterhead. In the town library are various relics discovered on the site of a 2nd- to 4th-century Roman fort excavated in Borrans Park. Tiny 18th-century Bridge House contains a National Trust information centre. About 1 mile south of Ambleside is the enchanting woodland garden of Stagshaw (NT) (open) with superb views of the lake from informal surroundings. In early times the floors of domestic and public buildings were covered with dried rushes that were replaced as they became soiled, and every July the town has a rush-bearing ceremony as a reminder of the days when everybody in the community collected rushes for the church floor. This very practical idea may have stemmed from Roman harvest thanksgiving celebrations.

Leave Ambleside with SP 'Keswick' to join the A591 and drive through pleasant mountain scenery to reach Rydal, near the Rydal Water.

RYDAL, Cumbria

Close to Rydal is the little River Rothay, which links the east end of peaceful Rydal Water with the vast expanse of Lake Windermere. The poet William Wordsworth lived at Rydal Mount (open) from 1815 until his death in 1850, and must have been inspired by the glorious views over two beautiful lakes that can be enjoyed from the 4½-acre gardens. Nowadays the house is a sort of historical shrine to the poet, preserving many personal relics from his lifetime. Dora's Field was given by Wordsworth to his daughter, and is famous for its daffodils. Nearby Nab Cottage is associated with the writers Thomas de Quincey and Hartley Coleridge. The whole area is dominated by the rugged heights of Nab Scar and Loughrigg Fell.

Leave Rydal and drive past the shores of Rydal Water and Grasmere, with Rydal Fell rising to the right. Continue for ¼ mile beyond Grasmere to reach Dove Cottage.

DOVE COTTAGE, Cumbria

After William Wordsworth had lived in this tiny 17th-century cottage from 1799 to 1808 it became the home of the writer Thomas de Quincey, who occupied it for 26 years. A Wordsworth Museum which now adjoins the house preserves several manuscripts and first editions of the poet's work.

Leave Dove Cottage and turn left on to the B5287 to reach Grasmere.

HIGH LAKELAND PASSES

Fell and dale scenery at its most impressive can be enjoyed from this route, but it should be remembered that the roads in this part of Lakeland are particularly severe. Hard Knott and Wrynose passes have gradients up to 1 in 3 and should not be attempted unless both car and driver are fit.

GRASMERE, Cumbria

The idyllic setting for this tiny stone village is between the tranquil waters of Grasmere Lake and the jagged heights of Helm Crag and Nab Scar. Close by is a beautiful natural arena where the famous Grasmere Sports are staged every August, perpetuating such traditional events as Lakeland wrestling and the guides footrace. The latter follows an arduous course up a steep crag and along a ridge before descending through rough country to end in the arena. Important sheepdog trials are held in the village at about the same time, and the two events make a colourful high spot to the summer. A local rush-bearing ceremony involves the carrying of elaborately decorated bundles of rushes to the church, after which each of the bearers is rewarded with a piece of delicious local gingerbread.

Tranquil Rydal Water contrasts with the constant bustle and activity of Lake Windermere. Both waters are renowned for their excellent fishing, and are the homes of many wildfowl.

In Grasmere turn left on to an unclassified road SP 'Langdale' and follow a winding, bumpy road along the west side of Grasmere Lake. In 1½ miles begin the ascent of Red Bank passing through woodland, and climb to the summit. Turn right here, descend through picturesque moorland, and at Chapel Stile bear right SP 'Dungeon Ghyll' to join the B5343. Drive along Great Langdale, passing through magnificent mountain scenery below cliffs that tower high above the road. Ahead are Langdale Pikes.

Dove Cottage in Grasmere, once the simple home of poet William Wordsworth, is now a museum containing examples of his work and various personal belongings.

Among the many traditions preserved in Grasmere is that of gingerbread making.

LANGDALE PIKES, Cumbria

Harrison Stickle and Pike O'Stickle soar to respective heights of 2,403ft and 2,323ft above the secluded green dales and sparkling little tarns of the area. Collectively known as Langdale Pikes, they are separated by a deep cleft which contains the roaring waters of Dungeon Ghyll Force. This spectacular Lakeland feature is well worth a visit and can be easily reached by footpath from the New Hotel.

Drive ¾ mile beyond the New Hotel and turn sharp left on to an unclassified road. Continue through a narrow pass with several steep climbs and a number of hairpin bends. Views from the road extend back to Great Langdale, and the lovely waters of Blea Tarn can be seen from the summit of the pass. Descend steeply, with views of the picturesque Little Langdale Valley, then turn very sharp right to climb the steep Wrynose Pass.

WRYNOSE PASS, Cumbria

All around this high pass are the steep sloping peaks of the Cumbrian Mountains. Just below the 1,281ft summit is the Three Shires Stone, where the boundaries of Lancashire, Cumberland, and Westmorland used to meet before the national county reorganization. The summit itself affords spectacular views over the surrounding hills and moors.

CUMBRIAN MOUNTAINS, Cumbria

Lakeland's highest passes cross the ancient Cumbrian Mountains, a range made up of several major groups separated by deep lake and river-filled valleys. At the geographical centre of the district are 3,210ft Scafell Pike, which is the highest mountain in England, the 3,162ft bulk of Sca Fell, and 2,960ft Bow Fell. To the north-west rise the Great Gable and Pillar groups, and Langdale Pikes to the east. Climbing parties test their skills on many of the peaks, and the high country holds many scenic rewards for the energetic fell walker.

Descend sharply from the summit of Wrynose Pass. Views ahead extend over the valley to Hard Knott Pass, where the mountain road can be seen snaking across ridges and dropping away into hidden folds in the landscape. Continue along Wrynose Bottom alongside the River Duddon, with steep scree slopes on either side.

Drive from Boot to the Woolpack Inn, where the waterfall of Birker Force can be seen to the right, and in 1½ miles begin a steep ascent through the tortuous hairpin bends of Hard Knott Pass. In places the road reaches a maximum gradient of 1 in 3.

HARDKNOTT PASS, Cumbria
The road that runs through this high pass to its 1,291ft summit is surfaced, but is considered one of the most difficult in the Lake District. Cars and drivers who attempt it should be in peak condition, and its passage should be regarded as something of an adventure rather than ordinary day-to-day driving.

The famous Pikes dominate Langdale.

A typical Lakeland cottage at Blea Tarn, one of the wilder and less frequented areas of Lakeland.

RIVER DUDDON VALLEY, Cumbria
Close to the Three Shires Stone in Wrynose Pass is the source of the River Duddon, a beautiful water that chatters down to Wrynose Bottom, through Seathwaite and the Dunnerdale villages to Ulpha. Its entire course is through attractive scenery immortalized by Wordsworth in no less than 35 individual sonnets.

In 2 miles turn left SP 'Broughton, Duddon Valley', with 2,129ft Harter Fell prominent to the right. Continue past a deep river gorge on the right. Pass the Dunnerdale Picnic Area, with the 2,631ft Old Man of Coniston to the left, and continue to Seathwaite.

DUNNERDALE FOREST, Cumbria
Walks from a riverside carpark provided by the Forestry Commission lead through the lovely and secluded countryside of Dunnerdale Forest, a haven for many different species of wildlife. A particularly scenic path leads to 2,129ft Harter Fell, providing excellent views over the Duddon Valley, Eskdale, and the Hard Knott Pass from its high route. Just below Birk's Bridge the Duddon flows through an impressive gorge.

SEATHWAITE, Cumbria
A remote Dunnerdale village in attractive surroundings, Seathwaite is well known as a walking centre and was beloved of the poet Wordsworth. His *Excursion* describes both the village and its 18th-century parson Robert Walker, whose grave can be seen in the local churchyard. About ½ mile north of Seathwaite is the Walna Scar Track, which leads 5 miles across the fells to Coniston.

Leave Seathwaite and continue, passing the peak of 1,735ft Caw on the left, to reach Hall Dunnerdale. At Hall Dunnerdale turn right and drive under a thickly wooded ridge, then in 1½ miles at Ulpha turn right with SP 'Eskdale' and ascend through more thick woodland. Follow a narrow winding road over Birker Fell for magnificent views to Sca Fell, Scafell Pike, Bow Fell, and the cone-shaped bulk of Harter Fell. Reach the King George IV Inn and turn sharp right with SP 'Boot, Langdale'. Follow the picturesque valley of Eskdale to reach Dalegarth Station, on the Ravenglass and Eskdale Railway.

RAVENGLASS AND ESKDALE RAILWAY, Cumbria
Established in 1875 to carry iron ore, this fascinating little narrow-gauge railway has been revived to carry passengers through 7 miles of enchanting countryside between Dalegarth in Eskdale to Ravenglass,
on the coast. Other stations allow the line to be joined at Eskdale Green and Beckfoot. The railway operates both steam and diesel locomotives, and provides a very convenient way by which to enjoy some of the district's best scenery.

ESKDALE AND STANLEY FORCE, Cumbria
At its lower end this beautiful valley has a pastoral aspect, with bankside footpaths following the course of the River Esk through gentle farmlands. Beyond the villages of Eskdale Green and Boot it turns north and becomes wilder as it forges between the rocky flanks of Sca Fell and Bow Fell. Opposite Dalegarth Station is the starting point for the Stanley Gill Nature Trail, which leads to a lush valley and the stunning 60ft cascade of Stanley Force. Many of the paths in the dale are more suited to climbing than walking.

Leave Dalegarth Station and continue on an unclassified road to Boot.

BOOT, Cumbria
A good starting point for walks along the heathery foothills of Eskdale, this beautifully situated village is surrounded by some of the highest mountains in the Lake District. Lovely Dalegarth Hall is a quaint old farmhouse with round chimney stacks that were once typical of the Lakeland region in general.

HARDKNOTT CASTLE, Cumbria
Just before the summit of Hardknott Pass are the remains of a Roman fort (AM) known as Hardknott Castle. Built in the 2nd century AD, the ruins include surviving fragments of corner watchtowers and a bath house. It was sited in this improbable and isolated position to guard a route from the port of Ravenglass.

Begin the steep descent from the summit of the pass, negotiating very sharp hairpin bends, and in 1 mile bear left and drive along Wrynose Bottom before climbing over the steep Wrynose Pass. Descend, with excellent views over Little Langdale, and follow the valley with Little Langdale Tarn visible to the right. Pass the Three Shires Inn, and in 1 mile meet a T-junction and turn right SP 'Coniston'. In ⅓ mile turn left on to the A593 SP 'Ambleside', and drive through Skelwith Bridge to reach Clappersgate.

CLAPPERSGATE, Cumbria
Magnificent views are afforded by the White Craggs Garden (limited opening) in Clappersgate, and in the gardens are splendid displays of heathers, rhododendrons, azaleas and many other plants.

Leave Clappersgate and cross the river bridge, then turn left for the return to Ambleside.

THE NORTHERN LAKE DISTRICT

This is a district of beautiful mountains and lakes, heathery slopes dotted with sheep and boulders between valley woodland and the misty blueness of windswept crags. Much of the countryside is owned or protected by the National Trust, whose codes of conduct should be respected.

KESWICK, Cumbria

This touring centre is close to some of Lakeland's finest scenery and attracts thousands of visitors every year. In Victorian times it was beloved of poets and artists, including such notables as Wordsworth, Coleridge, Southey, Ruskin, and Walpole. Many of their works and personal possessions are preserved in the fascinating Park Museum, which also features an impressive scale model of the Lake District and a variety of exhibits relating to the local area. Both Coleridge and Southey lived in Greta Park at different times, and there is a memorial to John Ruskin close to the town on the spectacular viewpoint of Friar's Crag (NT). Moot Hall is a handsome building that was reconstructed in the early 19th century. The superb 529ft viewpoint of Castle Head (NT) is within easy reach of Keswick.

Before starting the main route it is possible to take two rewarding detours to interesting areas close to the boundaries of Keswick. The first of these can be taken to Crosthwaite by driving through Keswick on the A5271 'Cockermouth' road before keeping forward on to the B5289 to reach the village.

CROSTHWAITE, Cumbria

Keswick's lovely 11th-century and later parish church is sited here, and is well worth a visit. Among its many treasures are several fine monuments, 21 consecration crosses, and the churchyard grave of poet and writer Robert Southey.

For the second detour, continue along the B5289 from Crosthwaite for ½ mile, bear left, then turn left to join the A66. Again a further ¼ mile turn left again on to an unclassified road SP 'Portinscale' to enter Portinscale village. Here turn right to reach Lingholm Gardens.

LINGHOLM GARDENS, Cumbria

The superb landscaped gardens of Lingholm (open), the home of Lord Rochdale, are laid out in a charming situation on the wooded western shores of Derwent Water. In spring the ground is golden with the famous Lakeland daffodils, and later in the year the banks of rhododendron bushes and azaleas blaze with colour.

DERWENT WATER, Cumbria

Typical of everything that is beautiful in the Lake District, this broad lake is ringed by mountain peaks and dotted with mysterious little tree-clad islands. It measures 3 miles long by 1½ miles wide at its widest point, and is best appreciated from the lofty Friar's Crag Viewpoint (NT), back along the route. At the foot of the crag is the start of a nature trail that runs for about 2 miles along the shoreline of the lake.

To start the main tour, leave Keswick on the B5289 'Borrowdale' road and pass the Friar's Crag Viewpoint (NT) on the right. Drive beneath Castle Head (NT) on the left and reach the eastern shores of Derwent Water. Steep wooded slopes rise to the left, and farther on the road runs beneath the cliffs of the Falcon Crag Viewpoint. A detour can be taken from the main route to Ashness Bridge and Watendlath by reaching Falcon Crag and then turning left on to a winding unclassified road.

ASHNESS BRIDGE, Cumbria

Thousands of visitors come here every year to admire the unique and enchanting combination of a single-arched packhorse bridge with beautiful falls on the little mountain stream which it spans.

Continue this detour by following the unclassified road to Watendlath.

Derwent Water is known as the queen of the lakes, deriving much of its beauty from the many islands.

WATENDLATH, Cumbria

A small beck which rises close to this delightful little hamlet (NT) threads its way through a pretty valley and joins Watendlath Tarn, which lies in the shadow of 1,588ft Armboth Fell.

On the main tour, drive forward on the B5289. Continue, with excellent views of the lake, and in 1 mile reach the Lodore Swiss Hotel and the impressive Lodore Cascade.

LODORE CASCADE, Cumbria

Views of this spectacular waterfall, which is situated at the southern extremity of Derwent Water, can be enjoyed from the carpark of the Lodore Swiss Hotel.

Drive through the short, green valley of Borrowdale, keeping to the left bank of the River Derwent, and in 1½ miles pass Grange village on the righthand side of the road.

GRANGE, Cumbria

A double-arched bridge spans the River Derwent in this lovely little Borrowdale village. Superb views of the dale can be enjoyed from the summit of Grange Fell, which is known as King's How (NT).

Leave Grange and in ½ mile pass a track leading left to the Bowder Stone.

BOWDER STONE, Cumbria

Although this remarkable 2,000-ton boulder (NT) seems about to fall from its precarious perch at any moment, it is quite firm and makes a good vantage point from which to survey the surrounding countryside.

Continue through Borrowdale to Rosthwaite.

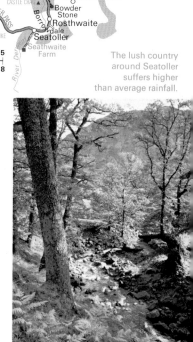

The lush country around Seatoller suffers higher than average rainfall.

ROSTHWAITE, Cumbria

As Borrowdale opens out on the approach to this tiny village the views widen into a spectacular panorama of the mountains ahead. Massive Castle Crag (NT) dominates a narrow pass known as the Jaws of Borrowdale, rising high above the valley floor to a 900ft summit.

BORROWDALE, Cumbria

Much of Borrowdale, the beautiful valley through which the last section of tour has just passed, is owned or protected by the National Trust. Its impressive crags and fells offer a challenge which draws climbers and walkers from many parts of the country, and its tiny unspoilt villages are an essential part of the tranquillity that underlies its scenic grandeur. The southern end of the dale is dominated by the summits of 2,560ft Glaramara and 2,984ft Great End, and the north by high fells.

Continue along the B5289 to reach the village of Seatoller.

SEATOLLER, Cumbria
During the 17th and 18th century this village was the centre of a busy mining industry. Seatoller is now known as a base from which walkers can ascend to the Sky Head Pass, in the south. Also south of the village is Seathwaite Farm (NT), one of England's wettest inhabited places.

A detour from the main route to Seathwaite Farm can be made by turning left in Seatoller on to an unclassified road and following a deep, steep-sided valley to the farm. On the main tour, continue along the B5289 and ascend Honister Pass.

HONISTER PASS, Cumbria
This part of the tour follows a steep, difficult road but offers some of the most spectacular scenery in the whole region. The summit of the pass is 1,176ft above sea level and affords distant eastern views of the craggy Helvellyn group, beyond the picturesque foreground of Borrowdale. Left towards Buttermere are the outstanding peaks of 2,479ft Red Pike and 2,644ft High Stile.

Descend between scree-covered slopes to the village of Buttermere.

BUTTERMERE, Cumbria
Well-situated between Crummock Water and the lake (NT) from which it derives its name, this pretty village stands in the heart of a spectacular landscape and is a popular base for walkers and climbers. Opposite the village curiously-named Sour Milk Ghyll tumbles down the flanks of lofty Red Pike. Scale Force, among the highest waterfalls in the Lake District, is nearby.

A detour from the main route to Newlands Hause and Moss Force can be made by driving to the outskirts of the village, turning right on to an unclassified road SP 'Keswick', and climbing steeply.

NEWLANDS HAUSE AND MOSS FORCE, Cumbria
Here the road climbs through the spectacular pass of Newlands Hause to a summit of 1,096ft, with an almost sheer drop plunging away into a deep valley on the left.

On the main tour, leave Buttermere village with the B5289 and follow the

Set amid mountains in one of Lakeland's most beautiful areas, Buttermere Lake is famous for the reflections that crowd its surface on calm days.

east shore of Crummock Water with views of the Loweswater Fell peaks on the far side of the lake. Leave the lakeside and after 2 miles meet a T-junction. Turn right SP 'Lorton, Cockermouth' and enter the broad expanse of Lorton Vale. Continue to the edge of Lorton and turn right on to an unclassified road SP 'Keswick'. Continue to High Lorton, turn left into the village, and at the end of the village turn right. Meet a T-junction and turn right again on to the B5292 and begin to ascend Whinlatter Pass.

WHINLATTER PASS, Cumbria
Drivers will find this one of the less taxing Lake District passes. Its gradients are reasonable and its bends are not quite as sharp as the others, but its 1,043ft summit affords views that are every bit as enjoyable as elsewhere.

THORNTHWAITE FOREST, Cumbria
Woodland walks planned by the Forestry Commission help the visitor to get the most out of this lovely area, the longest established national forest in the Lake District. Detailed information about all aspects of the forest is available from the Interpretative Centre near the summit of Whinlatter Pass.

Descend from the forest with fine views over Bassenthwaite Lake to the left. At the foot of the descent keep left into Braithwaite.

BRAITHWAITE, Cumbria
Climbers heading for the slopes and faces of 2,593ft Grisedale Pike generally start from this attractive village, which lies at the head of Coledale Valley.

Leave Braithwaite and take the 2nd turning left SP 'Cockermouth'. In ¼ mile turn left again on to the A66 and drive to the western shore of Bassenthwaite Lake.

BASSENTHWAITE LAKE, Cumbria
Opposite this wooded shore, towering above the peaceful waters of lovely Bassenthwaite Lake, are the stern slopes of 3,053ft Skiddaw.

After 2½ miles turn right on to the B5291 SP 'Castle Inn', then turn right again to follow the northern end of Bassenthwaite Lake. In 1 mile turn right SP 'Bothel', cross Ouse Bridge, and continue to Castle Inn. Meet a T-junction and turn right on to the A591. Take the 2nd turning left on to an unclassified road SP 'Bassenthwaite' and approach that village.

BASSENTHWAITE, Cumbria
Close to the lake in charming surroundings is the village church, which was restored in Victorian times and has a Norman chancel arch.

Do not enter the village on the main tour, but on its approach keep left (no SP) on to a narrow road and drive through pretty woodland. In 1¼ miles meet a T-junction and turn left SP 'Caldbeck', then ascend a winding road to pass Over Water and smaller Chapelhouse Reservoir on the left. After 2½ miles cross open moors and meet a T-junction. Turn right, and in ¾ mile keep forward on to the B5299. In 1¼ miles cross a cattle grid, and in ¼ mile keep left to reach Caldbeck.

CALDBECK, Cumbria
In 1854 the local folk hero of nursery song fame, John Peel, was buried in Caldbeck churchyard. According to tradition he was ruined by his obsessive love of fox hunting.

Drive forward on to an unclassified road and proceed to Hesket Newmarket.

HESKET NEWMARKET, Cumbria   NY33
At one time this charming village on the northern flanks of Skiddaw was an important market town. Nowadays it rests in quiet retirement as yet another of the Lake District's picturesque communities.

Drive to the end of the village and bear right SP 'Mungrisdale'. Continue through agricultural country and in ½ mile bear right. In 1 mile turn left on to a winding road and continue to the Horse and Farrier (PH). Just beyond the PH bear right on to moorland and drive below the sheer rock face of 2,174ft Carrock Fell. Continue through Mungrisdale, pass below Souther Fell, then meet a T-junction with the A66 and turn right SP 'Keswick'; 2,847ft Saddleback rises to the right. Continue to the outskirts of Threlkeld; the main village lies just off the main road to the right.

THRELKELD, Cumbria
No less than 35 local huntsmen are commemorated by a monument in the local churchyard, and it seems likely that the fanatical John Peel would have made many friends here. The village itself stands at the head of St John's Vale, on the banks of a stream that threads its way along the valley floor. North is the unusually shaped peak of Saddleback.

Continue along the A66 and pass the junction with the B5322. In ¼ mile turn left on to an unclassified road SP 'St John's in the Vale Church', and in 1 mile turn left again SP 'Stone Circle'. In ¼ mile turn left and ascend to the Castlerigg Stone Circle.

CASTLERIGG STONE CIRCLE, Cumbria
Situated in a superb mountain setting some 700ft above sea level, this prehistoric circle (AM, NT) measures over 100ft in diameter and is made up of 38 stones. An oblong space on the site contains another 10 stones.

Continue past the stone circle and descend to meet the A5271. Turn left and re-enter Keswick.

Castlerigg Stone Circle probably dates back to the bronze age.

BOUNDARY OF AN ANCIENT EMPIRE

Here the monumental ruins of Hadrian's Wall undulate across the rocky spine of Britain, still proclaiming the might of the Roman Empire many centuries after its collapse. South are the soft woodlands of the beautiful South Tyne Valley, the heart of rural Northumberland.

CARLISLE, Cumbria

During the Roman occupation Carlisle, then known as *Luguvalium*, was a strategic centre of the frontier that separated the largely Romanized peoples of the south from the wild northern tribes. Continued excursions from Scotland prompted William Rufus to build the town's sturdy castle (AM) in 1092; Queen Mary's Tower contains a fascinating museum devoted to the Border Regiments. During the Civil War the six western bays of Carlisle's small medieval cathedral were demolished to repair the town wall, but two surviving bays of the nave display Norman workmanship. The choir was restored in the 13th century and features a magnificent east window. In the cathedral grounds is a 13th-century pele tower known as the Prior's Tower. A museum occupies Tullie House a fine Jacobean mansion and contains exhibits relating to Hadrian's Wall.

Leave the centre of Carlisle with SP 'The South' on the A6 and in 3 miles reach the M6 junction roundabout. Take the 2nd exit SP 'Wetheral', and 1 mile beyond Cumwhinton pass a right turn leading to Wetheral Abbey. After a short distance enter the pleasant village of Wetheral.

WETHERAL, Cumbria

An ancient abbey gatehouse in this attractive village faces across the River Eden to the impressive pile of Corby Castle. Fine monuments by the sculptor Nollekens can be seen inside the local church.

Follow the main road through Wetheral village and in 1½ miles meet a T-junction. Turn right on to the A69 SP 'Newcastle' and cross the Eden. A detour from the main route to Corby Castle can be made by turning right immediately after the bridge on to an unclassified road and driving through pleasant countryside for 1½ miles.

CORBY CASTLE, Cumbria

In 1611 the local Howard family extended the old pele tower that had been guarding Great Corby since the 13th century, adding a long range that transformed it into a great L-shaped house. The present aspect of the building, set amid lovely grounds (open) in a particularly scenic area, owes much to further extension work carried out in the 19th century.

On the main tour, continue along the A69, skirt the grounds of Holme Eden Abbey, and enter Warwick Bridge.

WARWICK BRIDGE, Cumbria

The two small communities of Warwick and Warwick Bridge are separated by a fine bridge of 1837. Most of the notable buildings are off the main route in Warwick, including a superb Norman church with an outstanding 12th-century apse.

Leave Warwick Bridge and after a short distance meet crossroads. Turn right on to an unclassified road SP 'Castle Carrock' and in 50 yards turn left. Follow a quiet by-road and in 1 mile pass Toppin Castle, which incorporates a pele tower. In a further 1½ miles branch left SP 'Talkin', and 1 mile farther keep left, pass under a railway viaduct, and meet crossroads with the B6413. Drive forward over the main road and pass Talkin Fell on the right before entering Talkin.

TALKIN, Cumbria

Close to the high fells whose ownership was so hotly disputed for many centuries, this village has a lovely little church that has managed to preserve surprising evidence of its Norman origins. Work from that early period can be seen in the nave, bellcote, and chancel, and there are even traces in the pulpit and altar rail. Some 4 miles south-south-east of Talkin the summit of Cold Fell is surmounted by a cairn measuring 4ft high and 50ft in diameter.

Leave Talkin, and in ¼ mile turn right SP 'Hallbankgate'. Ascend, with views which extend left over the tree-bordered waters of Talkin Tarn and the great expanse of the Cumberland Plain. Reach Hallbankgate and turn right on to the A689 SP 'Alston'. Continue through Halton Lea Gate, then in just over 1 mile turn left on to an unclassified road SP 'Coanwood'. Descend to the steep wooded banks of the River South Tyne, cross the river, and ascend past Coanwood to meet crossroads. Turn left on to the 'Haltwhistle' road, in ¾ mile enter the hamlet of Rowfoot, and turn left SP 'Featherstone Park'. After ½ mile descend steeply to reach Featherstone Castle.

Carlisle Cathedral is impressive but small.

The River South Tyne chatters over its stony bed through the grounds of secluded Featherstone Castle.

FEATHERSTONE CASTLE, Northumb

Beautifully situated in large grounds beside the River South Tyne, this fine house dates from the 13th century and is now a children's activity holiday centre.

Leave Featherstone Castle on a secluded, picturesque road along the east bank of the River South Tyne. Meet a bridge and keep forward SP 'Haltwhistle', then in ½ mile ascend to a T-junction and turn left. In 1¾ miles reach Bellister Castle on the right.

BELLISTER CASTLE, Northumb

In the 16th century the ruined tower attached to this 3-storey building was known as a bastell house, which perhaps gives a clue to the origin of the name. The house itself dates from 1669 and displays a number of good architectural features, Peel tower open by appointment.

Leave Bellister Castle and after a short distance turn left to cross a river bridge and reach the outskirts of Haltwhistle. Turn right on to the A69 to reach the town centre.

HALTWHISTLE, Northumb
William the Lion founded this old mining town's church in 1178, and as it stands today the building is considered a particularly fine example of early-English architecture. There is no tower, and the sanctuary preserves three carved coffin lids which are thought to date from the 14th century.

Return along the A69 'Carlisle' and follow the railway for 2¾ miles. Turn right on to the B630 to reach Greenhead.

GREENHEAD, Northumb
This little village lies south of Hadrian's Wall, close to a series of attractive ravines known as the Nine Nicks of Thirlwall. The route of a Roman track known as the Maiden Way extends from here to Penrith.

Leave Greenhead on the B6318 SP 'Gilsland'. In ½ mile pass a section of Hadrian's Wall on the left.

A section of Hadrian's Wall at Gilsland.

HADRIAN'S WALL, Cumbria
Between AD 122 and 139 the Roman Emperor Hadrian ordered that a defensive wall should be built to discourage the independent Scottish tribes from marauding into the largely pacified territory to the south. Today this major engineering achievement still stands as a remarkable monument to the Roman occupation of Britain, stretching 73 miles from Wallsend-on-Tyne to Bowness. Its course was plotted from one natural advantage to the next, and it was built of the materials most readily to hand – stone in the east and turf in the west. Along its length were 20 or so major forts, interspersed with milecastles and signal towers close enough together to allow the quick transference of a warning by fire beacon. Much of the surviving structure is protected under the Ancient Monuments scheme.

Continue along the B6318 to Gilsland, and on the nearside of a railway bridge reach a left turn leading to the Roman wall's Poltross Burn Milecastle.

GILSLAND, Northumb
Gilsland has natural sulphur and chalybeate springs that once made it a popular spa resort, though it never developed to the rarefied fashionable heights achieved by its southern contemporaries. Part of the Poltross Burn Milecastle (AM) is incorporated in a railway embankment near by, and a section of the Roman wall (AM) stands east of the school.

Meet a T-junction in Gilsland and turn right. A detour from the main tour can be made to Upper Denton by turning left at the T-junction.

UPPER DENTON, Cumbria
It is thought that the Saxon builders of this fascinating little church may have used stone from Hadrian's Wall in its construction. Of particular note is the reconstructed Roman arch in the chancel.

Leave Gilsland by crossing the River Irthing. In ¼ mile turn left, and ascend with views of the Roman wall to the left. After 1 mile turn left on to an unclassified road SP 'Birdoswald, Lanercost', and in a further ½ mile pass Harrow's Scar Milecastle (AM) to reach Birdoswald.

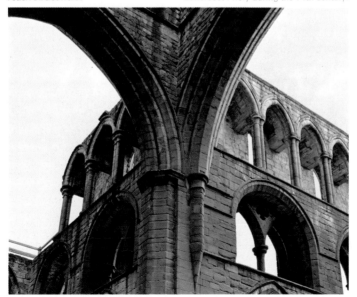

The excavated milecastle at Haltwhistle was one of several built at intervals along the length of Hadrian's Wall.

BIRDOSWALD, Cumbria
The Roman fort of *Camboglanna* (AM) occupies a 5-acre ridge-top site overlooking the gorge of the River Irthing near Birdoswald. Access to the remains, which include a particularly well-preserved angle tower and postern gate, is controlled by the farmer.

Leave Birdoswald and drive forward along the line of the Roman wall, passing two Roman turrets (AM) to reach Banks.

BANKS, Cumbria
Notable Roman sites in the area around Banks include Coombe Crag, Pike Hill (AM) and Boothby Castle Hill, and there is a milecastle (AM) with a section of the Roman wall here. One mile south-west lies the partly-ruined Augustinian, Lanercost Priory, founded in 1166. The nave is still in use. In the rebuilt Abbey mill is a craft workshop for the handicapped.

Raiding parties from the Scottish side of the border inflicted heavy damage on Lanercost Priory during the 14th century.

From Banks bear left, descend to the River Irthing, and continue to Lanercost.

LANERCOST, Cumbria
Extensive remains of a priory (AM) that was built with stones taken from the Roman wall can be seen here, including parts of a gatehouse showing 16th-century adaptations. The 12th-century nave serves as the parish church.

Pass the entrance to Lanercost Priory, cross the river, then immediately beyond the bridge turn left and ascend. After a short distance cross Naworth Park to reach Naworth Castle.

NAWORTH CASTLE, Cumbria
Pleasantly designed round a central courtyard, this 14th-century castle shows later additions and features a great hall, oratory, and rich tapestries. The building is open by arrangement.

At the castle entrance bear right and in ½ mile meet crossroads. Turn right on to the A69 SP 'Carlisle' to reach Brampton.

BRAMPTON, Cumbria
An unusual 8-sided moot hall stands in the cobble-flanked main street of Brampton, and the local church is the only ecclesiastical building known to have been designed by the inventive 19th-century architect, Philip Webb. The interior of the building is lit by a superb stained-glass window by the Victorian artist Burne-Jones.

Follow the A69 through Brampton, then keep forward on to the B6264 SP 'Carlisle Airport'. Proceed to Crosby-on-Eden.

CROSBY-ON-EDEN, Cumbria
The windows of the local church show the striking and original use of cut clear glass instead of stained glass. Other notable buildings here include Crosby House and High Crosby Farmhouse.

In 3½ miles turn left on to the A7 for the return to Carlisle.

THROUGH WEARDALE AND TEESDALE

Deep in the wooded outriders of the eastern Pennines are beautiful river valleys and spectacular waterfalls, attractive little dales villages, and the stream-fed waters of placid reservoirs. Everywhere is the sound of water falling from ledges, tumbling over boulders, and cascading down hillsides.

The fast-flowing River Tees becomes even more rapid as it nears High Force Waterfall.

Raby Castle was considerably altered during the 18th and 19th centuries.

BARNARD CASTLE,
Co Durham

The town of Barnard Castle stands in a picturesque setting on a clifftop overlooking the River Tees and is an ideal base from which to explore the lovely countryside of Teesdale. The first castle to stand here was built in the 12th century by Guy de Balliol, but this was rebuilt by his nephew Bernard – hence the Barnard element of the town name – and adapted throughout the centuries by various owners. During the Civil War it fell to the Cromwellian army, after which it was left to crumble away in peace. Today the site covers 6½ acres, and the extensive remains (AM) include the 3-storey keep and parts of a 14th-century great hall. In the town itself is a medieval bridge that is still in use, and many old houses and inns. It is thought that Charles Dickens may have written *Nicholas Nickleby* while staying here. Close to the town is the fascinating Bowes Museum of Art and the local countryside is dotted with picturesque little villages.

A short detour before the main route begins can be taken to Egglestone Abbey by driving south on the B6277 and turning off with SP on an unclassified road.

Egglestone Abbey is now a romantic ruin.

EGGLESTONE ABBEY,
Co Durham

These lovely ruins (AM) date from the 12th century and occupy a beautiful rural site beside the River Tees. Close by the Thorsgill Beck is spanned by a medieval packhorse bridge and an attractive 18th-century road bridge.
On the main tour, leave Barnard Castle with SP 'Bishop Auckland' and at the edge of the town turn left to follow the A688 to Staindrop.

STAINDROP, Co Durham

Strongly associated with the Neville family of nearby Raby Castle, this long village is strung out along a single main street and has a fine green. The local church was once the family church of the Nevilles and contains fine monuments spanning many generations. It is of Saxon origin and carries a tower that was added in the 12th century, but its south aisle, porch, and nave all date from the 15th century. Inside is the only pre-Reformation screen surviving in County Durham.

Turn left by Staindrop Church and after 1 mile reach the entrance to Raby Castle.

RABY CASTLE, Co Durham

This impressive pile stands in a 270-acre deer park and exactly matches the popular conception of what a castle should look like, right down to its moat and nine great towers. It is known to have been in existence in one form or another from 1016, but its present distinctive appearance is largely due to 14th-century rebuilding and extension. Over the centuries Raby has played a major role in the politics of Britain. The huge Baron's Hall was the scene of plotting aimed at putting Mary Queen of Scots on the English throne instead of Elizabeth I, but when the scheme failed the castle was forfeited and passed into the hands of the Neville family. Later it became the property of the Vanes, Lords of Barnard; nowadays it is a valuable national asset which attracts many visitors each year. Inside are fine collections of furniture, paintings and ceramics, and among the many fine chambers is a curious octagonal drawing room. The kitchens display 14th-century rib vaulting and preserve a smoke-driven spit, while outside in the stables is a collection of carriages.

Leave Raby Castle and continue along the A688 for ¼ mile. Turn left on to an unclassified road SP 'Cockfield' and after ¼ mile keep straight on SP 'Butterknowle'. After another 2¼ miles turn left on to B6282 for Copley and continue to Woodland. Meet a T-junction and turn left, then after 300 yards turn right on to an unclassified road SP 'Hamsterley'. Descend, with good views over Hamsterley Forest.

HAMSTERLEY FOREST,
Co Durham

Fast becoming known as one of the most beautiful countryside recreation areas in the county, this large state forest is crossed by a road that is open to motorists. It can be explored via dozens of footpaths, and parking space is virtually limitless. Visitors are catered for with three picnic sites, drinking water, forest picnic furniture, and a visitors' centre. A special woodland trail has been laid out to help children identify various species of plants and animals, and the glades away from the busy areas are the homes of roe, fallow, and red deer.

After 3 miles turn left SP 'Wolsingham' and descend, then in ¾ mile meet a T-junction and turn left again to cross Bedburn Beck. After a short distance pass a left turn that gives access to Hamsterley Forest, and drive through woodland before emerging into open countryside and descending into Weardale. Cross the River Wear and continue to the edge of Wolsingham.

WOLSINGHAM, Co Durham
A good base from which to explore beautiful Weardale, this typical Durham town of stone-built houses holds a precarious balance between the needs of industry and the preservation of its charm. The result is the type of contrast seen between giant steelworks on the outskirts and the historic 12th-century tower of St Mary's Church, more towards the centre of the town. North of Wolsingham is the lovely Tunstall Reservoir, which was formed by the constriction of Waskerley Beck and has become the home of many water birds and other wild creatures with a liking for aquatic surroundings.
Turn left on to the A689 SP 'Stanhope' and continue to Frosterley.

FROSTERLEY, Co Durham
A local stone known as Frosterley marble is much prized for building and monumental sculpture, but centuries of quarrying have almost exhausted the supply. What little is left is being saved for purposes considered important enough for such a rare material. Many of the county's churches have fonts, memorials, pillars, and various other features fashioned from the stone, which is not really marble but a grey limestone that becomes black and reveals hundreds of tiny fossils when polished. A particularly fine example of the material can be seen near the door of the local church, bearing the inscription 'This Frosterley marble and limestone, quarried for centuries in this parish, adorns cathedrals and churches throughout the world'.
Leave Frosterley and continue along the A689 to Stanhope.

An unusual feature of Stanhope Churchyard is the fossilized stump of a tree.

STANHOPE, Co Durham
Stanhope churchyard features the fossilized stump of a tree that grew some 150 million years ago. The church itself dates from 1200 and contains a number of fascinating relics, including a Saxon font, two wooden plaques and a painting all thought to be Flemish. Close to the churchyard gate is the old town cross. West of Stanhope, in the high Weardale moorland, is a wooded gorge containing the famous Heathery Burn Cave. Bronze-age weapons and various artefacts proving the early domestication of horses in England were found here, and are now on display in London's British Museum.
Leave Stanhope on the A689 'Alston' road and continue to Eastgate.

The drama of Caldron Snout is well worth the difficult approach.

EASTGATE, Co Durham
Attractive Frosterley marble is shown to advantage by the font in Eastgate's 19th-century parish church. A feature of the beautiful moorland countryside around the village is the Low Linn Falls, where a burn tumbles over rocks in an area that is of particular interest to geologists and botanists.
Leave Eastgate and continue along the A689 beside the River Wear to reach Westgate.

WESTGATE, Co Durham
Both Westgate and Eastgate derived their names from the entrances to Old Park, which was once the hunting residence of the bishops of Durham. The village has a 19th-century church and an attractive watermill, and was once well known as a cock-fighting centre. Nowadays it has a strange claim to fame as the only place where a medieval thimble has been found.
Continue to Daddry Shield.
The high moorland of Weardale is within easy reach of Stanhope.

DADDRY SHIELD, Co Durham
Another old centre of cock fighting, this attractive Weardale village stands just north of a mountain rescue post.
Continue to St John's Chapel.

ST JOHN'S CHAPEL, Co Durham
This ancient market centre takes its name from the Church of St John the Baptist. The original foundation was probably created many hundreds of years ago, but the present building dates from 1752.
Turn left on to an unclassified road SP 'Middleton-in-Teesdale' and climb to 2,056ft on Langdon Common, part of the Pennine Chain.

THE PENNINE CHAIN
Popularly known as the Backbone of England, this great upland mass of hills, moorland, and mountains stretches north from Kinder Scout in Derbyshire to the Cheviot foothills on the Scottish border. A 250-mile footpath known as the Pennine Way traverses the range from end to end.

Descend into Teesdale, meet a T-junction, and turn left on to the B6277. In ½ mile reach the Langdon Beck Hotel, where a short detour can be made from the main route by turning right and driving along a rough track to the picnic area at Cow Green Reservoir. A private road (locked) and footpath (open) lead from here to the waterfall of Caldron Snout.

CALDRON SNOUT, Co Durham
More of a tiered cascade than a proper waterfall, beautiful Caldron Snout tumbles 200ft down a natural staircase formed by a hard rock known as dolerite. It used to be fed by a long winding pool called the Well, but this has now been incorporated in the Cow Green Reservoir. Downstream from the cascade is the spectacular High Force waterfall, and between the two are the remains of a slate mill.
Continue along the B6277 and after 2¼ miles meet the High Force Hotel. A footpath opposite the hotel leads to the High Force waterfall.

HIGH FORCE, Co Durham
Here one of England's loveliest waterfalls plunges 70ft over the menacing black cliff of the Great Whin Sill, to be caught in a deep pool surrounded by shrubs and rocks.
Continue along the B6277 through Newbiggin to reach the town of Middleton-in-Teesdale

MIDDLETON-IN-TEESDALE, Co Durham
Strong Quaker influence is evident in the no-frills orderliness of this stern little town. This is because local lead mines, the mainstay of Middleton's economy until they were closed at the start of this century, were run by that denomination. The local church dates from the 19th century and shares its churchyard with various remains of a predecessor.
Leave Middleton-in-Teesdale and turn right on to a road SP 'Scotch Corner'. Cross the River Tees and in ⅓ mile keep left SP 'Barnard Castle'. Continue for ¾ mile, rejoin the B6277, and continue through Mickleton and attractive Romaldkirk.

ROMALDKIRK, Co Durham
The attractive houses of this perfect little Teesdale village are interspersed with greensward that transforms an already good villagescape into a splendid one.
Leave Romaldkirk and continue along the B6277 to Cotherstone.

COTHERSTONE, Co Durham
Beautiful and dramatic scenery surrounds this pleasant village, which stands at the junction of Balder Beck and the River Tees. Close to the watersmeet are slight remains of a Norman castle.
Leave Cotherstone, recross the River Tees, and return to Barnard Castle.

ALNWICK, Northumb

This attractive and historic town is a convenient touring centre situated in attractive countryside only 4 miles from the coast. Its splendid castle was once a stronghold of the dukes of Northumberland, and over hundreds of years has been extended to cover some 7 acres of ground. It was founded by the Percy family in the 12th century, but was ruined during a particularly violent phase of border warfare and was not restored to military effectiveness until the 14th century. The major features of its design date from this time, although a great deal of maintenance work was carried out in the 18th and 19th centuries, and today it ranks as one of the most magnificent buildings of its type in the country. The gateway is guarded by an impressive barbican, and the outline of its massive keep, walls and towers completely dominates the town's horizon. Parts of the castle open to visitors are the armoury in Constable's Tower, a museum of British and Roman antiquities in the Postern Tower, the keep, and many of its beautifully furnished state rooms. The town itself has several good churches and several good Georgian buildings. St Michael's echoes the castle with its battlemented tower and is said to preserve some of the best 15th-century workmanship in the county. Among the treasures inside are numerous fine monuments and a Flemish carved chest that dates from the 14th century. Remains of Alnwick Abbey stand on the northern outskirts of the town and include a well-preserved 14th-century gatehouse. The 18th-century Town Hall has shops in its arcaded ground floor. The annual Alnwick fair is held on the last Sunday in June, when the townsfolk dress in period costumes. The fair lasts for 7 days. Some 3 miles north-west of Alnwick in Hulne Park are the remains of 13th-century Hulne Priory.

Follow SP 'Morpeth', then 'Bamburgh B1340' and cross the River Aln via Denwick Bridge. Pass through Denwick, turn right on to an unclassified road SP 'Longhoughton', and after 2¼ miles turn left to join the B1339. Enter Longhoughton, then after another 1 mile turn right and in ½ mile drive forward on to an unclassified road SP 'Howick'. Continue for 1 mile to pass the entrance to Howick Hall, then turn right and after another ½ mile keep left to reach the edge of Howick.

HOWICK, Northumb

Situated where the Great Whin Sill outcrop meets the sea in 120ft cliffs of black rock, this hamlet is also a good base from which to tour the fine 18th-century mansion (open) standing in beautiful grounds (open).

In 1¼ miles meet crossroads and turn right through an archway to the fishing village of Craster.

196

AN UNDISCOVERED COAST

Much of Northumberland's coast is unvisited and unspoiled. North of Alnwick it is designated an Area of Outstanding Natural Beauty, while to the south the lovely River Coquet meets the sea after winding past the religious foundations and mighty castles of bygone ages.

Crabbing boats at Craster are still built to the traditional Northumbrian design.

CRASTER, Northumb

Craster is known for its oak-smoked kippers and splendid cliff scenery. The former can be sampled at many places in the district, and the latter is best appreciated from a 1¼-mile walk leading to Dunstanburgh Castle. Above the village is the Georgian house of Craster Tower, which incorporates the remains of a medieval building from which it takes its name.

Restoration in the 19th century preserved Bamburgh Castle's imposing presence on the Whin Sill outcrop.

DUNSTANBURGH CASTLE, Northumb

The great rocky promontory that juts into the sea here would be impressive in any circumstances, but crowned with the picturesque ruins of Dunstanburgh Castle it is magnificent. Remains of this essentially 14th-century structure (AM, NT) cover 11 acres of ground and are enclosed by massive defensive walls. This particular section of coast is in a designated area of outstanding natural beauty.

Return from Craster for ¼ mile and turn right SP 'Embleton'. In another ¾ mile meet a T-junction and turn right for Embleton.

EMBLETON, Northumb

One of the main buildings in this pretty village is the 14th-century fortified vicarage, which incorporates a pele tower. Military precautions in buildings ideologically devoted to peace are not uncommon in this area which was racked by war between Scots and English for centuries.

Keep left and drive to the church, then turn right on to the B1339. In 1¼ miles keep forward on to the B1340, and 1¼ miles farther turn right. In another 1⅓ miles meet crossroads and turn right again for Beadnell.

BEADNELL, Northumb

Close to this small fishing village are several 18th-century lime kilns (NT). Safe bathing and a sandy beach make it attractive as a resort, and the surrounding countryside is beautiful.

Continue to Seahouses.

SEAHOUSES, Northumb

During the late 19th century a harbour was built here to serve north Sunderland, and the village that grew up to house the port workers has changed little to the present day. It is a pretty place with plenty of boat traffic, including a service that runs to the offshore Farne Islands.

FARNE ISLANDS, Northumb

It is said that St Aidan came to this group of 25 small islands (NT) to meditate in the 7th century, and that St Cuthbert stayed in a little hermitage here until he was reluctantly persuaded to become Bishop of Lindisfarne (see tour 92) in the same period. Nowadays the group is best known for its bird sanctuary, and ornithologists of the Bird Observatory study from a converted 16th-century pele tower.

At Seahouses turn right, reach a war memorial, and turn left to follow the coast road to Bamburgh.

BAMBURGH, Northumb

Grace Darling was born in this unspoilt fishing village in 1815, and is buried in the graveyard of the mainly 13th-century church. She became instantly famous in 1838 when she sailed with her father from a lighthouse on Longstone Island, in the teeth of a gale, to rescue survivors from the wrecked ship *Forfarshire*. The RNLI has founded a local museum to her memory. Immediately obvious to the visitor is Bamburgh's huge Norman castle (open), once the seat of the kings of Northumbria now restored to its original magnificence, it includes the Armstrong Museum of Industrial Archaeology. During the 18th century it became a charitable institution, with schools, accommodation for shipwrecked sailors, and a hospital.

Branch right on to the B1342 SP 'Belford' and in 2½ miles meet a T-junction. Turn left, then after another 1¾ miles reach Belford Station and drive over a level crossing. In 1 mile cross over the A1 on to the B6349 for Belford.

Statues guard the barbican at Alnwick Castle.

ROTHBURY, Northumb
The Victorian Cragside House was the first house in the world to be lit by electricity generated by water power (open), it stands in a 900-acre country park. The surrounding area is rich in various prehistoric remains.

Keep forward and in ½ mile bear right on to the B6334 SP 'Morpeth'. After 3½ miles it is possible to take a short detour from the main route by turning right to Brinkburn Priory.

BRINKBURN PRIORY, Northumb
Beautifully set in a loop of the River Coquet, and is surrounded by rhododendrons in a wooded setting, this 12th-century foundation was created by Augustinian Canons and has one of the best priory buildings (AM) in the country. This status is largely due to sensitive 19th-century restorers.

On the main route, continue for 1½ miles and turn left on to the A697 SP 'Coldstream'. Reach the edge of Longframlington and turn right on to the B6345, then continue to Felton. Cross the River Coquet, keeping on the B6345 SP 'Amble'. After another 1¾ miles turn left and continue through Acklington. Turn left again at Broomhill village on to the A1068 for Amble.

AMBLE, Northumb
North of this attractive little resort is a stretch of coast that has been designated an area of outstanding natural beauty. Eider ducks breed on Coquet Island, which lies offshore from Amble.

Turn left and follow SP 'Alnwick', then in 1½ miles meet a T-junction and turn right into Warkworth.

WARKWORTH, Northumb
At the top of the main street in Warkworth are the impressive remains of a 12th-century and later castle (AM) that was probably built by the 1st Earl of Northumberland. Its keep, gatehouse, and hall are particularly notable. The view along the main street as it climbs towards the ruins between buildings of many periods is unforgettable. The mainly Norman Church of St Lawrence has an outstanding stone spire which is one of only two ancient examples to be found in the county, and the famous Warkworth Hermitage is a rock-cut chapel (AM) dating from the 14th century.

In 3¾ miles meet a roundabout and drive forward. A short diversion can be made from the main route by taking the 3rd exit from the roundabout and visiting Alnmouth.

ALNMOUTH, Northumb
This holiday resort was once a major grain-shipping port, but nowadays it deals mainly with yachtsmen and other small-boat sailors.

On the main drive, return along the A1068 via Lesbury to Alnwick.

BELFORD, Northumb
In coaching days this small market town on the Great North Road was a popular stop where passengers could stretch their legs and take refreshment at local inns. Belford Hall (not open) is a large building designed by James Paine in 1756.

Continue on the B6349 SP 'Wooler', and after another ¾ mile turn left again on to an unclassified road SP 'Chatton'. In 3 miles meet a T-junction and turn right on to the B6348, then descend from Chatton Moor to reach Chatton village. Drive to the end of the village and turn left on to an unclassified road SP 'Chillingham'. After another 1½ miles reach Chillingham Post Office and turn left; cross a ford into the village.

CHILLINGHAM, Northumb
During the summer months the grounds of 14th- and 17th-century Chillingham Castle (not open) are accessible for people wishing to see the remarkable Chillingham wild cattle. The animals in this herd are the descendants of wild oxen believed to have been trapped when the park was created in 1220.

Return to Chillingham Post Office and turn left, then pass an unclassified left turn leading to Ros Castle. This offers a pleasant detour from the main route.

ROS CASTLE, Northumb
Local people will insist, with some justice, that the views from this 1,036ft hill (NT) are better than any others in the county. The magnificent panorama stretches east to the coast and the Farne Islands, west to the Cheviot Hills, and embraces the romantic medieval outlines of both Bamburgh and Dunstanburgh Castles.

On the main tour, continue for 3 miles and drive forward to join the B6346 for Eglingham.

EGLINGHAM, Northumb
The multi-period church in Eglingham is a charming, if heavily restored, asset to the villagescape. Eglingham Hall (not open) dates from the early 18th century.

On the nearside of Eglingham turn right on to an unclassified road SP 'Beanley' and 'Powburn', then in 1 mile bear left SP 'Glanton'. After another 2¼ miles cross a main road for Glanton, then turn right and take the next turning left for Whittingham.

Atlantic seals bask under Longstone lighthouse in the Farne Islands, offshore from Bamburgh.

WHITTINGHAM, Northumb
Attractively grouped on both banks of the River Aln, this pretty village was once famous as the location of a large fair. A lovely stone bridge spans the river, and the local church shows evidence of Saxon origins in its tower and nave. A 15th-century pele tower survives here.

Cross the River Aln, turn right SP 'Callalay', and after 2 miles skirt the grounds of Callalay Castle.

CALLALAY CASTLE, Northumb
The Callalays are the last of three families to have successively owned this estate since Saxon times, and the manor house is one of the best in the county. Most of the present building (open) dates from the 17th to 19th centuries, but the 15th-century pele tower which it incorporates is evidence of a much earlier building.

In 2½ miles turn left SP 'Thropton', ascend, then descend into Coquet Dale at the edge of Thropton. Meet a T-junction and turn left on to the B6341 for Rothbury.

197

AMONG THE BORDER FORESTS

The fascinating remains of Hadrian's Wall can be seen at their best over the vast coniferous plantations and wild moorlands of the Kielder and Redesdale Forests, parts of the Border Forest Park. Special Forestry Commission roads allow motorists to enjoy this area right up to the Scottish Border.

Bewcastle's ancient cross is decorated with intricate carvings and Runic inscriptions.

BELLINGHAM, Northumb
The focus of life in North Tynedale, this small market town once had a flourishing iron industry but nowadays is best known as a gateway to the great moors and forests of Nortumberland. Its ancient Church of St Cuthbert has a unique roof, barrel vaulted with six-sided stone ribs instead of the usual timber, probably as a precaution against fire. In the churchyard is a well whose waters are traditionally held to have healing powers.

Leave Bellingham on the B6320 with SP 'Hexham', and in ⅓ mile turn left and cross a river bridge. Take the next turning right on to an unclassified road SP 'Kielder', then drive through picturesque North Tynedale.

NORTHUMBERLAND NATIONAL PARK, Northumb
Extending from Hadrian's Wall in the south to the Cheviot Hills in the north, this 400-square-mile national park occupies the whole western corner of Northumberland and joins the Border Forest Park along its western boundary. Much of the district is high moorland, with rugged hills and summits that afford superb views of the local countryside, but towards the east its character changes to a gentler landscape where the valleys of the Coquet, Redesdale, and North Tyne meander through beautiful woodland. Walking and pony-trekking are two popular ways in which visitors explore the park.

Continue for 4 miles, cross a river bridge, then turn right and continue to Stannersburn. After a while enter the Kielder Forest and drive to Kielder Reservoir.

KIELDER FOREST, Northumb
Really part of the Border Forest Park, this great sea of conifers blankets the slopes of the Cheviot Hills with the varied greens of larch, spruce, Scots pine, and lodgepole pine. It was planted by the state to meet the needs of industry and has matured as a valuable addition to the Northumbrian landscape.

BORDER FOREST PARK, Northumb, Borders
So called because it crosses the border into Scotland, this vast area of woodland incorporates three forests and is the largest area of its type in Britain. In the east its vast landscapes merge with the open moorland horizons of the Northumberland National Park, making a staggering 600 square miles

of beautiful, wild, and essentially unspoiled countryside in all. Both parks are crossed by the 250-mile Pennine Way footpath, and the Kielder, Redesdale, and Wauchope forests offer many planned walks and nature trails. Various leisure activities are catered for.

KIELDER RESERVOIR, Northumb
The largest reservoir in Western

Europe, situated in the heart of the Border Forest Park, offers a variety of activities. Within Tower Knowe is a Water Authority's Information Centre.

Continue through the Kielder Forest to the village of Kielder.

Much of the Border Forest Park has been planted with softwood species to supply the timber industries. Their dark ranks echo the forests of the past.

KIELDER, Northumb
This and several other villages were developed as the area's forestry industry became established, and nowadays they make handy bases from which to explore the local countryside. Kielder Castle is an 18th-century shooting lodge that now serves as a Border Forest Park information centre and a Forest Museum.

Continue for 3 miles and cross the Scottish border, then in 3¼ miles turn left on to the B6357 SP 'Newcastleton' and follow the attractive Liddel Water. In 6¼ miles reach a junction with the B6399. A detour from the main route to Hermitage Castle can be made by turning right on to the B6399, driving for 4 miles, then turning left on to an unclassified road.

HERMITAGE CASTLE, Borders
Romantically associated with Mary Queen of Scots, this brooding castle (AM) punctuates the desolate moorland landscape with four great towers and grim walls that entirely suit their windswept situation. It was a stronghold of the Douglas family in the 14th century, and much later became the property of Mary's lover Bothwell.

On the main route, bear left with the B6357 to reach Newcastleton.

Map labels: PEEL FELL, SAUGHTREE FELL 1424, Saughtree, ARNTON FELL 1484, Hermitage Castle, SCOTLAND, LARRISTON FELLS, Newcastleton, TINNIS HILL 1326, Tinnisburn Forest, Kershope Forest, Doe and Burn, Newcastleton Forest, LESTONE FELL 1569, GLENDHU HILL, Black Lyne, White Lyne, SIGHTY CRAG 1701, LONG CRAG 1510, Border Forest Park, Kielder, Kielder Reservoir, Kielder Forest, BLACK KNOWE, Stannersburn, Northumberland National Park, ENGLAND, BELLINGHAM, Wark, River North Tyne, Wark's Burn, Wark Forest, Spadeadam Forest, Bewcastle, River Irthing, Greenlee Lough, Broomlee Lough, Housesteads, Hadrian's Wall, Carrawbrough, Chollerford, mls 0 1 2 3 4 5 6 7, kms 0 2 4 6 8 10, Birdoswald, Gilsland, Greenhead, Twice Brewed Inn (PH) (Information Centre), Banks East Milecastle, Haltwhistle, B6318, N

NEWCASTLETON, Borders
Before the forestry industry became such an important influence on local life this attractive village was a flourishing weaving centre. Its position affords views of beautiful Liddesdale from almost anywhere in or around the village, and beyond Newcastleton Forest are the magnificent 1,678ft Larriston Fells. This part of the Border Forest Park was planted in 1921.

Drive to the far end of the village and turn left on to an unclassified road (no SP). Cross a river bridge and turn right SP 'Brampton', then after 3 miles cross Kershope Burn to enter the English county of Cumbria. Ascend a winding road through the Kershope Forest, then after ¾ mile reach the Dog and Gun Inn and turn left SP 'Carlisle'. In 4 miles turn right, and in another ¾ mile drive forward on to the B6318. Take the next turning left on to an unclassified road and drive to Bewcastle.

BEWCASTLE, Cumbria
Several ancient remains can be seen in the bleak open moorland that surrounds Bewcastle. Materials from a Roman fort that was once an outpost of Hadrian's Wall were used to build a castle (AM) here, but this too has succumbed to the ravages of time and cottage builders, leaving just a few fragments. In the village churchyard is the famous Bewcastle Cross, which dates from the 7th century and is intricately carved with Runic inscriptions and patterns.

At Bewcastle turn right (no SP) and cross a river bridge. In 5 miles cross the B6318, and in 2½ miles meet a T-junction. Turn left SP 'Birdoswald' and follow the line of Hadrian's Wall for ½ mile to reach Banks.

HADRIAN'S WALL, Northumb, Cumbria
This mighty engineering achievement was built in the 2nd century AD and is the most impressive monument to the Roman occupation in Britain. It runs for 73 miles across the entire width of northern England and is remarkably well preserved along several sections. It was part of a complex defence system designed to keep the marauding Scottish tribes out of the Romanized south, and included two broad ditches and a series of milecastles interspersed with turrets and signal towers. The Romans finally abandoned the wall in AD 383, but it survived in a reasonably complete state until quarried by road builders in the 18th century. Well-preserved forts can be seen at Chesters, Housesteads, Vindolanda, and Birdoswald, while the most complete section of wall stands to the west of the River North Tyne. Walks along the wall are most enjoyable and can be very instructive.

The northern frontier of Roman Britain still forms a barrier as it follows the high ridges of Whin Sill.

One of the best-preserved of the original 17 Hadrian's Wall forts has been excavated at Housesteads, revealing many facets of Roman life.

BANKS, Northumb
A turret (AM) on the Roman wall here was once manned by troops garrisoned at the nearest milecastle. A footpath leads east to the Pike Hill signal tower, part of a beacon system by which a warning of attack could be sent the length of the wall with surprising speed. One mile south west lies the Augustinian, Lanercost Priory (AM) which was founded in 1166 and its nave is still in use. In the rebuilt Abbey Mill, is a craft workshop for the handicapped.

Continue to Birdoswald.

BIRDOSWALD, Cumbria
Large and impressive outer defences of a Roman fort (AM) known as *Camboglanna* can be seen here beside the River Irthing, and well-preserved sections of Hadrian's Wall (AM) extend east and west. Close by are the substantial remains of Harrow's Scar Milecastle (AM).

In ½ mile ascend, then turn right on to the B6318 SP 'Gilsland' and in 1 mile turn right to reach Gilsland.

GILSLAND, Northumb
Sulphur and chalybeate springs brought brief fame to this small place as a spa resort, but it is much better known for its excellent Roman remains. Hadrian's Wall runs south of the village and includes the Poltross Burn Milecastle (AM), a fascinating and well-preserved survivor from the occupation. Close to the village is an attractive waterfall.

From Gilsland turn left along the B6318 and in 2 miles meet a junction and turn left to enter Greenhead.

GREENHEAD, Northumb
Close to Greenhead is a dramatic series of ravines known as the Nine Nicks of Thirlwall. Near by are the ruins of Thirlwall Castle, which was built in the 14th century, and the route of a Roman track known as the Maiden Way runs through the area.

Turn left on the B6318, ascend, and in 5 miles reach the Twice Brewed Inn.

TWICE BREWED INN, Northumb
Slightly away from the site of the original building, this famous inn now houses a useful Northumberland National Park information centre. Close by, at Winshields, the Roman wall (AM) reaches its highest point of 1,230ft above sea level.

Continue along the B6318 to reach Housesteads, where there is a reasonable carpark.

HOUSESTEADS, Northumb
The best-preserved fort (AM, NT) on Hadrian's Wall can be seen here. Once known as *Vercovicium*, it follows the typical Roman pattern of rectangular walls with rounded corners, and was built to house up to 1,000 infantrymen. Relics found during excavations in the area are displayed in a well laid-out museum, and close to Housesteads the wall itself reaches its highest point as it follows the high ridges of the Great Whin Sill rock outcrop. Marvellous views from the ridge extend west and take in several little lakes, including the lovely Crag Lough.

Continue for 5 miles to reach Carrawborough.

CARRAWBOROUGH, Northumb
One of the very few Mithraic temples to be found in Britain has been excavated here. Probably dating from the 3rd century, it was a very small building containing three dedicatory altars to the deity Mithras, and a figure of the Mother Goddess. Close by is the Roman fort known as *Brocolitia*.

Continue along the B6318 to reach Chollerford.

CHOLLERFORD, Northumb
Housesteads may be the best preserved of the Roman wall's forts, but *Cilurnum* (or Chesters) is by far the most interesting and best excavated. It was a large stronghold housing 500 troops. Digging has revealed fascinating details of the fort itself, plus the remains of a bath house and central heating system. Relics from this and other sites can be seen in the interesting local museum, and traces of the Tyne bridge that the fort was built to guard have been found downstream of the present 18th-century crossing.

Meet a roundabout and take the 1st exit on to the B6320 SP 'Wark, Bellingham'. Enter the North Tyne Valley to reach Wark.

WARK, Northumb
Access to this picturesque huddle of cottages and houses is by an iron bridge over the River North Tyne. The woodlands of Wark Forest stretch away to the west.

Continue along the B6320 for the return to Bellingham.

PEACE IN THE BORDER LANDS

Green rounded hills and unspoilt miles of coastline betray nothing of the centuries of human violence that once made this lovely area a place to avoid. Now the only battles are between nesting gulls, and the only invasions are of migrant birds seeking the haven of a largely unpopulated countryside.

BERWICK-UPON-TWEED, Northumb

A busy seaport and now England's northernmost town, Berwick was alternately held by Scottish and English forces during the bitter border struggles that began with the Romans and persisted until the 15th century. Remains of a castle built here by the Normans in the 12th century include three towers and ancient sections of wall that were later incorporated in the medieval town defences. During Elizabethan times the town walls (AM) were restored to full defensive effectiveness, and they have survived as a complete 2-mile circuit round old Berwick. Their rebuilding was done with gun warfare very much in mind, and in their present condition they represent the earliest examples of their type in northern Europe. The approach to the town itself is dominated by three famous and attractive bridges over the River Tweed. Berwick Bridge dates from the 17th century and has 15 elegant arches, the Royal Border Bridge of 1880 was built to carry a railway into the town, and the Tweed Road Bridge is a good example of modern architecture dating from 1928. It is said that the town has more buildings scheduled for preservation than any other place of comparable size in England, and a walk round the lovely old streets would certainly seem to confirm that. The parish

church, one of the few to be built during Cromwell's Commonwealth, is of exceptional architectural interest and was extended in the 19th century. In 1717 Vanbrugh built Britain's earliest barracks here, and today these incorporate the well laid out Museum of the King's Own Scottish Borderers. The Georgian period is represented by the Town Hall (open by arrangement) and several fine houses attractively sited by the quay. Relics from the town's past can be seen with collections of paintings and ceramics in Berwick Museum, and the lovely local countryside includes a coastal area of outstanding natural beauty. Every May Day the traditional ceremony of Riding the Bounds, reaffirming the parish boundaries, takes place here.

Leave Berwick on the A1167 with SP 'Edinburgh', and in ½ mile bear left on the A6105 SP 'Kelso'. In a further ½ mile turn left A1 then after ½ mile turn right B6461 after 1 mile enter the old Scottish county of Berwickshire. In ¾ mile keep left, and after another 1½ miles turn left on to an unclassified road SP 'Norham'. Later cross the River Tweed by the Union Suspension Bridge and re-enter Northumbeland. In ½ mile meet a T-junction and turn right, then in 1¼ miles turn right again and continue to Norham.

Berwick's 17th-century bridge was built across the estuary in 1611 to connect the town with Tweedmouth.

NORHAM, Northumb

One of the two triangular greens in this attractive village features a 19th-century cross, and together they form a focal point for the solid little stone-built houses that surround them. At the east end of the main street the massive Norman keep of a 12th-century castle (AM) towers above the River Tweed from a rocky outcrop, proclaiming a strength that resisted the efforts of Scottish forces for many hundreds of years. The army of Robert the Bruce unsuccessfully assaulted its walls for nearly a year, and 12 months later the castle resisted a siege that was immortalized by Sir Walter Scott in the poem *Marmion*. The hero of the occasion was Sir William Marmion, an English knight who accepted a lady's challenge to take command of the most dangerous place in Great Britain as proof of his love. On February 13 the opening of the salmon season is marked by a ceremony known as the Blessing of

the Nets, after which the Tweed can be fished for salmon by anyone with the right or money to do so.

Leave Norham, meet a main road, and turn left on to the B6470 SP 'Cornhill'. In ½ mile turn right on to an unclassified road, then in ¾ mile turn right again on to the A698. After a further 2 miles cross (with care) the picturesque Twizel Bridge.

The keep of Norham Castle dates from c1160.

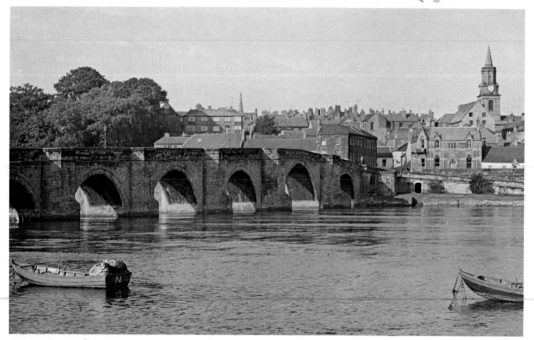

TWIZEL BRIDGE, Northumb

This beautiful 15th-century bridge spans the River Till with a single elegant arch of 90ft. Views from the bridge into the deep wooded glen are enchanting, and the ivy-covered folly of Twizel Castle enhances the scene from a nearby ridge. Many such 18th-century conceits were left unfinished, but this was genuinely never completed.

Leave Twizel Bridge and continue to Cornhill-on-Tweed.

CORNHILL-ON-TWEED, Northumb

The Scottish poet and folk hero Robert Burns entered England for the first time when he crossed the River Tweed here in 1787. This and other events are recorded on a plaque at nearby Coldstream.

A detour can be made from the main route to Flodden Field from Cornhill: meet a roundabout in the village and take the 1st exit on to the A697, then after 1⅓ miles turn right on to an unclassified road and proceed to Branxton for Flodden Field.

FLODDEN FIELD, Northumb

In 1513 one of the bloodiest battles ever witnessed on English soil was fought at Flodden Field, just a few hundred yards south of Branxton village. A monument inscribed 'To the brave of both nations' now marks the spot where James IV of Scotland was killed when the English army of 26,000 defeated a huge invading force of 40,000. Both sides suffered appalling casualties, with as many as 1,600 deaths between them.

A second detour from the main route at Cornhill to the village of Coldstream can be followed by taking the 2nd exit at the roundabout on to the A697 and driving for 1¾ miles.

COLDSTREAM, Borders

John Smeaton built the 5-arched bridge over the River Tweed here in 1766 to replace a ford that had been used for many hundreds of years, often by the armies of Scotland and England. A plaque on the bridge records the poet Burns' first crossing of the river into England, and one near the market commemorates the raising of the Coldstream Guards to fight in Cromwell's New Model Army.

On the main tour, meet the roundabout in Cornhill and take the 2nd exit on to the A697. Take the first turning left on to an unclassified road SP 'Learmouth', then in 1¼ miles meet crossroads and drive forward. Take the 2nd turning left SP 'Yetholm' and in 2½ miles meet crossroads. Turn left on to the B6352 SP 'Wooler' and in ¼ mile bear right to follow the Bowmont Water, then 2 miles farther turn right on to the B6351. Cross a river bridge, meet a T-junction, and turn left to follow the foot of the Cheviot Hills. Pass the edge of Kilham and drive to Kirknewton.

KIRKNEWTON, Northumb

Kirknewton's church has a chancel and south transept that were obviously built for defensive as well as religious purposes, a reminder of the centuries of unrest suffered by this and many other border villages. The valley of the College Burn leads from the village to the 2,676ft summit of The Cheviot via a narrow constriction known as Hen Hole. The lovely countryside hereabouts is best appreciated on foot.

Continue along the B6351 to Yeavering.

YEAVERING, Northumb

The Saxon King Edwin had his capital here in the 7th century, and excavations in a field near the River Glen have revealed traces of wooden halls and amphitheatres from his ancient town. It was Edwin who, according to tradition, allowed the monk Paulinus to convert the people of Northumbria to Christianity. One of the largest hillforts in the border country can be seen to the south of the village, on the 1,182ft summit of Yeavering Bell.

From Yeavering continue along the foot of the Cheviot Hills.

Winter in the Cheviot Hills can be a beautiful but lonely season.

THE CHEVIOT HILLS, Northumb

Much of this lonely range forms the border between Scotland and England. Its grassy flanks and mountainous summits are cropped smooth by the famous Black Face and Cheviot sheep, hardy breeds that can find food in the most unlikely places and survive with the minimum of interference from man. The countryside between the hills and Hadrian's Wall forms part of the Northumberland National Park, and the arduous northern section of the 250-mile Pennine Way brings the footpath to an end here. North-east of the great mass that is The Cheviot itself lies the picturesque College Valley, and the equally attractive Harthope Valley lies to the east. Auchope Cairn, rising to 2,382ft, straddles the border between England and Scotland.

After 1½ miles turn right on to the A697 to reach the edge of Wooler.

WOOLER, Northumb

Situated north-east of the Cheviot, this attractive little place makes a natural base from which to explore the open landscapes of the Cheviot Hills. Close to the village is a stone which commemorates the Battle of Hamildon Hill, when an English army led by Henry Percy defeated a huge Scottish army under the command of the Earl of Douglas.

Leave Wooler, turn left on to the B6525 SP 'Berwick' and continue to the village of Doddington.

The Priory at Holy Island was an important religious centre for centuries.

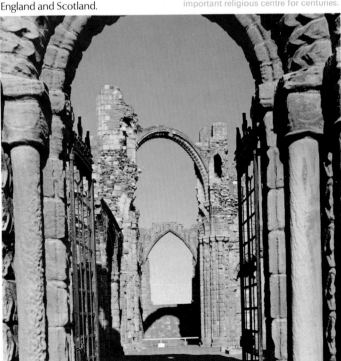

DODDINGTON, Northumb

Features of this village include a ruined pele tower of 1584 and a 13th-century church containing a Norman font. The local countryside is very rich in prehistoric remains, including earthworks and stones bearing the enigmatic cup-and-ring marks of ancient cultures. South is the iron-age hillfort of Dod Law, where a natural crag known as the Lateral Stone features curious carvings and vertical grooves. Below this is a cave known as Cudy's Camp; Rowting Lyn Camp is situated in a miniature gorge near by.

Leave Doddington and drive forward for 5 miles, then branch right on to the B6353 to reach Lowick. Pass Fenwick, meet the A1, and turn left to reach the Plough Hotel in West Mains; a detour from the main route can be taken by following a side road to the right by the hotel and driving to the village of Beal.

BEAL, Northumb

Most of the beautiful coastline near Beal is included in a national nature reserve, and the horizon to the south-west is dominated by the low summits of the gentle Kyloe Hills. A causeway exposed at low tide leads to Holy Island, but visitors should take careful note of the tide tables displayed all round the village to avoid being cut off.

To continue the detour, cross to the Holy Island of Lindisfarne via a causeway that is exposed for about 2 hours before and from approximately 3½ hours after high tide.

HOLY ISLAND (LINDISFARNE), Northumb

Historically known as Lindisfarne, this Cradle of Christianity is only an island at high tide but offered sufficient isolation to please the missionaries who were led here from Iona by St Aidan in the 7th century. About 150 years later their monastic foundation was sacked and destroyed by Danish marauders, but in 1082 the Benedictine order built a fine priory on the same site. Its gaunt ruins (AM) still stand today, and various relics found during excavations can be seen in a local museum. The island's restored 16th-century castle (NT) contains antique oak furniture. Examples of the needlework for which the islanders are justly famous can be seen in the 13th-century parish church. Christianity has been at Lindisfarne for a long time, but a reminder of more ancient days is the Petting Stone. A legend attached to this was that brides who jumped over the stone would have a happy marriage – a tradition with more than a hint of paganism. The nature reserve on Holy Island is an important haven for an enormous variety of wildfowl and wading birds.

On the main tour, leave the Plough Hotel in West Mains and continue along the A1. Passing Scremerston, at roundabout take 2nd exit A1167 and return to Berwick-upon-Tweed.

Scotland

The awe-inspiring Black Cuillin mountains dominate the view from the old bridge at Sligachan on Skye. Some of Scotland's finest and most spectacular scenery is formed by the wild loch and mountain landscapes of this, the largest offshore island in Scotland.

SIR WALTER SCOTT'S COUNTRY

A romantic glow cast by the great novels of Sir Walter Scott suffuses the wild and beautiful landscapes of the Border country. High in the Eildon Hills is the viewpoint from which he drew particular inspiration, and all round are tiny hamlets, remote castles, and the magnificent ruins of ancient abbeys.

Some of the original architectural splendour is preserved in ruined Melrose Abbey.

KELSO, Borders

This bustling Border town was described by Sir Walter Scott, who once lived here, as 'the most beautiful, if not the most romantic, village in Scotland'. Its abbey (AM) was the largest and most splendid of all the Border abbeys. Fine Norman workmanship can be seen in the surviving fragments of the abbey church. The cobbled town square features the elegant Town House of 1816, and John Rennie built the town's splendid Tweed Bridge in 1803. Not far from the bridge is the distinctive Turret House (NTS, not open). Floors Castle (open), home of the Duke and Duchess of Roxburgh, stands about 1 mile to the north-west of the town.

Leave Kelso on the A699 'St Boswells' and 'Selkirk' road, cross the River Tweed, and turn right. Cross the Teviot and in ¼ mile reach Roxburgh Castle.

ROXBURGH CASTLE, Borders

Roxburgh's Royal Burgh was a major town in the 13th century, but the town has completely disappeared and only the castle mound remains.

ROXBURGH, Borders

Roxburgh's famous name now belongs to a small hamlet lying 2½ miles south-west of the castle site, on the banks of the River Teviot.

From Roxburgh Castle drive on the A699 for 7 miles to reach Maxton.

MAXTON, Borders

Maxton Church has been considerably altered and restored, but originally dates back to the 12th century. A curious old cross shaft in the village marks the spot where the men of the barony assembled for war. A ruined tower remains from an old seat of the Ker family.

From Maxton continue on the A699 for 1¼ miles and meet the A68. Turn right, then right again on to the B6404 to enter St Boswells.

ST BOSWELLS, Borders

Once a famous centre for livestock sales, this village faces across a 40-acre common to St Boswells Green, centre of the Buccleuch Hunt.

Continue on the B6404 and in 1 mile cross the River Tweed. In ¼ mile turn left on to the B6356 SP 'Dryburgh', then drive through pleasant riverside scenery and in 1¼ miles reach Dryburgh Abbey.

DRYBURGH ABBEY, Borders

One of a famous group of 12th-century Border monasteries founded by David I, Dryburgh (AM) was repeatedly attacked by the English and badly damaged in 1544. The cloister buildings have survived in a remarkably complete state, and though the church itself has not fared so well its west front, parts of the nave, and the chapter house can still be seen. This is the resting place of Sir Walter Scott.

Return along the B6356 and in ½ mile turn left to pass the Wallace Statue.

WALLACE STATUE, Borders

This massive statue to Sir William Wallace overlooks magnificent Tweed Valley scenery.

Proceed on the B6356 to reach Bemersyde House on the left.

BEMERSYDE HOUSE, Borders

Traditional home of the Haig family, this house (not open) was frequently visited by Sir Walter Scott. It incorporates an ancient tower which was burned in a raid during 1545.

In ¼ mile turn left, then in ½ mile reach Scott's View.

SCOTT'S VIEW, Borders

This AA viewpoint on Bemersyde Hill faces west across the winding Tweed to the three conical peaks of the distinctive Eildon Hills.

In ½ mile drive forward on to an unclassified road SP 'Melrose' and descend through woodland to cross Leader Water. In ¼ mile turn right SP 'Jedburgh' and meet the A68. Turn left to cross the River Tweed, then immediately right to join the B6361. Continue to reach Newstead.

NEWSTEAD, Borders

Standing on the south bank of the River Tweed, this old-world village faces across the water to the slopes of Leaderfoot Hill. To the east of the village, a Roman-style altar marks the site of the Roman army camp of Trimontium.

Continue on the B6361 to Melrose.

According to legend the Eildon Hills were cleft into three by a wizard.

MELROSE, Borders

Border raids in the 14th and 16th centuries destroyed most of David I's beautiful Cistercian abbey (AM) at Melrose. Parts of the nave and choir remain, but the most spectacular survivals are the red sandstone windows with their rich tracery. The heart of Robert Bruce is buried somewhere within the abbey. A nearby museum of carved stones and treasures from the abbey and the Trimontium Fort is contained in the 15th-century Commendator's House. The town preserves a 17th-century cross with the arms of Scotland.

From Melrose follow SP 'Galashiels' to join the A6091 and after ¼ mile reach the B6494 left turn leading to Darnick. This can be taken as a detour.

DARNICK, Borders

The romantic Tweed-side setting of old Darnick Tower (not open) belies its turbulent past. Originally built in 1425, it was burned by the English, and rebuilt in 1569.

On the main route, continue along the A6091 SP 'Galashiels' and keep forward over 2 roundabouts, taking the B6360 to reach Abbotsford House.

ABBOTSFORD HOUSE, Borders

Internationally famous as the home of Sir Walter Scott, this fine building (open) was designed by the writer himself and he died here in 1832. It has been preserved in his memory, and the library contains a staggering collection of some 20,000 rare books.

Return to Melrose, meet a roundabout, and turn right on to the B6359 SP 'Lilliesleaf' and 'Hawick'. Ascend to a 814ft road summit, with views ahead of the Cheviots. After 3 miles meet the B6398 on the left, which leads to Bowden.

Scott's writing materials are preserved at Abbotsford House.

BOWDEN, Borders

A Conservation Area, features of Bowden are a laird's loft in the 17th-century church and the 16th-century market cross which serves as a war memorial.

On the main tour, continue with the B6359 and drive forward over the crossroads with the A699 and continue for 3 miles. Turn left to cross Ale Water, then right on to the B6359 and proceed to Lilliesleaf.

LILLIESLEAF, Borders

The parish church in this little village was built in 1771, but since then has been considerably extended. Some 2 miles south-west is a 19th-century tower on an old motte.

Leaving Lilliesleaf turn left with the B6359 SP 'Denholm'. Proceed to Hassendean.

HASSENDEAN, Borders

The song *Jack o'Hazeldean* is associated with this small village.

In Hassendean turn left on to the B6405, passing the twin peaks of the Minto Hills. In 1½ miles reach an unclassified left turn that offers a detour to Fatlips Castle.

FATLIPS CASTLE, Borders

High on the summit of the steep Minto Crags stand the ruins of this curiously-named castle, which was built in the 16th century for the Lockhart family.

On the main route, continue along the B6405 and cross the River Teviot to enter Denholm.

DENHOLM, Borders

Two literary figures were born in this small River Teviot village. James Murray (original editor of the *Oxford English Dictionary*) and Scott's poet friend John Leyden. Westgate Hall is an attractive 17th-century building near the village green, and Text House is the weird creation of a local eccentric, Dr Haddon.

In Denholm meet the junction with the A698 and turn right SP 'Hawick'. After 3½ miles turn left on to the A6088 SP 'Bonchester Bridge, Newcastle'. A detour from the main route can be made by keeping forward on the A698 to the old woollen town of Hawick.

HAWICK, Borders

John Hardie, a pioneer of Hawick's woollen industry, is buried in St Mary's Churchyard. The rebuilt church dates from the 13th century, and in Moat Park is probably the motte of a Norman castle. The battle of Flodden Field was a disaster for Hawick in 1513, when nearly all the men of the town were killed; they are commemorated by the Horse monument in the High Street. Wilton Lodge Museum and Art Gallery features the growth of the town's woollen industry.

This typically ornate entrance hall was part of Sir Walter Scott's design for his home, Abbotsford House.

On the main tour, continue along the A6088 through Kirkton to reach Bonchester Bridge.

BONCHESTER BRIDGE, Borders

Rule Water flows under this bridge and beneath the slopes of 1,059ft Bonchester Hill, eventually to join the Teviot farther north. Wauchope Forest lies to the south.

Continue on the A6088, passing Bonchester Hill on the left, to reach Southdean.

SOUTHDEAN, Borders

Souden Kirk stands in ruins to the south of Southdean, a little village beside the Jed Water. The building was a church in the 13th century, and the meeting place for Scottish leaders before the battle of Otterburn in 1388. A superb miniature altar only 9¼ inches long with fine carved crosses has been excavated from the site.

Jedburgh Abbey, although damaged and burned by the English, retains enough of its character to make it one of Scotland's finest medieval buildings.

Continue on the A6088 and ascend to the A68. Continue to Carter Bar.

CARTER BAR, Borders

Scotland meets England at this 1,370ft viewpoint in the Cheviot Hills. Lush pastures and trim plantations spread out to the north, with the Eildon Hills in the distance, and the Roman camp and earthworks of Chew Green lie to the east. The lonely tree-clad Rede Valley and Border Forest Park provide a wild southerly prospect.

Return along the A68 SP 'Jedburgh' and descend to the wooded valley of Jed Water to reach Ferniehurst Castle.

FERNIEHURST CASTLE, Borders

Scene of frequent Border skirmishes, this fine 16th-century castle was once the seat of the Border family of Ker. Their arms can still be seen on panels in the castle, but the most impressive part of the interior is the huge fireplace in the great hall. In today's more peaceful times the castle serves as a youth hostel.

Continue along the A68 to Jedburgh.

JEDBURGH, Borders

A popular walking, climbing and riding centre, Jedburgh stands as a gateway to Scotland. Its finest attraction is the abbey (AM), which is roofless and in ruins but nevertheless magnificent. It was one of David I's Border abbeys and was burned in 1523. Mary Queen of Scots is associated with the town, and the 16th-century Mary Queen of Scots' House is now a museum devoted to her life. The castle at the top of Castlegate is a 19th-century construction on the site of the 12th-century stronghold built by Scottish kings. Inside, rooms have been constructed to show the 'reformed' system of the early 19th century. The medieval custom of Candlemas Ba' takes place in Jedburgh every Shrove Tuesday, when a game of handball is played through the streets between Uppies born above the mercat cross — and Downies, born below it.

Leave Jedburgh on the A68 SP 'Edinburgh' and in 2 miles meet the A698. Turn right for Crailing.

CRAILING, Borders

The fine Regency mansion of Crailing House (not open) is the main feature of this pleasant small village.

Continue on the A698 and in 1 mile meet an unclassified road on the right. A short detour can be taken along this road to Eckford.

ECKFORD, Borders

A pair of 18th-century jougs — iron collars used to punish wrongdoers — is preserved in the church. An old watch-house stands in the churchyard to guard against body-snatching, once a common crime.

On the main tour, continue along the A698 and re-enter Kelso.

BORDER VALES AND MARSHES

This lonely, unpopulated land was the scene of border strife and bloody warfare for many centuries, but it was also the inspiration for some of Burns' poetry and the goal of eloping couples. The peace of its river-threaded dales and gentle grandeur of its hills belies its turbulent history.

LOCKERBIE, Dumf & Gall

In the late 17th century this pleasant little town was a major centre for horse and lamb trading. Lamb Hill takes its name from a market that has been held here since 1680, and everywhere there are signs of Lockerbie's agricultural affiliations. However, it has not always been as peaceful as it seems today. In 1593 one of the last Border family feuds ended in a fierce battle at which the Johnstones killed Lord Maxwell and some 700 of his followers. Wealth from the China tea trade came to local landowners and manifested itself in several great mansions that appeared in the area.

From Lockerbie follow signs Glasgow to join the A74 and drive through Annandale. In 7 miles cross Johnstonebridge.

JOHNSTONEBRIDGE, Dumf & Gall

This picturesque bridge spans the River Annan, which flows south through the lovely countryside of the Annandale valley.

In 6 miles turn left on to an unclassified road for Beattock.

BEATTOCK, Dumf & Gall

Beattock stands in hilly country on the Evan Water, in lovely Upper Annandale. Close by are four prehistoric forts, and farther north along the Evan Valley, on the way to the famous Beattock road and railway summits, are the picturesquely ruined towers of Blacklaw, Mellingshaw, and Raecleuch.

Turn left, pass under a railway bridge, and in 1 mile turn right on to the A701 'Dumfries' road. Continue to the hamlet of St Ann's and cross the Kinnel Water.

ST ANN'S, Dumf & Gall

The bridge here dates from c1800, and the picturesque ruins of Lochwood Tower from 1592. A little to the north-west of the hamlet are the lovely Raehills Glens.

Continue to Amisfield Town.

AMISFIELD TOWN, Dumf & Gall

Amisfield Tower 1 mile north-west is the ancestral home of the Charteris family, who have been associated with the area since the 12th century. It was built in the 16th century and is one of the best and most beautiful buildings of its type in Scotland.

Continue through Locharbriggs to Dumfries in Lower Nithsdale.

DUMFRIES, Dumf & Gall

Affectionately known as Queen of the South by the Scots, this ancient Royal Burgh was combined with its sister community of Maxwelltown in 1929. The two districts are linked by five bridges across the River Nith, and they hold much of their history in common. The central point of the town is an 18th-century complex of buildings known as Mid Steeple, comprising the old municipal buildings, courthouse, and prison. An inscribed tablet of distances on the

Ruthwell Cross, housed in a special apse, has been exceptionally well preserved since the 8th century.

wall of the building is a reminder of times when Scottish cattle drovers herded their animals the length of England to reach the lucrative markets of London. The 15th- and 16th-century remains of Lincluden College (AM), including the fine collegiate church and provost's house, can be seen just outside the town. Relics from this and other periods of the burgh's history are preserved in Dumfries Museum. Many famous people have visited or lived in the town, but it is the two Roberts who are best remembered. Robert the Bruce changed the course of Scottish history when he stabbed the Red Comyn in the former Greyfriars monastery, and

some 500 years later in 1791 the poet Robert Burns made his home here. Burns wrote some of his most famous songs while living in the town, and the house where he died has been made into a Burns Museum in his honour. On display are personal possessions and some of his manuscripts, and the road in which the house stands has been renamed Burns Street. Other relics associated with the poet can be seen in the Hole in The Wa' Tavern and the Globe Inn. The family grave and mausoleum are together in St Michael's Churchyard. There is a Burn's interpretation centre at the Old Town Mill.

At the roundabout turn right SP 'Stranraer' then shortly turn left SP 'Carlisle' and drive alongside the River Nith. At the end turn left then right, SP 'Glencaple' on to the B725 and continue along the B725 to Glencaple.

Devorgilla's Bridge, which was built in 1426, is one of five that span the River Nith at Dumfries.

GLENCAPE, Dumf & Gall
In his novel *Guy Mannering* Sir Walter Scott refers to this little Nith-estuary village as Portanferry. To the local people it is the Auld Quay.

Continue alongside the Nith estuary, with 1,868ft Criffell prominent across the water to the right, after 3 miles the ruins and estate of Caerlaverock Castle lie ¼ mile to the right.

CAERLAVEROCK CASTLE & NATURE RESERVE, Dumf & Gall
A fortified building has stood here since the early 13th century, but the triangular structure (AM) that now occupies the site owes most of its existence to the 15th century. As a Maxwell stronghold Caerlaverock had a stormy history. In 1638 a fine Renaissance-style block was put up but in 1640 the castle was seriously damaged in a 13-week siege by victorious Covenanters and it became a ruin. The Maxwell crest and motto can still be seen between two splendid towers over the gateway. The estate is now part of a 13,000 acre nature reserve with outstanding hide facilities and an observatory tower. The saltmarsh and sandy foreshore between the River Nith and Lochar Water is the winter haunt of the barnacle goose and other wildfowl.

Continue to Bankend and turn right SP 'Ruthwell'. Cross flat and often marshy countryside, and after 4¾ miles turn right on to the B724. After ¼ mile an unclassified left turn offers a detour to Ruthwell Church. (Ruthwell village lies to the right).

Robert Burns is commemorated in Dumfries, where he died in 1796.

RUTHWELL, Dumf & Gall
The 18ft cross at Ruthwell Church dates from the 8th century and is one of the most remarkable dark-age monuments (AM) to have survived in Europe. This archaeological treasure is preserved in a special apse and is heavily inscribed with early written phrases in the Northumbrian dialect of English. These make up the *Dream of the Rood*, which may have been written by the Saxon poet Caedmon; other inscriptions on the cross are in Runic characters. At Ruthwell village is the Duncan Savings Bank Museum.

Continues along the B724 to the village of Cummertrees.

CUMMERTREES, Dumf & Gall
Scott describes the district around this village in *Redgauntlet*. The full effect of the Solway Firth's notorious spring tides can be observed from nearby Powfoot.

Continue for 3 miles and turn right on to the A75 to enter Annan.

ANNAN, Dumf & Gall
Sited on the River Annan and the Solway Firth, this pleasant touring centre is noted for its shrimps and is within easy reach of beautiful countryside. Famous names connected with the town include Robert Stevenson, who built the fine bridge in 1826 and Thomas Carlyle who attended the old grammar school and later described it as Hinterschlag Gymnasium in his *Sartor Resartus*. North of Annan are the cooling towers of the Chapelcross Nuclear Power Station.

Cross the River Annan, meet traffic lights, and turn left on to the B722 'Eaglesfield' road. In 2 miles turn left again on to an unclassified road SP 'Ecclefechan', then after 2½ miles cross the Mein Water and turn right to Ecclefechan. Turn right on to the B725 to enter the village.

ECCLEFECHAN, Dumf & Gall
The Arched House (NTS) was the birthplace in 1795 of the writer and philosopher Thomas Carlyle, and now contains a collection of his personal possessions. Both he and his parents are buried in the village churchyard.

In Ecclefechan turn right and in ½ mile join the A74 'Carlisle' road. After 2½ miles pass a junction where a detour to Kirtlebridge can be taken.

KIRTLEBRIDGE, Dumf & Gall
Close to Kirtle Water, a little to the south-east of Kirtlebridge, are several old towers. The one known as Robgill was built in the 16th century and now forms part of a recent mansion, and the ancient Irving stronghold of Bonshaw Tower still has its ancient clan bell. About ½ mile south-east is the fine Merkland Cross, an interesting wayside monument that dates from the 15th century.

Until 1940 English couples could be married in Scotland without their parents' consent. The blacksmith's shop at Gretna Green preserves the anvil over which the ceremony was performed.

On the main route, continue along the A74 and after 2 miles reach a junction where a short detour to Kirkpatrick Fleming can be taken.

KIRKPATRICK FLEMING, Dumf & Gall
A cave which lies to the west of this village is popularly held to be the place where Robert the Bruce was given a lesson in perseverance by a spider. The event is also claimed by several other places in Scotland and Northern Ireland.

On the main route, continue along the A74 and after 3¼ miles branch left on to an unclassified road SP 'Gretna Green' to reach Springfield.

SPRINGFIELD, Dumf & Gall
Founded by weavers in 1791, this village became famous for elopement marriages that were performed here in the 19th century.

A short detour can be taken from the main route here by turning right for Gretna Green.

GRETNA GREEN, Dumb & Gall
For 100 years Gretna Hall and the smithy at Gretna Green were the first places over the Scottish border where runaway lovers could be married without parental consent. Clandestine marriages of this nature were prevented in England by an 18th-century law, but in Scotland it was only necessary for the couple to make a witnessed declaration that they wished to become man and wife. A law passed in 1856 made it a requirement that either the man or woman should have lived in Scotland for a minimum of three weeks, and more legislation in 1940 prevented the village smith from performing the ceremony.

On the main route, continue along the unclassified 'Longtown' road into England and cross Solway Moss. In 1542 the Moss was the site of a battle in which the Scots were defeated by the English. After ¾ mile turn left on to the A6071 and later join the A7 to enter Longtown.

LONGTOWN, Cumbria
At one time the main Carlisle to Glasgow road ran through Longtown, but this was superseded when the present A74 was built by way of Sark Bridge in 1830. To the north is Netherby Hall, made famous by the romantic elopement of the Graham heiress with Lochinvar in Sir Walter Scott's *Marmion*.

Return via the A7 and turn right SP 'Galashiels'. Follow the River Esk and return to Scotland at Scots Dyke. In ½ mile turn right on to the B720 for the village of Canonbie.

CANONBIE, Dumf & Gall
Before the Scots Dyke was built in 1552 the Debateable Land, an area close to Canonbie between the Rivers Sark and Esk, was held by anybody who had the force of arms to do so. The dyke formed an effective new boundary and put an end to the troubles. The village itself stands 2 miles from this new border and was once the site of an important priory. It was also a coaching stop, and an interesting old inn has survived from those days. Liddesdale, to the north-east is associated with Scott's novels.

Turn right on to the B6357, cross the bridge then turn left with the B720. Later rejoin the A7. Continue through the wooded, narrowing valley of Eskdale to Langholm.

LANGHOLM, Dumf & Gall
This angling resort and wool centre stands at the junction of Wauchope Water and the River Esk, with the lovely Ewes Water flowing in from the north. An annual border-riding ceremony that was instituted in the 19th century still takes place in the town. A monument to General Sir John Malcolm stands on 1,163ft Whita Hill, which rises to the east. The forbears of Neil Armstrong, the first man to walk on the moon, came from this area.

Leave the town on the B709 'Eskdalemuir' road and in 2 miles reach Craigcleuch.

CRAIGCLEUCH, Dumb & Gall
The Scottish Explorers' Museum has hundreds of colonial artefacts housed in a baronial mansion.

Continue along the B709 to Bentpath.

BENTPATH, Dumf & Gall
The brilliant engineer Thomas Telford was born in a shepherd's cottage near Glendinning Farm in 1757; his tablet stands ½ mile beyond the hamlet.

After 2 miles turn right and cross the River Esk then climb into the Castle O'er Forest. Proceed to Eskdalemuir.

ESKDALEMUIR, Dumf & Gall
This hamlet is on an important junction of roads in an area that abounds with prehistoric remains.

Cross the river and turn right then left on to the B723 for Lockerbie.

KIRKCUDBRIGHT, Dumf & Gall

This ancient burgh stands in the heart of an area known as the Stewartry and was once a bustling port. Much of the local history is displayed in the Stewartry Museum, and the town is dominated by the handsome ruins of 16th-century Maclellan's Castle (AM). Close to the 17th-century mercat cross is the old Tollbooth, once a prison for John Paul Jones. A fine collection of pictures by E A Hornel can be seen in 18th-century Broughton House (gardens and library open). South of the town the wooded peninsula of St Mary's Isle separates the Dee estuary from Manxman's Lake.

Leave Kirkcudbright on the A755 SP 'Gatehouse of Fleet' and cross the River Dee. In 6½ miles turn right then left across the A75 to join the B727. Skirt the Fleet Forest and enter Gatehouse of Fleet.

GATEHOUSE OF FLEET, Dumf & Gall

This town was the inspiration for Scott's otherwise fictitious town Kippletringham, in *Guy Mannering*. In the town is a huge granite clock tower of 1871, and the local countryside includes isolated moorland where the poet Burns once composed some of his works. To the north-west the Water of Fleet runs through a beautiful glen, and south are the contrasting features of Fleet Bay and deciduous Fleet Forest. Cally Palace Hotel, close to the town in fine parkland, was designed by architect Robert Mylne in 1763.

Go forward on the B796, and after 1 mile turn right on to the Stranraer road A75. After a short distance pass the ruins of Cardoness Castle to the right.

CARDONESS CASTLE, Dumf & Gall

This section of the drive follows one of the most beautiful roads in the south of Scotland. The picturesque ruins of the 15th-century tower house at Cardoness (AM) stand in a superb situation overlooking Fleet Bay, Murray's Isles (NT), and the Islands of Fleet.

Continue, and in ¾ mile reach an unclassified right turn that can be followed for a detour to the hamlet of Anwoth.

ANWOTH, Dumf & Gall

Anwoth Church is a ruined 17th-century building which has retained a number of good features, including a medieval bell. In the churchyard are a cross from the dark ages and the remarkable 8ft-high tomb of a member of the Gordon family who was buried here in the 17th century.

On the main route, continue along the A75 to follow the scenic coastline, passing below Barholm Castle to the right.

208

AMONG THE GALLOWAY HILLS

North of the empty beaches and bird-haunted estuaries of the Solway Firth are high forests, secret little lochs hidden between ridged outriders of the Galloway Hills, and dozens of green river valleys carved through hill flanks to the sea.

Kirkcudbright used to be one of Scotland's major ports, but it gradually declined in the 17th century. Today it is a small harbour at the mouth of the Dee.

BARHOLM CASTLE, Dumf & Gall

Close to the main road below this ruined tower (not open) is Dirk Hatteraick's Cave, the hiding place of the smuggler captain in Scott's *Guy Mannering*. The castle itself was once a place of refuge for the religious reformer John Knox, and is beautifully set overlooking Wigtown Bay.

Continue, and after a short distance pass Carsluith Castle to the left.

CARSLUITH CASTLE, Dumf & Gall

An unusual feature of this roofless 16th-century tower house (AM) is its L-shaped plan, brought about by the addition of a staircase wing in 1568.

Continue along the A75 to Creetown.

CREETOWN, Dumf & Gall

This former granite port overlooks the Cree estuary and the wide expanse of Wigtown Sands. The Gem Rock Museum here has gemstones and minerals from all over the world. To the north-east the Moneypool Burn runs through a charmingly wooded valley.

Continue through Creetown and after 3½ miles reach the hamlet of Palnure.

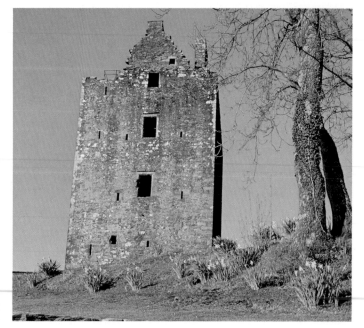

PALNURE, Dumf & Gall

A charming and worthwhile excursion can be made from this village to follow the clear Palnure Burn to Bargaly Glen. To the north-east rises Cairnsmore of Fleet (2,331ft) which is associated with John Buchan's spy novel *The Thirty-Nine Steps*.

Continue on the A75, and in 3 miles at a roundabout take 3rd exit A714 to enter Newton Stewart.

NEWTON STEWART, Dumf & Gall

In the 18th century this lovely Galloway market town was a centre for the weaving, spinning, and carpet-making industries. Nowadays these local skills can be seen in the production of mohair rugs and scarves at the Glencree Mill (open). Between Newton Stewart and Minnigaff the River Cree is spanned by a fine granite bridge built in 1813 by John Rennie. Galloway Forest Park, famous for its many historical and archaeological sites as well as for its great natural beauty, lies to the north.

Leave Newton Stewart with SP 'New Galloway (A712)', cross the Cree Bridge, and pass the edge of Minnigaff. In 1 mile turn left on to the A712 'New Galloway' road. Continue through attractive woodlands of the Galloway Forest Park, with splendid views of the high Galloway Hills to the north and south, along the A712 to reach Murray's Monument.

MURRAY'S MONUMENT, Dumf & Gall

This obelisk commemorates Dr Alexander Murray, who grew up near by as a shepherd boy and eventually became Professor of Oriental Languages in Edinburgh University. Near the monument the Grey Mare's Tail burn plunges in two waterfalls. Nearby on the crags of Talnotry an interesting wild goat park can be seen from the road.

Continue along the A712 and after 4½ miles reach the shores of Clatteringshaws Loch.

CLATTERINGSHAWS LOCH, Dumf & Gall

Part of the Galloway power scheme, this great reservoir was created by the obstruction of the Black Water of Dee. On the eastern shore are the battle site of Rapploch Moss, where a granite boulder (NTS) marks the spot where Robert the Bruce defeated an English force in 1307, and the Galloway Deer Museum. The River Dee runs from the loch to join the sea at Kirkcudbright, and the views in this area are magical. To the right of the main road is the 1,616ft Black Craig of Dee, and the Fell of Fleet rises to 1,554ft in the south.

Continue along the A712 and after 6 miles enter New Galloway.

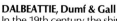

NEW GALLOWAY, Dumf & Gall
This noted angling centre on the River Ken is Scotland's smallest Royal Burgh. Kells Churchyard, sited a little to the north of New Galloway, features the grave of a Covenanter who was shot in 1685. Also here is the curious but attractive Adam and Eve Stone.

Turn right on to the Kirkcudbright road A762 and after 1 mile pass Kenmure Castle on the left.

The River Dee provides an attractive setting for isolated Threave Castle.

Stones from the old abbey were used to build much of Dundrennan village.

KENMURE CASTLE, Dumf & Gall
A little of the original 16th- and 17th-century work can still be seen in the ruins of this Gordon family stronghold, but most of the structure is more recent than that. The hero of Sir Walter Scott's poem *Young Lochinvar* sprang from this family.

After a short distance reach the shores of Loch Ken.

LOCH KEN, Dumf & Gall
Formed by damming the rivers Ken and Dee, this reservoir is partly bordered by rich woodland and is a picturesque addition to the landscape. Some 5 miles south-east of New Galloway the Black Water of Dee enters the loch after flowing through the lovely woodlands of Cairn Edward Forest.

Continue along the A762 and skirt the shores of Woodhall Loch to reach the hamlet of Laurieston.

LAURIESTON, Dumf & Gall
The works of writer S R Crockett are based on this area, and there is a monument to him in the village. Coniferous Laurieston Forest lies to the west, and south-west the waters of Loch Mannoch are overlooked by the Glengap Forest.

Continue through attractive hill country to Ringford.

RINGFORD, Dumf & Gall
During his bloody campaign of persecution the notorious Sir Robert Grierson of Lairg murdered five Covenanters here in 1685. A memorial to the victims stands 2 miles north of the village, on the tour route.

Turn left on to the A75 'Dumfries' road. In 4 miles, shortly after crossing the River Dee, reach a track that leads left to Kelton Mains for Threave Castle.

THREAVE CASTLE, Dumf & Gall
Built in the 1360s by Archibald the Grim, 3rd Earl of Douglas, this castle (AM) is beautifully sited on an island in the River Dee. The locally-forged and nationally famous Mons Meg cannon was used by James II to overcome the rebellious Douglas family here in 1455; this impressive piece of ordnance can now be seen in Edinburgh Castle. In 1640 the stronghold was captured by Covenanters, who sacked it and vandalized its interior.

Continue along the A75 towards Castle Douglas. Before the tour route enters this town it passes an unclassified right turn which offers a short diversion to the Threave Estate.

THREAVE ESTATE, Dumf & Gall
Threave Estate includes the house and grounds, and is the National Trust for Scotland's School of Practical Gardening. The house is not open to the public, but the Wildfowl Refuge and lovely gardens are. Visitors flock here in the spring to see the estate's vast and very beautiful display of daffodils.

On the main route, pass alongside Carlingwark Loch and enter Castle Douglas.

CASTLE DOUGLAS, Dumf & Gall
Once the commercial capital of its county, this pleasant old town is beautifully sited near the shores of Loch Carlingwark. In 1765 the loch was drained, revealing the remains of several prehistoric lake-dwellings known as crannogs, and a number of Bronze-Age artefacts.

At the far end turn right on to the A745 'Dalbeattie' road and after 5 miles descend past granite quarries then turn left on to the A711. Cross the Urr Water to reach Dalbeattie.

DALBEATTIE, Dumf & Gall
In the 19th century the shiny grey granite of which this lovely place is built was shipped from quays on the Urr Water to all parts of the world. South of the town are the green ranks of Dalbeattie Forest, while 2½ miles north is the Mote of Urr—one of the finest Saxon fortifications anywhere in Britain.

Leave Dalbeattie by returning along the A711 and re-cross the Urr Water, then turn left SP 'Auchencairn' and continue along the A711 to Palnackie.

Dalbeattie's quarries are famous for superb granite

PALNACKIE, Dumf & Gall
This attractive whitewashed village stands on the Urr Water north of the Rough Firth, which is an inlet of the Solway Firth. About 1 mile south on an unclassified road is 16th-century Orchardton Tower (AM), one of only two circular tower houses existing in the whole of Scotland.

Continue on the A711 to Auchencairn.

AUCHENCAIRN, Dumf & Gall
A short way offshore from this Auchencairn Bay village is Hestan Island, which was featured as the Isle of Rathan in S R Crockett's book *Raiders*. It is the site of a lighthouse.

Continue on the A711 to Dundrennan.

DUNDRENNAN, Dumf & Gall
Stone from the ruins of 12th-century Dundrennan Abbey (AM) was used to build many of the houses in this village. The foundation itself has sad associations with Mary Queen of Scots, for it was here that she spent her last night on Scottish soil before sailing from Port Mary to England and eventual imprisonment. The port is south of Dundrennan.

Continue along the A711 for the return to Kirkcudbright.

209

AYR, Strath

As well as being a popular resort with miles of safe, sandy beach, this Royal Burgh is also a fishing and commercial port and flourishing centre of industry. Here the spirit of Burns is never very far away. The poet was christened at the Auld Kirk, his statue stands near the station, and relics of his life and work can be seen in the Tam O'Shanter Museum. Ayr's famous Twa Brigs over the River Ayr were built in the 13th and 18th centuries respectively, but the later structure has been replaced by a modern road bridge. The early crossing was renovated in 1910 and is now used by pedestrians only. The town's oldest building is 16th-century Loudon Hall, which was extensively restored in 1938, but earlier incomplete fragments, such as ancient St John's Towers can be seen elsewhere in the area. Ayr is well known for its fine parks and gardens and a fine racecourse. Landmarks of the town are the 126ft high steeple of the Town Hall and the 113ft-high Wallace Tower. Also of interest are the Maclaurin Art Gallery and Rozelle House Museum on the Alloway road.

Leave Ayr on the A719 'Maidens' road and climb past Butlin's Holiday Camp to a height of over 300ft. Skirt Dunure, which lies to the right below the main road.

DUNURE, Strath

This attractive little fishing village is overlooked by a ruined castle on a clifftop site. During the 16th century the stronghold was notorious for the cruel treatment to prisoners and for the roasting alive of the Crown Factor of Crossraguel Abbey. Close by is an old dovecote in which pigeons were once raised to keep the castle supplied with fresh meat.

Continue for 2 miles to reach the Electric Brae.

ELECTRIC BRAE, Strath

A curious optical illusion caused by

THE LAND OF ROBERT BURNS

Scotland's most famous poet was born and raised in this area of cliff-fringed coast and lovely river valleys. His characters still seem to populate the stern little towns, charming villages, and enchanting countryside between the sea and the beautiful reaches of wooded Glen Trool.

Robert Burns was born in this cottage at Alloway in 1759. It now houses a commemorative museum.

the lie of the surrounding countryside makes the road through this area appear to be descending when it is actually climbing.

In 2 miles turn right with the A719 and follow a wooded valley to the entrance of Culzean Castle.

CULZEAN CASTLE, Strath

An ancient tower that was once a Kennedy stronghold forms the centrepiece of this splendid castle (NTS), which was designed by the talented Robert Adam in 1777. Everything about the building prompts superlatives, but the Round Drawing Room and magnificent staircase are probably its finest

features. Many of the rooms have beautifully decorated plaster ceilings. The grounds include the extensive Culzean Country Park.

CULZEAN COUNTRY PARK, Strath

Scotland's first countryside park was created in the 565-acre grounds of Culzean Castle this century, but the lovely walled garden was established in 1783 and the buildings of the Home Farm were designed by Robert Adam while he was extending the castle. The farm has been adapted as a reception and interpretation centre for the park.

Continue along the A719 to reach the village of Maidens.

MAIDENS, Strath

Just inland of this Maidenhead Bay resort is Shanter Farm, which was the home of Douglas Graham, the original of Burns' Tam O'Shanter. The bay has a good sand and shingle beach and a modern harbour for fishing and sailing.

Leave Maidens on the A719 to reach thhe golf resort of Turnberry.

TURNBERRY, Strath

Traces of Turnberry Castle and also a lighthouse stand on Turnberry Point, an attractive promontory to the north of the resort's famous championship golf course. Legend

has it that the castle was the birthplace of Robert the Bruce in 1247, and history records that he certainly landed here in 1307 to win his first battle against the English. On a clear day views extend to lonely Ailsa Craig, a rocky little island 12 miles away that rises to 1,110ft from the sea, and to the Isle of Arran.

In Turnberry village turn left on to the A77 'Ayr' road to reach Kirkoswald.

KIRKOSWALD, Strath

Kirkoswald Churchyard contains the graves of two of Robert Burns' best loved characters, Tam O'Shanter and Souter Johnnie. In real life Tam was Douglas Graham of Shanter, who supplied grain to an Ayr brewery, and his crony 'Souter' was a village cobbler named John Davidson. Davidson's thatched 18th-century cottage (NTS) now houses a Burns' museum. There are life-size figures of these characters in the garden.

From Kirkoswald continue along the A77 to reach Crossraguel Abbey.

CROSSRAGUEL ABBEY, Strath

Originally founded as a Cluniac monastery by the Earl of Carrick in the 13th century, this abbey (AM) was inhabited by the Benedictine order from 1244 to the 16th century. Many superb examples of 15th-century architecture can be seen amongst the extensive ruins.

Continue along the A77 and enter the town of Maybole.

MAYBOLE Strath

Maybole was once the seat of the very powerful Kennedy family, who were the Earls of Cassillis. Their town house was 17th-century Maybole Castle, whose picturesque turret and oriel windows make a charming architectural contribution to the town's High Street. Nowadays it is used as administration offices for the Kennedy estates. Other family connexions exist with the Tollbooth, which was one of their mansions and incorporates fragments of a much older building.

From Maybole turn right on to the B7023 'Crosshill' road and drive to Crosshill village. Turn right here with the B7023 'Dailly' road, then in 1 mile join the B741 and continue through the Water of Girvan valley. After 3 miles meet an unclassified left turn SP 'Barr'. A detour from the main route can be taken to Dailly by continuing along the B741 for 1 mile.

DAILLY, Strath

The 18th-century church in New Dailly features lairds' lofts, and the romantic 16th-century ruin of Dalquharran Castle stands to the north. Two miles south-west on the unclassified Old Dailly road are the Bargany Gardens (open), where fine displays of flowers and shrubs can be enjoyed.

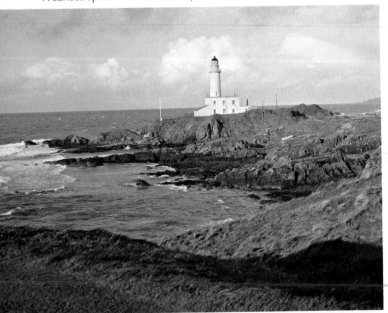

Views from the magnificent golf course at Turnberry extend past a lighthouse to distant Ailsa Craig.

Culzean Castle's Round Drawing Room is a superb example of Georgian elegance.

On the main tour, take the unclassified road SP 'Barr' and drive through moorland for 5 miles, cross the River Stinchar and turn right to follow the river to Barr.

BARR, Strath
Changue Forest, part of the huge Galloway Forest Park, lies close to this little River Stinchar angling resort. Craigenreoch Hill rises to the south-east.

Meet a T-junction and turn right then shortly turn left on to the B734 SP 'Barrhill'. In 6 miles meet the A714 and turn left SP 'Newton Stewart' to reach Pinwherry.

PINWHERRY, Strath
Ruins of a one-time Kennedy stronghold stand near the junction of the River Stinchar and the Duisk River at Pinwherry.

Turn right with the A714 Barrhill road and cross the Duisk Water. Continue up the valley to Barrhill.

BARRHILL, Strath
Desolate, open moorland surrounds this pleasant little village, relieved only by the green banks of the Duisk valley.

Continue along the A714 to Bargrennan and turn left on to an unclassified road SP 'Straiton'. Drive into the Galloway Forest Park.

GALLOWAY FOREST PARK, Dumf & Gall
A third of this huge 110,000-acre park is planted with trees, and its boundaries encompass five complete forests and 10 hills rising to over 2,000ft. Because this is a commercial enterprise as much as anything else, the predominant species of trees in the park are Douglas fir, Scots pine, Norwegian spruce, and other fast-growing conifers. This industrial aspect does not detract from its scenic value however, and each summer sees the arrival of more visitors to enjoy the tranquillity of its woodlands and exhilarating openness of those places that have not been planted. One of the finest areas is Glen Trool Forest.

Drive through Glentrool village and meet a right turn that offers a short detour from the main route to attractive Loch Trool.

Part of Loch Trool is a site of special scientific interest.

LOCH TROOL, Dumf & Gall
A campsite near the Martyr's Stone on the south-western side of this beautiful lake is the start of a 4½-mile circuit of its pleasantly wooded banks. Woodland and water-margin wild life can be seen. Above the northern shore a granite memorial records the defeat of an English force by Robert the Bruce at the eastern end of the loch in 1307.

Prominent to the north are the Rhinns of Kells and the Merrick, while Lamachan Hill rises to the south.

On the main tour, continue through the forest park and in 8 miles branch right. Climb to a road summit of 1,420ft, then descend through the Tairlaw Plantation of Carrick Forest into the Girvan Valley. Drive to the village of Straiton.

STRAITON, Strath
A good pre-Reformation aisle can be seen in the restored church of this attractive little village, and the old mansion of Blairquhan (not open) stands west near the Water of Girvan. The glen of Lambdoughty Burn lies east of the Dalmellington road and is known for its lovely waterfalls.

Go forward on to the Ayr road B7045 following the Water of Girvan to Kirkmichael. Continue with the B7045 and in 4 miles turn right on to the A77 then take the next turning left unclassified (no sign). In ¼ mile turn

Brig O'Doon frames the Burns Monument at Alloway.

right then in ½ mile turn right again into the B7024 SP 'Alloway'. Three miles farther cross the River Doon to enter Alloway.

ALLOWAY, Strath
The two-roomed clay and thatch cottage in which Scotland's national poet was born in 1759 contains many furnishings and domestic implements used in his day. Adjoining the cottage and set in pretty gardens, is the Burns Museum. This has an interesting exhibition of original manuscripts, a copy of the Kilmarnock edition of poems, and other of Burns' possessions, including his family Bible. The Auld Brig described by Burns still spans the River Doon here. It is possible that the bridge dates from the 13th century, and above it is the 19th-century Burns Monument. It was built to a fine design by Thomas Hamilton Junior with sculptures of characters in Burns' poems by a self-taught artist, James Thorn.
Bibles belonging to the poet and Highland Mary are kept inside the memorial. There is also a Land O'Burns Interpretation Centre. Situated in landscaped gardens, where audio-visual, multi-screen presentations show the life of Robert Burns. A roofless building near by is the haunted Kirk Alloway mentioned in one of his many works.
From Alloway continue on to the B7024, and after 1½ miles join the A79 to re-enter Ayr.

ON THE KINTYRE PENINSULA

The coast road of Kintyre opens up superb seascapes to the Western Isles and coast of Northern Ireland as it follows the peninsula's dramatic shore to the westernmost point in Scotland. Inland is a spine of rugged little hills scored by fertile valleys and dotted with the relics of ancient man.

KINTYRE, Strath

This tour is contained entirely within the Kintyre peninsula, a narrow tongue of wilderness that stretches south towards Ireland from the west coast of Scotland. At one point it is only 12 miles from Ireland's eastern shores. Down the middle of the peninsula is a backbone of rocky hills that culminate near Saddell with 1,491ft Beinn an Tuirc, and at its northern boundary Kintyre is almost completely divided from the Knapdale district by West Loch Tarbert. The farthest point south is the Mull of Kintyre, where there is a lighthouse.

TARBERT, Strath

Situated on a tiny isthmus between East and West Loch Tarbert, this fishing town and resort, once a centre of the Loch Fyne herring industry, is one of the main towns on the lovely Kintyre peninsula. According to legend the Norse prince Magnus Barefoot dragged his ships overland from loch to loch here, claiming the whole peninsula as one of the Hebridean islands and therefore the property of his father King Olaf. Norse ownership ceased after the Battle of Largs in 1263, and Tarbert later acquired a 14th-century castle that was to become the stronghold of both Robert the Bruce and James II. Remains of the castle still overlook the harbour it once guarded, but the only invasion that threatens the town today, is that of summer holiday-makers in search of the fine beaches and safe bathing.

Tarbert is a good base from which to explore the scenery beyond West Loch Tarbert. The B8024 along the often hilly north shore offers glimpses of the Sound of Jura and Loch Caolisport, and passes impressive Kilberry Castle (not open). This was the seat of the Campbells of Kilberry for 500 years and has fascinating sculpted stones dating form late medieval times. A83 which follows the loch's attractive south shore eventually joins the rugged west coast of Kintyre, affording views across the South of Gigha.

Leave Tarbert on the A83 'Campbeltown' road and drive alongside West Loch Tarbert to Kennacraig.

KENNACRAIG, Strath

Situated on beautiful West Loch Tarbert, Kennacraig is a terminus of car ferries that operate between the mainland and the island of Islay.

Continue on the Campbeltown road to reach the west coast of Kintyre and Tayinloan.

TAYINLOAN, Strath

A passenger ferry crosses the Sound of Gigha from here to the island of Gigha.

ISLE OF GIGHA, Strath

Although only 6 miles long by 1½ miles wide, this flat little island off the Kintyre coast has an impressive rocky shoreline and several interesting features. Among these is

Achamore House of 1884, whose 50-acre gardens were the inspiration of Sir James Horlick who gave them to the National Trust, and seem to justify Gigha's claim to be the most fertile of all the Scottish Islands. High belts of trees protect azaleas, rhododendrons, hydrangeas, and a host of ornamental shrubs from the destructive Atlantic winds. Also on the island is the 13th-century ruin of Kilchattan Church, and Gigha parish was the birthplace of Gaelic scholar Dr Kenneth MacLeod. Just off the south tip of the island is the tiny islet of Cara, popular with seabirds.

Continue along the peninsula to Killean.

KILLEAN, Strath

Close to the modern church in Killean are the remains of its ancient predecessor, from which it acquired its fine double window.

Continue to Glenbarr.

GLENBARR, Strath

Beyond modernized Glenbarr Abbey the pretty Barr Water meets the sea, and inland the Barr Glen leads deep into isolated hill country.

Continue along the A83 to Campbeltown.

CAMPBELTOWN, Strath

The chief town of southern Kintyre, Campbeltown stands at the head of a sheltered bay and has a rocky shore that is popular with sea anglers. Nowadays it is a resort known for its good facilities and unusually mild climate, but at the end of the 19th century it was a bustling centre of commerce and industry with 30 distilleries and a herring fleet of more than 500 boats. Reminders of the area's very early history, when lone Irish missionaries braved the Atlantic to lead Britain out of the dark ages, are everywhere in place names and ancient religious sites. About 3½ miles south-east near Auchinhoan Head is St Kieran's Cave, which is a mere 25ft above

St Columba's footprints near Keil are said to mark the saint's landing place on Kintyre.

high-water mark and may be the earliest Christian chapel in Scotland. It is thought that St Kieran, whose name can be recognized in the Kilkerran area of the peninsula, arrived in Scotland even before St Columba. Relics from these and prehistoric times can be seen in the town's museum, and an echo of Celtic culture is in the 16th-century cross standing at Old Quay Head. Offshore from the resort is isolated Davaar Island.

DAVAAR ISLAND, Strath

Boats can be hired to cover the short distance to this island, which is famous for the Crucifixion scene painted inside a natural cave by the 19th-century artist Archibald Mackinnon. It was designed so that the only illumination required is a shaft of light from a hole in the rock. It was retouched by a local artist in the mid 1950s.

It is possible to make several detours from the main route in Campbeltown, driving to such places as Machrihanish, Southend, Keil, and the Mull of Kintyre, all of which are worth visiting. Details follow: to visit Machrihanish turn right with the A83 and in 1½ miles go forward on to the B843.

MACHRIHANISH, Strath

One of the main attractions in this one-time salt producing village is its beach, which offers 3½ miles of sand on an otherwise rocky coast. Among the resort developments prompted by this natural asset is an excellent golf course that was laid out in 1876. Services from the nearby airport link with Glasgow and the Isle of Islay.

To visit Southend, Keil, and the Mull of Kintyre, leave Campbeltown on the Machrihanish road A83 and in 1½ miles turn left on to the B842 and drive south to reach Southend.

The southern area of Kintyre is peat moss, partially drained for forestry.

Ruins of an ancient chapel survive at Skipness.

The early lighthouse at the Mull of Kintyre is Scotland's closest approach to Ireland.

A small fishing fleet uses Carradale's modern harbour.

SOUTHEND, Strath
This small resort offers two sandy beaches facing Sanda Island across the narrow waters of Sanda Sound. Pleasantly isolated coastline is accessible by a short walk. direction.

From Southend follow an unclassified road to Keil.

KEIL, Strath
Tradition has it that a ruined chapel here marks the place where St Columba landed to begin his 6th-century mission in Scotland. He and his disciples were pledged to convert the Picts to Christianity; local evidence suggests that this site was a pagan place of sanctity long before the chapel was built. The impressions of two right feet on a flat stone known as St Columba's Footprints, may have been carved to mark the place where pagan chiefs took their initiation vows. Only 100 yards away are the remains of a druidical altar. Sparse remains of Dunaverty Castle, whose 300 occupants were slaughtered by Covenanters, survive in the neighbourhood.

For the Mull of Kintyre keep forward and in 1 mile turn left on to a narrow road.

MULL OF KINTYRE, Strath
The southernmost tip of the peninsula and Scotland's closest point to the Irish coast, this wild headland offers some remarkable views. Rathlin Island rises from the sea a mere 12 miles away, and behind it is the dark line of the Northern Irish coast. On both sides the shore has been torn ragged by the full force of the Atlantic Ocean, and inland the 1,405ft mass of Beinn na Lice isolates the headland from the rest of Kintyre. An early lighthouse built near the South Point in 1788 was later remodelled by Robert Stephenson.

On the main route, leave Campbeltown on the B842 SP

'Carradale' and follow the east coast of the peninsula. Continue to Saddell.

SADDELL, Strath
Interesting remains of an abbey and castle survive in this attractive village. It is thought that the former was founded by Somerled, the first Duke of the Isles, for Cistercian monks in the 12th century. Remains include boundary walls and sculptured Celtic tombstones in the churchyard. One of the recumbent effigies preserved here may be Somerled himself, the ancestor of the Clan Donald. Battlemented Saddell Castle dates from the 16th century and was once the residence of the bishops of Argyll. Lovely Saddell Glen is part of the South Kintyre Forest, a wild and beautiful area that merges with Carradale Forest farther north. To the west the Kintyre Hills are dominated by the peak of 1,491ft Beinn an Tuirc.

Continue through hill country where open stretches reveal fine views of the hills on the Isle of Arran; particularly prominent is 2,345ft Beinn Bharrain. Skirt the shore of Kilbrannan Sound and later reach the B879 junction

which can be taken for a short detour to Carradale.

CARRADALE, Strath
Situated opposite the Isle of Arran, this small resort has a sheltered fishing harbour. Close to the pier are the remains of Aird Castle, and the narrow spit of Carradale Point to the south protecting the sandy Carradale Bay carries an oval vitrified fort. Carradale House has beautiful gardens (open) with flowering shrubs.

On the main route continue along the B842 to Grogport.

GROGPORT, Strath
This small village stands on a secluded little bay in the Kilbrannan Sound, facing the Isle of Arran's mountainous outline.

Continue to Claonaig.

CLAONAIG, Strath
During the summer this hamlet is the terminus for the Arran car ferry.

A short detour to Skipness can be taken from the main route by turning right on to the B8001.

SKIPNESS, Strath
Features of this charming little place include the remains of an ancient chapel and a large 13th-century castle. Local views extend seaward across the Sound of Bute to the northern part of Arran.

On the main tour, keep forward on to the B8001 SP 'Tarbert'. Climb, then descend with views of Knapdale and West Loch Tarbert. Continue to Kennacraig and turn right on to the A83 for the return to Tarbert.

213

TARBET, Strath
Situated on a narrow neck of land between Lochs Lomond and Long this resort offers good views eastwards to the magnificent peak of Ben Lomond, 3,192ft.

LOCH LOMOND, Strath
Popularly known as the Queen of Scottish lakes, 24-mile Loch Lomond is the largest expanse of fresh water in Britain and is sheltered by wooded mountains that climb dramatically from its eastern shores. In the south it is bordered by a gentler landscape of soft green hills, and the isolation of its many beautiful islands was as much of an attraction for 5th-century Irish missionaries as it is for visitors today. One particular example is Inchmurrin, which is believed to have been the site of St Mirren's monastery in the 6th century and now features the ruins of Lennox Castle. Five of the islands in the south-eastern corner of the loch are included in a national nature reserve, and much of the east shore is cloaked by the lovely Queen Elizabeth Forest Park. The famous song *Loch Lomond* is said to have been composed by one of Bonnie Prince Charlie's followers on the eve of his execution.

Leave Tarbet on the A82 'Crianlarich' road to reach Inveruglas.

INVERUGLAS, Strath
Overlooked by 2,785ft A' Chrois and 3,004ft Ben Vane, Inveruglas is the site of a hydro-electric power station that receives its water by tunnel aqueduct from Loch Sloy.

From Inveruglas continue on the A82 to reach Ardlui.

ARDLUI, Strath
Situated at the northern tip of Loch Lomond, this beautiful village stands at the entrance to picturesque Glen Falloch and features a curious pulpit hewn out of the rock face.

Continue from Ardlui through Glen Falloch, past the Falls of Falloch, to reach Crianlarich.

CRIANLARICH, Central
The superb mountain scenery round Crianlarich has made it a natural resort for visiting walkers and climbers. Loch Dochart, with its pretty wooded island enhanced by the picturesque ruins of an old castle, lies to the east.

In Crianlarich turn left with the A82 'Fort William' road and drive along Strath Fillan. In 2¼ miles reach St Fillan's Chapel.

ST FILLAN'S CHAPEL, Central
Fragments of this 14th-century chapel can be seen to the east of Fillan Water. Robert the Bruce dedicated the place as a thanks offering for his victory at Bannockburn.

Continue on the A82 to reach the resort of Tyndrum.

BESIDE LOCH LOMOND
Many centuries ago Irish missionaries were attracted to the enchanting isolation of Loch Lomond's tiny wooded islands. Today the loch, set against a backdrop of gentle hillsides and wooded mountains, is still acknowledged as one of Scotland's loveliest expanses of fresh water.

Beautiful Ben Lomond, seen from the shores of Loch Lomond.

TYNDRUM, Central
Tyndrum is an angling and climbing resort in Strath Fillan, near its junction with Glen Lochy on the edge of the Grampian mountains. The legendary Brooch of Lorne was reputedly lost by Robert the Bruce during an ambush south-east of the village. It is now kept at the Macdougall mansion of Dunollie, near Oban.

Leave Tyndrum and turn left on to the A85 'Oban' road. Drive through Glen Lochy to reach Dalmally.

DALMALLY, Strath
The River Orchy flows through this Strath Orchy village on its way to Loch Awe. A monument has been erected to the Highland poet Duncan Ban MacIntyre, some 2 miles south-west of Dalmally, near a viewpoint on the old Inveraray road.

Leave Dalmally and in 1¾ miles turn left on to the A819 'Inveraray' road. For a detour to Kilchurn Castle keep

Some of the finest views of Loch Lomond can be enjoyed from Tarbet.

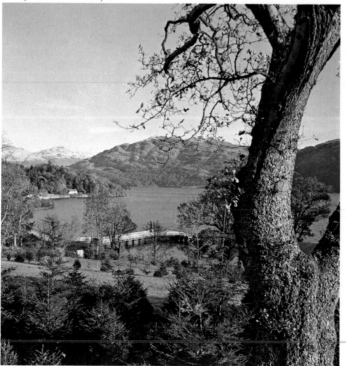

forward on the A85 for ¼ mile to a track on the left of the road.

KILCHURN CASTLE, Strath
Beautifully situated in mountainous country at the upper end of Loch Awe, Kilchurn Castle (AM) dates from the 15th century and stands on ground that was once an island. Major additions were made in the 16th and 17th centuries, but in 1879 it was damaged by dreadful gales that also caused the destruction of the Tay Bridge. However, even in its ruined state this former Campbell stronghold is one of the finest baronial castles in Scotland.

Continue on the A819, following the shore of Loch Awe for 4 miles, then turn inland across open country and ascend before the descent through Glen Aray. Pass Inveraray Castle on the left before entering Inveraray.

INVERARAY, Strath
Picturesque woodland provides a backing for this smart Royal Burgh, where white-walled buildings make an attractive cluster on the banks of lovely Loch Fyne. At one time the village site was near the ancient castle that can be seen near by, but after burning down it was replaced by the existing town and castle in the 18th century. The present castle (open), which had to be restored after another fire in 1975, houses many historic relics, including some of Rob Roy's possessions and several fine portraits. Architecturally the building is a very early example of the neo-gothic and Scottish baronial styles. A cannon from the sunken Spanish Armada vessel *Florida* is on display in the grounds. A fine Celtic burial cross, removed to the town from Iona, stands at the junction of Front and Main Streets. In the parish church is an unusual dividing wall which was built to allow simultaneous services in the English and Gaelic languages. The 126ft-high Bell Tower (open) is an excellent viewpoint. South-west of the village at Dalchenna is the comprehensive Argyll Wildlife Park.

Leave Inveraray on the A83 'Glasgow' road to reach Glen Shira.

GLEN SHIRA, Strath
A charming 18th-century ornamental bridge spans the little River Shira at the entrance to this beautiful glen. Although best appreciated on foot, the glen is also accessible by a narrow road that runs through forest past the ruined house of Rob Roy to the Lochan Shira dam.

Continue on the A83, beside the shores of Loch Fyne and pass the end of Glen Fyne.

GLEN FYNE, Strath
Threaded by the River Fyne, this picturesque glen leads north-east from the head of Loch Fyne. On the eastern side is the impressive Eagles Fell waterfall.

Continue along the shores of Loch Fyne to reach the edge of Cairndow.

Mighty snow capped summits dwarf Loch Awe and the once-isolated ruins of magnificent Kilchurn Castle.

Castle can be taken here by turning right with the B839 and driving to Lochgoilhead.

LOCHGOILHEAD, Strath
Standing on the shingly shores of Loch Goil, this pleasing little Victorian burgh of whitewashed houses is set against the dark background of the Cowal Hills.

To continue the detour, leave Lochgoilhead and join the unclassified road which runs west of Loch Goil. In 5 miles reach Carrick Castle.

CARRICK CASTLE, Strath
The ruined 14th-century Carrick Castle, once a royal stronghold, was destroyed by fire in 1685.

From Carrick Castle return to Lochgoilhead and thence to the junction with the B828 at the foot of Hell's Glen. From here continue the alternative route by keeping forward on the B828 SP 'Glasgow' through a small part of the Argyll Forest Park.

ARGYLL FOREST PARK, Strath
The huge forest park of Argyll covers 37,000 acres of beautiful mountain scenery from Ben Ime in the north to the Ben More ridge in the south. It is divided into two distinct areas: the large southern part stretches from Benmore Forest to Glenbranter Forest near Strachur, and the smaller northern section contains the Ardgoil and Ardgartan Forests between Lochgoilhead and Arrochar. The whole area is vast enough to provide an endless variety of gentle rambles, ambitious walks, and difficult climbs. It offers many things, from the pleasures of outdoor activities to the simple seeking out of solitude and peace in the mountains.

Continue along the B828 to reach Rest and Be Thankful and turn right on to the A83 to rejoin the main tour.

The 'Rest and Be Thankful' stone.

Forestry is a major industry in Argyll.

CAIRNDOW, Strath
Binnein an Fhidhleir 2,658ft dominates the township of Cairndow. Just outside, near Loch Fyne, is the excellent modern mansion of Ardkinglas House, which was built by the Scottish architect Sir Robert Lorrimer. The gardens (open) of Strone House to the south feature a 190ft tree that is claimed to be the tallest growing anywhere in Britain.

Leave Cairndow and continue on the A83 to make a long and easy ascent through Glen Kinglas to the 860ft road summit and 'Rest and Be Thankful' stone. An alternative route may be taken from Cairndow to the Rest and Be Thankful summit by leaving the township on the A83 and in 1 mile turning right on to the A815 SP 'Dunoon'. Continue for 2½ miles, then turn left on to the B839 SP 'Lochgoilhead' and drive through Hell's Glen.

HELL'S GLEN, Strath
The rocky and lonely glen with this unpleasant name lies between 2,402ft Stob an Eas and 2,001ft Cruach nam Mult and affords views down to the swirling waters of the River Goil.

Continue the alternative route on the B839 to meet the junction with the B828. A detour from the alternative route to Lochgoilhead and Carrick

REST AND BE THANKFUL, Strath
Near here the steep old road through Glen Croe, no longer used except for motor trials, reached a 800ft summit marked by a rough stone seat inscribed 'Rest and Be Thankful'. The seat has gone and the reconstructed road has been more gently graded for modern traffic, but the inscribed stone survives. The summit of 3,318ft Ben Ime can be reached by a long climb from the pass.

From Rest and Be Thankful continue along the A83, descending through Glen Croe and round Loch Long to reach Arrochar.

ARROCHAR, Strath
This little yachting and touring centre at the head of Loch Long makes a fine base from which to visit the mountains and forests of the Argyll Forest Park. To the north-west are Beinn Narnain 3,036ft, A'Chrois 2,785ft and Ben Arthur 2,891ft, popularly known as The Cobbler, and to the west above the Ardgarten Forest is The Brack 2,580ft.

Leave Arrochar and follow the A83 for the return to Tarbet.

215

STRONGHOLDS IN THE HIGHLANDS

High above the fishing quays of Oban is an unfinished replica of the Colosseum, a fascinating folly built to relieve unemployment. Inland are the castles and towers of the Campbells and MacDougalls, grim ruins of serious intent in the spectacular loch and mountain scenery of the Highlands.

Carnassarie Castle has been in ruins since the Argyll rebellion of 1685.

OBAN, Strath

In the 200 years of its existence Oban has become a major centre in the West Highlands. Its busy port offers ferry services to the islands of Lismore, Mull, Colonsay, Coll, and some of the Outer Hebrides, making the town a thriving tourist resort. One of its most remarkable buildings is McCaig's Folly, which was begun in 1897 to relieve local unemployment but never finished. It was intended to be a replica of Rome's Colosseum and to house a museum and art gallery. The inside courtyard is landscaped, and the folly shines bravely in floodlights that bathe the summit of Battery Hill at night. Oban's museum is housed in Corran Hall, and the little granite St Columba's Cathedral near by was built by Sir Gilbert Scott. The Island of Kerrera stands just offshore from Oban and features the ruined MacDougall stronghold of Gylan Castle. The town is a popular golfing resort, and the fine 18-hole course lies to the east. Macdonald's Mill, ½ mile south of the town centre on the A816, mounts a fascinating display of the story of spinning and weaving. The Caithness Glassworks is also of interest with demonstrations of paperweight making. On the shore north of the town is the ruined 12th- or 13th-century McDougall stronghold of Dunollie Castle. A modern mansion nearby contains Robert Bruce's Brooch of Lorne.

Leave Oban on the A816 'Campbeltown' road and after 4½ miles join the shores of Loch Feochan. In 2¾ miles reach a junction with the B844. *A detour can be made to Seil by turning right here and driving to Kilninver.*

KILNINVER, Strath

This small village on Loch Feochan faces north-west across the wide Firth of Lorne to the mountainous Island of Mull.

Turn right with the B844, and cross a bridge. In 4 miles reach Clachan Bridge.

CLACHAN BRIDGE, Strath

Telford built this attractive hump-backed bridge in 1792. It spans Seil Sound, a narrow arm of the Atlantic to link with the island of Seil.

Cross the bridge onto the island of Seil and continue to Balvicar. Here turn right for Easdale.

ISLAND OF SEIL, Strath

Slate used to be quarried here and on the much smaller island of Easdale. Of interest are the An Cala Garden (open), and the Easdale Island Folk Museum records the quarrying industry there. Luing Island to the south of Seil is accessible via the Cuan Ferry.

On the main tour continue along the A816. In 2½ miles a detour can be made to Loch Scammadale by turning left on to an unclassified road through Glen Euchar to reach lovely Loch Scammadale.

LOCH SCAMMADALE, Strath

This attractive loch lies in Glen Euchar, surrounded by hills.

On the main tour, continue along the A816 and drive through wooded Glen Gallain. Descend to reach Kilmelford.

KILMELFORD, Strath

This quiet angling village stands near the head of Loch Melfort which is sheltered by islands in the Firth of Lorne. The Pass of Melfort, north of the village off the A816, is a picturesque area which includes a small hydro-electric dam.

From Kilmelford continue along the A816 to follow the shores of Loch Melfort and reach Arduaine Gardens.

ARDUAINE GARDENS, Strath

Many rare trees and shrubs have been collected in theis 21-acre garden (open), which is especially famed for its spring displays of rhododendrons and azaleas. The attractive layout includes water and rock gardens, and superb views extend over Loch Melfort and the Sound of Jura.

Oban's busy port serves as the gateway to the Western Isles.

Continue on the A816 for 3½ miles. A detour from the main route to Craignish Castle can be taken here: turn right on to the B8002 and drive alongside Loch Craignish through Ardfern to Craignish Castle.

CRAIGNISH CASTLE, Strath

The 16th-century keep of Craignish Castle (not open) stands amid a fine rhododendron garden facing the Sound of Jura.

On the main tour, continue along the A816 to reach Kintraw.

KINTRAW, Strath

This attractive little hamlet offers magnificent views of the beautiful sea loch of Craignish, with its scattered islands.

Proceed on the A816 to the junction with the B840. Ahead along the A816 a road to the right, after ¼ mile leads to Carnassarie Castle.

CARNASSARIE CASTLE, Strath

Ruined Carnassarie Castle (AM) stands high on a hill about 1 mile north of the village of Kilmartin. It was built for the Bishop of the Isles in the 16th century, but was captured and partially blown up during the Duke of Argyll's ill-fated rebellion in 1685.

On the main route turn left on to the B840 and proceed to Ford, passing Loch Ederline to the right.

FORD, Strath

Sandwiched between huge Loch Awe and tiny Loch Ederline, Ford is a small angling resort. The surrounding countryside is ideal for walking.

At the Ford Hotel go forward on to an unclassified road SP 'Dalavich' with Loch Awe on the right.

TAYNUILT, Strath

Taynuilt is a small resort at the foot of Glen Nant, facing the lovely waters of Loch Etive. Ben Cruachan rises magnificently in the east, and the situation enjoyed by the village affords marvellous views of the mountains which overlook Upper Loch Etive. Lord Nelson is somewhat unexpectedly commemorated by a standing stone in the village.

A detour can be made from the main route to visit Bonawe: in Taynuilt village turn right on to the B845, then after ½ mile turn right again on to an unclassified road and enter Bonawe.

This isolated standing stone near Kintraw, stark against a background of hills, is thought to be of bronze-age date.

LOCH AWE, Strath

The Campbells of Inveraray had many occasions to be grateful for the protection given against attack from the north by this long natural moat. Reminders of its part in Scotland's turbulent history are scattered along the shores of the loch today. Ruins of a castle stand near Fincharn at the southern end, and the wooded islet of Fraoch Eilean in the north conceals remains of another. Early religious stirrings are recalled by ancient chapels built on some of Loch Awe's islands by holy men seeking isolation. In the south is the Innis-Sherrich Chapel, which was dedicated to St Findoc c1257 and stands near several 14th- or 15th-century carved slabs. Another foundation can be seen on Inishail, in the north. Today the loch forms part of Scotland's largest hydro-electric scheme and is a paradise for anglers and walkers. The lovely countryside of Inverliever Forest borders the loch and features several marked nature trails, some of which lead to notable viewpoints. At its northern end the loch is dominated by the twin peaks of 3,689ft Ben Cruachan.

Continue through Inverliever Forest to reach New York.

NEW YORK, Strath

A marked contrast to its famous namesake, this tiny hamlet faces across the peaceful expanse of Loch Awe to an ancient chapel at Portinnisherrich.

Leave New York and continue to the new forestry village of Dalavich, then after a short distance cross the River Avich. Continue through Inverinan Forest, meet the B845, and turn left to enter Kilchrenan.

KILCHRENAN, Strath

A granite block in the churchyard here commemorates 13th-century Mac Cailean Mor, clan hero and founder of the Argyll fortunes.

At Kilchrenan a detour can be taken from the main route to visit the gardens at Ardanaiseig by turning right on to an unclassified road.

ARDANAISEIG GARDENS, Strath

Superb views of Loch Awe can be enjoyed from these beautiful gardens (open), which are full of rare shrubs and trees. In the early part of the year banks of rhododendrons and azaleas burst into a magnificent display of colour.

On the main tour, continue on the B845 from Kilchrenan SP 'Taynuilt' and drive through Glen Nant. Meet the A85 and turn left to reach Taynuilt.

Telford's unusual Clachan Bridge is known as the 'Bridge over the Atlantic' because it actually spans a creek of that ocean.

BONAWE, Strath

During the 18th century a thriving iron industry developed in the unlikely Highland setting of picturesque Bonawe. The furnace, casting house, and workmen's cottages (all AM) used at that time have all been painstakingly restored.

On the main tour, continue along the A85 and later follow the shores of Loch Etive to reach Connel.

CONNEL, Strath

Cantilevered Connel Bridge is the largest of its kind in Europe, after the Forth Bridge, and is a splendid example of its type. Beside the bridge is a remarkable sea-cataract known as the Falls of Lora.

Continue on the A85 to Dunbeg for an unclassified right turn leading to Dunstaffnage Castle.

DUNSTAFFNAGE CASTLE, Strath

The castle (AM) on a bay north-east of Oban is a ruined four-sided 13th-century Campbell stronghold with a gatehouse, two round towers and walls 10ft thick. It was once the prison of Flora MacDonald.
The chapel near the castle was the burial place of the Campbells.

Continue on the A85 to re-enter the port of Oban.

Loch Etive is a sea loch of quiet seclusion and home of many seabirds.

EDINBURGH, Lothian

Scotland's finest city and its capital since 1437, Edinburgh stands on seven hills between the waters of the Firth of Forth and the 2,000ft summits of the Pentlands. Until 200 years ago this great centre of culture and learning was little more than a cluster of houses along the Royal Mile, a cobbled slope that followed a windy ridge from Castle Hill to the Palace of Holyroodhouse. The foremost building here is the castle (AM), which overlooks the picturesque streets of the Old Town from its lofty summit and has a history that stretches back at least 1,000 years. Its old name *Duneadain*, meaning Fort on a Slope, aptly describes its site on Castle Rock and refers to a previous stronghold that may have had iron-age origins. Many of Edinburgh's oldest buildings stand on even older sites along the Royal Mile, which has been admirably restored in recent years and has a distinctive aura of age. Canongate Tolbooth dates from 1591, 15th-century John Knox's house was built by goldsmiths to Mary Queen of Scots, and 17th-century Gladstone's Land features rooms decorated with fine tempera paintings (all open). Lady Stair's House is a restored 17th-century building housing a museum, and off Canongate is 16th- and 17th-century Holyroodhouse (AM) – Scotland's finest royal palace. Ruins of the 12th-century Chapel Royal foundation adjoin the palace. Here and there the splendour of the city is relieved by more down-to-earth domestic architecture, like the old White Horse Inn and the mercat cross. The 14th-century stronghold of Craigmillar Castle is associated with Mary Queen of Scots, and the 17th- to 19th-century Parliament House is where the Scottish parliaments met before the Union of 1707. Famous George Heriot's School dates from 1628 and was founded by the Jingling Geordie of Scott's *Fortunes of Nigel*. Near the Castle Mound are the Royal Scottish Academy and the National Gallery of Scotland, where many fine paintings by artists from various schools can be seen, and in Chambers Street the Royal Museum of Scotland exhibits one of the most comprehensive general displays in Britain. The National Library of Scotland comes close to Oxford's famous Bodleian in the richness of its contents, and the museum of the Scottish Records House, Charlotte Square. There are many other fascinating museums, galleries, workshops, and studios in the city, most of which will be listed in the local guides. Every year since 1947 Edinburgh's concert halls, theatres, galleries, and public halls have opened their doors to the arts of the world in the International Festival, a cultural extravaganza that takes place in late summer.

Among the other features of particular note are the Royal Observatory Visitor Centre at Blackford Hill, whose wide range of different astronomical exhibits

THE CITY ON SEVEN HILLS

Seven hilltops guarded by a massive castle carry Edinburgh, the Athens of the North. Just a few miles from its ancient heart are the rugged cliffs of the wild North Sea coast and the breathtaking scenery of mountains that were old before much of Britain was formed.

Edinburgh Castle stands high on a rock that may once have been the site of an iron-age hillfort.

include discoveries in the exploration of the Universe, whilst The Scottish National Zoological Park, one of the finest zoos in Europe set in eighty acres of grounds, contains a superb collection of mammals, birds and reptiles. The Zoo offers a further bonus with its magnificent panoramic views of Edinburgh and the surrounding countryside.

Leave Edinburgh city centre with SP 'Galashiels' and in 2 miles drive forward onto the A701 SP 'Peebles'. Drive through Straiton and Bilston then in 1 mile turn left on the B7003 SP 'Roslin'.

ROSLIN, Lothian

Scott mentioned this former mining village's famous Rosslyn Chapel in the *Lay of the Last Minstrel*. It was founded in 1446 by William Sinclair and contains many fine stone carvings, including the exquisite Prentice Pillar. Nearby Roslin Castle overlooks the North Esk River and picturesque Roslin Glen.

On the main route, continue to Rosewell, meet a T-junction, and turn right on to the A6094. In 2¼ miles turn left on to an unclassified road and cross Cauldhall Moor. In 1¾ miles meet crossroads and turn left on to the B6372, then 1¾ miles farther turn right on to an unclassified road SP 'Peebles'. In 1¼ miles pass a left turn leading to Gladhouse Reservoir.

GLADHOUSE RESERVOIR, Lothian

This attractive reservoir is set amid beautiful scenery below the summits of the Moorfoot Hills.

On the main route, continue for 3 miles and descend, then turn left on to the A703 to reach Eddleston.

EDDLESTON, Borders

This tiny hamlet lies in the valley of the Eddleston Water, with the 2,137ft summit of Blackhope Scar rising from the Moorfoot range to the east. On the Peebles road to the south of the village is a memorial to George Meikle Kemp, who served as an apprentice here in the 19th century and later designed the famous Scott Monument in Edinburgh.

At Eddleston turn right with SP 'Lyne via Eldons' and climb an unclassified road to 900ft. Descend and in 1¼ miles bear left. A short detour from the main route to visit Lyne can be made by bearing right, then driving for ½ mile and turning right to continue along the A72.

LYNE, Borders

One of the smallest churches in Scotland can be seen here. Inside are a pulpit and two pews of Dutch workmanship. Close by are the remains of a Roman camp of AD 83.

On the main route, continue for ¼ mile and turn left on to the A72 SP 'Peebles', driving alongside the Lyne Water and the River Tweed. In 1¾ miles a detour can be taken from the main route by turning right on to an unclassified road and crossing the Tweed to follow Manor Water to the village of Manor.

MANOR, Borders

Made famous by Scott's work *The Black Dwarf*, this small village stands at the foot of the long and beautiful Manor Valley. A little churchyard near Manor Water preserves the tomb of David Richie, on whom Scott modelled his Black Dwarf or Bowed Davie character.

On the main tour, continue along the A72 and after a short distance pass Neidpath Castle on the right.

NEIDPATH CASTLE, Borders

Originally a stronghold of the Fraser family, this 15th-century castle (open) is beautifully positioned above the River Tweed and is an attractive feature of the local countryside.

Proceed along the A72 to Peebles.

PEEBLES, Borders

Anglers come here to fish for the great Tweed salmon, but this attractive old Royal Burgh also offers facilities for golf, tennis, and pony-trekking. It has been the home of such famous people as the author Robert Louis Stevenson and Mungo Park, whose exploration helped to open up Africa. William Chambers and his brother Robert, publishers of the first Chambers' encyclopaedias and dictionaries, were born here and donated the Chambers Institute, a library, and a museum to the town. Relics of the town's history include the ruins of 13th-century Cross Kirk and the old shaft of a former parish cross. Old local inns include the 17th-century Cross Keys and early 19th-century Tontine. The woodlands of the Glentress Forest lap the outskirts of Peebles.

GLENTRESS FOREST, Borders

One of the first state forests to be established in Scotland, the Glentress comprises over 2,000 acres of fast-growing conifers such as Douglas fir, Norway spruce, and Sitka spruce.

Continue along the A72 SP 'Galashiels' to Innerleithen.

Edinburgh's Charlotte Square is a gem of Georgian architecture.

Neidpath Castle was restored after severe damage by Cromwell's artillery.

Traquair House has seen centuries of beer-brewing.

INNERLEITHEN, Borders

Sir Walter Scott popularized this small wool town in his novel *Ronan's Well*. To the south is the fine mansion of Traquair House (open), which can trace its history back to the 10th century and is the oldest inhabited house in Scotland. In its time it has played host to 27 English and Scottish monarchs, and its interior is packed with treasures and relics from many generations. A unique 18th-century brewhouse here is licensed to sell its own beer, and the grounds feature attractive woodland walks.

A detour from the main route can be taken by keeping forward on the A72 and driving to Walkerburn.

WALKERBURN, Borders

This Tweed Valley village was created in 1854 by the Ballantyne family as a weaving centre. They established a woollen mill here which was able to process raw wool to finished cloth in the one location. Today it is the home of the Scottish Museum of Wool Textiles. Here the fascinating history of the woollen industry is revealed, showing how it evolved from a cottage industry, through the Industrial Revolution, to the present day. Spinning demonstrations can be seen in the old weaver's cottage and a number of hand and power operated weaving machines are on display. A history of the art of dyemaking is of particular interest as are the examples of early wool and cloth patterns including tartans and shepherd check.

On the main route, leave Innerleithen by turning left on to the B709 SP 'Heriot' and drive alongside Leithen Water for 4 miles. Leave the main river behind and climb to a road summit of 1,250ft over a narrow pass, then descend to the Dewar Burn. In 2 miles drive forward on to the B7007 and follow a gradual ascent to a 1,324ft summit at the back of the Moorfoot Scarp. In good weather views from here take in the Pentland Hills, the 1,900ft summits of Scald Law and Carnethy, Arthur's Seat in Edinburgh, and the waters of the Firth of Forth. In 3¾ miles turn right on to the A7 SP 'Galashiels'. Continue along the A7 for 1¼ miles and turn left on to the B6367 SP 'Pathhead'. Continue to Crichton.

Peebles enjoys a delightful setting by the salmon-rich River Tweed.

CRICHTON, Lothian

Crichton Castle (AM) stands south-west of the actual village and is more elaborate than is usual in Scotland. It overlooks the River Tyne from a high and desolate site, and the Italianate lines that were the legacy of the Earl of Bothwell in the 16th century are certainly out of keeping with the dour practicality of conventional castle design. The medieval church features a quaint bellcote.

Turn left, then right along the B6367 to Pathhead.

PATHHEAD, Lothian

Close to this little village are two fine houses. Oxenfoord Castle stands beyond the Tyne Water and now serves as a school, and 18th-century Preston Hall which dates from 1791.

At Pathhead turn right on to the A68 then left SP 'Haddington' to rejoin the B6367. In 2 miles turn right on to the A6093. In 1 mile a detour can be taken from the main route by turning left on to the B6371 for Ormiston.

ORMISTON, Lothian

Situated on the Tyne Water, this village boasts a fine 15th-century cross (AM) mounted on steps.

On the main route, continue along the A6093 to Pencaitland.

PENCAITLAND, Lothian

This village is divided into two parts. Wester Pencaitland has an old mercat cross, and Easter Pencaitland is centred on a notable 13th-century church.

Meet crossroads and turn left on to the B6355 SP 'Tranet', then take the next turning right on to the B6363 SP 'Longniddry'. In 3 miles a detour can be taken to the village of Gladsmuir by meeting crossroads and turning right on to the A1.

GLADSMUIR, Lothian

In early times this area was notorious for witchcraft, but the village is more famous for its associations with the Battle of Prestonpans in 1745.

On the main route, drive over the crossroads on the B6363 and continue to Longniddry.

LONGNIDDRY, Lothian

Between 1643 and 1647 John Knox, the religious reformer, was a tutor here. The village itself is attractively sited just inland from the coast.

Turn right on to the A198 and follow SP 'North Berwick'. In 1 mile meet a T-junction and turn left on to the B1348 to Cockenzie and Port Seton.

COCKENZIE AND PORT SETON, Lothian

A large power station makes an unsightly blemish on the otherwise attractive appearance of Cockenzie, a quaint little fishing village close to the resort of Seton. Features of the latter include 2 miles of sandy beach, a fine 14th-century collegiate church (AM), and Robert Adam's Seton Castle of 1790.

After 2 miles pass the site of the Battle of Prestonpans on the approach to Prestonpans.

BATTLE SITE OF PRESTONPANS, Lothian

In 1745 the forces of Prince Charles Edward defeated Sir John Cope's entire army here in an astonishing 10 minutes.

PRESTONPANS, Lothian

Former prosperity is evident in this town's splendid 17th-century mercat cross (AM), Hamilton House (NT), and several other notable survivors from that period. The name Prestonpans originated from a salt-extraction industry operated by the monastic community from Newbattle Abbey in the 12th century.

Drive for 1½ miles beyond Prestonpans, meet a roundabout, and take the 3rd exit on to the A1. Return to Edinburgh through Musselburgh.

MUSSELBURGH, Lothian

This manufacturing town on the sandy Esk estuary has a 16th-century Tolbooth which preserves an ancient clock given by the Dutch in 1496. Jacobean Pinkie House (open) incorporates a 14th-century tower but mainly dates from c1590. A fine painted ceiling can be seen in the Long Gallery, and the building now forms part of Loretto School.

BETWEEN THE FORTH AND TAY

This narrow tongue of land between the Firth of Forth and Firth of Tay offers a contrasting landscape of exposed shores and sheltered estuaries. Here the rich farmlands of the Howe of Fife climb towards the high landward barrier of the Lomond and Ochil Hills.

ST ANDREWS, Fife

Historically this ancient Royal Burgh is one of the most significant places in Scotland. The cathedral (AM), which was founded in 1160, had grown to become Scotland's largest church by the time the finishing touches were made in 1318. Sparse remains include parts of the east and west gables, a section of the south nave wall, and the Precinct Wall (AM). Close by is small St Rule's Church (AM), which was built c1130 and is one of the best of its type in Scotland. The Church's famous square tower, after mounting 158 steps, affords a panoramic view of the town. St Andrews University was founded in 1412 and is the oldest in Scotland. Its Chapel of St Salvator carries an octagonal broach spire and contains the tomb of its founder, Bishop Kennedy. Also to be seen here is the oldest Sacrament House in a Scottish church, and a pulpit from which John Knox preached while leading his Protestant Reformation. St Andrew's Castle (AM) dates from the 13th century and overlooks the North Sea from a craggy eminence. The other reminder of the city's old defences is the West Port, which spans South Street on the course of the town walls. Today St Andrews is a popular summer resort on a cliff-girt coast, close to the four very famous golf courses of St Andrews Bay.

Leave St Andrews on the A91 SP 'Tay Bridge' and after a short distance pass the Royal and Ancient Golf Course on the right.

THE ROYAL AND ANCIENT GOLF COURSE, Fife

Written records of the Old Course, which is the oldest in the world, date back to the 15th century. The Royal and Ancient was founded in 1754 and is the ruling authority on the game throughout the world.

Continue to Guardbridge.

GUARDBRIDGE, Fife

One of the keystones of the attractive old bridge bears the shield of arms and pastoral staff of Bishop Wardlaw, who built it in the 15th century.

Cross the River Eden and turn right on to the A919 to reach Leuchars.

LEUCHARS, Fife

The fine Norman church that stands here was built by the de Quincy family and is one of the best of its type in Scotland. Its chancel and apse are original, and it contains some good monuments.

Continue for 1¼ miles to St Michael's Hotel and turn right on to the B945 to the port of Tayport.

TAYPORT, Fife

This one-time ferry port has a good church that was rebuilt in the 18th century. Some 47 acres of the local countryside have been taken over by the Tentsmuir Nature Reserve, including Morton Lochs.

St Andrews Castle.

The collapse of the original Tay railway bridge killed 75 people.

Leave Tayport on the B946 and drive beneath the new Tay Road Bridge into Newport-on-Tay.

NEWPORT-ON-TAY, Fife

A 42-span road bridge, the second longest in Europe, links this busy small town with Dundee – on the north side of the Firth of Tay.

Continue to Wormit.

WORMIT, Fife

The 2-mile railway bridge that spans the Tay here was built in 1885 to replace the famous one that collapsed, with great loss of life, during a freak gale in 1879.

Continue inland on the B946 and after ½ mile pass an unclassified right turn that offers a detour to Balmerino Abbey.

BALMERINO ABBEY, Fife

Founded in 1226 and built by monks from the great religious centre of Melrose, this abbey was suppressed during the Reformation and is now in ruins (NTS). Among its remains is a 15th-century Chapter House.

On the main tour, shortly branch left on to an unclassified road SP 'St Andrews' and after another 1 mile meet a roundabout. Take the 2nd exit and in another 1½ miles turn right on to the A92 to return to St Michael's Hotel. At the crossroads turn right SP 'Cupar' and continue through Balmullo, then after a further 2 miles join the A91 to enter Dairsie. Turn left on to an unclassified road SP 'Pitscottie', in 1 mile cross the River Eden, then turn right with views of Dairsie Castle on the north bank. Continue along the picturesque Dura

Glen, which is noted for its fossils, to Pitscottie. Turn left and immediately right on to the B939 SP 'Kirkcaldy' and continue to Ceres.

CERES, Fife

Some call this the prettiest village in Scotland. Old cottages surround a charming green, and the villagescape is completed by a medieval hump-backed bridge and the church.

After another 1½ miles reach Craigrothie and turn right on to the A916, which passes the entrance to Hill of Tarvit Mansion.

HILL OF TARVIT, Fife

Standing in spacious grounds overlooking the Howe of Fife, this fine Edwardian mansion (NTS) contains collections of furniture, paintings, tapestries, and porcelain. It occupies the site of a 17th-century house. On a nearby hill is the ancient Scotstarvit Tower (AM) keys for which are at Hill of Tarvit.

Continue along the A916 and descend into the Eden Valley to join the A92 for Cupar.

CUPAR, Fife

Cupar is a Royal Burgh and the market centre for the fertile Howe of Fife. Its parish church has a good 15th-century tower, and the mercat cross in the town is picturesquely adorned with the figure of a unicorn.

Follow SP 'Kincardine' to leave Cupar on the A91, and at the end of the town turn right on to the A913 SP 'Perth'. After another 1¾ miles turn right on to an unclassified road SP 'Luthrie'. Meet a junction with the A914 and turn left, then in ¼ mile turn right on to another unclassified road for Luthrie. After a further 1 mile bear left with the route, then later meet a T-junction and turn left to follow the Firth of Tay. Meet a junction with the A913 and turn right into Newburgh.

NEWBURGH, Fife

Situated on the south shore of the attractive Firth of Tay, this small Royal Burgh is near the ancient remains of Lindores Abbey. Close to the water is 18th-century Mugdrum House, opposite a tiny island which preserves the 1,000-year-old Mugdrum Cross.

Continue along the A913 to Abernethy.

Burleigh Castle stands near Loch Leven.

ABERNETHY, Tayside

One of the main features of this one-time Pictish capital is the remarkable 12th-century round tower (AM) of its parish church. This type of construction is more commonly found in Ireland, and the 74ft-high example standing here is one of only two in Scotland.

Continue past Aberargie and turn left on to the A912 SP 'Forth Road Bridge'. After 1½ miles turn right on to the B996 and drive through Glen Farg to reach Glenfarg village.

GLENFARG, Tayside

Glenfarg is a popular tourist resort in a sheltered position, and makes a good base from which to explore the beautiful scenery of Glen Farg.

In 2½ miles meet a T-junction and turn right on to the A91, then turn left on to the B919 'Glenrothes' road. In 1¾ miles reach Balgedie and join the A911 for Kinnesswood, with Loch Leven on the right.

KINNESSWOOD, Tayside

Poet Michael Bruce was born here in 1746, and his cottage at Portmoak is now a museum containing relics of his life and work. The landscape here is dominated by prominent Bishop Hill and White Craigs.

The Chapel Royal at Falkland Palace was formerly a banqueting hall.

LOCH LEVEN, Tayside

Romance and beauty mingle with an interesting history to make the very special atmosphere which surrounds Loch Leven. Its 14th- or 15th-century castle (AM), brooding on an island site, was the prison of Mary Queen of Scots until she made a sensational escape. The loch is often the venue for fishing competitions, and in winter its ice provides ideal conditions for curling. Some 300 acres of mixed habitats on the south shore make up the Vane Farm nature reserve, where there are nature trails and an official RSPB observation centre.

Continue to Scotlandwell.

SCOTLANDWELL, Tayside

The springs that give this village its name bubble up into a 19th-century stone cistern at the end of the main street.

Turn left and continue to Leslie.

LESLIE, Fife

A church on the green in this small industrial town is claimed to be the scene of a 15th-century poem entitled *Christ's Kirk on the Green*. Leslie House, a 17th-century seat of the earls of Rothes, stands east of the town.

Pass the church in the main street and after 300 yards reach the Clansman (PH). Turn left on to an unclassified road for Falkland.

Bishop Hill in the Lomonds rises behind the village of Kinnesswood.

FALKLAND, Fife

Old weavers' cottages and charming cobbled streets characterize this lovely little Royal Burgh, but it is chiefly known for the historic Falkland Palace (NTS). This was a favourite seat of the Scottish Court from the reign of James V, who made considerable improvements to the building before his death in 1542. The extensive gardens include Britain's oldest tennis court, c 1539.

Meet a T-junction and turn right on to the A912, and in ¼ mile turn left on to the B936 SP 'Freuchie'. Continue through Newton of Falkland to Freuchie, and at the end of that village meet crossroads. Drive straight on to an unclassified road and meet a junction with the A92. Turn right here, then turn immediately left on to the 'Kennoway' road. In 4½ miles turn left to enter Kennoway. Meet a main road and turn right, then immediately left SP 'Leven' and continue for 2 miles to reach the outskirts of Leven.

LEVEN, Fife

Formerly a weaving village, this resort and maritime town on Largo Bay is well known for its golfing facilities.

Turn left on to the A915 'St Andrews' road and drive past Lundin Links.

LUNDIN LINKS, Fife

Excellent fishing and sea bathing have made this a popular resort. Three prehistoric standing stones can be seen on the western outskirts of the town.

Continue to Upper Largo.

UPPER LARGO, Fife

The 17th-century spire of the church at Upper Largo rests entirely on the arched roof of the chapel and is unique in Scotland.

Follow the A915 SP 'Crail' and in 1½ miles turn right on to the A917 for Elie.

ELIE & EARLSFERRY, Fife

Sailing, fishing, and fine sandy beaches are offered by these twin resorts. They lie between Chapel Ness and Elie Ness, and are known for their good golf courses.

Follow the A917 'Anstruther' road along the East Neuk coastline, passing St Monans.

ST MONANS, Fife

Old houses cluster near the water's edge in this lovely little port, famed for its boat-building. The beautiful Old Kirk of St Monance dating from the 14th century but restored in 1828, stands almost on the foreshore. To the south-west of the village are the ruins of 17th-century Newark Castle.

Continue to Pittenweem.

PITTENWEEM, Fife

Some of the best architecture in this picturesque little Royal Burgh and fishing port has been restored by the National Trust for Scotland. The ruined priory dates back to the 12th century and the tower of the parish church is dated 1592. Some 3 miles north-west of town is Kellie Castle (NTS), a fine example of 16th- and 17th-century architecture.

ISLE OF MAY, Fife

Many species of sea bird use this isolated lighthouse station as a sanctuary.

ANSTRUTHER, Fife

Anstruther Easter and Wester, both Royal Burghs in their own right, stand each side of the harbour and make this an attractive resort. At the old harbourside of this fishing port; in a collection of historic buildings, is the Scottish Fisheries Museum. The museum provides a unique record of Scotland's fishing trade which includes examples of some old boats in the harbour.

Continue on the A917 to Crail.

CRAIL, Fife

The oldest Royal Burgh in the East Neuk district, this picturesque fishing town was once the haunt of smugglers. Its many lovely old buildings cluster round quaint streets and the harbour in a way that has attracted artists for generations. A curious weather vane depicting a salmon surmounts the 16th-century Tolbooth, and the mercat cross carries the figure of a unicorn.

Leave Crail on the A917 and drive through Kingsbarns and return to St Andrews.

221

STIRLING, Central

This Royal Burgh makes an ideal touring base as the 'Gateway to the Highlands', as it is popularly known, but is also worth visiting for its own sake. All round the foot of the rocky crag which carries its imposing castle (AM) are hilly streets of stone buildings, a quaint switchback area where it is difficult to find even the smallest patch of level ground. The castle itself seems to grow from the stone on which it is built. Its 250ft site has been fortified for many centuries, but the oldest parts of the present building date back about 500 years to the reign of James III. Magnificent views can be enjoyed from the viewpoints known as Queen Victoria's Lookout and Lady's Rock, extending far into the rugged Highlands in really good weather. Below the castle ramparts is the King's Knot (AM), one of the earliest ornamental gardens in Scotland, now all grass, but with the outline of the original garden still visible. Down the hill in the Old Town are many good examples of 16th-to 18th-century domestic architecture, interspersed with such fine public buildings as the Guildhall, the Tolbooth of 1701, and the 15th-century and later Chapel Royal where Mary Queen of Scots and the baby James VI were crowned soon after being born. The Argyll Lodgings is a 17th-century mansion that is today a youth hostel. Its exterior (AM) is considered the most impressive of its style and period in Scotland. Unfinished Mar's Wark (AM) in Broad Street was begun in 1570 and intended as a town house for the Regent Mar, and the town's 15th-century Old Bridge (AM) was rebuilt in 1749 after having been blown up during the '45 Rising. About 1 mile east of Stirling are the beautiful ruins of Cambuskenneth Abbey (AM), c1147 and the scene of Robert the Bruce's parliament in 1326. Stirling University (founded in 1967) is Scotland's newest university.

Leave Stirling on the A811 SP 'Erskine'. In 5¾ miles reach an unclassified road where a left turn can be taken as a short detour to Gargunnock.

GARGUNNOCK, Central

Situated in flat countryside traversed by the serpentine course of the River Forth, this village is an attractive little place with a fine 16th- to 18th-century mansion (not open).

On the main route, continue for 3 miles and turn right on to the B882 SP 'Thornhill'. A short detour can be followed from the main route to visit Kippen by turning left on to the B822.

KIPPEN, Central

An unusual aspect of this lovely south-facing village is the fame it attracted by the great Kippen Grape Vine. Claimed to be one of the largest in the world, it clearly liked the sun and soil conditions here and in its 70 years of life managed to cover an area of 50,000 square feet. The reason for its eventual demise is obscure, but before that time it

GATEWAY TO THE HIGHLANDS

Stirling stands in a bend of the River Forth and for years was the battleground of Scottish and English forces. Now it is a peaceful and historic centre from which to tour the beautiful Trossachs, the high country of the Campsie Fells, and the lovely Queen Elizabeth Forest Park.

Stirling Castle, home of Scottish kings, stands on a 250ft crag overlooking the Forth Valley.

managed to produce a staggering 1,000,000 bunches of grapes. A fine old dovecote (NTS) has been preserved in the village, and the local church of 1825 is considered one of the best examples of its period in Scotland. Treacherous Flanders Moss, a wild peat bog that is probably the site of an old forest, lies north of the River Forth.

On the main drive, continue along the B822 'Thornhill' road and in ½ mile cross the River Forth. Keep left and cross the Goodie Water, then at Thornhill join the A873. Keep forward with the B822 towards Callander, then pass through Torrie Forest and join the A81. Continue to Callander.

CALLANDER, Central

Callander's excellent position near the Trossach Hills and Loch Katrine makes it an ideal touring centre and resort. An inscribed sundial of 1753 is an attractive feature of South Church Street, and the Roman Camp Hotel has associations with the author Barrie. Other literary connections exist with Scott, who was a frequent visitor to the town. A road to the north-west leads through the beautiful Pass of Leny, where the River Leny rushes through a narrow gorge in a fine display of natural power. Close by is the Kilmahog Woollen Mill (open), where blankets and tweed cloth are made by hand. Some 3½ miles from the town and easily accessible to climbing enthusiasts is the severe 2,873ft peak of Ben Ledi.

Follow the A84 'Crianlarich' road and in 1¼ miles turn left on to the A821 SP 'Trossachs'. Cross the River Leny, then drive alongside lovely Loch Venachar with Ben Ledi overlooking Brig O'Turk to the right. Continue to Brig O'Turk.

BRIG O'TURK, Central

This particularly beautiful Trossachs village is splendidly situated between Lochs Venachar and Achray, and is a popular base for anglers. The Turk or Finglass Water is spanned here by a rustic old bridge described in Sir Walter Scott's ballad *Glenfinglas*. In the early 19th century Queen Victoria often came here, and during her visits she enjoyed the company of a famous innkeeper called Kate Ferguson. Then, as now, the area attracted many artists who strove to capture the timeless quality of 'typical' Scottish scenery.

Leave Brig O'Turk and enter the Queen Elizabeth Forest Park by driving alongside Loch Achray. After a short distance reach the romantically-set Trossachs Hotel.

THE TROSSACHS, Central

A bewildering combination of mountains, lochs, rivers, and thick woodlands makes up the outstanding landscapes for which this beauty spot is famous. The name means Bristly Country, but the nature of the land is not as unfriendly as this would suggest and has inspired such romantic works as Scott's *Lady of the Lake*. Most of the area is in a wooded gorge between Loch Achray and Loch Katrine.

Continue for ¼ mile beyond the Trossachs Hotel. A detour can be made from the main tour route to visit Loch Katrine by keeping forward to a pier at the eastern end of the lake.

LOCH KATRINE, Central

There are no public roads to disturb the peace of lovely Loch Katrine, but the summer steamer *Sir Walter Scott* which runs from the pier at its east end and gives visitors an appreciation of some of the Trossachs' most secret and beautiful places. After disembarking at Stronachlachar passengers can visit the birthplace of folk hero Rob Roy, but the area will always be most remembered for Scott's *Lady of the Lake*. The lady was Ellen Douglas, her lake was Katrine, and many of the places mentioned in the poem can still be identified. The modern world is not entirely shut out, however, and the 'Silver Strand' that was once opposite Ellen's Isle has been submerged since the water was raised to improve Glasgow's water supply. Ben Venue rises 2,393ft to dominate the whole scene, from Loch Katrine to the Pass of Achray.

On the main drive, continue on the 'Aberfoyle' road and drive through the Queen Elizabeth Forest Park.

Wooded Loch Achray leads gently into the mixed landscapes of lakes, rivers, mountains, and woodland which form the picturesque Trossachs.

Salmon are sometimes seen jumping the Falls of Leny near Callander.

Queen Elizabeth Forest Park was named in 1953.

QUEEN ELIZABETH FOREST PARK, Central

This National Forest Park covers 45,000 acres of lovely countryside from Loch Venachar to Loch Lomond, including the lofty summit of Ben Lomond. Both wild and planted areas can be enjoyed best by walking along the numerous marked trails that have been cleared for that purpose, though motorists are well catered for with carparks and stopping areas. A viewing shelter has been built for visitors by the Carnegie Trust.

Descend to Aberfoyle, passing the AA viewpoint of David Marshall Lodge.

ABERFOYLE, Central

The tiny hamlet of Aberfoyle, associated with Rob Roy and Scott's poem of the same name, has little in common with the development of the present village. During the 19th century devotees of Scott's works came here in crowds, and the resort soon eclipsed what was left of its tiny neighbour. A plough coulter hanging from a tree by the old site recalls a scene from the book.

From Aberfoyle it is possible to take an exceptionally scenic detour along the B829 for Inversnaid, on Loch Lomond: to follow it, drive alongside Lochs Ard and Chon, and 2 miles beyond the head of Loch Chon meet a T-junction. A brief visit can be made to the village of Stronachlachar by turning right here, but the main detour is left.

STRONACHLACHAR, Central

A lonely path leads from this village to isolated Glengyle, where Rob Roy was born. This famous freebooter was immortalized by Scott in 1871.

On the main detour, turn left at the T-junction and continue to Inversnaid along an unclassified road, passing Loch Arklet.

INVERSNAID, Central

A fort built here in 1713 was once under the command of General Wolfe, of Quebec Heights fame, but this tiny village is best known for its spectacular surroundings. On the far side of lovely Loch Lomond are the towering summits of 3,318ft Ben Ime, and 3,092ft Ben Vorlich.

On the main tour route from Aberfoyle, continue with the A821 'Stirling' road and after 1 mile branch left on to the A81 SP 'Callander'. After another 2⅓ miles reach the Lake of Menteith on the right.

LAKE OF MENTEITH, Central

Inchmahome Priory (AM) was founded on one of three tiny islands in this lake during the 13th century, and for a time was a refuge for the infant Mary Queen of Scots. The lake itself is the only large expanse of fresh water in Scotland not called a loch, and on its west side it lies peacefully beneath gentle slopes of the 1,289ft Hills of Menteith. The Port of Menteith stands on its shore.

Drive for 1 mile beyond the lake and turn right on to the B8034 SP 'Arnprior'. After a short distance pass the passenger ferry terminus for Inchmahome Priory, on the right by Menteith Church. Continue to Arnprior.

ARNPRIOR, Central

Here there is a fine Georgian mansion set in superb woodland gardens, which are unfortunately not open to the public.

At Arnprior turn right on to the A811, then turn left on to an unclassified road SP 'Fintry'. After 2 miles cross moorland below the Fintry Hills and turn right on to the B822 to Fintry.

FINTRY, Central

Fintry occupies a central position in the ancient territory of Lennox, with the bare Fintry Hills to the north-east. Culcreuch Castle, which stands a little north of the village, dates from the 14th century.

From Fintry turn right on to the B818 'Killearn' road, then in 5¼ miles join the A875 'Glasgow' road to Killearn.

KILLEARN, Central

George Buchanan, the historian and scholar who became tutor to James VI, was born here in 1506 and is commemorated by an obelisk. Killearn House is a 19th-century edifice 1½ miles south-west.

Drive for 2 miles beyond Killearn, keep left on to the A81, and continue through Blanefield to Strathblane.

STRATHBLANE, Central

This small resort is charmingly situated on the Blane Water, beneath the Strathblane Hills and the Higher Campsie Fells.

From Strathblane turn left on to the A891 and proceed to Campsie.

CAMPSIE, Strath

Above this Campsie Glen village are the summits of the Campsie Fells, which offer good walking country to the energetic. Excellent views can be enjoyed from the Crow Road, which runs through the glen, and nearby Earl's Seat.

Continue along the A891 to Lennoxtown.

LENNOXTOWN, Strath

Originally known as the Clachan of Campsie, this small industrial town stands in the ancient district that once came under the control of the Lennox family. The local churchyard features the Lennox vault and a number of 17th-century stones.

At Lennoxtown turn left SP 'Fintry' on to the B822, then climb out of the valley and pass the head of Campsie Glen. Cross the open moorland of the Campsie Fells, reaching a road summit of more than 1,000ft, and descend into the valley of the Endrick Water. Turn right on to the B818 SP 'Denny', then later run alongside the Carron Valley Reservoir. Drive for 1¾ miles beyond the dam and reach the Carron Bridge Inn, then turn left on to an unclassified road SP 'Stirling'. In 1¾ miles pass the small Loch Coulter Reservoir on the right, and after another 2¼ miles meet a T-junction and turn left. Later cross the M9 motorway, then in ¾ mile turn right then left to join the A872. Immediately to the left is the Battlefield of Bannockburn.

The bronze statue of Robert the Bruce at Bannockburn symbolizes Scotland's rebellion against English monarchy.

BATTLEFIELD OF BANNOCKBURN, Central

It was this battle, fought in 1314 for the possession of Stirling Castle, that established Robert the Bruce on the Scottish throne. Bruce won against odds of nearly three to one, and earned the fear of his enemy as well as the respect of his people. An open-air rotunda encircles the Borestone, in which a bronze equestrian statue marks Bruce's command post. This site is owned by the NTS.

Return to Stirling via the A872 and A9.

THE SIDLAW AND OCHIL HILLS

Scott immortalized the wild beauty of the countryside round Perth in his novels, and his praise is as justified today as it was then. Here the flanks of the Sidlaw and Ochil Hills sweep down to deep wooded straths, or valleys, where the enchantment of running water is never far away.

PERTH, Tayside

Once known as St Johnstoun, the fair city of Perth is an old Royal Burgh set at the head of the Tay estuary between the meadows of the North and South Inch. In early times the area attracted the attention of English forces, and the town was taken and fortified by Edward I in 1298. Its single year as the capital of Scotland ended with the murder of James I at a former Blackfriars monastery in 1437. In 1559 John Knox effectively started the Protestant Reformation here with his emotive sermon against church idolatry. Cromwell's parliamentarian army took the city a little under a century later, and it came into the Jacobites' hands in the Risings of the 18th century. One of the most important buildings to have survived all this turmoil is famous St John's Kirk, a fine medieval and later church that has been attended by many members of English and Scottish royalty. Perth's associations with Sir Walter Scott are numerous. The 14th-century heroine of the *Fair Maid of Perth*, Catherine Glover, lived in a house on the site where the present Fair Maid of Perth's House now stands (open). Also of interest are the Perth museum and art gallery, and the regimental museum of the Black Watch, which is housed in Balhousie Castle. A survival of early industry exists in the city's 19th-century dye- and glassworks, and the bridge which spans the Tay here was built by Smeaton in 1771.

Before the main route begins it is possible to take a short detour on the A85 SP 'Crianlarich', to Huntingtower Castle.

HUNTINGTOWER CASTLE, Tayside

Formerly known as Ruthven Castle, this great stronghold (AM) has a permanent place in Scottish history as the site of the Raid of Ruthven. In 1582 the 16-year-old James VI came here at the invitation of the Earl of Gowrie, ostensibly to hunt. When he tried to leave he found himself prevented by Protestant nobles, who demanded the dismissal of the young king's favourites. The conspirators held the young king for a year while they wielded power in his place. The 15th-century mansion that stands here today has been restored and contains fine painted wooden ceilings.

On the main route, follow SP 'Braemar' across the River Tay to leave Perth on the A93, and in 2 miles pass the grounds of Scone Palace.

SCONE PALACE, Tayside

Scone Palace, the home of the Earl of Mansfield, is a 19th-century mansion that stands on the site of the old Abbey of Scone. This was founded c1114 by Alexander I, and before it was destroyed by a mob of John Knox's reformers in 1559 it was the coronation place of all the Scottish kings up to James I. By tradition the kings were crowned on a stone that was brought to the ancient mote-hill of Scone by Kenneth Macalpine in the 9th century. This, identified with both Jacob's Pillow at Bethel and the Stone of Destiny at Tara in Ireland, was removed from the site and placed under the Coronation Chair of Westminster Abbey by Edward I in 1297. This token of conquest did little to improve relations between the two countries. The present mansion (open) contains various relics and objects of art.

Continue to Old Scone.

OLD SCONE, Tayside

As the abbey developed it attracted a little satellite community that grew into the village of Scone. In 1805 this was moved by the Earl of Mansfield to improve the landscape, and only the village cross and graveyard remain to mark its old site.

Continue through Guildtown, then after 1½ miles reach Stobhall.

Kinnoul Hill rises steeply above the Tay to the south-east of Perth, and provides outstanding views over the valley.

STOBHALL, Tayside

This picturesque group of buildings (not open) is centred on a courtyard and was once the home of the Drummond family. It is picturesquely sited on the banks of the Tay and comprises the house, chapel, and tower. Much of the structure dates from the 15th century.

Later cross the Bridge of Isla to reach the grounds of Meikleour House, continue alongside the fine beech hedge that follows the estate boundary, and at the end turn left on to an unclassified road for Meikleour.

Meikleour Mercat Cross dates from 1698.

MEIKLEOUR, Tayside

The 600-yard beech hedge passed on the way to this charming old-world village belongs to the local manor house and was planted in 1746. A focal point of the village is the mercat cross of 1698, opposite which is an old place of punishment known as the Jougs Stone.

Join the A984 'Dunkeld' road and drive through Spittalfield to Caputh.

CAPUTH, Tayside

An attractive bridge spans the salmon-rich Tay here, and across the river to the west is 16th-century and later Murthly Castle (not open) in grounds which feature huge specimens of Sitka spruce and Douglas fir. Some 3 miles east is the Roman camp of Inchtuthill.

Continue, driving through attractive and well-wooded Strath Tay to reach the town of Dunkeld.

DUNKELD, Tayside

Telford spanned the Tay with a fine bridge here in 1809, but this delightful small town is best known for the lovely ruins of its ancient cathedral (AM). It was founded in the 9th century, was desecrated in 1560, and considerably damaged in the 17th-century Battle of Dunkeld.

Nowadays the 14th-century choir has been restored and is in use as the parish church. East of the town is the Loch of Lowes Wildlife Reserve, where a variety of species can be watched from special hides, and 1 mile south-west is the restored 18th-century folly of Ossian's Hall. Near by the River Braan plunges over a rocky lip as the Falls of Braan, close to Hermitage Bridge (NTS).

Leave Dunkeld on the 'Crieff' road and cross the River Tay into Little Dunkeld. Turn right then left on to the A822 and ascend. After 7½ miles turn left to join the A22, then continue to Amulree.

Weaving is one of several cottage industries which still thrive in Scotland.

AMULREE, Tayside
The lovely countryside around Glen Quaich and Loch Freuchie, and in Glens Cichill and Almond, can be explored from here.

Enter Glen Almond and follow one of General Wade's military roads through lonely Sma' Glen.

GLEN ALMOND, Tayside
Rugged and mountainous at its beginning near Loch Tay, this beautiful glen gradually widens out to become a broad fertile valley after Newton Bridge. One of its many interesting features is a large prehistoric burial cairn.

SMA' GLEN, Tayside
Heatherclad Sma' Glen is a famous beauty spot that has attracted generations of admiring visitors. A partly-vitrified fort tops 1,520ft Dun Mor on the east side, and below it between the river and the road is a glaciated boulder known as Ossian's Stone, possibly named after Ossian the 3rd-century bard and warrior.

Continue to Gilmerton skirting the fine park of Monzie Castle.

GILMERTON, Tayside
Some 5½ miles east of this little village are sparse traces of 13th-century Inchaffray Abbey.

Turn right on to the A85 and continue to Crieff.

CRIEFF, Tayside
Beautifully situated in a hillside position overlooking Strath Earn, Crieff is a popular touring centre in one of Tayside's most scenic areas. To the north of the town the River Earn is joined by Turret Water, which flows from lovely Loch Turret and plunges downhill in a series of picturesque waterfalls. The town itself is old, with many interesting features. Close to the Town Hall is an octagonal cross of 1688, and the old Market Cross incorporates a 10th-century cross-slab made of red sandstone and decorated with Celtic patterns. Iron stocks that were last used in 1816 are kept in the 17th-century Tolbooth. About 4 miles south-east of the town is the ruin of 17th-century Innerpeffray Castle, and near by in Innerpeffray Library (open) is one of Scotland's oldest and most valuable collections of books.

Leave Crieff on the A822 'Stirling' road, and in 2 miles reach the grounds of Drummond Castle on the right.

DRUMMOND CASTLE, Tayside
Built by the 1st Lord Drummond in 1491, this fine castle has been considerably altered over the centuries and shows the work of several periods. The formal gardens (open) are laid out in the form of St Andrew's Cross.

Continue to Muthill.

MUTHILL, Tayside
Surviving fragments of Muthill's abandoned church (AM) include a splendid Romanesque tower that dates at least from the 12th century. Other remains are mostly of 15th-century date.

In 1¾ miles turn left on to the A823 SP 'Dunfermline'. In 3 miles a detour can be made from the main route by turning left on to an unclassified road and continuing to Tullibardine.

The elegant Long Gallery is the highlight of the 19th-century palace at Scone.

Famous roadbuilder and soldier General Wade constructed the highway through Sma' Glen.

TULLIBARDINE, Tayside
Founded in 1446, the collegiate chapel (AM) at Tullibardine is one of the few in Scotland to have been finished and left unaltered.

On the main route, continue for 1 mile and pass the entrance to Gleneagles Hotel.

GLENEAGLES HOTEL, Tayside
Gleneagles is situated on moorland near Auchterarder and is one of the best-known golfing resorts in Scotland, a country famed for its excellent courses.

Cross the A9 and follow the A823 through Glen Eagles, drive into the heart of the Ochil Hills and enter Glen Devon to reach the village of the same name.

GLENDEVON, Tayside
An excellent touring base for exploring the lovely glen from which it takes its name, this village stands on a road that affords fine views north over Strath Earn to distant ranges of mountains.

After 2 miles turn left on to the B934 towards Dunning, then re-cross the Ochil Hills for Dunning.

DUNNING, Tayside
The church in this pretty village has been rebuilt but retains a typical 13th-century tower.

In Dunning turn right with the B934, then keep left and follow SP 'Perth'. In 1¾ miles turn right with SP 'Bridge of Earn' on to the B935, then immediately keep left and continue to Forteviot.

FORTEVIOT, Tayside
This village stands just south of an attractive confluence where the Water of May joins the River Earn. It was once a Pictish capital. To the north 19th-century Dupplin Castle stands in wooded grounds east of Dupplin Loch, and the splendid early-Christian Dupplin Cross can be seen close to Bank Farm on the summit of The Earn.

Continue to Forgandenny.

FORGANDENNY, Tayside
Culteuchar Hill, also known as Castle Law, rises to a 1,028ft summit south of this village and preserves the remains of an old fort.

Continue to Bridge of Earn.

BRIDGE OF EARN, Tayside
This village stands in the wide Strath of Earn and fragments of its original medieval bridge can still be seen, and the 16th-century mansion of Balmanno lies 2½ miles south-east. Fine views are available from nearby Moncrieffe Hill.

At Bridge of Earn turn left on to the A912 'Perth' road, then cross the River Earn and turn right on to an unclassified road towards Rhynd. In 2¾ miles meet a T-junction and turn left, then after 1 mile reach a track that leads to the right for Elcho Castle.

ELCHO CASTLE, Tayside
More accurately a fortified mansion, ruined Elcho Castle (AM) was the ancestral seat of the earls of Wemyss and is noted for its tower-like wings. It dates from the 16th century.

Continue, with views of the River Tay and city of Perth from the road. Meet a junction with the A912, turn right, and return to Perth.

DUNDEE, Tayside

One of the largest cities in Scotland, Dundee covers some 20 square miles of hillside above the north bank of the Firth of Tay. Clashes between English and Scottish forces punctuate its history. Its strong seafaring tradition dates back to when local men went whaling to Iceland and the north as early as the 12th century. The only surviving gate of the strong walls that protected the town in medieval times is the Cowgate Port. One of the oldest buildings is 15th-century St Mary's Tower, the only surviving part of St Mary's Church, now a viewpoint and museum (temporarily closed). Also of interest are the Mills Observatory (open), and the comprehensive local collections shown in the City Museum and Art Gallery. Exhibits relating to natural history and geology can be seen in the Barrack Street Museum. Victoria Dock contains Captain Scott's HMS *Discovery* and the 19th-century HMS *Unicorn*, the only floating wooden warship in the country. Nearby Camperdown Park comprises 400 acres of landscaped gardens around the neo-classical Camperdown House. Nowadays Dundee is an important centre of industry, with 35 acres of dockland and a reputation for fine jam made with fruit from the fertile Carse of Gowrie. The renowned Dundee marmalade was first made by Mrs Keiller in 1797 and is still enjoyed on breakfast tables throughout the world.

Before leaving Dundee on the main route it is possible to make a 4-mile detour: leave the city on the A930 and drive to Broughty Ferry.

BROUGHTY FERRY, Tayside

Originally an old fishing village and ferry terminus, Broughty Ferry has developed into a residential suburb of Dundee and is a popular holiday resort. Broughty Castle (AM), a 15th-century castle rebuilt as an estuary fort in the 19th century, stands on a rocky headland and houses a fascinating whaling museum. Claypotts Castle (AM) is one of the most complete examples of an old tower house in existence, the dates on the tower of the latter are 1569 and 1588, and it still has its roof.

On the main tour, leave Dundee on the A92 with SP 'Aberdeen', and drive through agricultural country to Muirdrum. A short detour can be made from the main route to Carnoustie by turning right on to the A930 and continuing for 2 miles.

CARNOUSTIE, Tayside

Carnoustie is a popular holiday resort with sandy beaches and a championship golf course considered one of the best in the world. There is also another good course here, the Buddon Links course which has fine coastal views.

On the main route, continue with the A92 and in 5 miles turn right under a railway bridge to enter Arbroath.

ON THE ANGUS COAST

Fishing ports and popular holiday resorts fringe the surprisingly gentle North Sea coast of old Angus, where weathered cliffs of red sandstone guard sandy bays and narrow rock strands. Inland are the rugged heights of the Grampian Mountains and the fertile Howe of Mearns.

ARBROATH, Tayside

Best known for its smokies, delicious haddock flavoured and browned by smoke from an oak fire, this fishing port has a harbour at the mouth of the Brothock Water and has become a popular holiday resort. Various recreational facilities supplement the natural advantages of good sands and safe bathing, and the local countryside offers pleasant walks. Distinctive red sandstone cliffs known for their caves fringe the beach to the north-east. The town itself has been a Royal Burgh since 1599 and has an important place in Scottish history. After the Battle of Bannockburn, in 1320 Robert the Bruce signed Scotland's Declaration of Independence at Arbroath Abbey Considerable 13th-century remains (AM) of this important foundation have survived.

Continue along the A92 'Aberdeen' road to a point just north of the town. A short detour can be made by turning left on to an unclassified road and driving to St Vigeans.

ST VIGEANS, Tayside

One of the finest collections of early-Christian and medieval memorial stones in Scotland is housed in St Vigeans' Cottage Museum (AM). Many of these beautiful monuments take the form of Celtic crosses, invariably carved with elaborate interlacing decorations on the front and groups of animals, figures, and symbols on the back.

On the main route, continue along the A92 for ¾ mile to a point where another detour can be made, this time by turning right on to an unclassified road and driving to Auchmithie.

AUCHMITHIE, Tayside

Perched on a rocky sandstone cliff 150ft above a sandy beach, this precarious and exceptionally picturesque little fishing community can trace its history back to the 11th century. The cliffs extend north-east to impressive Red Head and Lang Craig, which overlook Lunan Bay. Dickmont's Den and the Forbidden Cave are just two notable examples of the many caves in the area.

On the main route, continue along the A92 to Inverkeilor.

INVERKEILOR, Tayside

A tiny place remarkably unspoilt, its notable attractions include its church which contains a good 17th-century pew, and the 15th-century and later pile of Ethie Castle standing two miles to the south-east. Remarkable singing sands, whose grains vibrate against each other when walked on, lie to the east on Lunan Bay.

From Inverkeilor a 2¼-mile detour can be made to Lunan by turning right on to an unclassified road, driving for 1½ miles to a T-junction, and turning left to Lunan.

A superb view of the city can be enjoyed from Dundee Law.

LUNAN, Tayside

Ruined Red Castle stands beside the sandhills in Lunan Bay. It may have been built to counter raids from Danish pirates in the 15th century, but an earlier fort on the site was given by Robert the Bruce to his son-in-law in 1328.

On the main route, leave Inverkeilor on the A92 to cross Lunan Water. Continue, later enjoying views into the Montrose Basin before crossing the River South Esk to enter the town of Montrose.

MONTROSE, Tayside

Here the South Esk River forms a 2-mile square tidal lagoon known as the Montrose Basin, which is popular with many different species of wader all the year round and is a wintering place for pink-footed Arctic geese. The town itself is a pleasant market and holiday centre popular with sailors, golfers, and anglers. A fine sandy beach is complemented by a grassy belt that parallels the spacious High Street and is known as The Links. Leading from the High Street to the town's charming old heart are narrow, twisting 18th-century closes lined by quaint old houses.

Beyond Montrose keep forward with the A937 SP 'Laurencekirk'. Continue for 4½ miles and turn right under a railway bridge before crossing the River North Esk to reach Marykirk.

MARYKIRK, Grampian

Marykirk is well situated at the edge of the Vale of Strathmore, near the point where it merges with the Mearns country, and is a good touring centre for these lovely districts. Its own villagescape is enhanced by the North Esk River.

Turn left on to the B974 SP 'Fettercairn', reach a junction with the A94, then turn right and left to stay on the B974. Continue for 3¼ miles and turn right on to the B966 for Fettercairn.

FETTERCAIRN, Grampian

Set in woods and fields at the edge of the Howe of Mearns, this 18th-century village boasts a great 19th-century royal arch that was built to commemorate an incognito visit made by Queen Victoria and Prince Albert. The village square has a 17th-century cross which is notched to show the length of the Scottish ell, a measurement that is roughly the same as the English yard. It remains to be seen if the memory of the yard will remain as strong as this in the age of metrication. Fettercairn House dates from the 17th century and was erected by the 1st Earl of Middleton, who was Lord High Commissioner to the Scottish Parliament. About 1 mile south-west of Fettercairn is 16th-century Balbegno Castle (not open).

Leave Fettercairn on the B966 'Edzell' road. In 3½ miles it is possible to make a detour from the main route, adding 31 miles to the tour, by turning right on to an unclassified road and driving to beautiful Glen Esk.

GLEN ESK, Tayside

The road through the superb scenery of long Glen Esk accompanies the River North Esk into the fastness of the Grampian Mountains. It is a truly memorable drive for anybody who has the time to take it. The following route instructions and entries detail the countryside from end to end.

On the detour, follow the unclassified road for 9½ miles to reach The Retreat.

THE RETREAT, Tayside

This one-time shooting lodge is now a museum of local country life and handicrafts.

Still on the detour, continue to Tarfside.

The Medicine Well at Montrose was a popular 18th-century spa.

The River North Esk enters the Howe of Mearns at Gannochy.

TARFSIDE, Tayside

Beautifully set in the foothills of the Eastern Grampians, this highly attractive village stands near the confluence of the North Esk River and the Water of Tarf. Mount Battock rises to 2,555ft in the north-east.

Still on the detour, continue to Loch Lee Church and the end of the Glen Esk road.

LOCH LEE, Tayside

Shortly before reaching the end of this lovely glen the road passes the picturesque ruins of Invermark Castle. At the end of the glen, south-west of the little local church, is the lovely expanse of Loch Lee. Queen Victoria and Prince Albert climbed the 3,077ft bulk of Mount Keen, which rises to the north-west of the glen, in 1861. Their visit is commemorated by the Queen's Well beside the Mounth Track, which follows a lovely route cross-country to Aboyne.

If the detour has been taken, rejoin the main route by returning along the entire length of Glen Esk to the B966. On the main tour, continue along the B966 and cross the River North Esk before reaching Edzell.

EDZELL, Tayside

From the south this little inland resort is approached through a fine 19th-century arch raised to the memory of the 13th Earl of Dalhousie. Early 16th-century Edzell Castle (AM) lies to the west of the main village and was visited by Mary Queen of Scots in 1562. One of its major features is a fine 17th-century garden surrounded by a wall which displays unique heraldic and symbolic decoration. The village itself lies between the lovely countryside of Strathmore and the fertile Howe of Mearns, which is situated just west of the North Esk River.

Continue for 3½ miles and meet the A94 'Perth' road. Turn right here, then in ¼ mile turn left on to the B966 for the town of Brechin.

BRECHIN, Tayside

Rising steeply from the banks of the South Esk River, this lovely old cathedral town of red-sandstone buildings stands against a backdrop of hills that gradually rise to the great dark chain of the Eastern Grampians. The old cathedral dates from the 12th century and parts of the original building still exist as proof of the foundation's great antiquity. It was partly rebuilt in the 19th century, but the lovely Maison Dieu Chapel (AM) is preserved as a particularly fine example of 13th-century workmanship. Attached to the church is an 87ft-high round tower (AM) that dates from the 10th or 11th century, with the addition of a spire in the 14th century, and is one of only two such examples existing in Scotland. The other is at Abernethy, and both buildings are similar in shape and decoration to those built by the Celts in Ireland. They were generally used as watchtowers and places of refuge for whole villages. Brechin Castle, the seat of the earls of Dalhousie, was rebuilt in 1711.

Follow SP 'Arbroath' to leave Brechin on the A933 and cross the River South Esk. Skirt the private Kinnaird deer park and Montreathmont Moor Forest, then after 7 miles meet the A932 and turn right SP 'Forfar'. Continue for 1¾ miles and pass the grounds of inhabited Guthrie Castle on the right.

GUTHRIE CASTLE, Tayside

Very occasionally open to the public, this castle has been the home of the Guthrie family ever since it was built by Sir David Guthrie in 1468. The lovely Spring Garden is best seen in early spring.

Continue on the A932, passing Balgavies Loch and the larger Rescobie Loch, and enter Forfar.

FORFAR, Tayside

Forfar lies in charming surroundings in the flat Howe of Angus, between the little Lochs Forfar and Fithie at the north-east end of the Vale of Strathmore. In the 11th century there was a Royal residence here, and an ancient octagonal turret marks the site of the castle where King Malcolm conferred surnames and titles on the Scottish nobility at a parliament in 1057. The castle itself was destroyed many years later by Robert the Bruce. His son was buried near Loch Fithie in Restenneth Priory (AM), a 12th-century foundation in beautiful surroundings. Forfar's Town House preserves a gruesome pronged bridle that was used to silence victims before and during execution, and is associated with so-called witches who were burned here during the 17th century. Forfar is perhaps best known for the 'Forfar Bridie', a half-moon shaped meat and onion pastry.

Leave Forfar on the A929 'Dundee' road, passing through agricultural country and crossing the low Sidlaw Hills on the return to Dundee.

GLEN LYON LANDSCAPES

On either side of the River Lyon's lovely and often spectacular glen are the wooded flanks and high rugged summits of the Breadalbane Mountains. Below them are the beautiful reaches of Loch Tay, attractive lochside villages in small river valleys, and the cascades and falls of numerous streams.

Meall Luaidhe, to the south of Bridge of Balgie, rises to 2,558ft.

PITLOCHRY, Tayside
Fine woodland graces the countryside round this attractive little resort and touring centre. It lies in the lovely valley of the River Tummel and is the site of a huge hydro-electric power station that, although built for obvious economic and practical reasons, has turned out to be a popular and unusual tourist attraction. When the station was built the river was blocked to form the artificial Loch Faskally, and a fish ladder had to be included to help springing salmon follow the old course of the river to their spawning beds in its upper reaches. Visitors can watch the brave efforts of these fish from an observation chamber in the exhibition centre. Various plays and concerts are staged at the Pitlochry Festival Theatre, also known as the Theatre in the Hills, during the summer months.

Leave Pitlochry on the A924 'Perth' road and in ½ mile turn right on to an unclassified road SP 'Festival Theatre'. Cross the Aldour Bridge and turn right with SP 'Foss' on to a narrow road. Pass the theatre and in ¼ mile turn right on to the Inverness road A9. In

¾ *mile turn right again on to an unclassified road and proceed alongside Loch Faskally and pass the Clunie Memorial Arch.*

CLUNIE MEMORIAL ARCH, Tayside
A bronze, horseshoe-shaped memorial at the end of the 2-mile water conduit between Loch Tummel and the Clunie generating station, this arch is the same shape as the conduit and commemorates men who died during its construction in 1946.

Continue alongside Loch Faskally to reach the Linn of Tummel.

LINN OF TUMMEL, Tayside
Once known as the Falls of Tummel, the Linn of Tummel (NTS) is a well-known feature where running water lends its own particular enchantment to lovely countryside. The name of the area was changed when the raising of the water level in Loch Faskally reduced the height and impressiveness of the waterfall. Walks starting from the Linn can be taken alongside the River Garry to

Queen Victoria was particularly attracted to the beauty of Loch Tummel.

Romantic ruins of Finlarig Castle stand just north of Killin.

the Pass of Killiecrankie, and to the magnificent viewpoint of Queen's View, named in memory of a visit by Queen Victoria.

Continue through magnificent scenery along the south bank of the River Tummel and Loch Tummel. After 12 miles turn left on to the B846 SP 'Aberfeldy'. A detour from the main route can be made to Kinloch Rannoch by turning right to stay with the B846; follow the River Tummel to Kinloch Rannoch.

KINLOCH RANNOCH, Tayside
Situated in an area of great scenic beauty, this little angling resort stands on the River Tummel at the east end of lovely Loch Rannoch. Magnificent views extend from the village to distant peaks that guard the entrance to Glencoe, and on the southern shores of the loch the famous Black Wood of Rannoch recalls the primeval Caledonian pine forests that covered the Highlands.

On the main drive, continue along the B846 'Aberfeldy' road and climb out of the Tummel Valley to a road summit of over 1,270ft above Loch Kinnardochy. There are good views

to the right of the 3,547ft quartzite peak of Schiehallion. On the descent pass the Glengoulandie Deer Park on the right.

GLENGOULANDIE DEER PARK, Tayside
Red deer, Highland cattle and endangered species can be seen here in natural surroundings.

Continue along the B846 and descend through the valley of the Keltney Burn to reach the Coshieville Hotel.

COSHIEVILLE, Tayside
An old inn from which this area and its hotel take their names once stood at the junction of roads from Aberfeldy, Fortingall, and Rannoch. It was a favourite stopping-off place for 18th-century cattle drovers on their way to Falkirk and Crieff.

Turn right on to an unclassified road and continue to Fortingall.

FORTINGALL, Tayside

Old thatched cottages and the attractive River Lyon are the main scenic features of this lovely little village, which is separated from the north end of Loch Tay by the wooded bulk of Drummond Hill. A huge yew standing in the local churchyard is thought to be the oldest living tree in Britain. Its girth was measured at 56ft in 1772, and the village tends its one remaining live stem with great care. Earthworks to the south-west of the village are often referred to as the Roman outpost of *Praetorium*, but they are more likely to have survived from a medieval fortified homestead. According to legend Pontius Pilate was born in the area.

Drive for ½ mile beyond Fortingall and turn right SP 'Glen Lyon' to follow the River Lyon into its valley.

GLEN LYON, Tayside

Measuring a full 32 miles in extent, this is the longest and one of the loveliest glens in Scotland. Its Gaelic name means Crooked Glen of Stones, and there is a tradition that the heroic Fingal of Celtic mythology had twelve castles here. Some of the castle, may be explained by the Iron Age ring forts that survive in the area.

Continue through Glen Lyon to Innerwick (not signed).

INNERWICK, Tayside

Isolated amongst the picturesque hills of Glen Lyon, this lonely village has a church which preserves an ancient bell.

Continue, and after 1 mile at Glen Lyon Post Office turn left (no signs) and cross the Bridge of Balgie.

BRIDGE OF BALGIE, Tayside

The attractive Bridge of Balgie is situated on the Glen Lyon road at a point where it meets the steep (1 in 6) mountain road to Killin.

Continue along the narrow Glen Lyon road and ascend through moorland to 1,805ft as the route crosses the Breadalbane Mountains. Descend, with views to the right of Lochan na Lairige and to the left of Ben Lawers.

BEN LAWERS, Tayside

At 3,984ft this grand old mountain of the Breadalbane district is the highest for many miles around. About 8,000 acres of its flanks and summit are protected by the National Trust for Scotland, and the abnormally large number of Alpine plant species growing on its lower slopes makes it an area of considerable scientific interest. Views from the summit, which can be reached quite easily, extend over the whole of the Breadalbane country and much of the Grampian range. Local history and details of the area's many outstanding features can be studied at the visitors' centre (NTS).

Continue past the Ben Lawers Mountain Visitor Centre, then after 2 miles turn right to join the A827 along the north side of Loch Tay.

Killin, on the River Dochart, is dominated by Ben Lawers.

LOCH TAY, Tayside

Overlooked at its western end by Ben Lawers and surrounded on all sides by breathtaking scenery, this superb loch was a favourite place of the poet Sir Walter Scott. He composed a beautiful word picture that captures the essence of its loveliness in his poem the *Fair Maid of Perth*. Below Ben Lawers the 120-mile-long River Tay flows towards Aberfeldy, carrying the greatest volume of water of any British river and providing an inland route for the famous Tay salmon.

Continue along the A827 to Killin.

KILLIN, Central

During spring and summer this all-year-round resort offers fishing and walking, while in the winter months it provides après-ski facilities for people who come here to ski on the slopes of Ben Lawers. The village is situated at the eastern end of mountain-encircled Glen Lochay, on the excellent game-fishing Rivers Dochart and Lochay. One of two small islands near Dochart Bridge adjacent to the attractive Falls of Dochart is the traditional burial ground of the Clan MacNab, and their 17th-century seat of Kinnell House faces the village from the south side of the river.

In its grounds is a well-defined circle of standing stones. Just north of Killin is ruined Finlarig Castle, a one-time Campbell stronghold described by Scott in his *Fair Maid of Perth*.

At the end of Killin cross the River Dochart, then turn right and take the next turning left on to an unclassified road SP 'Ardeonaig'. Continue along the south side of Loch Tay and pass through the hamlets of Ardeonaig and later Acharn. In 1½ miles go forward on to the A827 SP 'Aberfeldy'. To the left of the route at this point is the small resort of Kenmore.

KENMORE, Tayside

Robert Burns admired the lovely views from an 18th-century bridge that spans the Tay here, where the river leaves Loch Tay, and set his impressions down in verse. This little snippet of local history is recorded in the parlour of the hotel, a venerable establishment first licensed over 400 years ago. William and Dorothy Wordsworth left their beloved Lake District long enough to visit Kenmore, and nowadays the village is a charming and popular resort.

Salmon fishermen flock to the River Tay at Kenmore, a village praised by the poet Robert Burns.

Continue along the A827 in the Tay Valley, with views of Drummond Hill Forest and Taymouth Castle on the left.

TAYMOUTH CASTLE, Tayside

Once the seat of the Breadalbanes, Taymouth Castle was visited by Queen Victoria in 1842. The present building dates from the early 19th century and houses a school.

Proceed on the A827 to Aberfeldy.

ABERFELDY, Tayside

A 5-arched bridge that spans the River Tay in this little market town and touring centre was built by General Wade in 1733. The General built roads and bridges all over Scotland after the Rising of 1715, so that troops could be rushed to trouble spots with the minimum loss of time. Of all his works this bridge at Aberfeldy is thought to be among the finest still standing.

At Aberfeldy turn left on to the B846 SP 'Kinloch Rannoch'. Cross Wade's military bridge and proceed to Weem.

WEEM, Tayside

Weem Hotel, said to date back to 1527, displays a sign commemorating a visit by General Wade in 1733. Castle Menzies (open) stands in fine grounds just west of the village. This 16th-century stronghold was the clan's chief seat and is is now the Clan Centre. Monuments to the Menzies can be seen in the local church. Overlooking the village is the 800ft-high viewpoint of the Rock of Weem.

Turn right on to an unclassified road SP 'Strathtay', and follow the north bank of the river to Strathtay. A detour from the main route can be made here by turning right to cross the Tay and driving into Grandtully.

GRANDTULLY, Tayside

Grandtully Castle (not open), 2 miles south-west dates from the 16th century and is the ancestral home of the Stuarts of Innermeath. Canoe slaloms are held in the village, which is pronounced Grantly.

On the main route, keep straight on for 1¼ miles and turn left to join the A827 'Ballinluig' road. Continue to Logierait.

LOGIERAIT, Tayside

Interesting sculptured stones can be seen in the churchyard here, plus reminders of the macabre body-snatching exploits of Burke and Hare in the shape of several mortsafes. These were once placed over new graves and locked. At one time the crime was common in Britain.

At Logierait turn left on to an unclassified road for Dunfallandy. Follow the west bank of the River Tummel for 4 miles, then turn right to re-cross the Aldour Bridge. On the far side of the bridge turn left on to the A924 and re-enter Pitlochry.

BALLATER, Grampian

The Ballater Highland Games are internationally famous and have been drawing large audiences for over a hundred years. Traditionally held in August, they include many old Scottish sports and the arduous Hill Race to the summit of Craig Cailleach. The town itself is a popular summer resort, even without the attraction of the games, set in beautiful Grampian countryside. Lochnagar rises to 3,786ft in the south-west, and just north of the town the pretty Pass of Ballater is threaded by the old Deeside road as it passes beneath the flanks of Craig-an-Darroch. The long and lovely valley of Glen Muick lies south-west below 3,268ft Broad Cairn, and was a favourite of Queen Victoria. Edward VII bought the fine 18th-century house that stands 1 mile south-west of Ballater in Glen Muick while he was the Prince of Wales, and it is now used by HM the Queen Mother. To the east of Glen Muick is the Forest of Glentanar, which includes the 3,077ft bulk of Mount Keen.

Leave Ballater on the A93 'Aberdeen' road and drive along the Dee Valley to the Cambus O'May Hotel, then in ½ mile turn left on to the A97 SP 'Huntly'. Drive past Lochs Kinord and Davan, then turn left again to remain on the A97. Pass through Logie Coldstone and climb through moorland, with the 2,862ft peak of Morven to the left to a road summit of 1,213ft, then descend to Deskry Water and later the River Don. Turn right with the A97. A 2½ mile detour can be taken from the main route to visit Strathdon by turning left here on to the B973.

STRATHDON, Grampian

Here the trout-rich River Don is joined by the Water of Nochty, which flows down from the Ladder Hills. The river and hill country round the village is particularly lovely, and the village itself is a charming place with a church spire that can be seen for miles around. A little to the south-west the Don is spanned by a fine 18th-century bridge, and to the south-east Colquhonnie Castle was begun in the 16th century but never completed. In mid-August Strathdon is usually the venue for the Lonach Highland Gathering.

On the main route cross two river bridges and continue alongside the River Don. After 1¾ miles pass Glenbuchat Castle on the left.

GLENBUCHAT CASTLE, Grampian

Ruins of this ancient Z-plan tower house (exterior AM), considered one of the finest extant, form a major feature of lovely Castle Park. The building was erected in 1590 and is known for its variety of unusual architectural features.

Continue to Glenkindie.

CASTLES OF THE LADDER HILLS

This is a place of large pine forests and purple moors, of windy summits and glens guarded by ancient castles that once symbolized the strength of their clans. Here in the picturesque valley of the Dee is Balmoral Castle, the private country home of the Royal Family.

Dufftown lies within easy reach of broad expanses of moorland.

GLENKINDIE, Grampian

Close to Glenkindie House in the upper Don Valley is a remarkable weem, or ancient Pictish house. In a churchyard about 1 mile away on the other side of the river, near the remains of Towie Castle, is an ancient sculptured cross.

Continue for 2¼ miles to pass the ruins of Kildrummy Castle on the left.

KILDRUMMY CASTLE, Grampian

Built in the 13th century and extensively repaired since, this ruined castle (AM) stands at 800ft above sea level and is guarded on two sides by precipitous ravines. It has seen more than its share of stormy Scottish history, and in 1306 was the scene of a famous and gallant defence by Sir

Balvenie Castle is one of the largest in north Scotland.

Nigel Bruce. The remains are extensive and the most complete of this period in Scotland. One of its great towers is almost equal in size to the superb example at Bothwell, and it preserves a complete layout of domestic buildings, hall, kitchen, solar, and a chapel with a triple lancet window. There is a Japanese Water Garden in the lovely grounds.

Drive on to the hamlet of Mossat and turn left, then continue to Lumsden. Two miles further turn left on to the B9002 SP 'Dufftown'' and pass Auchindoir Church, then Craig Castle, on the left.

AUCHINDOIR CHURCH, Grampian

One of Scotland's finest medieval churches, roofless but otherwise complete, can be seen here. The main features of the ruins (AM) are a carved 12th- or 13th-century doorway and an interesting Sacrament House.

CRAIG CASTLE, Grampian

Patrick Gordon, who was killed on the battleground of Flodden Field in 1513, built the tower that first stood on this site 3 years before his death. It stands on the attractive waters of the Burn of Craig.

From the castle climb across bleak moorland to 1,370ft and later turn left on to the A941. Gradually descend, passing through the hamlet of Cabrach into the upper valley of the River Deveron.

CABRACH, Grampian

The countryside round Cabrach, dominated by the 2,368ft Buck of Cabrach in the south-east, is a place of contrasts. Flourishing deer forests fringe barren moorlands, and the lonely source of the River Deveron is hidden in the heathy slopes of the surrounding hills.

Continue along the A941 and drive alongside the River Deveron for a short distance before continuing over moorland. On the approach to Dufftown cross the River Fiddich and in 1½ miles reach an unclassified right turn that offers a ½-mile detour to Auchindoun Castle.

AUCHINDOUN CASTLE, Grampian

Prehistoric earthworks surround this ruined Gordon castle (AM), situated on a hilltop above the River Fiddich. It is thought that the stronghold was originally founded as early as the 11th century, but much of the existing structure was built by Thomas Cochrane in the reign of James III.

On the main route, continue to Dufftown turning left then shortly left again for the town.

DUFFTOWN, Grampian

This pleasant town was laid out by James Duff, the 4th Earl of Fife, in 1817 in the form of a right-angle cross. In the middle of the square is a Tolbooth tower. The town has a small museum with items from Mortlach Kirk (AM) to the south. The area is well known for its many whisky distilleries, including the famous Glenfiddich plant (open).

On the A941 just north of Dufftown are the ruins of Balvenie Castle.

BALVENIE CASTLE, Grampian

Originally built by the Comyn family, this great moated stronghold (AM) later came into the hands of the Black Douglases and subsequently the Atholls. It was the latter family who created the appearance of the building as it stands today, by demolishing the entire south-east front and replacing it with a 3-storey Renaissance tower house known as the Atholl Building. Edward I visited the castle in 1304, and it was occupied by the Duke of Cumberland in 1746.

Leave Dufftown on the B9009 'Tomintoul road and follow Dullan Water through Glen Rinnes.

Queen Victoria adored the romantic River Dee near Balmoral.

summer is popular with anglers, who come to fish here and south-west of the village, where the Avon is joined by the Water of Ailnack. There is a local museum in the square. The A939 road from Tomintoul to Grantown-on-Spey provides excellent views of the Grampian foothills.

Continue along the A939 through a landscape that becomes bleak and desolate as the route skirts the Ladder Hills. Climb to a 2,090ft summit on the Lecht Road.

LECHT ROAD, Grampian
An old carved stone on the Well of Lecht commemorates the building of this military road by the 33rd Regiment under Lord Charles Hay in 1745. The road summit of 2,090ft is the second highest on any classified road in Britain but is still dwarfed by the surrounding mountains which

tower house (AM) of Corgarff played a large part in the 18th-century Jacobite Risings.

In 2½ miles turn right with the A939 SP 'Braemar' and re-cross the River Don. Cross open moorland reaching the Glas-Choille summit, 1,138ft and descend to the fine old Gairnshiel Bridge. Cross the River Gairn and branch right with the B976, crossing further moorland, then after 5 miles reach Royal Deeside and a junction with the A93. Turn left on to the 'Aberdeen' road. After a short distance pass the road to Balmoral Castle on the right, across the River Dee and Crathie Church on the left.

BALMORAL CASTLE, Grampian
In 1852 Prince Albert bought this beautiful Royal Deeside estate for £31,000, and had the existing castle rebuilt in the romantic Scottish baronial style. Later Queen Victoria added Ballochbuie Forest to the grounds, and since 1855 Balmoral has been the private holiday home of the Royal Family. It is beautifully situated in a curve of the River Dee in the district of Mar, with Glen Gelder leading to the Balmoral Forest area and the White Mounth hills in the south. The glen provided a picturesque route for Queen Victoria and Prince Albert when they climbed Lochnagar on ponies in 1848. Appropriately, the Gaelic rendering of Balmoral is *Bouchmorale*, meaning Majestic Dwelling. The grounds, gardens and castle ballroom (works of art) are open in the early summer.

Continue, and after a short distance pass Crathie Church on the left.

GLEN RINNES, Grampian
This lovely glen is surrounded by fine mountain scenery. Ben Rinnes rises to 2,755ft in the north-west, and the south is dominated by 2,563ft Corryhabbie Hill.

Later pass Glenlivet Forest to reach Auchbreck (not signed). A 1¾-mile detour can be taken from here to visit the village of Glenlivet by turning right on to the B9008.

GLENLIVET, Grampian
Whisky has been distilled in this area for a great many years, and the famous Glenlivet distillery has been producing its fine unblended malt since 1824. Guided tours and a visitor centre are available. The Glen itself stretches south-east from the village towards the Ladder Hills and offers some good walks. Just south of the village are the remains of Blairfindy Castle, and a picturesque ruined bridge spans the Livet Water north at Bridgend.

On the main route, keep left on to the B9008 (no SP). Proceed along Glen Livet and pass through Tomnavoulin before climbing to reach the Pole Inn at Auchnarrow.

AUCHNARROW, Grampian
Near Chapelton in the Braes of Glenlivet, some 3½ miles south-east, is the old Scalen Seminary. This interesting Christian foundation was built in the mid-17th century and burned down during the Rising of 1745. Today its ruins form an

The Royal Family usually spends a summer holiday at Balmoral.

interesting feature of the local landscape.

Continue through forestry to a height of 1,285ft. Descend to crossroads and turn left on to the A939 'Braemar' road. A short detour from the main route into Tomintoul can be made by keeping forward here.

TOMINTOUL, Grampian
Claimed to be the highest village in the Highlands, Tomintoul is stretched out along a 1,160ft sandstone ridge between the Glen of Avon and the Conglass Water. It is also a winter skiing resort and in

have become a very popular winter sports area. During the winter deep snow often makes it impassable.

Continue, and descend by a series of steps to Cock Bridge.

COCK BRIDGE, Grampian
This picturesque bridge carries the Lecht Road across the River Don and is situated 1,330ft above sea level.

Continue with ruined Corgarff Castle on the right.

CORGARFF CASTLE, Grampian
The twice-burned 16th-century

CRATHIE CHURCH, Grampian
Queen Victoria laid the foundation stone of this church in 1895, and the Royal Family attend services here when in residence at Balmoral. The grave of John Brown, Queen Victoria's personal retainer for many years, lies in the churchyard of the present building's ruined predecessor.

Continue with the A93 alongside the River Dee and pass through attractive woodland on the return to Ballater.

THE SCOTTISH RIVIERA

Crescents of firm sand backed by high sandstone cliffs arc between rocky headlands east of the sheltered Moray Firth. Busy resorts are interspersed with coastal villages and miles of empty shoreline, where local craftsmen come to gather the mineral serpentine for sculpting into souvenirs.

Buckie boatyards produce some of the finest vessels in the Highlands.

BANFF, Grampian

Built on a series of cliff terraces rising high above the old harbour, this ancient seaport stands at the mouth of the River Deveron and is a popular holiday resort and sailing centre. Among its many fine buildings is the notable Duff House, built by William Adam in 1735 and eventually given to the town by the Duke of Fife. Its beautiful grounds now form a public park adjoining the Duff House Royal golf course. The 18th-century Town House incorporates an earlier tower, and the shaft of an old cross stands in the area known as Planestones. A few 17th-century houses and the remains of an old church can be seen elsewhere in the town, and an interesting cameo of local history is represented by the Biggar Fountain. This stands on the site of gallows where James Macpherson, a Highland freebooter in the 18th century, showed his contempt for authority by playing the fiddle as he was led to execution.

Leave Banff on the A98 ''Inverness'' road and after 1¾ miles turn right on to the B9038 for Whitehills.

WHITEHILLS, Grampian

This little fishing village stands on a sandy and rocky bay sheltered by the scenic promontories of Stake Ness and Knock Head.

At Whitehills turn left (no SP) on to the B9121 and in ½ mile at crossroads turn right on to the B9139 SP 'Portsoy'. In 3 miles reach Boyne Castle.

BOYNE CASTLE, Grampian

Beautiful woodland surrounds this picturesque ruin, which overlooks the Burn of Boyne. The stronghold dates from 1485 and was once held by the Ogilvie family.

In 1¼ miles turn right on to the A98 to the village of Portsoy.

PORTSOY, Grampian

The prized Portsoy marble for which the area round this little resort and former fishing village is known is actually a variety of serpentine. When worked and polished the mineral reveals unsuspected shades of translucent green and pink. Louis XIV of France used it for two of the chimney pieces in the magnificent Palace of Versailles, and local craftsmen have been working it for centuries. Even today the area's shop windows are adorned with finely wrought serpentine paper weights, chessmen, and other small objects.

Continue along the A98, parallel to the coast, and pass the fishing village and resort of Sandend. Continue to Cullen.

CULLEN, Grampian

Rocky Scar Nose and Logie Head extend out to sea on respective sides of this pleasant resort, sheltering the sandy beach and forming an attractive part of the local seascape. On the shore are three isolated rocks known as the Three Kings of Cullen. The town built on two levels, separated by attractive former railway viaducts offers many holiday facilities and preserves a number of good features. The original settlement was a mile inland around the 16th-century and later Cullen House (not open). Close by the house is St Mary's Church, which was founded by Robert the Bruce and became collegiate in 1543. Inside is the laird's pew of the Seafield line of Clan Grant, and a large monument to a member of the Ogilvy family.

Continue along the A98 'Inverness' road and in 1¼ miles turn right on to the A942 for Portknockie.

PORTKNOCKIE, Grampian

During the late 19th century a deep water harbour was constructed to service the flourishing local herring industry, but nowadays the fishing has declined and the quays are almost deserted. Along the coast to the east of this picturesque little place is the spectacular Bow Fiddle Rock.

Follow SP 'Inverness Coast Road' and pass the village of Findochty.

The double harbour at Portsoy is characteristic of this part of the coast.

FINDOCHTY, Grampian

On each side of this attractive village is a rocky, empty coastline that makes excellent walking country. The beach at Findochty is of fine sand and is ideal for bathing.

Continue to Portessie.

PORTESSIE, Grampian

Portessie is yet another of the many attractive little fishing villages for which this coastline is justly famous. It is unspoilt and retains many of its old cottages.

Continue to Buckie.

BUCKIE, Grampian

High above the rooftops of this straggling port is the elegant and very prominent twin steeple of St Peter's Catholic Church, acting as a landmark from both sea and land. The harbour here is the busiest on the Moray Firth, and many of the town's long maritime associations are recorded in the Buckie Museum and Art Gallery. The town's war memorial is considered to be one of the finest in Scotland.

Pass the harbour and turn right with the A990. Continue for 2 miles to Portgordon.

PORT GORDON, Grampian

The now disused grain exporting and fishing harbour here was built by the Duke of Richmond and Gordon in 1797.

Turn left with the A990 and after 1¼ miles meet a junction with the A98. On the right is a building which is revered as the Banffshire Bethlehem.

ST NINIAN'S CHAPEL, Grampian

After John Knox's hysterical and often bloody Reformation, many Scots who had been Catholic changed to the Protestant faith under pressure from the new regime. In the old Banffshire area the influence of the Gordon Clan was such that the local people clung persistently to the traditional faith, even when the clan chiefs played them false and forsook the religion which they had supported for generations. Following the Jacobite Risings Scotland was swept by a wave of hatred against anything Catholic, and the 1,000 or so faithful in Banffshire were hounded from one secret church to the next until they were given an old cottage-cum-byre that had been converted for sheep. It was this property of the Laird of Tynet that served as their place of worship through the troubled times and became known as the Banffshire Bethlehem. Even today the white walls under a grey slate roof appear to be nothing more than a farm building, but the interior has been carefully restored and is still in use.

Turn right then immediately left on to the Keith road B9016. In 1¾ miles a short detour can be made by turning right on to an unclassified road and driving for ½ mile to St Ninian's Kirkyard.

ST NINIAN'S KIRKYARD, Grampian

A decade or so after the Protestant Reformation, before the Jacobites created the need for such hideaways as the Banffshire Bethlehem, the faithful of this area built a new church in an ancient churchyard dedicated to St Ninian. This was the first Catholic place of worship to have been built since John Knox's religious crusade, but after the Jacobite Rising it was attacked by an armed band of Protestants and completely wrecked. Its site beside the Tynet Burn is marked by a cross raised to the memory of 18th-century Bishop Nicholson, who was the first Vicar Apostolic of Scotland.

On the main route continue with the B9016 for 4¾ miles, meet a junction with the A96, then turn left on to the 'Aberdeen' road. In 1 mile turn left on to the A95 and continue to the town of Keith.

KEITH, Grampian

Narrow lanes criss-crossing between the three parallel main streets of this Strath Isla market centre give it a quaint, timeless character all of its own. It stands on the River Isla,

The seashore near Gardenstown is picturesque but rocky and precipitous.

which is spanned by two bridges connecting the town with its close neighbour Fife of Keith. The early crossing dates from 1609 and the later from 1770. At one time Keith was famous for its fair, but nowadays it is better known as the site of the Strathisla Distillery. This was founded in 1785 and is the oldest working malt whisky distillery in Scotland.

Leave Keith on the A95 SP 'Banff' and follow Strath Isla. After 5 miles turn right on to the B9117 with SP 'Rothiemay'. In 2½ miles turn right then immediately left, and after ¾ mile follow the B9118 to Rothiemay.

ROTHIEMAY, Grampian

Remains of Rothiemay Castle stand beyond the River Deveron in fine gardens, and the river itself is spanned here by a fine old bridge. A monument at Milltown of Rothiemay commemorates James Ferguson, an early 18th-century astronomer.

Continue forward on an unclassified road, cross the River Deveron, and turn left. Continue along a narrow road through the well-wooded countryside of the Deveron Valley, and after 5¼ miles turn right on to the A97 'Huntly' road. In ½ mile turn left on to an unclassified road SP 'Inverkeithny'. After 1½ miles keep left and descend to Inverkeithny

Macduff harbour is the base for the town's important herring fleet.

hamlet, at the junction of the Burn of Forgue and the River Deveron. Climb above the river, then leave the valley and cross open country to a junction with the B9024. Turn left on to the 'Turriff' road and in 6 miles turn left again on to the A947 towards 'Banff' for Turriff.

TURRIFF, Grampian

In 1639 this thriving little market town was the scene of the Trot of Turriff, when Covenanters met Royalists in battle. A church of the Knights Templar stood here, and the old Market Cross was re-erected in 1865. Turriff stands on a plateau overlooking the confluence of the Deveron and the Water of Idoch and is the centre of a district particularly rich in castles and tower houses. Pleasant woodland to the east of the town surrounds the great tower house of Delgatie Castle (open by written application only) a seat of the Clan Hay that has been in the family's possession for nearly 700 years. It was founded by the Hays of Delgatie in the 13th century and shows alterations up to the 16th century. Inside are various relics and pictures, but among its best features are its fine painted ceilings of c1590. Towie Barclay Castle (open by appointment only) built around 1587 is completely Gothic and medieval in inspiration and consists of a single high rib-vaulted chamber in two bays.

Stay on the A947 'Banff' road and in 2 miles turn right on to the B9105 towards 'Fraserburgh'. After 2½ miles pass Craigston Castle on the right.

CRAIGSTON CASTLE, Grampian

Remarkable woodcarvings are preserved in this early 17th-century castle, which was built by John Urquhart and has hardly been altered since (not open).

Continue through Buchan countryside and in 3½ miles turn right on to the A98. In another 2½ miles turn left on to an unclassified road SP 'New Aberdour'. After another 2½ miles turn left again towards 'Pennan', then continue along a winding road to meet a junction with the B9031 at the coast. Drive over the crossroads and descend steeply into the village of Pennan.

PENNAN, Grampian

Pennan Head dominates the rocky and precipitous shore of Pennan Bay, and the pretty Troup Burn joins the sea near the village. Farther west is the bold outline of Troup Head. The village itself has housed generations of fishermen and is typical of many along this coast.

Return to the B9031 and turn right towards 'Banff'. Continue along a hilly road with occasional coastal views. Short detours from the main route towards the coast lead to the attractive villages of Crovie and Gardenstown.

CROVIE, Grampian

Crovie Head shelters this community, which stands at the base of high red cliffs on Gamrie Bay.

GARDENSTOWN, Grampian

Picturesque cottages and houses rise in tiers above the lovely old harbour of Gardenstown, a fishing village on the shores of Gamrie Bay. To the west near Mhor Head, on the Hill of Gamrie Mhor, is a ruined church that was founded to commemorate a local victory over the Danes. The date given for this event is recorded on the gable of the building as 1004, but it is unlikely that the existing structure is as early as that. West and east of the village are ranges of spectacular cliffs.

On the main route, continue for 8¾ miles (from Pennan) and turn right on to the A98 towards 'Inverness'. Continue to Macduff.

MACDUFF, Grampian

Steep streets of attractive houses lead down to a superb harbour in Macduff, an important Banff Bay town known for its fishing industry. It has one of the most pleasing waterfronts in Scotland, very picturesque and bustling with activity and very fine views of the area can be enjoyed from the war memorial on top of the Hill of Doune.

Cross the River Deveron and return along the A98 to Banff.

233

AVIEMORE, Highland

In the 1960s the village of Aviemore, situated in the heart of the British winter sports area, became transformed into one of Scotland's major inland resorts. This amazing change was brought about by the building of the Aviemore Centre, a massive complex of shops, restaurants, luxury hotels, and entertainment facilities with a definite après-ski flavour. Superb sporting facilities include ice-rinks for skating and curling, a go-kart track, a dry ski slope, and a swimming pool. Various events are staged at the theatre and concert hall, and for people who dislike hotel rooms there are numerous well-appointed chalets. The local granite and timber of which the complex is built is in keeping with its site at the foot of the great rock of Craigellachie. Steam-hauled trains operate on a revived railway which runs along the Spey Valley to connect Aviemore with Boat of Garten, some 5 miles away. Another feature of the area is a 600-acre nature reserve.

Leave Aviemore on the 'Perth' road B9152 and in 2 miles keep forward. Later skirt the shores of Loch Alvie and the village of Alvie.

ALVIE, Highland

Alvie Church is a homely focal point for this pleasant hamlet. Nearby Geal Charn Mor stands at 2,703ft and rewards anybody who climbs it with one of Scotland's finest views of the Cairngorm Mountains.
On Tor of Alvie Hill to the south is the Waterloo Cairn and Monument to the last Duke of Gordon.

Continue through Kincraig to reach the Highland Wildlife Park.

HIGHLAND WILDLIFE PARK, Highland

This was opened in 1972 and is based on an interesting historic theme, to illustrate the wildlife that has existed in Britain from the ice ages to the present day. Among the inhabitants displayed in one of the most fascinating collections in the country are bears, wolves, lynx, wildcats, and European bison.

Continue and in 3½ miles go forward on to the A86 to enter Kingussie.

KINGUSSIE, Highland

A popular pony-trekking centre surrounded by the wooded countryside of Strath Spey, Kingussie was chosen as the site for the superb Highland Folk Museum when it was moved from its place of foundation on Iona. Exhibits relate to the everyday life of the Scottish people and include farming implements, domestic tools, dress, tartans, relics of old crafts, and several much larger items such as a complete cottage furnished in traditional style, a mill

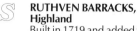

BELOW THE CAIRNGORM SUMMITS

Here are the best winter-sports facilities in Britain, mountain walks that are unequalled elsewhere in the country, and the forested depths of beautiful Glen More. Superb views are afforded by ski lifts that operate all the year round, riding high above granite crags and tree-shrouded lochs.

Superb facilities for ski-ing exist around Aviemore, including a wide variety of nursery slopes and many more difficult runs.

from the Isle of Lewis, a traditional islander's black house, and a curious clack mill. A visit here will provide the type of understanding that can only enrich the tourist's enjoyment of Scotland in general, and the Highlands in particular. Some 2½ miles north-east of Kingussie, off the Aviemore road, is the 18th-century mansion of Balavil. This was built by James Macpherson, who was born in the area and later became a translator of Ossianic poetry.

Before leaving Kingussie it is possible to take a detour from the main route by keeping forward on the A86 for 3 miles to Newtonmore.

NEWTONMORE, Highland

Highland ponies can be hired for rides into the bleak Monadhliath Mountains from a centre to the west of this town, which was the first place in Britain to offer pony-trekking as a recreation. Overlooking the site of a clan battle fought near by in 1386 is 2,350ft Craig Dhu, the ancient gathering place of the Clan Macpherson. Macpherson House Museum features clan history and relics of the 1745 Jacobite Rising.

On the main tour, turn left on to the B970 SP 'Ruthven, Insh' and drive over a level crossing. Continue to Ruthven Barracks.

RUTHVEN BARRACKS, Highland

Built in 1719 and added to by General Wade 'the road builder' in 1734, these old barracks (AM) were adopted to house anti-Jacobite troops between the Risings of 1715 and 1745. They were captured and demolished by the followers of Bonnie Prince Charlie in 1746.

Continue and in 1¾ miles cross the River Tromie at Tromie Bridge and turn left SP 'Kincraig'.

INSH, Highland

AA Celtic handbell that was once used to call people to worship is preserved in an 18th-century church above Loch Insh near Kincraig. It pre-dates the building by at least 1,000 years, and the site occupied by the church is even older.

In 2¼ miles keep forward with the 'Rothiemurchus' road and later cross the River Feshie at Feshiebridge.

FESHIEBRIDGE, Highland

Excellent all-weather footpaths extend along the Glen of Feshie towards Deeside from here. Some of the most scenic areas are where the valley penetrates the hill ranges of attractive Speyside.

Continue along the B970 and drive through attractive Inshriach Forest to reach Rothiemurchus.

ROTHIEMURCHUS, Highland

At one time the woodland round this hamlet formed part of the primeval Caledonian Forest that covered most of the Scottish Highlands. Much of it is contained within the boundaries of Rothiemurchus Forest, which is accessible by attractive paths and tracks. Part of the area is protected as a nature reserve and there is a visitor centre.

Just beyond Rothiemurchus it is possible to make a short detour from the main route by turning right on to an unclassified road and driving to Loch an Eilean.

LOCH AN EILEAN, Highland

Noted for its odd triple echo, this beautiful loch was once the bolthole of the Wolf of Badenoch, a clan leader who was notoriously bloodthirsty. The island ruins of his castle add a sinister note to the otherwise innocent enchantment of the lochside area.

On the main tour, continue along the B970 to Inverdruie.

INVERDRUIE, Highland

Situated here is the Whisky Museum with an audio-visual display, museum, tasting room, shop and a visitor centre.

Turn right for Coylumbridge.

The splendid Cairngorm Mountains rise to the north of attractive Loch Morlich.

The wild cat is a fierce native of the Scottish Highlands.

COYLUMBRIDGE, Highland
This ski resort on the River Druie is a key point of access to the peaks and valleys of the Cairngorms. A Forestry Commission road which starts here leads into the range, passing through Queen's Forest to the shores of Loch Morlich, where there is a youth hostel. After the recreational centre of Glenmore a further stretch of ski road ascends to the Cairngorms carparks and chairlift terminals. Views from the carparks extend for miles over the Glen More Forest Park.

GLEN MORE FOREST PARK, Highland
Some 3,300 acres of coniferous forest and 9,200 acres of mountainside make up this beautiful and often spectacular national forest park. At its heart is Loch Morlich, which lies in a hollow 1,000ft above sea level and has sandy beaches fringed by descendants of the old Caledonian pines that once covered the Highlands. Rock and heather take over where the trees stop, and all round the horizon are the serrated outlines of mountain peaks. Rare wildlife found nowhere else in Britain lives here, and species that are uncommon elsewhere abound. Walkers using the Forestry Commission trails may see the blue hare or stately red deer, the turkey-like capercaillie that was re-introduced to the Highlands several years ago, or the ptarmigan that never quite died out. Also here are grouse, golden eagles, the elusive osprey, and roe deer. Reindeer are being farmed in the area, so the walker who comes face to face with one of these magnificent creatures should not fear for his sanity.

From Coylumbridge follow SP 'Nethy Bridge' along the B970 to continue along Strath Spey. After 6¼ miles a ½-mile detour can be taken from the main route by following an unclassified left turn to Boat of Garten.

BOAT OF GARTEN, Highland
The curious name of this village is derived from a ferry that used to cross the Spey from here before the present bridge was built in the 19th century. It is the northern terminus of a 5-mile steam hauled railway which runs along Strath Spey to the winter sports and recreation centre of Aviemore.

On the main tour, continue along the B970 for a further ½ mile and turn right on to an unclassified road SP 'Loch Garten' to enter the Abernethy Forest. Continue to the banks of Loch Garten.

LOCH GARTEN, Highland
Visitors to the RSPB observation point here can watch many species of birds, including the rare osprey.

Pass Loch Garten and after ¼ mile keep forward on to the 'Nethy Bridge' road. In 2¼ miles turn right to rejoin the B970 and enter the resort of Nethy Bridge.

NETHY BRIDGE, Highland
Winter-sports enthusiasts come here for the ski-ing, and later in the year it is a popular centre for walkers and anglers. North of the village on the B970 are the ruins of Castle Roy, a great fortress that was a stronghold of the Comyn.

Cross the River Nethy then turn right on to an unclassified road (no sign) and in ½ mile drive over crossroads SP 'Tomintoul'. Ascend onto moorland, and after 4½ miles turn right on to the A939 towards Tomintoul. Proceed, with the Hills of Cromdale on the left and the dark outlines of the Cairngorms to the right. Ascend to a road summit of 1,424ft, then descend to the Bridge of Brown. Climb again then descend and cross the Bridge of Avon, then turn left on to the B9136 SP 'Craigellachie'. Follow Strath Avon and in 8½ miles cross the River Livet at the hamlet of Glenlivet.

GLENLIVET, Grampian
Fine malt whisky has been distilled in this small village for many years, and although there is a modern distillery here (open to visitors) the method has not changed much.

Beyond the Livet bridge turn left SP 'Whisky Trail' to join the B9008. After 4 miles reach the Delnashaugh Inn and turn left on to the A95 Grantown Road.

DELNASHAUGH INN, Grampian
Close to this famous landmark is Ballindalloch Castle, which was begun in the 16th century and bears the arms of the Macpherson-Grants. Beyond its picturesque grounds is the junction of the River Avon with the River Spey.

After a short distance re-cross the

River Avon, with the grounds of Ballindalloch Castle to the right, and continue to the hamlet of Toremore.

TOREMORE, Highland
In 1960 the first distillery to be built in the Highlands this century was opened here. The building, which at the time was described as 'the most beautiful industrial structure in the Highlands', was designed by Professor Sir Albert Richardson.

Continue along the south side of the Spey and pass through the hamlet of Cromdale. Continue to the resort of Grantown-on-Spey.

GRANTOWN-ON-SPEY, Highland
A local landowner planned this essentially residential resort in 1776, and the elegance of the 18th century has persisted to the present day. It is set in the lovely surroundings of Strath Spey and has become a major centre for anglers seeking the excellent Spey salmon. There is also considerable local involvement with the Scottish winter-sports industry. Castle Grant, a mansion that is the seat of the Earls of Seafield, stands about 2 miles north of the town.

Leave Grantown on the 'Perth' road A95 and continue to Dulnain Bridge.

Loch Garten is nationally famous as a breeding ground for the osprey.

Continue on the A938 and follow the valley of the River Dulnain to Carrbridge. Here turn left on to the Aviemore road B9135 for the village.

CARRBRIDGE, Highland
The award-winning visitor cente in this Highland resort is claimed to be the finest in Europe. It offers all kinds of information about the Highlands, including an exciting audio-visual display that covers some 10,000 years of history. In winter Carrbridge is a popular ski-ing centre.

Continue on the B9153 and in 2½ miles go forward on to the A95. Later take the B9152 to re-enter Aviemore.

ROAD TO THE ISLES

Reminders of Bonnie Prince Charlie and the ill-fated Jacobite
Rising are everywhere in the west Highland countryside.
Ben Nevis towers over lochs and glens, moors and hillsides,
known for the bloody battles and long-drawn-out feuds
enacted there in the past.

Snow-capped Ben Nevis forms a popular excursion from Fort William. On a clear
day views from the summit extend for 150 miles.

FORT WILLIAM, Highland
The first fort built here was a wattle-
and-daub structure erected by
General Monk in 1655, but the town
takes its name from a stone
stronghold that replaced it by order
of William III. It was besieged by
Jacobites in the Rising of 1715, but
they failed to take it and General
Wade was commissioned to
strengthen it. His engineering talents
were proved in 1745, when the
second Jacobite Rising failed to
capture it. The fort was garrisoned
until the mid 19th century, by which
time its redundancy was obvious
and it was demolished to make way
for the railway. Relics from these and
earlier days can be seen in the West
Highland Museum including a
curious picture of Prince Charles
Edward that can only be seen in its
reflection on a curved and polished
surface. The town itself is a major
resort and touring centre for the
West Highlands, situated near the
west end of Glen More and the head
of Loch Linnhe. Towering above the
town is the massive bulk of Ben
Nevis, while the comparatively low
summit of 942ft Cow Hill affords
lovely views into lower Glen Nevis.
One of the major features of the
local landscape is the white quartzite
peak of Sgurr a' Mhaim, which rises
like a snow-capped Alp to the south,
while north-east of the town another
is an aluminium smelting works
which makes use of hydro-electric
power.

BEN NEVIS, Highland
An enormous expanse of
countryside round Fort William and
the Lochaber area, including a large
part of Glen More, is dominated by
4,408ft Ben Nevis. It is the highest
mountain in the British Isles, and
round its south and west flanks is
Glen Nevis, one of the most beautiful
valleys in Scotland. At the far end of
the glen the River Nevis rushes
through a steep wooded gorge, but
closer to Fort William its waters can
be crossed to reach a mountain path
starting at Achintee Farm. The
mountain can be climbed from here,
but the path is only suitable for
properly equipped walkers. The
energetic explorer will find many
enchanting and often impressive
natural features to reward his efforts,
such as the Allt Coire Eaghainn
waterfalls plunging from their
hidden corrie, the waterfall of
Steall in its wild setting at the end of
Glen Nevis, and the spectacular
narrow arrête that links the Ben with
the upper slopes of Carn Mor Dearg.

*From Fort Wiliam follow SP
'Inverness' to take the A82
northwards out of the town and pass
Inverlochy Castle.*

INVERLOCHY CASTLE,
Highland
Thought to date from the 13th
century, this ruined Comyn
stronghold (AM) stands by the River
Lochy and is well-preserved. The
largest of its circular towers is named
after the family and has massive 10ft-
thick walls enclosing rooms that are
a full 20ft across. A Civil War battle
between a royalist force led by the
Marquess of Montrose and a
Covenanters' army under the
command of the Duke of Argyll
took place near here in 1645.

*Beyond the castle turn left to join the
A830 'Mallaig' road — the famous
Road to the Isles. At one time this was
notoriously difficult, but has been
much improved. Cross the River
Lochy, then the Caledonian Canal,
and enter Banavie.*

BANAVIE, Highland
Telford came here in the 19th
century to build a chain of eight
locks, known as Nepture's Staircase,
on the Caledonian Canal, and his
brilliance in solving difficult civil
engineering problems can still be
seen.
Continue to Corpach.

CORPACH, Highland
A little to the west of Corpach is
Kilmallie Churchyard, where an
obelisk was raised to Colonel John
Cameron after he fell in the Battle of

Quatre Bras during the Waterloo
Campaign of 1815. The town is well-
known for the large paper and pulp
mill.
*Continue along the A830 and follow
the picturesque shore of Loch Eil to
Kinlocheil.*

KINLOCHEIL, Highland
Nowadays this is a peaceful little
place, but it must have been full of
tension when Prince Charles Edward
came here after unfurling his father's
standard at Glenfinnan in 1745.
Continue to Glenfinnan.

GLENFINNAN, Highland
More than 1,000 clansmen mustered
here under the Stuart banner to
begin the second Jacobite Rising in
1745. The place where the standard
is said to have been unfurled is
marked by a tall castellated tower
(NTS) with an inner staircase leading
to a 19th-century statue of a
Highlander at the top. There is also a
visitor centre. Each year Highland
games are held on the site in
memory of those who died for
Bonnie Prince Charlie. Views from
here extend along 18-mile Loch
Shiel.

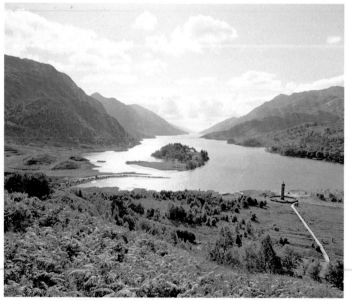

LOCH SHIEL, Highland
Many visitors consider Loch Shiel to
be the most picturesque expanse of
fresh water in the Highlands. At its
north end it is framed by spectacular
mountain scenery, and parallel
ranges of rocky hills border Glen
Finnan to the north of the '45 Rising
monument. Below the massive bulk
of Ben Resipol are the narrows of
the loch and the little island of
Eilean Fhionain, which used to be a
burial ground many centuries ago.

*Continue, then pass Loch Eilt on the
way to Lochailort.*

LOCHAILORT, Highland
Situated in a lovely position at the
head of the sea loch Ailort, this
village stands against a backdrop of
high hills in which 2,877ft Rois
Bheinn is prominent. At the seaward
end of the loch is the tiny island of
Eilean nan Gobhar, where the
French ship that brought Bonnie
Prince Charlie anchored in July of
1745.

*From Lochailort a 39-mile detour can
be taken to Mallaig by continuing
along the A830 alongside Loch Ailort,
then Loch nan Uamh.*

LOCH NAN UAMH,
Highland
Worth visiting for its own sake, this
picturesque loch is best known for its
associations with Bonnie Prince
Charlie and the Jacobite Rising of
1745. Borrodale House was the
scene of a fateful meeting when the
whole issue of the Jacobite cause
came into question, and although it
was burnt after the Battle of
Culloden it still preserves much of its
original structure. After the '45 Rising
had degenerated into a disorganized
bloodbath the Prince returned to
Loch nan Uamh with a fortune on his
head, and he had to hide in the
woods of Glen Beasdale before
escaping to the isolation of the
Outer Hebrides.

*Still on the detour, continue to Arisaig
with views across the Sound of Arisaig
to the little islands of Rhum and Eigg.*

Wild Loch Shiel echoes with memories
of Bonnie Prince Charlie at Glenfinnan.

ARISAIG, Highland

A memorial clock in the Roman Catholic church here commemorates the most revered of all Scots Gaelic poets, Alisdair MacMhaigstir Alasdair, who took part in the Rising of 1745. South-east are the gardens of Arisaig House Hotel.

Still on the detour, continue to Morar.

MORAR, Highland

Loch Morar is the deepest inland water in Britain, and the Falls of Morar have been harnessed in a local hydro-electric scheme on the River Morar. The white sands of a bay formed by the river's estuary are famous. The hamlet itself is situated on a narrow neck of land between the loch and the Sound of Sleat.

Continue on the detour to Mallaig.

CASTLE TIORAM, Highland

One of the most romantic and beautifully situated ruins in the Western Highlands, this 13th-century castle is perched on a spit of land that becomes isolated when the tide rises. It was built by the Macdonalds of Clanranald who, after they realized that the 1715 Rising was doomed to failure, burned it rather than let it fall into enemy hands.

Continue on the A861 to Acharacle.

Neptune's Staircase of 8 locks at Banavie raises the Caledonian Canal 64ft in 1 mile.

ACHARACLE, Highland

This little angling resort stands on the west tip of Loch Shiel.

Continue to Salen

SALEN, Highland

The small fishing resort of Salen stands on Loch Sunart, a narrow ribbon of sea that separates Ardnamurchan from the traditionally MacLean territory of the Morvern district. It is little more than a cluster of cottages round a hotel, but its surroundings are a superb mixture of mountain, moorland, and pine plantations.

LOCH SUNART, Highland

At the head of this beautiful sea loch is an amphitheatre of hills where the Ardgour and Morvern districts meet.

A 50-mile detour can be made from Salen to Kilchoan and Ardnamurchan Point: take the B8007 (a narrow, winding road) west along the loch and drive inland through the Ardnamurchan Peninsula, returning to the coast at Kilchoan. To reach Ardnamurchan Point and lighthouse (a further 6 miles) continue along the B8007 for another 4 miles and turn left on to an unclassified road to Ardnamurchan Point.

KILCHOAN AND ARDNAMURCHAN POINT, Highland

Situated on the rocky Ardnamurchan coast, this remote little village has a pier that is the starting point of a passenger ferry to Tobermory, on the Island of Mull. Ardnamurchan Point, the most westerly point in mainland Britain, is a wild and lonely area populated by seabirds.

On the main tour, leave Salen and continue along the A861 SP 'Strontian' beside the northern shore of Loch Sunart to the village of Strontian.

STRONTIAN, Highland

Strontium, a rare mineral that used to be mined in the district, is named after this village. To the north the River Strontian carves its way between the mountains of Sunart and Ardgour before emerging from its glen to join Loch Sunart in an area that used to be mined for lead. Close by is the Ariundle Forest nature reserve, one of the few places where the true Scottish wildcat survives.

Keep right and continue along the A861 through Glen Tarbert. Later pass through Inversanda to reach the shores of lovely Loch Linnhe.

LOCH LINNHE, Highland

Situated at the extreme west end of the Great Glen, or Glen More, Loch Linnhe is divided into the Inner and Outer Loch by the Corran Narrows. Loch Leven joins it beyond the Narrows, which are crossed by a car ferry between Ardgour and Corran.

Continue along the west shore of Loch Linnhe to Ardgour.

ARDGOUR, Highland

This name applies generally to a wild and rugged district between Loch Shiel and Loch Linnhe, and particularly to a small village on the Corran Narrows.

From the ferry point at the Ardgour Hotel the main route crosses the narrows by the Corran Ferry and at Corran turn left on to the A82 for the return to Fort William. A detour (23 miles) by way of the west shore of Loch Linnhe and Loch Eil can be made by keeping forward with the A861 to Camusnagaul.

CAMUSNAGAUL, Highland

Excellent views extend over Loch Linnhe to Fort William that ever-popular resort with tourists and climbers alike, dominated by the towering summit of Ben Nevis. Close by the loch bends west to become Loch Eil.

Continue along the A861 to follow the shore of Loch Eil, then round the head of the loch and turn right on to the A830 for Kinlocheil and the return to Fort William.

MALLAIG, Highland

Facing the Isle of Skye from the rocky shores of north Morar, this major fishing port stands at the western end of the Road to the Isles and is the mainland terminus of the islands' ferry. Cars can be taken from here to Armadale, on Skye.

On the main route, at Lochailort turn left on to the A861 SP 'Ardgour' and follow the eastern shore of the loch and the Sound of Arisaig. Later turn south to reach Loch Moidart and Kinlochmoidart.

KINLOCHMOIDART, Highland

Here, where the River Moidart flows through woodland to the head of Loch Moidart, survive 5 of the 7 beech trees planted to commemorate 7 local men who were among Bonnie Prince Charlie's most constant companions.

Continue along the A861 and after 6 miles reach an unclassified right turn. A detour can be made from the main route to Castle Tioram here.

During the season Mallaig harbour is packed with fishing boats.

KYLE OF LOCHALSH, Highland

This busy fishing and shipping village stands at the west end of Loch Alsh and is the railhead on a line from Inverness. It is also the main ferry stage for Skye, and the shores of that beautiful island lie just a few hundred yards away across the Kyle Akin waters. Fine views from Kyle of Lochalsh encompass the Cuillin range on Skye, the Crowlin Islands, and Raasay to the west. East is the vast Balmacara Estate (NTS).

Take the Skye ferry across the narrow strait to Kyleakin.

KYLEAKIN, Highland

Ruined Castle Moil stands on the shore a little to the east of this small fishing and car-ferry port. It is thought that its small Highland keep may have been built by the daughter of a Norwegian king but it is known to have served as a lookout post and fortress against Norse raiders for centuries. During most of this time it was a stronghold of the Mackinnons of Strath. Behind the village is the 2,396ft bulk of Beinn na Cailleach.

Drive along the A850 and pass through Breakish to reach Broadford.

BROADFORD, Highland

Broadford is a convenient touring centre for south Skye. It stands by Broadford Bay on a junction of roads from the ferry ports of Armadale, Kylerhea, and Kyleakin, overlooked by the granite screes of the Red Hills. Prominent in the range is 2,400ft Beinn na Caillich, the site of the largest hill cairn in Scotland. Tradition has it that a Norwegian princess was buried here, where the winds of Norway could blow over her grave, in the 13th century. Offshore to the west is the Island of Scalpay.

From Broadford a detour can be made along the A881 to reach Torrin and Elgol.

TORRIN, Highland

In front of this crofting township is Loch Slapin, and the majestic Red Cuillin range rises in the north-east. Across the loch on the Strathaird peninsula is the great Black Cuillin peak of 3,044ft Bla Bheinn and a precipitous rocky ridge known as Clach Glas. The latter is popular with experienced rock climbers.

Still on the detour, continue to Elgol.

ELGOL, Highland

Magnificent views from this Loch Scavaig hamlet extend north to the Cuillins and south to the mountainous little islands of Canna, Rhum, and Eigg. Motor-boat trips can be taken from here to Loch Coruisk, which lies amongst the wild Cuillin peaks in a landscape of lochs and mountains more scenic than any other in the British Isles. The loch can also be reached by way of footpaths, one of which runs along the lovely and mountainous north shore of Loch Scavaig.

THE ISLE OF MIST

History and legend join hands in the misty no-man's land that is Skye's romantic, often turbulent, past. Old castles guard the shoreline, and some of the most spectacular mountains in Scotland encircle the magical scenery of hidden inlets and unsuspected lochs.

On the main drive, continue on the Portree road, and skirt the island of Scalpay then Loch Ainort with views of 2,649ft Garbh-bheinn to the left.

Castle Moil at Kyleakin commands breathtaking views up Loch Alsh

CUILLIN HILLS, Highland

Unrivalled for scenic splendour anywhere in Britain, the Black and Red Cuillins are the most famous landscape features of this outstanding island. A 6-mile arc of black peaks, 15 of which exceed 3,000ft in height, curves across the south-west part of the island as the Black Cuillin range; on the other side of Glen Sligachan, in spectacular contrast to its jagged neighbours, are the softly rounded summits and glowing pink granite of the Red Cuillins. The black peak of 3,309ft Alasdair and rough pinnacled mass of 3,167ft Sgurr nan Gillean attract experienced climbers, while the determined walker heads for the fastnesses of hidden corries and surprising little valleys in the red hills. Both ranges are prone to sudden mists and can be deadly, even to experienced people. Local advice

Portree offers a pleasant harbour for steamers to Raasay

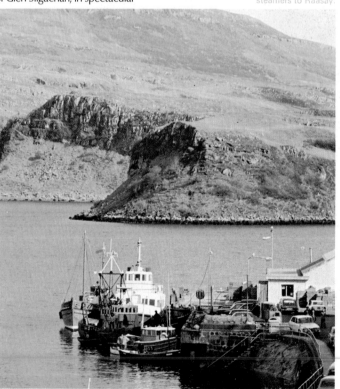

should be sought before attempting to explore either.

Ascend from Loch Ainort with Red Cuillin summit of 2,542ft Glamaig to the left of the road. Later descend with views of the island of Raasay on the right to reach Sconser.

SCONSER, Highland

Parts of an inn where Dr Johnson and Boswell stayed while visiting the island in 1773 have been incorporated in the Sconser Lodge Hotel. The hamlet itself is sited at the mouth of Loch Sligachan.

Proceed to Sligachan.

SLIGACHAN, Highland

Well known for its salmon and sea trout, this hamlet stands on the River Sligachan near the head of the loch of the same name. The U-shaped glacial valley of Glen Sligachan extends south into the Black Cuillins, with the 3,167ft peak of Sgurr nan Gillean prominent to the left. Several high peaks and spectacular Loch Coruisk can be reached via a path through the glen.

Drive north along Glen Varragill and descend to Portree Loch to reach the harbour town of Portree.

PORTREE, Highland

Skye's pleasant little capital town of whitewashed houses stands on Portree Bay, which is sheltered by high cliffs on three sides. Well situated as a touring centre for the island, the town has a charming harbour and receives all kinds of light boat traffic at its pier. Opposite, across the Sound of Raasay, is the wooded island of Raasay. This isolated place is of particular interest to botanists and geologists.

Turn right on to the A855 and later pass the reservoirs of Loch Fada and Loch Leathan, both of which are incorporated in a hydro-electric scheme. To the left are the Trotternish Ridge and the precipices of The Storr.

THE STORR, Highland

Extending the length of the wild Trotternish peninsula of Skye, a 10-mile backbone of rock is dominated by the 2,360ft conical peak of The Storr. Here is a grand and disturbing landscape of sudden cliffs and jagged crags, where the Old Man of Storr pinnacle rises to 160ft like a giant's tower in a child's story. It has posed a challenge for centuries, but was not climbed until 1955. The Storr'lochs are harnessed to a hydro-electric scheme.

Continue, passing Lealt Falls and the well-known Kilt Rock near Loch Mealt, to reach Staffin.

STAFFIN, Highland

Opposite this village in the curve of sandy Staffin Bay is the gull-populated isolation of Staffin Island. One mile south-east is the Kilt Rock, so named because its columnar and horizontal beds of basalt suggest the pleats in a Highland kilt.

Continue, passing the Quiraing on the left.

The Cuillin Hills form Skye's most dramatic aspect.

Gaunt ruins of Duntulm Castle stand exposed on the headland.

Dunvegan Castle is steeped in legend.

QUIRAING, Highland
This strange wilderness of rocks is one of the most peculiar sights on Skye. It is a remarkable group of stone stacks and pinnacles bearing such descriptive names as Needle Rock, The Table, and The Prison, including a grassy natural amphitheatre and a rugged group known as Leac nan Fionn.

Continue and skirt Flodigarry.

FLODIGARRY, Highland
Flora Macdonald, known for her part in Bonnie Prince Charlie's escape after the collapse of the Jacobite cause at Culloden, spent the early years of her marriage here. She escorted the Prince, disguised as her maid, from Benbecula in the Outer Hebrides to Portree. Her house adjoins a local hotel.

Continue to Duntulm.

DUNTULM, Highland
Crumbling Duntulm Castle dates from the 15th century and was once the seat of the Macdonalds of Sleat and Trotternish. The promontory of Rubha Hunish extends beyond the shore of Score Bay north of Duntulm, and views north-west across the waters of the Minch encompass the mountainous Outer Hebridean island of Harris.

Continue along the coast road to Flora Macdonald's burial place and the Skye Cottage Museum.

SKYE COTTAGE MUSEUM AND FLORA MACDONALD MONUMENT, Highland
Traditional Highland furniture and relics from the island's past can be seen in the four well-restored crofters cottages here. This type of dwelling and the Black Houses were traditional amongst the islands, though few good examples now survive. Close by is the old burial ground of the Macdonalds, Martins, Macarthurs, and Nicolsons. In 1790 Flora Macdonald was buried here, wrapped in a sheet in which Bonnie Prince Charlie had slept at Kingsburgh. Over her grave is a great Iona cross inscribed by Dr Johnson.

Proceed beyond Kilmuir and descend Idrigill Hill, with fine views over Uig Bay. Turn left on to the A856 for Uig.

UIG, Highland
Situated on a fine bay, this picturesque little hamlet of scattered crofts faces across Loch Snizort and its islands to the Vaternish peninsula. The steamer pier is used by car ferries to the Outer Hebrides. In 1746 Flora Macdonald and Bonnie Prince Charlie landed here after a much more difficult and dangerous voyage from those islands.

Continue to Kensaleyre on the shore of Loch Eyre, an inlet of Loch Snizort Beag, and in another ½ mile turn right on to the B8036. After another 1½ miles meet a T-junction and turn right on to the A850 to follow the shores of Loch Snizort Beag and Loch Greshornish to Edinbane. To the right of the road are views of the Outer Hebrides. Continue to Dunvegan.

DUNVEGAN, Highland
Dunvegan Castle north of the village is the seat of the Macleod chiefs. Dating from the 15th to 19th centuries, it is claimed to be the oldest continuously inhabited castle in Scotland. Views from the ramparts extend across island-studded Dunvegan Loch to the distant ranges of Harris. Its greatest treasure is a fragment of silk which is known as the fairy flag and was probably woven on the Island of Rhodes in the 7th century. According to tradition a fairy gave the flag, and various magical properties, to the 4th clan chief in the 14th century. Other relics include the great broadsword of the 7th chief, the ancient Dunvegan Cup of Irish silver that was given to the 11th chief, and various items related to Bonnie Prince Charlie. Features of the building itself include a 15th-century dungeon with a high slit window opening on to the kitchen stairs, no doubt as an additional torture for the hungry prisoners. South-west of Dunvegan is a pair of flat-topped basalt mountains known as Macleod's Tables.

From Dunvegan take the A863 'Sligachan' road, which affords good views of the Cuillins ahead, and on the approach to Struan pass Dun Beag on the left.

DUN BEAG, Highland
Extensive remains of a 2,000-year-old Pictish broch stand here. Once a 40ft look-out post and refuge, the ruins include 12ft-thick walls, several rooms, and parts of a stone staircase.

Cross high ground above Loch Harport and descend to Glen Drynoch. A detour can be made from the main route here by turning right on to the B8009 and driving first to Carbost, then to Port-na-Long.

CARBOST, Highland
The well-known Talisker Whisky Distillery is sited here, on the west shores of Loch Harport.

Still on the detour, continue to Port-na-Long.

PORT-NA-LONG, Highland
This tiny weaving village has become famous for Harris Tweed.

On the main route, continue to Sligachan and turn right on to the A850 for the return to Kyleakin, where the ferry is taken back to Kyle of Lochalsh on the mainland.

239

TOUR 111   119 MILES

FROM THE CAPITAL OF THE HIGHLANDS

Close to Inverness are some of Scotland's best-known features. The Moray Firth offers sheltered boating and fishing, Loch Ness broods with mystery in the bottom of the Great Glen, and the engineering prowess of the 19th century is proved by the locks and cuts of the Caledonian Canal.

Early Victorian Inverness Castle occupies a commanding position above the town.

INVERNESS, Highland

Inverness, often referred to as the capital of the Highlands, is situated amid beautiful scenery with views across the Beauly and Inverness Firths. Buildings of interest include the early Victorian castle commanding a fine position overlooking River Ness, with a monument to Flora MacDonald; the High Church, parts of which date from the 13th century; Cromwell's citadel clock-tower; 16th-century Abertarff House, northern headquarters of the NTS; An Comunn Gaidhealach, the headquarters of the Gaelic Language Organisation with a permanent exhibition and sales centre on Highland culture; 19th-century St Andrew's Cathedral; the 130ft high Tolbooth Steeple of 1791, and Dunbar's Hospital, an almshouse of 1668. Also of interest are the Library, Museum and Art Gallery, the modern Eden Court Theatre and the Gothic-style Town House. A good viewpoint is at the cemetery on Tomnahurich Hill between the river and canal. Craig

Phadraig, to the west, is crowned by a vitrified fort. North of the town is the impressive Kessock bridge, carrying the A9 over the Beauly Firth. It has an overall length of 3,260ft, main span of 744ft and height above high water of 90ft.

On the main tour, leave Inverness by the A862 SP 'Beauly' and after 1 mile cross the Caledonian Canal.

CALEDONIAN CANAL

Created in the 19th century to provide passage between the Irish and North Seas, this 60½-mile waterway along the remarkable Great Glen uses 22 miles of canal to link lochs and virtually split Scotland in two. Without it the sailing boats of the day would have had to risk the passage round Cape Wrath.

Continue along the A862 to skirt the south shore of Beauly Firth, and after 7 miles a detour to Moniack Castle can be made by turning left on to an unclassified road then in ½ mile turning left again and taking the next turning right.

MONIACK CASTLE, Highland

This former Lovat stronghold (open)

St Andrew's Cathedral was built in 1866-69 at a cost of £20,000

Urquhart Castle was ruined before 1715.

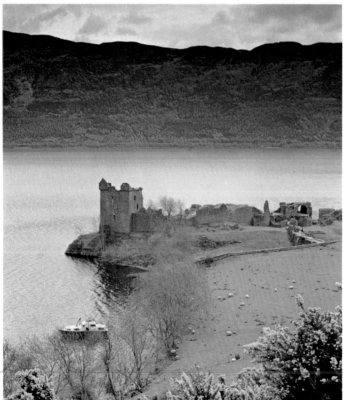

is now a major wine-making centre.

On the main route continue on the A862 and in 3 miles cross the River Beauly at Lovat Bridge then branch left on to the A831 SP 'Cannich' and continue to Kilmorack.

KILMORACK, Highland

South-east of this village is 19th-century Beaufort Castle, seat of the Chief of Clan Fraser. Near by are the ruins of an earlier stronghold. Although the castle is not open to the public it can be seen from foot and bridle paths that cross the Beauly River.

Continue along thickly wooded river banks and reach Crask of Aigas. Just past this hamlet, on the other side of the River Beauly, is Eileanaigas House.

EILEANAIGAS HOUSE, Highland

Situated in lovely gardens between two arms of the River Beauly, this house (not open) was the home of Lord Lovat in 1697 and that of Victorian prime minister Robert Peel. It is also associated with the Sobiéski brothers, who claimed direct descendancy from Prince Charles Edward.

Continue along the Beauly Valley, passing Erchless Castle before crossing Struy Bridge.

STRUY BRIDGE, Highland

Near this bridge the River Farrar joins the Glass to form the Beauly River. Beautiful walks along Glen Strathfarrar penetrate deep into mountain country from here, eventually reaching the lovely expanse of Loch Monar.

Continue through Struy and along Strath Glass to reach Cannich.

CANNICH, Highland

Cannich is a charming stone-built Highland village in a beautiful woodland setting at the south end of Strath Glass. The area is popular with walkers.

Pleasant detours from Cannich lead through Glen Cannich and Glen Affric, each of which is penetrated by about 10 miles of road. At the end of each glen turn round and return to the main route in Cannich.

240

GLEN CANNICH, Highland
The woodland scenery in this glen is outstanding. After passing under the slopes of 2,120ft Beinn a'Chairein the road enters densely forested hill country and follows the River Cannich to tiny Loch Carrie. After skirting the banks of Carrie the road reaches Loch Mullardoch, an attractive water which backs up behind the main dam of the Cannich hydro-electric scheme.

GLEN AFFRIC, Highland
In many ways Glen Affric is very much like its neighbour Cannich. After the hamlet of Fasnakyle, where a power station is situated, the road passes the Dog Fall and emerges amid birch and pine trees that surround Loch Beinn a'Mheadhoin. Magnificent scenery accompanies the road as it nears its end by the isolated expanse of Loch Affric, with 3,401ft Sgurr na Lapaich rising above the water.

On the main tour, continue along the A831 'Drumnadrochit' road to climb away from Strath Glass and enter Glen Urquhart. Pass Loch Meiklie and follow the River Enrick between pine-clad slopes, through Milton to Drumnadrochit.

DRUMNADROCHIT, Highland
Situated on the River Enrick and the west side of Loch Ness, this village is a popular centre for walking, angling, climbing, and pony-trekking. The Official Loch Ness Monster Exhibition located here has exhibits and audio-visual displays and now includes the International House of Heraldry and also glass-blowing.

Turn right on to the A82 SP 'Fort William' and in 2¼ miles enter the Great Glen and pass Urquhart Castle on the left.

URQUHART CASTLE, Highland
Ruined Urquhart Castle overlooks Loch Ness from a lonely promontory and is one of the largest castles in Scotland. It dates from the 14th century and has had a long and violent history. Many sightings of the Loch Ness Monster have been reported from this part of the loch.

LOCH NESS, Highland
One of a chain of lochs connected by the Caledonian Canal in the Great Glen, Loch Ness extends 24 miles from near Inverness to Fort Augustus and in places is over 700ft deep. It is world famous as the reported home of the Loch Ness Monster or Nessie as it has become known. Sightings of the creature have been reported since the 7th century, but these have swelled from a trickle to a flood since the road along the wooded west shore was opened in 1933. Investigation is hampered by the almost opaque quality of the water, which is stained brown by the peat-laden streams that feed the loch.

Continue to Invermoriston.

INVERMORISTON, Highland
This small town at the east end of Glen Moriston faces Loch Ness and is bordered to the north by the Hills of Invermoriston.

Turn right on to the A887 'Kyle of Lochalsh' road, enter wooded Glen Moriston, and climb gradually beside the river to cross Torgyle Bridge.

TORGYLE BRIDGE, Highland
The reach of the River Moriston spanned by this bridge is known for its fine rapids. Torgyle Power Station can be seen to the left.

Continue through the glen to meet the 'Fort William' road and turn left on to the A87. Climb on to bare mountains beside Loch Loyne, and continue with spectacular views before passing an AA viewpoint and descending beside Loch Garry. Here a single-track road to the right leads 22 miles west to Loch Quoich and Kinloch Hourn, passing through some of the wildest scenery in Scotland. On the tour, continue along the A87 to pass the Falls of Garry.

FALLS OF GARRY, Highland
At the east end of Loch Garry the River Garry plunges over rocks and ledges in a series of beautiful waterfalls. It is now part of a hydro-electric scheme. The forests to the west of this area can be explored by means of planned walks, nature trails, and woodland paths.

Beautiful Glen Moriston forms part of a large hydro-electric scheme.

Proceed to Invergarry.

INVERGARRY, Highland
South of this little hamlet, on the shores of Loch Oich, are the impressive ruins of Invergarry Castle. It was once the seat of the MacDonells of Glengarry and replaced castles destroyed in 1654 and 1689. Bonnie Prince Charlie stayed here before and after the battle of Culloden, and the 'Butcher' Duke of Cumberland had the building burned in reprisal. Just north of the ruins the River Garry flows into Loch Oich, and the whole area is framed by spectacular Highland mountain scenery.

Turn left on to the A82, skirting the north end of Loch Oich.

LOCH OICH, Highland
Small but beautiful, this is the highest of the Great Glen lochs in the Caledonian Canal chain. Bonnie Prince Charlie rallied his clansmen at Aberchalder Lodge, near the north end, before crossing the Corriveyairack Pass on his way to Edinburgh and England. The road that runs along the east shores of the loch was built by General Wade as a military way.

Telford spent from 1803 to 1847 building the Caledonian Canal.

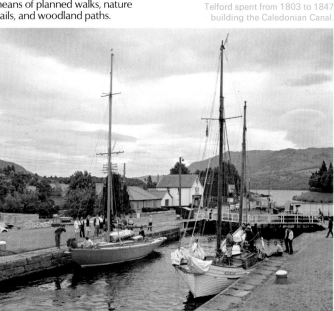

Continue to Fort Augustus, crossing the Caledonian Canal.

FORT AUGUSTUS, Highland
Wooded hill country surrounds this hamlet, which stands at the south-west end of Loch Ness in the Great Glen. It takes its name from a Hanoverian outpost that was built against the Jacobite Highlanders after the first Rising in 1715. General Wade built the first fort in 1730 and it was named after William Augustus, the Duke of Cumberland, who was later to become known as the Butcher of Culloden. In the second Rising of 1745 the Highlanders actually captured the fort and managed to hold it until the Prince's defeat at Culloden marked the end of the Jacobite cause. The site of the fort is now occupied by a 19th-century abbey and a Catholic boys' school. The Great Glen Exhibition in Fort Augustus relates the history and traditions of the area.

Turn right on to the B862 'Whitebridge, Dores' road and follow a former military road which eventually leads to Inverness. Climb steeply through Glen Doe and enjoy magnificent scenery to the north, then pass Loch Tarff and pass through forested areas to reach Whitebridge.

WHITEBRIDGE, Highland
Here the River Foyers is joined by the River Fechlin, which flows from remote Loch Killin in the hills rising to the south-east.

Proceed for 1 mile and turn left on to the B852 SP 'Foyers'. Descend through woodland to the east shore of Loch Ness to reach Foyers.

FOYERS, Highland
This village on the eastern shores of Loch Ness is best known for the beautiful Falls of Foyers. The uppermost of these drops 30ft and the lower 90ft, but their scenic impact was considerably reduced when they were starved of water by the opening of Britain's first hydro-electric scheme in 1896.

Continue alongside Loch Ness, with fine mountain views to the west, and reach Inverfarigaig.

INVERFARIGAIG, Highland
A permanent Forestry Commission display and several marked trails have been provided here to help the public understand the industry and wildlife of the area.

Continue to Dores.

DORES, Highland
Dores stands in Strath Dores at the point where it meets Loch Ness and is well situated for walking and angling. Aldourie Castle lies 2 miles north off the B862 and has been a seat of the Frazers since 1750. The first castle was built here in 1626, but the earliest work evident today dates from the 18th century.

Join the B862 and follow Strath Dores, then the River Ness, for the return to Inverness.

HELMSDALE, Highland

This small fishing town at the mouth of the River Helmsdale has a natural harbour which offers a safe anchorage and sandy beaches.

Leave Helmsdale on the A9 'Wick' road and climb on to moorland before descending steeply to the village of Berriedale.

BERRIEDALE, Highland

Red-deer antlers decorate the post office and old smithy of this pleasant village, which is situated at the mouth of Berridale Water. Remains of a 14th-century castle stand here, and the house of Langwell stands in fine gardens where a variety of plants grow in exposed conditions (gardens only open). Langwell Water rises on a distant slope of the 2,313ft Morven and meets Berriedale Water here.

Ascend from Berriedale and continue, with good views along the rocky coast. Pass Dunbeath Castle on the right and descend to Dunbeath.

DUNBEATH, Highland

This scattered fishing village probably derives its name from an ancient Pictish broch which lies about ½ mile north-west and is called Dun Beath. The castle of the same name (not open) perches on a lofty promontory 1 mile south and, despite having been enlarged in the 19th century, retains much of its original 15th-century work. It was besieged and captured by Jacobites during the Risings. To the north-east of Dunbeath is the Lhaidhay Croft Museum in an early 19th-century Caithness longhouse.

Continue to Latheronwheel.

LATHERONWHEEL, Highland

Latheronwheel is the residential half of a partnership with its sister community of Latheron and has a small but attractive harbour at the bottom of a steep lane.

Continue to Latheron.

LATHERON, Highland

Sister village of Latheronwheel, Latheron is at the centre of a district which is well known for its ancient remains. A homestead of early Iron-Age date is the latest of several ruins recently excavated about 1 mile north at The Wag. A hill above the local church is surmounted by a tower which houses the church bell.

Proceed to Lybster.

LYBSTER, Highland

This is the largest of several attractive fishing villages that manage to make a living on this wild and rocky coast. Its church, built with locally dressed flagstones, has a west door and chancel entrance that are typical of an ancient design used in the area. A road east of the village leads to The Grey Cairns of Camster (AM), which are two chambered tombs from the prehistoric megalithic period.

Continue to Mid Clyth.

NORTH TO DUNNET HEAD

The rocky, wave-torn headland of Dunnet Head extends far into the stormy Pentland Firth to become the northernmost point on the British mainland. Along the coast are rocky cliffs and small sandy bays where seals bask in the sun, high dunes hiding smothered villages, and ferry points for the Orkneys.

The small port of Helmsdale is famous for its lobsters.

MID CLYTH, Highland

Appropriately named the Hill of Many Stones (AM), the slopes behind this village feature 22 prehistoric rows containing 192 stones. They are unique in Scotland, but similar structures exist elsewhere.

Continue along the A9 to Thrumster.

THRUMSTER, Highland

Many prehistoric remains survive in the area round Thrumster, particularly in the vicinity of Loch Yarrows. These include brochs, cairns, and various scattered stones, and there is a standing stone just south of the village school.

Continue to Wick.

WICK, Highland

Situated on Wick Bay at the mouth of the Wick River, this ancient Royal Burgh is a market town and fishing port with two good harbours. One of these was initially designed by Thomas Telford and later improved by Stephenson. Wick is famous for the Caithness Glassworks (open) and there is also a town Heritage Centre. The ruined Castle of Old Wick (AM), also known as Castle Oliphant, stands 1½ miles south-east. Close by are the curious rock stacks known as Brig O'Tram and Brough.

A detour can be made from the main route by leaving Wick on the unclassified Ackergill Street and

driving 3 miles, passing Wick Airport and the castles of Girnigoe and Sinclair to reach Noss Head.

CASTLE GIRNIGOE AND CASTLE SINCLAIR, Highland

Close together in a striking situation at Noss Head are these two picturesquely ruined castles, both abandoned in the mid 17th century.

On the main route, leave Wick on the A9 SP 'John O' Groats' for Reiss.

REISS, Highland

Reiss stands at a road junction a little inland from Sinclair's Bay, which has one of the longest stretches of sand on this coast. On the shore is modernized Ackergill Tower, which claims to be one of Scotland's oldest inhabited castles.

Turn right with the main road and skirt Sinclair's Bay to the right. Continue to Keiss.

KEISS, Highland

The remains of the 16th-century Keiss Castle stand on the coast to the north of this Sinclair's Bay fishing village, near its modern replacement.

Continue to Freswick.

FRESWICK, Highland

The transition from land to sea near this village is a gentle affair of green slopes and broad sands around Freswick Bay. Close by are the ruins of 15th-century Bucholly Castle.

Continue along the A9. On the approach to John O' Groats a short detour can be made from the main route by taking an unclassified right turn to Duncansby Head.

DUNCANSBY HEAD, Highland

Here, at the extreme north-eastern point of the Scottish mainland, spectacular sandstone cliffs soar to over 200ft above the sea in a massive display of strength that must have alarmed would-be invaders in times past. Remains of an ancient watch tower still stand on the head, close to a lighthouse, and the great chasm of Long Geo runs inland from the sea.

On the main tour, continue to the end of the A9 at John O' Groats.

JOHN O' GROATS, Highland

The shortest distance by road between this village and Land's End in Cornwall is exactly 877 miles. Its name is derived from that of a Dutchman who came to Scotland in the 15th century, and its beach is famous for the attractive little seashells known as Groatie Buckies.

Return along the A9 for ½ mile and turn right on to the A836 SP 'Thurso'. After 2 miles a detour can be made from the main route along an unclassified left turn to Canisbay.

CANISBAY, Highland

The most 18th-century church in this village contains a number of interesting monuments, including one to members of the de Groot family. Jan de Groot gave his name to John O' Groats.

Berriedale Water flows through a long valley to join the sea.

The stacks of Duncansby rise to the south of John O' Groats.

A salmon leap is provided at the Bridge of Forss.

On the main tour, continue along the A836 to reach Mey, with views over the Pentland Firth to the right. Various access roads lead to the shoreline from the tour route.

MEY, Highland
Grey seals are a common sight in the little coastal bays of the Pentland Firth, and views across the water from this village take in the distant Orkneys. One of the best vantage points in the area is in the gardens (open occasionally) of the Castle of Mey, famous as the summer residence of HM the Queen Mother since 1952. The building dates from the mid 16th century.

Proceed to Dunnet.

DUNNET, Highland
Dunnet Church has a saddleback tower and is thought to date from the 14th century. The village itself overlooks Dunnet Bay to the south. St John's Loch, nearby, is popular with trout fishermen.

A detour can be made from the main route at Dunnet by turning right on to the B855 to reach Dunnet Head.

DUNNET HEAD, Highland
Fine views from this, the most northerly point in Britain, extend across the rough seas of the Pentland Firth to the Orkneys and the 450ft rock stack of the Old Man of Hoy. A lighthouse stands on the headland.

On the main route, skirt the sands of Dunnet Bay to reach Castletown.

CASTLETOWN, Highland
This village was founded in 1824 to house workers employed in a nearby quarry once famous worldwide for its paving stones. It has a picturesque little harbour and stands close to the 2-mile long sands of Dunnet Bay.

Continue to Thurso.

THURSO, Highland
An expanding resort and residential town on the sandy shores of Thurso Bay, this charming place is the most northerly town on the British mainland. It stands on the River Thurso, which is well known for its salmon and flows into the bay between the craggy cliffs of Holborn Head and Clardon Head. Close to the harbour are well-restored houses dating from the 17th and 18th centuries, and ruined St Peter's Church stands on a site occupied since the Vikings. The remains that stand here today are of a 17th-century building. Thurso's interesting museum maintains good collections of plants and fossils, and boasts a lovely little Runic cross. Roofless Thurso Castle, birthplace of the 18th-century statistician and agriculturalist Sir John Sinclair, stands ½ mile north-east of the town. Beyond this is Harold's Tower, which was erected over the 12th-century grave of Harold, Earl of Caithness, and has subsequently been used as the clan's burial place. Sir William Smith, founder of the Boys' Brigade, was born at Pennyland in 1854.

Leave by the A836 'Tongue' road and after a short distance reach the A882 junction. This offers a detour to Scrabster.

SCRABSTER, Highland
A ferry from Stromness in the Orkneys crosses the Pentland Firth to Scrabster, which stands on sandy Thurso Bay and is sheltered in the north-east by the remarkable Holborn Head. This headland is split from top to bottom by several chasms, the largest of which is open to the sea and spanned by two natural rock arches. Near by the precipitous rock of Clett rises 150ft from the sea.

On the main tour, continue along the A836 to reach Dounreay.

DOUNREAY POWER STATION, Highland
The world's first prototype fast-breeder reactor was constructed at the experimental nuclear power station here in the 1950s. A visitor centre with guided tours of the plant is open from May to September.

Continue to Reay.

REAY, Highland
Situated near the head of Sandside Bay, this village has a good 18th-century church that can be considered typical of the area. It has an external staircase leading to the belfry, and there is a carved Celtic cross slab in the churchyard. The bay's broad sands, appreciated by the holiday-maker today, were the death of the old village that was overwhelmed by them in the 18th century.

Continue and in 4½ miles turn left on to the A897 'Helmsdale' road to enter Strath Halladale. Pass through the small angling resort of Forsinard and cross bleak moorland. Leave by passing little Loch an Ruathair to reach the edge of Kinbrace village.

KINBRACE, Highland
Two burns meet near this lonely crofting village to form the River Helmsdale, and the local countryside is rich in prehistoric remains. Several chambered cairns can be seen near the Kinbrace Burn. In 1877 the 3rd Duke of Sutherland devised a local reclamation scheme to increase his holding of arable land.

Continue along the A897 beside the River Helmsdale and pass through the Strath of Kildonan to reach Kildonan.

KILDONAN, Highland
At some time in the 19th century small quantities of gold dust were found in Kildonan Burn, but the minor gold rush that resulted from the discovery fizzled out when efforts to extract it failed. Prehistoric rows of stone stand north-west on Leirable Hill.

Descend through the Strath of Kildonan and return to Helmsdale.

243

The wild moorlands near Forsinard, in the sparsely populated far north of Scotland, are overshadowed by the peaks of rugged Ben Griam Beg and its lofty neighbour Ben Griam Mor.

'Auld Lang Syne' manuscript at Burns' Cottage Museum, Alloway.

A magnificent old ship's figurehead in Buckler's Hard Museum.

C

Amongst many treasures in Brecon Cathedral is this fine Norman font.

Interior decoration at Watts Memorial Chapel, Compton.

The Clan graves at Culloden serve as reminders of a great battle.

The Abbot's Kitchen at Glastonbury Abbey has been preserved intact.

This field gun stands inside the walls of Pevensey Castle.

St Mary's Church at Rye carries this ornate clock.

Coverlet by Mary Queen of Scots at Traquair House, Innerleithen.

THE NATIONAL GRID

The National Grid map references which appear after the place and county names throughout this book can be used to pin-point those places on any Ordnance Survey based map.